Mastering the SAP® Business Information Warehouse, Second Edition

Mastering the SAP® Business Information Warehouse, Second Edition

Leveraging the Business Intelligence Capabilities of SAP NetWeaver

Kevin McDonald
Andreas Wilmsmeier
David C. Dixon
W.H. Inmon

Wiley Publishing, Inc.

Mastering the SAP Business Information Warehouse, Second Edition

Published by
Wiley Publishing, Inc.
10475 Crosspoint Boulevard
Indianapolis, IN 46256
www.wiley.com

ISBN-13: 978-0-7645-9637-7
ISBN-10: 0-7645-9637-3

10 9 8 7 6 5 4 3 2 1

For general information on our other products and services or to obtain technical support, please contact our Customer Care Department within the U.S. at (800) 762-2974, outside the U.S. at (317) 572-3993 or fax (317) 572-4002.

Library of Congress Cataloging-in-Publication Data is available from the publisher.

For

Theodora and Malcolm

Rita, Theresa, and Arne

Karl

About the Authors

 **Kevin McDonald** is a consultant and entrepreneur. He co-founded and was the CEO of COMPENDIT, Inc., a consulting services firm acquired by Inforte Corp. in 2004. He was an Ernst and Young Entrepreneur of the Year regional finalist and was recognized by *Entrepreneur* magazine for having created a "Hot 100" fastest-growing new business. He has instructed, implemented, and designed enterprise decision-processing systems for dozens of clients. Prior to co-founding COMPENDIT, Kevin was the Director of New Dimension Technology and a corporate spokesperson for SAP, where he had worked in both America and Germany. He was program manager during the successful market launch of SAP Business Information Warehouse (SAP BW), and he authored the SAP BW product map that was first used to define the scope and development direction for the software.

Kevin started his career at Baxter Healthcare, where he held positions in both IT and finance functions. He has authored numerous articles about SAP's Business Intelligence Solution for The Data Warehouse Institute's newsletter, and he has made presentations on business intelligence at DCI's Data Warehouse World, HP World, ERP World, TDWI conferences, ASUG, SAP TechEd, SAP Sapphire, Decision Processing 98 and 99, and Informatica World. Kevin is an advisor to the Cognos Innovation Center and may be contacted at `kevin.mcdonald@renditionx.com`.

Andreas Wilmsmeier is a managing director of Inforte Deutschland. Andreas has been a member of the initial SAP BW core development team, where he has been responsible for designing and implementing parts of the Staging Engine (for example, the Staging BAPI). Andreas has been consulting SAP BW clients since the initial customer shipment of SAP BW 1.2A in early 1998 and has continued to contribute to the development of SAP BW by providing feedback from the field and to the development of business content for the financial services and defense industries.

After receiving his diploma in computer science and business economics, Andreas started his career in developing data warehouse and Internet solutions. Prior to working for Inforte, Andreas ran the German subsidiary of COMPENDIT until its acquisition by Inforte in early 2004.

His knowledge of data warehousing, data mining, and knowledge management has been showcased at numerous international conferences, including SAP Sapphire, SAP TechEd, ASUG, Cebit in Hanover, Germany, and Systems in Munich, Germany. Andreas has authored articles in the *SAP Technical Journal*, (now featured on `intelligentERP.com`) and the German-language *E/3 Magazine*. Andreas may be contacted at `andreas.wilmsmeier@inforte.com`.

David Dixon is a vice president with Inforte's SAP Practice, where he is responsible for ensuring the quality of Inforte solutions and project deliveries. A recognized authority in business intelligence, he has extensive full-lifecycle project experience in architecting and implementing complicated global solutions for Fortune 100 companies. David has also worked with the SAP SEM and SAP BI development teams on numerous occasions in support of the latest products.

Prior to joining Inforte, David worked for COMPENDIT, a consulting firm acquired by Inforte in March 2004, where he was a founding team member. Prior to joining COMPENDIT, he was a Platinum Consultant with SAP. David started his career as a Financials and Controlling (FI/CO) consultant with SAP in 1995, specializing in all of the SAP reporting and analysis applications and tools. An accomplished speaker, he has presented at industry-leading SAP and BI events, including SAP TechEd, ASUG, and TDWI. He may be contacted at `david.dixon@inforte.com`.

 **Bill Inmon** is thought of as the "father of the data warehouse" and is co-creator of the "corporate information factory." He has more than 28 years of experience in database technology management and data warehouse design. He is known globally for his seminars on developing data warehouses and has been a keynote speaker for every major computing association and many industry conferences, seminars, and trade shows. Bill has written about a variety of topics on building, usage, and maintenance of the data warehouse and the corporate information factory. More than 500 of his articles have been published in major computer journals such as *Datamation*, *ComputerWorld*, and *Byte* magazine. Bill is currently a columnist with *Data Management Review* and has been since its inception. He has published 39 books.

Bill founded and took public a Silicon Valley company, Prism Solutions, in 1991. Prism Solutions became Ardent Software, which was acquired by Informix, renamed Ascential Software, and acquired by IBM. The software he created is still used by hundreds of companies today. More recently, Bill decided to publish his vast data warehousing information resources on his Web site at www.billinmon.com. The Web site has now grown to support millions of visitors a month. Bill consults with a large number of Fortune 1000 clients, offering data warehouse design and database management services.

Credits

Executive Editor
Robert Elliott

Development Editor
Kevin Shafer

Technical Editor
Bryan Katis

Production Editor
Angela Smith

Copy Editor
C.M. Jones

Editorial Manager
Mary Beth Wakefield

Production Manager
Tim Tate

Vice President and Executive Group Publisher
Richard Swadley

Vice President and Publisher
Joseph B. Wikert

Compositor
Maureen Forys,
Happenstance Type-o-Rama

Illustrator
Jeff Wilson,
Happenstance Type-o-Rama

Proofreading
Jennifer Larsen, Word One

Indexing
Johnna VanHoose Dinse

Contents

Foreword

Today's challenging business environment calls for a flexible approach to business processes that integrates and embeds analytics. In 1997, SAP started developing its own enterprise data warehouse and business intelligence solution, the SAP Business Information Warehouse. Nine years later, these capabilities find themselves at the center of SAP NetWeaver. This new breed of software not only provides mature business intelligence capabilities; it openly enables organizations to flexibly *model*, expose, and optimize business processes.

The Business Intelligence capabilities of NetWeaver now play a central role in nearly every solution brought to market by SAP. SAP NetWeaver enables customers to accurately forecast and strategically analyze information for better customer service, optimized business operations, and improved corporate performance. By embedding these analytic capabilities and advanced technologies, SAP customers may realize maximum benefits as quickly as possible while maintaining the flexibility to change their business processes over time.

The writing and publishing of this book's second edition reflects the success of and the growing adoption of SAP NetWeaver. Thousands of customers are already using the business intelligence capabilities in productive applications — sourcing data from SAP and non-SAP systems alike, some with thousands of users and terabyte-sized databases.

Mastering the SAP Business Information Warehouse links theoretical enterprise data warehousing concepts to customer requirements, and details the options for implementing powerful analytic engines. It speaks to data warehousing specialists, as well as those who have implemented ERP solutions. The authors of this book all have long-term experience in data warehousing, reporting, and analytic applications. Their perspective on SAP comes from years of implementations and working with our development teams on enhancing the offering.

Integral to the success of any business scenario is the availability of resources and guides that describe how to successfully deploy professional solutions. You need this information from people who have been in the trenches, who have implemented successful projects, and who can speak from experience, not simply theory. This book provides you with the best of three worlds: an understanding of business intelligence, application of these concepts to SAP NetWeaver, and the authors' own expertise in setting strategies and deploying solutions.

So, sit back, enjoy this book from cover to cover, and use it as a reference during your implementations.

—Dr. Heinz Haefner
Senior Vice President SAP
NetWeaver Development
SAP AG, Walldorf

Acknowledgments

From the first edition: First, we would like to thank Bob Elliott and Emilie Herman of Wiley for their guidance and patience through the authoring process and for providing us the opportunity to share what we have learned about SAP in this book. The copyediting team at Wiley has helped create a common voice and a consistency throughout the chapters that we may not have been able to accomplish on our own. We would also like to thank our co-author, Bill Inmon, who joined the authoring team shortly after the project started. He provided the needed stimulus to take the project to completion.

Writing a book about a software component that has hundreds of people dedicated to evolving the product as quickly as possible presented an interesting challenge. There were many individuals and teams at SAP AG, SAP Portals, SAP America, and SAP International that provided invaluable feedback and support, without which this book may never have happened. The list below does not come close to acknowledging all the people who supported us in our lives, careers, and on this project.

A special thank you goes to Klaus Kreplin, Dr. Werner Sinzig, and Lothar Kallweit for their guidance and mentoring through the years. The SAP BW development and product management teams, namely Heinz Häfner, Lothar Henkes, Claudia Weller, Gunther Rothermel, and from the marketing department, Sabine Eggl, provided great support in straightening out the SAP BW architecture sections in the book. We'd also like to thank Mark A. Smith for his eleventh-hour briefing on the SAP Business Intelligence Solution and his insight over the years as we have often debated the future of the industry.

For the second edition: First, we would like to thank Bob Elliott, Kevin Shafer, and the rest of the Wiley team for providing us with the opportunity and support needed to write a second edition to this book, as well as to Bryan Katis for allowing us to convince him that he had time tech edit this edition. We could not have completed this edition without his near-daily support.

Writing this book presented an interesting challenge. Much like an artist painting the horizon, every time we wanted to get closer to our subject matter, it kept moving away from us. There were many individuals at SAP helping us to accurately detail our horizon. A special thank you goes to Marc Bernard, Scott Cairncross, Heinz Häfner, Tobias Hagen, Lothar Henkes, Rainer Höltke, and Stefan Sigg. The SAP Regional Implementation Groups (RIGs) have rounded out our thoughts in several areas related to system administration and performance. Finally, thank you to Chris Reitz for sharing his EDW project experience and contributing to Chapter 5.

A very special thank you to Julia for her support, Theodora for keeping her little fingers off the keyboard, and Malcolm for sleeping through the night; and to Rita, Theresa, and Arne for their support and patience throughout the authoring process. Stefan Krauskopf and Mohammad Mazhar — we couldn't have done it without you. A lifetime's worth of thank you to Karl H. Dixon for his teachings, written examples, and the loving memories he has left his family and friends.

A final thanks to the readers of the first edition for your kind words and insightful suggestions.

Introduction

While we have seen only a few IT shops that rely exclusively on SAP software, the percentage of business processing conducted via SAP software has steadily increased. More and more corporations have successfully implemented SAP. These organizations may have started their projects in isolated divisions, but over the past decade, larger portions of the business are being run on SAP software. We see many organizations adopting IT philosophies that have SAP software as the default solution. It is not uncommon to hear a CFO comment, "You better have a very good reason not to use the SAP software we already paid for." These organizations have moved beyond automating and integrating business processes and want to optimize their business performance, reduce the slack in their supply chains, and realize the potential value of their customer relationships.

Parallel to the ERP and business process reengineering evolution was the evolution of informational processing, now commonly referred to as business intelligence. The explosive growth in data captured by organizations (in part because of the rapid adoption of Internet technologies) has made available an increasing amount of business information. This, combined with the increased pace in the way business is conducted, has created significant demand for efficient decision-making processes. The data warehouse was conceived to enable such processes.

SAP has brought to market NetWeaver software that has created a tremendous opportunity for organizations to lay a common technical foundation on which flexible business processes may be defined, executed, and altered as part of larger composite applications. The line between transaction processing and decision processing has disappeared. SAP NetWeaver was the eraser. Organizations that implement SAP NetWeaver will find they are able to quickly deploy business processes that span systems and company boundaries, that embed predictive analytics and apply prescriptive business rules, and that increase the velocity and effectiveness of decision-making.

Why did we write this book? At the time we wrote the first edition, many books on SAP focused on step-by-step instructions for accomplishing a given configuration task and spoon-fed readers with checklists, transaction codes, and code samples. Our goal was to bridge the gap between these low-level books and the high-level books that focused on data-warehousing architectures but did not necessarily explain how SAP software could be used to realize such architectures. Our goal, then, was to create a reference that exposed the various implementation options available in SAP BW by defining the fundamental architecture and concepts to enable readers to understand and use those options. With the second edition, we have updated the content to cover the BI capabilities of NetWeaver2004s.

This second edition should inspire readers to implement these options in order to strategically analyze information and accurately forecast optimized operations, better customer service, and improved bottom-line performance. SAP BI has richness in functionality that extends beyond the capacity of any one person to know in detail every option available in the software and the potential consequences that implementing one option may have on another. The product's maturity and importance to SAP NetWeaver compelled us to update the first edition and once again share our knowledge from within the industry.

We have taken the approach that technology is there to serve business and have counterbalanced technical sections with commentary on how a particular option may be used to drive business value. *Mastering the SAP Business Information Warehouse* looks at options for modeling, deploying, populating, accessing, analyzing, presenting, planning, and administering data and information in SAP NetWeaver. This book is our contribution to accelerating the search for actionable information.

Who Should Read This Book

We are assuming that you, the project team member, are familiar with mySAP ERP, although you may not be as familiar with data warehousing, business intelligence, or SAP NetWeaver.

Business and IT professionals of large organizations who are considering implementing SAP will also find this book useful, as the BI capabilities in NetWeaver are the underpinning for every business solution that they sell.

How This Book Is Organized

As we note in the "Acknowledgments" for the second edition, writing about SAP software is extremely difficult because it is constantly changing. Not only is functionality added in new releases, but features, functions, and even entire products are renamed, repositioned, or morphed into new offerings. This is very much the case with SAP BW. SAP BW is now referred to as a capability (or, more specifically, as a business intelligence capability) of SAP NetWeaver. We have (as a matter of convenience and comfort to the reader) continued to use the term "SAP BW" when addressing BI capabilities. As we wrote the second edition, we made difficult choices on what to include and not include as it relates to the broader NetWeaver platform. We decided to add a chapter dedicated to detailing the platform. The content in the second edition has been updated to reflect NetWeaver2004s and the embedded SAP BW version 7.0.

This book may be thought of as consisting of four parts, meant to reflect the process an organization goes through during an implementation of the software. We begin with an introduction to business intelligence and SAP NetWeaver, which is meant to provide a backdrop for readers who may come from more of a mySAP ERP implementation background than a data warehousing background. Chapter 1 is an introduction to business intelligence and how enterprises tackle such challenges as:

- Extracting data from online transaction processing systems

- Eliminating poor data quality

- Structuring data in such a way that history may be recorded and recalled

From these needs arose the idea of combining both traditional data with documents to offer organizations a collaborative platform for analyzing information and optimizing business performance. Today, this is called *business intelligence*.

While business intelligence is not new, the toolsets available to realize such are constantly changing. We have entered a time when technical integration is a worry of the past, and semantic and process integration are at the forefront.

In Chapter 1, we examine SAP's offerings. You will quickly see what SAP realized around 1996: that ERP systems are not designed for analytical processing. We explain the challenges of reporting and analyzing data in the ERP system.

Readers familiar with data warehousing, the evolution of SAP, and information processing may wish to start reading the book at Chapter 2, where we discuss SAP NetWeaver and all of its capabilities. In this chapter, we define the major architectural components and set the context for the business intelligence capabilities described throughout the remainder of the book.

From data extraction to the analysis of information and creation of Web applications, readers will start to understand the breadth and depth of functionality in SAP while reading Chapter 3. We also map SAP to the corporate information factory (CIF). You will quickly see the characteristics SAP has in common with non-SAP data warehousing platforms, as well as the unique features found in NetWeaver.

The second part of this book focuses on metadata and the options available to information modelers as they work to deliver value data. Chapter 4 explains the information model and how this collection of metadata objects (which describe business processes, business objects, information containers, and their mutual relationships, as well as how the scope, granularity, and semantics of information available in the system) are important parts of a proper deployment of a business intelligence solution.

New to the second edition is Chapter 5, where we define and compare the layers found in enterprise data warehouse implementations. We look at the characteristics of each layer, including the staging area, ODS, Data Warehouse, and InfoMart, and detail the differences among them. The modeling options, as well as example topologies, are also elucidated. We end the chapter with a section on governance and the organizational design needed to support an enterprise data warehouse.

The third section of the book focuses on the services available in the SAP BW used to realize such an information model (Chapters 6 through 10). These include the following:

- Extraction, transfer, and loading (ETL) services

- Data storage services

- Information analysis and distribution

- Services supporting integrated planning and information presentation

Chapter 6 leads readers through identifying the SAP sources of data, extracting data from these sources, applying the transformations required, and storing the transformed data in a way that best supports reporting and analysis. In other words, this chapter presents the functionality provided by the ETL aspects of the business intelligence capabilities of NetWeaver. This is often the most time-consuming part of building a data warehouse solution. In the CIF framework, this is referred to as "sourcing and manufacturing of data and information." The options described in Chapter 6 will enable readers to take an information model and instantiate it in SAP software. Chapter 6 also describes how to integrate and transform data so that it may be stored in the various constructs (such as DataStore Objects, InfoCubes, and Master Data).

Chapter 7 picks up the information logistics process where Chapter 6 leaves off and highlights the main services provided in SAP BW that access data, turn it into meaningful business information, and deliver it to the analysis services. The chapter has been organized in three main sections: SAP BW information access, analysis services, and distribution services. We also have included a section on the application programming interfaces (APIs) options, with which custom applications or third-party tools may interface. A significant section of this chapter has been dedicated to the analytic process designer and the predictive analytics capabilities found therein.

Chapter 8 describes the Business Explorer tools, including BEx Report Designer, BEx Analyzer, BEx Mobile, and BEx Web Application Designer.

Chapter 9 is an entirely new chapter that covers the concepts of integrated planning. Here we discuss the concepts of planning, including some of the best and worst practices we have seen. The chapter covers three main areas of planning: process, data, and technology.

Because NetWeaver is a platform for building analytic applications, we have reformulated and dedicated a chapter to business analytics in the second edition, whereas the first edition included two chapters (one on Business Content and one on analytic applications). This reformulated Chapter 10 details the architecture and three different examples of analytic applications. The three analytic applications covered are customer relationship analytics, supply chain analytics, and financial analytics. We use the analogy of building blocks to help describe Business Content, in the sense that Business Content includes the extraction for data sources, transformation of that data, storage in a schema, and the queries and applications that access and present the information. These building blocks are foundational to analytic applications. The usability of Business Content is assessed and the challenges to its growth critiqued.

The last section focuses on the administration and performance options for the software component (Chapters 11 and 12). In this section, administration tasks — both process-oriented tasks and system-oriented tasks — are described.

Chapter 11 begins by describing process-oriented tasks, which consist of application processes such as scheduling, monitoring, and troubleshooting of data loads, as well as archiving. System-oriented tasks consist of security measures, transports, and upgrades. There are many different application processes besides data loading, such as index maintenance, building aggregates, and batch scheduling of reporting jobs. All these application processes can have complex dependencies.

Also in Chapter 11, SAP BW security is explained from a design perspective, detailing the decisions to make when building authorizations, such as making them user-based versus role-based, or object-centric versus data-centric. We continue the administration section by describing the options in the change management system with specific attention on the transportation of metadata from a development system to quality assurance and production. We conclude Chapter 11 by looking at the considerations for a multilayered application environment when performing an upgrade.

From an end user's perspective, the data warehouse is only as good as the last query. Performance should be carefully planned and given constant attention. However, because of the discontinuous, unpredictable user behavior characteristic of an information consumer, this may prove to be a challenging task. In Chapter 12, we describe the performance management process and the BI Accelerator. We have divided this discussion into two parts: performance planning and performance management.

During the system development process, performance planning is essential. Performance planning lays the foundation for overall system performance. It involves reviewing information models; designing an appropriate information logistics model and system landscape; implementing efficient transformations; defining parallel, collision-free data loads and data maintenance process chains; and managing user expectations.

Performance management, on the other hand, is part of production system administration. It entails monitoring all processes and resources in the system. We describe how the system may be tuned by defining aggregates, adjusting operating system parameters, determining database management system settings, and configuring hardware. Like many of the options that we describe in the book, performance planning and performance management deal with trade-offs. The trade-offs in this case are among disk and memory space, flexibility, loading time, and retrieval time.

Throughout the book, we have included images, lists, notes, and tips to help you implement your own solutions. This book is not a step-by-step list of configuration settings, and it is not intended to be a substitute for hands-on learning. You do not become a black belt in karate by reading a book. The same is the case with mastering SAP. We encourage you to log in to a test system, configure the services described in this book, and assess the trade-offs.

What's on the Web Site

The accompanying Web site for this book can be found at `www.wiley.com/compbooks/mcdonald`. It contains updates to the technology and the book.

From Here

In the third century B.C., Greek writer Plutarch may have put it best when he wrote, "The mind is not a vessel to be filled, yet a spark to be lighted." It is our hope that readers of this book will discover the options available in SAP NetWeaver and uncover a new means to improve business performance. We hope you enjoy the book as we open with Chapter 1 and an introduction to business intelligence.

Mastering the SAP® Business Information Warehouse, Second Edition

The Origins of Business Intelligence

The origins of business intelligence may be traced to the first data-processing applications such as accounts payable and receivable. These applications ran on sequential technology (such as magnetic and paper tapes). Using sequential media for storage meant the entire file had to be accessed, even if only a fraction of the file was needed. Oxide often stripped off of magnetic tapes, and entire files were lost. These issues led to the need for a new way to analyze information.

   This chapter discusses how enterprises tackled the challenges of extracting data from online transaction-processing systems, dealing with poor data quality, and structuring data. This discussion describes what a data warehouse is from its data model, table structure, granularity, and support of historical data and how it fits into a broader intellectual concept called the *corporate information factory* (CIF). While the CIF was evolving, so was SAP, until finally the two converged.

Evolution of Information Processing

The computer profession is historically immature. Other professions have been around for millennia. In caves in Chile, bones have been found showing that humankind practiced medicine (in at least a crude form) as long as 10,000 years ago. In Rome, walls and streets are used today that engineers built before the time of Christ. In Egypt, hieroglyphs on the walls of the tombs indicate that an accountant declared that wheat was owed the Pharaoh 3,000 years ago.

On the contrary, the computer profession has been around a measly half a century or so, depending on when you start counting. So, comparing the maturity of the IT profession is a mismatch; IT professionals are infants in comparison to their other professional brethren.

Data-Storage Advancements

The early beginnings of the computer profession featured wired boards and paper tape. These crude forms of programming allowed the programmer to route and reroute data as it passed from paper tape (or punched cards) to reports. To even the most ardent technologists, early boards and paper tape were crude. Soon came computer languages such as Assembler, Fortran, and Cobol. These languages allowed people to perform complex logic, something not possible with early forms of computing.

And with early forms of computing came magnetic tape. Magnetic tape could store massive amounts of data. Also, magnetic tape was reusable. Once someone wrote on a tape, the tape could be rewritten. Magnetic tape was a leap ahead from punched cards and paper tapes. And with this leap ahead came programs and systems, unleashing a flood of computing.

But magnetic tape was not without its limitations. It had to be read sequentially. With magnetic tape, you had to access 100 percent of the data to find the five percent you really wanted. Magnetic tape had the nasty habit of shredding. When shredding occurred, all the oxide on the tape came off, and with the stripping of the oxide, data was permanently lost. And, as a last issue, magnetic tape required a significant amount of manual manipulation.

Nevertheless, with magnetic tape, the gates of commercial computing opened.

But around the corner was disk storage. *Disk storage* was data stored on a spinning drum read by read/write arms. With the disk eternally spinning, data was, for all purposes, directly accessible. No longer was it necessary to read all the data to get five percent of what was needed. With disk storage, data could be accessed directly.

With disk storage came the notion of a database. A *database* was data stored on disk that could serve multiple purposes. With older magnetic files, data was stored in a *master file*, which essentially had a single purpose — to satisfy the needs of the application for which the master file was built. But with a database and disk storage, it became possible to build databases used in multiple applications.

Transaction Processing Dominates

Soon, applications that centered on the database sprung up everywhere. But a new usage of disk storage soon became a possibility: the advent of *online transaction processing* (OLTP). With online transaction processing came possibilities never before possible. Prior to OLTP, computation was done in terms of reports, batched transactions, and overnight processing. The length of time it took to conclude a transaction limited the usage of the computer in the business. In those days, accounts payable, accounts receivable, and human resources were the primary applications that a shop had automated. But with online transaction processing, it became possible to use the computer in ways intimately tied to the business.

With OLTP (where there is consistent two- to three-second response time), applications such as bank-teller processing, airline-reservation processing, insurance-claims processing, telecommunications operator assistance, and so forth became the norm. For the first time, the computer became one of the cornerstones of business. When the computer was interrupted, of course, business immediately felt the stoppage.

With online systems, the computer became an essential part of business. And businesses everywhere began to use the computer in ways never before imagined.

In fact, applications — batch and online — became so pervasive that soon they were everywhere. And with this explosive growth in applications came some unforeseen and unanticipated problems. Soon the problem of *unintegrated data* reared its ugly head. Unintegrated data occurred because with so many applications, the same unit of data was found in many places. The problem was that, in each place, the unit of data had a different value. In some ways, this was worse than having no data at all. The organization was confused, the customers were confused, and decisions were based on factors other than data and information — a dangerous way to make decisions.

The applications were known as "spider web systems." The applications and the data inside them were tied together in a structure reminiscent of a spider web.

In many ways, the unintegrated data found in the spider-web environment was more insidious than other challenges that the IT community had met. Prior to the spider-web environment, when a problem occurred, there was always a new technological advance to bail everyone out. But no such easy technological fix existed when it came to solving the spider-web problem. For the first time, an architectural solution was needed.

Extract Files Appear

The first reaction to the challenge of not having corporate data was to create an *extract file*. An extract file would be created by a database from one application and shipped to another application, so it seemed that data could be shared and corporate data could be created. Extracts became very popular, and soon there were a lot of them. Every new extraction exacerbated the problems of the spider web. Adding extractions made matters worse, not better. The problems of the spider web included the following:

- **Data integrity** — The same element of data appeared in many places. In one place, the element had a value of 25. In another place, the element had a value of 67. In still another place, the element had a value of 135. No one really knew what the right value was.

- **Data redundancy** — The sheer redundancy of data was enormous. The same data was shuffled from one place to the next; the burden of massive amounts of data being repeated over and over began to add up to significant amounts of storage and processing power.

- **Timeliness of data** — While shuffled around the system, data was aging. In one day, the value of a unit of data may change five or six times. The extract processing simply was not capable of keeping up with the speed with which data changed.

- **Multiple *silo* of data were created** — A *silo system* is not easily integrated with other systems. The use of the term comes from the cylindrical towers found in Middle America, where corn or feed is stored in an air-tight manner. Many versions of the same data exist in various silos, which violates the idea of a single "truth." Silos are sometimes also referred to as *data islands* or *stovepipe applications*. Each silo was its own operating domain with no coordination or integration with outside silos. One part of the organization found itself making decisions contrary to the interest of other parts of the organization.

- **The extract processing froze an already moribund system** — Online transaction applications were difficult to change in any case. But wrapping lines of extraction around the online applications glued those applications into a permanent position.

- **Data became much more inaccessible** — The extract processing placed coordination requirements on the environment, which ensured that accurate data was impossible to obtain and so forth.

Of particular interest is the lack of historical data. Online applications value current data. How much is a bank account balance right now? Where is a shipment right now? What is the status of an insurance claim right now? Online applications optimize the "right now" aspect of information processing. As soon as data became dated, it was discarded. Lots of historical data clogged the arteries of efficient online processing. Therefore, online data and processing required that older data be jettisoned as soon as possible.

But there is real value in historical data. With historical data, organizations can start to see the forest *and* the trees. With historical data, organizations can start to understand their customer base, because customers are creatures of habit.

Because there was no corporate integrated data or historical data, data was difficult to access. Even if accessed, data was not trustworthy, so it is no wonder organizations began to grow frustrated with an inability to find and process information. Department after department would say, "I know the data is somewhere in my corporation; if I could only get at it."

The frustrations of the end user with data locked in the spider-web environment resulted in the realization that there were different kinds of data. There was an essential difference between *operational data* and *informational data*. Table 1-1 outlines those differences.

Table 1-1   Characteristics of Operational versus Data Warehouse Systems

OPERATIONAL	DATA WAREHOUSE/DSS
Modest amount of data	Immodest amount of data
Can be updated	Snapshot records; no updates allowed
Accurate up to the second	Timestamp on each record
Used for clerical purposes	Used by management and analysts
Built based on requirements	Built from data model
Supports small uniform transactions	Supports mixed workload
Yields two- to three-second response time	Yields 30- to 24-hour response time
Data designed for optimal storage	Data designed for optimal access
Very current data	Mainly historical data
Data is application oriented	Data is integrated
Data designed around functional usage	Data designed around subject areas
Referential integrity is useful	Referential integrity is not useful
High availability is normal	High availability is nice to have

A fundamental split exists between *operational information* and *informational information*. Operational information is used to support the daily operations of a business. Informational information is commonly called *decision support system* (DSS) information. The foundation for DSS processing became an architectural structure known as the data warehouse. A *data warehouse* is a place physically distinct from the online operational application. The following sections describe the data warehouse and how it enables analytic information.

The Data Warehouse Is Conceived

The needed solution was a split in database types. Prior to this point, it had been widely held that a database was a place for all processing against the data. But the spider-web problem was so difficult that a new approach to understanding what a database should be was needed. Thus, the data warehouse was born.

And indeed there are many more significant differences between the data warehouse and an operational database.

The advent of a new database type sent the database theoreticians of day into a tailspin. It was once heresy to suggest that there should be anything but one database type for all purposes. But the database theoreticians of the day got over it.

What Is Data Warehousing?

Since the beginning of the movement toward data warehousing, data warehouses have been defined as:

- **Subject oriented** — Data is organized around a major object or process of an organization. Classic examples include subject-area databases for customer, material, vendor, and transaction.

- **Integrated** — Data from various subject areas should be rationalized with one another.

- **Nonvolatile** — Data in a data warehouse is not updated. Once a record is properly placed in the warehouse, it is not subject to change. This contrasts with a record of data in an online environment, which is indeed very much subject to change.

- **Time variant** — A record is accurate only as of some moment in time. In some cases, the moment in time is a single moment. In other cases, it is a span of time. But in any case, the values of data found in a data warehouse are accurate and relevant only to some moment in time.

■ **Decision making** — Data warehouses were created for the purpose of management decisions.

In addition, the data warehouse provides the following:

■ Detailed or granular data

■ Integrated data

■ Historical data

■ Easy-access data

The data warehouse is at the center of the business-intelligence environment. The data warehouse represents the single version of truth for the corporation and holds data at a granular level. In addition, the data warehouse contains a robust amount of historical data. The need for a data warehouse is as true within the confines of SAP as it is outside SAP. And the elements of a data warehouse are as valid for SAP as for the non-SAP environment.

The data warehouse emerges from these requirements and supports the process of moving data from source systems and transforming and cleansing data so that it may be stored in an integrated data model at an atomic level of granularity. Many factors influence the design of a data warehouse and the structure in which data records are stored. The following sections discuss some of these factors.

The Data Model

The design of the data warehouse begins with a *data model*. At the highest level, the data model is known as an *entity relationship diagram* (ERD). The ERD represents the abstraction of the granular data found in the data warehouse. *Granular data* refers to very low-level detailed records. Note that for the purposes of data warehouse design, the ERD represents only granular data, not derived data. *Derived data* is created from other data elements. This distinction is important because it greatly limits the size and complexity of the data model. There are, of course, other data models outside the data warehouse environment that do attempt to take into account derived data and atomic data. Granular data is discussed more a bit later in this chapter.

The ERD consists of entities and relationships. Each entity represents a major subject area of the corporation. Typical subject areas are customer, product, transaction, and vendor. Each entity is further defined at a lower level of data modeling called the *data item set* (DIS). The DIS specifies a lower level of detail than the entity does, encompassing such things as keys and attributes, as well as the structure of those things. The DIS is further broken down into a low level of design called the *physical design*. At the physical level of design, the physical characteristics of the data are created.

The data warehouse is now specified and defined to the database management system (DBMS) that will house it. Other physical aspects of database design (such as partitioning, loading, indexing, storage media, and timestamping) are determined here as well. Figure 1-1 shows the design of the data warehouse from the different components of the data model.

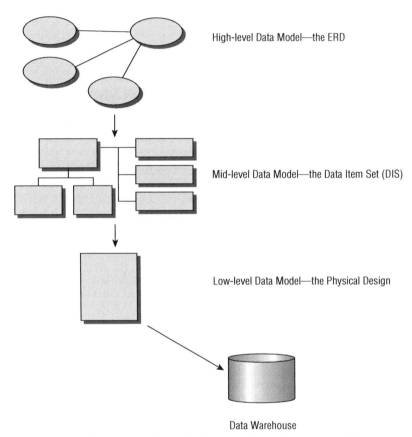

High-level Data Model—the ERD

Mid-level Data Model—the Data Item Set (DIS)

Low-level Data Model—the Physical Design

Data Warehouse

Figure 1-1   The data warehouse is designed from the data model

Different Physical Tables

The data warehouse is made up of interrelated tables or physical databases. Within the data warehouse, different physical tables represent different subject areas or even subsets of subject areas. One table relates to another by means of a shared-key or foreign-key relationship. The data warehouse typically has several areas, including the following:

- Customer
- Product

- Shipment
- Vendor
- Order

Each subject area resides on a separate physical table or database. Collectively, the different tables along with their relationships form a data warehouse.

Integration and Transformation Processing

One of the most important and most difficult aspects of data warehouse development and population is the movement and conversion of data from the operational/legacy source environment. It is estimated that for the first iteration of development, at least 75 percent of the resources required for development will be expended here. During extraction, data is pulled from the legacy environment and moved into the data warehouse environment. This data is pulled from a variety of sources, such as mainframe order-entry systems, proprietary shop flow-control systems, and custom-built payroll systems.

But data is not merely moved from the legacy environment to the data warehouse environment. Instead, data undergoes a thorough transformation as it is moved, including:

- Converting data into a common format
- Reformatting data
- Realigning encoded values
- Restructuring data
- Assigning default values
- Summarizing
- Resequencing
- Converting keys
- Converting from one DBMS to another
- Converting from one operating system to another
- Converting from one hardware architecture to another
- Merging different record types
- Creating metadata that describes the activities of conversion
- Editing data
- Adding a timestamp

Metadata

One of the essential aspects of the data warehouse is metadata. *Metadata* is information about the contents of what has come to be termed the corporate information factory (CIF). Every application has its own metadata, which is distributed across the entire landscape of architectural components. Metadata has two functions:

- To describe data found in the architectural component
- To exchange metadata with other components

Metadata in the data warehouse plays several roles. One role is describing what data resides where for normal usage. It also acts as a coordinator between different services from extract/transfer/load (ETL) software to information access. (ETL is discussed in more detail later in this chapter in the section titled "Extraction Transformation Loading.") The services of the architecture have very different foundations and functions. Some serve under one DBMS, others under another DBMS. Some services operate under one type of multidimensional technology, and other services operate under other multidimensional technologies. And each service has a very different function. For the services to operate in unison, there must be coordination from one service to the next. Coordination is achieved through metadata being passed from one architectural layer to another.

There are distinctly different kinds of metadata, including the following:

- **Technical metadata** — This describes the structure and content of the different types of data. This type of data has been housed in data dictionaries and repositories for a long time.

- **Operating metadata** — This represents the metrics generated by the day-to-day operation of the data warehouse. Metrics such as records passed from one software component to another, length of operation of a program, number of records in a database, and so forth make up operating metadata.

- **Business metadata** — This is couched in terms that the businessperson understands. Business definitions, business formulae, and business conditions all make up business metadata.

All three types of metadata are needed for controlling the operation of a data warehouse.

One concern is the metadata's integrity. To maintain control and believability of metadata when it is distributed across many different components, a certain protocol is necessary. To maintain integrity of metadata across a distributed environment, each unit of metadata must be unique and have one owner. The owner of the metadata is the only person or organization that has the right to update, create, and delete a unit of metadata. Everyone else becomes a sharer of the metadata. As metadata is passed from one node to the next, a careful track of ownership must be kept.

Granular Data

Data found in a data warehouse is very *granular*. This means that data is placed in the data warehouse at a very low level of detail. Data may then be reshaped by an application so that it can be viewed in a distinct manner.

Sometimes called the *atomic data* of the corporation, granular data makes up the "single version of truth" that is at the basis of reconciliation for informational processing. Having granular data at the core of the data warehouse provides many benefits. A primary advantage is that the same data can be viewed in different ways. Figure 1-2 shows that marketing looks at data one way, sales looks at it another way, and finance yet another way. But all three departments have a single source of reconcilability.

Usually, each grain of information in the data warehouse represents some finite unit of measure or business activity for the corporation. For example, a grain of information might represent details of the following:

- **A sale** — The amount, the date, the item sold, the location of the sale, or the customer
- **An order** — The date of the order, the product ordered, or the amount of the order
- **A telephone call** — The time of the call, the length of the call, the calling party, or the person called
- **A delivery of a product** — The date of the delivery, the location of the delivery, or the person making the delivery

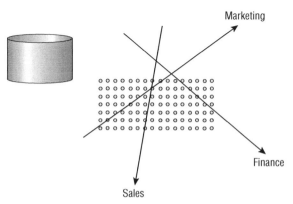

Figure 1-2 Granular data allows the same data to be examined in different ways

Each grain of information can be combined with other grains to provide a different perspective of data.

In addition to allowing data to be viewed differently by different parties, another benefit is that granular data may lie in wait in the data warehouse for unknown and future requirements. Then, when a requirement becomes known, granular data can be shaped immediately to suit the new requirements. There is no need to go to the operational/legacy environment and pull data out. This means that the data warehouse puts the corporation in a proactive rather than reactive position for new needs for information.

Historical Data

One of the most important characteristics of a data warehouse is that it contains a robust amount of *historical data*. Figure 1-3 shows a data warehouse that contains five years of history. Such an amount of history is typical. However, some data warehouses may contain even more historical data, and other data warehouses may contain less data, depending on the business needs of the corporation.

| 2006 | 2005 | 2004 | 2003 | 2002 |

Figure 1-3 The data warehouse contains robust amounts of historical data

Although historical data has many applications, perhaps the most potent is the ability to step backward in time and perform what-if analysis. Doing so allows you to gain insights that cannot be achieved any other way.

Timestamping

The units of data stored inside the data warehouse are *timestamped* so that each unit of data has some element of time associated with the record. The time-stamping of data-warehouse data signifies that the unit of data is accurate as of the timestamp.

In general, there are two ways that a record is stored in the data warehouse: discretely or continuously (see Figure 1-4). In a *discrete record*, there is one instant in time for which the record is accurate. In a *continuous record*, there is a span of time for which the record is accurate. These records form a larger definition of information over time.

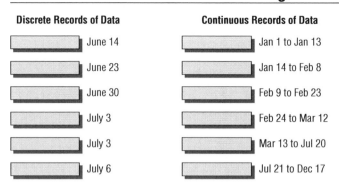

Discrete Records of Data		Continuous Records of Data	
	June 14		Jan 1 to Jan 13
	June 23		Jan 14 to Feb 8
	June 30		Feb 9 to Feb 23
	July 3		Feb 24 to Mar 12
	July 3		Mar 13 to Jul 20
	July 6		Jul 21 to Dec 17

Figure 1-4   Timestamped records are either continuous or discrete

Usually, discrete records are used for a large number of fast-changing variables. Continuous timestamps are used for a small number of variables that change slowly and for which there is value in knowing information over time.

Data Relationships

The different types of data found in the data warehouse relate to each other by means of *foreign keys* pointing to *actual keys*. For example, suppose customer ABC places an order. There would be a customer record for customer ABC, as well as a separate order record for the order. The order record, in its body, would have a foreign-key reference to customer ABC.

Data relationships found in the data warehouse are special in that they are delimited by time. When a relationship is indicated in the data warehouse, the relationship is intended to be valid only for the moment in time indicated by the timestamps found on participating records. This interpretation of a relationship is quite different from that found in the online environment. Online environments enforce *referential integrity* (where the values of one data set are dependent on the existence of a value or values in another data set).

Generic Data versus Specific Data

One design issue that arises in every data warehouse is how to account for generic data and specific data at the same time. *Generic data* applies to all instances of a subject area. *Specific data* applies only to certain occurrences of a subject area.

The generic database stores customer information along with related tables, including a wholesale customer table, a European customer table, a long-term customer table, and a preferred customer table. Each of the outlying tables contains information specific to the class of tables that meet the criteria. For example, a preferred wholesale customer would have data in the generic customer table, in the preferred customer table, and in the wholesale customer table.

In such a manner, data of different types can be represented efficiently in a data warehouse.

Data Quality

Data quality is an important issue for the data warehouse environment. As shown in Figure 1-5, data quality is addressed in three places:

1. At the point of data entry to the legacy/operational environment
2. At the point of ETL processing
3. Once the data resides inside the data warehouse itself

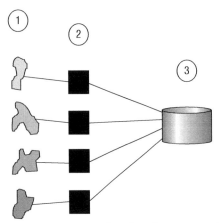

Figure 1-5 Base data for all customers is kept in one table; specific data for different types of customers is kept in separate, unique tables

For example, raw data entry is addressed inside the legacy/operational environment. The problem is that the budget for doing tasks such as mainte-nance here has long gone away. In addition, no shop is eager to go poking around old, fragile, undocumented legacy applications, lest something unto-ward and unexpected happens. Therefore, not much data-quality activity occurs in the legacy/operational environment. The adoption of ERP systems has greatly improved data quality at the time of data entry.

Most data-quality activity occurs at the moment of ETL, which does not require that older applications be manipulated or touched in any way. Data that comes out of the legacy application can be isolated. And data coming from different applications can be integrated. Data is in transit in any case, so this becomes an ideal place in which to examine and audit it and to make changes if needed.

The third place where data quality can be applied is once the data has arrived in the data warehouse. Over time, data changes, and what was accurate and proper one year is not accurate and proper the next. So even if the data is loaded perfectly into the data warehouse, there still is a need for periodic adjustment of data based on changes in business conditions that have occurred over time.

Volumes of Data

The volume of data grows beyond any expectations in a data warehouse. Once terabyte (about 1,000 gigabytes or GB) data warehouses were a dream; today they are a reality. In fact, it is not unheard of to build petabyte (about 1 million GB) data warehouses.

As data volumes grow large, approaches to their management change. One of the most important characteristics of a data warehouse's growth is the appearance of *dormant data* that just sits there taking up space and costing money. When the data warehouse was small, all or nearly all of the data that resided in it was used. But as the data warehouse grows large, increasingly large amounts of data reside in the warehouse in an unused state.

When a data warehouse is around the 100 GB range, there may be only 10 to 20 percent dormant data. But as a data warehouse approaches a terabyte, it is not unusual for the dormancy ratio to increase to 50 to 75 percent. And, as a data warehouse goes beyond several terabytes, the amount of dormant data frequently approaches 90 to 99 percent.

It is wasteful for a corporation to continue to increase the size of a data warehouse when the proportion of dormant data increases as well. In addition, increasing the size of a data warehouse when there is much dormant data grossly hurts performance.

Removing Dormant Data

Dormant data must be periodically removed from disk storage and placed on another media. Active data is placed on disk storage and is managed and accessed in a normal manner, while inactive data is placed in a physically separate facility, sometimes called *alternate storage* or *near-line storage*. (Near-line storage is discussed in detail later in this chapter.) This causes the cost of the data warehouse to drop dramatically and the speed with which data can be accessed to increase.

To make the marriage between dormant data and actively used data residing on disk work well, a technology called a *cross-media storage manager* (CMSM) may be utilized. The CMSM sits between disk storage and alternate storage and manages the traffic between the two environments so that the end user is presented with a seamless view of the data residing in the data warehouse.

Architected Solutions

The data warehouse concept was just the beginning of the split between operational and informational databases. Soon there were all sorts of other database types. There were personal computer databases. There were Online Analytic Processing (OLAP) multidimensional databases. There were customer databases gleaned from national marketing and sales efforts. There were statistical databases. And with these new database types came all sorts of other applications and uses of data. There were *data marts,* which were statistical databases such as *exploration* and *data mining warehouses.* There was a hybrid structure known as an *operational data store* (ODS). There were adaptive data marts. There were change data capture files. There were Web databases full of click-stream data.

> **NOTE** Data marts, ODS, and exploration warehouses are all discussed in detail later in this chapter.

In a few short years, there was a bonanza of data, architecture types, and new and innovative applications. And with this bonanza came new users — users who in an earlier day and age had been neglected and whose information needs had not been served. There became a real need for tying together all of these different forms of data. Into the arena came the corporate information factory (CIF).

Corporate Information Factory

The CIF was an architecture that weaved together the many different architectural components. The CIF accounted for the many information needs of the organization. The CIF is widely used by vendors and corporate IT shops alike to describe how the different components of architecture fit together. Figure 1-6 shows the progression from the earliest technologies to the CIF.

The CIF is a long-term architectural blueprint for business intelligence. Like any good blueprint for the future, there will be features not be needed now but perhaps needed at some point in the future. Whether or not you use all of the features, there is a certain comfort in knowing that those features are integrated should you need them. The CIF is not static. Every three or four years, different components are added to the CIF, as technology and common business use warrant.

But there are other advantages to having a full architecture laid out, such as that specified by the CIF. One advantage of an architecture is to see how other people who have gone before you have solved the same problems that you are facing. Nothing is worse than feeling as though you are facing problems that no one has ever encountered. (Rarely is that the case.) There is a certain comfort in knowing that someone, somewhere, has faced the same problem and has found a solution. Even though the issues are still in front of you, the fact that you are not facing a unique and insurmountable problem is of some comfort.

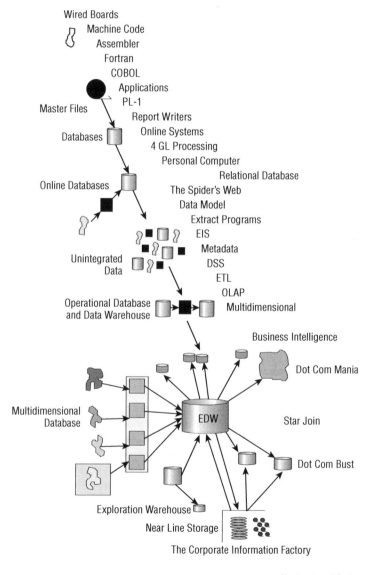

Figure 1-6 From paper tape to the CIF

And a blueprint can do just that. You look at the blueprint, you see where other people have addressed the same problem, and you don't feel quite so alone. Another use of a blueprint is that it helps you plan. The blueprint allows you to see all that is in front of you and to make a rational decision as to the order that architectural components should be addressed. Blueprints, then, are a very useful planning tool. Figure 1-7 shows a blueprint and the CIF architecture.

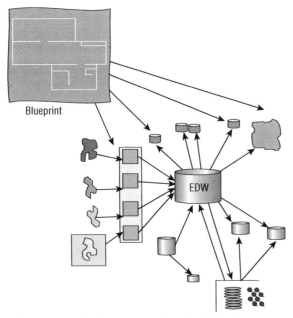

Figure 1-7   The long-term value of a blueprint

Enterprise Data Warehouse

At the heart of the CIF architecture that has been described is the data warehouse (sometimes called the *enterprise data warehouse* or the EDW). The data warehouse acts — in many ways — like a terminal (such as Grand Central Station). In a terminal, data arrives, is stationed there for a while, and eventually moves on to its ultimate destination. Unlike a terminal, in which a person has a single destination, data in a data warehouse has multiple destinations.

For example, a woman sitting in Grand Central Station wants to go to New Haven, CT. If she is going to New Haven, she is not also going to Baltimore, MD, at the same time. But a unit of data in the data warehouse does not have the same restrictions. A unit of data sitting in the data warehouse may have as its ultimate destination two data marts, an exploration warehouse, and near-line storage all at the same time.

As previously described, data in the data warehouse is at the lowest level of granularity. This low level of granularity is the most important factor to the success of the data warehouse. With data at a low level of granularity, many different forms of data can be created. One person can summarize data by the day, another by the week, and another by the month. One person can look at data by sales region, another by product, and another by package. When data is at a low level of granularity, it can be shaped and reshaped many ways. The fact that the information entering the EDW is transformed into an integrated data set means that lots of people may look at the same data in lots of ways.

Not only can integrated, granular data serve today's need for data, but integrated, granular data can serve future, unknown needs. With a body of integrated, granular data available, the business analyst is prepared for tomorrow's needs for information, even though tomorrow's needs have not been articulated.

An EDW contains a lot of historical data. Unlike almost anywhere else in the IT environment, historical data is welcomed in the data warehouse. Consider historical data and the OLTP environment. The OLTP environment centers on performance during the inserting and updating of records. And one of the most basic ways that OLTP developers achieve performance is to remove historical data from the transaction-processing environment. Historical data acts like cholesterol in slowing high performance. For these reasons, the OLTP systems programmer typically jettisons historical data as fast as possible. But in the data warehouse, historical data is welcomed. Two years, three years, or even ten years of historical data can be found in a data warehouse.

Extraction Transformation Loading

It is important to remember that in the beginning there was just the data warehouse. The data warehouse by itself was a significant accomplishment. But it was very quickly recognized that the data warehouse was difficult to build because there was no way to create the interface programs between the legacy environment and the data warehouse, other than to write them by hand. But with the innovation of extract/transfer/load (ETL) software, which automatically creates the interfaces needed to bring data into the data warehouse, the floodgates for the building of data warehouses were opened.

One of the real benefits of ETL processing is that data enters the ETL process in a specific application mode and exits in an integrated enterprise mode. The processing that occurs inside ETL software allows data to be integrated and metadata about the transformations to be cataloged.

Operational Data Store

After the data warehouse was built, another type of architectural structure was needed — the ODS.

> **NOTE** The operational data store (ODS) is a hybrid structure that has characteristics of both the data warehouse and operational systems. Because the ODS is a hybrid structure, it is difficult to build and operate. The ODS allows the user to have OLTP response time (two to three seconds), update capabilities, and DSS capabilities.

In truth, not all organizations needed an ODS. If an organization had a need for integrated operational processing, or if the organization needed online transaction response time for access to integrated data, there was a need for an ODS.

Other architectural entities began to appear. One of those entities was the *virtual operational data store* (VODS). The VODS was a temporary structure where data from a variety of sources was pulled together to form an analysis. The VODS is very inexpensive to construct, and with the right technology, the VODS can be constructed very quickly. However, the VODS provides only a fleeting glimpse of data. If a VODS report is constructed at 11:43 A.M., the analysis is valid only for that moment. In other words, if the same analysis is constructed at 12:03 P.M., the organization could not expect to get the same results, since the underlying data may have changed between 11:42 A.M. and 12:03 P.M. Chapters 4 and 5 discuss the various classes of ODS in greater detail.

Data Marts

Shortly after the ODS was discovered, data marts came into being. A *data mart* is a departmental manifestation of the data warehouse. While the data warehouse was built for the entire enterprise, the data mart is built for one group of like-minded users (such as the finance department, the sales department, the marketing department, and so forth). The data mart collected data from the data warehouse and reshaped the data to create a form and structure of data applicable to the department that uses it. Data marts made widespread usage of multidimensional technology, which happened to fit the needs of data-mart processing.

In addition, *adaptive project marts* (sometimes called *adaptive data marts*) began to appear. An adaptive project mart was a highly flexible temporary structure. The difference between a data mart and an adaptive project mart is that once built, a data mart becomes a permanent structure, while an adaptive project mart is never a permanent structure. The adaptive project mart can evolve into a full-fledged data mart over time, but it is not the nature of an adaptive project mart to become a permanent structure.

Hub and Spoke

The architecture that resulted from the adoption of data marts was called *hub-and-spoke architecture.* Similar to the flight plans and strategies used by the commercial airline industry where a city acts as the hub and enables connections to various destinations through routes, the data warehouse sits at the hub, and various analytic applications and data marts act as destinations. The process of delivering information to the destinations is analogous to the routes or spokes.

Exploration Warehouse

The next structure added to the CIF was the *exploration warehouse* or *data mining warehouse*. The exploration warehouse is a place where data miners or exploration analysts go to do statistical analysis of data or to create hypotheses and assertions. By isolating the statisticians from the data warehouse, several benefits accrued.

First, there was no performance conflict between the statistician and the normal user of the warehouse. Second, on occasion, the exploration analyst performed heuristic processing. There may have been a need to "shut off" the flow of fresh data to verify the results of changing an algorithm. By having a separate warehouse, the analyst could "shut off" new data from the statistical-analysis environment.

Near-Line Storage

As data warehouses grew, they started to exhibit some characteristics not previously seen. With the growth in data volume, the data inside the data warehouse divided itself into one of two classes: *frequently used data* and *infrequently used data*. In fact, in most large data warehouses, far less data was being used than was not being used. It made no sense to keep unused data in expensive, high-performance storage. A new architectural component started to grow out of the desire to optimize storage investments. The component is referred to as *near-line storage*.

Near-line storage is not the same physical storage type as disk storage. Typically, near-line storage is sequential storage controlled by robots. Near-line storage is suitable for storing large, bulky data that does not need to be updated, because it is only accessed infrequently. This description of near-line data fits perfectly with the need to store infrequently accessed data from a data warehouse. In many ways, the near-line storage component becomes a form of "overflow" storage for the data warehouse.

Government Information Factory

On September 11, 2001, the world changed. One of the many changes that occurred that day was the awareness that government information systems needed to be altered. Prior to September 11, government information systems were typified by what can be called *stovepipe systems*. Stovepipe systems are individual and do not share data. One agency gets one piece of data, another agency gets another piece of data, and yet another agency gets another piece of data. And there is no way to piece all this data together to form a useful and meaningful picture.

The events of September 11 proved to the government and the public in general the weakness of stovepipe information systems.

Unfortunately, correcting the difficulties of stovepipe systems is a hard task. Correcting stovepipe systems requires not a new technology, not a new methodology, and not a rebuilding of systems. To solve the problems of stovepipe systems, there must be a change in architecture and a change in basic attitudes of the agencies collecting and using data. Without both of these changes, there can be no victory over the tyranny of stovepipe systems.

From an architectural standpoint, the CIF evolved into the *government information factory* (GIF) as a result of the events of September 11. Figure 1-8 shows the evolution from the CIF to the GIF.

The GIF in many ways is similar to the CIF. Indeed, about 60 percent of the architecture is the same. But there are some interesting and significant differences between the GIF and the CIF, as explained in the following sections.

Integration Among Agencies

The GIF requires integration among agencies; the CIF does not require the same level of integration.

To see how the CIF is different, consider a commercial data warehouse. Chevron builds a data warehouse for its own purposes. Chevron does not build a data warehouse to share data with Bank of America. Chrysler builds a data warehouse to suit its own information needs. Chrysler does not build a data warehouse to share information with Burlington Northern. Citicorp builds a data warehouse for its information needs. Citicorp does not build a data warehouse to share information with Pepsi Cola and so forth.

In the commercial world, data warehouses are built to suit the needs of the entity that owns the data. This is not so in government. If the government is ever to break out of the mold of stovepipe systems, there *must* be true sharing of data among agencies. This means that the FBI must share data with the CIA; the Immigration and Naturalization Service (INS) must share data with the Internal Revenue Service (IRS); the Health Care Finance Administration (HCFA) must share data with the Social Security Administration (SSA) and so forth.

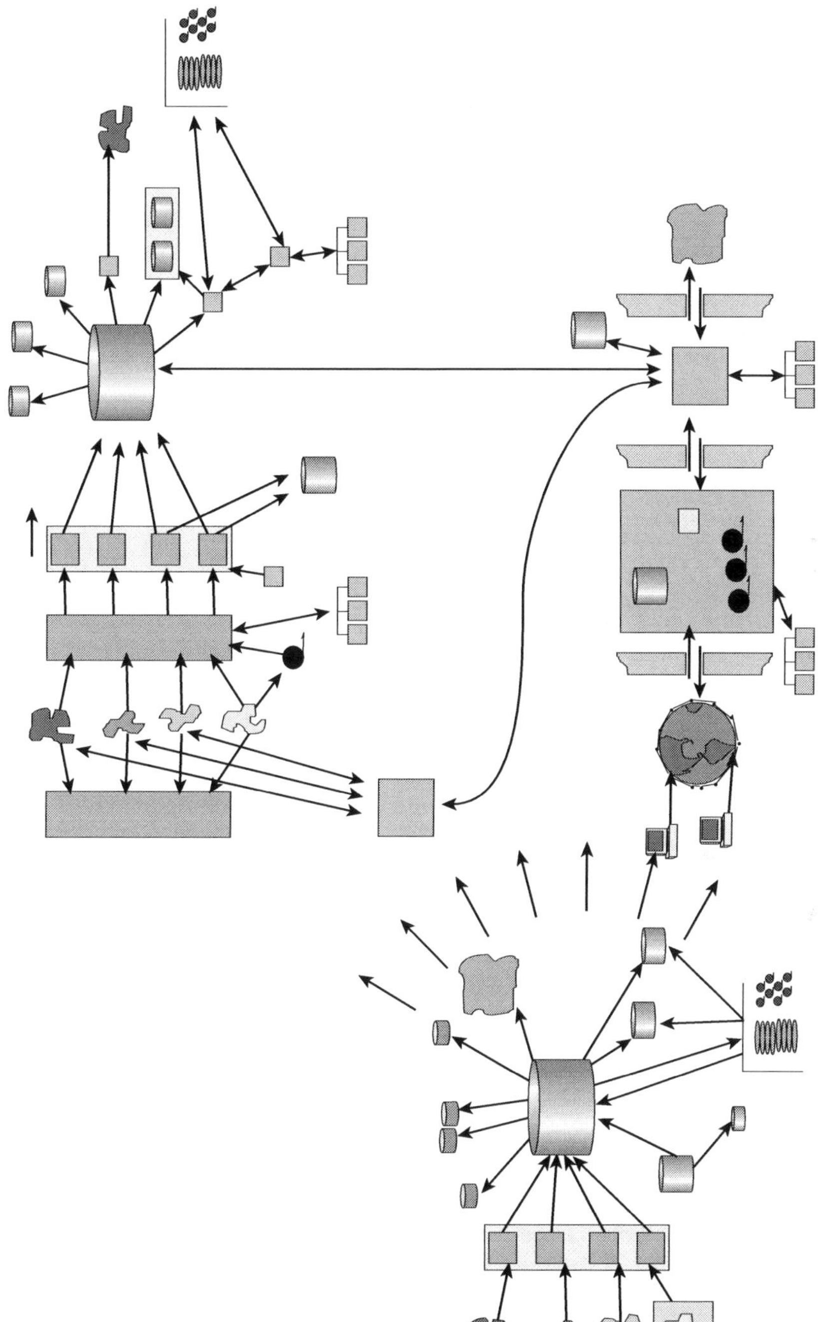

Figure 1-8 From the CIF to the GIF

The mentality of sharing data across agencies is required to remedy the stovepipe attitude. And the architecture that supports that sharing is a big part of the picture. For these reasons, then, the GIF is significantly different from the CIF, because the CIF assumes no agency-wide sharing of data.

Security

The CIF calls for security. But in truth security in the CIF environment is almost an afterthought. In the GIF, however, security is paramount.

In the world of the CIF, if security is breached, someone loses money. But in the world of the GIF, if security is breached, someone may die. So there is a significant difference between emphasis on security in the two environments.

For example, both active and passive security are found in the GIF. *Active security* is designed to keep someone from having unauthorized access to certain data. *Passive security* is not designed to stop anyone from doing anything. Instead, passive security keeps track of what has been done, should there be an unauthorized access of data. And security is found at many places in many forms in the GIF environment,

Longevity of Data

Data lives longer in the government environment than in the commercial environment. For this reason, bulk-data management, near-line storage, and archival processing all have a very important role in the GIF.

Evolution of SAP

The CIF represents the progression of thought and development that occurred with informational processing. This progression occurred in the same timeframe that SAP and Enterprise Resource Planning (ERP) were developing and maturing. It was inevitable that the worlds of SAP/ERP and data warehouse/corporate information factory would merge.

From the standpoint of timing, the CIF was intellectually articulated before SAP Business Information Warehouse (SAP BW) became available. However, this fact hardly means that the business world went out and built the CIF immediately. Yet, that SAP BW followed the intellectual establishment of the CIF in no way diminishes or tarnishes the value of the SAP BW product. Indeed, SAP BW provides an easy path to the actualization of the CIF for many organizations.

In many ways, the CIF is like a city plan. A city plan takes years and decades to develop. In the case of grand cities built from a plan (such as Washington,

D.C.), it may take decades for the city plan to be realized. Thus it is with the CIF. The CIF is a blueprint and, as such, may require many years for implementation. The CIF in a robust state is illustrated in Figure 1-9.

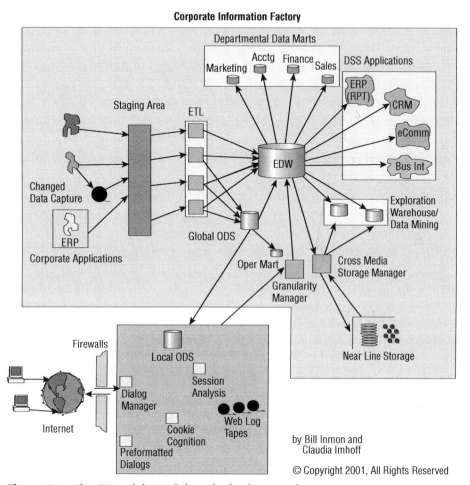

Figure 1-9 The CIF and the Web-based e-business environment

The progression of SAP started with the early vestiges of R/2, the mainframe predecessor to its client/server brother SAP R/3. What made SAP so enormously successful and set it on the road to dominating the ERP market? Was it the support of complex business processes without writing specific application code for each variation of a business process? Was it the technological advancements of so-called lock objects? Was it SAP's heavy investment in its proprietary Advanced Business Application Programming (ABAP) language? Was it the partnering with the big consulting firms? Was it business-process reengineering or Y2K? Perhaps it was the elimination of the cap on the commissions that SAP sales people could earn. Whatever the reason, today the letters SAP are synonymous with Enterprise Resource Planning (ERP), and there are many indications that SAP will also become synonymous with business intelligence (BI).

SAP and ERP have developed from early applications that ran financial transactions to a complete solutions set serving the needs of entire vertical markets. More recently, SAP extended the product line to e-business, customer relationship management, supply chain management, and enterprise portals.

NOTE SAP markets solutions that contain components. For example, the mySAP Business Suite consists of the MySAP ERP, MySAP CRM, and NetWeaver, which includes the business-intelligence capabilities discussed throughout this book.

The advent of SAP occurred over a three-decade period. Movement was afoot for organizations to build a solid applications base well before the year 2000, but there is no question that the challenges to the world of information technology posed by the turn of the century gave impetus to the need for revamping the enterprise software applications. Many organizations decided to completely replace their legacy applications, rather than go back into older applications and refurbish them to handle the year-2000 problem. But there were problems with the older applications other than those posed by the year-2000 dilemma. Some of the problems included the following:

- **Older applications had long ago ceased to be documented** — No one knew what the application really did or how it worked.

- **The applications were brittle and fragile** — Corporations were afraid to go into an application and make changes unless something completely unexpected and unrelated happened.

- **The applications were written in older technology** — Applications were designed to store data efficiently, rather than in an easily accessible way. Consequently, data was hard to get to.

- **The applications were not integrated** — Often acquired by merger, purchase, or other means, older legacy applications were never designed to run in an integrated manner.

- **The staff that built the older legacy applications left** — This means that no one has the knowledge or skills to update older legacy applications.

ERP applications promised not only to be the panacea for Y2K and business-process reengineering, but they also promised to provide an integrated view of a corporation's information. Once the ERP solution was implemented, however, organizations discovered that solving the problems of transaction processing was different from solving the problems of informational processing. In truth, this was the same discovery that had been made previously by the non-ERP community, the result of which was the advent of data warehousing.

There still was the need for information in the face of a successful ERP implementation. Once the ERP environment was created, the corporation asked, "Where's my information?" It simply wasn't there or could not be accessed.

Why is there a need for information in the ERP environment even when there is a solid application foundation? There are several reasons:

- ERP applications are not designed to store history. Applications store current information, and many powerful forms of analysis need history.

- ERP applications create an integrated environment when *all* the applications are under the ERP umbrella. But often only some of the applications are ERP based. In this case, there is still a need for integration.

- The technology optimal for running ERP processing is optimized on the efficient running of transactions. Informational processing does not run well on this kind of technology (that is, predictable processes are found in the transaction-processing world, while unpredictable requests are made in the analysis world).

- ERP applications often have thousands of tables collecting data in a highly normalized schema that may be difficult to access and to make available to the informational analyst.

- ERP applications require their own processing windows. These processing requirements are often for real-time information, while informational processing may tolerate latency.

There are a host of reasons why a need still exists for informational processing even after a successful implementation of ERP. One of the more common questions we are asked by data-warehousing savvy professionals is this: "Why did SAP create a data warehouse and business intelligence toolset when there are several vendors with mature tools in the marketplace with whom they could have partnered?" The answer is really quite simple when you look at SAP's history of development in the areas of reporting and analysis and data management. It already had several years of experience developing such tools as part of SAP R/3. A brief look back to the origins of SAP reporting and analysis may shed some light on the decision-making process.

Evolution of SAP Reporting and Analysis

The first approach taken by SAP was to make reports easier to obtain. SAP accomplished this by creating an information systems layer within the SAP R/3 product. The information systems layer was built directly in the SAP R/3 in releases as early as 2.0. The information systems layer differed throughout the different application areas in the SAP R/3 product. For example, the Logistics Information System (LIS) had its own set of information access tools called standard and flexible analysis, whereas the Human Resources Information System (HRIS) had its own set of query tools. Each of these tools was developed by its respective development team. While this leveraged the deep domain expertise of application developers, it created challenges for implementing organizations.

The first challenge was that the different information systems needed to be configured in totally different ways. Where the LIS utilized InfoStructures, Communication Structures, and Copy Methods, the HRIS utilized Infotypes, Logical Databases, and ABAP Queries. These configuration and administration differences created a need for specialists to configure the information systems, because the data structures and update mechanisms varied widely.

The second challenge was for information consumers or end users. End users were forced to learn different tools for accessing information depending on the application area the information was originally processed in. In many cases, seemingly simple cross-application reporting requirements were satisfied only by creating multiple reports or custom-written ABAP programs. These differences caused a tremendous amount of frustration and waste because end users were requesting information that crossed modules. A seemingly simple request to view purchase orders' line items with accounts payable to a vendor would more than likely be satisfied with two different reporting tools.

Figure 1-10 Legacy-reporting environment

Source: Hashmi, Naeem, *Business Information Warehouse for SAP* (Prima Tech 2000, ISBN 0-7615-2335-9)

The original development work that had been done in SAP R/3 in the online analytic processing (OLAP) area was originally called a *research processor*. In the early 1990s, the tool was used initially by the *Controlling Profitability Analysis* (CO-PA) development team as a means of reporting profitability across numerous dimensions by allowing the end user to interactively navigate through a virtual cube of aggregated data. This tool is found in SAP R/3 and is referred to as *Drill-Down Reporting*. The customer demand for multidimensional analysis caused the different development departments to start to adopt the Drill-Down Reporting tool in other aspects of SAP R/3.

SAP found itself with a handful of very powerful analytic tools developed in the SAP R/3 application, a dissatisfied customer base hungry for information processing, a thriving partner ecosystem consisting of vendors of maturing business-intelligence tools, and a fair amount of knowledge on how to architect a separate data-warehousing solution. This combination led to SAP cofounder Hasso Platner's mandate that SAP create a reporting server. Thus, the SAP Business Information Warehouse (SAP BW) was conceived.

SAP BW and the New Dimension Applications

When SAP BW was designed, it may never have been a consideration to use a third-party OLAP engine. More than likely, it was a very quick decision to port the concepts from SAP R/3 to SAP BW and leverage its development experience. Two examples of tools developed years ago as a core part of SAP R/3 that have found their way into SAP BW (not the code but the concepts) are the *Early Warning System* and the *Report-to-Report Interface* (RRI). In highlighting the reuse of R/3 tools, we are not saying that specific code was ported from one product to the next but only that SAP has had many years of experience in business intelligence and OLAP.

The Early Warning System, developed as part of the LIS in SAP R/3, has also found its functionality (not its code) in SAP BW as the reporting agent. Setting thresholds for conditions and exceptions, and announcing the findings to a user or group of users, is by no means a development revelation, but an evolution from R/3. A common use of the reporting agent is monitoring vendor-managed inventory. The quantity of inventory at a customer's location may be the vendor's responsibility to restock. This process may be managed with the assistance of the reporting agent. The vendor in this case would set an alert in SAP BW that is to be evaluated at regular intervals to make certain that when inventory levels of the product reach a reorder amount, the category manager is automatically notified so a replenishment order is shipped.

The RRI and the reporting agent are just two examples of many functions originally developed in R/3. SAP BW is built on the same base technology as SAP R/3: the SAP Web Application Server (WAS). (This technology is examined further in Chapter 2.) SAP has significant experience gained over many years solving business problems with OLAP and data-management technologies that predate SAP BW.

SAP has been developing software according to its city plan, or, as they refer to it, a *solution map*, for the past ten years. Like a city plan, SAP's solution maps do provide the general direction in which SAP is heading with the software releases they are providing. More or less according to plan, SAP has evolved from its enterprise resource planning (ERP) origins into a complete business software solutions company covering areas such as customer-relationship management, supply-chain optimization, and business intelligence. Now, SAP is once again evolving. This time it is leading the change process.

The Road to Business Process Integration

Throughout the past decade, the IT industry has evolved from proprietary technologies and interfaces to open standards that are independent of any one vendor's technical architecture. One of the outcomes of this evolution is known as *Web services*. Web services are programs that perform a function using open standards that enable the application to be self-contained and described. Once deployed, a Web service may be discovered and invoked by other Web services and applications.

For this type of integration to occur, quite a few standards needed to be agreed upon by the software vendors and industry leaders. The following contains a list of common Web-service standards:

- **Hyper Text Transfer Protocol (HTTP)** — Enables the exchange of various file types over the World Wide Web.

- **Extensible Markup Language (XML)** — Provides the structure and semantics for definition, interpretation, validation, and transmission of data.

- **Simple Object Access Protocol (SOAP)** — XML-based framework that describes what is in a message and how to process a given instance of application-defined data types.

- **Universal Description Discovery and Integration (UDDI)** — A directory that provides a standard way of describing Web services and finding already published services.

- **Web Services Description Language (WSDL)** — The language the UDDI directories use to describe how to access a service, as well as the operations the services will perform.

The general acceptance of these standards is only the first step toward dynamically assembled business processes that span trading partners. So-called *Service*

Oriented Architectures (SOAs) have grown out of the ability to provide and consume Web services.

An analogy commonly used to describe the challenge of integrating applications is that of verbal communication. To communicate verbally, people must first have an agreed-upon alphabet. The Web-service standards act as an alphabet. It is clear that more is needed to communicate verbally; for example, words and the definitions of those words must be agreed upon as well.

The software industry has been defining its vocabulary. This vocabulary is commonly referred to as *business objects*. Business objects have a set of characteristics and functions that describe them and their behavior. For example, the Customer object may have characteristics (or attributes) such as Company Name, Address, Credit Limit, and so on. As well, the Customer object supports a set of functions (or methods) such as Create Customer, Display Customer, and so on. The standards for these so-called business objects are primarily driven by vertical industry leaders and their supply-chain business partners. Table 1-2 lists the organizations driving standards for describing business objects by industry.

Table 1-2 Driving Industry Standards

ORGANIZATION	INDUSTRY
1SYNC	Consumer products manufactures and retail
RosettaNet	High-tech manufacturing
CIDX	Chemical
Extensible Business Reporting Language (XBRL)	Accounting (cross industry)
Automotive Industry Action Group (AIAG)	Automotive OEM
Standards for Technology in Automotive Repair (STAR)	Automotive retail
papiNet	Paper
Petroleum Industry Data Exchange (PIDX)	Petroleum
Association for Cooperative Operations Research and Development (ACORD)	Insurance
Health Level Seven (HL7)	Healthcare
SWIFT	Banking

These organizations are not only driving standards for business-object definition but also for business-process standardization. The standardization of business processes and the individual tasks within a business process will provide the quantum leap in productivity for organizations able to effectively manage, monitor, and modify them. Alongside the process of defining standards for processes is the process for defining standards for how to define and invoke tasks within a business process.

As organizations define and publish services that adhere to a common set of technical and semantic standards, the next challenge becomes effectively utilizing these Web services. It is not a trivial problem. Keeping in mind that the goal of exposing these Web services is to be able to flexibly adapt business processes (especially when a business process crosses an enterprise's boundaries and becomes an integral part of a business partner's business process) integrated with business partners, difficult problems emerge.

If we look to a common business process such as canceling a customer order, an ugly set of problems emerge when the individual tasks within the business process "cancel order" are performed by business partners. The canceling of an order would trigger events such as stopping production, purchasing of component parts, crediting the customer's accounts, adjusting the commissions because of the referring channel partner, and so on.

This is where having an Enterprise Services Architecture (ESA) enters the IT landscape. Many times, business processes are not able to be undone by calling a single Web service. Much like drilling a hole into a piece of wood, there is no un-drill function. Granted there are some tasks in business processes that may be one-way in nature, but others are bidirectional and require either synchronous or asynchronous responses, If/Then/Else-style routing, and so on. Organizations may no longer hardwire their business processes and remain competitive. ESA raises the level of intelligence from a SOA in that it enables complete business functions to be managed, monitored, secured, and modified in real-time.

Let's look at the cancel order example a bit further. Some of the tasks in canceling the customer order are fairly straightforward and conform to conventional ERP thinking. Stopping the sales order is integrated into the production planning and purchasing systems within the organization canceling the order.

Now, imagine that the business partners are as forward-looking as we are and they are able to provide sub-assembled components for our production orders. In fact, we automatically send two vendors a component-availability request and await a reply from both vendors. If only one vendor replies to our request, we use that vendor. If both vendors reply, we automatically decide which supplier to use for a customer's order based on a set of business rules that include shipping date and proximity to our customer's desired shipping location. Canceling such an order may require a message to be sent to the supplying vendor. The vendor may (manually or in an automated fashion) check a set of contractual conditions before confirming the cancellation of our purchase order and calculate the appropriate cancellation penalty.

As we describe further in Chapter 2, SAP has evolved into a provider of a business process integration platform that enables an ESA to be actualized on its SAP NetWeaver software. You may be asking yourself what this has to do with business intelligence. Everything. The adoption of ESA in organizations allows for analytics to truly be embedded into business processes and the results of analytic processes to alter the tasks in an instance of a business process. Henry Morris's vision back in the mid-1990s when he coined the term *analytic application* is now bound for ubiquity.

ANALYTIC APPLICATIONS

Dr. Henry Morris of IDC coined the term *analytic application* in 1997 as packaged software that meets three criteria:

1. **Process support:** Packaged application software that structures and automates a group of tasks pertaining to the review and optimization of business operations or the discovery and development of new business.

2. **Separation of function:** The application functions independently of an organization's core transactional applications yet can be dependent on such applications for data and may send results back to these applications.

3. **Time-oriented, integrated data:** The application extracts, transforms, and integrates data from multiple sources, supporting a time-based dimension for analysis of past and future trends.

(Source: IDC Bulletin 1997)

During the past five years, information-based services have become a critical part of business processes in the financial services industry (think fraud protection and anti-money laundering). You could foresee a whole new set of information-based business services being made available as the adoption of ESAs continues.

One not-so-far-fetched example could involve eBay. Imagine you are purchasing a digital camera on eBay. With the entire historical marketplace data that eBay collects on sales of digital cameras, they could train a predictive model to evaluate the probability of a specific digital camera selling for less than the amount you have just entered as your maximum bid. Based on very low probability of the camera auction closing at a lower price, eBay could offer price-protection insurance to bidders. The insurance coverage and premium would scale up and down based on the results of the historically trained model with all its variables (day, time of day, merchandising options, auction closing rates, and so on) and the real-time marketplace data for other cameras currently being offered. Of course, not every camera being auctioned would qualify for price-protection insurance.

This type of real-time adaptability (which auctions qualify for the insurance offer and at what bid prices) could enable the auction site an opportunity to increase revenue, while not upsetting their sellers with ever-increasing posting fees, and increase buyer satisfaction by providing peace of mind that they are not irrationally overbidding.

Summary

In the beginning were simple applications, followed by online applications. Soon a spider web of systems and data was created. With the spider web came many difficulties, such as redundancy of data, lack of integrity, and the inability to make changes.

In parallel it was recognized that there was a fundamental difference between operational data and informational (or DSS) data, requiring a change in architecture. The spider-web environment needed to be split into two kinds of processing: operational processing and informational processing. Operational processing was done out of an ERP system like SAP, and informational processing was done out of a data warehouse, which became the "single version of truth" for the corporation at the most granular level.

Data warehouses — whether from SAP environments or non-SAP environments — share some common elements:

- **Data model** — The ERD determines what the major subject areas are. The data item set determines what the attribution and keys will be.

- **Different physical tables or databases linked by a common key structure** — The different tables are built in an iterative manner. It is patently a mistake to build the data warehouse in an all-at-once manner or a "big bang" approach.

- **ETL processing** — ETL processing accesses legacy/operational data and prepares the data for entry into the data warehouse. ETL processing represents the point of integration for data found in the data warehouse.

- **Granular data** — Granular data can be examined in many ways, and it sits in wait for unknown requirements.

- **Robust history** — Typically, five years' worth of data is found in the data warehouse environment.

The data warehouse sets the stage for the many different forms of business intelligence and is the central component in the CIF. The adoption rate of industry standards is enabling adaptive business processes to be managed at a task level, with analytics and business intelligence being embedded into business processes.

Chapter 2 discusses the components of SAP NetWeaver and examines how it may be used to drive business analytics.

The SAP NetWeaver Integration Platform

This chapter begins with a short explanation of the development path SAP has taken over the years and how it has led to today's SAP NetWeaver BI capabilities. The focus then turns to the two main components of the solution: The Portal and SAP BW. The Portal and its knowledge management (KM) capabilities, along with the SAP BW software components, create a broad foundation for organizations on which to build analytical applications and collaborative business intelligence solutions. The remainder of this book focuses on the options available to those implementing the SAP BW component. However, we must first place the SAP BW into the SAP NetWeaver BI context and set the stage for subsequent chapters.

The Architectural Roots of SAP NetWeaver

SAP was among the first software development companies to fully adopt a multi-tier client/server model (see Figure 2-1) and move away from traditional host-based solutions for business software. This was the beginning of the SAP R/3 success story back in the early 1990s.

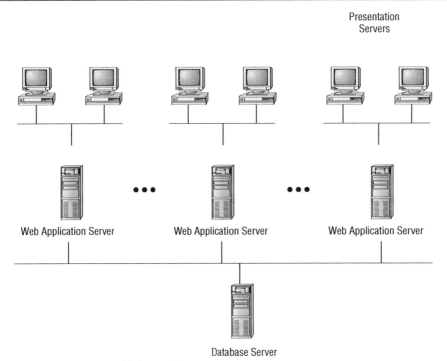

Figure 2-1   SAP multi-tier architecture

To fully utilize the existing mainframe R/2 business applications (to a large extent implemented in the ABAP programming language), SAP had not only to implement a high-performance development and runtime environment but also a lot of tools available on host computers at the time:

- Transaction-based application server concept
- Job scheduling and monitoring tools
- Dynamic UIs
- Secure communication software (a business-driven authorization concept)
- A database abstraction layer

The result of this development process was the SAP Basis software or Basis Component (BC). All SAP application modules, including Financial Accounting (FI), Controlling (CO), and Sales and Distribution (SD), were originally developed using the BC functionality. Additional common functionality such as Application Link Enabling (ALE), Intermediate Documents (IDocs), Business Application Programming Interfaces (BAPIs), the handling of currencies and units of measure, documentation, and translation tools were developed separately and distributed in a separate application component called Cross Application (CA).

The traditional SAP R/3 Basis component allowed you to develop applications using the ABAP programming language and was able to communicate with other systems using a proprietary protocol named *Remote Function Calls* (RFC). During 1999, the mySAP.com platform included Web awareness through the Internet Transaction Server (ITS) for the first time, added XML support through the SAP Business Connector, and allowed for object-oriented software development using ABAP objects.

In the year 2000, the development of the SAP Basis software toward Internet technologies finally resulted in changing the name from SAP Basis Component to *SAP Web Application Server* (WAS). This evolution is shown in Figure 2-2, focusing on the most relevant developments.

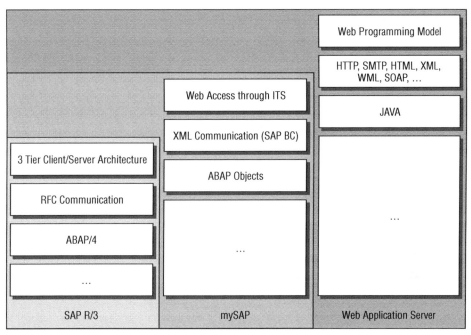

Figure 2-2   Web Application Server evolution

While the ITS and the SAP Business Connector have been separate software systems interfacing with core R/3 functionality, the SAP WAS provided an integrated server platform, fully aware of all relevant protocols and standards (such as HTTP, SMTP, XML, SOAP, and .NET). Around the same time that SAP was developing the ABAP WAS, the InQMy Java application server was quietly acquired by SAP in 2001. It has been the cornerstone of SAP's Java strategy and allows application development using Java, including Enterprise JavaBeans (EJBs), Java 2 Enterprise Edition (J2EE), and Java Server Pages (JSPs). Of course, SAP also allows application development using ABAP in all its flavors (ABAP, ABAP Objects, and Business Server Pages).

During the year 2003, SAP bundled its technology infrastructure along with components to support people, information, and process integration. This bundle was named *SAP NetWeaver Integration Platform* or simply *NetWeaver*. A large portion of this chapter is dedicated to describing the components and services available in NetWeaver. By the completion of this chapter, you should have an understanding of where the SAP Business Information Warehouse (BW) fits into the platform and how it may interact with the other components of the NetWeaver platform.

NetWeaver Overview

SAP has been using the so-called *refrigerator slide* for the past several years to depict the components and services available in SAP NetWeaver. Figure 2-3 will act as our guide for the discussions throughout this chapter.

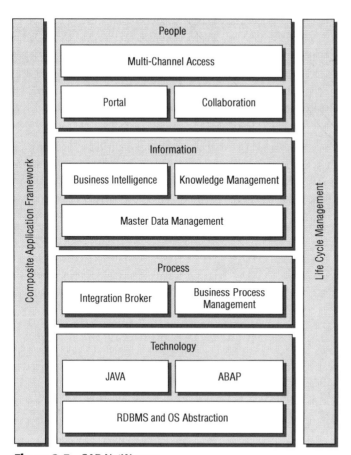

Figure 2-3 SAP NetWeaver

Based on copyrighted material from SAP AG

This chapter looks at the components and services included with NetWeaver, including the following:

- Application Platform (Technology)
- Process Integration
- Information Integration
- People Integration
- Composite Application Framework

Application Platform (Technology)

This section examines the following features of the Application platform:

- Application Server Architecture
- Front-End Technologies
- Mobile Infrastructure
- System Landscape
- Security
- Administration

DEFINITION

A *framework* is an extensible structure for describing a set of concepts, methods, technologies, and cultural changes necessary for a complete product design and manufacturing process. Framework products are most prevalent in the areas of electrical and electronic design. Frameworks provide a mechanism that guides users through a proper order of steps, applications, and data conversions via a common interface to the process being followed.

(**Source:** `http://cedar.web.cern.ch/CEDAR/glossary.html`)

Application Server Architecture

The SAP technology is no longer just a platform for SAP applications. It has now evolved into a serious multipurpose business-application development and runtime environment with its own complex architecture, as shown in Figure 2-4. The technology evolved so much during past releases that it deserved a new name: NetWeaver. You will see us using NetWeaver and NetWeaver AS (Application Server), depending on how broad the context of its usage is during our writing. The Netweaver AS is essentially WAS re-branded.

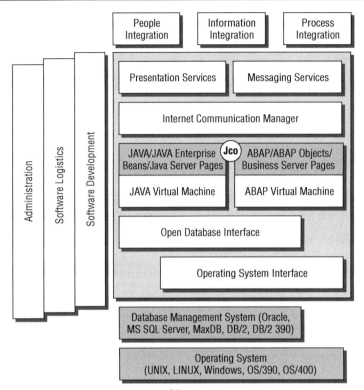

Figure 2-4   NetWeaver AS architecture

The following sections provide an overview of the most important components from an SAP BW point of view.

Core Components

The *operating system interface* allows the NetWeaver AS to be installed on several different hardware and operating system platforms, including UNIX/ Linux, OS/390, OS/400, and Microsoft Windows. It hides the details of the different operating systems and provides an abstract layer for access to operating system functionality. The operating system interface provides shared process services, including dispatching of application requests, shared memory services, and synchronization services (enqueue/dequeue).

The *open database interface* enables SAP BW to utilize database functionality from different vendors (including Oracle, IBM, and Microsoft), as well as the MaxDB database offered by MySQL. Besides hiding the implementation details of different database systems, the open database interface allows application-specific caching of database requests and provides buffer synchronization among multiple application servers using the same database server.

NOTE The special multidimensional requirements of SAP BW provoked some significant enhancements of the open database interface and forced the SAP BW development team to develop its own additional database abstraction layer on top of the open database interface.

The *Java Virtual Machine* (JVM) supports the execution of Java programs, Java Server Pages (JSPs), and JavaScripts and integrates with Enterprise Java-Beans. With the integration of the JVM into the SAP Netweaver AS, SAP opened its platform to a whole new world of application developers.

The *ABAP Virtual Machine* has been in place right from the beginning of SAP R/3 development. Originally a functional programming language, ABAP has been extended by object-oriented software-development features (ABAP objects) and Web-enabled objects (Business Server Pages or BSPs). The ABAP Virtual Machine precompiles the ABAP code into a byte code, which is then stored in the database and used for execution. While to date most of the core business functionality developed by SAP is implemented in ABAP, a lot of the more front-end and modeling-tools development will be done in Java.

The *Internet Communication Manager* provides support for open Internet standards and protocols (including HTTP, SOAP, HTML, XML, and WML), as well as traditional SAP communication protocols such as RFC. The Internet Communication Manager has an integrated Web server, allowing external applications and front-end systems to use the HTTP protocol for communicating with the NetWeaver AS.

The *presentation services* integrate with the SAP Portal infrastructure, offering iViews and other Portal infrastructures from third-party vendors. The presentation services support several types of front-end systems, including the traditional SAPGUI for Windows, the SAPGUI for Java, and the SAPGUI for HTML. The messaging services allow the exchanging of data with other applications using the SAP protocols and open protocols such as SMTP and SOAP.

DEFINITION

Simple Object Access Protocol (SOAP) is a lightweight message format for exchanging information in a distributed, heterogeneous computing environment. Based on XML, SOAP consists of three parts: The Envelope (which contains what is in the message and how to proceed), Encoding Rules (for how to instantiate instances of data-types found in the Envelope), and a method for Remote Procedure Calls (as well as responses to be communicated).

SOAP, UDDI, and WSDL are the standards that create a foundation for Web services and their continuing proliferation. This set is often the preferred standard for exchanging information via Web services.

Software Development

One of the key success factors for SAP has been the integrated software-development tools that allow customers to adapt the system to their specific requirements by implementing their own custom ABAP programs or enhancing programs delivered by SAP. The software-development platform of SAP, called the *ABAP Workbench*, integrates various editors such as an ABAP editor, a screen painter, and SAP query with a data dictionary, allowing you to share common definitions of data types and table structures. Debugging functionality is available, allowing you to debug both custom and SAP code. Open interfaces (the BAPIs) allow access to SAP functionality by reading and writing data and metadata, as well as by executing business processes.

SAP now offers its own Java development environment, thanks in large part to IBM. It is called the *NetWeaver Developer Studio*. In 2001, IBM donated the Eclipse Platform to the Open Source community where the Integrated Development Environment (IDE) may be used royalty-free. The donation was anything but altruistic. It may, in fact, prove to be a significant under-the-radar, tax-deductible blow to two large competitors: Microsoft and Oracle. At the time, it was not clear what would become of the newly founded `Eclipse.org`. While the IDE was widely used by the Java development community, it was lacking significant enterprise functionality.

SAP has greatly enhanced the Eclipse IDE by utilizing the base platform's Extension Points to create new environment Perspectives. The NetWeaver Developer Studio is SAP's IDE for all NetWeaver components. Figure 2-5 shows the components of the Developer Studio. It is used to create Java programs and associated table definitions. It supports local development and testing via a local Java Runtime Environment (JRE) while coordinating larger projects with multiple developers by using a so-called Design Time Repository (DTR) and Component Build Service (CBS). The naming and versioning of Development Objects is managed via a check-in/check-out function. For example, if a table already exists, the programmer will be notified in order to either use the existing table or rename the table as new. The CBS allows for building and confirming sources and verifying with the development of other developers' resources.

SAP's enhancements to the Eclipse Platform are profound and include the following new Perspectives:

- **Web Dynpro** — Used to create client-independent Java and ABAP user interfaces. Web Dynpro ensures the separation of presentation, processing logic, and data access.

- **Web Service** — Starting point for creating and consuming EJB, Java Class, and Web services.

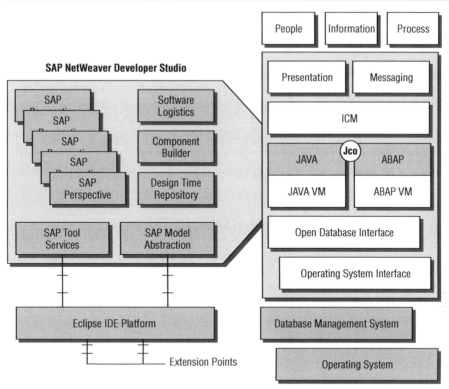

Figure 2-5 SAP NetWeaver Developer Studio and the Eclipse Platform

- **Dictionary** — Centralized repository that enables local developers to define, create, and modify database objects. This is not a full-blown data dictionary like that found in the ABAP dictionary. Note that for-eign-key definitions and domain concepts are not supported. The dictionary does allow for database independence and the support of Structured Query Language embedded in Java (SQLJ) and Open SQL.

- **Design Time Repository (DTR)** — The DTR shows both active and inactive workspaces, along with the properties of selected objects, while indicating whether objects exist locally or centrally. Integration conflicts are categorized. Errors and failures are displayed in the command out-put view.

- **Configuration** — Lists all open and completed DTR activities in either Local or Team View.

- **Development** — Creates a common entry point for creating and editing J2EE development objects.

Now Java programmers may enjoy the same features and enterprise-strength development concept that ABAP programmers have used for around two decades. In addition, Java development maybe done locally and tested on local JRE, which is not possible in the ABAP Workbench.

Both the ABAP and Java development environments contain very similar functionality regarding the management of programs, table definitions, and the like. While the environments are different from a look-and-feel (as well as semantic) perspective, they perform essentially the same functionality.

Development Objects are tables and files that a programmer creates. They may be stored as a version in the source DTR. Several Development Objects may be assigned to a Development Component. The components are then assigned to Software Components. In a case where the development is part of a larger, team-based development project, a team leader would be responsible for this level of build and for determining what is to be delivered in a particular installation or upgrade. There is a higher-level element called a Product in the Development Studio. The Product is a collection of Software Components that may be shared across multiple software Products.

Front-End Technologies

There is no shortage of front-end presentation tools in NetWeaver. The remainder of this chapter (and the book) refers to the user interfaces (UIs) and tools SAP has developed.

SAPGUI

The graphical user interface (GUI) that SAP has historically used to present screens for online entry and display is called SAPGUI. The SAPGUI is installed on the client and is used to render screen layouts, menus, and the graphical elements to be organized when an ABAP program event is triggered. Every ABAP program has the capability to describe screen layouts as well as the procession logic for each layout.

The processing logic is triggered by the input received from the user as he or she interacts with the screen layout or after the application logic of the ABAP program is executed but prior to the creation of the screen layout. The process logic is triggered either by the process before output (PBO) or process after input (PAI) events.

This separation of presentation, process logic, and business logic is at the heart of NetWeaver AS. The separation enables screen layouts to take on many differing views based on the process and application logic directed by the end user's interactions with the application. Collectively, this process is referred to as a dynamic program (Dynpro).

Web Dynpro

Web Dynpro is targeted for use by professional developers with application requirements for a zero-footprint, browser-based UI. It is used for both Java and ABAP user-interface creation. The model-driven approach of Web Dynpro reduces the amount of actual coding by the developer while supporting sophisticated runtime services such as screen updates without browser reloads.

Like its older sister, SAPGUI Dynpro, there is a separation of presentation, process, and business logic. This separation exists whether or not the underlying application is built in the Netweaver Developer Studio (Java) or the ABAP Workbench.

Web Dynpro supports the popular user-interface concept referred to as the *Model View Controller*. The View is the layout of an application that consists of UI elements (such as buttons or menus for example) and is used to create a consistent look and feel throughout the interface. The Controller aspect of the concept is responsible for the graphical navigational flow and automatic context data transfer from one view to the next. The Model is a data handling application object such as a Web service, ABAP function, or Java program. Developers are able to convert the user interfaces created via the ABAP Screen Painter (SAPGUI Dynpros) to Web Dynpro without loss of functionality. The opposite, however, does not hold true. That is, Web Dynpro user interfaces may not be converted and edited with the ABAP Screen Painter.

BEx Web Application Designer

This is a tool used to create Web applications that access SAP BW Queries and Query Views. The BEx Web Application Designer is a primary focus of Chapter 8.

Visual Composer

This is a visual modeling tool that enables content development for the Portal. The Visual Composer is entirely Web-based and provides debugging, testing, and the creation of documentation. SAP is converging many of the front-end presentation tools into the Visual Composer, but for the time being, the Visual Composer is used by the business-analyst type rather than the professional developer. Like the Web Application Designer, SAP BW Query Views may be incorporated into an application built by the Visual Composer.

Interactive Forms (Abode Designer)

SAP has entered into an OEM relationship with Adobe. An outcome of the agreement between the companies is that Adobe Designer is now available to create and deploy interactive forms. The interactive forms are used to collect business data, be that a salesperson's weekly expense information or a cost-center manager's budgeting information.

Both the NetWeaver Developer Studio and the ABAP Developer Workbench are integrated with the Form Designer, allowing a consistent form design to be created and deployed, regardless of the type of application or development environment used to create the application or user interface. Form-layout information and data in the layout are stored in XML documents, thereby creating a separation of content and presentation elements.

Mobile Infrastructure

SAP has provided an optional mobile infrastructure (MI) that, when embedded into the NetWeaver platform, supports business scenarios such as order entry and inventory availability as part of a broader mobile-asset-management solution that includes field service and scenarios. The compelling aspect of the mobile infrastructure is not remote data entry or inventory looks, not even the synchronization of multiple remote devices with the backend server. The real compelling aspect of the MI is that it may be integrated into the backend systems for optimized routing of field-service personnel. While many of the features in MI may be found in standalone mobile applications available in the marketplace, the integration into the backend SAP systems is still one of SAP's most profound advantages.

The goal of MI is to provide a platform and network-independent infrastructure for running mobile applications. To accomplish this, SAP embraced open standards such as HTTP and Java to create applications containing a user interface, business logic, and database storage on a variety of handheld devices. The compelling aspect of MI is that the application must be created only once, and it is deployable to multiple platforms. As shown in Figure 2-6, the following components are available within MI.

SAP Mobile Client

Installed on the mobile device as a lightweight footprint, this is a Web server, database, and business-logic engine. The mobile applications may take advantage of the client's ability to process business logic, thereby reducing dependency on constant network availability. Although there is a business-logic engine, note that the engine is not yet capable of running a local (offline) Analytic Processing Engine but is able to provide online analysis. Chapter 7 provides more details on the Analytic Processing Engine.

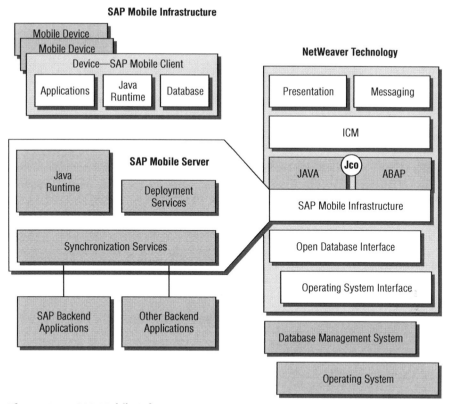

Figure 2-6 SAP Mobile Infrastructure

SAP Mobile Infrastructure Server

The server component consists of a JVM and enables the development and runtime environments for mobile applications. The applications themselves may be written as JSPs or Java 2 Mobile Edition (J2ME).

Synchronization and Replication

This process is performed by a piece of SAP middleware that queues and dispatches synchronization requests. The middleware is executed over HTTP with Secure Sockets (HTTPS) and uses standard connection types such as Global System for Mobile Communications (GSM) and its General Packet Radio Service (GPRS). It is also possible to synchronize or replicate data via traditional LAN, wireless LAN, and physical hardware cradles. There are options for conflict resolution, delta determination, and user assignments.

Mobile Deployment and Development Kit

Applications written with these tools may run in either a mobile browser or a client-specific user interface. Once the application is written, it may be deployed to run on a variety of mobile devices from a central control point.

System Landscape

Through the Systems Landscape Directory (SLD), technical and business systems are defined and viewed, along with software products/components and development. The SLD provides three primary services: landscape directory, component repository, and development namespace reservations.

The SLD is where you may add, maintain, delete, or list technical systems. Following are the five primary types of technical systems:

- ABAP AS
- Java AS
- Exchange Infrastructure
- Standalone Java
- Third-party

NOTE Functions within the SAP Business Suite run on one or the other SAP provided Netweaver Application Servers. For example, the Portal runs on the Java platform, and mySAP ERP runs on the ABAP platform.

The SLD contains the definitions for all SAP installations (system name and host name) including the definition of the SDL itself. Technical systems, once named, also record the applications, services, libraries, and interfaces deployed on them into the SDL. For software components (installed or not) and any SAP Java Connectors (JCo) in the landscape, their destinations are also recorded in the SLD.

Once the SLD is established, it enables change management and deployment of the applications through the landscape. Tracking of SLD entries is done via services that highlight upgrade dependencies. The namespace reservation assures developers that components they create will not be in conflict with components from other developers (including SAP).

Software Logistics

The NetWeaver AS includes sophisticated software-logistics support for software development objects, metadata, and customization data based on the

Transport Management System (TMS). The TMS performs the following major tasks around managing software development and distribution:

- It tracks all changes to development objects under its control, whether these are delivered by SAP or developed by the client. Objects under control of the TMS include programs, database tables, all metadata objects, and customized data.

- The TMS provides sophisticated software-distribution mechanisms to manage complex application-development landscapes, including separate multistaged development, test, and production systems.

- It allows the upgrading of running systems and applying support packages. It automatically identifies modified objects and allows you to manually handle modifications during the upgrade or update process.

Landscape Considerations

It is good practice to keep separate instances of the systems on which you are running business applications — especially for development, testing, and production purposes. SAP systems (including SAP BW) have always supported these activities with the TMS. The TMS captures changes in many types of objects, including the following:

- All programming objects (including ABAP programs, function groups, types, classes, includes, and messages)

- All dictionary objects (including tables, views, data elements, and domains)

- All customization tables (including currency translation types, application components, printer definitions, user profiles, authorizations, profiles, and calendars)

- All metadata of other SAP systems (such as mySAP ERP, PLM, SCM, and so on)

- All SAP BW metadata objects (including InfoObjects, InfoCubes, InfoSources, Data Sources, queries, Web applications, and process chains). Chapter 3 describes these objects in greater detail.

All development objects logically belonging together are assigned to *packages* (formerly known as *development classes*). These objects are referenced in a directory table in the SAP database; the TMS now keeps track of changes by simply assigning the key values of such an object to a task, which itself is assigned to a transport request.

Once all tasks are completed and released by the users assigned to them, the request is released — effectively exporting the current versions (all table contents, not just the keys) of all objects tracked in that request into a file. Using the TMS, you can import this file into any SAP system, usually the test system, where special before- and after-import programs take care of additional actions after importing the objects. After testing is complete, you can import the same file into the production system for productive use.

The TMS not only keeps track of changes in development systems; it also keeps track of changes in the test or production system. Or, depending on global system settings, the TMS prevents users from changing anything in these systems at all. This type of scenario is well known to SAP users and larger organizations for complex custom software development and mainte-nance. The same paradigm and the same technology are used by SAP BW to ensure stable and highly available software systems. The TMS allows you to define and maintain complex system landscapes for application development, as shown in Figure 2-7.

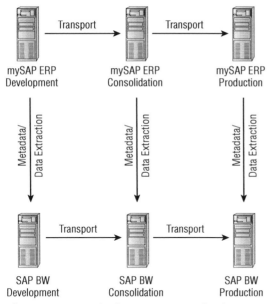

Figure 2-7   Standard SAP BW system landscape

Two complete system landscapes are shown in Figure 2-7: one for mySAP ERP and one for SAP BW. There could be even more than two, if additional SAP systems such as CRM and Advanced Planner and Optimizer (APO) are used in an organization. These systems must be in sync as well, for two major reasons:

■ Development of an application usually requires customization of exist-ing or additional data-extraction programs and sometimes, depending on specific requirements, even changes to the customization of business processes. Both development paths must be kept in sync over the whole system landscape so that you can efficiently develop, test, and deploy the application.

■ In typical development systems, testing is nearly impossible because of poor data quality. One reason for poor data quality is that development systems are normally sized according to development needs and do not allow mass testing or even just storing mass data. Another reason is that data in development systems is often modified manually to provide test data for specific development-test cases.

However, some development activities may not be conducted in the test system but rather done in the production system. These may include the definition of ad-hoc queries, ad-hoc Web applications, definition of load procedures, and others. The TMS allows you to define exceptions for these types of objects — but this implies that the TMS no longer tracks changes to these objects.

Note that talking about system landscapes does not necessarily mean talking about multiple physical systems. Today's high-performance parallel servers with many CPUs, large amounts of main memory, and access to storage networks allow you to install multiple instances of mySAP ERP or SAP BW systems on a single physical system. Even smaller physical systems today allow you to run a development system and an integration-test system on one physical server in smaller organizations where development and testing frequently are consecutive processes so that there are few testing activities in intense development phases and vice versa.

Keeping that in mind, there's actually no reason to go for a poor man's system landscape like the one shown at the top of Figure 2-8. However, it is possible, in early stages of prototype development projects or with very small exploratory implementations, to use the complete SAP BW functionality delivered with mySAP ERP because it may reduce costly prototyping and evaluation expenses. Implementation of this type should not be put into production without approval from SAP.

A more complex system-landscape scenario has proven useful in global rollouts, where a central development team works on a global template system, which is then localized and tested locally. Figure 2-9 shows the *global rollout system landscape.* The point here is that objects from the global development system are first transported into a global test system, where the system may be tested prior to being rolled out to several local development systems. The local development systems are used to adapt the global template to local needs to some extent (language, local legal requirements, and local business requirements). Keeping track of local changes to global objects, the TMS supports identification and synchronization of global and local objects. Once the localization of the application is complete, it may be transported to the local test and production systems.

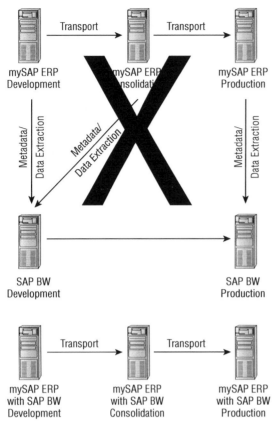

Figure 2-8   Poor man's SAP BW system landscape

> **NOTE** SAP is actually using a similar scenario to roll out support packages and new releases of its new software to customers. The same (or similar) mechanisms for identifying and synchronizing changes to global (in this case, SAP-defined) objects are used to maintain the system's integrity. The SAP software itself can be considered a template for a local (in this case, local means customer-specific) rollout developed by SAP. Although the system landscape at SAP is more complex than the one shown in Figure 2-9, the basic principles remain the same.

Other complex application-development projects might also require using a software-integration system landscape (as shown in Figure 2-10), where objects from several different development systems meet in a central development landscape for integration work, final testing, and productive use.

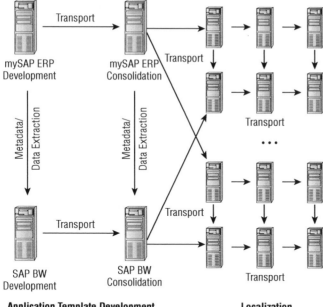

Application Template Development   Localization

Figure 2-9   Global rollout system landscapes

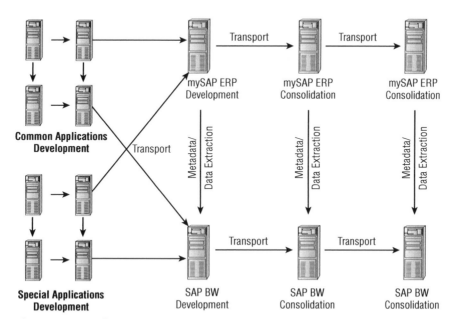

Figure 2-10   Software-integration system landscape

The actual system landscape chosen in a particular situation largely depends on the complexity of the development work and the complexity of the rollout. Investments in hardware and system setup pay off in the long run through ease of development, integration, and testing. Experience has shown a return on investment through achieved increase in information accessibility and quality.

Security

A key issue often neglected (or at least not implemented at a sufficient level of sophistication) in custom data warehouse solutions (and sometimes even standard data warehousing tools) is security. Protecting the information in the data warehouse is as important as protecting the data in your operational system against unauthorized access. NetWeaver security relies on the application server, which uses Secure Network Communications (SNC) to provide single sign-on (SSO) and centrally managed user stores based on the Lightweight Directory Access Protocol (LDAP).

The SAP authorization does not simply rely on authorization concepts provided by operating systems and database systems. Instead, it comes with its own application-authorization concept, allowing for very detailed adjustments of authorizations in operational and data warehouse systems to the policies of any organization. Authorization checks are executed and defined by the SAP application using application-server functionality.

Following are three objects that must be defined to understand the SAP security concept:

- **Users** — These are individuals or automated processes that have a unique identifier, allowing them to log on to and use a specific system.

- **Authorizations** — An authorization warrants a specific user the right to perform a specific action or retrieve a certain bit of information from a system.

- **Roles** — The role concept resembles the role or function that individuals have in an organization. Examples of such roles include a purchasing manager role, a sales representative role, and the CEO role. In the same way as in an organization, roles can be assigned to multiple individuals simultaneously (such as there may be multiple sales representatives), and the assignment of roles to individuals may change over time without affecting the definition of the role itself (a purchasing manager will always be expected to manage the purchasing process, regardless of the individual filling that role).

To ease the task of administering a large number of users on such a detailed level, the whole authorization concept is role based. Roles can consist of several profiles, which are collections of authorizations required to perform a specific task. Roles may be assigned to multiple users, and users may have different roles assigned. Profiles may include other profiles and normally do include a couple of authorizations. Each authorization is an instance of an authorization object, describing exactly which operations are allowed for a certain object. Figure 2-11 provides an overview of authorization.

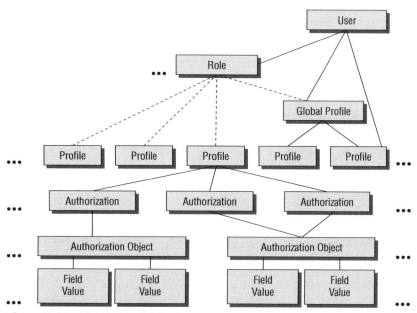

Figure 2-11   The SAP authorization concept
Based on copyrighted material from SAP AG

NOTE Roles are not used only to collect all authorizations required to execute on a specific business role; they are used also to provide easy access to menus or complex personalized applications in a Portal environment.

Administration

SAP administration covers the whole range of functionality required to run complex online applications and batch processes — including job control and job monitoring, user and authorization management, performance monitoring and performance optimization, output management, and archiving.

Most of the functions related to the more technical aspects of administering an SAP system are integrated in the *Computing Center Management System* (CCMS). Frequently used functionality such as printing and job scheduling and monitoring are available from nearly all transactions.

Chapter 11 covers general administration strategies for SAP BW in greater detail, and Chapter 12 includes a discussion of the CCMS functionality for performance monitoring and optimizing an SAP system (especially an SAP BW system).

Process Integration

Process integration in NetWeaver is covered by a software component called the *Exchange Infrastructure* (XI). The mission of XI is to enable the integration of SAP and Non-SAP software systems. The integration platform may be used to support application-to-application as well as business-to-business scenarios in asynchronous or synchronous communications, thus supporting cross-component and inter-enterprise business process management. It is important to note that SAP has stated its intention to use XI as the foundation for its business applications.

Before looking at the components of XI, it is important to understand how central this component is to SAP's software strategy. For more than a decade, organizations have been deciding to implement ERP software from SAP because of its tight integration between applications when compared to its chief competitors. This key differentiator for SAP was also its Achilles' heel. In other words, a monolithic, complex application would need to be deployed for the most basic functionality to be put into production. It's a bit like undergoing open-heart surgery when proper diet and exercise would do the trick.

Now, with the arrival of XI, SAP is looking to insert an architected solution where spider webs exist in its ERP applications. Such an architected solution based on the XI backbone enables applications to be assembled based on small service components. To create software based on a service concept and utilize XI, SAP may very well rewrite the most fundamental of application functionality (for example, currency conversion, general ledger postings, and so on). The other competitive knock SAP would take was that its software was not easily extensible. As described shortly, that objection is addressed in XI.

XI is set to take advantage of the maturation and broadening adoption of Web services by utilizing the shared classification and discovery of businesses and services through its support for UDDI. Loose coupling via XML messaging allows XI to take asynchronous communication as far as possible and to use synchronous communication when absolutely required.

Figure 2-12 shows XI's main components. To sum matters up in one sentence, "The Exchange Infrastructure acts as the messaging middleware for service communication, connectivity, transformation, and portability" (copyright SAP AG 2005, CAF Core Overview, Volker Stiehl & Will Carlton, page 7).

While it may sound simple to configure message routings and mappings needed to trigger a process, wait for responses, and send outbound messages, XI is a deceptively powerful component. The following sections describe the key features of XI because it will become an instrumental component in *business activity monitoring* (BAM), as well as the embedding of business intelligence into business processes (be that an interactive process or automated via a set of ever-learning predictive models).

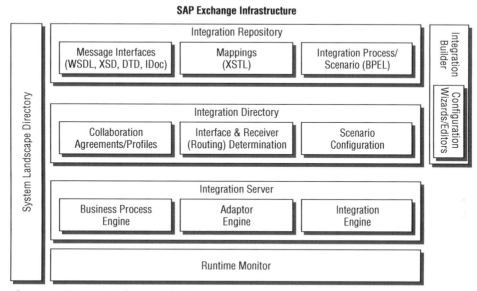

Figure 2-12   SAP Exchange Infrastructure

DEFINITION

"Applistructure" is a term coined by a JP Morgan Analyst used to describe the convergence of applications and infrastructure. It is believed that the maturity of Web services and reusable components is blurring the lines between business applications and technical infrastructure.

Many in the enterprise software industry believe there is a race to see who will win the Applistructure contest. The old saying about technology appears to be holding true: "Every new layer on the technology stack commoditizes those beneath it." Much like the browser wars of yesteryear, the battle has moved up the software stack to the business-process level. The leaders in the race will secure a customer base for the next decade and, if done correctly, will create a thriving ecosystem of independent software vendors building adaptors, services, and embeddable subprocesses that will create greater reliance on the platform providers.

SAP XI is at the heart of SAP NetWeaver and thus their Applistructure offering. It is designed to be used where integration scenarios, business processes, Web services, interfaces, mappings, and routing rules come together to create a common shared understanding of how collaborative business processes work from an enterprise's perspective. It is not only where the definitions come together; it is also where distributed execution of said processes is managed.

Integration Builder

The Integration Builder is a set of design-time tools for creating messages, processes, and mappings. The builder creates metadata that represents scenarios, conditions, mappings, interfaces, and processes stored in the Integration Repository. Many of the tools in the Integration Builder are Editors or Wizards to ease the creation process.

Integration Repository

The Integration Repository houses the metadata for scenarios, processes, mappings, and messages. There are three noteworthy categories of metadata:

- Message interfaces
- Mappings
- Scenario/process integration

Each category of metadata is stored in an industry-standard format. A *message interface* would be described in the repository using WSDL, XML Schema Definition (XSD), and Document Type Definitions (DTDs). A *mapping* would be stored in the repository as Extensible Style Sheet Transformations (XSLT). Business *process definitions* are currently stored as Business Process Execution Language (BPEL). Note that message interfaces defined as representing SAP systems often use the Intermediate Document format (IDoc) that is proprietary to SAP.

Integration Directory

The Integration Directory stores the configuration for the business scenarios, processes, routing rules (such as receiver determination and interface determination), along with the associated mappings and business partner security agreements. The key difference between the Integration Directory and Repository is that the Repository stores the metadata and the Directory stores how that metadata will be used at runtime.

Consider an analogy of a digital video recorder (DVR). The DVR wish list contains all of the programs with the time and channel information so that they may be recorded. The DVR also has stored your wish lists and favorite programs. In this analogy, the DVR is the Repository. Not until you program the DVR with your wish list, tell the DVR at which time it may use your connection line to retrieve the current programming schedule, and instruct it on how long to keep each recording (and whether you want to record only first-run shows and/or repeats) will the DVR actually run. This type of runtime configuration is stored in the Integration Directory.

Integration Server

The Integration Server is the runtime environment for XI. It consists of three parts: The Business Process Engine, Adaptor Engine, and Integration Engine. The Integration Server utilizes the configuration found in the Integration Directory and executes it.

A simplified way to think of the Integration Server is to imagine it listening for messages sent from systems. The Integration Server determines for which business process the message is bound. Once the business process is determined, the Integration Server figures out whether the message must be mapped to the interface of the business process or step within the business process. It determines which instance of a business process the inbound message is intended for and decides if the relevant business process rules are satisfied before continuing the execution of that business process. If the rules are not satisfied, it decides what should happen next. Finally, it determines who or what service should receive an outbound message and in what format that message should be sent.

The communication between XI and a system sending or receiving messages may be done synchronously or asynchronously with built-in error processing. From a technical perspective, XI transports messages via HTTP or HTTPS and utilizes the SOAP.

Besides the management of the business process (through the Business Process Engine) and the runtime of the Integration Engine, the Integration Server has an Adaptor Engine. The Adaptor Engine manages the security and queuing of messages as they arrive and are dispatched to a resource adaptor. The resource adaptor is developed specifically for connecting XI to a specific third-party application or marketplace. The resource adaptors are based on the Java Connector Architecture (JCA) and are certified by SAP. SAP provides an adaptor development kit.

Runtime Monitor

While integration scenarios are brokered and business processes managed by XI, there is an active alert monitor watching it all happen. The SAP Alert Framework monitors business alerts as well. The CCMS is alerted when any component of the XI system fails. Inbound XML messages are checked, and, because they are part of a process, the outcome of the check is recorded in the monitor. The monitor allows for processes to be viewed and managed from either a message's perspective or a process's perspective.

Information Integration

The next key component of NetWeaver is Information Integration. This component consists of these main ingredients:

- Business intelligence
- Master data management
- Knowledge management

Business Intelligence

There are some common misunderstandings about SAP BW being just another application module comparable to FI, CO, or SD.

While SAP BW is technically delivered as part of the mySAP ERP solution and is installed on the same physical server and may run on the same logical database instance, it is recommend to be installed as a separate SAP instance and should use its own separate database with its own application servers. SAP started developing the SAP BW in late 1996, based on an SAP system with just the technology basis and cross-application components installed. It was conceived as a completely separate architecture, optimized for reporting and analysis purposes.

SAP has bundled and rebundled its software several times during the past few years to maximize revenue and market share. SAP's solution approach to selling simply means that when a solution is purchased, the necessary software components to realize the solution are delivered by SAP. The SAP BW software component is delivered with nearly every solution sold by SAP, because it is one of the more mature software components in the NetWeaver integration platform. In fact, as of this writing, the SAP BW software component is no longer sold independently from NetWeaver.

Historically, the SAP business intelligence solution was a bundle including the Portal with its knowledge management capabilities and the SAP BW components. The current software release has seen the convergence of these parts into NetWeaver. NetWeaver creates a broad foundation for organizations on which to build collaborative analytic applications that may be embedded into business processes. In traditional SAP fashion, they deliver prebuilt applications.

Master Data Management

In a break from SAP's historical practice of not acquiring technology, SAP master data management (MDM) is a product from the acquisition of A2I Inc.

The acquisition allows SAP to now meet requirements for product information catalogs and Web publishing of said catalogs, while maintaining the core data-management feature set that includes master data consolidation, synchronization, and distribution.

While software acquisitions always raise the question of how tightly integrated the software is, it should be noted that the "new" MDM 5.5 has a number of options for integrating with XI and the Portal. However, the administration of MDM (as of this writing) does not "feel" like an SAP product. In time, MDM and other SAP software components will have their administration functions converge into a uniform set of security and user administration, as well as other system services.

There are two primary business scenarios that MDM supports. One is referred to as Rich Product Content and the other is Global Data Synchronization. *Rich Product Content* is a scenario where parametric searches on product data may be performed via a Web site against the entire product catalog. The scenario of Global Data Synchronization enables trade-item information to be exchanged with a data pool such as 1SYNC (formerly Transora and UCCNet).

There are three IT scenarios that SAP has historically supported with MDM:

1. Master data consolidation
2. Master data harmonization and synchronization (and harmonization)
3. Centralized master data management

As we describe in Chapter 1, it is not uncommon for larger organizations to have multiple databases storing the same or similar information. The idea behind *master data consolidation* is that master data records (for example, a customer's records) may need to be cleansed and have duplicates eliminated (*de-duping*) as records from multiple databases are pulled together to create a common view of the customer across an entire organization. This scenario may be implemented in a variety of ways.

For example, in conjunction with the business intelligence capabilities of NetWeaver, an organization may import data, consolidate it, and send it back to the original source system. This scenario may be used as basis for cleansing vendor information and providing cross-company expense reporting. Another possibility would be to import data from a system like Oracle Financials (which is run at a subsidiary), consolidate it with the corporate SAP Financials, and send it to a NetWeaver system for enterprise reporting. This scenario may be used to find duplicates and create cross-reference information about the mapping, of, say, general ledger accounts, in your BI system.

Master data synchronization is a bit more challenging. In this scenario, master data changes must be tracked. The additions and changes to master data may occur in any of a number of systems. Once one system is updated, it tells the MDM server so that the other interested systems may be updated. XI is used to support scenarios where multiple ERP systems are implemented in an organization.

The idea behind *central master data management* is as it sounds. Master data is maintained in a central location and only in the central location. All systems that require master data receive the equivalent of a read-only copy of it. This scenario helps to ensure a high standard of data quality.

MDM Runtime Server

Figure 2-13 shows the software components and services that compose the MDM solution. The centerpiece of the MDM product is the *MDM runtime server*. You may think of this as an in-memory database or abstraction layer that takes care of the locking and synchronizing of master data. The server is written in the generic C programming language and is not dependant on either the ABAP technology stack or the Java technology stack found in NetWeaver (although we anticipate this changing in future releases). The server may be installed on a number of different operating systems and hardware platforms.

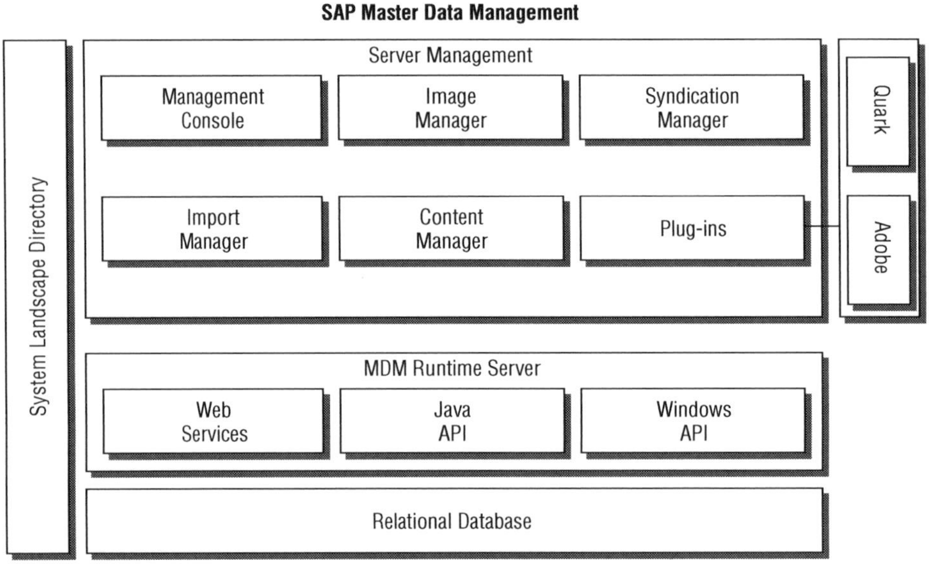

SAP Master Data Management

Figure 2-13   SAP master data management (MDM)

Master data is managed within a repository. Repositories are physically stored in one and only one database, but the database may contain multiple repositories. A repository is mounted onto an MDM server. A repository may be active/loaded on only one server at a time, although it may be mounted (but inactive) on several servers at the same time.

NOTE The following is an unfortunate selection of terminology for describing MDM servers. Seeing how it is not our intent in this book to emancipate all of the oppressed servers out there in IT shops, we will use SAP's chosen terminology.

The master-slave concept is central to how MDM handles repositories — be that when referring to the databases they reside in or the services they are mounted onto. *Slaves* are read-only copies of a *master*, and slaves are created in unique databases. Therefore, the slave is a new repository that may be used by one or more applications needing to search and retrieve master data information. The master knows nothing about its slaves, which makes us question the appropriateness of the term "slaves." Slaves are responsible for initiating a synchronization request, and such a request may be done manually or automatically.

The master-slave concept enables MDM to scale or, to be more specific, provides the option to *scale-in* or *scale-out*. Scaling-in is supported by mounting several repositories to the same MDM server but on different ports. This is not unlike adding work processes to the NetWeaver AS under the same dispatcher. Scaling-out is accomplished by mounting repositories on different servers. While there are pros and cons to both scaling methods, there is the ability to scale and handle high volumes of searches.

The MDM server has standardized APIs that support a variety of consumers who may wish to access it. For example, the MDM server and its master data may be accessed by a client-side interface delivered as part of MDM or with a so-called input manager, syndicate, or third-party component that accesses the server's APIs.

Management Console

The Management Console takes care of essentially three things:

- Catalog structure
- Catalog security
- Catalog administration

The Console has client software that must be installed on Win32-compatible operating systems. There is also an API that may be used to invoke the MDM server. The MDM server does not distinguish the client mode from the batch API mode. All of the Console commands you enter from the client interface are executable via the API.

The Console is where tables and relationships are created within repositories and form a catalog. Updating indexes, defragmenting databases, creating slaves, and normalizing (emancipating slaves) are all functions made available via the Management Console. Master-slave synchronization is managed in the

Console, along with the associated mounting/dismounting, locking/unlocking, deleting, verify/repair, and other administrative functions.

> **NOTE** Use the `update indexes` **command after loading a catalog and re-index when repository structures change.**

The Console is where users and roles are maintained. Note that this is not exactly the same user-role concept found in other NetWeaver components, but it is similar enough that it is easy to learn. Security is supported via LDAP but not SSL or SSO as of this writing. (We anticipate this to be addressed in the near-term by SAP.) The Console also provides a place for the management of user tasks, validations, notifications, and change approvals to be grouped into a workflow or to create a work list.

Import Manager

The Import Manager is just that: a tool used to manage the importing of external data into MDM. It, too, has a Win-32-dependant client and a batch mode with API. While the tool is able to aggregate and transform data as it is imported, this is a rather rudimentary "manager," because it currently is unable to selectively import records.

Consider a load via the Import Manager to be an all-or-nothing venture. The Input Manager uses a table-level locking operation for tables accessed during imports. Importing via the API allows for inserts, updates, and deletes because it only locks the row within a table.

It is also important to note that the Import Manger cannot concurrently load multiple files into a single repository. So, while you are able to run two Import Manager sessions concurrently against the same server, table-level locking prohibits a parallel update to the same table. On the bright side, the Import Manager is most commonly used only during the initial implementation of the MDM server, and writing to the API eliminates many of the limitations.

Content Manager

The Content Manager is where master data and its attributes are created, as well as updates searched and categorized. This tool also has a client and batch mode. Each master data record is searchable with corresponding family information for each record (parents, children, brothers). The validation rules, workflows, search selections, and Web information are also available via the Content Manager.

Hierarchy and taxonomy searching and selection are possible, along with pick-list and attribute-searching functionality. While MDM was "not invented here" (that is, by SAP), SAP wasted no time integrating the search functionality of the MDM Content Manager into the Portal, creating a consistent user experience.

Several views are possible for master data. The record view is very common and shows the detailed characteristics of a master data record, along with any associated images or documents. Taxonomy, hierarchy, and family views of master data are also possible to aid in the record search process. Note that MDM now feels more like a catalog management system than its earlier versions.

Image and Syndication Managers

The Image Manager allows for the creation of data-driven page layouts and dynamic print publishing. A layout view provides a pallet for laying out a catalog design. The ability to publish the catalog to desktop publishing tools is also possible.

The Syndication Manager handles the exporting of repositories to non-MDM systems. Processes such as defining the target file's output destination, format, and schema and setting the field mappings from MDM to the output format are managed here. The Syndication Manager is one of the integration touch-points between MDM and XI that enable SAP to provide business scenarios, including ERP-based models for customer, vendor, material, and employee master data.

Knowledge Management

The Portal found in SAP NetWeaver contains a set of services for knowledge management. Knowledge management (KM) provides efficient document management, automatic classification, check-in/check-out, subscription, feedback, versioning, and retrieval of documents and unstructured data.

The knowledge management functionality delivered is not a document management system or Web content management system like Vignette, Interwoven, or EMC's Documentum. The platform is designed to harmonize these tools under one enterprise knowledge management platform, regardless of the data's physical location. The platform consists of several areas that work together on unstructured content:

- Repository Framework
- Classification and taxonomy engines
- Index and search engines

Repository Framework

The Repository Framework is at the center of KM capabilities in the Portal. The content of documents and the corresponding attributes of documents are managed here. Content may physically reside in any number of places, including pure play document or Web content management subsystems. The Repository Framework is an integration layer used to communicate with the subsystems that physically hold the documents. The subsystem may be a file system, document management application, or database. In fact, NetWeaver has its own set of document-management services. A Repository Manager is defined for each content source or subsystem. The Repository Manager's role is to integrate the repositories of each content source. The Repository Manager utilizes APIs to access the functionality of subsystems. So, if an administrator would like to interface with Documentum and take advantage of Documentum's capability to lock documents, he or she may do so programmatically through the APIs.

Classification and Taxonomy

Two primary classification techniques are available in the KM: *manual classification* and *automatic classification*. The KM services organize content in folders, or tree structures, analogous to the folder structure found in Microsoft Windows Explorer. This allows, for example, folders for Wine to have subfolders for Varietals, Regions, Glassware, and so on. In addition, the subfolder Varietals may have subfolders of its own such as Cabernet, Zinfandel, Malbec, Viognier, and Pinot Noir. The platform supports the automatic generation of taxonomies, as well as traditional manual classification. A folder structure may be automatically generated after the classification engine is "trained." The training process weighs different subjects according to an organization's preferences and is similar to the training of a data mining method (a concept discussed in Chapter 7).

Once content is classified, it is made available in a few different ways. Documents have a *home folder* that may be navigated to by expanding and collapsing the folder tree, or each document may be accessed by a URL. The URL enables documents to be linked to other documents that may be categorized in different logical folders. This provides end users the option of navigating the treelike structure to find information, as well as the ability to jump to associated information based on links.

Index, Search, and Retrieval

In the area of text indexing and retrieval, SAP has stuck to the built-versus-buy heritage and created an indexing service called *TRex*. TRex is an acronym for

Text, Retrieval, and Extraction. TRex can index Web sites, corporate directories, local directories, and other file-management systems. TRex creates an index for both structured and unstructured information and supports Java and .NET services. Three primary search features are available: basic, linguistic, and fuzzy. The *basic search* is a standard Boolean search. A *linguistic search* retrieves words of the same family (for example, a search for "grapes" may return documents about wine, raisins, farming, and so on). A *fuzzy search* is best applied when the spelling of a word is unknown.

NOTE TRex is also at the center of the SAP BW High Performance Analytics (HPA) offering, which provides linear scalability and is suitable for grid computing environments. Chapter 12 addresses HPA in more detail.

People Integration

One of the last areas in organizations left to be automated is that of people integration. Many business processes are performed in an ad-hoc manner, within a set of flexible boundaries that require collaboration and input from numerous individuals. Automating a process like the launch of a new drug for a pharmaceutical company has to date been confined to subtasks within in the launch process. SAP now has a platform for managing and supporting such processes. SAP accomplishes this type of process automation by offering components and services that enable collaboration, multichannel access, and a Portal that enables flexible business processes to be guided rather than hard-wired.

The idea behind multichannel access is that there are numerous ways to connect people to other people as well as to enterprise systems. Communication channels such as interactive voice response (IVR) and radio frequency identification (RFID), in addition to the traditional Web/GUI, are indeed the methods in which people access information. There are also messaging and mobile access channels that we've described in preceding sections of this chapter. SAP has delivered a handful of components and services to support people integration. This section explores the Portal, Business Unification, and Collaboration.

Portal Framework

The goal of the Portal is to create a common entryway into corporate applications and information, as well as into applications and information that may exist outside of the enterprise. Portals are generally described as "Yahoo! for corporate information." While this description is valid, it is incomplete.

Sure, the Portal from SAP includes services for security and SSO; personalization of content and applications; offering, indexing, categorizing, and retrieving documents via its KM; workflow approvals; and online collaboration; as well as the ability to execute applications. But the Portal component takes this a step further.

The Portal contains an optional Business Unification layer that enables the dynamic integration of both applications and information from various sources. This is often referred to as *Drag and Relate technology*. The unification services expose the relationships between objects and tables and allow the Portal end user to dynamically link information and applications with a few clicks. Not unlike a data warehouse implementation, Portal projects define metadata repositories and spend a fair amount of time on data integration in order for end users to make only a few clicks.

Unification is discussed in greater detail shortly, but you should first note that, unlike earlier versions of Business Unification, the current release of the product no longer needs to run on a separate server from the Portal. It is now tightly integrated with the Portal, runs on the Java side of the NetWeaver AS, and utilizes relational database technology. This is a positive and significant evolution in the product.

A common question often asked is, "Are we able to utilize the Business Unification component with our existing non-SAP Portal?" Unfortunately, the answer is no. One way to think about the relationship between Business Unification and the Portal is to think of it as you would a VCR and a television. The television enables you to watch programming without a VCR, but the VCR provides little value without being attached to a television.

Figure 2-14 shows the architecture of the Portal.

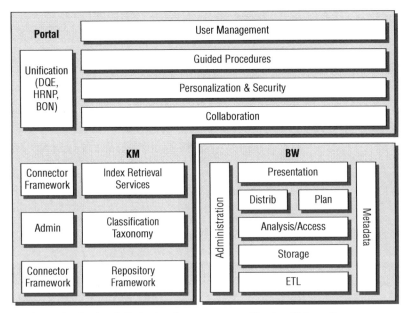

Figure 2-14   Portal and SAP BW

Portal Runtime Environment

The Portal Runtime Environment consists of both Portal Components and Services. The Components are the Page Builder, Containers, and Administration tools. The Services (which may be exposed as Web services) include User Management Services, Navigation Services, Content Management Services, and the Portal Content Directory (PCD) services.

The PCD is the heart of the Portal, and at the center of the PDC are *iViews*, which are like frames within a page on the Portal that may be customized on a per-user basis for a given application or information source. These iViews are analogous to Plumtree's Gadgets (acquired by BEA Systems Inc.) or Share-Point's (Microsoft) Web Parts. An iView may contain information from any source, be it text, graphics, reports, table listings, or charts, to name a few.

An end user may interact with an iView (for example, if a list of orders is displayed in a table format, a single order may be selected to review the order line items). A Portal user may drag information from an iView to any number of components on the Portal page. This is referred to as the *work area*. The components in a work area are not limited to SAP systems but include other systems from other enterprise application vendors or custom systems. External Web services (such as FedEx for shipment tracking) may be launched and context-sensitive information passed about a business object.

An administrator of the PCD designs the layout of a *workset*, which is a series of tasks that may be performed by an end-user community. Worksets are made of Portal pages that include one or more iViews. They exist primarily because of the lack of screen real estate available in Web browsers. Worksets are assigned to roles and then roles to users. The PCD includes the roles and the systems with which the Portal is to interact. This enables flexible security schemes to be deployed that deliver the appropriate applications and information to a set of users.

The NetWeaver Portal has a collection of predefined worksets that may be downloaded from the SAP Developer's Network in the form of content portfolios. The Web site contains both certified and noncertified content packages in the form of Portal archive repositories (`.par` files) to ease importing and activation. Worksets are not unlike Business Content in that their goal is to speed an implementation to the realization of business value. Also, like SAP BW Business Content, there is still integration work for project teams to make the worksets function according to an organization's specific requirements.

Business Unification

An optional Portal component is called *Business Unification*. Business Unification enables the creation of a unified object model so that a Portal user may dynamically integrate applications and information from various sources.

Business Unification maintains a model for the business objects of the back-end systems and their relationships to one another. Different back-end systems may be correlated to one another and presented to end users as if they were in the same system. This is a type of front-end information integration. Business objects may include tables in a database, business objects from the Repository of mySAP ERP (BOR), or InfoObjects from SAP BW.

The unification server enables business objects from these various, technically unrelated applications to be queried with a common set of qualifiers. This enables Portal developers to create composite applications that query multiple back-end systems with one SQL statement, as shown here:

```
*Database Table
(<System Alias>.<Table>.<Column>)
*R/3 System
(<System Alias>.<BusinessObject>.<Column/Attribute>)
*BW System
(<System Alias>.<Table/InfoObject>.<Column/Attribute>)
```

This functionality may best be described with an example. Imagine that a manager logs on to an intranet. Navigating to a page full of various iViews, the manager displays a list of sales orders that have been entered for a particular division. The manager sees a unification icon next to each sales order, which lets him or her know that a relationship exists between this sales order and another object in this or another system. In this case, an object is defined that represents customer master data in a separate, say, non-SAP, CRM system. The manager can drag any part of the sales order from the iView to the object representing the customer, and the unification technology will relate the sales order to the details of the corresponding customer.

The unification concept was perhaps the primary benefit of SAP's acquisition of TopTier Software in the spring of 2001, aside from the talented human capital. Unification uses logical business objects from component systems to create a unification object model of sorts. This object model is stored in the repository, and a mapping links objects to one another. Through the use of the unification server, users are able to dynamically pass content from one information source or application to another.

Unification within SAP components is reasonably straightforward, because SAP has developed its application components, for the most part, on a consistent business object model. These logical business objects represent such things as purchase orders, vendors, or even users of a system. Let's look at the aforementioned sales order example.

The sales order has different attributes such as the customer's PO number, the document date, the product ordered, the quantities being purchased, the customer requesting the order, the price, and so on. These attributes may be used as input for various transactions. The customer placing the sales order may only be displayed by perhaps a unique identifying number. Most users will not know which customer the number is associated with, unless they go to the transaction to display the master data for the customer that placed a specific order.

Since the repository contains an object representing the customer and an object representing the purchase order, along with the relationship between the two objects, unification is possible. The so-called *unifier* is stored in the Business Object Repository (BOR). This enables a Portal user who may be picking products to fill the sales order to take the order and drag it to the customer master data display transaction within the Portal page and release. The customer number, along with the other attributes of the sales order object, would be passed as input parameters to the receiver, in this case, the master data display transaction. This Drag and Relate utilizes a Hyper-Relational Navigation Protocol (HRNP), which passes the information about the object, as well as the object key.

For example, a sales order object in the BOR may be referenced by BUS2012. An instantiation of the order object (that is, a specific sales order) may be given the number 12345. The HRNP would enable the association of the specific sales order as it is displayed on the Portal page. This is seen by the Portal user as a draggable link displayed as a unification icon. The hypertext markup for this would look like the following (assuming this unifier is available through port 3500):

```
<href a="hrnp://mysystem.mydomain:3500/BUS2012/OBJECTKEY/12345">
```

All of the sales orders in a system will have the same draggable link as seen in the preceding code snippet. However, the last five digits would represent each unique purchase order. Since the object is dragged as a whole, it does not matter which attributes are specifically dragged to the master data display transaction. The object model and underlying relationships between the objects will take care to determine the appropriate values to pass. Therefore, you may drag the customer number, the sales order number, or perhaps even an item within the sales order to display the customer transaction and the correct customer master data.

The business objects of a component system are mapped within their respective BOR. These relationships are defined with the correlater wizard. The wizard evaluates the business objects within the repository and finds potential objects that may be related. It is possible to manually establish relationships not picked up by the wizard. Relationship-resolving is the way a source navigates to a target. There maybe implied relationships that connect a source object to a target object in a Drag and Relate scenario.

Note that a unifier project is necessary per component system. Each project is then defined within the Portal as a data source. For example, mySAP ERP would be defined in the Portal as a data source so that the business objects found in mySAP ERP may be included in a unifier project. Within the data source definition, users are mapped to their appropriate component user IDs. This can be done using either certificates or standard user mapping. Once this linkage is established, the unifier project is assigned to a role, and the role is assigned to a Portal user.

An important aspect of unification is the *connector*. A connector provides an interface to communicate with the component system whether that system is an SAP component or non-SAP component. A connector must be installed or activated for a unification project. In the case of unifying non-SAP systems, databases take the place of SAP business objects.

The unification server now includes business object navigation (BON) along with the HRNP, as well as a Distributed Query Engine (DQE). BON enables drill-down to a business object's details via a context menu. Upon clicking a field in an iView, the context menu will display a list of potential targets that the field may be related to (more accurately the object the field is an attribute of). BON uses this type of context-sensitive menu to display objects based on the user's role, too.

The DQE is an equally powerful part of the unification services. It breaks queries into subqueries and sends those queries to the respective back-end source system for processing. Once the results of all the subqueries are returned, the DQE assembles the results and presents them in a unified manner to the Query iView on a Portal page.

The DQE utilizes the metadata from business objects found in the back-end systems. The enterprise information system collects the metadata for the business objects in those back-end systems and enables a class I ODS to be created virtually. As briefly discussed in Chapter 1 (and to be discussed in Chapter 5), the VODS is technique for realizing real-time access to information inside and outside of an organization, across various databases without copying or pre-processing the data.

Guided Procedures

Guided procedures provide a set of boundaries for modeling business processes that span multiple back-end systems, while supporting ad-hoc runtime collaboration. As stated earlier in this chapter, not all business processes may be hard-wired. The collaborative aspects of a task in a business process are often ad hoc and highly dependant on the culture of an organization. For example, if you look at a financial budgeting process, discussions and haggling often occur prior to finalizing a figure. The budgeting business process is not as simple as, "Here is the spreadsheet. Fill in your figures and send it to corporate so we may roll them up." Guided procedures allow the nondeveloper to configure business processes that trigger online application services (as well as supporting offline forms) in an intuitive graphical interface that takes advantage of reusable patterns.

Guided procedures may be thought of in three distinct ways:

- Design time
- Runtime
- Administration

The *design time* environment provides a gallery of reusable components and processes that may be modeled to create collaborative applications. The components consist of *callable objects*, which are essentially services that have been exposed by enterprise applications, process flows, and roles. The callable objects are assembled into a process flow where context is persistently maintained. *Work items* may be created and assigned to users or roles for processing tasks within a business process. These work items appear in a user's work list for processing. The workflow runtime is that same as the BPM runtime discussed earlier in this chapter.

Guided procedures may be maintained in various so-called *perspectives*. For example, the flow control perspective illustrates the steps in the procedure and how they are sequenced for execution, which could include parallel steps and/or parallel work-item paths. There are also perspectives to illustrate the data flowing between work items, as well as the resources (think human resources) to perform a given work item. The administration aspect of guided procedures allows for the monitoring and managing of the instantiated work processes. It also supports software logistics in that guided procedures may be transported to other installations of the Portal.

User Management and Personalization

The Portal utilizes the LDAP to retrieve user entries and attributes stored in the directory. Several vendors, including Microsoft and Novell, support the LDAP standard. The Portal requires an LDAP-compatible directory. The Portal may use any LDAP directory already in place within a corporation, or the Novell eDirectory delivered by SAP with NetWeaver may be implemented. LDAP is a standard method by which to access a user directory. The directory is similar to a database in many ways, but it is designed to support reading information more so than writing, and, as such, it lacks many of the rollback-restore features of a conventional database.

The Portal uses the directory to store users and their information (such as full name, password, and address). The mapping of each user to the various component systems is also stored in the directory. The directory may include passwords to each of these systems as well. Access is controlled by the directory server.

Many corporations already have some kind of directory deployed. It is possible to synchronize the LDAP-compliant directory delivered as part of the SAP Portal with one or many existing corporate directories. In the end, SAP customers have a choice of using the directory delivered by SAP, a non-SAP directory, or a combination of both. The goal is to support SSO to corporate applications and information sources. The Portal makes this possible by the use of a certificate that may be loaded into a corporate application (SAP BW, for example). Once the certificate is loaded, a user in the Portal may be granted access to the system.

Collaboration

Collaboration services enable communication within an organization, as well as with trading partners. Services such as virtual rooms, integration with groupware applications, and Web-conferencing tools are all supported by the Portal. Among the more common features is the entry of personal notes for any given document stored in the Portal. A collection of feedback and rating forms is also available. The feedback and polling information may be used as a preference during the automatic classification and categorizing of new documents or the reclassifying of existing documents. The collaboration services allow, for example, a document to be published to a specific business workflow process for approval. The collaboration services are pervasive throughout NetWeaver components.

SAP has taken instant messaging (IM) from the playground to the workplace. People-centric services are available for inclusion in collaborative applications. They include such services as a common method for rendering people that indicates their status and ability to perform various tasks. This people-picker service is designed to reduce the email traffic that often starts with subject lines such as, "I don't know if you are the person to ask about this, but I'll ask anyway…" or "Do you know who is responsible for…."

Another collaborative option is the so-called Synchronous Collaboration Framework (SCF). The SCF is used to integrate tools such as NetMeeting and WebEx into the Portal. For the most part, the SCF is a set of APIs that enable a developer to integrate aspects of the Portal such as the team calendar with the online meeting tools. It also enables integration with the KM services so that the meeting's content is retrievable in an asynchronous manner as well.

Composite Application Framework

The Composite Application Framework (CAF) is a collection of tools and methods for assembling applications from the services exposed by existing applications. The goal of the CAF is to be able to create an application from existing applications without having to write code. There are three layers to the CAF architecture: Process, UI, and Persistence/Services. Figure 2-15 illustrates the layers of the associated components and the services within each. You may be asking yourself, "How is this different from guided procedures?" In fact, guided procedures are one of the tools used to create composite applications.

Composite Application Framework

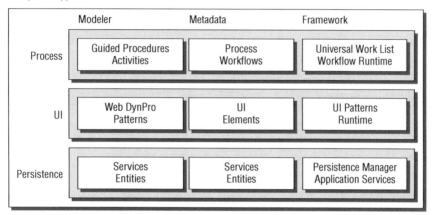

Figure 2-15 Composite Application Framework

The real value in the CAF is that it provides not only a place to view and assemble services from application services, but it also creates a persistence layer for instantiating new applications from those services. It also enables business logic to be implemented around the services and provides for a common user interface. The unified business object model enables not only an object persistency layer but also provides for an abstraction of business process steps and user interface elements by so-called *actions*. This separation, along with object-model persistence, makes it possible for nontechnical users to model new processes and user interfaces and then activate them.

The entity services and application modelers are two of the tools available to the creator of composite applications. These tools are used to define entity and application services and their corresponding attributes. The entity modeler will create the tables and underlying data dictionary elements as well as the methods for the entities (that is, read, write, and search). The application modeler is responsible for creating the composite application's business logic and connecting services to the user interface. As you might expect, the user interface may be built from *patterns*, which are simply commonly used user interface templates and elements.

As more and more applications are developed to support ESA, the greater the need for "development" or assembly platforms. In time, business processes will be adjustable with a few simple commands.

Summary

SAP, with its mySAP ERP, has long been a force in the IT industry. SAP has evolved its offering beyond just ERP into an "applistructure" provider. Along with its customer relationship management, supply chain optimization, and business intelligence solutions, SAP has created a technical infrastructure to support ESA called NetWeaver. This transformation has been driven by customer demand, industry adoption of Web-service standards, and technological innovation.

NetWeaver consists of a core technology stack that supports both an ABAP and a Java technology stack and is referred to as the NetWeaver AS. The technology platform is accompanied by tools and components that support process, information, and people integration.

In Chapter 3 and throughout the remainder of this book, we describe business intelligence capabilities, its architecture, and the options available within NetWeaver to those implementing the software to solve business challenges.

SAP Business Information Warehouse Architecture

SAP entered the data warehouse market when the market started maturing and has been able to take advantage of the experience available and avoid many mistakes made by early adopters. To those familiar with other data warehouse solutions and custom data warehouse development, as well as anyone following discussions about data warehousing, the high-level SAP Business Information Warehouse (SAP BW) architecture looks familiar.

Being part of the SAP NetWeaver integration and application platform, SAP BW takes advantage not only of the service-oriented architecture of SAP NetWeaver but also of complete software-development environments for both ABAP and Java, a comprehensive set of systems-management tools, and a variety of additional functionality and tools (such as unit or currency conversion, authorizations, locking, monitoring, and so forth).

SAP BW is fully integrated with other SAP NetWeaver components such as the Enterprise Portal the Exchange Infrastructure (XI), master data management (MDM), or knowledge management (KM). Portal integration, for example, provides advanced information-distribution features, while KM capabilities are used to store and document metadata objects as well as actual data used in SAP BW.

This chapter provides an overview of the SAP BW architecture and its metadata concepts.

SAP BW Architectural Components

Figure 3-1 shows a high-level view of the SAP BW architecture, with eight main building blocks organized in the typical six-layer architecture of an end-to-end data warehouse accompanied by two administrative components:

- Metadata and document management services, featuring metadata maintenance and management of unstructured documents
- Design, administration, and monitoring services, combining design time, administrative, and process-monitoring features
- A data-acquisition and transformation layer, providing functionality to extract and transform data from different sources
- A data-storage layer, including services for storing, managing, and archiving data
- A data-access and analysis layer, offering services to access and analyze data stored in SAP BW
- A planning layer, supporting planning applications
- An information-distribution layer, with functionality for distributing information to information consumers — end users, analysts, or other applications
- A presentation layer, offering different options for presenting information to end users and analysts

It is no surprise to see that SAP BW is completely based on an integrated metadata management concept. SAP BW still is one of the few data warehouse products that offer an integrated, one-stop-shopping user interface for design, administration, and monitoring: the Data Warehousing Workbench (DW Workbench).

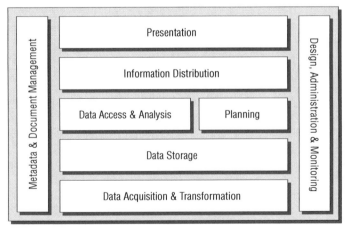

Figure 3-1 SAP BW high-level architecture

Metadata and Document Management

Like other data warehouse solutions, SAP BW is based on metadata or data about data. Three types of metadata can be distinguished: *business*, *technical*, and *operational*, with the first two commonly referred to as just *metadata*. While business data describes data from a business perspective (such as business rules or semantics) and technical metadata describes the technical aspects of data (such as data types, valid values, and so on), operational metadata relates to processes. SAP BW metadata objects are used to model and maintain business and technical metadata, while operational metadata is generated by data warehouse processes and is available through scheduling and monitoring components. Structured metadata can be enhanced with unstructured information using the document management capabilities of SAP BW.

SAP BW comes with predefined metadata, called *Business Content*. Business Content includes complete data warehousing scenarios, from data acquisition, transformation to reporting and analysis, and is introduced in Chapter 2. Chapter 10 provides a more detailed discussion of Business Content in the context of business analytics.

Metadata Management

The SAP BW *Metadata Management* services provide both an integrated *Metadata Repository* (where all metadata is stored) and *Metadata Management services* (which handle all requests for retrieving, adding, changing, or deleting metadata). A variety of different metadata objects describe all relevant objects and processes — definitions and more detailed descriptions of these objects are part of the discussions of the architectural components of SAP BW later in this chapter. Figure 3-2 shows the metadata services layer architecture.

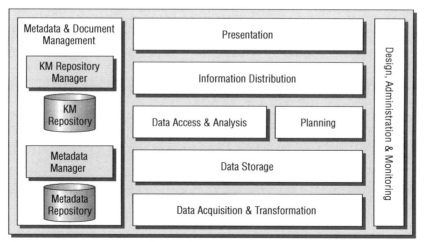

Figure 3-2   SAP BW Metadata and Document Management architecture

All functionality available to access the Metadata Repository shown in Figure 3-3 is integrated into the DW Workbench. The Metadata Repository provides an online hypertext documentation of metadata objects in use and the metadata objects included in the Business Content. You can export this hypertext documentation to a set of HTML files and publish it on a Web server, where it may also serve as an online and automatically updatable project documentation.

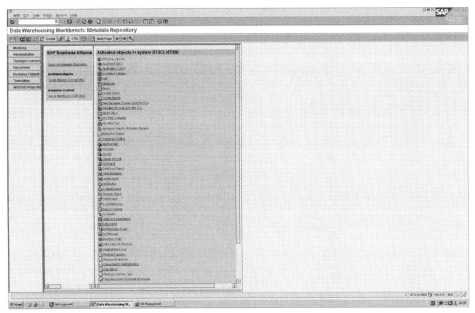

Figure 3-3 SAP BW Metadata Repository
Copyright © SAP AG

The Metadata Manager allows exchanging metadata in XML format with SAP BW systems or other systems compliant to the Common Warehouse Metamodel Interchange (CWMI) specified by the Object Management Group (www.omg.org).

Document Management

Besides fundamental metadata needed by data acquisition, transformation, and analysis processes maintained by SAP BW itself, any kind of documentation maintained in the *Knowledge Management Repository Framework* may be linked to relevant metadata objects. The KM Repository stores unstructured information and allows you to find and use this information efficiently.

Examples for such documents include word-processor documents, spreadsheets, or presentations.

This enables you to attach additional comments, descriptions, and documentation to static metadata objects, as well as to dynamic query result sets (or even single cells within these result sets) and have these instantly available in the DW Workbench, the Business Explorer, and on the Web.

Integration with the KM Repository provides an integrated view of structured and unstructured information to the end user.

Elementary Metadata Objects

Definitions of the most elementary metadata objects — the InfoObjects, InfoObject Catalogs and InfoAreas — are provided here up front to establish a basis for discussing the remaining architectural components and their metadata objects.

InfoObjects

InfoObjects are the core building blocks for all other data warehouse-related metadata in SAP BW (for example, data sources, transformations or queries). InfoObjects implemented in SAP BW provide a powerful basis for setting up complex information models supporting multiple languages, multiple currencies with automated translations based on the same sophisticated currency conversion rules as in mySAP ERP, multiple units of measure, multiple hierarchies, multiple versions of hierarchies of any type, and time-dependent master data.

An InfoObject is the SAP BW representation of the lowest-level business object used to describe business processes and information requirements. Four types of InfoObjects are available in SAP BW: key figures, characteristics, unit characteristics, and time characteristics.

Key figures are used to describe any kind of numeric information. Low-level numbers (such as sales quantities or sales revenues) and high-level key performance indicators (such as customer lifetime values) are all modeled using SAP BW key figures. SAP BW distinguishes six different types of key figures:

- **Amount** — Key figures of type *amount* are numeric values with an associated fixed or variable currency. SAP BW enforces a consistent representation composed of both the key figure and the currency through the whole staging and reporting/analysis process. Variable currencies are specified by unit characteristics (discussed later in this section), whereas fixed currencies are specified by currency codes stored in the InfoObject description.

- **Quantity** — Key figures of type *quantity* are numeric values with an associated fixed or variable unit of measure. As with amount key figures, SAP BW enforces a consistent representation of the key figure and the unit of measure. Variable units of measure are specified by unit characteristics (discussed later in this section), and fixed currencies are specified by codes for units of measure stored in the InfoObject description.

- **Number** — Key figures of type *number* are used for storing numbers in a floating-point or fixed-point format with no dimensions (currencies or units of measurement) associated.

- **Integer** — Key figures of type *integer* are used for storing numbers in an integer format with no dimensions (currencies or units of weight) associated.

- **Date** — Key figures of type *date* are used for storing date information. In contrast to date representations as characteristics, date key figures can be used for date computations (for example, actual date - planned date = delay).

- **Time** — Key figures of type *time* are used for storing time information. In contrast to time representations such as characteristics, time key figures can be used for time computations (for example, end time - start time = duration).

The *properties* of a specific key figure stored in the Metadata Repository include a technical description of the key figure (for example, the data type) and a business description (such as the unit of measure, currency, aggregation behavior, and display properties used in the Business Explorer).

Characteristics are used to describe the objects dealt with in business processes. These can be anything from core business objects such as customers, products, and accounts to simple attributes such as color, zip code, or status. While key figures from a database point of view simply describe a single field in a database base table, characteristics are more complex. The description of a characteristic includes a field description as it does for key figures, but it may also include the description of a complete set of master data tables storing attributes, texts, and hierarchies associated to that field. An InfoObject definition includes the following:

- Technical field descriptions such as data type, length, and conversion exits

- Display properties such as display keys/texts, filter properties, value help, relevance for authorization checks, and properties for geographical representations

- Data transfer routines executed whenever data records referencing this InfoObject are uploaded

- Master data descriptions such as a list of attributes (which themselves are InfoObjects of any type), time dependency of attributes, availability of attributes for query navigation and filtering, text properties (short, medium, long texts, time and language dependency), properties of hierarchies associated with the InfoObject (time and version dependency, among others), and a list of characteristics used in a compound key required to uniquely identify a certain instance of this InfoObject

Chapter 4 provides a more detailed description of some of the properties, as well as the data model used for storing master data.

Unit characteristics are used to store either currencies or units of measure in conjunction with key figures of type amount and quantity. Unit characteristics have a reduced set of properties compared with regular characteristics.

Time characteristics are predefined and used to represent date or time. Time characteristics are used in the obligatory time dimension of InfoCubes to express the time reference of business events. Time characteristics in SAP BW are internally treated in a special way. Table 3-1 shows time characteristics currently available in SAP BW.

Table 3-1 Time Characteristics in SAP BW

TIME CHARACTERISTIC	DESCRIPTION
0CALDAY	Full date in YYYYMMDD format
0CALMONTH	Month in YYYYMM format
0CALMONTH2	Month in MM format
0CALQUART1	Quarter in Q format
0CALQUARTER	Quarter in YYYYQ format
0CALWEEK	Week in YYYYWW format
0CALYEAR	Year in YYYY format
0FISCPER	Fiscal period including fiscal year variant in YYYYMMM format
0FISCPER3	Fiscal period with fiscal year in YYYYMMM format
0FISCVARNT	Fiscal year variant in VV format
0FISCYEAR	Fiscal year in YYYY format
0HALFYEAR1	Half year in H format
0WEEKDAY1	Day of week in D format

InfoObject Catalogs

An *InfoObject catalog* is a directory of InfoObjects used to catalog all Info-Objects defined in the system. InfoObject catalogs are very useful in organizing project work in large SAP BW implementations; typically, hundreds of different InfoObjects are used in several business contexts (for example, an InfoObject *Product* would be used in production, sales, and marketing).

Separate types of InfoObject catalogs are used for key figures and regular characteristics. InfoObjects can be assigned to several InfoObject catalogs simultaneously. A standard way of cataloging InfoObjects is to define two InfoObject catalogs (one for key figures and one for characteristics) for every business context and to assign all InfoObjects used in that business context to these InfoObject catalogs. InfoObject catalogs for unit and time characteristics are predefined by SAP.

InfoAreas

An *InfoArea* is a directory of InfoProviders (see the section "Data Storage," later in this chapter, for a definition) and InfoObject catalogs used in the same business context. Every InfoProvider or InfoObject catalog belongs to exactly one single InfoArea. InfoAreas are grouped in a hierarchy and, in the same way as InfoObject catalogs, help organize project work in large SAP BW implementations.

Obsolete Metadata Objects

Over time, some of the metadata objects available in SAP BW have become obsolete. While SAP BW still supports the use of these objects, their relevance for actual implementations will diminish. These include the following:

- **Event Chains** — Replaced by process chains
- **InfoPackage Groups** — Replaced by process chains
- **Reporting Agent Scheduling Packages** — Replaced by information broadcasting
- **Reporting Agent Settings** — Replaced by information broadcasting
- **InfoSpokes** — Replaced with the new transformation concept
- **MOLAP Aggregates** — Obsolete with introduction of the BI accelerator, no longer supported

Design, Monitoring, and Administration

Figure 3-4 shows the architecture of the design, monitoring, and administration components of SAP BW. This section addresses the primary features of this component.

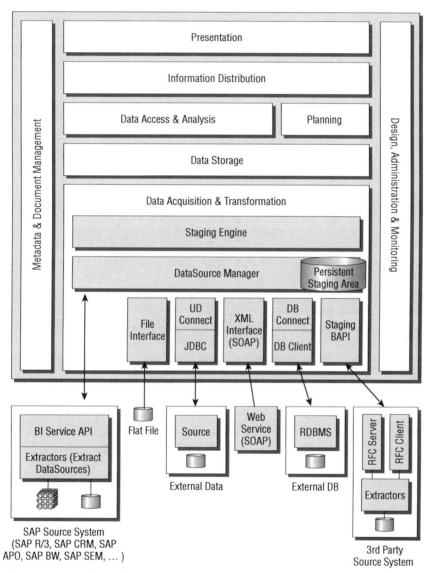

Figure 3-4   Design, administration, and monitoring architecture

With the DW Workbench shown in Figure 3-5, SAP BW provides a single point of entry for all design, monitoring, and administration, as well as document-management activities. As shown on the left-hand side of Figure 3-5, the DW Workbench itself is divided into the following six different areas:

- **Modeling** — Modeling of SAP BW metadata objects and processes

- **Administration** — Administrative and monitoring functionality

- **Transport Connection** — Transport of SAP BW metadata from development environments to test and production environments

- **Documents** — Maintenance of documents and their links to metadata objects

- **Translation** — Support functionality for the translation of metadata descriptions in a multilanguage environment

- **Metadata Repository** — Information portal for all SAP BW metadata, including technical details, cross references, and documentation

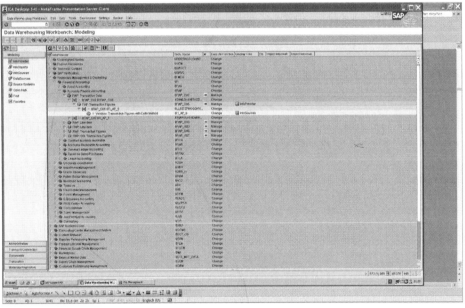

Figure 3-5   DW Workbench
Copyright © SAP AG

Design

The design and modeling functionality shown in Figure 3-5 is the most important part of the DW Workbench. It supports designing the information model, as well as all processes related to data acquisition, data staging, and information distribution through the DW Workbench. Figure 3-5 shows an InfoCube (FIAP: Transaction Data) with its complete data flow. Accounts-payable information is acquired from a mySAP ERP system, transformed, and staged into a DataStore Object from where it is then transformed and staged into the InfoCube. Chapters 6 through 9 provide a more complete discussion of the design functionality. The following discussion focuses on the most prominent metadata objects used in design and modeling.

InfoCubes

An *InfoCube* is a multidimensional data container used as a basis for analysis and reporting processes. SAP BW supports two classes of InfoCubes: *standard InfoCubes* and *real-time InfoCubes*. Standard InfoCubes are optimized for read access, allowing for scheduled uploads initiated by SAP BW. Real-time Info-Cubes have been developed for use by applications that must directly write data into the InfoCube, such as Integrated Planning or SAP Supply Chain Management (APO).

Regardless of which classes they belong to, InfoCubes always consist of key figures and characteristics, the latter organized in up to 16 dimensions. Three of these dimensions are predefined by SAP: the time dimension, the unit dimension, and the data packet dimension. While the *time dimension* can be directly customized by adding time characteristics to the InfoCube, the *unit dimension* is automatically maintained based upon the unit characteristics assigned to the key figures included in an InfoCube. The *data packet dimension* uniquely identifies data packages loaded into the InfoCube (supporting the data-quality efforts of SAP BW administrators) and cannot be modified or removed.

The terminology SAP uses to describe InfoCubes has caused some confusion in the data warehouse community. In that community, "dimension" is commonly used for what SAP calls a characteristic, whereas "dimension" is used by SAP to refer to a *collection* of characteristics. This explains why a maximum of 13 dimensions in SAP BW is not actually a serious restriction; one single dimension in SAP BW may be composed of more than 250 different characteristics.

InfoCubes can also include navigational attributes. *Navigational attributes* are not physically stored in the InfoCube; instead, they are attributes of characteristics included in the InfoCube definition and made available for navigation purposes (drill down, filtering, and so on). From an end user's perspective, characteristics and navigational attributes are used in exactly the same manner. However, navigational attributes differ from characteristics in two ways:

- The use of navigational attributes results in slightly more expensive data-access paths at query-execution time.

- Characteristics and navigational have different semantics in reporting and analysis.

Chapter 4 provides a more detailed discussion of both topics.

NOTE While you cannot define custom characteristics treated as time characteristics, you can define characteristics of data type **date** or **time** and use those to store additional date or time information. These characteristics cannot be assigned to the standard time dimension but must be assigned to a custom dimension. See Chapter 4 for a more detailed discussion of characteristics and dimensions.

Aggregates

Most of the requested result sets of reporting and analysis processes consist of aggregated data. In SAP BW, an *aggregate* is a redundantly stored, aggregated view on a specific InfoCube. Aggregates can significantly increase query performance by providing pre-aggregated data, avoiding access to the total number of records stored in the underlying InfoCube. In SAP BW, aggregates are available for InfoCubes and are stored in relational database tables utilizing the same data model and sharing some of the actual database tables used with InfoCubes.

Aggregates are still among the most powerful means that SAP BW provides to optimize the performance of reporting and analysis processes. Not only does SAP BW automatically take care of updating aggregates whenever necessary (for example, after uploads of master or transaction data); it also automatically determines the most efficient aggregate available at query-execution time. Chapter 12 provides a more detailed discussion of aggregates.

In the SAP NetWeaver 2004s release, classic aggregates are supplemented by the BI accelerator introduced in the "Data Storage" section, later in this chapter.

DataStore Objects

A *DataStore Object* is a data container with a flat structure used for reporting and data cleansing, data harmonization, and data-quality management. A DataStore Object consists of key figures and characteristics organized into key and data fields, with key figures unavailable for use as key fields. In previous releases of SAP BW, DataStore Objects have been known as Operational Data Store (ODS) Objects. To avoid confusion with the architectural concept of an ODS, SAP has decided to rename ODS Objects.

Three different types of DataStore Objects are available: standard DataStore Objects, direct-update DataStore Objects, and write-optimized DataStore Objects. *Standard DataStore Objects* are used as building blocks for the operational data store. They play an important role in designing a data warehouse layer, and from an end-user point of view, standard DataStore Objects made available for reporting purposes appear very similar to ordinary InfoCubes. *Direct-update DataStore Objects* are comparable to real time InfoCubes and are used for analytic applications such as the Analysis Process Designer (APD) that require direct updates. *Write-optimized DataStore Objects* are optimized for uploading large volumes of data but do not support automatic delta determination.

A more detailed discussion of the role of DataStore Objects in the context of the corporate information factory and the differences between DataStore Objects and InfoCubes can be found later in this chapter. Modeling aspects of DataStore Objects are discussed in Chapter 4.

InfoProviders

An *InfoProvider* is a physical or virtual data object available in an SAP BW system. As its name suggests, an InfoProvider provides information. InfoProvider is a generic term subsuming all metadata objects providing information (such as InfoCubes, DataStore Objects, InfoSets, and master data tables). InfoProviders are generally available for reporting and analysis purposes.

MultiProviders

A *MultiProvider* is a union of at least two physical or VirtualProviders available in an SAP BW system. A MultiProvider itself is a VirtualProvider. MultiProviders allow combining information from different subject areas on the fly at reporting/analysis execution time.

VirtualProviders

VirtualProviders are InfoProviders referring to data physically stored on a remote SAP BW, mySAP ERP, or third-party/custom system, made available to SAP BW by one of the following three methods:

- **Direct access through data-transfer process** — These VirtualProviders refer to sources of data available through standard SAP BW data transfer processes (discussed in Chapter 6).

- **BAPI-based virtual InfoCubes** — BAPI-based VirtualProviders refer to data stored on a remote system supporting the remote InfoCube BAPI. This type of VirtualProvider is used for third-party and custom data.

- **Function-module based virtual InfoCubes** — Function-module based VirtualProviders refer to data stored on a remote system available through a user-defined function module on an SAP system.

InfoSets

An *InfoSet* is a VirtualProvider implementing an additional abstraction layer on top of the SAP BW Metadata Repository. InfoSets allow defining joins of multiple InfoCubes, DataStore Objects, and master data tables. SAP BW InfoSets differ from classical InfoSets known from other SAP business solutions in that they are designed to support SAP BW InfoProviders.

Keep in mind that InfoSets and MultiProviders are not the same. MultiProviders implement a union of the underlying InfoProviders, while InfoSets define joins of the underlying InfoProviders.

Monitoring

Monitoring data-warehouse-related processes (as well as system stability and performance) is crucial in large data warehouse implementations. SAP BW monitoring provides configurable overview cockpits showing statistical information about data loads, query performance, aggregates, system loads, alerts, universal work lists, and others, in addition to detail-analysis transactions.

For example, the Data Load Monitor shown in Figure 3-6 supports troubleshooting by providing access to detailed protocols of all activities related to loading, transforming, and storing data in SAP BW — allowing you to access single data records and to simulate and debug user-defined transformations. Other processes monitored include DataStore-Object activation, master data attribute activation, hierarchy activation, aggregate rollup, realignment and readjustment jobs, InfoCube compression jobs, database-index maintenance, database-statistics maintenance, and data exports.

Administration

Administration includes all services required to administer an SAP BW system, such as the following:

- **Transport** — The *transport connector* supports consistent transports of development objects and settings in complex system landscapes with development, test, consolidation, and production systems by evaluating cross references between development objects and collecting objects in transport requests.

- **Information Lifecycle Management** — In addition to traditional archiving, SAP BW now supports moving dormant data to near-line storage (NLS) systems, keeping it available for reporting purposes while increasing performance of data load and reporting processes for frequently used data.

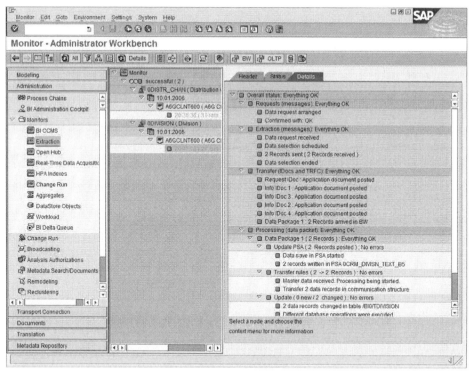

Figure 3-6   Overview cockpit and Data Load Monitor
Copyright © SAP AG

- **Authorizations** — SAP BW includes a sophisticated authorization concept allowing you to define standard authorizations to control access to metadata objects and analysis authorizations to control access to data stored in these metadata objects.

- **Analysis and repair services** — Consistency checks and corresponding repair programs are provided in one single transaction.

- **Remodeling** — Remodeling is new with the SAP NetWeaver 2004s release of SAP BW. Remodeling allows for changing the structure of standard InfoCubes without having to reload data.

- **Other settings** — A variety of administrative settings are available to control how SAP BW performs certain tasks, such as the number of parallel processes to be used for a single data-extraction process, the size of data packages in data extraction, and so on.

The following sections describe some of the metadata objects used in administration.

Users

Users are individuals or automated processes that have a unique identifier allowing them to log on to and use a specific SAP BW system.

Authorizations

An *authorization* warrants a specific user the right to perform a specific action (access or modify a metadata object) or retrieve a certain bit of information from an SAP BW system. SAP BW utilizes the technical infrastructure known from mySAP ERP to implement standard authorizations to control the actions performed on metadata objects. Analysis authorizations, on the other hand, are fully integrated into the analytic engine of SAP BW to provide a sophisticated framework for controlling access to information while keeping technical overhead low. Chapter 11 provides a more detailed description of SAP BW authorizations.

Roles

As implemented in SAP BW, the *role* concept resembles the role or function individuals have in an organization. Role definitions in SAP BW are composed of a collection of menu items (referring to queries, transactions, or documents), authorizations, and a set of users assigned to a given role.

Examples of such roles include a purchasing manager role or a sales representative role. In the same way as in an organization, roles can be assigned to multiple individuals simultaneously (such as there may be multiple sales representatives), and the assignment of roles to individuals may change over time without affecting the definition of the roles themselves (a purchasing manager will always be expected to manage the purchasing process regardless of the individual filling that role).

Currency Translation Types

Currency translation types are used to define how to convert currencies from a source to a target currency and which currency exchange rates to use for this conversion in transformations or in reporting and analysis processes.

Quantity Conversion Types

Quantity conversion types are used to define how to convert quantities from a source to a target quantity in transformations or in reporting and analysis processes.

Data Acquisition and Transformation

The *Data Acquisition and Transformation* layer of the SAP BW architecture includes services for data extraction, data transformation, and data loading. It also serves as a staging area for intermediate data storage for quality-assurance purposes. The major enhancements with the SAP NetWeaver 2004s release include the addition of the Universal Data Connect interface, major performance improvements of the Web Service (XML) interface, and a completely new data transfer and transformation process, including a new data-source concept. Figure 3-7 shows the architecture of this layer.

With the Universal Data Connect interface, SAP BW now supports a widely adopted standard for physical data access and has closed the gap of not being able to directly access non-SAP databases and data formats. That gap had stirred persistent discussions about the openness of the product and its ability to handle non-SAP data, although with the Staging BAPI, SAP did (and still does) provide an open interface that many third-party extract/transfer/load (ETL) tool vendors used to connect with SAP Business Intelligence.

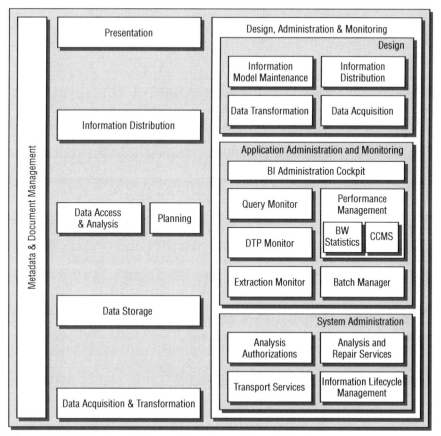

Figure 3-7 Data Acquisition and Transformation architecture

Significant performance improvements in the Web Service (XML) interface now allow for mass uploads of data (for example, using the SAP NetWeaver XI product or third-party tools with similar functionality). On the background of the general trend of using XML-based approaches in building interfaces between systems, the importance of the Staging BAPI will decrease in the long term.

The new data-transfer process is explained in more detail in Chapter 6. The main improvements here include a new data-source concept with improved data-staging performance, increased flexibility by being able to independently connect and load different types of sources of data to different InfoProviders, enhanced error-handling functionality, and a completely new graphical (and more intuitive) user interface for defining transformation rules. Figure 3-8 shows a comparison of the classic and the new data-staging processes.

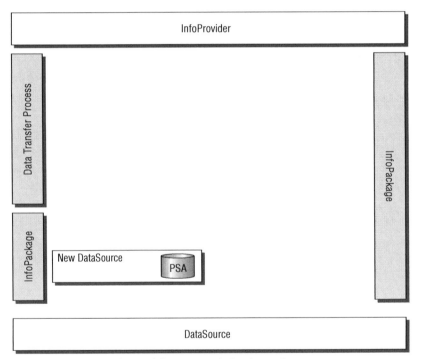

Figure 3-8   Comparison of the new and classic staging processes

Most Important Metadata Objects

The main differences between the classic and the new data-staging processes are examined as part of the discussion in the following sections defining the most important metadata objects of this layer. Note that the classic data acquisition and transformation scenarios are still fully supported in the SAP

NetWeaver 2004s release or later releases. However, SAP encourages SAP BW customers to use the new functionality for new implementations and, as of this writing, is preparing to offer migration tools to support migration efforts for existing applications.

Source Systems

A *source system* is a definition of a physical or logical system providing data to an SAP BW system. Six types of source systems are available:

- SAP NetWeaver-based business solutions equipped with the SAP BI Service API (including SAP BW itself), allowing you to extract data from other SAP BW systems or from objects stored in the same SAP BW system.

- Flat-file source systems, used for uploading flat files in ASCII, comma-separated variables (CSV), or binary format.

- DB Connect source systems providing access to external database systems.

- Third-party systems using the Staging BAPI interface. These can either be standard ETL tools supporting the Staging BAPI interface (such as Ascential, ETI, or Informatica) or custom programs.

- XML source systems accepting XML data streams.

- Universal Data Connect (UD Connect) source systems providing access to all types of external data through the JDBC interface, the OLE DB for OLAP interface, the XML for analysis interface or the SAP Query interface. Additional connectors for the UD Connect interface may become available over time.

All types of source systems except the flat-file source system include references to some physical source system or service. This reference typically includes network or service address information (such as the RFC destination) to allow SAP BW to automatically connect to the source system and retrieve metadata or request data extractions. The description of a flat-file source system simply consists of a name and a description of the source system. Requests for data loads are executed by the SAP BW server itself in this case.

DataSources

A *DataSource* describes a specific source of data on a specific source system from a technical point of view. The DataSource description includes information about the extraction process and the data-transfer process, and it provides the option to store data transferred to SAP BW in the persistent staging area (PSA).

SAP BW distinguishes between classic DataSources supporting the classic data-staging process as described earlier and the new DataSources supporting the enhanced data-staging process. Four different types of DataSources are available: transaction data (or flexible staging), master data attributes, texts, and hierarchies. As of this writing, DataSources for hierarchies are available only as classic DataSources. Figures 3-9 and 3-10 provide illustrations of both DataSource concepts. Chapter 6 contains a detailed description. Throughout this book, the term *DataSource* is used generically wherever a distinction between a classic and a new DataSource concept is not required.

DataSource descriptions are source-system specific, because different source systems may provide the same data in different specifications, technical formats, or with a different level of detail. Source systems may provide a list of fields available for the DataSource, which may be replicated to the SAP BW Metadata Repository, as shown on the lower left-hand side of Figures 3-9 or 3-10. Or DataSources may have to be maintained manually, as for DataSources for flat-file source systems (lower right-hand side of Figures 3-9 and 3-10).

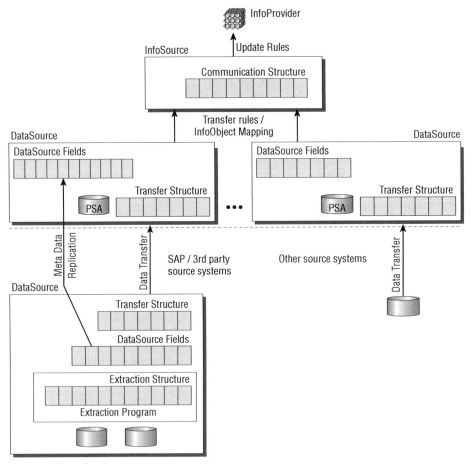

Figure 3-9 Classic DataSource concept

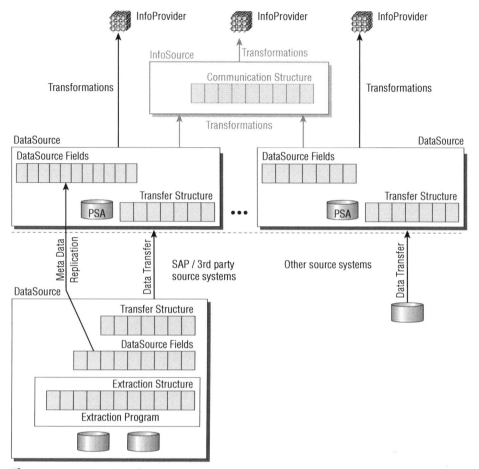

Figure 3-10 New DataSource concept

Note that regardless of the type of source system, the DataSource definition itself is always controlled by SAP BW, while the extraction process and the technical specifications of the extraction program are defined by the source system.

The PSA is a set of database tables for storing data uploaded to an SAP BW system prior to applying transformation rules. The main purpose of the PSA is to store uploaded data for data-quality and consistency maintenance. Once stored in the PSA, data is available for multiple updates into multiple InfoProviders at different points, avoiding multiple extraction runs for the same set of data.

The PSA can be accessed using a published API. It supports error handling and simulation of data updates. A complete error-handling scenario based on the PSA includes identifying and tagging invalid records as part of the upload process, manually or automatically correcting the tagged records utilizing the PSA API, and restarting the upload for the corrected records. The simulation feature includes debugging options and has proved helpful in developing transformations.

Application Components

An *application component* is a directory of DataSources and InfoSources. Just as InfoAreas are used for organizing InfoProviders, the application hierarchy helps to organize DataSources and InfoSources. Neither type of object can be assigned to more than one node in the application hierarchy.

InfoSources

An *InfoSource* describes a source of business information (business events or business-object description) available in one or multiple source systems. The core part of an InfoSource definition is the communication structure composed of a set of InfoObjects.

An InfoSource is not designed to store data. Instead, it is an intermediary between the technical implementation of the data-transfer process and the specific business requirements modeled into the InfoCubes, DataStore Objects, and master data. Figure 3-9 shows a classic InfoSource and its communication structure.

In the reality of actual SAP BW implementation projects, where there is a general trend toward implementing a layered data warehouse, the role of the Info-Source as an intermediary between technical and business aspects of the staging process has diminished. Consequently, InfoSources are now an optional part of the staging process and will be used mostly for structuring complex staging processes.

Transfer Rules

Transfer rules are a set of transformations defining the mapping of fields available in a specific DataSource to the fields used in an InfoSource definition. You create transfer rules by assigning a DataSource to an InfoSource and assigning InfoObjects to the fields of the extract structure (InfoObject mapping). The main purpose of transfer rules is converting the source-system-specific representation of data into an SAP BW-specific view and eliminating technical or semantic differences among multiple source systems providing the same data. Typical transformations used for this purpose include data-type conversions, key harmonization, and addition of missing data. Transfer rules allow you to check the data loaded for referential integrity — enforcing that all characteristics values sent by the source system are already available in the corresponding master data tables. In conjunction with the PSA, you can also use transfer rules to check and ensure data integrity.

SAP BW offers several ways to actually define a specific transformation:

- Simple field assignments, where a field of the transfer structure is assigned to a field of the InfoSource

- Constant value assignment, where a constant value is assigned to a field of the InfoSource

- Formulas, where predefined transformation functions can be used to fill a field of the InfoSource

- Routines, which allow you to implement custom ABAP code for complex transformations

> **NOTE** Transfer rules are available only for classic DataSources; for new DataSources, *transformations* are used instead.

A *transfer structure* is data structure that describes the technical data format used to transfer data from a source system to an SAP BW system. The transfer structure can be regarded as an agreement between the SAP BW system and its source system on how to transfer data and what data to transfer. Transfer structures effectively are a projection view upon the fields of the DataSource, because they usually are made up of a subset of those fields.

Multiple DataSources can be assigned to a single InfoSource, allowing you to extract the same kind of data from different source systems (for example, sales orders from different operational systems used in different regions) or to extract different flavors of the same kind of data from one single source system (for example, standard material master data and material classification data from a mySAP ERP system). A DataSource can only be assigned to one single InfoSource; assigning a DataSource implicitly assigns a source system to that InfoSource.

Update Rules

Update rules connect an InfoSource to an InfoProvider (InfoCube, DataStore Object, or a master data table), allowing it to specify additional transformations from a business point of view.

Update rules establish a many-to-many relationship between InfoSources and InfoProviders. An InfoSource can be used to update multiple InfoProviders, and an InfoProvider can be updated from multiple InfoSources. While transfer rules are used to eliminate technical differences, update rules are used to perform transformations required from a business point of view. For example:

- Perform additional data validity and integrity checks

- Perform data enrichment (for example, adding fields read from master data tables)

- Skip unnecessary data records

- Aggregate data

- Dissociate data provided in a single data record into several records in the InfoCube (for example, dissociate plan and actual data delivered in one record)

- Convert currency and unit of measure

Update rules support the same types of transformations as transfer rules, plus an automated lookup of master data attributes that, for example, allows you to assign a material group value read from the material master data table to the material group characteristic of an InfoCube. Update rules automatically take care of mapping the logical data flow to the physical implementation of the InfoProvider, including generation of surrogate keys.

> **NOTE** Like transfer rules, update rules are only available for classic Data-Sources; for new DataSources *transformations* are used instead.

Transformations

Essentially, *transformations* descend from the update rules known from the classic DataSource concept, replace the combination of transfer and update rules, and enhance their functionality and performance. Transformations connect sources (for example, DataSources, DataStore Objects, InfoCubes, Info-Sets, and so on) to targets (for example, InfoProviders) of a data-staging process and establish an n:m relationship between these two in the same way as update rules establish an n:m relationship between InfoSources and Info-Providers. The most important improvements with transformations include (but are not limited to) the following:

- End Routines, in addition to the existing start routines, allow modifications to the whole data package after all other transformations have been applied.

- Expert Routines allow the implementation of complex transformations independent of the restrictions of the standard data-transformation process.

- Transformation Groups replace the key figure specific updates of the update rules of the classic data-transformation process.

- Use of ABAP objects as a framework for ABAP-based transformations.

Chapter 6 provides more information on transformations.

Formulas

Formulas are a convenient means of implementing simple transformations that cannot be accomplished by direct assignments of InfoObjects or constant values, avoiding the need to code such transformations in the ABAP programming language. Formulas are available in transfer rules, update rules, and transformations.

NOTE In early versions of SAP BW, formula performance has been very poor, leading to long load times for even simple formulas. This has been improved dramatically starting with the SAP NetWeaver releases of the software, so that formulas are now actually usable in many transformation scenarios. For complex formulas, however, an implementation in ABAP should still be considered.

InfoPackages

All scheduling and monitoring functions for classic data-transformation processes are based on *InfoPackages*, which are defined per DataSource and source system. In the new data-transformation process, the role of InfoPackages is restricted to defining the data-acquisition process; acquired data is stored in the PSA and made available for further processing using the new data transfer process (DTP). The following list shows an overview of all properties of an InfoPackage:

- **Selection criteria** — Selection criteria are similar to the standard ABAP select options. Fields available in the InfoSource and tagged as selection fields can be used to restrict the amount of data extracted from the source system, provided that the source system supports field selections. Selection parameters can be specified as fixed or variable values. Hierarchies do not support selections based on field values. Instead, the selection screen for hierarchies allows you to select one of the hierarchies available in the source system for the current InfoSource for upload.

- **External filename, location, and format** — These options are available only for uploads from a file source system and specify the details about the file to be uploaded.

- **Third-party parameters** — Third-party parameters are required by third-party extraction programs (ETL tool or custom program). These parameters heavily depend on the actual source system and typically include usernames and passwords.

- **Processing options** — Processing options depend on the definition of the transfer rules. If the transfer rules are PSA enabled, the processing options allow you to specify how the PSA should be used during the upload process. These options are not applicable to new DataSources.

■ **Data target selection** — Data target selection allows you to select which of the InfoProviders available for the InfoSource should be updated by the upload process and how to handle existing data in the data target (keep data, delete based on selection criteria, or delete all data). These options are not applicable to new DataSources.

■ **Update parameters** — Update parameters are used to request full or delta loads and for defining basic error-handling parameters. These options are not applicable to new DataSources.

■ **Scheduling** — Scheduling parameters allow you to specify exactly when and at what frequency a specific data upload is supposed to be executed. Options for specifying the time of an upload include immediate upload, upload at a specific time, upload after completion of a specific job, and upload at a certain event.

InfoPackages are fully integrated into the SAP BW job control functionality around process chains, discussed in detail later in this chapter.

Data Transfer Process

A *data transfer process* (DTP) performs a data transformation from source to target in a similar way as InfoPackages in the classic data-transformation process. DTPs define more advanced parameters of the transformation process including the following:

■ The extraction mode allows for full and delta extractions from the source.

■ Error handling has been improved in the new DTP allowing three different options in case of invalid data records in a data request:

  ■ *No update, no reporting*

  ■ *Update valid records, no reporting*

  ■ *Update valid records, allow reporting*

■ The data package size defines how the request for data is segmented in data packages by defining the maximum size of a data package.

■ Selection criteria on field level now allow for selective updates of targets within SAP BW.

■ Restarting parameters allow you to define how a certain extraction can be restarted. Temporary storage can be used to facilitate restarting processes.

■ The degree of parallelization can be defined to control system performance and utilization.

Process Chains

A *process chain* is a defined sequence of interdependent processes required to perform a complex task in an SAP BW environment. Tasks are not restricted to uploading data. Aggregate maintenance, index maintenance, master data activation, DataStore Object activation, and a variety of other jobs are required to update data, guarantee best-possible performance, and maintain data integrity. Typical SAP BW implementations have complex interdependent networks of jobs in place that run every night, week, or month. Figure 3-11 shows a simple example of a typical job network, including standard and custom processes.

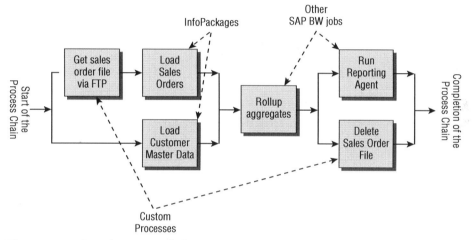

Figure 3-11   Sample process chain

Process chains allow you to define complex job networks consisting of standard SAP BW jobs as well as custom jobs. They support visualizing the job network and centrally controlling and monitoring the processes.

Staging Engine

The core part of the ETL services layer of SAP BW is the *Staging Engine*, which manages the classic and the new staging process for all data received from several types of source systems. The Staging Engine generates and executes transformation programs, performing the transformations defined in the DW Workbench. It interfaces with the scheduler and monitor for scheduling and monitoring data-load processes. The type of source system is transparent to the Staging Engine; the same staging process is applied to SAP data as well as non-SAP data.

The actual implementation of transformations will differ, however, for different types of systems, simply because different systems may deliver data about the same business events (for example, sales orders) using different record layouts, different data types, and different characteristics values for the same business semantics. In addition, different systems may provide different levels of data quality. Chapter 6 provides a detailed discussion of the staging process.

DataSource Manager

The Staging Engine is supported by the *DataSource Manager*. The DataSource Manager manages the definitions of the different sources of data known to the SAP BW system and supports six different types of interfaces:

- BI Service API
- File interface
- Web Service (XML) interface
- Universal Data Connect (UDConnect) interface
- DB Connect interface
- Staging BAPI

The DataSource Manager also allows capturing and intermediate storing of uploaded data in the PSA. Data stored in the PSA is used for several purposes:

- **Data quality** — Complex check routines and correction routines can be implemented to make sure data in the PSA is consistent before it is integrated with other data sources or is uploaded to its final data target.

- **Repeated delta updates** — Many extraction programs do not allow you to repeat uploads of *deltas*, which are sets of records in the data source that have been inserted or updated since the last upload. Repeated delta uploads are required in cases where the same delta data has to be updated into multiple data targets at different points of time.

- **Short-term backup data source** — A short-term backup data source is required in cases where update processes fail for some technical reason (such as insufficient disk space or network availability) or where subtle errors in the transformations performed on the data-warehouse side are only discovered at a later time. Once stored in the PSA, data may be read from the PSA and updated into the final data target at any time and as often as required.

- **Supporting development** — Based on data in the PSA, SAP BW allows you to simulate transformations and debug the implemented transformations.

BI Service API

The most important interface supported by the DataSource Manager in SAP environments is the *BI Service API*. The BI Service API is available in all SAP NetWeaver-based systems, including SAP BW itself. ERP-type systems usually provide operational data, while SAP BW-type systems allow the creation of complex information-flow scenarios with cascading SAP BW instances.

The BI Service API provides a framework for data replication from SAP systems, including generic data extraction, sophisticated delta-handling, and online access to extraction programs via the VirtualProviders. It handles all communication between the source system and the requesting SAP BW system and makes a wide range of predefined extraction programs (encapsulating application know-how) available to SAP BW. It is included in all SAP business solutions.

Extraction programs either are part of Business Content (from where they may be enhanced according to client requirements) or they are custom extraction programs (defined by the client using the generic extraction technology). Generic extractors allow accessing any table or database view available in the SAP ABAP dictionary. Used in SAP BW-based systems, the BI Service API provides access to data stored in master data tables, DataStore Objects, and InfoCubes.

File Interface

The *File interface* allows loading flat files of three different types into SAP BW:

- **ASCII files** — The File interface reads ASCII files with fixed field lengths and variable record lengths, filling missing fields with blanks and ignoring extra fields at the end of data records.

- **Comma-separated variables (CSV) files** — CSV files are text files using a variable field delimiter (usually ";" or ",") and variable field and record length. They are commonly used to exchange data among different applications.

- **Binary files** — The File interface can import binary files that comply with the physical data format used by ABAP programs writing data in binary format (documentation on the physical format used can be found at `http://help.sap.com`).

Web Service (XML) Interface

The *Web Service (XML) interface* accepts XML data streams compliant with the Simple Object Access Protocol (SOAP). While all other SAP BW interfaces follow the pull philosophy (meaning that SAP BW pulls data out of these systems by initiating data-load requests), the Web Service (XML) interface follows a push philosophy (where the actual data transfer is initiated by the source system).

Data loads through the Web Service (XML) interface are always triggered by an external Web service using SOAP to send XML format data to an SAP BW system, where data is temporarily stored using the delta queue mechanism. SAP BW pulls data out of the delta queue using the same scheduling mechanisms as for other interfaces. The Web Service (XML) interface is used by the SAP NetWeaver Exchange Infrastructure (SAP NetWeaver XI) to push data into SAP BW. Early versions of the interface suffered from serious performance problems, limiting the use of the Web Service (XML) interface to a relatively small number of records. These problems have been solved in the SAP NetWeaver 2004s release of the software.

Universal Data Connect

The *Universal Data Connect* (*UDConnect*) interface relies on the Java-based Universal Data Integration (UDI) infrastructure to access data on non-SAP (and SAP) systems. UDI currently supports the connectors listed here and is extendable by adding additional third-party or SAP connectors using the J2EE connector architecture:

- **JDBC Connector** — Non SAP relational
- **OLE DB for OLAP connector** — Non SAP multidimensional, SAP BI
- **XML for Analysis connector** — Non SAP multidimensional, SAP BI
- **SAP Query connector** — SAP

With uniform connection management and monitoring, UDConnect provides integrated access to virtually all available types of data sources.

DB Connect Interface

The *DB Connect interface* connects to a remote database and provides access to its database tables to an SAP BW system. The DB Connect interface uses core parts of the SAP database interface layer and the database client software (which must be installed separately if the remote database system differs from the local database system) to connect to the remote database. The DB Connect interface can read the remote data dictionary, replicate table, and view metadata into the local SAP BW Metadata Repository, and it allows extraction of data from those tables and views. The DB Connect interface supports all database systems supported by SAP BW.

Previous releases of SAP BW have come with a similar interface called *DB Link*. The DB Link interface has become obsolete with the introduction of the DB Connect interface and the UD Connect interface.

Staging BAPI

The *Staging BAPI* is an open interface based on the BAPI technology. Available from the first official release of SAP BW, the Staging BAPI allows third-party ETL tools (as well as custom programs) to connect to SAP BW, exchange metadata with SAP BW, and transfer data to SAP BW.

Systems using the Staging BAPI must implement a simple Remote Function Call (RFC) server program that waits for and schedules SAP BW data-load requests, starts executing extraction programs accordingly, and returns the resulting data set to SAP BW using RFC-client functionality. SAP has published detailed information about this open interface and has provided a sample extraction program implemented in Microsoft Visual Basic to showcase the use of the Staging BAPI.

As mentioned earlier in this chapter, the Staging BAPI has been widely adopted by third-party ETL tool vendors such as Ascential Software (now a part of IBM), ETI, Informatica, and others. A complete list of third-party ETL tools certified for use with SAP BW can be found on the SAP Web site (www.sap.com). Considering the general trend toward using XML as a data-exchange standard, applications of the Staging BAPI will lose significance.

Data Storage

The Data Storage layer (also known as the SAP BW Data Manager) manages and provides access to the different InfoProviders available in SAP BW, as well as classic aggregates and BI accelerator aggregates. The Data Storage layer offers information lifecycle management through a near-line storage (NLS) adapter as an extension to classic archiving of dormant data (data used infrequently or no longer used at all). Figure 3-12 provides an overview of the components of the Data Storage architecture layer.

Master Data Manager

The *Master Data Manager* generates the master data infrastructure consisting of master data tables as well as master data update and retrieval routines according to the definition stored in the Metadata Repository. It maintains master data and provides access to master data for SAP BW reporting and analysis services. Chapter 4 takes a closer look at the SAP BW master-data data model and discusses metadata that describes master data.

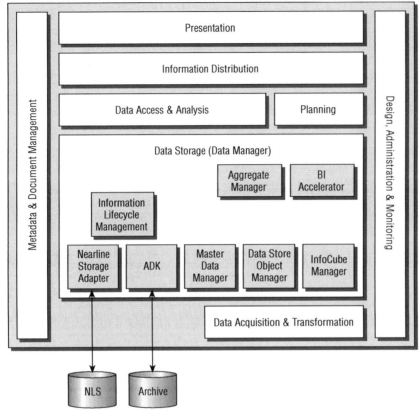

Figure 3-12 Data Storage architecture

The task of maintaining master data includes the following:

- Handling master-data uploads
- Finding or generating surrogate keys
- Handling time windows for time-dependent master data
- Ensuring the technical correctness of master-data hierarchies
- Providing a generic user interface for interactive master-data maintenance
- Activating master data, a process that copies modified data in master data tables from a modified version (which is not visible in reporting and analysis) to an active version (which is visible in reporting and analysis)

From an output point of view, the Master Data Manager provides access to master data for use by SAP BW reporting components (for example, the BEx Analyzer), as well as for exporting to other data warehouse systems via analysis and access services.

Data Store Object Manager

The *Data Store Object Manager* generates the DataStore Object infrastructure, which, for standard DataStore Objects, consists of an active data table, a change log, and an activation queue, as well as update and retrieval routines according to the definition stored in the Metadata Repository. It maintains DataStore Object data, creates a change log for every update applied as part of the activation process, and provides access to DataStore Object data for SAP BW reporting and analysis functionality.

The DataStore Object Manager allows real-time updates to direct update DataStore Objects through the corresponding API. Closely related to that, the DataStore Object BAPI provides open read access to DataStore Objects. Chapter 4 provides the details on the DataStore Object data model.

> **NOTE** While BAPIs are documented and supported from release to release, an API is not necessarily documented or guaranteed to remain unchanged from release to release.

InfoCube Manager

The *InfoCube Manager* generates the InfoCube infrastructure (consisting of fact and dimension tables, as well as update and retrieval routines) according to the definition stored in the Metadata Repository. It maintains InfoCube data, interfaces with the Aggregate Manager (for classic aggregates and BI accelerator indexes), and provides access to InfoCube data for SAP BW reporting and analysis services. Chapter 4 provides more details on the InfoCube data model.

Aggregate Manager

The *Aggregate Manager* generates the aggregate infrastructure (consisting of fact and dimension tables, along with the update and retrieval routines) according to the definition stored in the Metadata Repository. Maintenance of aggregates implies keeping them in sync with updates applied to the underlying InfoCube or master data attributes and hierarchies used in these aggregates. An elaborate status concept ensures that aggregate maintenance is transparent to end users and that queries always provide correct results.

BI Accelerator

The *BI accelerator* is a recent addition to SAP BI and has shown some impressive performance gains, with typical improvement factors between 10 and 100.

Based upon the TREX (Text, Retrieval, and Extraction) search engine for unstructured data, it applies its technology to structured data stored in the InfoCubes of an SAP BI system.

The BI accelerator achieves these performance gains by applying a vertical decomposition algorithm to data and storing and indexing data by column (or attribute) instead of by rows (or *tuples*) as in traditional databases. An efficient compression algorithm reduces the size of these indexes by a factor of up to 20, allowing you to keep indexes in main memory rather than having to retrieve indexes from disk space at all times. Because the BI accelerator runs on a separate, highly parallel blade server, it profits from its parallelized indexing and retrieval algorithms.

In many applications, classic aggregates will be sufficient to provide good performance for query execution. Typically, the BI accelerator will be deployed in cases with very high data volumes, erratic query requirements, or very high expectations regarding average query runtimes because of the additional investment in the hardware required.

Information Lifecycle Manager

The *Information Lifecycle Manager* supports classic archiving of data as well as hierarchical storage models in connection with an NLS subsystem. Classic archiving is achieved by interfacing with the archive development kit (ADK) also used for mySAP ERP archiving. Data is archived and deleted from SAP BW; for reporting purposes, data has to be reextracted from the archive.

The NLS adapter introduced with SAP NetWeaver 2004s provides access NLS. Data can be removed from the productive system — improving both load and query-execution performance — while keeping rarely used data available in the NLS for online reporting purposes at a different service level (response times) without having to retrieve data from an archive.

Both options not only store raw data but also keep track of relevant metadata (such as the layout of InfoCubes or DataStore Objects) that may change over time.

Data Access and Analysis

The Data Access and Analysis layer provides access to analysis services and structured information available in SAP BW. Figure 3-13 provides an overview of the components of the Data Access and Analysis layer. Relevant metadata objects that have not yet been introduced are discussed in following sections.

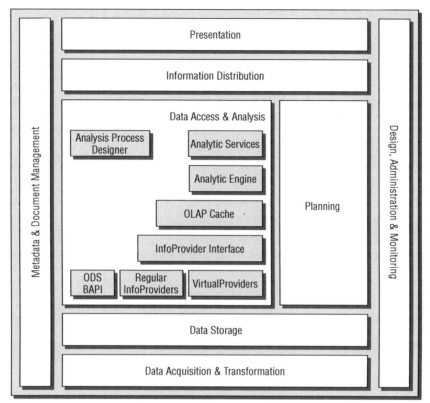

Figure 3-13   Data Access and Analysis architecture

InfoProvider Interface

The *InfoProvider interface* has been introduced to generalize access to data available in SAP BW. The InfoProvider interface allows access to regular Info-Providers and VirtualProviders. Regular InfoProviders include InfoCubes, DataStore Objects, master data tables, and InfoSets physically available on the same system.

ODS BAPI

The *ODS BAPI* is a stable, published interface providing access to DataStore Objects for applications programmers, separate from the InfoProvider interface (which is for internal use only).

OLAP Cache

The *OLAP Cache* caches data that has been retrieved from InfoProviders to reduce the number of physical data read-access operations on the database. Different variants of caching are available: session-level caching, system-level caching, and precalculated queries. Recent enhancements include a delta mechanism for caching and caching for MultiProviders.

Analytic Engine

All planning, analysis and navigational functions (such as filtering, runtime calculations, currency conversions, and authorization checks) are provided by the *Analytic Engine*. The Analytic Engine retrieves query definitions from the Metadata Repository, generates or updates query execution programs if required, and finally executes queries by running the generated program. The Analytic Engine includes basic data-mining functionality for more advanced analysis through the Data Mining Workbench (see Figure 3-14). Supported algorithms include decision trees, scoring, ABC analysis, clustering, and association rules. Although the Data Mining Engine was originally designed for use in CRM applications, it is sufficiently generic to be used for all kinds of applications. All analytic services are provided through the Analytic Engine.

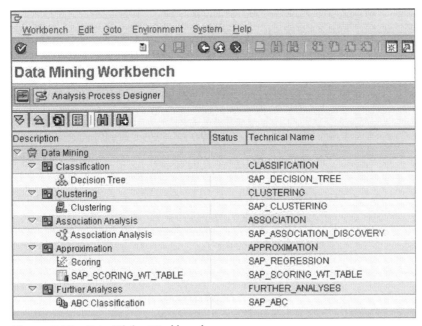

Figure 3-14   Data Mining Workbench

Analysis Process Designer

The *Analysis Process Designer* (see Figure 3-15) allows you to define complex analytic processes that source data from characteristics, InfoCubes, DataStore Objects, MultiProviders, Queries, flat files, or database tables; applying complex transformations, including filtering, aggregation, joining or merging multiple sources, sorting, ABAP routines or data-mining algorithms, and, finally, writing the results back to DataStore Objects, characteristics, OLTP systems (for example, mySAP ERP), or data-mining models.

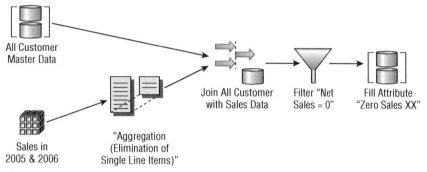

All Customer
Master Data

Sales in
2005 & 2006

"Aggregation
(Elimination of
Single Line Items)"

Join All Customer
with Sales Data

Filter "Net
Sales = 0"

Fill Attribute
"Zero Sales XX"

Figure 3-15   Analysis Process Designer

Information Distribution

The *Information Distribution* layer provides APIs for use by third-party systems or custom programs. It also provides functionality to actively distribute information to the Portal, other databases, and third-party and custom applications. Figure 3-16 shows an overview of the Information Distribution architecture.

Information Distribution Interfaces

Third-party and custom applications are able to access information stored in SAP BW using the *Information Distribution* interfaces described in the following sections. Examples of third-party tools optimized for use with SAP BW include Business Objects, Cognos PowerPlay, dynaSight by Arcplan, and others. A complete list of such tools certified for use with SAP BW can be found on the SAP Service Marketplace (`http://service.sap.com/bi`).

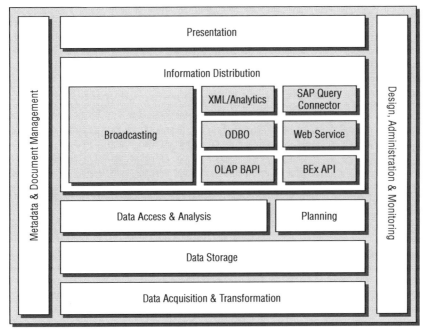

Figure 3-16 Information Distribution architecture

OLAP BAPI and the OLE DB for OLAP Interface

The *OLAP BAPI* provides an open interface for accessing any kind of information available through the Analytic Engine. The OLAP BAPI specification is based on Microsoft's OLE DB for OLAP interface specification, utilizing the MDX language definition and adopting the basic API layout (functions and interfaces available). The OLAP BAPI is used by both third-party front-end tool vendors and SAP clients to provide specialized front-end functionality for the SAP BW end user.

The OLE DB for OLAP interface (ODBO interface) is an industry standard proposed by Microsoft for accessing multidimensional data. The ODBO interface allows third-party front-end and analysis tools to connect to SAP BW and to provide display, navigation, and specialized analysis functionality to end users. For detailed information about OLE DB for OLAP, refer to `http://www.microsoft.com/data/oledb/olap`.

XML for Analysis

The OLAP BAPI also serves as a basis for the SAP implementation of *XML for Analysis*, an XML API based on SOAP and designed for standardized access to an analytical data provider (OLAP and data mining) over the Web.

Business Explorer API

The *Business Explorer API* connects the Business Explorer (BEx), the SAP BW reporting and analysis front-end solution, to the Analytic Engine, allowing access to all available queries. While the BEx API provides the most comprehensive functionality, it is not an officially published interface available for use by other applications.

Broadcasting

Information broadcasting is one of the most important recent additions to the product. The purpose of information broadcasting, put in simple words, is to distribute information from a specific source to a specific recipient or destination.

Potential sources for information broadcasting include queries, query views, Web templates, reports, or workbooks. Currently supported formats include different variants of HTML, including compressed files, URLs, output formats (PS, PCL), and PDF documents. Broadcasted information can be received by multiple recipients (or groups, distribution lists) via email, viewed in a Portal or collaboration rooms, or just picked up at a printer. Information broadcasting can be used to fill the OLAP cache, the MDX cache, or the precalculation store, where precalculated query results are available for immediate access. Information-broadcasting processes can be scheduled by administrators and (within certain limits) by end users.

Queries used for information broadcasting can be used for exception-reporting purposes. Exceptions can be added to the SAP NetWeaver alert framework and to the universal worklist (UWL). It replaces the reporting agent known from previous releases of SAP BW. The reporting agent will still be supported for compatibility reasons.

Presentation

The *Presentation* layer includes all components required to present information available in SAP BW in the traditional Microsoft Excel-based Business Explorer Analyzer (BEx Analyzer), in the BEx Web environment, or in the portal. Figure 3-17 provides an overview of the components of the Presentation layer.

Presentation Metadata Objects

The following sections discuss the most important metadata objects of the Presentation layer.

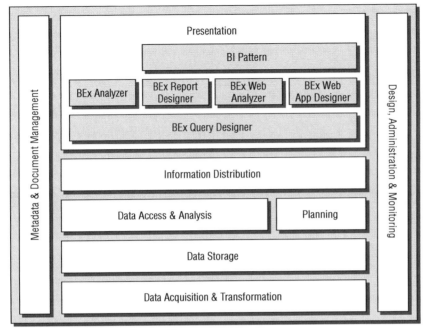

Figure 3-17 Presentation architecture

Queries

A *query* is a specification of a certain dynamic view on an InfoProvider used for multidimensional navigation. Queries are the most important basis for all kinds of analysis and reporting functionality available in SAP BW.

Queries are always based on exactly one InfoProvider. All characteristics, navigational attributes, and key figures available through that InfoProvider are available for use in query definitions. Queries effectively describe a usually aggregated subset of the data available in the InfoProvider. Query cubes define the degree of freedom available for query navigation in the Presentation layer (see Figure 3-18).

A query consists of query elements arranged in rows, columns, and free characteristics. While query elements assigned to rows and columns are displayed in the initial query view, free characteristics are not displayed but are available for navigation. Each navigational step (drill down, drill across, add, or remove filters) in the analysis process provides a different query view. Following are the available query elements:

- A *reusable structure* is a particular commonly used collection of key figures or characteristics stored in the Metadata Repository for reuse in multiple queries (for example, a plan/actual variance).

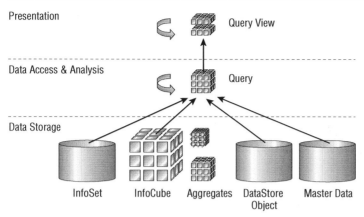

Figure 3-18   Queries and navigation

- A *calculated key figure* is a formula consisting of basic, restricted, or other calculated key figures available in the InfoProvider. Calculated key figures are stored in the Metadata Repository for reuse in multiple queries (for example, an average discount rate).

- A *restricted key figure* has an associated filter on certain characteristic values stored in the Metadata Repository for reuse in multiple queries (for example, year-to-date sales of the previous year).

- A *variable* is a parameter of a query. Usually, SAP BW determines the values of variables at query-execution time by running a user exit or requesting user input, but you may also choose to specify constant values as part of the variable definition. Variables are available for characteristic values, hierarchies, hierarchy nodes, texts, and formulas.

- A *condition* is a filter on key figure values with respect to a certain combination of characteristic values.

- An *exception* assigns an alert level from 1 to 9 (1 meaning lowest, 9 meaning highest) to a range of key figure values with respect to a certain combination of characteristic values. Alerts can be visualized in queries or in the alert monitor and can be used to automatically trigger a workflow (for example, by sending an email).

Queries are not device dependent or presentation-tool dependent. The same query definition may be used by the BEx Analyzer, in a Web environment, on a Portal, on a mobile device, for batch and exception reporting in information broadcasting, in formatted reporting, or in a third-party presentation tool.

Query definitions are created and maintained in the BEx Query Designer by simply dragging the available query elements into the rows, columns, free characteristics, or filter area and eventually defining additional properties.

The BEx Query Designer also integrates all functionality required to define the query elements in the preceding list. Query views are navigational states of queries stored in the metadata repository.

BEx Workbooks

A *BEx workbook* is a standard Microsoft Excel workbook with embedded references to query views and optional application elements built using Microsoft Excel functionality (for example, business charts or graphical elements such as pushbuttons and list boxes) and Visual Basic for Applications (VBA) code.

   Using Microsoft Excel as a query-execution option in SAP BW allows you to combine the functionality of multidimensional analysis on top of a data warehouse solution with the functionality of Microsoft Excel. In addition to the application-development functionality mentioned in the preceding definition, BEx workbooks allow for offline use of query results (and the applications built on top of that) embedded in a BEx workbook or for distributing BEx workbooks to a bigger audience via email or other file-distribution mechanisms. The most important addition to BEx workbook functionality includes extended formatting capabilities.

BEx Report

BEx reports are similar to queries but represent their result set in a flat (rather than multidimensional) structure and integrate advanced formatting features. Starting with the SAP NetWeaver 2004s release, SAP BW no longer has to rely on third-party vendors to provide formatted reporting. In conjunction with the information-broadcasting functionality and its PDF-rendering capabilities, SAP BW also includes a viable alternative for most printing requirements.

Report-Report Interface

The *report-report interface* is well known from mySAP ERP and has been extended to support SAP BW queries. It allows navigation across multiple queries, multiple systems, and mySAP ERP reports and transactions.

Web Templates

Web templates are collections of Web items connected to SAP BW data providers (for example queries) arranged on a Web page providing cockpit-like, Web-based access to the information available. Examples of available Web items include result tables, charts of various types, navigation blocks, drop-down boxes, tickers, ABC analysis, and so on. With increasing functionality of the Visual Composer introduced with SAP NetWeaver 2004s, Web templates will lose importance for cockpit-like application development — especially because of the lack of functionality to integrate BI and operational components in the final Web application.

BEx Analyzer and BEx Web Analyzer

The traditional SAP BW tool for actually invoking multidimensional reporting and analysis in SAP BW is the *BEx Analyzer*. The BEx Analyzer is implemented as an add-on to Microsoft Excel, combining the power of SAP BW OLAP analysis with all the features of Microsoft Excel. The BEx Web Analyzer provides very similar functionality but adds the AdHoc query designer.

BEx Query Designer

All multidimensional reporting and analysis performed in SAP BW is based on query definitions stored in the Metadata Repository. Queries provide access to multidimensional information providers (InfoCubes), as well as flat information providers (DataStore Objects, master data, or InfoSets). The *BEx Query Designer* provides easy-to-use (yet comprehensive) functionality for defining queries in an interactive standalone application.

BEx Report Designer

The *BEx Report Designer* is used to define Enterprise Reports with a user interface very similar to that of the BEx Query Designer enhanced by formatting capabilities. SAP BW still supports integration with Crystal Reports by Business Objects (and other third-party tools) to provide comprehensive pixel-level formatted reporting functionality on a cell-by-cell basis.

BEx Web Application Designer

The *BEx Web Application Designer* allows you to quickly design complex Web pages, including not only the traditional query elements (such as query results, navigation blocks, business charts, and maps) but also interactive components such as pushbuttons and drop-down boxes by simply dragging and dropping the required objects into the layout window, adding some additional text and graphics, adjusting the object properties, and publishing the new page to the integrated Web server. If required, users can also directly manipulate the generated HTML code. Web pages designed with the BEx

Web Application Designer provide all the functionality available in the traditional BEx Analyzer.

BI Patterns

BI Patterns basically are master templates for the HTML code, the layout, included Web items, and functionality that can be inherited by application-specific templates. SAP delivers a few samples for the usage types Information Consumer, Casual User, and Analyst.

Visual Composer

The *Visual Composer* is actually not an integral part of SAP BW. The Visual Composer is a development tool that allows composing applications (rather than coding applications) by connecting and configuring Web services and front-end elements (from simple fields and buttons to complex tables and charts).

By being able to combine Web services from different heterogeneous systems, it becomes possible to easily create applications combining transactional and analytic components in one single application. The Visual Composer is a core part of SAP's Analytics initiative.

Planning

With the SAP NetWeaver 2004s release, planning has become an integral part of the SAP BW suite. Changes to plan data can now directly be entered in queries in both Excel and the Web interface for planning purposes. Changes are written back to the server on request. Additional planning functionality is provided as part of the back-end and discussed in more detail in the following sections. Figure 3-19 provides an overview of the planning architecture, which is basically composed of extensions to the Analytic Engine, planning functions, and planning sequences. Chapter 9 provides a detailed discussion of planning.

Analytic Engine

The basic *Analytic Engine* has been discussed in the context of the Data Access and Analysis layer of the SAP BW architecture. For planning purposes, it has been extended by planning data services such as semantic rules defining relationships between different characteristics and a locking mechanism that prevents the system from trying concurrent, conflicting updates. A plan-data cache accelerates access to frequently used data. Aggregation levels are used to allow planning on aggregated data.

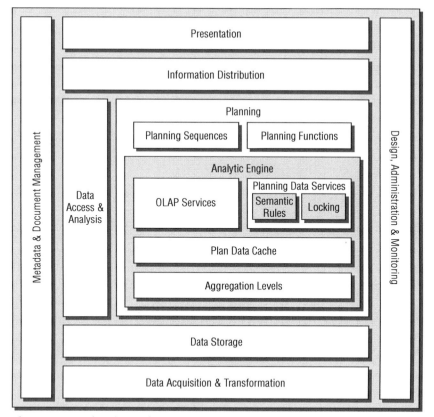

Figure 3-19 Planning architecture

Planning Functions

Planning functions support automated updates of plan data using a variety of different customizable functions, such as time distribution of plan data, user-defined formulas or routines (in the ABAP or FOX language), or copying, revaluating, or reposting data and forecasting.

Planning Sequences

Multiple manual or automated planning steps can be grouped in planning sequences to build complex planning scenarios.

Summary

SAP BW uses the usual layered architecture with a Data Acquisition and Transformation layer, a Data Storage layer, a Data Access and Analysis layer, an Information Distribution layer, and a Presentation layer, plus an additional Planning layer. SAP BW is completely based on metadata managed by the metadata services, and it is centrally controlled by the DW Workbench utilizing the administration services.

SAP-specific open interfaces such as the Staging BAPI, the OLAP BAPI, or Universal Data Connect (UDConnect) allow exchanging data and metadata with other systems and tools optimized for SAP BW. Industry-standard interfaces such as XML, XML for Analysis, and OLE DB for OLAP are supported, allowing easy access to data and metadata maintained in SAP BW for virtually every tool supporting those industry standards.

With knowledge of the SAP BW architecture and its most important metadata objects, you are now prepared to take a closer look at the physical data models used and the options SAP BW provides for modeling and developing applications, all of which are tackled in Chapter 4.

Information Modeling

In traditional data warehouse and database application software development, one of the most important tasks is developing a data model and a database design reflecting that data model. This often keeps the focus of the development process on technical details rather than on the information required. SAP BW comes with a predefined yet flexible data model, completely described and implicitly configured by business-level metadata stored in the Meta Data Repository. Using metadata to describe the contents of a data warehouse or any other database application is hardly new (see `http://www.llnl.gov/liv_comp/ metadata/index.html` for early research). However, SAP BW was the first commercial, integrated data warehouse product to be completely based on business-level metadata describing the entities relevant to business and analysis processes from a business rather than a technical point of view. Examples of such metadata objects include the following:

- Business objects such as customers, products, and sales organizations
- Business events such as sales orders and purchase orders
- Status information such as stock values and head counts
- Key performance indicators such as customer profitability, product profitability, vendor service quality, and return on investment
- Providers of information, such as InfoCubes and DataStore Objects
- Queries such as plan/actual comparisons and head count development

Business-level metadata has enabled data warehouse developers to evolve beyond data modeling and database design and to focus on information and the flow of that information into and out of the data warehouse. Therefore, the term *information model* will be used in this discussion instead of *data model* to describe the results of the modeling process.

An *information model* is a collection of metadata objects describing business processes, business objects, information containers, and their mutual relationships, as well as the scope, granularity, and semantics of the information available in the data warehouse system. The process of developing an information model is called *information modeling*. Transformations performed during the extraction or staging process are not part of the information model; the information model defines the target of transformations. An information model is not necessarily restricted to an implementation on a single physical machine but may be distributed across a complex system landscape and may include physical and virtual objects. Information modeling is at the core of the design process. Laying the foundations for staging, as well as reporting and analysis processes, information modeling is crucial to the success of any implementation project.

This chapter begins with a discussion of the prerequisites for information modeling before looking into the details of the actual physical data model used by SAP BW. Then the options available for dimensional modeling are discussed in detail. The chapter concludes with an introduction of modeling options using nondimensional metadata objects.

Information Modeling Prerequisites

The information model is the core deliverable of the technical blueprint development phase of an SAP BW implementation project, directly following the business strategy development/validation and the requirements-analysis steps in the overall project plan. The deliverables of those preceding steps providing the prerequisites for developing the information model include the following:

- **Business intelligence strategy** — Often neglected is a business intelligence strategy directly aligned with the overall business strategy of an organization; it defines what business information is needed (requirements and priorities) and how to technically deliver it (overall architecture and implementation approach). From a business perspective, more advanced business intelligence strategies not only incorporate the defining of core metrics (*historical reporting*) but also the process of explaining them (*descriptive modeling*), sensing them (*predictive modeling*), and acting on them (*prescriptive modeling*). From a technology perspective, more advanced business intelligence strategies incorporate the latest innovations and related architectural trends such as Web services and SOA.

- **Business processes and analysis requirements** — This refers to the complete set of detailed analysis requirements for the business processes in focus, including the key performance indicators (KPIs) used to monitor these business processes. KPIs may be anything from simple key figures describing a business event (such as revenue in a sales transaction) to complex derived key figures, eventually based on restricted key figures and calculated key figures (such as a customer lifetime value).

- **Relevant entities** — As a result of the requirements-analysis phase, strong and weak entities relevant to business processes are identified. Strong entities are those such as customer, product, account, and time, which are directly related to a business event; weak entities are related to a strong entity and describe the business event in more detail. Examples of weak entities include ZIP code, product groups, and other classifying information. In SAP BW, both strong and weak entities can be used as characteristics in an InfoCube and have master data attributes, texts, and hierarchies assigned to them.

- **Attributes of relevant entities** — Attributes provide additional information about an entity (such as address information or the customer group for a customer entity). Attributes available for display can be made available for navigation in queries (*navigational attributes*). The concept of navigational attributes is important for the information modeling process, because it allows handling the slowly changing dimension phenomenon in an elegant way (more on this later in this chapter).

- **Hierarchies of relevant entities** — Hierarchical relationships between different objects of the same kind (for example, cost center hierarchies) or between different objects of different types (for example, regional hierarchy grouping customers) are important for analysis purposes. Hierarchical relationships can be modeled as hierarchies or as (a collection of) attributes. Choosing hierarchies allows for more flexibility but is technically more expensive.

- **Dependencies between relevant entities** — Dependencies between relevant entities have a major impact on the information model and on the transformations required to populate an information model with data. This is not restricted to technical information captured in an entity relationship model but reaches out to how changes in business processes (such as reorganizations) actually affect the relationship of entities (for example, the relationship between a product group and a product or an employee and a cost center).

- **External information** — Measuring the performance of a company means comparing it to something else (for instance, to internal information such as budgets, plans, and previous year results but also to external information such as market shares or demographic data). External data sources (for example, address databases and credibility databases) can also be used to verify and enrich information in the data warehouse. While the actual origin of information is not relevant for the information modeling process, information from outside the enterprise can be very valuable in terms of benchmarking the development of the enterprise against industry trends.

- **Data Volume** — Information about the data volume must be considered for all entities from two different perspectives. From a static perspective, you need to know how much data will have to be stored and maintained; from a dynamic perspective, you need to know how many data records you need to process in a certain period of time.

- **Granularity** — The granularity of information defines the level of detail of the information provided. It may range from a line-item or schedule-line level in sales transactions, to highly aggregated management information. There is, of course, a trade-off between performance and granularity: The higher the granularity of a reporting object, the larger the data volume and, obviously, the longer query execution will take. Granularity typically differs among the different levels of the data warehouse architecture.

- **Timeliness** — The timeliness of transaction and master data is determined by the frequency in which InfoCubes, DataStore Objects, and master data are updated. In many cases, information in a data warehouse is updated on a daily, weekly, or monthly basis. Some applications, however, require more frequent updates or even real-time information (for example, Web-log analysis).

- **Functional requirements** — Functional requirements (as opposed to business requirements), include a description of user interfaces, systems to be available for extraction, Web servers for Web reporting, hardware, and software.

- **Nonfunctional requirements** — Nonfunctional requirements include (but are not restricted to) system properties, such as environmental and implementation constraints; performance; platform dependencies; maintainability; extensibility; and availability.

- **Information delivery requirements** — Information delivery is not restricted to making reports available to end users. In many applications, information is also exported to external companies (for example, market research transferred to ERP or legacy systems and planning results imported back into an operational system to control production).

- **Usability** — Although information modeling has little to do with designing front-ends and front-end tools, it still has an impact on the usability of the information system. A transparent, easy-to-understand information model helps end users understand predefined queries and define their own ad-hoc queries.

Understanding the SAP BW Metadata Model

Before diving deeper into the process of developing an information model, it is now time to take a closer look at the underlying data models of the metadata objects introduced as part of the architecture discussion in Chapter 3. Although the actual physical representation of these metadata objects does not have to be in the focus of information modeling, it is still helpful to have at least a basic understanding of the data models used to understand the information modeling options and their impact on performance or usability. The following paragraphs provide details of the master-data data model, the InfoCube data model, and finally the DataStore Object data model.

Master-Data Data Model

SAP BW distinguishes three categories of master data (attributes, texts, and hierarchies), each stored in different tables associated with the InfoObject. Figure 4-1 gives an overview of the tables involved in storing master data, using material master data as an example.

The SAP BW data model in general and the master-data data model in particular make extensive use of surrogate keys. Surrogate keys are automatically generated uniform keys uniquely identifying corresponding semantic (real-world) key values. As part of all data upload or maintenance processes, the system automatically generates a surrogate key for all new semantic key values and keeps track of the relationship between surrogate and semantic keys in so-called surrogate ID tables (*SID tables*), as shown in Figure 4-1, #1. In addition, SID tables are used to maintain information about where a specific SID is used.

Attribute tables (Figure 4-1, #2) are used to store attribute values that are independent of each other and can be flagged as either time dependent or time independent. Two separate tables are used to store time-dependent and time-independent attribute values, avoiding redundant storage of the same unchanged time-independent attribute values for different periods of validity. For time-dependent attributes, DateTo and DateFrom fields identify the period of validity of any given combination of time-dependent attributes. Records in attribute tables carry automatically maintained version information (active and modified version) used to maintain data integrity. An automatically generated database view provides all time-dependent and time-independent master data.

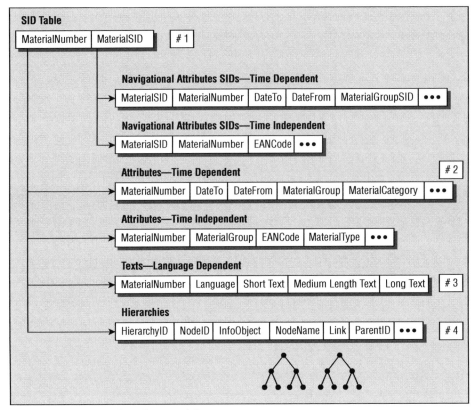

Figure 4-1 Master-data data model

> **NOTE** It is important to recognize that a period of validity is maintained for the combination of values of all time-dependent attributes, not just for a single attribute.

Navigational attribute SID tables are semantically similar to attribute tables. But instead of using real-world keys to store attribute values, they use corresponding SID values to speed up access to navigational attributes at query runtime. Navigational attribute SID tables store SIDs only for attributes flagged as navigational attributes.

Text tables (Figure 4-1, #3) are designed to store names and short descriptions assigned to key values (for example, the name of a product and its short description). There are three reasons for separating textual and attribute information in the data model:

- **Ease of implementation** — In most of the analysis and reporting requirements, end users want to see texts instead of key values. Text tables provide a uniform way of easily retrieving text information at query runtime.

■ **Performance** — Storing texts and attributes in the same tables would slow down text retrieval because database systems usually physically read complete data records (both texts and attributes), where just texts are required.

■ **Language dependency** — In a global business environment, you must be able to provide information in different languages. Both language dependency and time dependency (a feature rarely used for texts) are optional and can be turned on and off in the InfoObject maintenance dialogs.

In the same way as attributes, texts can be defined as time dependent or time independent. Defining texts as time dependent again adds the `DateTo` and `DateFrom` fields to the database table used to store text information.

Hierarchy tables (Figure 4-1, #4) are used to store hierarchical relationships. Hierarchical relationships modeled as hierarchies and stored in hierarchy tables are usually referred to as *external hierarchies* — as opposed to *internal hierarchies*, where a hierarchical relationship is modeled using attributes. The basic layout of hierarchy tables is the same for every InfoObject, varying with the properties of those hierarchies. Options for modeling hierarchies include version and time dependency for the whole hierarchy tree, time dependency for the hierarchy structure, and the use of intervals instead of single values to assign a range of values to a specific hierarchy node. Figure 4-1 shows a simplistic picture of the hierarchy data model, including only the most important fields of one out of four different tables used for storing hierarchies. The hierarchy data model provides a very flexible means to store balanced and unbalanced hierarchies, with different types of hierarchy nodes on different hierarchy levels.

NOTE While the example in Figure 4-1 shows a simple master data table with only one key field (the material number), SAP BW allows you to define master data tables with more than one key field by defining compound InfoObjects. For compound InfoObjects, SAP BW still uses a single SID field; however, the SID table and all other tables referring to the real-world key contain all real-world key fields.

All master data tables are automatically created during InfoObject activation according to the following naming convention:

```
/BI<C or digit>/<table code><InfoObject>
```

`<C or digit>`:	C = Customer-defined InfoObjects
	Digit = SAP-defined InfoObjects
`<table code>`:	S = SID table
	T = Text table

P = Time-independent master data attributes

Q = Time-dependent master data attributes

M = Union of time-dependent and time-independent master data attributes

X = SID table for time-independent navigational attributes

Y = SID table for time-dependent navigational attributes

H = Hierarchy table

K = Hierarchy SID table

I = Hierarchy SID structure table

J = Hierarchy interval table

`<InfoObject>`:   The name of the InfoObject without leading digits

To illustrate these naming conventions, Table 4-1 shows all possible master data tables for an SAP-defined InfoObject (`0MATERIAL`). Table 4-2 lists all possible master data tables for a customer-defined InfoObject (`HOUSEHLD`). Note that, depending on the actual definition of an InfoObject, some of these tables will not be available for that specific object.

Table 4-1   Master Data Tables for SAP InfoObject `0MATERIAL`

TABLE NAME	DESCRIPTION
/BI0/SMATERIAL	SID table
/BI0/TMATERIAL	Text table
/BI0/PMATERIAL	Time-independent master data attributes
/BI0/QMATERIAL	Time-dependent master data attributes
/BI0/MMATERIAL	A database view defined as the union of time-dependent and time-independent master data attributes
/BI0/XMATERIAL	SID table for time-independent navigational attributes
/BI0/YMATERIAL	SID table for time-dependent navigational attributes
/BI0/HMATERIAL	Hierarchy table
/BI0/KMATERIAL	Hierarchy SID table
/BI0/IMATERIAL	Hierarchy SID structure table
/BI0/JMATERIAL	Hierarchy interval table

Table 4-2   Master Data Tables for Customer InfoObjects HOUSEHLD

TABLE NAME	DESCRIPTION
/BIC/SHOUSEHLD	SID table
...	...
/BIC/JHOUSEHLD	Hierarchy interval table

The InfoCube Data Model

Standard InfoCubes are the relational SAP BW implementation of multidimensional data structures. The InfoCube data model is an extended star schema using surrogate keys (see definition earlier in this chapter) for referencing dimensions and characteristics (and through those also master data texts, attributes, and hierarchies).

As shown in Figure 4-2, #1, an InfoCube is composed of two separate fact tables (for compressed and uncompressed data-load requests) and up to 16 dimension tables. Three of the 16 dimension tables are maintained automatically: the time dimension, the unit dimension, and the package dimension, all to be explained in more detail later in this chapter. The remaining 13 dimensions are available for information modeling purposes.

Fact tables store detailed or aggregated key figures also known as facts (for example, revenue, quantity, and discount), illustrated in Figure 4-2, #2, and references to *dimension tables*. The fields of the dimension tables are filled with automatically generated and maintained surrogate key values known as *dimension IDs* (DIMIDs). The role of dimension tables is to group associated characteristics to reduce the number of fields in the fact table and to reduce redundancies in storing frequent combinations of characteristics values in a table. Examples of characteristics typically grouped into one dimension include Customer, Customer Group, and Zip Code grouped into a customer dimension or Material, Material Group, and Color grouped into a material dimension. Dimension tables hold SID values that refer to the associated characteristic values. This allows the master data to be shared across all InfoCubes.

A special case of a dimension is the line-item dimension, which is used for characteristics with very high cardinality. A typical example is the document number in a line-item-level InfoCube; the document number may or may not have master data associated with it. Another example of a high-cardinality characteristic is the customer number in industries that deal with many end customers, such as telecommunications, banking, and insurance. For line-item dimensions, SAP BW does not generate a dimension table or a separate DIMID but instead uses the characteristic's SID as a DIMID in the fact table (Figure 4-2, #3).

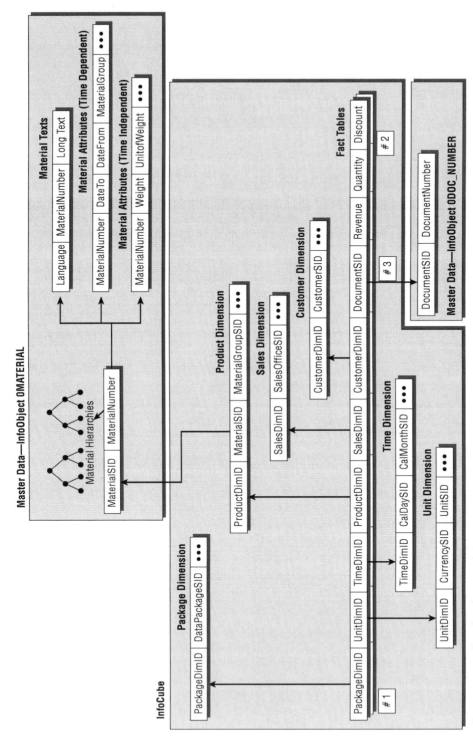

Figure 4-2 InfoCube data model

InfoCube tables are automatically created as part of the InfoCube activation process. The table names follow a specific naming convention. Table names for InfoCubes defined by SAP as part of the Business Content start with `/BI<digit>/`. Table names for customer-specific InfoCubes start with `/BIC/`. This prefix is followed by a one-character table code and the name of the InfoCube (without leading digits). This is then followed by the dimension code.

```
/BI<C or digit>/<table code><InfoCube><Dimension>
```

`<C or digit>:`	C = Customer-defined InfoCube
	Digit = SAP-defined InfoCube
`<table code>:`	D = Dimension table
	E = Fact table (compressed data requests)
	F = Fact table (uncompressed data requests)
`<InfoCube>:`	The name of the InfoCube without leading digits (if any)
`<dimension>:`	(only used for dimension tables)
	P = Package dimension
	U = Unit dimension
	T = Time dimension
	0-9, A, B, C = User-defined dimension tables

Table 4-3 lists tables for the Business Content InfoCube `0SD_C01`.

Table 4-3 Tables for Business Content InfoCube `0SD_C01`

TABLE NAME	DESCRIPTION
`/BI0/D0SD_C011`	Business Content-defined dimension table
`/BI0/D0SD_C012`	Business Content-defined dimension table
`/BI0/D0SD_C013`	Business Content-defined dimension table
`/BI0/D0SD_C014`	Business Content-defined dimension table
`/BI0/D0SD_C015`	Business Content-defined dimension table
`/BI0/D0SD_C01P`	Package dimension table
`/BI0/D0SD_C01U`	Unit dimension table
`/BI0/D0SD_C01T`	Time dimension table
`/BI0/E0SD_C01`	Compressed fact table
`/BI0/F0SD_C01`	Uncompressed fact table

Aggregates Data Model

Persistent relational aggregates are available for query performance optimization purposes. These aggregates are stored using the same relational data model used for InfoCubes, including both fact tables and the dimension table. Wherever possible, dimension tables created for the InfoCube are reused for the aggregate, thus avoiding redundant data storage and maintenance.

The DataStore Object Data Model

DataStore Objects are used for many purposes, including building an operational data store or an enterprise data warehouse layer of the CIF. Loading data into a standard DataStore Object is a two-step process. In the first step, all uploaded data records are stored in an *activation queue*. The second step, called *activation of data*, compares the active records with those in the activation queue, identifies changes (inserts or updates) to existing data, writes those changes to a change log, and updates the active record table with data from the activation queue. Note that records deleted from the source cannot be detected by this process. The change log is often used to address the lack of a delta capability in the source system.

The DataStore Object data model is based on two flat database tables, which are automatically created during activation of the DataStore Object. The names of the physical database tables follow a specific naming convention shown here. Note that the data model has changed compared to previous releases.

```
/BI<C or digit>/A<DATASTORE Object><Table code>
```

`<C or digit>:`	C = Customer-defined InfoObjects
	Digit = SAP-defined InfoObjects
`<DataStore Object>:`	The name of the DataStore Object without leading digits (if any)
`<table code>:`	00 = Active records (available for reporting)
	40 = Activation queue

Developing an Information Model

Usually, the answer to the question "What information do you need?" is simple: "I need everything!" In an ideal world, information modeling would be easy — just add all information available to a set of InfoProviders, make those available to end users, and have end users run queries against these Info-Providers. However, there is a fundamental dilemma in information modeling caused by conflicting objectives (see Figure 4-3). On one hand, business requirements need to be fulfilled. These often are in conflict with nonfunctional requirements such as performance or usability. There always is a trade-off between performance and the amount of information available, as well as a trade-off between the complexity of an information model and its usability for at least an occasional end user who wants to create and execute meaningful queries with consistent and complete result sets.

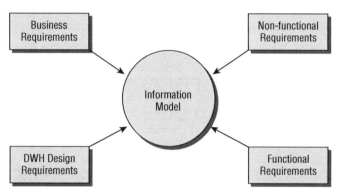

Figure 4-3   Conflicting objectives in information modeling

In addition, there are general data warehouse design requirements conflicting with both of the preceding objectives, such as the need for an enterprise data warehouse layer or the need for additional redundancies through the implementation of several InfoMarts providing correlated information. Sometimes, because of the predefined physical data model, the restrictions of standard software limit the degree of freedom in the information modeling process. Data warehouse design requirements are driven by the technical side of data warehouse development, by the people responsible for actually developing and maintaining the data warehouse. Though playing a less prominent role in information modeling, functional requirements should be considered part of it.

By laying out the options for information modeling and by illustrating the consequences of different choices, this chapter tries to help convert information modeling from an art to a reproducible, comprehensible process, leading to results that are close to an optimal compromise among all those requirements.

Multidimensional Modeling

It is no surprise that a major part of this discussion on information modeling concentrates on modeling InfoCubes as the most important and visible objects for reporting and analysis. One of the first design decisions to be made when starting the modeling process for an InfoMart relates to the scope of each InfoCube of that InfoMart. In the early days of SAP BW, complex reporting or analysis requirements involving several types of events (for example, sales orders and marketing campaigns for measuring the success of a campaign or sales orders and costs for calculating contribution margins) being reported and analyzed in a combined view compelled the definition of a complex InfoCube storing all required types of events, sometimes at different levels of granularity. Such InfoCubes tend to be complex to manage and make it more difficult for occasional users to define their own consistent queries. Since MultiProviders have been available as an additional information modeling option, it is now generally recommended to define smaller InfoCubes with reduced scope and either combining these using MultiProviders or using the report-report-interface or comprehensive Web applications to achieve the same results.

The following sections start with discussing the different modeling options for designing InfoCubes and master data before addressing the use of other types of InfoProviders (such as DataStore Objects or MultiProviders).

Dimensions

Modeling the dimensions of the InfoCube means first to define dimensions and second to assign all characteristics to one of these dimensions. The starting point for modeling dimensions is to collect all characteristics required for reporting and analysis based upon the InfoCube. SAP BW allows for a total of 16 dimensions, each holding up to 248 characteristics. Three of the 16 dimensions are predefined:

- **The time dimension** — All predefined time characteristics included in the InfoCube definition are automatically assigned to the standard time dimension. Characteristics of any other type cannot be assigned to this dimension, nor can customers define their own time characteristics. It is, however, possible to define characteristics with a data type `date` or `time` and add these to any customer-defined dimension to include additional time information in the InfoCube.

- **The unit dimension** — All unit characteristics (currencies and units of measure) assigned to the key figures included in the InfoCube definition are automatically assigned to the unit dimension. If none of the key figures has a unit of measure or currency assigned, the system will not generate a unit dimension. The unit dimension cannot be edited directly.

- **The package dimension** — The package dimension is a technical dimension supporting data-integrity maintenance by separating data from different data-load requests. The main information contained in the package dimension is the request ID and the data package ID, uniquely identifying a data package in a specific data-load request. The package dimension cannot be edited manually.

Defining Dimensions

Let's look at the simplified example of data records describing point-of-sale transactions of a retail company including the following characteristics and key figures to describe the basic steps of the dimensional modeling process:

- Date
- Product number
- Product group
- Outlet
- Region code
- Promotion number
- Promotion type
- Quantity sold
- Price
- VAT
- Discounts

The first step in developing a dimensional design is to identify the strong entities describing the transaction. In this example, these would be *date*, *product*, *outlet*, and *promotion number*. Consequently, the weak entities are *product group*, *region code*, and *promotion type*; they are describing the strong entities in more detail. For each of these strong entities, you now define one dimension and assign to it the corresponding strong entities. All weak entities are then assigned to the dimensions containing the strong entity they describe. This approach leads to an intuitively understandable design of dimensions shown in Figure 4-4, with every characteristic where it is expected to be by the occasional end user. Note the predefined package, unit, and time dimensions with the automatically assigned characteristics also shown in Figure 4-4.

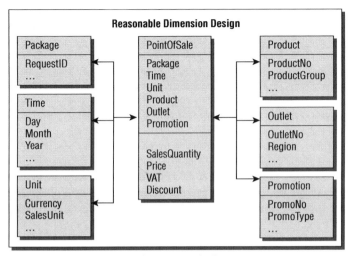

Figure 4-4   Reasonable dimension design

In contrast to the reasonable dimension design, Figure 4-5 shows a confusing dimension design assigning the promotion number to the product dimension and the promotion type to the region. Users will seldom look for promotion information in these two dimensions.

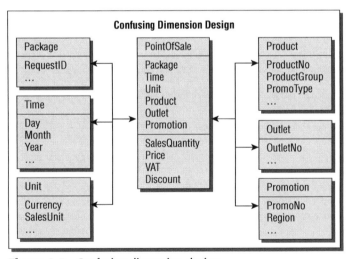

Figure 4-5   Confusing dimension design

Dimension Cardinality Considerations

A frequent effect of bad dimension design is *explosion* and has to do with the effects of assigning characteristics to dimensions on the cardinality of the dimension tables. Consider the dimension design shown in Figure 4-6 and have a closer look at the dimension called *explosion*.

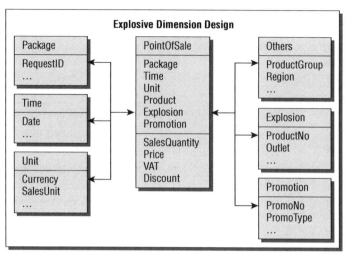

Figure 4-6 Explosive dimension design

The upper limit of the cardinality of the explosion dimension can be calculated easily by multiplying the number of products by the number of outlets. Assuming that the retailer is offering a total of 150,000 different articles in a total of 2,000 outlets, this upper limit would then be 300-million records. Admitting that not every outlet offers and sells every single article, let's further assume an average outlet offers and sells some 10,000 different products (including assortment changes over time). You still end up with 20-million records stored in the dimension table. With an average of 1-million line items a day, the fact table holding some 730-million records would have to be joined to a dimension table with 20-million records for queries asking for either a product or an outlet — an expensive database operation that can dramatically slow query-response times.

While the modeling approach just described avoids making obvious mistakes that lead to explosive dimensions, it is best practice to check every dimensional design for dimension cardinality to ensure that the cardinalities of all dimension tables are within certain limits. As a rule of thumb, the cardinality of a dimension table should not exceed a number in the low 100,000s or 10 percent of the size of the fact table for relatively small fact tables.

To estimate the cardinality of a dimension, you first must collect information about the cardinality of a certain characteristic. This allows you to compute the upper limit of the granularity of a dimension table by multiplying the cardinalities of all characteristics of that dimension. Looking at the product dimension of Figure 4-4, you find product number and product group assigned to this dimension. Assuming product number has a cardinality of 150,000 and product group has a cardinality of 150, the upper limit of the cardinality of this dimension would be 22.5 million. For the promotion dimension, on the other hand, this number would be much lower with an assumed number of 2,000 promotions and 50 promotion types.

For the promotion dimension, cardinality does not need further investigation, because the upper limit is within the range of reasonable dimension cardinalities. It does require, however, further investigation of the dependencies between the product and product group characteristics of the product dimension. The question to ask here would be: To how many product groups will a certain product typically be assigned to over the two-year reporting period?

This may reveal that each product is assigned a single product group, and this assignment changes only with a probability of 50 percent during the product lifetime. Considering this, you end up with an estimated cardinality of about 225,000 records. While 225,000 records in a dimension table exceeds the suggested limit of 100,000 records per dimension table, it is still reasonable to include both characteristics in this dimension; the product number alone already exceeds the 100,000-records limit, and adding the product group to the same dimension only adds little to that cardinality.

The bottom line is that the more uncorrelated the characteristics of a dimension are, and the higher the granularity of that characteristic is, the more likely it is to end up with an explosive dimension in your design. Typical (and frequently overlooked) examples of uncorrelated characteristics are dates and times detailing the different events that completed a business transaction (such as a "sold date," a "planned delivery date," and an "actual delivery date" in a typical sales order).

Line-Item Dimensions

There are cases, however, where the cardinality of a single characteristic significantly exceeds this limit. The document number of the point-of-sale transaction (assuming that an average transaction has five items) alone would have a cardinality of 146-million records; other examples include customer IDs in database-marketing applications in consumer-centric businesses such as telecommunications, banking, and insurance. Adding such characteristics to an InfoCube would lead to a type of dimension often referred to as *degenerate dimension*.

In SAP BW, degenerate dimensions can be modeled as so-called *line-item dimensions*. Line-item dimensions can be composed of only one characteristic, usually with a high cardinality (for example, a customer or document number), and needs to be flagged as a line-item dimension in the dimension properties dialogue shown in Figure 4-7. Dependent characteristics with lower cardinalities (for example, customer properties such as ZIP code, date of birth, or customer group) need to be assigned to a separate dimension. Note that the relationship between the characteristic in the line-item dimension and the dependent characteristics in the other dimension does not get lost; it is tracked in the records of the fact table. The less-intuitive dimension design resulting from splitting dimensions into a line-item dimension and another dimension both related to the same strong entity can be compensated for by defining a MultiProvider on top of the InfoCube that then has a proper, intuitive dimension design.

There is no separate dimension table for a line-item dimension; instead the SID of the high-cardinality characteristic (the document number) is used in place of the DIMID, as shown in Figure 4-2. Saving the dimension table does not only mean you save disk space; it also reduces a join of three large tables (fact, dimension, and surrogate key) to a join of two very large tables (fact and surrogate key).

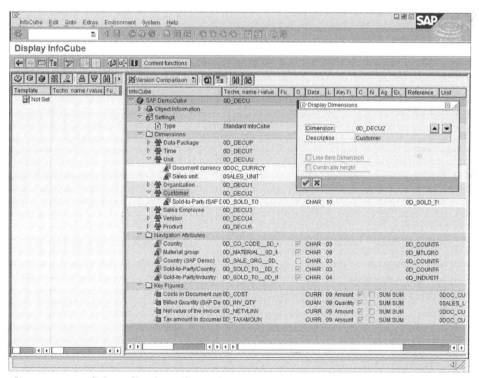

Figure 4-7   Defining a line-item dimension

Copyright © SAP AG

Flat InfoCubes

In cases where the total number of user-defined characteristics does not exceed the limit of 13 dimensions, the system will silently generate line-item dimensions for all characteristics, keeping the dimension layout as defined by the user, effectively creating what is called a *flat InfoCube* with no custom dimension tables at all. The only dimension tables for a flat InfoCube would be the package, unit, and time dimensions. Flat InfoCubes improve load, as well as reporting performance.

High-Cardinality Dimensions

In cases where line-item dimensions cannot be defined because of the 13-dimension limit, another option for dimensions with high cardinality is to flag them as *high-cardinality dimensions*. While this has no direct impact on the information model, it allows the system to optimize the definition of indexes or other database-specific parameters relevant to handling the dimension.

Key Figures

Key figures can be used in InfoCubes, DataStore Objects, and master data attributes; they don't have attributes of their own, though. Key figures can represent the outcome of a business event (such as sales revenue or a discount) or the current status of something (such as weight and volume of a material, size of an outlet or a plant in square feet, or the number of children of an employee). Five types of key figures are available for information modeling: amounts, quantities, numbers, date, and time. Each type has different semantics.

Amount key figures are closely tied to either a fixed currency defined in the key figure metadata or a variable currency defined by the value of a currency characteristic associated to the amount key figure by either a business event (for example, the document currency) or an entity relationship (for example, the local currency). By enforcing the use of currency information for this kind of key figure, SAP BW ensures consistent currency handling and makes the same highly flexible currency-conversion procedures available to all staging and reporting processes.

Quantity key figures are used to store any type of quantitative information that requires a unit of measure. In the same way as for amount key figures, SAP BW enforces a specific fixed unit of measure or a unit characteristic holding the actual unit of measure to be defined in key figure metadata. As of the SAP NetWeaver 2004s release, SAP BW provides complex unit-of-measure conversions similar to those for currency conversions. The physical data type of both — amount and quantity key figures — is either *packed decimal* or *floating point*.

Simple *numbers* are not connected to currencies or units as amounts and quantities are; numbers can be defined as *integer*, *packed-decimal*, or *floating-point* values. Typically, key figures of this type are used to store simple numerical values such as counters, percentages, scores, rates, or deviations.

There are several ways to store *date* and *time* information in InfoCubes: predefined date and time characteristics in the system-defined time dimension, user-defined date, time characteristics in user-defined dimensions, and, finally, date or time key figures. While modeling date and time as characteristics allows for drill-downs, time-series analysis, or all kinds of navigation on date and time information, modeling date and time as key figures allows for arbitrary computations (such as the number of days between two dates).

Aggregation Behavior

Another important categorization of key figures refers to the aggregation properties of the key figure. Common data warehouse literature distinguishes three categories:

- **Additive key figures** — These may be aggregated by summing up all available values to a total value, regardless of the dimension. Examples include sales revenues, discounts, or actual salary payments.

- **Semiadditive key figures** — These may be aggregated by summing up all available values to a total value for some dimensions but not for others (mostly the time dimension). Examples include head counts, stock values, or number of customers.

- **Nonadditive key figures** — These cannot be aggregated at all. Examples include market share or growth rates.

Table 4-4 shows an example of semiadditive key figures based on head-count data for several departments of a company. While adding up the head-count values for December 2005 for all departments returns a meaningful number of employees for all three departments of 82, adding up the head-count values for the accounting department of December and January would not return useful information. Defining the head count as semiadditive would ensure that the head count for the accounting department returns the sum of only the last month, regardless of the number of months returned by a query.

Table 4-4 Sample Head Count Data

DEPARTMENT	MONTH	HEAD COUNT
Accounting	12.2005	15
Sales	12. 2005	45
Marketing	12. 2005	22
Accounting	01. 2006	17
Sales	01. 2006	50
Marketing	01. 2006	25

SAP BW supports all three categories of key figures by associating an aggregation function with the key figure and by distinguishing between *cumulative* and *noncumulative* key figures. Cumulative key figures in combination with summation as aggregation function are used to model additive key figures. Semiadditive key figures where no aggregation over characteristics other than time is allowed are modeled as cumulative key figures with an exception aggregation (for example, maximum, first value, or counter) defined for the nonadditive characteristic. Figure 4-8 shows the key figure metadata maintenance dialog.

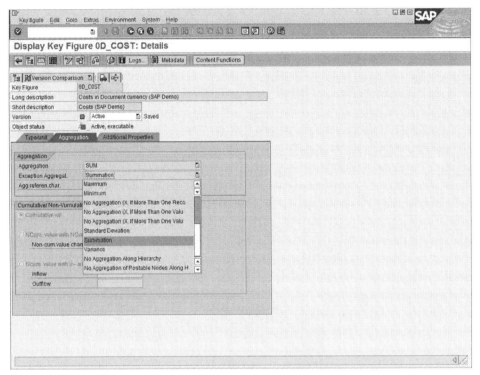

Figure 4-8   Key figure metadata maintenance
Copyright © SAP AG

The standard aggregation function of a key figure is used whenever there's no exception aggregation defined for that key figure or whenever the exception aggregation does not apply. The exception aggregation function is applied whenever a query aggregates over the exception aggregation characteristic (for example, day, month, year, customer number, or document number). Put another way, it is applied whenever the exception aggregation characteristic is not displayed or used as a filter in the query.

Semiadditive key figures where no aggregation over time characteristics is allowed are defined as noncumulative key figures. Finally, nonadditive key figures will be modeled as cumulative or noncumulative key figures with no aggregation function at all. Tables 4-5 and 4-6 show available standard and exception aggregation functions.

Table 4-5 Standard Aggregation Functions

FUNCTION	DESCRIPTION
Summation	The summation function is the default aggregation function in SAP BW. This function simply adds all the values retrieved for the key figure according to the characteristics included in the query.
Maximum	The maximum function always returns the maximum values retrieved for the key figure according to the characteristics included in the query.
Minimum	The minimum function always returns the maximum values retrieved for the key figure according to the characteristics included in the query.
No aggregation	This function does not perform any aggregation at all, if an additional condition applies. Three variants of this function, with three different additional conditions, are currently available: ■ More than one record occurs for the characteristics included in the query. ■ More than one different value occurs for the characteristics included in the query. ■ More than one different value unequal to 0 occurs for the characteristics included in the query.

Table 4-6 Exception Aggregation Functions

FUNCTION	DESCRIPTION
Average	The average function returns the average of the values retrieved for the key figure according to the characteristics included in the query. The average function comes in four different flavors: ■ Average of all values not equal to zero ■ Average of all values not equal to zero weighted with the number of calendar days ■ Average of all values not equal to zero weighted with the number of working days according to the SAP BW factory calendar ■ Average of all values

Table 4-6 Exception Aggregation Functions *conitnued*

FUNCTION	DESCRIPTION
Count	The count function returns the number of values retrieved for the key figure according to the exception characteristic (which is not included in the query; the query aggregates over the exception characteristic). The count function comes in two different flavors: ▪ Count all values unequal to 0 ▪ Count all values
First value	The first value function returns the first value retrieved for the key figure according to the characteristics included in the query.
Last value	The last value function returns the first value retrieved for the key figure according to the characteristics included in the query.
Standard deviation	The standard deviation function returns the standard deviation of the values retrieved for the key figure according to the characteristics included in the query.
Variance	The variance function returns the variance of the values retrieved for the key figure according to the characteristics included in the query.

The exception aggregation function is used whenever a query aggregates over the so-called exception aggregation characteristic; both are specified in the key figure metadata maintenance dialog. In the preceding example of the head-count query, this would be the *Month* characteristic, and the aggregation function used for exception aggregations would be the first variant of the "no aggregation" function.

NOTE Aggregation functions for key figures are relevant only for reporting and analysis; they do not apply to the staging process. SAP BW does not prevent nonadditive or semiadditive key figures from being aggregated during the staging process. Also, using standard aggregations other than "Summation" or using exception aggregations reduces the degree of flexibility when defining aggregates.

A noncumulative key figure in SAP BW always requires one or two cumulative key figures to be assigned for staging purposes (see Figure 4-8). While the noncumulative key figure itself stores the noncumulative values at a specific point in time (such as head counts or inventory), the cumulative key figures provide changes to these noncumulative values at a given point in time or over a period of time. Both the noncumulative and the associated cumulative key figures are included in the InfoProvider and are available for reporting purposes.

- If there is one single cumulative key figure associated with the noncumulative key figure, this key figure provides all changes (positive or negative) to the noncumulative value. If, for example, the noncumulative key figure is a head count, negative values of the associated cumulative key figure indicate employees leaving the company or department, while positive values indicate new employees in the company or recent assignments to the department.

- If two cumulative key figures are associated with the noncumulative value, one is used for positive changes, the other is used for negative changes, and both values are specified as positive values (see Figure 4-9). Note that in this scenario it is possible to report negative and positive changes separately by using the two assigned cumulative key figures.

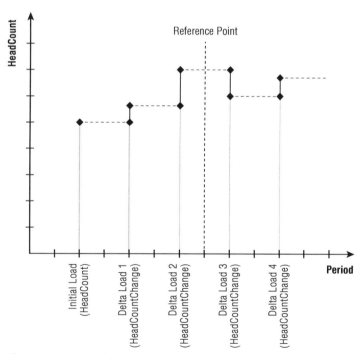

Figure 4-9 Use of noncumulative values

Storage for InfoCubes containing noncumulative key figures differs from storage for regular InfoCubes in that, in addition to the records uploaded to the

InfoCube, the values for the noncumulative key figures are physically stored for a certain point in time — the so-called *reference point*. A query requesting data for a point of time different from the reference point would first read data from the reference point and then read all the changes staged through the cumulative key figures associated with the noncumulative key figure and add them to (for changes later than the reference point) or subtract them from (for changes prior to the reference point) the values read from the reference point. In general, the more change records have been uploaded, the more expensive the query execution will be. Note that reference points can be moved in time as part of InfoCube compression; the system will automatically adjust the values according the changes stored in the InfoCube. Figure 4-9 illustrates the reference point as well as the relevant change records coming through the different data loads.

Generic Key Figures

Some reporting scenarios require a large number of key figures for analysis and reporting purposes. Looking at the retail example, there could easily be 100 or more different types of discounts available for price calculations, although only a few will be used in any specific sales transaction, and many will be rarely used at all. Choosing an information model with one key figure for each possible discount leads to an effect called *key figure sparsity*; many of the key figure values stored in the database are actually empty. On the other hand, whenever the business creates a new discount, the information model and the staging process will have to be modified. Both effects will still be acceptable, as long as there are not too many sparse key figures and as long as the number and semantics of key figures to report on are not changing too frequently. The modeling approach is called *specific key figure modeling* (sometimes also referred to as *key-figure-based modeling*).

An alternative approach that takes into account sparsity and frequent changes to the actual key figures required is what we call the *generic key figure modeling* approach (sometimes also referred to as *account-based modeling*). Instead of adding specific key figures for each discount to the InfoCube, just one key figure plus a specifying characteristic are included in the InfoCube definition. The key figure is generic in that it itself does not have a meaning without the value of the specifying characteristic. The specification characteristic can either be assigned to a dimension already available in the InfoCube, or it can be assigned to a separate dimension, using the same dimension-modeling considerations discussed previously. In this example, you would be defining a key figure called *discount* and a specifying characteristic called *discount type*. For multiple discounts, multiple records would be stored in the fact table to fully describe a sales transaction.

Figure 4-10 shows two different layouts of a fact table: one using specific key figures, the other using a single generic key figure in combination with the discount type characteristic. Tables 4-7 and 4-8 show sample contents of those two fact tables for the same set of sales transactions.

| TimeDimKe | ProductDimKey | CustomerDimKey | ••• | Revenue | CustomerDiscount | CampaignDiscount | BulkDiscount | ••• |

Fact Table with Specific Key Figures

| TimeDimKey | ProductDimKey | CustomerDimKey | DiscountTypeDimKey | ••• | Amount |

Same Fact Table with Generic Key Figure

Figure 4-10   Generic and specific key figures

Table 4-7   Specific Key Figures Example

PRODUCT	MONTH	REVENUE	CUST. DISCNT	CAMP. DISCNT	BULK. DISCNT
Apples	12.2005	224	22	26	0
Cabbage	12.2005	459	68	0	30
Peaches	12.2005	50	0	0	0
Bananas	12.2005	140	0	20	10

Table 4-8   Generic Key Figures Example

PRODUCT	MONTH	VALUE TYPE	AMOUNT
Apples	12.2005	Revenue	224
Apples	12.2005	CustomerDiscount	22
Apples	12.2005	CampaignDiscount	26
Cabbage	12.2005	Revenue	459
Cabbage	12.2005	CustomerDiscount	68
Cabbage	12.2005	BulkDiscount	30
Peaches	12.2005	Revenue	50
Bananas	12.2005	Revenue	140
Bananas	12.2005	CampaignDiscount	20
Bananas	12.2005	BulkDiscount	10

NOTE Note that in the generic key figure example, an aggregation over all value types returns the nondiscounted revenue: (discounted) revenue + customer discount + campaign discount + bulk discount.

Using the generic key figure approach provides a maximum of flexibility without modifications to the information model. Additional key figures can be added by just defining another value for the value-type characteristic and loading the data. However, this flexibility comes at a cost. In InfoCubes based on generic key figures, the number of records (while being shorter) can be significantly higher than in other InfoCubes. To allow end users easy use of the key figures, developers will have to define restricted key figures, calculated key figures, or templates in the query builder (more on that in Chapter 8).

There are other application scenarios where the generic key figure modeling approach should be considered, including planning and budgeting applications where actual values, different versions of plan values, budget values, and estimated budget values are required for reporting and analysis. In this case, the value type would include values such as *Actual*, *Plan*, *Plan Version 1*, or *Budget*. It is also possible to choose more than one characteristic to specify the actual meaning of a key figure (for example, value type and version).

Also note that the generic key figure modeling approach is not new or unique to SAP BW. Some data warehouse products and custom data warehouses actually use the generic key figure approach as their primary method of storing information, calling the key figure a fact and having dimensions and attributes describe this fact.

Conversion of Currencies and Units of Measure

The basic principles of currency conversions and conversions of units of measure are discussed in more detail in Chapter 7. From an information-modeling point of view, the question of conversion is a question of when and how to use the conversion mechanisms available.

Performing conversions during the staging process allows faster query execution but reduces the flexibility in choosing the type of conversion at query-execution time. Performing conversions at query-execution time, on the other hand, takes some extra time to retrieve details about the type of conversion and to actually convert the values, but it allows dynamically selecting the reporting currency or unit of measure. In the end, the choices made in a specific information model all depend on the degree of flexibility required at query-execution time and on query-performance expectations.

Master Data

Master data has largely not been thought of as a separate class of data in data warehousing but instead has been seen as an integral part of the multidimensional model. This has led to a couple of issues for OLAP tools and data warehouse suites, including how to handle slowly changing dimensions or unbalanced and other irregular hierarchies.

Right from its start, SAP BW has dealt with master data in a different way. The discussion of the master data model earlier in this chapter has already shown that there are completely different data models for master data, Data-Store Objects, and the multidimensional InfoCubes linked together through surrogate keys or, in case of DataStore Objects, through real-world key values.

Modeling Text Information

Master data texts are used to provide text information instead of or in addition to key values for characteristics. As already discussed earlier in this chapter, texts may be defined as language dependent and time dependant. Language-dependent texts (along with the multilingual implementation of the SAP BW software and the UNICODE option) allow international companies to implement truly multilingual information systems. Time-dependent texts help keep track of renaming of products and organizational units, among other tasks. Figure 4-11 shows the InfoObject maintenance transaction related to modeling text information.

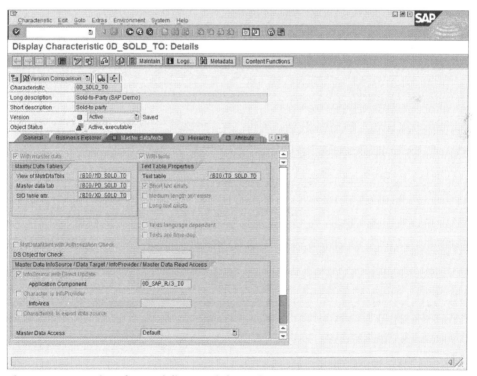

Figure 4-11 Options for modeling text information

Properties of Attributes

Attributes play a far more important role in information modeling than texts. SAP BW distinguishes between two types of attributes (see Figure 4-12):

- **Display attributes** — These can be used to display additional information in reports and queries. Examples include discrete information (such as street address, name of the city, customer phone number, and name of contact person) and scalar information (such as the weight and volume of a product).

- **Navigational attributes** — These can be used for display and for navigation and filtering in BEx queries. Use of navigational attributes, of course, is restricted to discrete information.

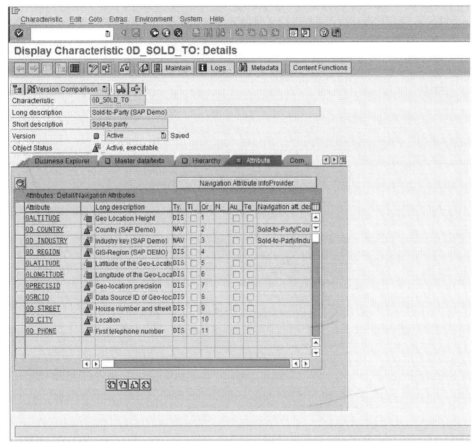

Figure 4-12   Options for modeling attributes

Copyright © SAP AG

While display attributes play a minor role in information modeling, comparable to that of texts ("define, use, and don't think about it"), navigational attributes play a very important role because they are available for filtering and drill-down operations in query navigation.

Attributes may individually be flagged as time dependent. As described in the *master-data data model* discussion, time-dependent and non-time-dependent attributes are stored in two different database tables. Every distinct combination of the values of time-dependent attributes of a characteristic has a distinct period of validity assigned, indicated by two database fields in the time-dependent attributes table: `DateTo` and `DateFrom`. Neither date is automatically maintained, but both have to be extracted from the source system or have to be derived during the staging process. The system does, however, take care of automatically adjusting validity periods of existing data records to avoid overlaps and makes sure to split validity periods once the combination of values changes during an existing `DateFrom` and `DateTo` interval.

Master Data Key Figures

SAP BW allows the use of key figures as attributes of any characteristic. Examples include the birth date of customers; the price, weight, and volume of a material; or the size of a plant in square feet. These master data key figures can be displayed in queries or can be used in calculations. Because master data key figures (or key figures in general) contain scalar information, they cannot be used as navigational attributes.

Hierarchies

In most reporting and analysis applications, hierarchies are an important means of defining aggregation paths and visualizing KPIs in a convenient way. In mySAP ERP, for example, there are hierarchies for cost centers, profit centers, accounts, customers, products, and many more. From an information-modeling point of view, you can distinguish several types of hierarchies:

- **Homogenous hierarchies** — Every node of the hierarchy except the root node is of the same type. For example, in a customer hierarchy, every node of the hierarchy itself refers to a customer.

- **Heterogeneous hierarchies** — Some nodes on a single level or on multiple levels of the hierarchy refer to different types of nodes (for example, a hierarchy describing the assignment of customers to profit centers).

- **Balanced hierarchies** — Every node of a single level of the hierarchy is of the same type, and every branch of the hierarchy has the same number of levels (for example, a product hierarchy where product assignments to product groups are tracked). Figure 4-13 shows an example of different versions of a heterogeneous hierarchy of products grouped into product groups.

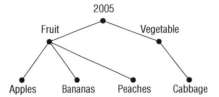

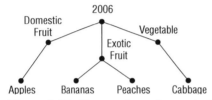

Figure 4-13   Two versions of a product group hierarchy

- **Unbalanced hierarchies** — There is a different number of hierarchy levels for the different branches of the hierarchy or for a specific hierarchy level referencing different InfoObjects in different nodes. Figure 4-14 shows an example of an unbalanced, heterogeneous hierarchy. Unbalanced hierarchies are frequently used in human resources applications, in the consumer products industry, or in project management.

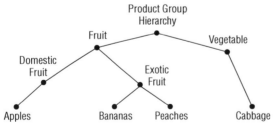

Figure 4-14   An unbalanced product group hierarchy

- **Network hierarchies** — A node has more than one parent node, as shown in Figure 4-15. Network hierarchies are often used in sales organizations.

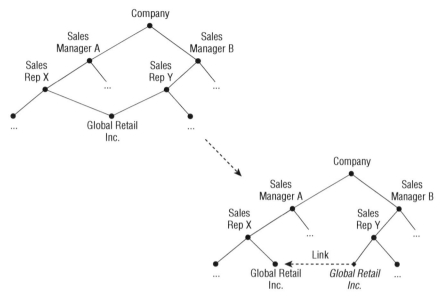

Figure 4-15   A sales network hierarchy

SAP BW provides two options for modeling hierarchies: *internal hierarchies* and *external hierarchies*. The internal hierarchy approach models hierarchical relationships simply by adding one characteristic per level of the hierarchy to an InfoCube dimension or DataStore Object or as a navigational attribute. This way it is easily possible to filter as well as drill down and across to navigate through the hierarchy. Whenever there is a homogeneous, balanced hierarchy with no significant changes of the structure of the hierarchy anticipated (while there may well be changes to the actual relationships between hierarchy nodes) and only a small number of hierarchy levels required, this is the approach to choose. An example of this type of hierarchy is the product group hierarchy shown in Figure 4-13. In all other cases, use of external hierarchies should be considered.

External hierarchies in SAP BW are called external because they are neither stored in InfoCube dimensions nor in a DataStore Object nor as navigational attributes. Instead, they are stored in separate hierarchy tables associated to the base InfoObject (for example, 0PRODUCT for a product hierarchy). Those hierarchy tables store a single record per hierarchy node that includes a unique node identifier and a reference to a parent node. Table 4-8 shows the most important fields of a hierarchy table, and Table 4-9 shows the data records storing our 2006 version of the product hierarchy in this format.

Table 4-8 Fields of Hierarchy Nodes Table

FIELD NAME	DESCRIPTION
HIEID	Unique hierarchy identifier
NODEID	Unique node identifier (unique within this hierarchy)
IOBJNM	Name of the InfoObject this hierarchy node refers to
NODENAME	Key value for the InfoObject this hierarchy node refers to
TLEVEL	Level of this hierarchy node
LINK	Link indicator for a hierarchy node (see the text that follows for more details)
PARENTID	Unique node identifier of the parent node of this hierarchy node
CHILDID	Unique node identifier of the first child node of this hierarchy node
NEXTID	Unique node identifier of the next node on the same level of this hierarchy node
DATEFROM	The starting date of the validity period of this hierarchy node record
DATETO	The end date of the validity period of this hierarchy node record
INTERVL	Flag: This hierarchy node is an interval node

Table 4-9 Storing the Product Group Hierarchy 2006

NODEID	IOBJNM	NODENAME	TLEVEL	LINK	PARENTID	CHILDID	NEXTID
1	0HIER_NODE	2006	1	-	-	2	-
2	0PROD_GRP	Domestic Fruit	2	-	1	3	4
3	0PRODUCT	Apples	3	-	2	-	-
4	0PROD_GRP	Exotic Fruit	2	-	1	5	7
5	0PRODUCT	Bananas	3	-	4	-	6
6	0PRODUCT	Peaches	3	-	4	-	-
7	0PROD_GRP	Vegetable	2	-	1	8	-
8	0PRODUCT	Cabbage	3	-	7	-	-

External hierarchies allow for storing multiple versions of the same hierarchy and for two types of time dependency. Time dependency in its simple form is just another kind of versioning in that it allows you to specify the validity period of a complete hierarchy, while the more complex and more flexible type of time dependency supports time-dependent assignments of nodes to their parent nodes. Additional features of hierarchies as implemented in SAP BW include interval nodes (allowing the representation of ranges of key values in a single hierarchy node) and link nodes (allowing you to model network type hierarchies). Properties assigned to hierarchy nodes provide a basic mechanism to modify aggregation behavior along the hierarchy; aggregated values or values assigned to a node with the reverse flag set changes their sign from + to - and vice versa. The `link` flag, finally, allows you to model network hierarchies, which, in fact, are not exactly hierarchies at all. Network hierarchies, for example, are found in sales organizations where large clients are managed by multiple sales representatives independently. Figure 4-15 shows such a network hierarchy for sales representatives.

Table 4-10 illustrates physical storage of such a network hierarchy. Note that there are two occurrences of the "Global Retail Inc." node, each assigned to a different parent node. Both nodes have the same value for the nodename field with different nodeids; the nodename serves as a secondary key. In addition to having a different `nodeid`, the second node has the `link` flag set to "X," identifying this node as a virtual node. When aggregating along the hierarchy, the analytic engine takes into account that the values for the node flagged, as a link must not be counted twice when computing the results for any node above the link node.

Table 4-10   Storing the Sales Network Hierarchy

NODEID	IOBJNM	NODENAME	TLEVEL	LINK	PARENTID	CHILDID	NEXTID
1	0HIER_NODE	Company	1	-	-	2	-
2	0EMPLOYEE	Sales Mgr A	2	-	1	3	100
3	0EMPLOYEE	Sales Rep X	3	-	2	4	…
4	0CUSTOMER	Global Retail Inc.	4	-	3	…	…
…	…	…	…	…	…	…	…
100	0EMPLOYEE	Sales Mgr B	2	-	1	101	…
101	0EMPLOYEE	Sales Rep Y	3	-	100	102	…
102	0CUSTOMER	Global Retail Inc.	4	X	101	…	…
…	…	…	…	…	…	…	…

From a query-performance perspective, external hierarchies are, of course, slightly slower compared to navigational attributes. Additional tables are maintained to speed up hierarchy access and utilize recursive join support of modern database systems to provide the best performance. Another option for keeping hierarchies small and effective is to create interval nodes specifying a range of key values instead of a single key value. Intervals are stored in a separate interval table not described here.

Compound InfoObjects

The earlier discussion on the data model behind the SAP BW master data concept does not actually cover InfoObjects with structured keys. The discussion implicitly assumes there is a single field identifying a business object described by the InfoObject. In many cases, however, more than just one field is required — for example, cost centers in mySAP ERP are uniquely identified only within a controlling area; products might have different sales prices in different sales organizations; different plants are producing the product at different costs.

All of the preceding examples require additional key fields to be assigned to the corresponding InfoObject. This is implemented as a so-called *compound InfoObject*, where the cost center InfoObject is compounded with the controlling-area InfoObject.

> **NOTE** The example given here can be viewed in the Business Content. The cost center InfoObject is called 0COSTCENTER; the controlling area InfoObject is called 0CO_AREA.

There is not much to discuss here from a data-model point of view; the data model discussed previously essentially stays the same, except that the SID table is composed of the SID and all real-world keys of all participating InfoObjects. The SID in these cases refers to a unique combination of key fields instead of just a single key field.

Reference Characteristics

SAP BW allows defining InfoObjects that reference other InfoObjects, effectively inheriting all properties of the referenced InfoObject except the technical name and textual descriptions. All other properties (including the physical master data tables of the referenced InfoObject) are reused for the referencing InfoObjects.

Think of a sales transaction where several organizations or organizational units act in different roles. Organizational unit A orders some products to be delivered to organizational unit C, which are paid for by organizational unit B. In another sales transaction, A orders, products are delivered to A, and A also pays. While you want to know who ordered, whom you delivered to, and who paid, you obviously do not want to keep separate customer master data in three different places (as an order customer, a shipment customer, and a paying customer). The Business Content, for example, provides multiple different customer InfoObjects: 0CUSTOMER to generically keep customer master data; 0SOLD_TO referencing 0CUSTOMER in the order customer role; 0SHIP_TO referencing 0CUSTOMER in the shipment customer role; and finally 0PAYER referencing 0CUSTOMER in the paying customer role.

Virtual Key Figures and Characteristics

Values of key figures and characteristics do not necessarily have to be stored permanently in an InfoCube or in a master data attribute table. Virtual key figures and virtual characteristics allow the dynamic computation or derivation of values for key figures and characteristics at query-execution time. Examples of using virtual characteristics include dynamic categorization of key figure values such as age groups and price ranges, where the basis for calculating the categorical values is variable (as for age). Another use of virtual characteristics is to compute complex compound values, possibly combining information read from the InfoCube with current information retrieved from other sources (for example, master data attributes).

Both virtual key figures and virtual characteristics are used only where there is no other way to achieve the same desired results, because they can affect query performance and the degree of flexibility in defining aggregates significantly.

Different Versions of Truth in the Data Warehouse

One of the most important — and difficult — discussions in the requirements-analysis phase is about what version of the truth is required in reporting and analysis. Three different versions of truth can be distinguished with respect to time:

- **Historical truth** — The historical truth provides information about the status of all entities related to a business event (such as customers or products) at the time that business event occurred (for example, something was sold or bought). Let's assume that apples had been assigned to product group *Fruit* in 2005. The historical truth for all sales transactions selling apples in 2005 would then be that apples are assigned to product group *Fruit*.

- **Current truth** — The current truth provides information about the status of all entities related to a business event as of today. If apples currently are assigned to product group *Domestic Fruit*, the current truth for all sales transactions selling apples in 2005 would be that apples are assigned to product group *Domestic Fruit* — even if at the time of the transaction they had been assigned to a different product group. Note that "current" in this context refers to the last update of master data attributes.

- **Truth of a specific point of time** — The truth of a specific point of time provides information about the status of all entities related to a business event as of any specified date. If, for example, there are plans to reorganize the product group assignments in the future, apples might be categorized in a completely different way.

SAP BW supports modeling and comparing all three versions of the truth. The historical truth is tracked in InfoCubes. All information required from a historical-truth perspective (in this case, the product group) needs to be stored in the InfoCube. The current truth can be modeled as non-time-dependent navigational attributes or as non-time-dependent hierarchies of the characteristics included in an InfoCube. The truth at a specific point of time can be modeled using time-dependent navigational attributes or time-dependent hierarchies of characteristics included in an InfoCube. Note that the current truth can also be considered a special case of the truth of a specific point in time: Today.

To illustrate the effect of these different versions of the truth, look at Table 4-11, which shows simplified sales data for the retailer stored in an InfoCube. Note that the assignment of product groups to products has changed on January 1, 2006. In 2006, sales of a new product "Grapes" has started in the new product group "Domestic Fruit"; "Apples" have been reassigned to the same new product group; "Peaches" and "Bananas" have been reassigned to the new product group "Exotic Fruit." The fact table of the InfoCube records product revenues in the given period of time, along with the corresponding product group assignment during that period of time — tracking the historical truth.

Table 4-11   Sales Facts in a Sample InfoCube

PRODUCT	PRODUCT GROUP	YEAR	REVENUE
Apples	Fruit	2005	100
Bananas	Fruit	2005	180
Cabbage	Vegetable	2005	130
Peaches	Fruit	2005	150
Apples	Domestic Fruit	2006	90
Bananas	Exotic Fruit	2006	170
Cabbage	Vegetable	2006	210
Grapes	Domestic Fruit	2006	160
Peaches	Exotic Fruit	2006	150

Queries asking for the historical truth about revenues per product group would yield the results in Table 4-12.

Table 4-12 Reporting the Historical Truth

YEAR	PRODUCT GROUP	REVENUE
2005	Fruit	430
	Vegetable	130
Subtotals		560
2006	Domestic Fruit	250
	Exotic Fruit	320
	Vegetable	210
Subtotals		780
Totals		1340

In 2005, the total revenue with products in the product group "Fruit" was 430. In 2006, this revenue was split in two different groups, "Domestic Fruit" and "Exotic Fruit," with the new product "Grapes" contributing to the revenue in "Domestic Fruit." Revenue in product group "Vegetables" increased by 80. But what happens if the product groups are not stored in the fact table but rather as an attribute of the product characteristic? Table 4-13 shows a new fact table, without the product group.

Table 4-13 Sales Revenue Facts in the InfoCube (Revisited)

PRODUCT	YEAR	REVENUE
Apples	2005	100
Bananas	2005	180
Cabbage	2005	130
Peaches	2005	150
Apples	2006	90
Bananas	2006	170
Cabbage	2006	210
Grapes	2006	160
Peaches	2006	150

Accessing current product group assignments as stored in the master data tables of the product characteristic (Table 4-14), the query returns a different result, shown in Table 4-15.

Table 4-14   Customer Group as Navigational Attribute

PRODUCT	PRODUCT GROUP
Apples	Domestic Fruit
Bananas	Exotic Fruit
Cabbage	Vegetable
Grapes	Domestic Fruit
Peaches	Exotic Fruit

Table 4-15   Reporting the Current Truth

YEAR	PRODUCT GROUP	REVENUE
2005	Domestic Fruit	100
	Exotic Fruit	330
	Vegetable	130
Subtotals		560
2006	Domestic Fruit	250
	Exotic Fruit	320
	Vegetable	210
Subtotals		780
Totals		1340

Note that access to navigational attributes is slightly slower than access to characteristics stored in the InfoCube. The Analytic Engine performs an additional join to actually determine the value of the navigational attribute. However, for lower cardinality characteristics (fewer than 100,000 records), this is usually not critical; for higher cardinality characteristics, additional indexes on the attribute SID tables can help to increase query performance.

So far, this discussion has focused on characteristics in non-time-dependent master data tables. As mentioned, SAP BW also provides time-dependent master data attributes. What is the effect of using product groups stored as a time-dependent attribute of the product in our query? Table 4-16 shows the results of a query, with October 1, 2005, as a reference date.

Table 4-16 Reporting the Truth as of October 1, 2005

YEAR	PRODUCT GROUP	REVENUE
2005	Fruit	430
	Vegetable	130
Subtotals		560
2006	Fruit	410
	Vegetable	210
	Not assigned	160
Subtotals		780
Totals		1340

"Grapes" have not been sold in 2005, and, therefore, the category had not been assigned to a product group, but revenue still must be reported. This is why revenue with "Grapes" is shown as "Not assigned." The access path for this query is the same as that of non-time-dependent master data queries, except that the reference date specified is used to select the navigational attribute value valid for that point of time. Using the current date as a reference date would deliver the same results as for non-time-dependent master data. Note that these scenarios can be combined and used in the same queries (for example, for comparison purposes).

Storing and handling different versions of truth is also referred to as the slowly changing dimensions problem first described by Ralph Kimball (*The Data Warehouse Toolkit*, 2nd Edition, Wiley Publishing, Inc., 2002). Kimball initially defined three types of slowly changing dimensions:

- **Type 1** — Storing current values with the facts. Slowly changing dimensions of type 1 are providing the current truth.

- **Type 2** — Storing historic values with the facts. Slowly changing dimensions of type 2 are providing the historical truth.

- **Type 3** — Storing current values and one previous value. Slowly changing dimensions of type 3 are providing the current truth and parts of the historical truth.

SAP BW does support all three types of slowly changing dimensions — and it goes beyond those by optionally storing all historical and current values using validity periods assigned to every specific combination of attributes. This option provides the current truth and all possible historical truths available in the database. However, this option should be used with care, because mixing these different versions of the truth can lead to confusing query results.

Realignment

In the context of the different versions of truth in data warehousing, a phenomenon closely related to the current truth and well known from mySAP ERP applications like CO-PA (Profitability Analysis), from custom data warehouse systems, and from other standard data warehousing software is called *realignment* — the process of realigning reporting structures to changes applied to master data attributes and hierarchies. Realignment usually is a very expensive process, not only in terms of process runtime and use of resources. Realignment potentially destroys a wealth of historic data in traditional information systems.

You can preserve the history by keeping the historic and the current truth separate in InfoCubes and navigational attributes. SAP BW is able to realign information at query-execution time without a significant performance impact, allowing more flexibility with regard to the version of the truth required for a certain query.

Realignment in SAP BW is required only for traditional aggregates whenever master data used in the aggregate is changed. (Chapter 3 includes a definition of aggregates.) The difference here is that there is no information loss, because historic data still is available in the InfoCube and reporting would still be possible while the realignment is in progress, although you won't be able to use the affected aggregates. (SAP BW would either read data from the InfoCube or from any other matching aggregate.)

Additional Information Modeling Options

Besides multidimensional InfoCubes, SAP BW provides a number of additional options for creating an information model: MultiProviders, DataStore Objects, real-time InfoCubes, VirtualProviders, and InfoSets are discussed in the following sections.

MultiProviders

MultiProviders are mainly used for the decoupling of queries or other information consumers from the actual design of the underlying InfoCubes, logical partitioning, and combining multiple InfoProviders into a single InfoProvider through a union operation.

Decoupling

It has become best practice to never directly define queries on physical Info-Providers but always define a MultiProvider and use that MultiProvider for query definitions. While the performance impact caused by the additional overhead is negligible, decoupling InfoProviders and queries serves four main purposes:

- Changes to the design of a physical InfoCube after Go Live can be implemented without having to delete the InfoCube and possibly all queries. In fact, a migration from an old version of an InfoProvider to a new version can be done by just redefining the MultiProvider to reference the new version of the InfoCube in production, thus allowing intensive testing with a limited user group before actually switching over.

- The dimensional design process may result in a nonintuitive dimensional design for technical reasons (for example, dimension cardinality). A MultiProvider on top of such an InfoCube will still allow presenting an intuitive dimension layout.

- A change of requirements between different versions of the truth (historical versus current) is easily possible by remapping the characteristic of the MultiProvider to the characteristic or navigational attribute of the underlying InfoCube.

Logical Partitioning

Logical partitioning refers to splitting a physical InfoProvider into multiple physical InfoProviders using a discriminating characteristic such as calendar year, region, or product group. The advantages of logical partitioning include the following:

- Logically partitioned physical InfoProviders are smaller and easier to manage than monolithic, large physical InfoProviders.

- Aggregates have to be rebuilt or changed only for those InfoProviders where data has actually changed. For example, in the case of logical partitioning by year, only aggregates for the current year are affected.

- Logical partitioning can be introduced after all queries have been designed and all data has been loaded by just adding another InfoCube to the MultiProvider definition.

Union of Multiple InfoProviders

MultiProviders are an alternative to modeling large (or, better, broad) physical InfoProviders holding all information required for a query in a single place. SAP BW will then execute a union (not a join) of all underlying InfoProviders to retrieve the query results. An example of such an application scenario is shown in Tables 4-17 through 4-19, with a contribution margin using Month and Material as common characteristics for calculating the union.

Table 4-17 Sales Revenue Facts in an InfoCube

MONTH	PRODUCT	REGION	REVENUE
200607	Apples	NorthEast	110
200607	Peaches	NorthEast	80
200608	Bananas	NorthEast	70
200608	Apples	NorthEast	150
200609	Peaches	NorthEast	300

Table 4-18 Procurement Costs in an InfoCube

MONTH	PRODUCT	VENDOR	COST
200607	Apples	1234	97
200607	Peaches	2345	80
200608	Bananas	3456	80
200608	Apples	1234	110
200609	Peaches	2345	200

Table 4-19 Contribution Margin Retrieved from the MultiCube

MONTH	PRODUCT	REVENUE	COST	MARGIN
200607	Apples	110	97	13
200607	Peaches	80	80	0
200608	Bananas	70	80	-10
200608	Apples	150	110	40
200609	Peaches	300	200	100

Slow-Moving Item Scenario

A frequent reporting scenario addressed by MultiProviders is that of the slow-moving item, where a query is required to identify products that have not been sold in a certain period of time. A standard query on an InfoCube would produce results only for items that have actually been sold, because only for these items would it find sales transaction records in the database. Merging the sales transaction InfoCube with the product characteristic (which contains all products) allows showing all items and their sales (see Table 4-20).

Table 4-20 Slow-Moving Items Report

MONTH	PRODUCT	REGION	REVENUE
200608	Bananas	NorthEast	70
200608	Apples	NorthEast	150
200608	Peaches	NorthEast	0

DataStore Objects

From a technical point of view, DataStore Objects are nothing more than a table, or, actually, a collection of two tables (but that, in fact, is irrelevant to information modeling), holding key fields and data fields, allowing you to track changes as well as perform analysis and reporting. They are used for modeling operational data stores, or data warehouse layers (discussed in more detail in Chapter 5), or as an intermediate data store for complex multilevel staging processes. Across these uses of DataStore Objects, keep the following high-level modeling guidelines in mind:

- A correct definition of the key fields of a DataStore Object is crucial. It not only affects the number of records stored but, more important, the delta-generation capability. Generally speaking, the key definition should contain the identifying InfoObjects of the business entity described by the DataStore Object, plus additional timestamps if tracking of history is required.

- Data dependencies and parent-child relationships between entities must be understood before starting to model a DataStore Object. Chapter 5 provides a more detailed discussion of modeling a data warehouse layer.

- Most DataStore Objects will be standard. However, for operational data stores, high-performance updates, or close to real-time analysis requirements, write-optimized or direct-update DataStore Objects may be more appropriate.

- Properties of a DataStore Object must be reviewed carefully; the SID-generation flag is especially critical. Refer to the SAP BW documentation for more information about these properties and how to use them.

Multilevel Staging Considerations

Typical requirements that lead to multilevel staging scenarios include status tracking and complex aggregations, as shown in Figure 4-16. Applications that require the different statuses of a business process must be able to update status values stored in the InfoMart. Given that InfoCubes do not allow direct updates, there are two ways to implement this functionality:

1. Implement a DataStore Object that updates statuses as required, and perform reporting and analysis using this DataStore Object.

2. Implement a DataStore Object that updates status and creates a change log that can be propagated to an InfoCube.

The first option would be used for small data volumes; the second would be used for large data volumes, taking advantage of the optimized data structure of the InfoCube.

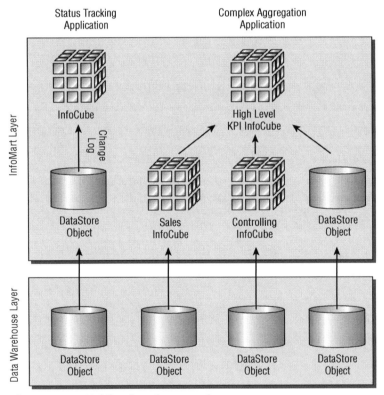

Figure 4-16   Multilevel staging scenarios

Other applications (especially management information systems and balanced scorecards) mostly require highly aggregated key performance indicators calculated using complex formulas. While SAP BW does not provide complex aggregation algorithms to be defined for stored aggregates or online aggregations, it does allow you to populate InfoCubes with data extracted from other InfoCubes and DataStore Objects. Complex calculations can then be performed in the update rules.

In general, precalculated aggregates do not affect information modeling. However, from a reporting-performance point of view, when you are modeling highly aggregated information from various sources, highly aggregated InfoCubes populated from more granular InfoProviders often are a better choice compared to a combination of MultiProviders and aggregates.

As Figure 4-16 also shows, SAP BW allows you to implement multiple stages of DataStore Objects. This is frequently used for merging data from different business processes into a single InfoCube or DataStore Object and, of course, in implementing more sophisticated, layered data warehouse architectures.

Real-Time InfoCubes

SAP BW supports real-time InfoCubes that can be updated synchronously using a special API. This functionality is used, for example, by SAP analytic applications such as SAP BW Integrated Planning, SAP APO, and SAP CRM. From an information-modeling point of view, these objects are handled the same way as traditional InfoCubes. However, keep in mind the following restrictions when using transactional data targets:

- Real-time InfoCubes are updated directly, without applying transfer and/or update rules.

- Updates to real-time InfoCubes are not monitored by the SAP BW monitor.

- Updated data is not visible for standard reporting without making it visible explicitly or using special query variables.

- There is no synchronous rollup for aggregates on real-time InfoCubes.

As mentioned earlier, direct-update DataStore Objects are similar to real-time InfoCubes, except that they do not represent a multidimensional object.

InfoSets

InfoSets essentially are joins of InfoProviders of other types, now including InfoCubes (new with the SAP NetWeaver 2004s release). The use of InfoSets allows combining data from multiple InfoProviders without having to have a sophisticated design or having to implement another staging/transformation process. But use of InfoSets is, therefore, also limited to what exists in your SAP BW system.

InfoSets are good for simple reporting needs with low data volumes and conservative performance expectations. Reporting of historic data or time series is also limited. InfoSets are best suited for snapshot-type reporting. They are often used in combination with VirtualProviders for data-reconciliation purposes.

VirtualProviders

VirtualProviders are useful whenever data residing on a remote system cannot (or should not) be copied to the local database. Sometimes external data cannot be copied to a local system for legal reasons (such as demographic or market research data). Other times, there is a design decision not to copy data from an operational system into the data warehouse. This approach is frequently used to provide controlled instant access to live data on an operational system. VirtualProviders can easily be defined for all SAP BW data sources available on SAP-based platforms but are available also for custom platforms supporting the corresponding API.

Summary

Standard software solutions for data warehousing such as SAP BW enable developers to turn their attention from data and technology to information and business. Modeling a data warehouse has become more and more a task of modeling information and information flows instead of dealing with the technical details of data warehouse implementation. Predefined information models contained in the Business Content add to that by taking some of the load of information modeling off the shoulders of developers. The Business Content offers best-practice information models that can be extended and customized to specific needs.

The core part of an SAP BW implementation project, however, still remains information modeling based on a thorough understanding of the business strategy, the business processes, and user requirements — and a thorough planning of the overall architecture and implementation approach discussed in more detail in Chapter 5.

Enterprise Data Warehousing

While the definition of a data warehouse has not changed since its conception, there are many definitions of enterprise data warehousing available out there. For purposes of this discussion, enterprise data warehousing is the sum of all processes and decisions around building a corporate or government information factory or enterprise data warehouse (EDW). While many of the processes can be distributed and many of the decisions can be made in a distributed way, they must follow certain rules and standards that typically are developed (or at least enacted) on a corporate or enterprise level to achieve the goal of enterprise data warehousing to provide structured information according to the following four objectives:

- **Reliability** — Once information is available, users must be able to rely on the availability of information at all times. Ongoing development, redesign, or maintenance activities must not compromise the quality of information, its timeliness, or any reporting or analysis processes relying on that information.

- **Consistency** — While information provided by any information system cannot always be completely correct, it must be provided according to certain defined levels of quality. Information must be as complete, integrated, harmonized, and consistent as possible.

- **Agility** — Often quoted but still true: The ever-increasing speed of change in modern business forces enterprises to make operational and strategic decisions based upon up-to-date, sometimes even real-time, information. Newly emerging requirements for information are a constant challenge that enterprise data warehousing must address.

■ **Efficiency** — Last but not least, information must be supplied in a cost-effective way. Every dollar spent on enterprise data warehousing must pay off in a reasonable time frame by helping either to reduce cost or generate more revenue.

Not surprising, these objectives are conflicting. Agility is required to quickly accommodate different analysis requirements from different parts of the business and may affect the reliability of the system or the consistency of data as a result of the changes applied. Sometimes it is more efficient to extract a well-known data set again, but then the additional (potentially uncontrolled) redundancy may compromise consistency.

The overall goal of a sound enterprise data warehousing initiative must be to find the right balance between these goals in your organization. The ingredients for this are a well-defined business intelligence strategy, a sound architecture, an appropriate system topology, a concept for addressing data integration and data quality, an approach for capturing the history of changed data, and, finally, a set of rules and policies as a framework for all development initiatives and for running the enterprise data warehouse.

Business Intelligence Strategy

There are a number of common misperceptions around data warehouse implementations in general and SAP BW implementations in particular:

■ **Misperception 1: Data warehouse implementations are IT projects** — Yes, of course, IT plays a major role in data warehouse implementations. The real value of a data warehouse, however, can only be achieved if its drivers are in line with the business strategy and priorities of the organization and if strong business sponsors support the data warehouse initiative. Many issues along the way of a data warehouse implementation are organizational, political, or business-process related, and many of these issues surface as a result of a data warehouse project. An IT-driven project tends to find technical solutions for what really needs to be solved on the business side.

■ **Misperception 2: "Quick-win" iterative implementations will lead to a successful data warehouse** — Quick wins help to create trust in the capabilities of a new software package but are very dangerous because they fuel the expectation that all new requirements will be available with the same speed. They effectively just migrate the departmental, isolated, stovepipe solutions to a central system — without realizing the value of a truly coordinated solution: reduced redundancy, increased consistency, and lower long-term cost. While an EDW initiative can use quick wins for internal project marketing purposes, it really needs to pursue a platform approach that focuses on building an integrated solution.

- **Misperception 3: Business Content is a proper solution to accommodate all BI demands** — Business content does provide a tremendous value to any SAP BW implementation, especially on the data-extraction side but also with closed-loop analytic applications. However, it does not cover all requirements, does not currently support a true data warehouse approach, and is not integrated across all business processes or industries. For many business processes, there is no competitive advantage in just following standard solutions. Many projects will, therefore, choose to not just activate the Business Content and use it as it is.

- **Misperception 4: Governance can be introduced later** — It can be very tough and expensive to introduce a development framework after a number of applications have been developed and are used productively. These existing applications will have to be migrated to new standards, and team structures and responsibilities will have to be changed. A lot of resistance will be put up against this. Still, introducing a framework too late is better than not having one at all.

- **Misperception 5: Operations is not so important** — Even the most successful implementation survives just a short period of time if no one ensures that data is being loaded and made available on time with a defined quality, that query runtimes are within the range of reasonable expectations, and that maintenance activities do not adversely affect the system.

Compare your enterprise data warehousing initiative to driving your car. A sound car has a powerful engine, a reinforced body, safe tires, comfortable seats, and so forth. But to actually go somewhere with your car, you require more. First of all, you need infrastructure (highways, roads, and local streets). You need traffic rules to safely use the infrastructure, and you need resources (gas) to keep your car running. Every once in a while you also need a skilled mechanic for regular maintenance on your car.

You can just enter your car and go to the grocery store without even thinking about it. For a longer journey, however, you must have a destination and a strategy (or map) you can use to determine the best way to get there. Only with all these things in place can you start your trip and be sure to finally get where you want to go. You may take detours, and things may break, but you'll still get there. You might even change your mind on where you finally want to go, but then you'll do so deliberately.

Transferring this back to the world of enterprise data warehousing, it is obvious that having a proper business intelligence strategy is crucial to the mid- and long-term success of your enterprise data warehousing initiative — or any serious reporting, analysis, and data warehousing initiative. Therefore, let us repeat the definition of the term *business intelligence strategy* from Chapter 4:

A business intelligence strategy defines what business information is needed (requirements and priorities) and how to technically deliver it (overall architecture and implementation approach). From a business perspective, more advanced business intelligence strategies not only incorporate the defining of core metrics (historical reporting) but also the process of explaining them (descriptive modeling), sensing them (predictive modeling), and acting on them (prescriptive modeling). From a technology perspective, more-advanced business intelligence strategies incorporate the latest innovations and related architectural trends such as Web services and SOA.

The actual instance of a business intelligence strategy for your organization will be driven by your business strategy; strategic and tactical business drivers; the size of your organization; how it is organized; the corporate culture; internal politics and balances of power; IT landscapes; and external factors such as market development, competitors, political environments, and so forth. Elements of a business intelligence strategy include the following:

- A definition of the scope of the business intelligence initiative and its alignment with the overall business strategy to grant sponsorship from senior management and create awareness across the organization

- A list of business requirements from a high-level perspective, including key metrics, scorecards, and a definition of the level of data quality required

- An assessment of the current data warehouse landscape and a gap analysis with respect to high-level requirements

- A plan for integrating the business intelligence initiative with other corporate initiatives such as master data management or an ERP implementation

- A definition of priorities and master project plans as a basis for development time lines and rollout strategies

- An approach to allocate cost to different parts of the business to avoid deadlock situations in fighting over the distribution of budgets

Starting an EDW initiative without a proper business intelligence strategy in place leads to a short-term solution focus with low overall reliability and flexibility, uncontrolled redundancy, inconsistencies between information from different sources, higher cost of ownership and, ultimately, falling short of the goals of enterprise data warehousing.

Architecture

Multiple architectural concepts have been introduced and discussed over time, mostly focusing on the layers of an EDW. The most well-known architectural concept is the corporate information factory (CIF), defined by Bill Inmon (see www.billinmon.com or *Corporate Information Factory, Second Edition,* Wiley Publishing, Inc., 2001), shown in Figure 5-1.

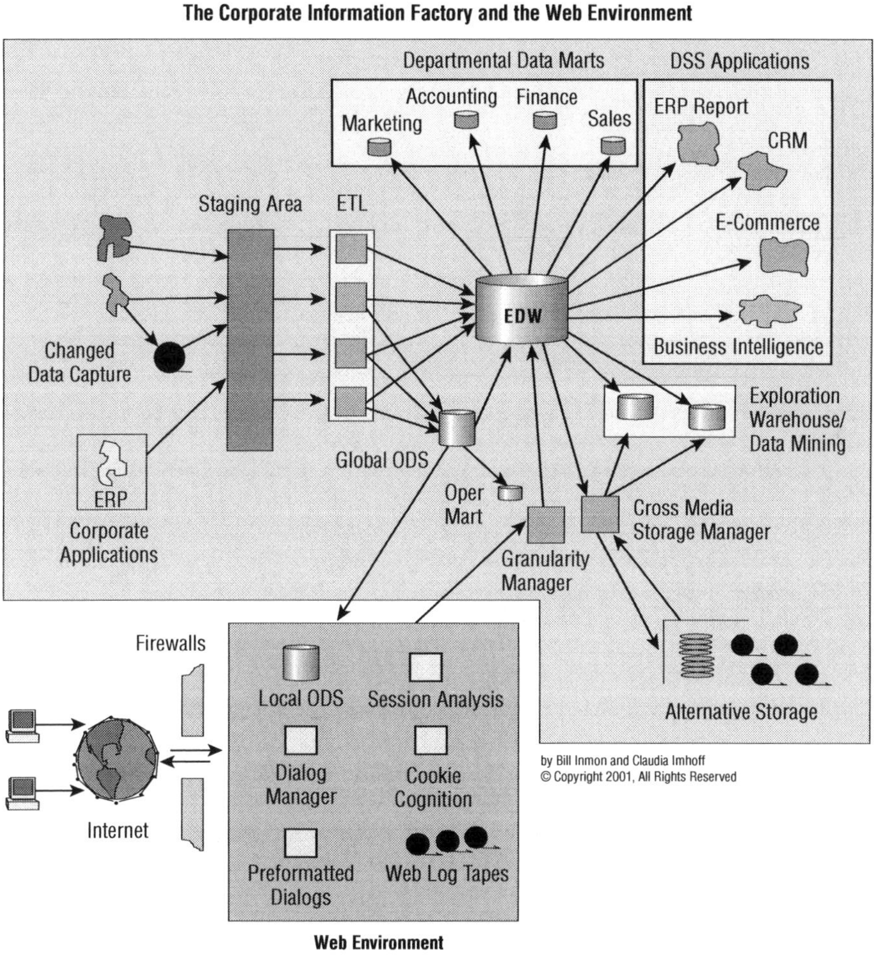

The Corporate Information Factory and the Web Environment

by Bill Inmon and Claudia Imhoff
© Copyright 2001, All Rights Reserved

Web Environment

Figure 5-1   The Corporate information factory (CIF)

Copyright © 2001 Bill Inmon, Claudia Imhoff

The following section extends the discussion around EDW architecture by including topological and system-landscape aspects. The discussion here focuses on laying out the options SAP BW provides to realize the chosen architecture.

Layers of an EDW Architecture

Organizing an EDW into different data layers helps in formalizing the data staging and integration process, provides a defined level of data quality on each of these layers, and allows controlled redundancy in optimized data structures for different purposes. As shown in Figure 5-2, four different layers are commonly used in enterprise data warehousing: the data staging layer, the operational data store, the data warehouse layer, and the InfoMart (or Data-Mart) layer.

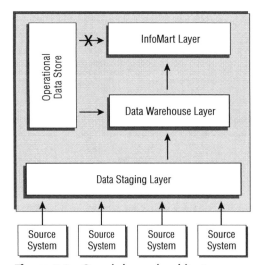

Figure 5-2   Generic layered architecture

Each of these layers requires a separate data model describing the objects of that layer and their relationships. The degree of correlation among the different data models determines the complexity of the mapping processes required to transfer data among these levels.

Data Staging Layer

The *data staging layer* serves as a backup for less-mature applications by decoupling extraction processes from staging, transformation, or reconciliation processes. The data staging layer is not necessarily identical with the Persistent

Staging Area (PSA) provided by SAP BW, although many clients choose to use the PSA as a data staging layer. The main difference between the PSA and a data staging layer implemented using DataStore Objects is that the latter allows reporting off of the objects of the data staging layer. While this type of reporting will, in most cases, not be available to end users, it can be used for technical and data-reconciliation purposes.

Data is usually loaded from once a day to real-time with high granularity but no history. Archiving is not required at this level. Data will typically be deleted after a period of two to four weeks (except for immature applications, where data-quality issues are anticipated) to avoid significant additional redundancy. Data is owned by the functional area (for example, finance or sales).

Operational Data Store

The Operational Data Store (ODS) is defined by Bill Inmon as follows (see www.billinmon.com or *Building the Operational Data Store, Second Edition* (Wiley Publishing, Inc., 1999):

The Operational Data Store (ODS) is a hybrid structure that has characteristics of both the data warehouse and operational systems. Because the ODS is a hybrid structure, it is difficult to build and operate. The ODS allows the user to have OLTP response time (2/3 seconds), update capabilities, and decision support systems (DSS) capabilities.

Bill Inmon distinguishes four types of operational data stores:

- **Class I** — The time lag from execution in the operational environment until the moment that the update is reflected in the ODS is synchronous (that is, less than a second).

- **Class II** — The time lag from execution in the operational environment until the moment that the update is reflected in the ODS is in the two-hour to four-hour range (that is, in a store-and-forward mode).

- **Class III** — The time lag from execution in the operational environment until the moment that the update is reflected in the ODS is overnight (that is, in a batch mode).

- **Class IV** — Data is processed in the data warehouse and fed back to the ODS in an aggregated manner.

Depending on the class of ODS, data is usually loaded from once a day to real-time with high granularity but no history. Archiving is not required at this level. Data will be typically be deleted within a period of six months to avoid significant additional redundancy. Data is owned by the functional area. The adoption of Web services has enabled virtual ODS to be realized whereby data is not physically moved into the ODS but retrieved via a Web service."

Data Warehouse Layer

As we touched on in Chapter 1 the *data warehouse layer* is intended to establish a single point of truth or corporate memory for all reporting or analysis-relevant information. The following description of a data warehouse layer is based on Bill Inmon's definition (*Building the Data Warehouse, Fourth Edition*, Wiley Publishing, Inc., 2005):

- **Subject oriented** — Data is organized around subjects rather than applications.
- **Integrated** — Data must be integrated and must provide a defined level of data quality.
- **Unflavored** — Data will not be changed in relation to the goals of particular requirements or applications.
- **Granular** — Data will not be aggregated or filtered.
- **Nonvolatile** — Data will not be deleted or modified. Instead, a complete history of changes is kept at the data warehouse level.

All data used for reporting and analysis must be staged through this layer on its way from the source to the InfoMarts. The data warehouse layer also allows instant rebuild of InfoMarts off of integrated data; it serves as a fallback line for unexpected ad-hoc reporting needs that cannot be served by existing InfoMarts and avoids redundant data loads and transformations.

Data is usually loaded from once a month to once a day; in some cases there are requirements for more up-to-date data. Archiving will be required for large data warehouses because data will not be deleted from or updated in this layer. Data is owned by a central data warehouse team.

InfoMart Layer

The final (and, from an end user's point of view, most visible) layer is the *InfoMart layer* from which most reporting and analysis requests are served. This layer provides most of the information available to end users in an integrated, aggregated, and application-specific manner. An InfoMart has the following properties:

- **It is dynamic and disposable** — InfoMarts may (but do not have to be) rebuilt dynamically or even disposed of, following adjustments driven by changing business environments. New or changed InfoMarts can be created very easily based on the data stored in the data warehouse layer.
- **It is volatile** — Data in an InfoMart may or may not be updated, depending on the analytical application. Pure reporting and analysis InfoMarts will be nonvolatile. InfoMarts used in other types of applications, such as planning (for example, Integrated Planning or SAP SCM) will be volatile.

■ **It is a subset of information for a specific audience** — InfoMarts focus on the reporting and analysis requirements of a specific, possibly cross-business-area audience inside or outside the organization and provide the subset of information required for this audience.

■ **It is persistent or virtual, multidimensional, or flat** — InfoMarts can be built using persistent or VirtualProviders using multidimensional or flat data models.

■ **It focuses on reporting and analysis** — InfoMarts are used primarily for reporting and analysis services, including analytical applications.

Again, data is usually loaded from once a month to once a day and typically kept for some three years. Requirements for more up-to-date data and for keeping data for longer periods of time are not unusual, though. Archiving may be required for auditing purposes. Data is owned by functional areas (for example, finance or sales).

Conclusion

As a summary of the discussion in this section, Table 5-1 provides a comparison of the properties of the different layers of an EDW. More information about modeling for the different layers can be found later in this chapter.

Not many organizations have consequently implemented all layers of the EDW architecture. While we strongly recommend that you do so, we realize that a lot of pragmatic decisions are made on the way of implementing an EDW architecture. However, whenever you decide to slacken your standards, ensure that it is a conscious decision and that you have thoroughly weighed the pros and cons of doing so.

Topology

The term "topology" in this context refers to the distribution of the different systems constituting an EDW by geographical and/or functional and/or architectural criteria. One central single instance of a data warehouse may not serve all purposes. Different companies have different corporate cultures, structures, and geographies and need different topologies to reach their goals in the most cost-efficient way. There is no silver bullet for choosing the right topology for your enterprise. There are, however, questions to ask before making a decision:

■ Does your company pursue a more centralized or a more decentralized management strategy?

■ What does your overall IT strategy look like? What topology did you choose for the rest of the IT landscape?

Table 5-1 Comparison of the EDW layers

LAYER	FREQUENCY OF DATA LOADS	DATA HISTORY	REPORTING	GRANULARITY	OWNER	UPDATES	ARCHIVING
InfoMart	Daily – monthly	Up to 3 yrs	Yes	Aggregated	Functional area	Limited	Yes
DWH	Daily – monthly	Multiple yrs	Limited	Granular	DWH team	No	Yes
ODS	Real-time – daily	0-6 months	Limited	Granular	Functional area	Limited	No
Staging	Real-time – daily	0-3 months	No	Granular	Functional area	No	No

- Who is your sponsor, and how much influence does he or she have in your organization?

- How are your users distributed across different locations, and what are the bandwidths of your communication channels?

- How heterogeneous are your source systems? What levels of data quality do they provide, and how much integration of data do you actually need in what place?

- Do you already have data warehouse solutions (SAP BW-based or other) somewhere? Do these need to be migrated or otherwise integrated with the EDW?

- What other major IT initiatives are currently under way (for example, a mySAP ERP implementation)?

- What cost restrictions are you facing?

- How different are the reporting requirements in different parts of your organization from a legal, geographical, organizational, or business point of view?

The following sections discuss different typical topologies found in today's SAP BW implementations. Note that, in reality, all kinds of combinations exist between the distinct scenarios described here to multiple levels of local data warehouses and mixes of template approach and local data warehouses.

Single Global Data Warehouse

With the *single global data warehouse* approach, all relevant data from different sources are staged into a single, integrated global EDW. Figure 5-3 shows this topology. Typically, single global EDWs store a large amount of data about different business processes, with many users accessing such data. Note that they might not be run on one single physical machine but actually distributed to multiple physical systems for better performance. They still logically remain a single global EDW.

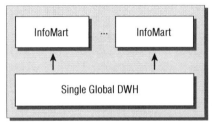

Figure 5-3   Single global data warehouse

This topology best supports the *single point of truth* or *extract once, deploy many* paradigms of enterprise data warehousing controlling redundancy at the corporate level. It ideally fits centralized organizations, where business processes are in line with (or are supposed to be in line with) a central business strategy. Implementing this approach is obviously easier the smaller or less complex or the more structured an organization is. Organizations with a single line of business, or organizations with an existing master data integration strategy, will most likely choose this topology.

Global Data Warehouse Feeding Local Data Warehouses

This topology can actually be considered an extension of the topology described previously in that there still is a global, integrated data warehouse that may or may not have its own InfoMarts. However, in addition to that, there are local data warehouses fed by the global data warehouse. Figure 5-4 illustrates this extended topology.

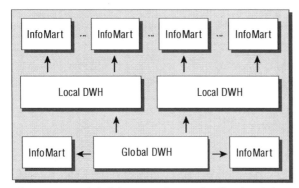

Figure 5-4   Global data warehouse feeding local data warehouses

Note that "local" in this context does not necessarily reflect a geographical concept but can be used in a broader sense, covering all kinds of segmentations (such as geographical, functional, or line of business). In many cases, this topology is also used to address (expected) performance issues with either the overall load of users or the bandwidth available for reporting and analysis. Other applications include local variations of reporting and analysis requirements (legal, functional, or other) that are just implemented locally but may be fed by a central integrated data warehouse instance.

Managing redundancy in such a scenario is relatively simple because all data is still integrated in a central data warehouse. However, local implementations must be managed closely according to global EDW standards to avoid uncontrolled redundancy.

Local Data Warehouses Feeding a Global Data Warehouse

The more decentralized or diversified a business is, the more it makes sense to evaluate a topology where most reporting and analysis is provided by a local data warehouse — following the same rules as a global EDW (see Figure 5-5). Multiple local data warehouses can exist by geography or, more typically, by business unit, forming a virtual EDW. To what extent data across different local data warehouses is integrated depends on the degree of autonomy the local business units have, as well as on technical, political, and financial factors.

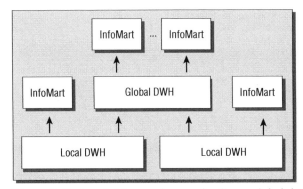

Figure 5-5   Local data warehouses feeding a global data warehouse

An additional global data warehouse (again following the same rules) serves as a consolidation point for enterprise-wide reporting requirements fed by the local data warehouses. The global data warehouse will typically hold an aggregated view of globally relevant information (for example, financial information). Similar to the global approach, data will need to be integrated on the way from the local data warehouses into the global data warehouse.

Template-Driven Local Data Warehouses

Another topology (closely related to the local data warehouse approach) is the template-driven local data warehouse topology (see Figure 5-6). From a topologic point of view, both are actually more or less identical. The approach of building the local data warehouses differs in how much of the local data warehouse is prescribed centrally.

In the template-driven local data warehouse, centrally developed templates for reporting and analysis applications are rolled out to all local data warehouses in very much the same way as SAP rolls out its Business Content for typical mySAP ERP reporting requirements. Depending on the degree of local autonomy, the local data warehouse teams can activate and use the template application, enhance the activated templates according to local requirements, or use the templates as examples.

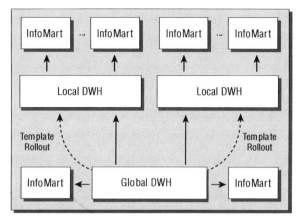

Figure 5-6   Template-driven local data warehouses

SAP BW supports the template approach by opening its Business Content development features to partner and customer development. The template approach uses this functionality to develop enterprise content and roll it out to local SAP BW data warehouses using standard transport functionality and Business Content activation features. SAP partners are using the same functionality to develop partner content in areas they specialize in. The SAP BW authorization concept can be used to control changes to the enterprise content.

Generally, this approach ensures metadata consistency across multiple local data warehouses and facilitates collecting local data from local data warehouses into a global data warehouse. Note that metadata consistency does not by itself guarantee data integration. Data integration still must be done at least on the way into the global data warehouse.

Virtual Data Warehouse

A recent trend discussed in the data warehouse community is *virtual data warehousing*, where not all data is actually moved among different systems but where a rich front-end tool (eventually in combination with a middleware) is used to retrieve data directly from sources and present analysis results directly or with limited on-the-fly calculations.

While this topology can be implemented with SAP BW (with the Analytic Engine as middleware, VirtualProviders as metadata objects, and the Business Explorer as the front end), data-integration requirements are usually hard to match in virtual data warehousing. Also, virtual data warehousing tends to open the back doors for uncontrolled development of reports and analysis based on unconsolidated data, leading to the same chaos that data warehousing was invented to address in the first place.

The virtual data warehouse topology is also known and discussed in the industry as a *federated data warehouse*.

Relevant SAP BW Interfaces and Technology

The key to implementing complex topologies is open interfaces, allowing not only the extraction of data from operational systems but also the bidirectional exchange of data with ERP systems, different data warehouses, external information, and so forth. SAP BW provides a collection of interfaces on both ends of the information introduced in Chapter 3 and explained in more detail in Chapters 6 and 7. These interfaces include the SAP Service API, the various BAPIs on both sides (BW and ERP), the VirtualProvider interface, the Universal Data Connect interface, the XML interfaces for staging via Web services, reporting and metadata exchange, and, finally, the Open Hub Service.

It is not useful to make general recommendations on how to design the topology or what interfaces to use to enable the data flow among the different systems constituting that topology. You must know the business, functional, and nonfunctional requirements, organizational details, user and system distribution, and details about the network, as well as the hardware and software environments in place. Actual decisions will have to be made on an individual basis.

System Landscapes

It has long been common sense in the SAP world to have separate environments for development, testing, and production purposes (see "Traditional System Landscape" in Figure 5-7). The higher investment on the hardware and software side is more than compensated by the advantages of ensuring that production is never compromised by any development.

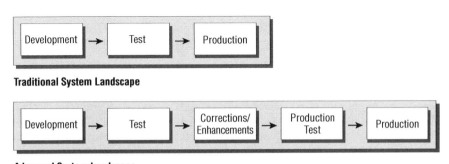

Traditional System Landscape

Advanced System Landscape

Figure 5-7   System landscapes

However, in more complex project situations such as large EDW initiatives, new challenges are presented. Small changes and enhancements that must be applied to the productive environment quickly (agility!) are in conflict with broader developments and cannot be productive without these. Handling this type of conflict can best be achieved by adding a fourth or fifth system to the system landscape, as shown in the "Advanced System Landscape" in Figure 5-7.

Initial development and development activities related to larger programs will be done in the development system; all development tests will be done in the test system. The corrections/enhancements system is used for all minor corrections and enhancements to the productive solution and for integrating these changes with the larger developments done in the development box. The production test system is used for final testing of both larger developments and minor enhancements and corrections before everything is moved to the production system.

Some clients choose not to install a separate production test system but use the corrections/enhancements system for these purposes. While this approach reduces the cost of infrastructure, it requires much more discipline when it comes to developing and testing enhancements and corrections.

In the initial stages of an SAP BW implementation, some clients actually go for a two-stage system landscape, skipping the separate test system. This is tolerable only in very small projects with just a few developers working closely together on a limited scope of projects. Additional systems are often added to the landscape for prototyping (sandbox) or training purposes.

Another aspect of system landscape comes into play with performance optimization by load distribution. Besides utilizing the traditional three-tier architecture with data base servers, application servers, and front-end systems that SAP provides, systems can also be split along the lines of the layers of the EDW with ultimately up to four different systems (or system landscapes) being used — one for each layer of the data warehouse. But, again, actual decisions on how to design the system landscape must be made individually.

Data Integration

Data integration is one of the most important (and commonly most expensive) aspects of any data warehouse initiative — but particularly for enterprise data warehousing, where data from all over the company must be brought together in one place and integrated so that meaningful reporting and analysis can be performed based on consistent data. Data integration has multiple aspects:

- **Technical integration** — Ensures that the same data formats are used by converting data types, performing basic calculations, and basic data-quality and plausibility checks (such as adding missing information using defaults or derived values).

- **Semantic integration** — Ensures that a common coding of values is used across all objects in the EDW (for example, that the gender is always represented as "M" for male, "F" for female, or "initial" for unknown). While the gender example is a simple one, implementing semantic integration can become very expensive in heterogeneous environments.

- **Process integration** — In many cases, business processes and their respective operational systems have to be enhanced or modified to fully support the requirements for integrated data in the EDW. For example, if a customer group is not maintained on a certain sales system, while it is crucial for analysis purposes, that system and the corresponding business processes must be enhanced to enforce maintenance of customer groups.

- **Analysis integration** — Ideally, the same objects or objects derived from one another are used in all reporting and analysis processes across all systems of the topology to ensure maximum integration.

First of all, data integration is a conceptual problem, not a technical problem. Political hurdles must be overcome, and business processes (or their implementation in operational systems) must be changed. Business users must learn new (or modified) processes. Extensive mapping rules must be defined. All of these activities are independent of the actual implementation or the technology used for that implementation. In many cases, there will already be a data integration initiative such as a master data management (MDM) program — many times driven by customer or supplier relationship management programs. As the name suggests, data integration in the context of enterprise data warehousing must be aligned with any global integration initiative.

Master Data Integration

Most data integration efforts are around master data. MDM is on the top of the list in many larger organizations around the globe, with passive MDM scenarios such as master data consolidation or active scenarios such as master data harmonization and distribution. Whenever an ongoing MDM initiative is in your organization, an EDW is a potential client.

On the other hand, many EDW projects are run without an existing MDM solution. Many aspects of at least master data consolidation must be considered, and solutions must be developed to ensure that data in your EDW is consistent and free of uncontrolled redundancies. Figure 5-8 shows a generalized sketch of the master data integration problem from a data warehouse point of view.

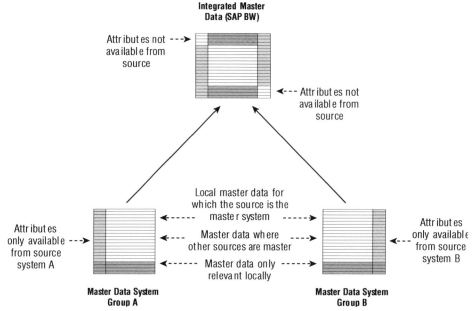

Figure 5-8 The master data integration problem

Generally speaking, you can distinguish four different segments of master data per source system (group):

- **Master data records only relevant locally** — In many legacy systems, data records are kept for technical or internal data management purposes, often in a special range of key values or predefined by the application. While a data warehouse is designed to keep a complete history of business events, these records do not add any value and should not be staged into the data warehouse.

- **Master data where other source systems are the system of record** — Often, master data is distributed among different systems (for example, in different geographies) and is partially or completely replicated among multiple systems. There should be one system that keeps the master copy of the data record — the system of record.

- **Master data records where the source system is the system of record** — When multiple systems are maintaining the same or overlapping sets of master data records, for each identifiable subset of records, one of these systems should be defined as the system of record.

- **Master data attributes where the source system is the system of record** — This is different from the others, because, in this case, master copies of certain attributes (but not the record, its key value, or other attributes) are kept in the source system. An example would be a marketing system that determines and keeps sophisticated customer classifications, whereas address data is kept in a different system.

The (seemingly simple) step from the source system view to the integrated view in Figure 5-8 is not at all easy in many cases. The primary challenge is to determine which system actually is the system of record, and, in many cases, multiple copies of the same record are kept in different places. This is where sophisticated algorithms are required to identify duplicates and to make (automated) decisions about which data records (or attributes) to use from which source. It is important to notice that master data integration must be thought through and implemented for all characteristics delivered by all source systems.

You should use a true MDM approach to master data integration wherever possible, but SAP BW and its transformation engine can be used to implement sophisticated master data consolidation scenarios that are sufficient for reporting and analysis purposes (see the section, "Modeling Support for Data Integration," later in this chapter).

Transaction Data Integration

Transaction data integration is not much different conceptually from master data integration. It is important to notice, though, that all integration efforts for master data must be applied in the same way to all transaction data. In addition, it is important to ensure that transaction data from different sources is disjunct (that is, the same transaction can only be recorded and uploaded to the data warehouse once, and the same business processes from different systems are aligned so that they can be measured using the same or comparable key figures). The same is true for inventory data, which, in many cases, can be derived from transaction data.

Data Quality

While data integration and data quality are closely related, data integration focuses more on issues related to matching data from multiple sources. On the other hand, data-quality management focuses on checking data for the following:

- **Invalid technical data formats** — Invalid or unrecognized date formats or fields with numeric values that actually contain letters or special characters.

- **Invalid values** — Data fields with values out of the range of admissible values according to the definition of the InfoObject.

- **Missing information** — Data fields that do not have a value or have an initial value.

- **Referential integrity** — Data fields with a reference to another data record that cannot be resolved (for example, a customer number that cannot be found in the customer master).

- **Plausibility** — For example, a birth date more than 120 years ago in your current customer master.

In some cases, data-quality issues can be corrected automatically (for example, by assuming reasonable default values for missing or invalid fields or by deriving correct information from other sources or from other parts of the data warehouse layer). Whenever an unrecoverable data-quality issue occurs, there are basically three options left:

- Filter and isolate invalid data and continue the update process.
- Filter and isolate invalid data and abort the update process.
- Just ignore the error.

While the latter sounds unreasonable, it actually doesn't have to be. The cost of eliminating the error may well exceed the cost of living with a certain degree of error in reporting and analysis. It is important, though, to make a conscious decision to ignore errors based upon an analysis of the consequences and the cost of fixing them.

Filtering and isolating invalid data that cannot be automatically corrected is mandatory. For all other cases, the question is, "What happens to the update process?" If you continue the update process, you will end up with incomplete data (for example, all revenues from invalid data records are missing completely) or incomplete updates of existing data (such as when a reclassification of customers is applied only for some of the customers). Generally, this will lead to confusion, incorrect reports, and, in the worst case, incorrect decisions based upon that information.

In any case, all data-quality issues must be logged as part of the regular data-load logs so that issues become transparent and can be addressed. The best way to deal with data-quality issues, however, is to include data quality as a high priority in all design and development activities. This allows adjusting business processes, optimizing source systems and extraction processes, and monitoring the transformation before any data-quality issues harm the consistency of the data warehouse.

Once an unrecoverable error has occurred, immediate action must be taken. This includes communication of the error to data/business-process owners, identification of the root cause of the error (many times this is not the data warehouse or the transformation process), and, finally, the elimination of the root cause of the error. Many times, modifications to existing data transformations must be made even though the error may not have been caused by these transformations.

Modeling the Layers of an EDW

Looking at the different purposes of the layers of an EDW, there are different approaches to modeling the objects that constitute the layers. These different approaches are discussed in upcoming sections of this chapter.

However, there's one common guideline that we have found to be of tremendous value in our implementation projects: Use completely separate sets of InfoObjects for each of the layers of an EDW to make sure that integrated and non-integrated, application independent and application specific data is not mixed up.

Modeling the Data Staging Layer

The most appropriate metadata object to use for modeling the data staging layer is the standard DataStore Object. Direct-update or write-optimized DataStore Objects can be used for high-update frequencies or real-time requirements. As far as the actual data model is concerned, the objects of the data staging layer normally follow the lines of the structures extracted from the source systems, in some cases enhanced by additional information. Current versions of the Business Content do not include a data staging layer but instead rely on the PSA functionality of SAP BW.

Modeling the Operational Data Store

SAP BW offers two main options when modeling operational data stores: DataStore Objects and VirtualProviders. While DataStore Objects are physically stored copies of data in the SAP BW system, VirtualProviders are references to data records stored on a separate system. By class of the ODS (as defined by Bill Inmon), we recommend using the following metadata objects:

- **Class I ODS** — As Class I ODS get closest to real-time requirements, direct update DataStore Objects in combination with SAP XI for real-time message passing provide the best results. A prerequisite of implementing this, however, is the ability to capture updates in the operational system and propagate those to the ODS in real-time — a feature rarely found in operational systems. VirtualProviders simulate rather than implement a true Class I ODS; this type of virtual ODS should be used with care.

Queries on VirtualProviders are actually run on the source system on data models that are not optimized for reporting and may cause significant additional load on those systems.

- **Class II ODS** — Either use direct-update DataStore Objects in combination with SAP XI or write-optimized DataStore Objects for quick updates without a delta mechanism. Standard DataStore Objects are of limited use for this class of ODS.

- **Class III ODS** — Use write-optimized DataStore Objects for quick updates without a delta mechanism. Standard DataStore Objects are of limited use for this class of ODS; direct-update DataStore Objects will not be required.

- **Class IV ODS** — Use write-optimized DataStore Objects for quick updates without a delta mechanism or standard DataStore Objects if deltas are an issue.

The actual data model of an ODS is similar to that of the data staging layer. It still is very close to the structures used for data extraction but is enhanced according the operational reporting needs addressed by the ODS.

Modeling the Data Warehouse Layer

How to model the objects of a data warehouse layer is a matter of intensive discussion in the industry. Proposed solutions range from modeling in third normal form (3NF) to using denormalized data models such as the star schema. We tend to use a pragmatic approach that results in something between 3NF and denormalized data models driven by considerations around the complexity and performance of the transformations required from the data staging layer into the data warehouse layer and from the data warehouse layer in to the InfoMart layer.

The main SAP BW metadata object for modeling the data warehouse layer again is the DataStore Object. As opposed to the multidimensional structure of InfoCubes, the essentially flat DataStore Objects provide all the flexibility required to implement all kinds of data models from normalized to denormalized, as shown in Figure 5-9. In most instances, a standard DataStore Object will do; for requirements closer to real-time data warehousing, write-optimized or direct-update DataStore Objects can be considered. However, given that direct-update DataStore Objects do not support transformations and monitoring, using them in the data warehouse layer will pose a high risk to data quality in the data warehouse layer. Table 5-2 shows a comparison of normalized and denormalized modeling as shown in Figure 5-9.

Normalized Sales Order DataStore Objects

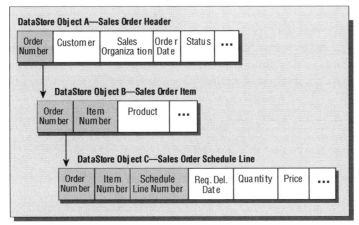

Denormalized Sales Order DataStore Object

Figure 5-9   DataStore Object modeling approaches

Table 5-2   Normalized Versus Denormalized DataStore Objects

PROPERTY	NORMALIZED DATASTORE OBJECT	DENORMALIZED DATASTORE OBJECT
Redundancy	Lower	Higher
Data volume	Lower	Higher
Number of records	Higher	Lower
Administration effort	Higher	Lower
Support for realignment	Good	Poor
Delta handling	Easy	Difficult

The administration effort for normalized DataStore Objects is obviously higher, because multiple objects must be maintained instead of just one denormalized object.

Support for realignment and delta-handling is better for normalized models, because fewer objects must be updated as part of the realignment process.

Look at the sales order example, where an order status is changed in the operational system (which typically uses a normalized data model to store orders). For a normalized DataStore Object, just one data record on the order level must be updated; for a denormalized DataStore Object, all records relating to the updated order must be identified and changed.

On the other hand, from a transformation point of view, the more normalized a data model is, the more complex the transformations from the data warehouse layer into an InfoMart tend to be. Complex joins are often required to retrieve additional information from the data warehouse layer.

On a final note, a data warehouse layer is not in large parts of current releases of the Business Content.

InfoMart Layer

Modeling for this layer mainly focuses on multidimensional objects and optimizing structures for reporting, analysis, and information-delivery purposes. The Business Content includes information models for all SAP solutions and supported industries. Refer to Chapter 4 for more details on dimensional modeling.

Modeling Support for Data Integration

With a sound conceptual basis, data integration on an enterprise level is still easier said than done, even in the ideal case where all source systems deliver harmonized or common coded data. A typical example is that as a result of an acquisition, a new system must be integrated that is not (yet) able to deliver common coded data. The best time to consider and address this issue is when you start modeling your EDW. This is what this section is about. Let's start with a couple of definitions:

- **Source system** — An operational or data warehouse system that provides data for the data warehouse.

- **Source system group** — A group of source systems that use the same common key values for a specific master data object.

- **Local Key** — The locally (for a specific source system or source system group) unique identifier of a master data object.

- **Qualified Local Key** — The globally unique concatenation or compounding of the local key and the source system group identifier.

- **Global Key** — A globally (independent of source systems or source system groups) unique identifier of a master data object.

It is recommended not to use a SAP BW supplied source system ID for data separation but instead to go for a custom source system group identifier to remain independent from the actual source system landscape and to be able to organize different, homogeneous source systems in groups.

Modeling with Global Keys

Modeling using global keys is fairly straightforward. Figure 5-10 shows a full example using books covering all layers of an EDW.

At the source-system level, obviously the local keys are used. Upon staging source data into the data staging layer, you should determine the global key value through some kind of key-mapping algorithm (more on mapping later in this chapter). There are two major reasons to perform the mapping on this layer. First, this allows staging the global key into the ODS without having to apply the mapping rules redundantly. On the other hand, there is a chance that the data in the data staging layer is reused in other staging processes, which may require the global key.

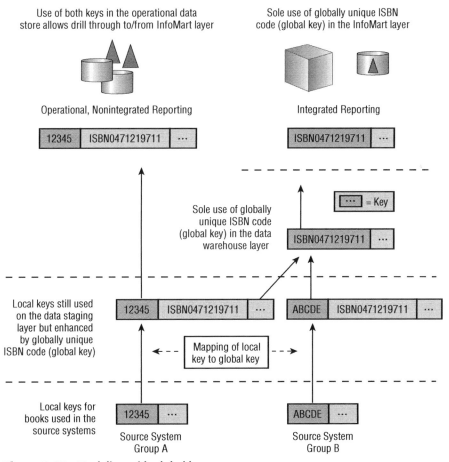

Figure 5-10 Modeling with global keys

On the ODS level, use the local key and add the global key to allow for navigating between the ODS and the InfoMart and data warehouse layers. In the InfoMart and data warehouse layers, only the global key is used.

An advantage of the global key modeling approach is that there is exactly one record per master data object (because the key is globally unique), so the total data volume just depends on the number of records and attributes of that master data object. Except for the determination of global keys (which can become quite complicated), the staging process is straightforward. A disadvantage is that any errors in the mapping routine are hard to correct because the global key will be used in multiple objects with a potentially large data volume. Every change in the mapping rules will require reloading the affected data records into all subsequent objects on all layers of the EDW. In many cases, orphaned records will remain in the system.

The global key modeling approach makes sense whenever you're dealing with trivial InfoObjects such as gender, language, or flags or with InfoObjects that represent a highly standardized or stable set of keys and mapping rules, such as the ISBN code used in Figure 5-10.

Modeling with Qualified Local Keys

In cases where data cannot be fully integrated or where future integration efforts are to be expected, physical separation of data in the same data model while maintaining the ability to report on integrated data provides an approach to the data integration challenge. This can be done by using qualified local keys instead of global keys.

Up to the data staging layer, the qualified local key modeling approach follows exactly the same guidelines as the global key modeling approach. Both approaches begin to differ where data integration starts. While the global key approach no longer separates integrated data, the qualified local key approach uses the same DataStore Objects to store data but separates data from different sources by always using the qualified local keys instead of one global key in the data warehouse and the InfoMart layers.

Figure 5-11 shows an example where an InfoObject with qualified local keys is used in modeling an InfoCube and is populated from an integrated Data-Store Object on the data warehouse layer. Another consolidated InfoObject using the global key value is assigned to this InfoObject as a navigational attribute, making the global key value available for reporting and analysis. This consolidated InfoObject itself might have consolidated attributes that can then be used for navigation and display.

The main advantage of this modeling approach is that errors or changes in the mapping rules can be accommodated very easily. Just change the mapping rules (or add mapping rules), reload the master data to apply the new mapping rules, and all other reporting objects will provide correct reporting based upon both the global key value and the qualified local key value. There is no need to realign or reload any other reporting objects such as InfoCubes or DataStore Objects.

The cons of this approach include more complex transformations along the staging process. In many cases, lookups will be required to determine missing field values (these can often be implemented as part of the mapping rules to make life easier). The overall data volume will obviously increase compared to that of the global key approach. In the worst case, there will be one data record per source system group, and, in many cases, the number of attributes will also be higher.

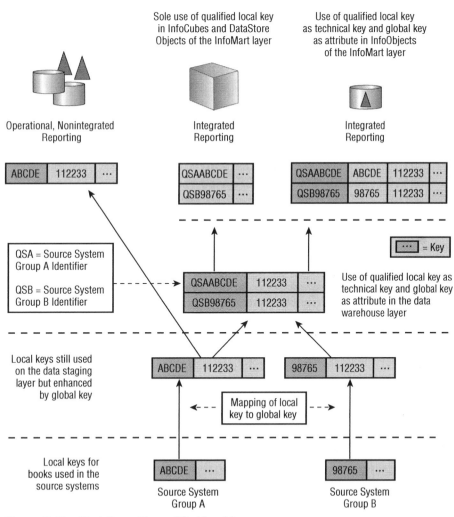

Figure 5-11   Modeling with qualified local keys

Still, the qualified local key approach is the way to go for unstable master data objects with multiple, potentially changing sources. Typical examples include `customer`, `vendor`, `material`, and so forth. In cases of extremely high cardinalities, you may want to revert to the global key approach, sacrificing the flexibility of qualified local keys.

Concatenation Versus Compounding

When it comes to creating qualified local keys, SAP BW provides two options: *concatenation* of key values and *compounding* of relevant InfoObjects. In the case of concatenation, the source-system group and the local key value(s) are concatenated. All fields will be made available in separate attributes so that they can be used independently for navigation and drill-through purposes. In the case of compounding, a compound InfoObject is defined, which uses the source-system group as one of its compound keys. Both approaches have their pros and cons. Generally, you should use concatenation for the following reasons:

- Concatenation has a limited effect on the activation and use of Business Content because it does not require any changes to the structure of keys; just the key length needs to be adjusted.

- Concatenation does not affect existing referenced objects (such as Info-Cubes, DataStore Objects, or other InfoObjects using the InfoObject).

- Concatenation can easily be implemented retrospectively — after having loaded master data or transaction data.

- Concatenation can potentially be dropped after implementation once global data integration has been realized (for example, in an MDM system).

- Concatenation makes life in reporting easier because there are no dependencies among the different parts of key, as there are for compound InfoObjects.

On the downside of concatenation, in order to allow drill-through support, additional InfoObjects will need to be introduced that hold the key values of the individual fields that constitute the key. Concatenation can affect overall reporting and data-load performance by increasing the size of the master data tables. Note that derived structures (such as InfoCubes) will not be affected because of the use of surrogate IDs.

Mapping Approaches

Mapping of local keys to global keys can be more than tricky; in many cases, a completely accurate mapping algorithm just cannot be defined and implemented. We've seen this happen especially with large data volume and poor data-quality scenarios (such as customer data integration or material master integration). Still, mapping approaches can be divided into four different categories:

- **Generic mapping table** — A generic custom database table is used to map the combination of the local key and the source-system group identifier to a corresponding global key value. Typically, the actual content of the mapping table would either be maintained manually or updated automatically on a regular basis. This mapping approach can be used for low-volume data sets with relatively stable mappings. A single generic function can be implemented to perform the lookup so that no extra coding is required.

- **Specific mapping table** — A custom database table is used to map a combination of the local key to the source-system group identifier and additional data fields to its corresponding global key value using a specific algorithm. The mapping table in this approach will normally be updated automatically on a regular basis. This approach can be used for low- to high-volume data sets with relatively stable mappings.

- **Mapping algorithm** — A specific algorithm is developed to perform the mapping, independent of mapping tables, often using data available in DataStore Objects or sometimes applying a (complex) calculation to the local key value, returning the global key value independently of additional data. This is often the case for very complex or unstable mappings (such as in large-volume customer data integration) but can also be used for simple mapping rules.

- **External mapping** — Mapping is performed in the source system or in a third-party tool such as Enterprise Architecture Integration (EAI), ETL, or data-quality management software.

Independent of the mapping approach chosen for a particular mapping, keep in mind that all mappings need administrative attention from initial preparation of the mapping tables via continuous (manual) maintenance of mapping tables, to continuous monitoring to identify mapping errors or other data-quality issues.

Modeling Support for Data Historization

Historization means ensuring that all relevant changes to master data and transaction data are tracked and recorded and that proper timestamps (depending on availability) are assigned to these changes. Historization is a prerequisite to achieving the goal of establishing the data warehouse as a corporate memory. Most data in operational systems is no longer available after a certain amount of time or has been archived; even worse, historical versions of most master data are not stored at all but are just overwritten by maintenance transactions or automated updates and get lost completely. The purpose of this discussion is to introduce the basic concepts for historization on the data warehouse level and how these can be implemented in SAP BW. Let's start with an introduction of the different points of time relevant to a business transaction:

- The time a change or an event occurred
- The time a change or an event was reported
- The time a change or an event was recorded in the system
- The time a change becomes effective (time valid from and to)
- The time a change or an event is recorded in the data warehouse

Figure 5-12 illustrates these points in time using the example of a customer moving to a new address. The example assumes that the effective time (valid from) is the same as the time of the move. From a data-warehousing perspective, all of these times can be relevant (if available). In many cases, operational systems do not record all of these times. Sometimes even the fact that something changed gets lost. Because operational systems are not changed easily (and for good reason), the task of tracking history is often assigned to the data warehouse team.

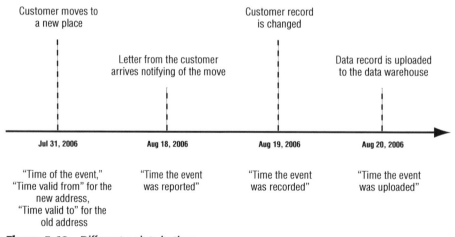

Figure 5-12 Different points in time

Tracking History of Transactional Data

In many operational applications, *transaction data* describes events and will never be changed (for example, in financial applications). These are easy to handle under historization aspects — just record all transactions in a DataStore Object on the data warehouse layer. This is not quite so easy, however, with transactional data that has a status updated multiple times until completion of the business process. Handling this type of transactional data is similar to handling master data explained in the next section. Inventory data can normally be derived from transactional data and does not need separate consideration from a historization point of view.

Tracking History of Master Data

To illustrate the process of tracking history in the data warehouse using SAP BW functionality, consider a simple scenario (shown in Figure 5-13) where, in the source system, a customer record is updated with a new ZIP code. Unfortunately, the source system does not track when the change has occurred or when it was reported or recorded, so you must "re-create" history based upon the upload of the changed record to the data warehouse, ideally when staging into the data staging layer.

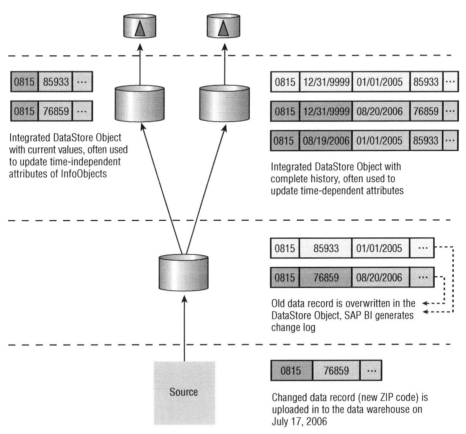

Figure 5-13   Historization process

On the data warehouse layer, the most comprehensive approach to tracking history involves two different DataStore Objects: one for all current values (shown on the left) and another one for the complete history of values (shown on the right). While the first essentially is a subset of the latter, separating these DataStore Objects can come in handy because many applications on the Info-Mart layer need only the current values. Transformations into the current-value DataStore Object are usually pretty straightforward.

For history DataStore Objects, this is a little more complicated:

1. A "Date Valid To" InfoObject must be included as a key field of the DataStore Object; a "Date Valid From" InfoObject is required as a data field.

2. Determine the load date and create a new record with "Date Valid To" as the day before the load date (use return tables or update groups). This requires a lookup on the history DataStore Object.

3. Update the existing record (with DateTo = '12/31/9999') to the new values.

4. Assign the old values to the new record.

Note that this is just one way to implement historization in SAP BW. You could use "Date Valid From" as a key field instead of "Date Valid To," or you could choose to go for higher granularity by using timestamps instead of dates. Finally, there are more complex scenarios where information is changed that has been derived via lookups in the data warehouse transformations or where the source system actually does deliver timestamps for changes, but these changes do not occur linearly but rather in the past or in the future, affecting multiple records in the history DataStore Object.

Be aware that whenever a DataStore Object in the data staging layer must be reloaded from the source or from PSA data, the real load date is typically no longer available or is available only from the SAP BW Monitor. You may want to track the actual load date of a data-load request in a custom table so that it is available if the data staging layer needs to be rebuilt. Making this table editable (for administrators) allows even more flexibility in defining the load date.

Governance

The best architectures and the best strategies are rendered useless without proper organization, policies, and standards. Governance, especially in EDW initiatives, often is something developed along the way, driven by immediate needs to fix an issue. Many of the topics discussed in this section are not new but are willingly neglected to save time and money in the short term. Templates and guidelines for some aspects of governance can actually be downloaded (for example, from the SAP Web site). The ASAP accelerators or the "How To Guides" also offer a lot of help for governance issues.

Think of this section as a reminder of what needs to be thought about and what needs to be done very early in the process of implementing an EDW. This is not meant as a comprehensive guide to project management in the EDW context.

Standards

Global, well-documented standards help streamline project work, ease the task of administering systems and users, and provide guidance to new team members or users. Standards should be set early in the development process, ideally before the first serious development efforts begin. Areas to standardize including the following:

- **Architecture, topology, and system landscape** — Yes, again, ensure that all development efforts adhere to the architecture, topology, and system landscape you defined. Exceptions should be rare and need to be controlled.

- **Documentation** — Establish standards for the layout and the structure of documents developed along the development process, for handover to operations or for actual operations tasks. Do the same for project marketing material such as presentations or white papers. Documentation should be comprehensive but concise; don't waste time and money on formalism.

- **Naming conventions** — A seemingly unimportant topic, naming conventions play a crucial role in organizing the work in large programs with multiple concurrent projects. These facilitate implementing sophisticated authorization concepts and maintaining authorizations for large numbers of objects and users.

- **Information-modeling guidelines** — Information modeling is often considered an art. Establishing guidelines helps take the art out of information modeling and convert it into a process that people can follow and that will lead to a proper design. In support of the guidelines, a set of modeling examples for different requirements proves helpful.

- **Authorizations** — A generic authorization concept with distinct roles for development, operations, and users must be defined, which can then easily be applied to new projects and applications. The larger the program or the number of projects in the program, the more restrictive these roles need to be.

- **Programming guidelines** — Nothing is more constant than change, and, unfortunately, that also applies to the team. Programming guidelines help structure programs and make it easier for new team members to get up to speed with existing code.

- **Code repository** — Reusable code should be kept in a central place and should be documented in a way that facilitates actually reusing it. Many times, reusable code is, in fact, never reused, just because it can't be found or understood easily.

Organization

The ideal organizational form of your enterprise data warehousing initiative depends on a number of factors, including your company culture, the availability of resources, and the chosen architecture and topology. As mentioned, the important thing is to view any EDW initiative as a platform-development initiative rather than a collection of loosely coupled projects that pursue a common goal.

To address the interdependencies among multiple concurrent and competing projects (the most important challenge), use an approach with decentralized project work that is tightly coordinated by a central instance in combination with a strictly separated operations team. All this must be based upon strict rules and processes. This leads to a project organization centered on a central center of competence (COC), coordinating all development activities; separate project teams for each project or application; and a separate operations team that keeps the productive system up and running.

Hiring experienced consultants will help to speed up the overall implementation process. Depending on internal capacities and long-term plans, you might want to consider anything from having external consultants kick-off activities or projects and do regular reviews, to completely outsourcing (parts of) projects. Regardless of the level of involvement of external consultants you choose, you must ensure that the people you finally get on board are actually qualified for what you hired them for and that the mix of skill sets in the consulting team matches your requirements. Not all consultants on your team will need multiple years of experience in implementing SAP BW or in enterprise data warehousing.

The following sections define the roles of these different groups, keeping in mind that there are other forms of organizations, additional groups such as steering committees, and so on. However, we leave a more detailed discussion to the library of project management books.

Center of Competence

The tasks of a center of competence (COC) include definition, refinement, and enforcement of the architecture, topology, system landscapes, global standards, and processes, as well as driving the review process. In many cases, the COC is also involved in the modeling and/or development of integrated objects in the data warehouse layer or is defined as the owner of the data warehouse layer. The COC also should drive training and knowledge sharing within and across the development and operations teams.

Project/Application Teams

Application development is best handled by dedicated teams understanding the business processes and the specific requirements of the application supported by the COC. As part of their work, these teams will locate additional data required; design and implement data-extraction processes accordingly; extend the data staging layer; design and build an ODS (optional); request enhancements to the data warehouse layer where it does not already provide the data required for the application; eventually design and implement these enhancements in coordination with the COC; and, finally, design and implement application-specific InfoMarts (including the required staging and transformation processes off of the data warehouse layer).

In a template scenario, the project teams would be responsible for designing, building, and rolling out the template. Responsibilities of the project teams are largely independent of the chosen system landscape of topology. In scenarios with local data warehouses, local project teams may have to take over certain responsibilities from the COC — depending on the degree of freedom these local organizations have with respect to building their data warehouses.

Operations

As mentioned, there should be a strict separation line between any development teams and the operations team with clearly defined hand-over and development-support procedures. For the most part, operations takes responsibility for keeping the data warehouse within the service-level agreement. Responsibility for operations is usually spread across separate teams: one for hardware and operating system, one for database management systems, one for the SAP application stack, and, finally, one for the actual SAP BW applications running on top of all this. The tasks of the latter group include job scheduling and monitoring (typically using process chains); monitoring data-load and reporting performance; monitoring the availability of the system; performing backups, repairs, and recoveries; applying upgrades and support packages; and coordinating maintenance activities.

Operations also plays an important role as part of quality assurance by making sure that applications go live only after thorough reviews and after sign-off by end users.

Processes

Supplementing standards, properly defined processes provide the framework to coordinate and monitor all activities related to developing and running an EDW:

- **Development** — Although data warehouse development has a much more iterative character than traditional software development, the process should be the same with defined project phases, milestones at the end of each phase, reviews, and go or no-go decisions at each of the milestones.

- **Maintenance** — Maintenance tasks range from small ad-hoc fixes to properly planned releases of new versions of the platform or its applications. Processes and responsibilities must be defined to coordinate these efforts and ensure undisrupted operations of the productive solution.

- **Transports** — Transports are part of development and maintenance; they are critical because every transport has the potential to (voluntary or not) disrupt operations by applying changes to productive objects. Transports should be closely monitored and carefully reviewed before they are imported into the production system.

- **Hand-over to operations** — Define standards and procedures for handing over an application to operations after final testing and sign-off by users. This is a crucial step, even if operations has been involved in development as recommended. They need to be brought up to speed on the specifics of the application being handed over to be able to monitor data loads and take actions in case any problems occur.

- **Roll out** — Once development is complete, the application is rolled out to its users. Data or application migration, planning the switch over, end-user training, and user communication are crucial parts of this phase.

- **Operations** — Tasks for operations include coordinating and monitoring data loads, managing users and authorizations, monitoring performance and addressing performance issues, and, finally, providing end users with a single point of contact for issues with the system.

- **Reviews** — While reviews have been mentioned before, it is important to emphasize that reviews should be taken very seriously and that the best and most experienced talent on your team should be involved in a leading role on all major reviews. Other parties involved are business owners (to ensure that all requirements are met), members of other teams (for learning purposes), and, of course, the project team.

Training

A sound plan for educating all different groups involved in building and using the EDW must be in place before the actual project is started. This includes training plans and template training material for occasional or regular end users, query builders, data analysts, and the development team.

On the user side, training should be composed of two different components: a generic part teaching the functionality of the tool and an application-specific part teaching the actual content the user gets to see in the system, the relevant parts of the data model, assumptions made as part of the development process, and so on.

Developers on the other side should receive comprehensive training across all different components of the software, about enterprise data warehousing, and about information modeling. Developers should also be encouraged to keep their knowledge up to date by reading additional material from the SAP Web site (such as "How To Guides" or documentation enhancements) and to participate in discussions on the SAP Developers Network (SDN).

Project Marketing

One of the decisive factors in the success on an EDW initiative is that it is accepted by its users. User acceptance is determined by the quality of data, performance, and how their requirements are matched by the system. What users ultimately do to judge a system is compare it to their expectations, some of which are created long before they ever touch or see the system.

This is why project marketing plays an important role in the success of an EDW initiative (or any other software development project, for that matter). Activities in project marketing start with communicating the plans for building an EDW. They include regular updates about project progress; release plans or changes; updates about new functionalities; as well as bad news (such as planned or unplanned downtimes). Especially the latter allows users to plan accordingly and avoid frustration with an unexpected unavailability of the service.

Finally, success stories (such as the ones the software vendors and consultants are distributing) are a valuable tool for promoting the EDW inside the organization and, in some cases, even outside the company. Give your project a name that resonates with your user community to increase identification with the initiative.

Summary

The key to successful enterprise data warehousing (or any significant business or IT initiative, for that matter) is to start with a sound strategy, strong business sponsors, a strong team, as well as with the understanding that a data warehouse is not built in one big step or in a short time but must be built iteratively and driven by business priorities and within technical limitations.

The right architectural choices are crucial not only from a technical point of view but also to help organize development activities in multiple concurrent projects using a common set of integrated data objects while competing for resources and attention.

Information modeling plays a crucial role not only for InfoMarts, as discussed in Chapter 4, but also in the other layers of the EDW. Important issues such as data integration and data historization can be addressed using the modeling approaches presented here, although all the hard issues cannot be solved generically.

All smart technical solutions are of little value without a framework of rules, policies, and standards in place, which must be defined before (or very early in) the development process.

Unfortunately, there is no silver bullet for the decisions that must be made on the way to an EDW. Constant training, research, and active participation in discussions in the data warehouse or SAP communities help to stay up to date and to verify design decisions.

Having a complete overview of the SAP BW architecture and how it integrates into the overall SAP NetWeaver framework and having knowledge of the information modeling options SAP BW provides, it is now time to take a closer look at the different architectural layers of the software, starting with the data acquisition and transformation layer, as discussed in Chapter 6.

Data Acquisition and Transformation

Identifying the right sources of data, extracting data from those sources appropriately, applying the transformations required, and storing the transformed data in a way that best supports reporting and analysis is usually the most time-consuming part of building a data warehouse solution. In the CIF framework, this is referred to as *sourcing and manufacturing of data and information*. More specifically, it involves extracting, moving, transforming, loading, and indexing data and information. All functionality required for the extraction, transfer, and loading processes is provided by the data acquisition and transformation services layer (also popularly known as ETL for "extraction, transformation, and loading"). Note that the term "extraction" generally connotes "pull," not "push." As real-time data acquisition becomes more prevalent and relevant, the term *data acquisition* is more comprehensive (for push and pull scenarios).

From an SAP BW point of view, the data acquisition and transformation services layer is composed of the following (see Figure 6-1):

- A Staging Engine
- A DataSource Manager supporting a number of interfaces to different types of source systems
- The persistent staging area (PSA)

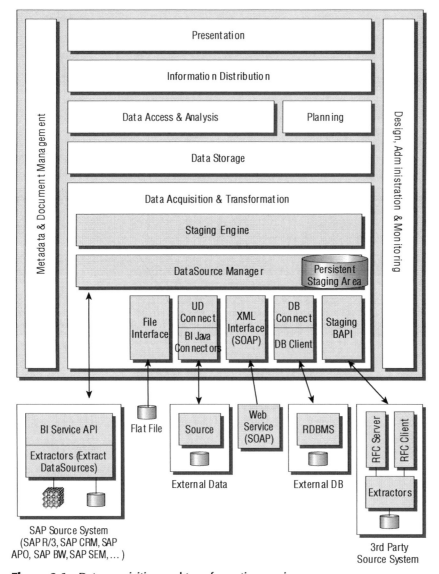

Figure 6-1 Data acquisition and transformation services

The extraction interfaces break down further into the BI Service API used for extracting data from SAP applications, including SAP BW systems, the Web Service interface, the DB Connect interface, the UD Connect interface, the File interface, and the Staging BAPI. The BI Service API supports a large number of extractors: generic extractors, generated extractors, or extraction programs specifically implemented by SAP. The BI Service API is the standard SAP BW extraction interface for all SAP applications. The SAP Application Link Enabling (ALE) technology is used as the standard for handling all communications between SAP source systems and SAP BW systems. Other standards are used for other types of source systems, which will be explained later in this chapter.

Staging in SAP BW encompasses the flow of information from the originating systems through the various stages of the SAP BW system landscape in the information supply chain. As information moves up the information supply chain, it becomes more integrated and usually more aggregated. Information becomes more granular and disparate toward the beginning of the information supply chain.

Before information can actually flow into and through SAP BW, the information supply chain must be defined and configured. The first step in configuration is creating a DataSource, which essentially describes the extraction side of things from an SAP BW point of view. The DataSource consists of a number of data fields in the metadata of the source system and a persistent database object known as the PSA (previously an optional layer but now mandatory). The exchange of data formats between source and target is no longer handled by a transfer-structure field to InfoObject mapping in the Data-Source; it is now handled directly by transformation rules. In fact, the concepts of a communication structure and transfer structure are now obsolete (although InfoSources are still in use and sometimes required). Similarly, the PSA is no longer associated with the transfer structure but rather the DataSource (and must be maintained from the DataSource). Although the DataSource resides in the SAP BW system, it is purely defined in the metadata of the source system and directly corresponds to a now mandatory PSA, as shown in Figure 6-2.

NOTE The PSA is of the same definition as the DataSource, except it also includes request, data packet, and record counter data as part of its key. In addition, SAP source systems have their own DataSource definitions (separate metadata definition from the SAP BW DataSource). When discussing BI Service API extractions, don't confuse the source-system DataSource with the SAP BW DataSource. In all other extraction interfaces, there is only the SAP BW DataSource definition.

From an SAP source system point of view, there are three types of extraction programs: the *generic extractor* (as used for many master data extractors), an *extraction program* generated based on SAP customizing (such as for CO-PA transaction data extractors), or a *specifically implemented extraction program* (as for many hierarchy- and application-specific extractors). The data structure used by the extraction program to extract data is called the *extraction structure*. The fields of this extraction structure are mapped to the fields of the SAP Source System DataSource (on the SAP source system side of the DataSource concept; technology has not changed in the new release).

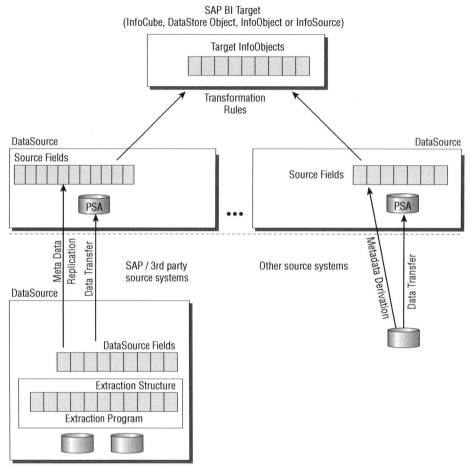

Figure 6-2   DataSources

The fields of the DataSource are maintained in the source system using the source-system DataSource definition transactions described later in this chapter and are replicated to SAP BW systems connecting to the SAP source system. Because an SAP BW system might acquire data from several SAP systems instances via the same Business Content extractors, there is one PSA per SAP DataSource and source-system combination. The source-system DataSource is an agreement between a specific SAP BW system and a specific SAP source system on how to actually transfer data and what data to transfer for an extraction. The source-system DataSource usually is composed of a subset of the fields of the Extraction Structure.

For non-SAP source systems, the fields of the DataSource may be replicated from a database catalog (as for the DB Connect interface), may have been uploaded using the Staging BAPI, or may have been entered manually (as with the File and Web Service interface). All structures are stored in the SAP BW Meta Data Repository. While the SAP BW DataSource fields may be maintained manually in SAP BW, the source system still effectively defines what fields are available in what format, and SAP BW defines which fields are required for the staging process.

Transformations connect the SAP BW DataSource to a target SAP BW object (that is, InfoCubes, DataStore Objects, or InfoObjects). Target SAP BW objects, in turn, can act as Data Sources for new Data Targets. In fact, this is how a typical EDW is modeled (using extraction Data Sources to load DataStore Objects as the EDW layer, which then have export DataSources that can load InfoCubes as part of a DataMart layer). The interface for loading SAP BW objects into themselves is known as the *DataMart interface.*

Certain transformation rules (master data lookups, currency translation, and unit conversions) require that the DataSource be sourced from the SAP BW system itself (that is, be composed of InfoObjects instead of the metadata of the source system). For these scenarios, an InfoSource can act as a virtual SAP BW layer on top of the DataSource, instead of using the DataMart interface as the intermediary. Two transformations are needed: one from the DataSource to the InfoSource and another from the InfoSource to the persistent SAP BW object. The second transformation is capable of performing master data lookups, currency translations, and unit conversions that the first transformation cannot. The InfoSource eliminates the need to persistently store the data once again in order to perform the InfoObject-dependent transformation rules.

InfoSources are particularly useful when common transformations need to be leveraged. There are two types of helpful scenarios: occasions when multiple source-system types need to be mapped to an InfoProvider or when multiple InfoProviders are targets of a transformation.

The InfoSource can be thought of as an additional layer on top of non-SAP BW source system DataSources (that is, completely composed of InfoObjects). In contrast, non-SAP BW source system DataSources are not composed of InfoObjects but rather source-system fields (that is, the metadata of the source system). The same DataSource can have multiple sets of rules for mapping to the same target SAP BW objects by defining multiple transformation groups. Each transformation group (there is always at least one referred to as the *standard*) consists of a complete set of transformation rules that map fields available in a DataSource to each of the InfoObjects used in the target definition. For key figures or data fields, additional transformation rules can be added to the transformation group for the same target InfoObject.

Many-to-many relationships can be established between DataSources and target SAP BW objects through transformations (that is, the same source can update multiple targets, and the same target can be updated by multiple sources). Even for a specific source-to-target transformation, multiple runtime load behaviors can be controlled via Data Transfer Processes (DTPs). DTPs control load behaviors such as what data is selected, what Data Target(s) is updated, and how it is updated (such as delta versus full loads). Multiple Data Transfer Processes can be defined per transformation, enabling different data sets to be passed through the same source, transformation, and target.

The remainder of this chapter discusses the information staging process in greater conceptual and technical detail, dividing it into three sections: data acquisition, transformation, and loading. Pseudocode logic and representative interfaces in ABAP code will illustrate the workings of the transformation processes. However, these discussions are kept at a high level; ABAP know-how is not required.

Data Acquisition

Since release 1.2, SAP BW has supported loading external data through its File interface and the Staging BAPI without actually making a distinction between SAP data and non-SAP data from a data transformation and storage point of view. Many ETL tool vendors (such as IBM, ETI, and Informatica) have adopted the Staging BAPI to allow SAP BW users to load data and metadata from many different databases and file formats. Nevertheless, SAP BW had a reputation for not being open or not open enough. SAP successfully addressed this reputation by adding interfaces (such as Web Services, DB Connect, and UD Connect interfaces) and by entering strategic partnerships with ETL vendors. For example, SAP had a reseller and co-development agreement with Ascential Software. The co-development with Ascential centered on interfaces such as the Staging BAPI and Open Hub API. Note that this reseller and co-development relationship terminated when Ascential was acquired by IBM. Subsequently, SAP has been working more closely with Informatica.

Although SAP BW can now connect virtually to any database through its UD Connect interface and has improved the user interface for more graphics-based configuration, it still benefits from the transformation and data-cleansing capabilities of third-party tools.

Regardless of the actual technological specifics of the data-acquisition process, it is important in any data warehouse implementation to have skilled staff understanding the specifics of the source systems involved — from both a business process and a technology point of view. Without a sound understanding of details of the underlying business processes, it is neither possible to define a proper information model nor to populate an existing information model with consistent data.

Once a first pass is made at information modeling, the core question is "We can build it, but can we fill it?" The conceptual part of this work (especially in a heterogeneous system environment) is definitely taking more time and effort than the actual technical implementation. This is why this chapter begins with a discussion of the basic principles of data extraction and a discussion of the specifics of typical operational systems. Related to that is a discussion of the metadata exchange between the source system and the SAP BW system, including a translation from the source system semantics to the BI-unified semantics of the SAP BW environment. In heterogeneous system landscapes, this is usually the biggest challenge of integration; issues of differing data quality and completeness levels, system availability, granularity, and business semantics must be solved. Besides being an information model for SAP BW implementations fed from SAP applications, SAP BW Business Content has proven to be very helpful as a basis for this kind of integration work as well.

While this discussion very much focuses on mySAP ERP many of the principles and problems discussed here also apply to other enterprise applications such as Oracle, IBM, Siebel, or legacy systems. mySAP ERP was chosen for three reasons:

- mySAP ERP showcases all the basic principles and problems discussed here.
- Many (not all) SAP BW customers use mySAP ERP as one of their source systems.
- A large number of predefined extraction programs are available for mySAP ERP as part of the SAP BW Business Content.

Other types of source systems introduced in Chapter 3 (such as Flat-file, XML, DB Connect, UD Connect, and Staging BAPI) are covered from an integration and interfacing point of view. Extracting data from these systems requires intimate know-how about these non-SAP systems and cannot be covered in this book.

Basic Principles

Generically discussing data acquisition for data warehouse applications is not an easy task, considering the many different ways data is physically stored in database systems or elsewhere, the many different data models used for storing the same data, and the many ways data may be used for data warehousing purposes. However, before going into the details of the extraction process itself, let's examine some basic principles related to different classes of data, to the data flow and integration in an ERP system, to the different dimensions of data extraction, and, finally, to data management technology.

Classes of Data

There are three basic classes of data in a typical ERP system like mySAP ERP: master data, transaction data, and configuration data.

Master data represents any business entity in an ERP system. Many times it represents organizational entities such as the company, a plant, a sales area, a cost center, or an account. Other times it represents external entities such as customers and vendors. Or it may represent things such as materials. Master data is an important concept to data warehousing, because it constitutes the dimensions or dimensional attributes of the data warehouse.

Master data itself can take on various forms. SAP BW categorizes master data into three forms: attributes, hierarchies, and texts. *Attributes* are any fields that describe a master data entity. *Hierarchies* are mostly separate tables that store parent-child relationships between master data entities (such as a cost-center hierarchy or a product hierarchy). *Text* tables simply contain the textual descriptions of master data and are usually stored in separate tables because they are language dependent.

The primary keys of master data tables, of course, differ by application. SAP BW usually handles multiple field keys through the use of compound InfoObjects (effectively defining compound keys), as noted in Chapter 4. Universal extended key concepts such as version and time dependency are handled by SAP BW through generated key fields such as 0DATETO and 0DATEFROM for time dependency. Different in each application is how this is reflected in extraction tables. For example, in HR-PA, master data records for personnel are stored with start and end dates in the primary key. In CO-CCA, cost-center date dependencies are stored with only the valid-to date in the primary key. In EC-CS, consolidation units are fiscal-period dependent and year dependent, but no date is stored; rather, the period and year make up the primary key.

Hierarchy tables tend to be more difficult to understand than master data attribute tables. First, the relationships of master data within hierarchies can be complicated. Second, the techniques for storing these hierarchical relationships can be different application by application. Many applications have unique tables and techniques for storing hierarchies. For example, the product hierarchy on the material master in mySAP ERP is a specific one. It stores the hierarchy as a string in an attribute field on the material master. Configuration settings allow parsing the string into user-defined categories and levels. In mySAP ERP accounting, general-ledger accounts are organized hierarchically as financial-statement versions stored in unique tables. In mySAP ERP HR, employees are created within a personnel development organization hierarchy, which is yet again technically stored in HR-specific tables.

There are hierarchy technologies that cross applications, however. Two of the most pervasive technologies in mySAP ERP are sets (commonly used in the Report Writer or for configurations like cost allocations) and drill-down hierarchies (used exclusively for drill-down reporting).

Transaction data describes a business event (such as a sales order) or the result of business processes (for example, the current in-stock quantity of a specific product). Transaction data contains the preponderant share of the key figures that will become your fact table in SAP BW InfoCubes.

There are two conceptual levels of transaction data: the document level and summary levels. The *document level* may consist of several tables. Most commonly, there are up to three levels of detail for the document level, such as headers, line items, and schedule lines. Header information normally contains information about the document itself — for example, the document type and the date it was posted. The line items consist of the details of the document, such as materials on a purchase order or general-ledger accounts on a financial transaction. Schedule-line details usually revolve around the delivery schedule, where a given quantity of a specific product ordered has to be broken into several scheduled deliveries. Because it provides the largest amount of information, usually the lowest level of granularity is the ideal source for extractions.

Dynamic *summary* tables are redundant summarizations of line-item data and primarily exist in the ERP system for reporting purposes. mySAP ERP's special ledger and logistics information systems are common examples. SAP BW steadily makes the summary level of mySAP ERP obsolete (except for summary-level-only transactions such as balance carry forward or planning).

In mySAP ERP HR, the distinction between master data and transaction data is blurred. HR Infotypes — a hybrid between master data and transaction data — store details such as personal data and payroll results as Infotype data.

Configuration data drives the ERP application logic. Typically, many configuration data tables can be found in an ERP system. The reality of a highly customizable enterprise-wide software solution was achieved through data-driven application logic. Of course, SAP NetWeaver has taken things a step further through metadata or model-driven application logic (but that's another topic beyond the scope of this chapter).

Although primarily used for defining the details of business processes, configuration data often is required for data warehousing purposes. For example, configuration data assigned to the type of a schedule line of a sales order defines whether that schedule line is relevant for production-planning purposes. This information is stored in the mySAP ERP schedule line type configuration table. Filtering this information on the extraction side would hide information from the data warehouse. Selecting sales orders according to this information in the analysis or reporting process allows analyzing information relevant for production planning.

NOTE In SAP BW, configuration data is modeled as characteristics and may have master-data attributes, texts, and hierarchies. SAP BW does not distinguish between configuration data and master data.

Configuration data, master data, and transaction data records all may contain fields relevant to reporting and fields not relevant to reporting. Often there are many fields of a very technical nature (used for controlling business processes or for tracking the individual who actually changed a specific record at what time) that are not relevant to BI and can be ignored. To be understandable to the data warehouse, some of the reporting-relevant fields may need conversion even prior to going through the transformation process in SAP BW. This is the case when operational or configuration information required to perform this conversion is available only in the operational system and cannot (or for some reason should not) be made easily available to SAP BW. Common examples include the order type in mySAP ERP SD, which changes depending on the language, and cost objects in CO depending on the application. The order type OR (English version), for example, gets stored in the database as TA. In the mySAP ERP controlling module (CO), cost center, internal orders, WBS elements, and production orders are all saved in the same field name (called *object number*) of the same tables (Business Content splits these tables into separate extractors per cost object) and are in a technical format that must undergo conversion before it is recognizable to the user (that is, internal CO object number to external cost center number conversion). Although most of the transformation will be done by SAP BW, there still may be important transformations to be performed during data extraction.

NOTE Other than changes to master data, changes to configuration data reflect changes to business processes and may also require a substantial redesign of the SAP BW information model.

Data Flow and Integration

mySAP ERP persists as a complex system with many applications using their own data model idiosyncrasies. As mySAP ERP grew, it experienced cycles of divergence and convergence until its mySAP ERP underwent mitosis, spawning new monolithic solutions such as mySAP Supply Chain Management, mySAP Customer Relationship Management, mySAP Supplier Relationship Management, and mySAP Product Lifecycle Management. Each of these enterprise applications has its own distinguishing characteristics, especially from an information-systems perspective. However, if you look at the bigger picture, you see that they are still integrated with each other; business processes or events in one application can cause other business processes or events in another. In addition, by looking at the components of each of these applications, you see that this is even more evident.

Understanding the process flows is important for cross-application information models and identifying where key figures should be sourced. For example, accounting postings often originate outside of the accounting application, such as in logistics, where more and different details are stored with the originating document. Decisions must be made regarding where to extract the information from. Many SAP BW clients debate whether to use the logistic extractors or CO-PA extractors for sourcing sales documents from mySAP ERP. The bottom line is that one of the biggest achievements of SAP BW-based reporting compared to mySAP ERP-based reporting is the comparable ease of cross-application analysis and reporting.

The following paragraphs present two common mySAP ERP processes to demonstrate how data is spread in the mySAP ERP system and to highlight the difficulties in extracting from these sources: Order-to-cash and purchase-to-pay. Each is briefly described and the corresponding relevant tables highlighted. While this discussion very much focuses on mySAP ERP, its business model, and even physical database tables, the same fundamental principal of a business event kicking off different business processes implemented in different application areas apply in other ERP packages and in legacy systems.

Order-to-Cash Business Process

Examples of analysis that require an understanding of the order-to-cash process include the following:

- **Bookings, billings, and backlog analysis** — This report evaluates sales orders (bookings) and invoices (billings), as well as the difference between quantities ordered and quantities delivered (backlog).

- **Sales commission calculations** — In some business environments, sales commissions are paid not only on sales but also on timeliness of customer payments. This requires a merge of sales-order data and aged accounts-receivable data and the availability of a sales representative reference in both types of documents.

- **Royalty payment analysis** — Obligations for paying royalties have to be tracked from sales orders until money is received on the bank account, at which time a royalty calculation prompts payments to royalty recipients.

- **Days sales outstanding (DSO) and days sales inventory (DSI)** — This analysis requires sales information, as well as receivables and inventory amounts. DSO calculation involves amounts from accounts receivable, while DSI involves quantities from inventory management.

Following is a simplified order-to-cash process in mySAP ERP:

1. When a sales representative enters a sales order in the mySAP ERP system, the system stores the transaction into three SD tables: VBAK (header), VBAP (line item), and VBEP (schedule line). This transaction has no direct financial impact, so no accounting documents are created.

2. A delivery due list is executed for all sales orders, and deliveries are created in tables: LIKP (header) and LIPS (line item). A goods issue is subsequently made updating tables MKPF (header) and MSEG (line item). This document does have an accounting impact, and the corresponding financial transaction tables BKPF (header) and BSEG (line item) are updated.

3. An invoice due list is then executed for all deliveries. After an invoice is created (updating tables VBRK and VBRP), it is released to accounting, which creates an accounting document (BKPF and BSEG) and sets up the receivable in table BSID (line item).

4. The receivable is cleared when a payment check is received. Another accounting document is created (BKPF and BSEG), the open receivable is cleared, and table BSAD (line item) is updated.

Procure-to-Pay Business Process

Following are some examples of analytics for the procure-to-pay process:

■ **Vendor evaluations** — This analysis involves assessing how well vendors are performing by measuring, for example, on-time delivery by comparing the requested delivery date of a certain purchase order with the actual time goods are delivered. The first event is generated in the purchasing application, while the second event is generated in the inventory management.

■ **Commitments, obligations, cost, and disbursements analysis** — This analysis evaluates how budget is committed (purchase requisitions), obligated (purchase orders), costed (goods receipt), and disbursed (invoice payment). This analysis sources its data from purchasing, inventory management, and accounts payable.

■ **Payment analysis** — This analysis involves ensuring that discounts and promotions are taken advantage of and that late fees and penalties are avoided. The pricing conditions on a purchase order or contract dictate the terms of the agreement, and the accounts payable holds the information of whether payment was made optimally.

Following is a simplified procure-to-pay process in mySAP ERP:

1. A purchase requisition is created, and table EBAN (line item) is updated.

2. The requisition is converted into a purchase order and tables EKKO (header) and EKPO (line item) are updated.

3. A goods receipt on the purchase order is made that updates tables MKPF and MSEG.

4. The invoice is then received, updating financial tables BKPF and BSEG, as well as setting up the payable in table BSIK (line item).

5. The invoice is paid via a payment run, the payable is cleared, and table BSAK is updated (line item).

Dimensions of Data Acquisition

Five dimensions are generally used to describe the different methods and properties of data acquisition processes:

- **Acquisition mode** — The extraction mode refers to the range of data extracted from the source system. There are two basic extraction modes: full extraction and delta extraction. *Full extraction mode* extracts all data records available in the source tables based on the acquisition scope defined (see the text that follows for more details). *Delta extraction mode* only reads updated or inserted records ("delta" refers to the set of updated or inserted records). From an SAP BW point of view, extraction mode is referred to as *update mode*.

- **Acquisition scenario** — Data can either be pushed into a data warehouse or pulled from an operational system. In a push scenario, the initiator of the data acquisition is the sender system or middleware. The Web Services interface is an example of a push data acquisition. In a pull scenario, the initiator is the data warehouse. The File interface is an example of a pull data acquisition. Note that the SAP Real-time Data Acquisition (RDA) via the use of a daemon is technically pull technology. It is near real-time because of the scheduled frequency of updates.

  The push-versus-pull concept has a connotation of directorship; in reality, information logistics deals more with initiators and receivers of information flows.

  A more meaningful way to convey the push concept is to connect it with the phrase *publish and subscribe*. Similarly, the pull concept could be ascribed to *request and response*.

- **Acquisition formats** — Data can be file versus database, relational versus multidimensional, or XML versus text versus binary.

- **Data latency** — Data latency refers to the timeliness of data acquisition. Whether or not an acquisition is synchronous (real-time), asynchronous (stored and forwarded), or asynchronous batch (on demand, event driven, or scheduled) determines the latency of the data.

- **Acquisition scope** — Acquisition scope refers to the specification of how data must be acquired from a projection (which fields), a selection (which records are required), and an aggregation (at what level of granularity) perspective.

The first SAP BW extractors available for mySAP ERP data mainly supported the full extraction mode in an asynchronous batch-pull scenario. Some extractors, like the Logistics Information System (LIS) extractors, did already support delta loads. This was the beginning of an evolutionary development toward supporting today's analytic applications such as planning with SAP SEM and SAP APO or customer analytics with SAP CRM that require delta extractions, push scenarios, and close-to-real-time updates in the data warehouse. Such applications involve a lot of development on both sides. mySAP ERP and SAP BW were required (and still are required) to support as many delta extractions as possible to support synchronous updates of data targets and to support RDA scenarios. As a general trend in mySAP ERP, extractions have steadily moved from dynamic summary tables to transaction tables, and delta change capture mechanisms have become more sophisticated and enabled to be scheduled more frequently for update.

The main problem in implementing delta extraction lies in identifying the deltas. There are two basic SAP approaches to delta loading (as opposed to snapshot comparisons): the use of delta queues and the use of timestamps (or datestamps). In many cases, the timestamp approach is used (that is, data-selection criteria), simply because it is easier to implement; often, the timestamp is not stored in the transaction itself but is logged in some external table. Using timestamps usually leaves a gap in time between the timestamp being logged and the transaction being updated, however. Hence, some documents may be missed if they have not yet been committed to the database. To mitigate this risk, SAP often uses a *safety delta* concept, setting back a user's timestamp selection for a few hours to avoid missing late updates.

A more expensive (but guaranteed) delta mechanism is the use of *delta queues*, as used in the mySAP ERP logistics extractors. A delta queue is similar to logs written by database management systems in their attempt to ensure consistent data even after serious system failures. Delta queues essentially are tables capturing the key values of changed or inserted records or the entire transaction records. The SAP implementation of delta queues actually tracks before-and-after images of changed data records, allowing you to identify and track every single change of a field value.

Other than the timestamp approach, the delta queue technology does not require any safety delta regardless of the extraction frequency. Another difference between the delta queue and the timestamp techniques is that the timestamp technique captures only the version actually stored in the database at extraction time. For low-frequency extraction (for example, once a month), intermediate versions of the document are missed and cannot be made available in SAP BW.

NOTE ALE change pointers also use a delta queue approach. ALE tracks the keys of all changed data records in a separate table. While avoiding the safety delta problem, ALE change pointers are only designed to deliver the latest version of a data record and do not allow you to identify changes on a field level. The ALE pointer approach is used for some master data extractors in mySAP ERP.

Another complexity in delta extraction, common to both techniques, is capturing changes in interdependent database tables. For example, you might want to indicate a change to a customer master data record when only the address details stored in a different database table have changed. Or perhaps a set of line-item-level documents must be reacquired because of changes applied to the header document. An additional challenge for managing delta extractions is when multiple systems extract data at different times using different selection criteria. Each of these systems expects a different delta data set, depending on when the last delta data set has been extracted and on the selection criteria used. Many extraction programs available for the BI Service API support those individual deltas for multiple target systems.

Additionally, delta extractions can either be pushed or pulled data acquisitions with various data latencies. For example the following scenarios can be found in today's SAP applications:

- RDA through scheduling a daemon to repeatedly "listen" for changes before acquiring deltas.
- Direct updates to a real-time InfoProvider through tools like Integrated Planning or applications like Business Consolidations (SEM-BCS).
- A business transaction event in mySAP ERP calls an SAP Advanced Planner and Optimizer (SAP APO) process interface to synchronously update SAP APO (push scenario).
- The sales order extractor of the mySAP ERP logistics extraction cockpit is available for periodically pulling sales orders.
- List reports downloading data to flat files, which, in turn, are pulled into SAP BW.

Currently, synchronous push scenarios to InfoProviders are not fully supported by SAP BW (for example, pushing deltas through a DataSource, transformations, and InfoProvider through to OLAP cache). Even real-time Web service push scenarios must update the PSA (InfoPackage scheduling) before being propagated on (DTP scheduling). While it is possible to synchronously update data into a real-time InfoProvider or DataStore Object for direct update (see SEM BCS and SAP APO examples in the preceding list), this update always bypasses the regular staging process. These updates do not apply transformation rules, nor do they run under the control of the SAP extraction monitor.

Push technology usually goes hand in hand with delta updates, while pull is used for full and delta extraction mode. Currently, the most pervasive technique in BI for true real-time reporting is via the use of remote InfoCubes utilizing extraction technology. The single biggest issue with this approach is performance, which can be mitigated through the use of MultiProviders. However, when real-time line-item data is needed, asynchronous extraction still is the way to go. The need for real-time data, for example, in Web-log analysis has increased the demand for push scenarios, so you can expect to see RDA and push technologies (like SAP XI) mature and become more widespread in future versions of SAP BW and the Business Content.

While the available extractors for mySAP ERP allow dynamic specification of selection (defined in the InfoPackage used to schedule the load process) and projection criteria (defined by the DataSource), only a few are suitable for configurable preaggregations (i.e., data summarization before extraction). For asynchronous extractions, you can usually compensate for this by actually aggregating data after it arrives in SAP BW, instead of preaggregating in the source system. For synchronous extraction through remote InfoCubes, however, this is not practical, because there is no data persistence.

OLTP Technology Considerations

The technology used to capture and read data independently of the application poses its own challenges to the data warehouse developer, since the data models and the storage technology chosen are optimized for use in OLTP environments, typically with short read and write transactions, pulling the database-performance requirements in two diametrically opposite directions. This section takes a closer look at how data is inserted and updated in an OLTP system, how data is read, and what the important technical implications are. Again, this section showcases approaches used in mySAP ERP to illustrate basic principles of modern ERP and legacy systems.

Physical Updates

Data is updated in mySAP ERP in two different ways: synchronously and asynchronously. *Synchronous updates* are performed by the application itself, while the user is waiting for his or her transaction to come back. *Asynchronous transactions* usually are committed near-real-time, without the user having to wait for the update to complete. These updates are termed V1 or V2 updates in mySAP ERP. *V1* denotes time-critical updates used for updating the actual transaction tables. *V2* denotes non-time-critical updates used for updating statistics tables related to the transaction tables. For example, after a sales order entry transaction is completed, the corresponding sales order tables would be updated in V1 mode, and the corresponding statistics tables would be updated in V2 mode. The longer the task queues, the longer the updates will take. Depending on system load, the physical update may take anywhere from a more or less immediate update to a couple of minutes.

From a data warehousing perspective, there are two fundamental ways data is written to database tables in operational systems: with a delta change capture mechanism and without. As discussed, the coverage of delta change capture mechanisms in mySAP ERP is growing. Both basic delta-capturing mechanisms have been implemented in mySAP ERP updates via two approaches: timestamps and delta queues.

Before SAP BW was introduced, there was already a growing need to split ERP into several instances, while still having data flowing between these instances. The business framework concept was developed where the original vision was to decouple all the applications and have them talk via ALE (ALE is discussed in detail later in this chapter). This business framework concept looked like the beginnings of the SAP NetWeaver and ESA concept but based on BAPIs and ALE instead of Web services and SOAP. Workflow also worked off of this business framework concept to allow for alerts or notifications or to pass onto another link in the transactional supply chain.

Even before ALE was introduced, a change log technology existed for audit purposes. BI leveraged this technology, and some of the early master data delta extractors used ALE change pointers to determine the delta. This wasn't enough, so other BI-specific techniques were developed.

The first delta extraction technique in LIS involved two additional tables that toggled each other for the extraction of delta records. This was replaced by the delta queue technology supplemented by an additional V3 update mode similar to the V2 update mode. The main difference is that V2 updates are always triggered by applications, while V3 updates may be scheduled independently. Many extraction programs available for SAP applications today use the generic and central delta queue technology to identify delta change records.

Another maturing option for capturing deltas is through transactions forwarded through Enterprise Application Integration (EAI) middleware such as SAP XI and updating the SAP BW delta queue through an SAP RFC or Web-service call.

An older approach is provided by the Business Add-in (BADI) technology. Essentially, BADIs are an evolution of the familiar customer exits, allowing you to hook customer-specific code into the standard application. BADIs can be used in various ways; often, they are used for application-specific updating. More explicitly, business transaction events (BTEs) allow hijacking the process and having it perform custom logic synchronously or asynchronously. BADIs technologically paved the road for real-time updates to consumer systems such as SAP BW.

Volatile Documents

Every business transaction in mySAP ERP goes through a lifecycle; it has an active phase and an inactive phase. During the active phase, a document can be continually updated with new or changed information, and any of these changes may have to be promoted to SAP BW. One of the more common examples of volatile business documents is status management; some mySAP ERP transactions (for example, sales orders) track document statuses during its lifecycle. Examples include (but are not limited) to CREATED, OPEN, RELEASED, COSTED, CLOSED, BLOCKED, and TECHNICALLY COMPLETE. These statuses, in turn, control what actions can be performed on a document, actions that may be relevant for reporting and analysis (such as the settling of costs to an internal order).

Similarly, subsequent data flows may be tied to a business document. For example, in the procure-to-pay business process flow, you might need to check the cycle time between order and delivery for evaluating a vendor. An active purchase order schedule line document is usually updated with the goods receipt date. In accounts receivable, a clerk might extend the grace period for a good customer who requests it on a specific payment. This change in payment date recalibrates all the dates and affects aging analysis.

Understanding the volatility of data is important for developing the SAP BW information model (for example, passing volatile data to a DataStore Object that supports overwrites) and when to archive the data in mySAP ERP (that is, when the data goes stale). After a business document becomes inactive, it may become less relevant for reporting. Data about inactive documents needs to be loaded only once into SAP BW and is typically used for historical-trend analysis. In some applications, the active and inactive thresholds are clearly defined. For example, when a document clears in accounts receivable and accounts payable, the information is deleted from one table and inserted into another (BSID to BSAD and BSIK to BSAK, respectively). In documents with status management, there are statuses (like TECO, for technically complete) indicating that the document can no longer be changed.

Other documents in the system have a long lifecycle (such as contracts in purchasing or outline agreements in sales). Some documents may have an indeterminate life (such as a long-standing internal order for specialty requests and its corresponding costs).

Reading Data

There have been third-party attempts to connect to SAP's database directly without going through the application layer. Although it's true that many of the database tables mySAP ERP uses for storing data are directly available, a couple of intricacies are still involved. First of all, just reading those tables completely ignores business logic that may have to be applied for reporting to provide meaningful data. Then there are some technical intricacies, such as the application server buffering data and locking data records above the database level. Handling these problems requires an intimate understanding of the technical details of the business processes involved and requires the functionality of the SAP Application Server.

Even when data is committed to the database, it may not actually be stored in an easily accessible database table. SAP uses a number of table concepts that you should be aware of. Some of these concepts deal with how data is technically stored (transparent tables, database clusters, pooled tables), while others deal with how information is presented (logical databases, database views).

- **Transparent tables** — Transparent tables are ABAP dictionary tables that have a one-to-one relationship with database tables stored in the underlying database management system.

- **Database views** — These are views in the ABAP dictionary that join tables for data-selection purposes.

- **Pooled tables** — In earlier days, mySAP ERP needed more tables than the underlying database management systems would allow and had to group tables together in pooled tables. In other words, table definitions are in SAP that act and behave as transparent tables, but on the database no single corresponding physical table exists. Technically, these pooled tables had the table name as its key, and data would be saved as a long raw string in a field in the database. When a pooled table is read, data is parsed back into the data structure of the SAP table it is supposed to represent.

- **Cluster tables** — SAP uses cluster tables, which are similar to pooled tables. The main difference is that in cluster tables, complex data objects in program memory can be saved to a cluster without any flattening operations (as would be necessary if this data had to be committed to a transparent table). Technically, data in clusters is saved as raw strings. Because of the requisite parsing and flattening transformations needed to read these tables, performance can be an issue. Many HR payroll tables are defined as cluster tables.

- **Logical databases** — This is a hierarchy of reporting structures populated with values via an ABAP program. The structures in the hierarchy may or may not represent actual tables. Logical databases are popular for reporting because developers who program against its structures do not have to invest any development time into designing the data retrieval to the actual tables. In ERP, logical databases are a popular reporting structure for SAP Query and InfoSets.

SAP Source Systems

The next few sections discuss the specific details of all available types of source systems and interfaces, beginning with a generic architectural overview of SAP source systems. Also note that the technology on the SAP source system has not changed, which adds considerations on the SAP BW-side of the Data-Source. If older-release DataSources (that is, release 3.x or below) haven't been migrated, but you want to leverage new BI capabilities (like DTP or transformations) they can be used as emulated DataSources. Otherwise, either the older 3.x BI capabilities (such as use of InfoPackages and transfer rules) must be used or the DataSource must be migrated to the new SAP BW DataSource concept.

Architecture

Figure 6-3 provides a detailed view of the extraction architecture. The BI Service API handles both metadata exchange and data extraction for SAP systems. It is composed of numerous smaller components not described here in full detail; the most relevant are metadata maintenance and transfer, data acquisition and transfer, and the request dispatcher. Metadata maintenance and transfer is called by SAP BW to return a selected set of metadata mainly consisting of the DataSource fields that define and automatically generate appropriate dictionary structures and data transfer programs. The request dispatcher is built on top of ALE technology and is called by the ALE layer when a data-load request arrives at the source system. It checks the request for consistency and correctness before passing it on to data acquisition and transfer. This component in turn calls the appropriate acquisition program, which acquires data from the corresponding database tables and sends both data packages and status information back to the calling SAP BW system.

The SAP BW Service API lets you acquire data from SAP application components such as mySAP ERP, SAP CRM, SAP BI, and SAP SEM systems. Note that the BI Service API also allows you to connect an SAP BW system to itself, allowing you to extract data from its own InfoCubes, DataStore Objects, and master data tables (that is, the DataMart interface). This feature is used to set up multilevel staging scenarios within a single SAP BW system.

Metadata Flow

The extraction structures used by extraction programs, and eventually customer extensions to those extraction structures, basically determine the mySAP ERP source system metadata. They describe fields in which technical formats are available through the extraction programs. This information is used as a basis for defining the fields of the DataSources in the DataSource maintenance dialog. Fields available in the extraction structure can be hidden, as shown in Figure 6-4, effectively defining a projection of the extraction structure to the fields of the DataSources. An application example for such a projection can be found in the public sector Business Content, which extends CO DataSources by grant, functional area, and fund. These fields are not projected unless explicitly defined.

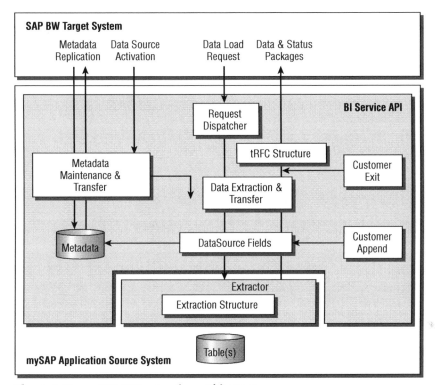

Figure 6-3   mySAP ERP extraction architecture

Figure 6-4   DataSource maintenance in SAP source systems

Similarly, fields that should be available for selection are controlled by a configuration switch, as shown in Figure 6-4 (Selection). The purposes of selecting a subset of data are saving resources required for running the extraction, saving bandwidth by reducing the number of records transferred, and keeping the data warehouse clear of unnecessary data. Business reasons for selecting data are again showcased in the Business Content. In many cases, an SAP BW implementation is run in waves, with increasing functionality and scope implemented in each wave. For example, the CO DataSource for actual line items partially replaced the CCA DataSource for loading actual data. The CCA DataSource is still needed for other value types (such as plan), however. As a result, if both DataSources are to be used, you must select the value type for the CCA totals extractor. The main reason to control the use of a field for selection purposes is technical; selections on fields without any index may result in very long run times for extraction programs.

As a rule of thumb, aggregation should normally be performed in SAP BW at query-execution time, not by the source system at extraction time, since aggregation always means losing information. The most granular data should be extracted from the source system and made part of the EDW layer of an SAP BW system. However, whenever remote InfoCubes are defined directly using an SAP source system extractor, this extractor should support preaggregation for performance reasons. The direct-access flag shown in Figure 6-4 defines whether an extractor supports remote InfoCubes and aggregation (2), supports remote InfoCubes but does not support aggregation (1), or does not support remote InfoCubes at all (0).

Most Business Content DataSources (in particular, line-item delta extractors) do not support aggregation for remote InfoCubes (although some support remote InfoCubes). DataSources typically are defined with a fixed level of aggregation as implemented in the extraction program; this may be a very granular level, as in the CO Actual Costs DataSource, or at an aggregated level, as in CO Costs and allocations.

Most of the extraction programs available in the Business Content have been developed by the same development teams that originally developed the application itself, since the members of those teams are most familiar not only with the typical business requirements but also with the technical details of the specific implementation of each application area. As a result, different extractors use different implementation approaches, sometimes even incorporating complex transformation logic. However, they all adhere to the same technical standards set by the BI Service API and follow high-level Business Content development governance (such as naming conventions) and best practices (incorporating DataStore Objects).

Once the required DataSources have been identified (if available in the Business Content), enhanced from the Business Content, or specifically implemented by the client, the next step is to make the metadata available to SAP

BW. As shown in Figure 6-3, SAP BW calls the BI Service API of the SAP source system to retrieve either the complete set of metadata available or to update metadata for a specific DataSource — a procedure called *metadata replication*. The DataSource is composed of a subset of fields available in the extractor and is used as the technical structure for transferring data from the source system to SAP BW. Definition and propagation of the DataSource complete the setup for a specific source system and allow for actually extracting data.

Data and Control Flow

To support fail-safe extraction and data transfer and to support detailed monitoring, SAP BW uses the ALE technology, originally designed to support exchanging data between distributed (but integrated) mySAP ERP systems. ALE is composed of communication, distribution, and application services and provides all seven networking layers specified in the ISO-OSI reference model (ISO Basic Reference Model for Open Systems Interconnection, www.iso.org): physical layer, data link layer, network layer, transport layer, session layer, presentation layer, and application layer. It is the last, topmost layer, the application layer, which is discussed further in this section, where SAP BW acts as the application.

ALE exchanges messages or data between two systems by way of intermediate documents (or IDocs). An IDoc is a container for passing data between systems via ALE. The different types of messages and the related types of IDocs basically define the language spoken between two different systems using the ALE technology. SAP BW automatically performs all necessary customizing required for setting up the IDoc infrastructure on the SAP BW side and, by calling the BI Service API, on the SAP source system side. Three types of message are used in the communication protocol between SAP BW and an SAP source system:

- **Request IDocs** — When an InfoPackage is executed, a data-load request is created and sent to an SAP source system as an outbound IDoc (see Figure 6-5). This IDoc is processed by ALE and passed on to the IDoc dispatcher, where it is checked for consistency and correctness. The request IDoc is tied to message type RSRQST and contains the following information:

  - Technical details about the request, such as a unique request identifier, DataSource, type of DataSource (transaction data, master data attributes, texts, or hierarchies), who scheduled it, and when (date and time).
  - Data-selection criteria as defined in the InfoPackage.

- The data transfer mode; ALE/IDoc or transactional remote function calls (tRFC).

- The update mode (or extraction mode). Possible modes include transfer of all requested data, transfer of the deltas since the last request, transfer of an opening balance for noncumulative values, repetition of the transfer of a data packet, or initialization of the delta transfer.

- **Status IDocs** — The status of every step in the extraction and data transfer process is logged by the source system by sending status IDocs to SAP BW. The status communicated in the status IDocs is used to update the SAP BW monitor. Figure 6-5 shows the different status IDocs that an SAP source system may send. Status IDocs are tied to message type RSINFO and contain the following information:

  - Technical details about the extraction, such as the unique request identifier, extraction date, and extraction time.

  - The current status (informational, warning, error) including a more detailed error message describing the error (only if available).

- **Data IDocs** — Because the PSA is now mandatory, the use of data IDocs are for limited scenarios (texts and hierarchies, primarily). Data IDocs are used to pass extracted data in the DataSource format back to SAP BW. Depending on the size of the extracted set of data, the data set may be split into several data packages (and usually will be for transaction data and larger master data extractions). Status IDocs are sent after a certain customizable number of data packages to keep the monitor up to date when extracting large sets of data. Data IDocs are tied to message type RSSEND and contain the following information:

  - Technical details about the request, such as a unique request identifier, the data packet identifier, the DataSource, the type of Data-Source (texts or hierarchies) who scheduled it, and when (date and time).

  - All data records in the data package in the format of the transfer structure.

- **Transactional remote function calls** — For transactional and master data attribute DataSources, SAP BW uses transactional RFC in place of data IDocs (but still uses the messaging IDocs for extraction monitor updates). The tRFC adheres to the same communication protocol as a data IDoc. The tRFC warrants safe asynchronous data transfer on a single data package level. Because only the tRFC method allows storing data in the PSA and provides better performance, it is not surprising that it completely replaces the data IDoc option for transaction and attribute data.

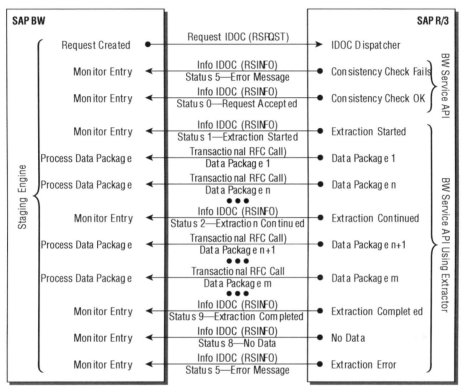

Figure 6-5   Data and control flow for SAP source systems
Based on copyrighted material from SAP AG

Understanding how SAP BW communicates with SAP source systems is relevant for gaining a better understanding of the extraction monitor (covered in more detail in Chapter 11). The following is a sample step-by-step extraction data and control flow for a successful data extraction:

1. An InfoPackage is scheduled for execution at a specific point of time or for a certain system- or user-defined event.

2. Once the defined point of time is reached, the SAP BW system starts a batch job that sends a request IDoc to the SAP source system.

3. The request IDoc arrives in the source system and is processed by the IDoc dispatcher, which calls the BI Service API to process the request.

4. The BI Service API checks the request for technical consistency. Possible error conditions include specification of DataSources unavailable in the source system and changes in the DataSource setup or the extraction process that have not yet been replicated to the SAP BW system.

5. The BI Service API calls the extractor in initialization mode to allow for extractor-specific initializations before actually starting the extraction process. The generic extractor, for example, opens an SQL cursor based on the specified DataSource and selection criteria.

6. The BI Service API calls the extractor in extraction mode. One data package per call is returned to the BI Service API, and customer exits are called for possible enhancements. The extractor takes care of splitting the complete result set into data packages according to the IDoc control parameters. The BI Service API continues to call the extractor until no more data can be fetched.

7. The BI Service API finally sends a final status IDoc notifying the target system that request processing has finished (successfully or with errors specified in the status IDoc).

NOTE Control parameters specify the frequency of intermediate status IDocs, the maximum size (either in kilobytes or number of lines) of each individual data package, the maximum number of parallel processes for data transfer, and the name of the application server to run the extraction process on.

Example of an Application-Specific Extractor

Many of the extractors found in SAP application components are complex, application-specific programs implicitly taking the underlying business logic into account. An example is the logistics extractor, which is shown in Figure 6-6 extracting transaction data from SAP logistics applications. Note that this is just one example of a real SAP extractor. Extractors for other business areas may and do use a different approach in extracting full and delta data sets.

Sales orders entered in the mySAP ERP SD application are not only stored in the VBAK and VBAP tables but also propagated to statistical tables in a separate step, if configured. These tables are used by the logistics extractor to provide delta initializations or full uploads. On the other hand, any changes are written to a delta queue utilizing the V3 update process discussed earlier in this chapter. The delta queue is used by the extractor to provide delta loads.

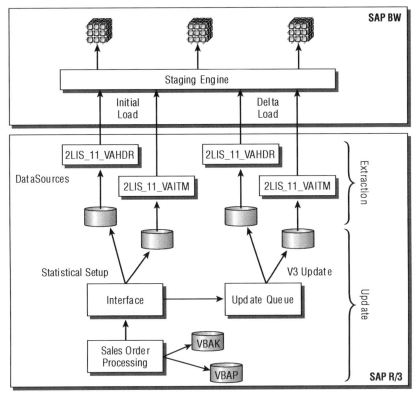

Figure 6-6   Logistics extractions

Client-Specific Data Extraction Options

Although the Business Content and the extractors supporting it have reached a significant coverage of the business areas covered by SAP applications, there are still reasons to enhance existing extractors or develop new custom extractors. Reasons can vary, such as customer-specific business logic, customer extensions to SAP data, custom tables, or missing fields in Business Content for standard tables. Many SAP systems have been enhanced; custom fields may have been added to SAP tables, or clients may have developed their own custom applications through what is now known as SAP NetWeaver. The resulting question is this: What are the options on extracting data from SAP source systems such as mySAP ERP and SAP BW? Depending on availability and coverage of the Business Content, and on the kind of data to be extracted, several options appear in the decision tree in Figure 6-7.

Figure 6-7   Decision tree for extraction methods

Although it is possible to write a custom ABAP report, extracting data from some dictionary tables and downloading those to a file (which then could be uploaded using the File interface), this should be the last resort for extraction from an integration, performance, and administration point of view. The first and best option to evaluate is utilizing the SAP extraction technology provided by the BI Service API. You should use the file-download approach only in cases where the SAP BW extractors cannot be installed on the SAP source system for some reason (for example, mySAP ERP release out of maintenance, SAP system freeze, lack of resources for installing and testing the plug-in).

The first thing to check is what the gaps are with SAP Business Content extractors. In most cases, the required extractors are already available but perhaps do not have all the fields needed. All Business Content DataSources are viewable via transaction SBIW. The corresponding extractors can be tested and traced with the ABAP debugger from within transaction RSA3. Once a matching DataSource is identified, it can be activated and used without further development work.

If the Business Content DataSource delivers only a subset of the information required, it can be extended. Extending a DataSource essentially means adding fields to the extraction structure. In many cases, just by adding the fields to the DataSource, it will automatically get filled (in these cases, the extractor has a MOVE-CORRESPONDING ABAP statement that dynamically maps all the fields from the standard source table to the extraction structure). If the fields are not automatically mapped, they can be filled with custom ABAP code in a customer exit for the extractor (customized in transaction CMOD).

This custom ABAP code can be anything from simple calculations or table lookups, to complex business logic requiring access to multiple database tables. In reviewing various SAP implementations over the years, the authors believe this extraction exit is often too heavily used or made overly complex (probably because programmers are more familiar with the mySAP ERP environment). In general, if the same logic can be effectively performed in a transformation within the SAP BW environment, it should be put there. The case is stronger if your SAP BW system is connected to multiple SAP systems on different releases, but all require similar logic, because this approach may force multiple implementations of the same thing (because of release-specific nuances) and may create transport complexities. Reserve this option for either simple data-lookup scenarios (where you don't want to necessarily bring the data into the SAP BW system and do the lookup there) or more complicated technical scenarios (where there is source-system-specific customer logic and there are useful source-system-specific function calls not available in the SAP BW environment, such as substitution or validation services).

Some ERP applications do not use fixed data structures for extraction but rather generated ones. These typically require a specific program to be run to generate the DataSource. Some examples are CO-PA operating concerns, classifications master data, Special Ledger, and LIS.

Whatever can't be handled by the Business Content DataSource can be resolved by creating custom generic DataSources for either transaction data and master data using either tables, database views (inner-joined tables), SAP Query InfoSets (reporting tool), or a function module (ABAP development). These custom generic DataSources can also support delta extraction if ALE change pointers (on tables or views), timestamps, or counters can be used.

NOTE The use of a XI and the Web Service Interface is another new option for pushing deltas to DataSources.

Generic DataSources are best used whenever there's a need to extract data from a single table or from a database view or from an InfoSet. The generic extraction technology does not distinguish between tables and views; however, Figure 6-7 illustrates all three options. Before opting for InfoSets-based generic extractors, you should evaluate using tables or views. Both provide higher performance and are usually easier to define.

Very rarely will you be able to use a table, however, as most tables do not store the currency or unit of measure with them, which is a requirement for the SAP BW extraction structure. In such cases, the currency key or unit of measure is stored on another table that must be joined into a custom view since tables cannot be extended via enhancement for extraction without physically appending them.

The advantages of SAP Query InfoSets are that they can read logical databases and handle complex and flexible joins (including outer joins and joins on nonkey fields), as well as complex selection logic. ABAP Query InfoSets support ABAP coding enhancements (even for data retrieval) for enriching the results without necessitating the extractor customer exit. The disadvantage is that SAP Query InfoSets can be slow. For better scalability and performance for complex extractions, the function-module approach is the best (SAP Business Content works in almost the same way, except its function module interface isn't simplified for customer use). Typically, the authors opt for the function-module approach over the InfoSet approach unless there is a dual need for reporting (such as for data reconciliation especially or when logical databases are involved).

Generic extractors can be defined in the SBIW transaction. Note that, in some cases, self-defined extractors based on generic extraction technology must be extended in the way described previously and that generic data extraction does not support extracting hierarchies.

The BI Service API and the generic extraction technology are also available in SAP BW systems. SAP BW adds generators generating export DataSources and corresponding extraction programs for a target BI object (InfoCube, Data-Store Object, or master data table).

File Interface

The File interface allows loading three different types of flat files:

- **Comma-separated variable (CSV) files** — CSV files are simple ASCII files where every record contains a certain number of fields separated by a field separator (usually a comma). Files of this type can be generated by many PC-based applications such as Microsoft Excel, Microsoft Access, and so forth. In the SAP BW context, these files are, in a misleading way, sometimes referred to as Excel files or Excel CSV files. The sequence and semantics of the fields of each record must match the definition of the DataSource in the SAP BI system. Missing trailing fields and characters are padded with blanks, and excess character fields and characters are cut off.

- **Fixed field length files** — These are ASCII files where every record contains fixed-length fields exactly matching the definition of the Data-Source. Missing fields at the end of the record are padded with blanks; excess fields or characters are cut off.

- **Binary files** — Binary files allow you to pass numerical data in binary format. For the technical format used for binary files, consult the ABAP documentation. The application uses the ABAP TRANSFER statement to read and interpret records from a binary file. For loading binary files, a control file is required that contains additional parameters for the upload.

Architecture

The architecture of the File interface is shown in Figure 6-8. Because there usually is no system providing metadata about the structure of a file, these have to be derived by the system and manually checked. The names of the fields in the structure are derived by the header (that is, first line) of the flat file. Metadata for the File interface is effectively reduced to the DataSource, describing the layout of the source file. In this case, the extraction structure is essentially synonymous with the DataSource fields.

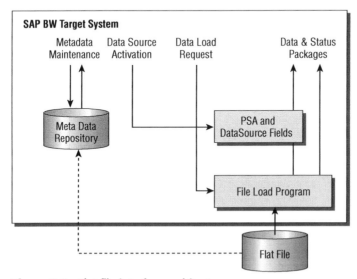

Figure 6-8   Flat-file interface architecture

When a data-load request is issued by SAP BW, the Flat-File interface dynamically generates and executes a flat-file load program, which reads the flat file from the application server or from the client workstation and creates data packages in DataSource format, finally passing these data packages on to the Staging Engine. The configuration for a Flat-File DataSource controls how the load program handles separators (such as data, thousands, and decimal points) and header records and where to get the file (directory path and filename from either the application server or presentation server). A preview function within the DataSource definition allows a sample set of data to be loaded before it is saved and data is to be loaded.

Data and Control Flow

The data and control flow protocol for the flat-file interface is essentially the same as for the BI Service API. However, SAP BW does not send any data IDocs; instead, it directly calls a generated transfer program. Figure 6-9 provides an overview of the data and control flow for the flat-file interface. Note that SAP BW does send status IDocs to itself for monitoring purposes.

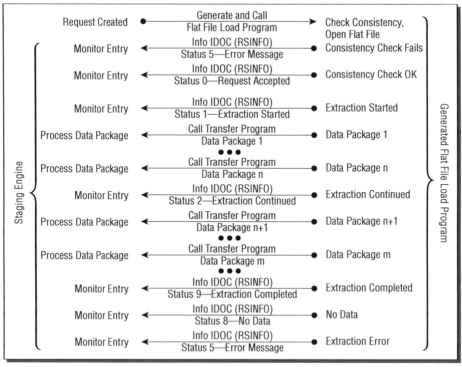

Figure 6-9 Data and control flow for the flat-file interface

Based on copyrighted material from SAP AG

DB Connect

An SAP BW system is connected to at least one database system: the one it's running on. This default database system that the SAP BW system runs on is already open and connected by the SAP kernel. All SQL called by ABAP is automatically routed through this connection. Through the same mechanism, additional connections to other external database systems can be created (as long as they are SAP-supported database systems). Once a new database source system connection is made, it can be accessed via regular SQL (open or native) in ABAP. To create new DataSources against DB Connect tables and views, source systems explicitly for DB Connect must be configured. DB Connect DataSources allow for the configuration of type conversions (from external database formats to SAP formats).

Architecture

The basic idea behind the DB Connect interface is to install the client software and the database shared library (DBSL) of the database management system that needs to be accessed (such as Oracle or SQL Server) on the SAP BW application server accessing it, thus making the database visible to the application server and to SAP BW. This is an additional installation activity, as the default DB client and DBSL normally come preinstalled. Once the new connections are made, the connection behaves similarly to the default; it acts as a bridge between SAP and the database management system.

The DB Connect interface supports all databases supported by SAP. Access to external databases is not restricted to the database management system used for running SAP. An SAP BI system running on Oracle would still be able to use the DB Connect interface to access a Microsoft SQL Server database on a Microsoft Windows server. Figure 6-10 shows the DB Connect interface architecture.

Defining a DataSource for a DB Connect source system follows similar steps as defining a DataSource for the BI Service API:

1. A source system must be created with a logical source system name but with additional details such as the database management system (DBMS), the DB user ID and password, and connection string info (DB-dependent parameters).

2. A DataSource is created against the DB Connect source system. From the extraction parameters for the database table adapter, the DB Connect interface retrieves a list of tables and views available from the remote database. After an entry is selected from this list field, information for the selected table or view is retrieved from the database catalog.

The selected fields are then used as a basis for generating the Data-Source definition, which is stored in the Meta Data Repository. The system will propose a list of type conversions from the DataSource definition. You can preview a sampling of what the data will look like in SAP.

After that, you can assign the DataSource to act and behave as any other DataSource.

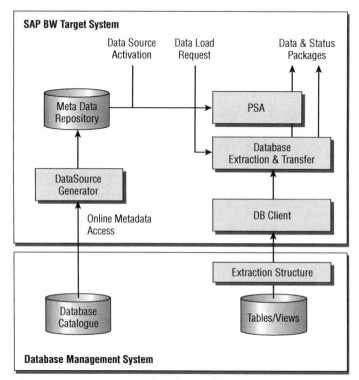

Figure 6-10   DB Connect interface architecture

Data and Control Flow

The data and control flow of the DB Connect interface is very similar to the data and control flow of the flat-file interface.

UD Connect

When SAP integrated a J2EE server into its application server, SAP was able to leverage the Java Connector Architecture (JCA) to access virtually any relational database management system (RDMBS), multidimensional source, and flat file that Java technology can connect to. Universal Data Connector (UDC) uses four JCA-compliant resource adapters that SAP has called BI Java Connectors: BI JDBC Connector, BI ODBO Connector, BI XMLA Connector, and SAP Query Connector.

These same connectors can be used by the BI Java SDK to develop Java applications on the SAP NetWeaver AS to read data from SAP BW itself or any external system to achieve universal data integration. UDC simply leverages the same connectors for data extraction.

The BI Java Database Connectivity (JDBC) Connector is for connecting to relational and flat-file sources. Practically all significant database or file formats are supported (for a definitive list, go to `http://developers.sun.com/product/jdbc/drivers`). As of this writing, there are more than 200 JDBC drivers.

The BI JDBC Connector can connect and read any data source that the flat-file interface and DB Connect interface can read and a lot more. However, SAP still recommends the use of the flat-file interface and DB Connect interface for better performance or easier administration. From a performance perspective, the gap is already closing, probably because of the strategic nature of universal data integration. However, UDC will always have an additional step (the JDBC driver itself) that the flat-file interface and the DB Connect interface skip, which gives them a performance disadvantage. From a source system connection perspective, the RFC connections must be created in both the J2EE Engine and the SAP BW environment and administered from both the SAP BW environment and the Visual Administrator for the J2EE Engine.

For multidimensional data sources, UDC can leverage either the BI ODBO Connector or the BI XMLA Connector. The ODBO Connector is based on a Microsoft Object Link Enabling (OLE) DB for OLAP standard. ADO (Active Data Objects) and ADO for MD (multidimensional) are needed in the SAP BW environment for this connectivity (that is, Windows 2000, NT, or XP). Any OLAP system that supports this standard (such as SAP BW) can be connected to via this connector. The BI XMLA Connector is based on the SOAP standard and XML messaging. Finally, there is the SAP Query Connector. This connector is more relevant to reporting and analysis than to data acquisition. As explained earlier, generic data extractors can be created against SAP Query InfoSets to acquire data. This direct approach is recommended over using the BI SAP Query Connector for data extractions; the connector is more suited for reporting and analysis scenarios. Figure 6-11 illustrates the UDC interface architecture.

Data and Control Flow

The data and control flow of the UDC interface is very similar to the data and control flow for the flat-file interface.

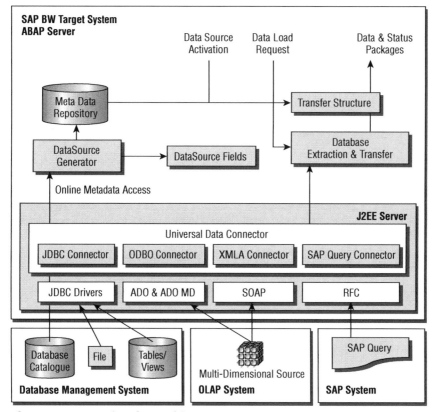

Figure 6-11 UDC interface architecture

Staging BAPI

The Staging Business Application Programming Interface (BAPI) is the only interface not supported in the new release from a DataSource maintenance perspective. It still works under the older technology and concepts. The Staging BAPI is an open interface for metadata and data exchange between SAP BW and third-party systems. Old DataSources can still be used as emulated DataSources, but any new DataSource should use the Web Service interface for open interface programming. The Staging BAPI is more suited for third-party vendor applications such as Ascential DataStage. Customers using the Staging BAPI to connect their own custom ETL applications should consider migrating to the Web Service interface. The Staging BAPI has mainly been used by ETL tool vendors to provide their customers access to a wider range of data cleansing and transformation capabilities and predelivered content.

Architecture

The Staging BAPI utilizes the BAPI framework that comes with the Web Application Server to provide an official, stable API for data and metadata exchange. A high-level overview of the Staging BAPI architecture is provided in Figure 6-12. Since release 2.0, the Staging BAPI provides complete metadata exchange functionality; in release 3.5, it was enhanced with Unicode support.

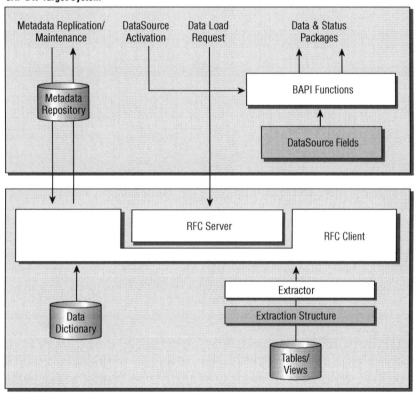

SAP BW Target System

Staging BAPI Source System

Figure 6-12   Staging BAPI architecture

The Staging BAPI not only allows you to read InfoSource metadata (as in SAP BW release 1.2) but also provides the ability to create DataSources, InfoObjects, and InfoCubes. However, the DataSource and the transformations still remain under the control of the SAP BW system. In the same way as for the file interface, there is no difference between the DataSource fields and the extraction structure; the actual extraction structure is known only to the extraction tool or program.

Staging BAPI source systems are required to implement an RFC server. This involves waiting for SAP BW to remotely call a specific function implemented as part of this RFC server to initiate a data-load request, as well as an RFC client extracting data and sending the resulting data set back to SAP BW by calling the Staging BAPI. The RFC client should check if the definition of the transfer structure as stored in SAP BW still matches the technical details of the extraction process, because someone might have changed the DataSource definition without adjusting the extraction process or vice versa. This check is mandatory for ETL tools to be certified.

More specific information on these BAPIs can be found in the SAP Developer Network (www.sdn.sap.com).

Data and Control Flow

Again, the data and control flow of the Staging BAPI is essentially the same as for all interfaces. However, the RFC client software does not need to know about the details of sending IDocs or calling the transfer program. All it needs to know is how to call the BAPI to send data and the definition of the transfer structure. The Staging BAPI takes care of all communication-protocol details and ensures monitoring support for data loaded through the Staging BAPI.

The administrator must ensure that the DataSource structure defined has the same format as the extraction structure provided by the extraction program. Most third-party clients do not allow automatically adapting their extraction programs to changes in the DataSource structure. However, some third-party clients do allow dynamic checks to verify if the DataSource structure still matches the extraction structure provided by the extraction process.

Ascential DataStage

As mentioned, many of the major ETL tool vendors support the Staging BAPI, allowing vendors to exchange metadata with and transfer data to an SAP BI system. The benefit for SAP not only lies in extending its offering with ETL capabilities but also in extending the reach of the Business Content by jointly providing integrated solutions for ERP and CRM solutions provided by other vendors, such as PeopleSoft, Siebel, and Oracle. This section briefly showcases the use of Ascential DataStage from an extraction technology point of view as a representative example.

Note that Ascential Software is used as an example because of its reseller and co-development partnership history with SAP. The SAP BW solution offered with Ascential Software's ETL package called DataStage is still relevant, but it is important to note that the partnership was dissolved in 2005, when IBM acquired Ascential.

From a technology point of view, the main advantage of ETL tools such as DataStage is that they not only provide access to disparate systems and technologies (less important now with UDC) but also powerful and flexible data cleansing and transformation logic, all defined using GUI designer software to facilitate design and maintenance.

The need for a robust transformation engine is greater when disparate source-systems data must be merged. When you are loading from single-instance SAP systems only, this is less of a necessity, since the system is integrated and shares common metadata. For example, all the applications in mySAP ERP reference the same table for common master data such as customer or vendor. In another system, there may be an entirely different list of codes for customer or vendor, as well as table structures. A tool must transform those records in a foreign system into a conformed set of master data codes. Further exacerbating matters, there may be more than one field that has to be considered in the mapping. For example, source systems might have one coding-block structure that represents the natural account and responsibility center. SAP would require you to split that coding block into G/L accounts, cost centers, or profit centers, where there may not always be a mapping for each or at different levels of aggregations. For those with experience, the task is daunting, especially without a tool with flexibly defined, easy-to-use, and reusable transformations. This is where Ascential DataStage can add value, especially if SAP NetWeaver MDM is not being used. An example scenario would be using Ascential DataStage to connect to Siebel data and load it into SAP BW. Siebel data is loaded through a transformer stage, which performs the actual transformations.

A transformer stage connects inputs (data sources like Siebel or an ODBC connection) to outputs (for the case of this discussion, it would be a load pack for SAP BW) via macros, functions, constants, routines, and transformations. DataStage, of course, allows much more complex transformation scenarios involving multiple inputs, multilevel staging, and multiple outputs.

Single transformations can be selected from a repository of predefined or custom-defined macros, functions, constants, or transformations. Reusing components already implemented makes transforming raw data from disparate sources into high-quality data for data warehousing purposes much easier and reduces the need to actually implement code.

Ascential DataStage and other third-party ETL tools do not fully replace SAP BW transformations, however. There still is a need for SAP BI transformation rules. As a rule of thumb, all enterprise-wide, business-level transformations and data-cleansing activities should to be defined in SAP BW. All transformations and data-cleansing activities specific to a DataSource should be implemented in the ETL tool.

More specifically, five data-quality levels have been defined for transformation processes, and a dividing line between levels Q1 and Q2 has been drawn by SAP and Ascential for when to use DataStage and when to use SAP BW for transformations. These data-quality levels are defined as follows:

- **Source system valid domain analysis (Q0)** — This check is performed by DataStage to validate that existing values in data records correspond to correct values in its domain (or check tables). For example, the gender value for male in the legacy system should have a value of either M or W. In the cases where it is X, DataStage converts the value to an M.

- **Completeness and validity (Q1)** — This check is also performed by DataStage to ensure that data is complete and accurate from the local source system perspective. For example, if any values are missing in any fields, DataStage would handle them. If the gender status field is left empty and must be derived, a value of G may be derived to ensure completeness of the data.

- **Structural integrity (Q2)** — All enterprise-wide cleansing and transformations are done by SAP BW transformations. For example, male and female have indicators of M and W, respectively, which does not conform to the enterprise domain values of M and F. A transformation is needed to make this translation.

- **Referential integrity (Q3)** — All referential integrity checks and data harmonization are also performed via transformations.

- **Business rules (Q4)** — All business logic routines for application-related InfoMarts are done via transformations.

Note that these data-quality levels not only apply for Ascential DataStage; in principle, the same considerations apply when extracting from mySAP ERP source systems or custom legacy systems.

Web Service Interface

The SAP XML interface has evolved and morphed into the Web Service interface. This interface opens the world of XML data exchange for SAP BW by allowing you to accept XML data streams. Implemented using the SOAP protocol, it is compliant to current open standards for XML data interchange.

Architecture

The new Web Service interface works in conjunction with the RDA Daemon, as shown in Figure 6-13. The old XML interfaces worked as a push technology into the delta queue and then used the BI Service API to extract data into a

DataSource. Now, the new Web Service interface writes directly to the Data-Source via the PSA. A special RDA Infopackage dictates the frequency to which to close the PSA request (so that pushed updates to the PSA can be collected into one request, which is better for performance than having a separate request per record updated). The RDA Infopackage should be optimized by coordinating its schedule with an RDA DTP (process chains can help ensure this). The RDA DTP loads data from the PSA into a DataStore Object but in an optimized way (less logging and activation processing known as "lean staging"). More on RDA and DTPs is covered in Chapter 11.

SAP BW Target System

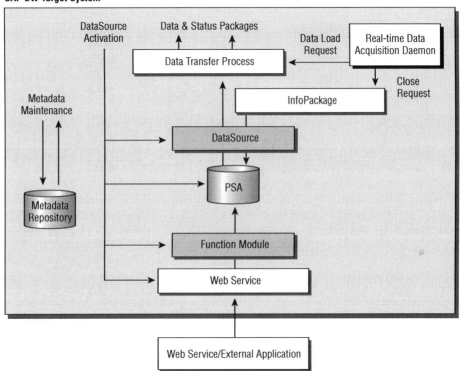

Figure 6-13 Web Service interface architecture

Earlier, the old XML interface could not interpret metadata incorporated into the XML data stream and propagate this information to the Meta Data Repository. The DataSource for the XML interface had to be generated based on a DataSource for the File interface. At this time, a function module interface was generated, but a Web Service interface was not (still had to be manually generated from the function module). Now, the Web Service interface is defined by its own source system and DataSource classification in the Data

Warehouse Workbench. Furthermore, the data structure may be segmented (hierarchical or deep structure, instead of a flat record) and this is defined in its own DataSource definition. Both the function module and Web service are generated at time of this DataSource activation. As a result, the SOAP Profile (Basic Authorization or Secure) must be first defined with the DataSource definition (which will pass through to the Web service definition).

The Web Service interface is designed for use with relatively small data volume pushed synchronously via a Web service. An accompanying File interface DataSource should be used for large-volume (full) asynchronous updates. The XML data streams need to comply with the metadata definition stored in the Meta Data Repository in order to be accepted by SAP BW.

Data and Control Flow

The data and control flow for the Web Service interface is basically the same as for SAP source systems, as both use the exact same technology. The data and control flow for pushing data into the PSA is compliant with the SOAP protocol.

Because easy-to-use SOAP-compliant controls are available for many PC-based development environments such as Microsoft Visual Basic, using the Web Service interface is also an appropriate way to implement custom solutions for loading smaller data sets.

Closing the Loop

SAP BW provides additional options for extracting data for use in interface programs feeding data streams into operational or analytic applications:

- **DataMart interface** — From a technical point of view, the DataMart interface is nothing more than the BI Service API discussed previously. The DataMart interface allows building complex information logistics models, as shown in the topology examples in Chapter 5 (assuming both local and global data warehouses are on SAP BW). All InfoProviders available are at the DataMart interface's disposal. However, use of the DataMart interface is restricted to SAP BW systems.

- **Retractors** — These are dedicated ABAP programs reextracting data from SAP BW into a mySAP ERP system. Retractors are a relatively new concept and are currently only available for a few applications, including SAP SEM-BPS and SAP CRM.

- **SAP BW Java Connectors** — This is an official API for executing queries and retrieving query results. Custom programs can access

OLAP cubes to retrieve query results for any purposes. By using the either the ODBO or XMLA interface through the Java SDK, any front-end applications in almost any programming language can access SAP BW query results. However, using OLAP results is not recommended for use with large result data sets, as it is optimized for interactive applications, not extractions.

- **Open Hub Services** — These allow you to define controlled and monitored data-export processes, exporting data target contents into a flat file, a flat database table, or an application for further processing.

Figure 6-14 shows the distinction among DataMart interface, retraction, and Open Hub interface information flows and their relationship to the architecture.

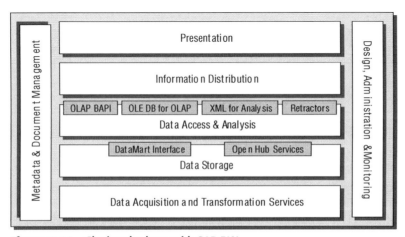

Figure 6-14 Closing the loop with SAP BW

Transformation

Modern ETL tools and data warehouse solutions have reduced the effort needed to actually implement and test transformations by providing intuitive GUIs and libraries of predefined transformations. However, most of the time is actually spent designing the transformations from a conceptual point of view.

How does SAP BI support data warehouse developers when implementing and testing the transformations identified? This section begins with a short discussion of commonly used transformations in data warehouse applications and then dives into the details of the staging architecture and the SAP BW-specific transformations.

Common Transformation Operations

There are two main drivers for implementing transformations on the data warehouse side: data integration and application logic. While *data integration transformations* aim at eliminating technical and semantic differences among data from disparate source systems, *application logic transformations* transform integrated data into an application-specific format optimized for a specific purpose.

Of course, categorizing commonly used transformation operations as in the following discussion does not mean that those operations cannot be applied in a meaningful way in other stages of the information supply chain. All of the transformation operations discussed are principally usable at any stage. There are also additional transformations not discussed here in detail that are typically used at other stages, such as low-level technical transformations performed at extraction time (handling different database systems, operating systems, or hardware) and the calculation of high-level key performance indicators upon information retrieval or presentation. Transformations in the loading process include generation of surrogate keys; luckily, SAP BW takes care of this task automatically, as you will see later.

The common transformation operations discussed in the following text will be showcased as part of the detailed discussion of transformation rules later in this section.

Data Integration Transformations

Following are the most important transformations involved in technical data integration:

- **Straight mapping** — Although a trivial transformation, straight mapping of two semantically and technically identical source and target fields is listed here for completeness.

- **Type conversions** — Data types used in the operational environment are converted to those used in the data warehouse environment. SAP BW automatically performs compatible type conversions without further notice, while incompatible type conversions usually require the more complex transformations to be applied.

- **Character set conversions** — Character sets used in the operational environment may include Extended Binary Coded Decimal Interchange Code (EBCDIC) character sets used in mainframe systems, and different local ASCII character sets (such as Latin or Kanji) need to be integrated into one single representation in the data warehouse (for example, Unicode character set).

SAP BW now supports using Unicode character sets and automatically converts incoming data from the source character set to the Unicode character set. Some character set conversions, however, such as EBCDIC to Unicode, still must be implemented explicitly.

- **Reformatting** — The technical representation of values may need to be reformatted on the way from the source to the target system.

  Dates represented as 01/31/2002 or 31.01.2002 may need to be converted to 20020131. Material numbers represented externally as 010-XYZ-9000 need to be reformatted to an internal format like 010XYZ9000. Customer key values may need to be converted from mixed-case "Duck Brothers" to uppercase "DUCK BROTHERS."

- **Missing values** — Sometimes not all source systems are able to provide meaningful data for all required fields. In these cases, constant default values or values retrieved from lookup tables have to be determined.

  It is common, for example, for non-SAP source systems to send date information without information about fiscal-year variants, since fiscal-year variants tend to be an SAP-specific data element.

- **Unit and currency conversions** — Unit and currency conversions are required wherever amount and quantity values need to be stored with a specific unified unit of measure or currency.

- **Semantic integration** — Semantic integration involves converting values to a common standard notation as defined for the data warehouse environment.

  The gender of a customer may be represented as M and F in one system and as 0 and 1 in another. mySAP ERP CO uses a value type of 4 for actual values, while LIS uses 10. Many times, a single field is mapped to multiple target fields or vice versa. In the purchasing Business Content, for example, the process key 001 is derived from a combination of the LIS event MA and the purchase order category of 1.

- **Cleansing** — More or less complex transformations may be required to make sure data stored in the data warehouse is correct. Cleansing transformations are most important in the data warehouse environment to ensure correctness and completeness of data. Cleansing transformations can range from simple value-range checks on a field level to complex sanity checks referring to data packages or the whole extracted data set and may involve extensive table lookups.

  Examples of cleansing include checking that the gender of a customer in the input record is always represented as M or F. Invalid values need to be flagged or replaced by meaningful defaults (for example, determining the most probable gender by analyzing the first name of the customer). A more complex example would be to check consumer sales records reported by mobile devices for plausibility by comparing the reported revenue for every customer with the average revenue and the standard deviation and to flag suspicious records. Or you may want to check if the customer key already exists under another key (or if it's still valid) by comparing postal addresses against public records after tokenizing and standardizing notations.

NOTE Cleansing scenarios are quite expansive and are part of the burgeoning functionality (and industry) around master data management spawning new niches such as customer data integration and product information management (for example, global data synchronization and data pools).

- **Referential integrity** — Ensuring referential integrity requires checking the existence of referenced data (such as a customer master data record for a customer referenced in a sales order) and eventually creating such a data record using appropriate default values.

Application Logic Transformations

Application logic transformations are driven by business requirements. Following are the most important operations used for this type of transformation:

- **Calculations** — More complex, high-level key figures may be calculated on the fly during the transformation process. Calculations may or may not require table lookups for reading additional information. In the staging process, calculations are frequently used in combination with aggregations or with other data read on the fly to achieve more comprehensive key figures. Of course, calculations are also daily functions in the information retrieval and presentation processes.

- **Joins** — These can be simple lookups off of other tables to enrich the data or more complicated mergers of data from two different data sets such as outer joins or conditional joins. For example, a list of all customers and their sales figures (whether or not they had sales) would require a left outer join on master data.

- **Splits** — A lookup that explodes the number of records based on the number of matches found. For example, a balance sheet adjustment process in SAP financials that explodes A/R and A/P open items (tables BSID and BSIK) by profit center (BFOD_A and BFOK_A) needs to be mirrored in a transformation. This is similar to de-aggregations, except a table key lookup is needed to do the de-aggregation.

- **Selections** — Selections play an important role where only parts of the data available are desired for a certain analytic application (for example, in cases where an InfoMart is set up to serve a specific part of the sales organization).

- **Projections** — Projections (effectively hiding fields) serve the same purpose as selections in that they hide information that would technically be available.

- **Aggregation** — Aggregation reduces the level of granularity, again reducing the amount of information available. Performance improvements through aggregations, of course, still are one of the most important reasons to aggregate data. However, SAP BW-persistent aggregates could be used for improving performance without losing the possibility to analyze data on the lowest-possible level of granularity.

- **De-aggregation** — De-aggregation distributes aggregated values to a certain range of characteristics values. Yearly sales forecasts, for example, may be distributed to 12 months according to historic seasonal sales patterns to provide monthly forecast values.

- **Normalization** — Normalization is a process where data is mapped from a denormalized into a normalized data model, usually reducing redundancy and sparsity but increasing the flexibility and complexity of the data model. Normalization is used, for example, wherever a source system provides data using specific key figures, whereas the information model uses generic key figures. (For a review of specific versus generic key figures, refer to Chapter 4.) Normalization is also used wherever denormalized master or transaction data is provided by a source system and needs to be populated into a normalized information model.

  Planning applications, for example, frequently use a record format where 12 key figures in a single record represent one plan value for each month of the planning year. Distribution would generate 12 data records with a year and month characteristic and one single plan key figure. For further information about normalization and various normal forms, refer to *An Introduction to Database Systems* by C. J. Date, 7th edition (Boston: Addison Wesley, 1999).

- **Denormalization** — Denormalization is the reverse process of normalization, usually merging several input data records into one output record. This usually increases redundancy and sparsity and decreases complexity, but also flexibility, of the data model.

  Denormalization is used where a small, fixed set of values (for example, different versions of costs — say, actual, plan, and budget) is required for reporting. A denormalized information model would use three different key figures to model this.

Reference Objects for Transformations

Another useful classification of transformations is based on the referenced object. Six different categories of transformations can be identified using this approach:

- **Field level transformations** — These use single fields of single data records as their input. Examples are straight mapping, type conversions, or reformatting.

- **Record level transformations** — These use multiple fields of single data records to determine or calculate values. A simple example is price calculation based on revenue and quantity. Other examples of record level transformations include table lookups and more complex calculations.

- **Logical unit level transformations** — These use multiple records belonging to a single logical unit (such as multiple line items belonging to a single sales transaction or records sharing the same semantic groupings). Logical unit level transformations are difficult to implement in SAP BW, because extracted data is split into several packages by the extraction programs; data records belonging to a single logical unit may be distributed to several data packages (even if the SQL uses a group by statement you want, records in the semantic groups maybe split into two data packages). Aggregation transformations with nontrivial aggregation functions (such as Maximum, Minimum, or counting of different material numbers) are examples of logical unit level transformations. On the other hand, integrated planning does this type of transformation quite well through the configuration of planning function parameters.

- **Data package level transformations** — These use a complete data package. Because data packages have arbitrary content-based package sizes (at least from an SAP BW point of view), these kinds of transformations are rarely useful and are mostly used for optimization purposes.

- **Extraction data set level transformations** — These use the complete extracted data set comprising multiple data packages. SAP BW supports extraction data set level transformations through the PSA API, where programs may read and modify data sets identified by request identifiers.

- **Full data set level transformations** — Rarely used for performance reasons, these transformations may be required for complex sanity checks (for example, in CRM applications where customer sales transactions may be checked against historic transactions of the same customer or customer group).

Data Transformation in SAP BW

The following sections provide an overview of the data transformation process in SAP BW, including multilevel staging and persistency considerations.

Architecture and Data Flow

Historically, older releases separated data integration and application logic transformations into two sets of transformations: transfer rules and update rules. In the new release, both transfer rules and update rules are displaced by one set of transformation rules. Some data integration transformations are handled by the DataSource (such as type, character set, and reformatting conversions), while the rest are handled by the new transformation rules.

Transformations connect DataSources to persistent target SAP BW Objects (such as InfoCubes, DataStore Objects, and InfoObjects) or virtual target BI Objects (specifically, InfoSources). Transformation rules involve mapping the fields of the DataSource to one specific InfoObject in the target. Transformation groups are a logical collection of transformation rules within a transformation that represents one complete mapping of source to target. Transformation rules are either global to all transformation groups or local to a specific transformation group. Globally defined transformation rules are maintained and referenced as part of a standard group. Local transformation rules are overtyped in each subsequent transformation group created. The transformation group concept replaces the key-figure based update rules where each characteristic mapping could be applied globally across all key figures or locally to one key figure. Transformation groups are more flexible because one or many can be created and include all InfoObjects (not limited key figures). No matter the number of transformation groups used, each transformation will only be called once during runtime to optimize performance.

At the other end of the data transfer process, transformations map to one or more target BI objects (InfoCubes, DataStore Objects, InfoSources, and master data) and take care of transforming technically integrated data into application-specific formats as defined in the information model. Note that hierarchy and texts are not targets that can be manipulated in a transformation. All single-staged or double-staged transformations (via an InfoSource) are in-memory transformations. A data package is passed from one of the staging interfaces discussed previously to the Staging Engine as an in-memory source package stored in an internal table. Up to this point, no transformations have been applied; the data still is in source-structure format. The transformation then applies the transformation rules defined, effectively converting the data records into the result or target format.

Multiple transformations may be called in parallel, one for each data target. The transformation applies the specific mapping and converts the resulting data records into a flattened target format implicitly defined through the target BI object definition.

A third generated program receives these data records, converts them into the physical data model used for the InfoProvider, and loads them into the SAP BW object accordingly. More details on this loading process are provided in the next section.

Persistency Considerations

SAP BW allows persistently storing data along the information supply chain in the PSA for InfoPackages and temporary storage or the error stack for DTPs. The PSA is mandatory, while the levels of detail for temporary storage are configurable within the DTP. Possible applications of the PSA and DTP temporary storage include the following:

- **Error handling** — Transformation rules allow flagging single data records as incorrect and logging the cause of this error in the SAP BW monitor. Records flagged as incorrect are separately stored in the PSA and the error stack for DTPs that can be used for later manual or automated correction and reloading. More details on error handling are provided later in this section and in Chapter 11.

- **Repeated transformation of raw data** — The PSA and DTP temporary storage allows repeatedly performing transformations based on stored data without having to reextract from the source system. Repeated execution of transformation is most useful for tracing and debugging user-defined transformation rules and, in some cases, for populating data targets from scratch. However, you should use the data warehouse layer for this purpose.

- **Decoupling extraction and transformation** — Some application scenarios involving multiple disparate systems require scheduling multiple extractions at different times, whereas transformations and updates into the target BI objects can be performed at different points of time because of, for example, system availability or resource availability restrictions in different time zones. Again, you should use the data warehouse layer for this purpose whenever possible but the functions of InfoPackages versus DTPs decouples extractions from transformations

- **Extraction data set level transformations** — This is a special application of decoupling extraction and transformation, allowing you to perform extraction data set level transformation of the data stored in the PSA using the PSA API. This is particularly useful for data-cleansing scenarios.

Taking into account that the PSA stores operational data in an operational data format, why not use the PSA for modeling the ODS (in traditional data warehouse speak)? First of all, one of the popular definition requirements of the ODS is that it allows reporting. The PSA does not directly support reporting; instead, an InfoSet would have to be defined, joining the PSA database tables into one single InfoSet that would be available for reporting purposes in the Business Explorer. However, the names of the PSA database tables are not fixed in that they are different on the development, test, and production systems. Every time the DataSource needs to be changed for some reason, SAP BW will add another table with the new structure to the PSA, causing the InfoSet to be invalid or at least incomplete. Second, the PSA does not allow any transformations to be applied, whereas DataStore Objects do allow transformations. As a result, DataStore Objects are better for use in modeling an ODS.

Multilevel Staging Considerations

So far, staging and transformation considerations have focused on single-level staging scenarios, where all staging processes end with updating a certain number of InfoProviders. SAP BW, however, allows implementing multilevel staging in the transformation process, as shown in Figure 6-15.

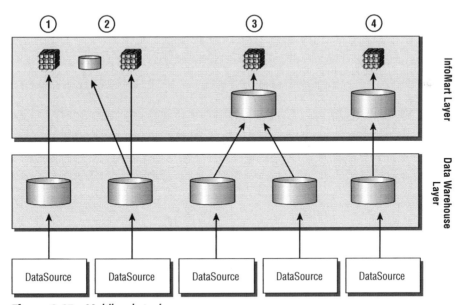

Figure 6-15 Multilevel staging

The most important reason for implementing multilevel staging is the implementation of a data warehouse layer, as shown in Figure 6-15. The data warehouse layer stores integrated consistent data. Populating the data warehouse layer usually requires complex data integration transformations handling all kinds of ways to harmonize data from different sources and only a little application logic in the downstream transformations. In contrast, the focus of populating the InfoMart layer (off of a harmonized data warehouse layer) is more centered on application-logic transformations. The role of the data warehouse layer is discussed in more detail in Chapter 5.

A general drawback of multilevel staging in SAP BW is losing the efficiency of in-memory transformations, as Figure 6-16 shows. Every additional level in a multilevel staging scenario requires persistently storing data in a target BI object and subsequently extracting data from the target BI object before going to the next staging level. At best, an InfoSource can be introduced as an in-memory intermediary staging level between a DataSource and a persistent target BI object. Otherwise, an expert routine transformation is needed to code the entire transformation so as to programmatically introduce as many in-memory transformations and staging levels needed.

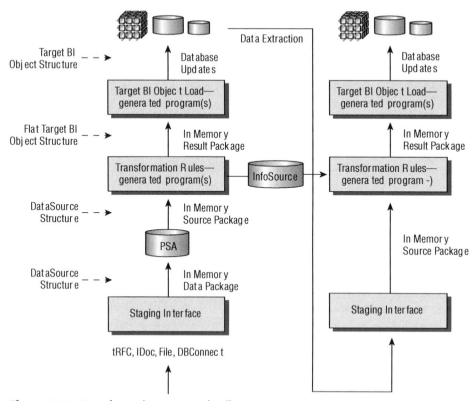

Figure 6-16 Transformation process details

While it is a deliberate decision to leverage the data warehouse layer by using it as a staging layer to feed transformation processes (see Figure 6-15, examples 1 and 2), additional multistage transformations may be required to match application-logic requirements (see Figure 6-15, examples 3 and 4). Such additional persistent staging layers degrade transformation performance and should be used sparingly unless many targets can consume the staged data (not depicted) or transformation complexity needs to be reduced. Although in many cases it is technically possible to collapse multistage transformations into a single stage, the transformations required may become excessively complicated and difficult to maintain. If more levels are needed, multistaged, write-optimized DataStore Objects or InfoSources are recommended for simplicity of design and understandability. For very high load volumes and complex transformations, sophisticated ETL tools allowing multistage in-memory transformations (such as Ascential DataStage or Informatica PowerCenter) might also be an option.

A practical example has already been sketched earlier in this chapter. Calculating *days sales outstanding* (DSO) requires sales information as well as accounts receivable information. One option to model a DSO InfoCube is to feed sales and accounts receivable information into the DSO InfoCube via an intermediate DataStore Object (see Figure 6-15, example 3). Another example of application logic requiring multistage transformations is sales-order-status tracking. A sales-order record keeps changing its status during its lifecycle from CREATED to COMPLETED in several steps, each adding information. Because InfoCubes do not allow updates of characteristic values, it is not easily possible to adjust the InfoCube to changes of sales-order statuses. Adding a DataStore Object as an intermediary stage (see Figure 6-15, example 4) allows utilizing the DataStore Object change-log functionality to automatically adjust the InfoCube.

There are no technical limits to the number of stages in an end-to-end transformation. However, the more stages there are, the more time is required to finally update the ultimate data target. Note that since release 3.0, there is no longer a significant difference between staging transaction data and staging master data with the introduction of flexible InfoSources, except that SAP BW still supports special master data DataSources for compatibility reasons.

Transformation Rules

Having examined the transformation process from a concept perspective, let's now take a closer look at the options provided to implement transformations in SAP BW. The new transformation design has been conceptually simplified and genericized. In the past, transformations were logically split up into specialized pieces. For example, update rules were designed for shared application logic, while transfer rules were for source-system-specific data integration logic. For InfoCubes, routines were divided by characteristics and key figures (by key figure), while for DataStore Objects they were divided by key fields and data fields (by data field).

Now the transformation logic is unified. Irrespective of the source and the target, the transformation is pretty much the same. Instead of grouping transformation rules by key figure or data field, it is grouped by a more generic concept called a *transformation group* representing a collection of source-to-target mappings within a transformation. Figure 6-17 shows a standard transformation group.

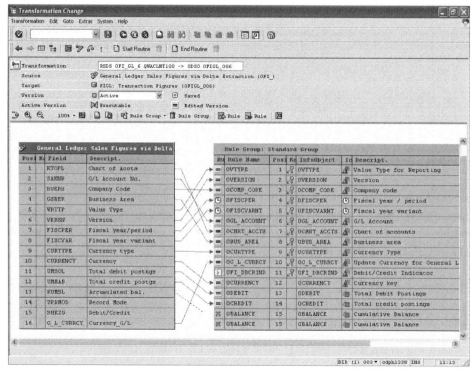

Figure 6-17 Standard transformation group

In turn, each transformation group is composed of *transformation rules* that are unique to each InfoObject in the target. Note that key-figure transformation rules can be copied in the transformation group so that it can be updated twice (generating an additional record similar in functionality to copying key-figure update rules for those of you who have used this feature). The transformation rules define the rule type and which source field(s) if any will be used for the rule. Conversion routines can be specified for source and/or target fields in the transformation rules to support data integration.

Conversion routines are not native to SAP BW and have been a concept long part of SAP (described in more detail shortly). If the rule is for a key figure, a currency or unit conversion must be specified along with an aggregation behavior. The aggregation behavior controls how the load program will update the key figures. Currency translation and unit conversions are possible only if the source is an InfoSource. The various other rule types will be covered shortly but should be similar to concepts employed by the earlier update and transfer rules. How they are conceptually organized and grouped is new, however. In addition, the routines that can be programmed have been extended with new concepts such as the end routine and the expert routine.

Conversion Routines

A conversion routine can be defined to reformat the display output of a field. In general, conversion routines apply reformatting rules on input and output operations, converting internal representations to external representations on output and external to internal representations on input. SAP BW data loads from non-SAP source systems are considered input operations. Data loads from SAP source systems already provide the internal format; therefore, no conversion routines are applied in this case. Conversion routines can be assigned to either an InfoObject (as part of the InfoObject definition) or explicitly for non-SAP DataSources in the transformation rules. Readers familiar with mySAP ERP might already have come across conversion routines there. Examples of conversion exit routines are "ALPHA" (adding leading zeros on input and removing leading zeros on output) and "SDATE" (converting external date formats into internal data formats and back based on date formats defined in the current user's profile).

Conversion exits should not be confused with a transformation rule. If a conversion exit is defined on an InfoObject level, the Business Explorer automatically applies the output conversion exit when displaying values.

NOTE A number of predefined conversion routines are available in the system. In addition to those, it is possible to create custom conversion exits. To do so, two function modules have to be implemented according to the following naming conventions:

- **For input exits** — CONVERSION_EXIT_XXXXX_INPUT

- **For output exits** — CONVERSION_EXIT_XXXXX_OUTPUT

where XXXXX **is the five-digit name of your custom conversion exit identifier.**

Aggregation

The way key figures are updated in an InfoCube or the data fields are updated in a DataStore Object is controlled in the transformation rule. If the target is an InfoCube, summation, minimum, and maximum are the selectable aggregation behaviors. If the target is a DataStore Object or master data, the options are overwrite or sum. For both targets, there is also the option of not updating. Not updating a key figure or data field is required to avoid overwriting existing values in cases where multiple DataSources each provide only a subset of the key figures or data fields required by the data target (leading to data sparsity).

If a transformation rule is for a key figure, the options offered in the transformation rule include source key figures, formulas, and routines. While source key figures and formulas work in the same way as already described, key-figure routines add additional options discussed later.

Finally, there are options for selecting automatic currency conversions to be performed wherever applicable. These are explained later as part of rule types.

Rule Types

A transformation rule is defined per InfoObject in the target structure of a transformation rule. There can be multiple source fields per target InfoObject but only one target InfoObject per transformation rule. There are a variety of transformation rule types that control how to update an InfoObject in the target structure:

- Initial
- Constant value
- Direct assignment
- Time update
- Reading master data
- Currency translation
- Unit conversion
- Formula
- Routine

Initial

This leaves the InfoObject in the target unfilled. For sparse data models, this can be a commonly used transformation rule (or, in this case, lack of one).

Constant Value

Missing information may sometimes be replaced by meaningful default values. It is common, for example, for non-SAP source systems to send date information without information about fiscal-year variants, because fiscal-year variants tend to be an SAP-specific data element. A constant value defining the fiscal-year variant to use would typically be assigned in InfoSource transformations, since this is the place to ensure technically integrated data.

To reduce the maintenance effort in case of changing business rules (and subsequently changing default values), you may also choose to implement constant value assignments in the InfoObject transformations.

Direct Assignment

The direct assignment option performs a straight mapping of a field in the source to an InfoObject in the target. The direct assignment option implicitly defines a type conversion from the source data to the target data type of the InfoObject definition. Note that the generated type conversions may fail at runtime, since SAP BW is not able to check the correctness of type conversion at definition time (for example, whether a character field is convertible into a numeric field depends on the field content).

An example of a mismatching type conversion includes a 13-character material number from a non-SAP source system being mapped to the chosen data warehouse standard of 18 characters. In this case, you must define how to fill the remaining five characters (for example, keep blank or add leading zeros). Even worse, if the input field is actually longer than the output field, a situation may arise that causes the transformation to lose information. Handling these kinds of situations either requires using one of the options listed in the text that follows or adapting the information model. More complex type conversions would have to be implemented using either the formula or the routine option.

Time Update

Time characteristics have the same transformation options as regular characteristics, plus an additional option for automatic conversions and time distributions. Note, however, that these functions are not available for DataStore Objects where time characteristics are treated as data fields. Because there are a variety of formats representing fixed time InfoObjects (like the difference between OFISCPER and OFISCYEAR), the system will do an automatic type conversion if disparate time InfoObjects are mapped. For example, if OFISCPER is mapped to OFISCYEAR, the period is truncated (that is, 012/2007 -> 2007). These conversions are automatically determined if a default exists in the systems. The mapping can also work the other way, thereby creating an automatic time distribution that spreads facts evenly across a more detailed slice of time.

Put differently, the time distribution option is a de-aggregation method allowing distribution of values from a lower granularity source time dimension (such as calendar month) to a higher granularity target time dimension (such as the calendar day) based on the calendar or a factory calendar. (*Factory calendars* carry additional factory-specific information about local bank holidays, factory holidays, and so on.)

Assume, for example, that the value of 0CALMONTH is 200712 (December 2007) in a source-package record. That record will be broken into six records, each record representing a week. The first record will contain 1/31th of the original key-figure amount. That is because December 1, 2007, is a Sunday and the week starts on a Monday. That means the first week (0CALWEEK = 200747) has only one day (December 1, 2007). The weeks that follow are full weeks (each of the weeks 200748 through 200751 receive 7/31st of the original key-figure amount) except for the last week (0CALWEEK = 200752), which receives the remainder of 2/31st of the original key-figure amount.

Simple time conversions are generated automatically wherever possible. For example, the calendar day can be set to the end of the month using an automatic routine. Calendar month is derived from the InfoSource and is automatically converted to fill the quarter (QYYYY format), year (YYYY format), month (MM format), and quarter (Q format).

Reading Master Data

This option is available only where the source structure consists of InfoObjects (since the target InfoObject is derived from a source structure InfoObject). The target InfoObject in the target must be the same InfoObject that exists in the attributes of one of the source InfoObjects. In addition, all compound InfoObjects must also exist in the source structure. If these preconditions are met, candidate InfoObjects ready for assignment will appear in selection to be mapped. This transformation rule is helpful when navigational attributes need to be stored as a dimensional attribute in order to be able to report on its transitive attributes (that is, navigational attributes of navigational attributes).

For time-dependent master data, an option for determining how to calculate a datestamp for selecting a time-dependent attribute must be parameterized. Options available for reference dates are using the current system date, a constant date, or a date derived from an InfoObject of the source (using either the start or end date of the period specified by that InfoObject). If, for example, the POSITION of an employee needs to be derived using the 0EMPLOYEE characteristic of the InfoSource, the calendar month can be used as the reference time period.

When using this option, be sure that a process chain is designed to load the reference master data before the transaction data is loaded, to avoid lookup of obsolete data.

NOTE It is not yet possible to perform transitive attribute derivations (master data derivation of a master data derivation). If, for example, the date of birth of an employee (InfoObject 0EMPLOYEE) is required, the person identifier must first be looked up on the employee master data table before being able to look up the date of birth in the person master data table. A routine would have to be coded to perform such a transformation.

Currency Conversion

Currency conversions can be performed at runtime via a BEx query (explained in Chapter 7) or in the staging process. The currency conversion type hasn't significantly changed, but there are some new options. The currency conversion type controls how currency translation is performed. The conversion type needs to be configured to determine how the source currency is to be determined, how the target currency is to be derived, and which exchange rate to use.

The most popular option for determining the source currency is from the data record itself. Other options include explicitly setting the currency in the conversion type, deriving it from master data (provided the master data InfoObject is in the source and that InfoObject has a currency InfoObject assigned to it), or deriving it via a BEx variable.

Similarly, the target currency can be derived via the same options. If the master data option is used, it can be restricted only for use in transformations (that is, not reporting). In addition, there is an option to specify the currency at runtime, which is relevant only to reporting. Lastly, the target currency can be determined by an SAP BW InfoSet and works similarly to the master data option. SAP BW InfoSet table and field aliases are mapped to the conversion type under this option.

The exchange rate can be supplied by the data record itself (in which case the InfoObject with the exchange rate needs to be specified in the conversion type) or from a BEx variable or via an exchange rate type (standard table TCURR lookup). If an exchange-rate type is specified, date-determination logic must be configured. Some of the options for date determination are specifically query related (key date of the query or runtime selection). Other date determinations can be done during the staging process (such as system date, date from BEx variable, date derivation from the source record, or date via an InfoSet).

The source currency, target currency, and exchange rate are all controlled by conversion type configuration. Figure 6-18 shows the key inputs for a currency conversion type.

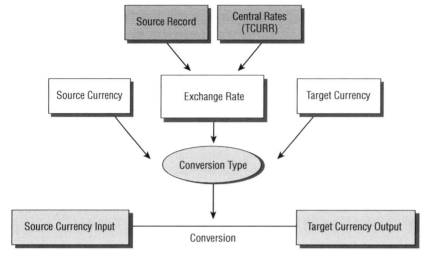

Figure 6-18 Currency conversion types

Unit Conversion

Unit conversions historically needed a routine written to handle more complicated BI business scenarios. The technology was based on ERP unit conversion functionalities centered on the central units of measure table (table T006). A limitation of this table and the corresponding conversion types was that the conversions couldn't be cross-dimensional (each unit of measure is categorized within a dimension and can only convert with its dimension). For example, converting pieces to grams or boxes to cubic meters was not possible. In addition, unit conversion factors by material or product grouping were not possible, since the central units of measure table is fixed.

The advantage of using this central table is that it can be uploaded from SAP source systems. The disadvantage is that it cannot be modified. As a result, the new release of SAP BW has added the capability of introducing a custom DataStore Object to replace or be used in conjunction with the central units of measure table. The configuration for looking up conversion factors controls whether the central table is used or a DataStore Object is used for determining the conversion factor (or both, either looking up on the DataStore Object first and if it's not available then on table T006 or vice versa).

Unit conversions are controlled via a piece of configuration called the *conversion type*. Conceptually, unit conversion types are very similar to currency conversion types (without the explicit time dependencies). They control what unit to use as a source, what unit to use as a target, and which conversion factors to apply. Figure 6-19 shows the key inputs for a unit conversion type.

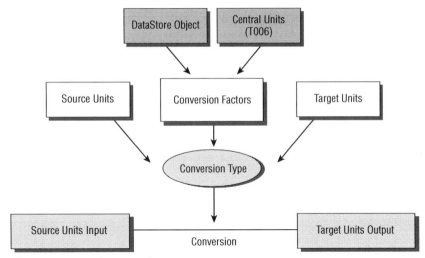

Figure 6-19   Unit conversion types

The most popular means for determining the source of the unit of measure for a quantity is from the source-data record itself. However, there are other options in the conversion type to determine the source unit. The data record can be overridden by explicitly fixing a source unit, using a BEx variable, or reading master data (provided there is a quantity attribute on an InfoObject that is in the source-data record).

The options for determining the target unit of measure are similar in that the target unit can be explicitly fixed, derived via a BEx variable, or read from master data (again provided that the InfoObject is part of the source for the transformation). However, there are other options. First, determining the target unit from the source-data record doesn't make logical sense and is not an option. The target unit can be specified at runtime for reporting, but this option doesn't make sense during staging transformations. Lastly, there is an additional option to derive the target unit of measure from an SAP BW Infoset. This conceptually works the same as the master data lookup option. Infosets generate table and field aliases that must be referenced in the conversion type configuration.

For deriving the conversion factors, they can either be dynamically determined (from T006 or a custom DataStore Object) or from a specified InfoObject in the DataSource record. If the conversion factor is not already provided in the staging process, it must be derived. Using the central table for conversion factors (T006) does not need any additional preparation (other than loading the table via replication). Using a custom DataStore Object for conversion factors requires proper configuration, a reference InfoObject, and proper parameterization and assignment of conversion types. The reference InfoObject definition itself (for example, 0MATERIAL) must be updated with a unit of measure and the name of the DataStore Object to house the corresponding conversion factors. A characteristic can only have one custom conversion factor DataStore Object assigned to it. Because of the tight dependency of the reference InfoObject with conversion factor DataStore Object, the DataStore Object cannot be maintained outside of the maintenance of the reference InfoObject. From a process-loading perspective, the reference InfoObject must be loaded before the custom DataStore Object for referential integrity. To help ensure this data integrity, an additional consistency check has been added to the analysis and repair monitor (transaction RSRV).

Formula

Release 3.0 introduced the Formula Editor, and it behaves the same way in the new release. The formula option provides access to the formula library, where several types of elements can be used to create complex formulas:

- More than 50 predefined functions from different categories (such as string functions, mathematical functions, date functions, and logical functions)
- Standard arithmetic and logical operators
- Important system variables (such as current date and time, factory calendar day, and username)
- Constant values of different data types
- Fields of the transfer structure
- Custom functions

All of this could, of course, be implemented as an ABAP routine (explained next). However, using formula routines does not require programming skills and makes life easier by saving programming and, more important, testing effort. Routines are still available for more specialized needs that formulas do not cover.

NOTE Formulas are not a novel concept in SAP. The SAP Report Painter offers a similar concept with the calculator function. SEM BPS offers something called formula extension (also known as FOX). Visual Composer delivers something similar called dynamic expressions.

The formula library is a repository of predefined functions but is also extendible. Customers can use the BADI technology to implement their own custom functions that can be used anywhere a formula can. The formula library also is the starting point for a growing set of reusable custom functions commonly used by SAP BW customers. SAP development performed a survey of what type of custom routines customers are using and found a preponderant share of those routines redundant and eligible for standard delivery as a formula.

Routine

As a last resort, there is a programming option for transformations. There are two different kinds of routines for transformation rules: one for characteristics and one for key figures. In addition, a transformation can have other routines outside the transformation rules (such as a start routine, end routine, and an expert routine). The topic of routines and their respective interfaces will be covered next in more detail.

Transformation Routines

Routines allow you to implement any kind of transformation that can be coded in the ABAP programming language and that cannot be defined using the Formula Editor (such as nontrivial database lookups and calculations).

Some examples of where routine transformations might be used are master data lookups on nonkey fields, lookups on transitive attributes, merging time-dependent master data, hierarchy lookups, record splitting, record reversals (for realignments), deleting records (for complex filtering), or some custom combination. For example, probably one of the more complex coding challenges is merging time-dependent transitive attributes in order to build hierarchical relationships (which requires using ABAP logic such as the PROVIDE command).

Routines are similar to business add-ins or user exits in that they are called from within the generated transformation program. In the new release, these transformation routines use an object-oriented interface instead of the form-based interface of the earlier releases. Their interfaces will be explained later in this chapter.

There are several types of routines (as depicted in Figure 6-20): start routine, characteristic routine, key-figure routine, end routine, and expert routine. Each routine is an object method (generated for characteristics and key-figure routines). The data structure definitions to be used as source and target are generated as a type definition in the routine class. The implementation of the generated method is where all the custom logic is coded.

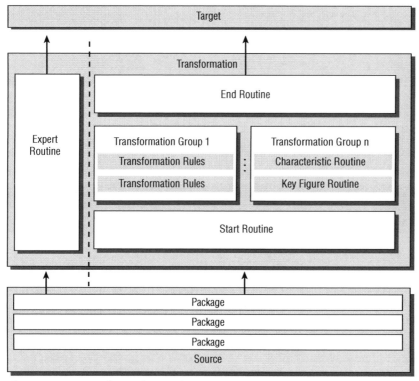

Figure 6-20   Transformation routines

In summary, SAP BW automatically generates a framework for the transformation routine, broken into the following sections:

■ **Public section in the routine class definition** — Generated types for source and target are delivered by the system.

■ **Private section in the routine class definition** — As a default, type-pools, custom global data declarations to be used across all routines (as a custom insertion), and the method declaration are defined here. These data declarations can also be used in the public section if you decide that your data structures or methods should be accessible outside the class.

■ **Implementation of the class routine** — Local custom code (the actual individual transformation routine logic).

Although some of this code may become release dependent, it helps to illustrate the transformation process and to lay out the options in defining transformation routines. Note that the following discussion is intended to showcase the structure of transformation routines rather than explain the details of ABAP code.

NOTE Complex calculations in leading ETL tools always require custom coding. While some tools allow coding to be created in Java or C, many tools have proprietary scripting languages. Creating a script is not much different from creating ABAP code.

You should implement nontrivial, reusable transformations as separate ABAP logic (such as includes or classes) and then include this reusable programming in the object method. This reduces maintenance efforts (especially if the same logic is used in many transformations). If a transformation gets deleted, the logic is not lost. The only additional step is to ensure that the global logic (include or class) is transported before the routines.

What follows is a more detailed explanation of each transformation routine and respective method interface.

Start Routine

Start routines are created as part of the transformation independent of the transformation rules. Start routines are executed prior to applying the transformation rules. The interface passes all the records in the source data package (not the entire extracted data set but a series of data packets). The most practical use of start routines is to preload tables into memory or to do some preprocessing before using that memory in a characteristic or key-figure routine. Start routines can also stand alone (such as applying complex record filters to the data package). However, you must take care not to break the memory limits of the application server, especially keeping in mind that multiple parallelized data packages will each consume their own memory areas.

For every routine, the DTP load request identifier and data package identifier (a sequential counter) are imported as parameters into the interface. With the request ID, you can derive usual information about the load (the name of the source and target, the time of load, the selections used for the load, and so on). The data package number is useful if you need to access data across data packages (not usually recommended, because of the additional memory this consumes), such as finding the offsetting entry for a financial posting that got separated into two data packages.

Additionally, the source data package is passed into the start routines and can be manipulated in the implementation of the method. The structure of the source data package is typed (ty_t_SC_1) in the public section of the routine via a generated listing of each source field of the DataSource and the respective data element types. If an error occurs in the routine, the transformation can be aborted by raising the exception cx_rsrout_abort, and messages can be logged to the DTP monitor by appending the monitor internal table. This monitor internal table is an export-only parameter. The method definition just described is as follows:

```
METHODS:
  start_routine
    IMPORTING
      request                    type rsrequest
      datapackid                 type rsdatapid
    EXPORTING
      monitor                    type rstr_ty_t_monitors
    CHANGING
      SOURCE_PACKAGE             type_ty_t_SC_1
    RAISING
      cx_rsrout_abort.
```

Characteristic Routine

A characteristic routine is a type of transformation rule. It must have only one target InfoObject but can have many source fields used in the routine. Instead of passing the entire source data package (as in the start routine), each record of the data package is passed to the characteristic routine interface (and only a selection of source fields from that record). The source fields available within the routine are configurable in the transformation-rule definition. These specified source fields will then be part of the imported parameter (SOURCE_FIELDS) for the routine interface (generated ABAP type ty_s_SC_1).

As with all transformation routines, the request ID and data package counter are also imported into the routine. The target characteristic to be updated in the transformation rule is an exported parameter (RESULT) with a data type of the target InfoObject. Exception handling is just like the start routine, except there is an additional exception class to exit the routine without aborting (cx_rsrout_skip_record). Recall that this routine is within a data package loop, while the start routine is not. This exception class allows you to skip to the next data package record in the loop without aborting the whole transformation process. The characteristic routine method interface is generated (the method is given the name routine and a numeric identifier) and is as follows:

```
METHODS:
  ROUTINE__4_1
    IMPORTING
      request                    type rsrequest
      datapackid                 type rsdatapid
      SOURCE_FIELDS              type ty_s_SC_1
    EXPORTING
      RESULT                     type ty_s_TG_1-BUS_AREA
      monitor                    type rstr_ty_t_monitor
    RAISING
      cx_rsrout_abort
      cx_rsrout_skip_record.
```

Key-Figure Routine

Key-figure routines can be defined exactly the same way as characteristic routines. Instead of updating a target InfoObject of type characteristic, the key-figure routine updates a key figure. The generated method interfaces look identical, except the type for the result parameter is a key figure instead of characteristic. However, there are two additional variations. In the transformation rule for a key figure, the corresponding unit of measure or currency key (if any) must be specified in the target fields and must be mapped. This mapping can be via conversion type or via the routine itself (for custom currency translations or unit conversions). If the currency or unit of measure is to be derived via routine, an additional export parameter is added to the method interface for currency or unit, respectively. The following interface example is for a currency key derivation; if it were for a unit of measure derivation, the parameter CURRENCY would be replaced with UNIT. The interface for filling an amount key figure is provided as an example.

```
METHODS:
  ROUTINE__12_1
    IMPORTING
      request                 type rsrequest
      datapackid              type rsdatapid
      SOURCE_FIELDS           type_ty_s_SC_1
    EXPORTING
      RESULT                  type_ty_s_TG_1-AMOUNT
      CURRENCY                type_ty_s_TG_1-CURRENCY
      monitor                 type rstr_ty_t_monitor
    RAISING
      cx_rsrout_abort
      cx_rsrout_skip_record.
```

Note that in the older technology of update rules it was possible to specify a result table instead of a result in a key-figure routine to explode records in the format of the target. This has been replaced by transformation groups or the end routine explained next.

End Routine

While the start routine runs before the transformation rules are executed, the end routine runs afterward. Whereas the start routine manipulates the source data package, the end routine manipulates the target data package. The source data package is in the structure of the DataSource, while the so-called result package is in the structure of the target SAP BW object. The result package is an internal table defined by a generated type (ty_t_TG_1 for the internal table of the target structure). The rest of the interface should be similar to the rest of the routine methods. The end routine is similar in concept to the key figure result table routine in the older update rule technology.

```
METHODS:
   end_routine
      IMPORTING
         request                    type rsrequest
         datapackid                 type rsdatapid
      EXPORTING
         monitor                    type rstr_ty_t_monitors
      CHANGING
         RESULT_PACKAGE             type ty_t_TG_1
      RAISING
         cx_rsrout_abort.
```

Expert Routine

If an expert routine is used, the entire transformation is skipped and all source-to-target data transformations must be made via the expert routine in its place. Expert routines are helpful if complex or better-performing transformations are needed. For example, start routines are typically used to load data structures into memory so as to access them later in characteristic or key-figure routines deeper into the call stack. Expert routines do not require as much memory overhead in the call stack and can eliminate the need for loading large data sets that are data-package dependent into program memory for later lookup and processing (which themselves are additional steps).

The interface is quite simple and straightforward. A part of the inbound interface is the data package for the DataSource (again, it is referenced as a generated table type). Part of the outbound interface is the data package for the target BI object (also referenced as a generated table type). Instead of filling an internal table for monitor entries, object methods from a logging class (`cl_rsbm_log_cursor_step`) have to be called. This instantiated object is passed into the expert routine interface.

```
METHODS:
   expert_routine
      IMPORTING
         request                    type rsrequest
         datapackid                 type rsdatapid
         SOURCE_PACKAGE             type_ty_t_SC_1
         log                        type ref to cl_rsbm_log_cursor_step
      EXPORTING
         RESULT_PACKAGE             type ty_t_TG_1.
```

Rules of the Game

All of the transformations discussed in the preceding text are executed in a certain order before the whole transformed data package is passed on to the target BI object.

Having discussed all the options of defining transformations, let's now take a step back and look at the whole picture from a higher-level point of view. The following pseudocode shows the highly simplified procedural logic for executing the transformations:

```
Transformation Logic Steps
*** STEP 0 - Extract by data package and load into memory the DataSource
structure after applying conversion exits.

*** STEP 1 -
Execute start routine for source_package.

*** STEP 2 - Record by record processing of the source package
Loop at source_package.

*** STEP 3 - Standard transformation group rules for all fields
(characteristics and key figures).
    Determine common transformation rules (as shown below).

*** STEP 4 - Apply transformation rules for remaining
***           transformation groups
    Process characteristics or key fields of target.
      If source field directly assigned to current field.
        Assign source field value to target field converting data types.
      End.
      If constant value assigned to target field.
        Assign constant value to target field.
      End.
      If formula assigned to target field.
        Execute formula.
        Assign result to target field.
      End.
      If routine assigned to target field.
       Execute routine.
        Assign result to target field.
      End.
      If master data attribute assigned to target field.
        Retrieve master data attribute.
        Assign result to target field.
      End.
    End.
    Convert unit / currency.

*** STEP 5 - Collect data record into result package
    Collect data record(s).

*** STEP 6 - Apply transformations to result package if any.
Execute end routine for result_package.

*** STEP 7 - Call InfoProvider update with result_package in
***           target format passing result package in memory.
Call InfoProvider physical update program.
```

Table 6-1 shows a sample data package in source format, containing 12 sets of key figures for planned sales revenue and discounts (in percent) for a specific material in 2007. The set of key figures represents calendar months.

Table 6-1 Source Package

MATERIAL -DISNCT 3	YEAR	PLAN 1	PLAN 2	PLAN 3	...	DISCNT 1	DISCNT 2	...
M01	2007	12	14	15	...	10	9	8
M02	2007	50	60	70	...	6	6	6
M03	2007	60	50	40	...	9	10	10

The approach in this example is to update an InfoCube with the material, year, and month as characteristic values (instead of a set of 12 key figures) and to have only two key figures (one for planned sales revenue and one for discount). As a result, 12 transformation groups will be applied for each set of plan values, effectively normalizing the source records. Each of the 12 key figures of the source is mapped to the same corresponding target key figure (either plan sales revenue or discounts) but with a different characteristic constant for the calendar month.

When each of these 12 groups is created, all key-figure rules of the standard transformation group are overtaken as reference rules into each new group. At runtime, the reference rule is executed only once, and its result value is passed to each of the 12 transformation groups. Only the explicit changes in the transformation rules of each of the 12 transformation groups are applied afterward. In our example, a rule of type `constant value` is specified for the month in each transformation rule. The other rules remain untouched (using references rules from the standard transformation group).

In summary, Step 2 initiates the record-by-record processing of the source package. Step 3 determines all transformation rules for all fields that are part of the standard group, following the same procedure as in Step 4 (all remaining transformation groups). Again, this is an optimization, avoiding multiple determinations of the same values for standard transformation rules across transformation groups.

> **NOTE** In transformation groups, it is possible to copy a key-figure transformation rule, which effectively doubles the records (one record for the original key figure and another record for the copy). This might be helpful for creating two different versions of data. By copying a key-figure transformation rule, you create the possibility of using different transformation rules for the same target key figure within the same transformation group (none in this example). For those familiar with earlier releases of the application, this is similar to the old concept of copying key figure update rules, which generates additional records for the same key figure.

For simplicity and clarity, note that the specific execution order within data records, key-figure transformation rules, and characteristic transformation rules is not defined in the pseudocode logic provided.

When applicable in Step 4, the value of the key figure itself is determined by applying the transformation rules, as well as unit or currency conversions. This example requires 12 transformation groups to be able to normalize the data record. The collected result package for the plan revenues looks like Table 6-2.

Table 6-2   Result Table in Data Target Format

MATERIAL	YEAR	MONTH	PLAN	DISCNT
M01	2002	01	12	10
M01	2002	02	14	9
M01	2002	03	15	8
...				
M02	2002	01	50	6
M02	2002	02	60	6
M02	2002	03	70	6
...				
M03	2002	01	60	9
M03	2002	02	50	10
M03	2002	03	40	10
...				

In many simple update scenarios, a single source record generates a single entry in the target. This is the case when all characteristic values are the same for all key figures, so that aggregation is able to aggregate those multiple records of the nonaggregated table into a single record of the final aggregated table. Specifying different characteristic transformation rules per transformation group provides another option for normalizing data records, because different characteristic values prohibit aggregation of the internal result table. This way, multiple data entries are written to the data target.

Step 8 finally passes the internal result table in target format to the generated target update program that controls the loading process of SAP BW.

Loading

Loading data into an InfoProvider is the last step of the staging process. So far, data has always been passed in some flat-record format. Loading data into a target SAP BW object involves transforming this flat-data structure into the data-target-specific format and generating or retrieving surrogate keys wherever necessary. Although SAP BW completely automates this process by generating and using data-target-specific data-load programs, you should still understand what's going on behind the scenes when defining or optimizing an information model.

Additional topics related to data loading are covered in more detail in Chapter 11.

Master Data Loading

The three types of master data supported by SAP BW (attributes, texts, and hierarchies) all are modeled slightly differently and require different loading procedures. Before going into the details of these different processes, you may want to have another look at the discussion of the master-data data model in Chapter 4 and particularly note Figure 4-1.

Generally, it does not make a difference in what order attributes, texts, and hierarchies are loaded. You should load texts first, since this is usually the quickest load and will generate all required surrogate IDs, effectively speeding up subsequent load processes, unless the master data check option is turned on when loading transaction data.

However, it does make a difference if master data or transaction data is loaded first. You should load master data first and not just for performance reasons. Loaded master data allows using the master data check functionality and ensuring that no transaction data records referring to unknown master data (via lookup update rules) are updated into any data target with obsolete values.

Master Data Attributes

Loading flat master data attribute records affects several tables of the master-data data model. First, SIDs must be retrieved from the SID table or generated if not available. Second, attributes have to be mapped to either the time-dependent or non-time-dependent attributes table. Finally, SAP BW has to retrieve or generate SIDs for navigational master data attributes and store those SIDs in the attribute SID tables. The following code fragment shows a highly simplified master data attributes update algorithm:

```
Master Data Attribute Update Algorithm
*** STEP 1 - Process data package record by record
Loop at data package.

*** STEP 2 - Surrogate key handling
  Retrieve/Generate surrogate key.
  Update SID table.

*** STEP 3 - Non time dependent master data.
  Retrieve existing non time dependent record.
  Insert/Update non time dependent attributes.
  Retrieve surrogate keys for attributes.
  If not all SIDs available.
    If master data check requested.
      Log error, start error handling.
    Else.
      Generate new SID.
    End.
  Insert/Update attribute SID table

*** STEP 4 - Time dependent master data.
  Retrieve existing time dependent records.
  Check for validity period overlaps.
  Adjust overlap records accordingly.
  Insert/Update time dependent attributes.
  Retrieve surrogate keys for attributes.
  If not all SIDs available.
    If master data check requested.
      Log error, start error handling.
    Else.
      Generate new SID.
    End.
  Insert/Update attribute SID table
End.
```

Several items are important to note:

- SAP BW automatically maintains all surrogate keys (see Steps 2, 3, and 4).

- SAP BW automatically handles overlapping periods of validity in master data updates (see Step 4). Note, however, that it handles overlaps only between the data load and already existing records. It does not handle overlaps within the load itself and will end in error.

- SAP BW allows you to update a subset of the attributes from one DataSource without compromising existing values by updating only available fields. In other words, if half the attributes are available in the DataSource, it will not overwrite the other half with blank values but rather merge the values.

- Duplicate keys abort the load process, and SAP BW would not be able to tell which record to use for updating the data target. Using an incorrect sequence would result in inconsistent data. This feature can be turned off, though.

NOTE Automated SID maintenance also provides some protection from accidentally deleting SIDs. Before deleting master data, SAP BW always ensures that the corresponding SID is not used in any other data target.

Master Data Texts

Loading text records is similar to (yet simpler than) loading attribute records, because there are no additional SID tables to update:

```
Master Data Text Update Algorithm
*** STEP 1 - Process data package record by record
Loop at data package.

*** STEP 2 - Surrogate key handling
  Retrieve/Generate surrogate key.
  Update SID table.

*** STEP 3 - Non time dependent master data texts.
  Retrieve existing non time dependent record.
  Insert/Update non time dependent texts.

*** STEP 4 - Time dependent master data texts.
  Retrieve existing time dependent records.
  Check for validity period overlaps.
  Adjust overlap records accordingly.
  Insert/Update time dependent texts.
End.
```

Master Data Hierarchies

Characteristic hierarchies all generate their own unique SIDs to improve reporting performance. There are actually four different hierarchy tables generated if an InfoObject uses hierarchies as discussed in Chapter 4 (the H, K, I, and J tables). Hierarchies are different from other data loads in that an extracted hierarchy is valid only in its entirety; it is not possible to update just a selection of the records of the hierarchy without compromising the hierarchy structure. It is, however, possible to load consistent hierarchy subtrees, as the following pseudocode logic illustrates:

```
Master Data Hierarchy Update Algorithm
*** STEP 1 - Check hierarchy consistency
If hierarchy subtree loaded.
  Merge subtree into existing hierarchy.
Endif.

*** STEP 2 - Check hierarchy consistency
Check for duplicate nodes.
Check for loops.
Check for orphans.

*** STEP 3 - Update hierarchy
Write hierarchy into hierarchy table
Write hierarchy intervals into hierarchy interval table

*** STEP 4 - Create SIDs
Write hierarchy SID tables
```

Recently added options in hierarchy loading include the following:

- Loading hierarchy subtrees
- Loading hierarchies into the PSA
- Additional attributes can be assigned to hierarchy nodes
- A sign can be assigned to a hierarchy node, allowing for applications such as net-profit calculations in an account hierarchy in the Business Explorer

InfoCube Loading

Understanding the details of the InfoCube load process requires understanding the InfoCube data model, which is explained in detail in Chapter 4 and illustrated in Figure 4-2.

The fact tables and dimension tables primarily consist of surrogate keys. The fact tables contain the key figures, plus all the dimension identifiers to link them to the dimension table. The dimension tables use SIDs to link characteristic values to the dimension table. All of these SIDs are automatically retrieved or generated during data loads. The following pseudocode logic shows the basics of the InfoCube update algorithm:

```
*** STEP 1 - Process data package record by record
Loop at data package.

*** STEP 2 - Surrogate key handling
  Retrieve SIDs.
  If not all SIDs available.
    If master data check requested.
      Log error, start error handling.
    Else.
      Generate new SID.
    End.
  End.
  Insert/Update SID tables

*** STEP 3 - Dimension key handling
  Retrieve/Generate DIMIDs.
  Insert/Update DIMID tables.
  Assign DIMIDs to related fields of the fact table.

*** STEP 4 - Key figure handling.
  Assign key figure values to related fields of the fact table.
  Insert/Update fact table.
End.
```

Loading DataStore Objects

Loading DataStore Objects is a two-step process: Load data into an activation queue and then activate that data. Upon activation, the contents of the activation queue are compared to the active data records, changes are tracked in the change log, and current records are written to the active data table of the DataStore Object. Both processes are illustrated in Figure 6-21. As of release 3.0, DataStore Object load and activation processes can be parallelized due to a parallel inserting algorithm.

The standard DataStore Object itself consists of three underlying ABAP dictionary tables: activation queue, change log and active data. The activation queue is where transformed data is first loaded. It is unaggregated (each loaded record is separated by request, data package, and record number called a *technical key*). While activating the data, these data packages are aggregated into the *semantic key* (combination of characteristics that unique identify the record) of the active table (used for reporting). In parallel, before and after images are recorded in the change log per technical key (used for downstream delta change data transfer processes). As data is loaded into the change log and active table, it is deleted from the activation queue.

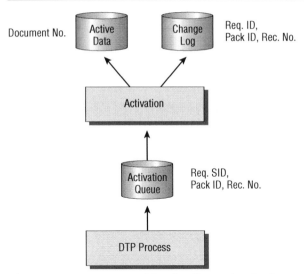

Figure 6-21 DataStore Object loading and activation

The following two pseudocode fragments show the basic procedure for loading data into a DataStore Object and subsequently activating the data from the activation queue:

```
*** STEP 1 - Data Load
For every technical key data package.
     Insert technical key data package into activation queue.
Endfor.

*** STEP 2 - Process Activation Queue
Loop at activation queue
*** STEP 3 - Build Semantic Key Data Package.
     Build semantic key data package
     For every semantic key data package
*** STEP 4 - Generate surrogate keys if DataStore object is BEx-enabled
          Create SID's if requested and store as intermediate result.
     Endfor
Endloop
*** STEP 5 - Delta change processing
For each intermediate data package
     Loop at data package
          Read active DataStore record with same key.
               If record does not exist.
                    Insert into active data records.
                    Insert into delta queue.
               Else.
                    Invert existing record.
                    Insert inverted record into change log.
                    Insert new record into change log.
```

```
                                     Update active data records with new record.
                           End.

        Endloop
     Endfor
```

Even with the optimizations and recently changed logic for DataStore Object loads, further performance gains can be achieved by using write-optimized DataStore Objects in lieu of standard DataStore Objects. Loading a write-optimized DataStore Object eliminates the overhead of data activation and SID generation (and corresponding activation queue and change log tables). Data is only loaded into the active reporting table.

The key of the table is technical, not semantic (similar to the standard activation queue, the key of the write-optimized active table is request, data package ID, and record number). As a result, data does not aggregate when loading into a write-optimized DataStore Object, which may generate logical duplicates if uniqueness is not checked (defined in the DataStore properties). Only new records get loaded into this DataStore Object. The data then gets propagated to downstream target SAP BW objects by request (instead of the change log mechanism).

Write-optimized DataStore Objects are useful for fast load scenarios that do not require a lot of reporting such as an intermediary staging area (to reuse particular transformations in an information supply chain) or for use as an EDW layer.

DataStore Objects for direct update are similar to, but different from, write-optimized DataStore Objects. They are similar in that they also consist of only one active reporting table (which supports BEx by generating the necessary SIDs at query runtime). Write-optimized DataStore Objects are different in that DataStore Objects for direct update cannot be updated via data-transfer processing but rather via an API for direct update (such as an Analysis Process Designer or SEM applications). In addition, DataStore Objects for direct update use a semantic key rather than a technical one.

Summary

Data acquisition, transformation, and loading not only remain the most time-consuming and resource-consuming parts of a data warehouse project but also remain the most critical parts, as accurate, integrated, and comprehensive information is one of the key success factors for every information system. This chapter not only lays the foundation for understanding the extraction processes in mySAP ERP, it also provides valuable insight for implementing extraction processes in other operational-system environments, whether another ERP system or a custom legacy system.

SAP BW supports different interfaces, providing access to data stored in SAP systems, in flat files, and in external database systems and accepts XML data streams. Data acquisition and transformation is complemented by an open interface for standard ETL tools (such as Ascential DataStage, Informatica PowerCenter, and others).

SAP BW nearly eliminates the need to think about how data is technically loaded into the different data targets. All the details of the load processes (such as mapping flat data records to a complex data model and handling surrogate keys) are automatically handled by update programs generated according to the metadata definitions of the target BI object.

Whereas this chapter has been about to how to get data into a BI system, Chapter 7 is about how to get data out. Data transformations and calculations do not stop with the Staging Engine; the Analytic Processing Engine offers a further opportunity to transform data into information (but at runtime instead of background preprocessing). Our focus will now shift from data acquisition, transformation, and loading and move toward information access, analysis, and distribution.

Data Access, Analysis, and Information Distribution

Chapter 6 described how to integrate and transform data so that it may be stored in constructs such as DataStore Objects, InfoProviders, and master data. This chapter picks up where Chapter 6 left off. This chapter has been organized into three main sections: data access, analysis, and information distribution. The discussion highlights the main services provided in SAP NetWeaver that access data and turns it into meaningful business information. Then the topics of information distribution via the Broadcaster are examined, as well as programming interface options available to tools that present said information.

Data Access

Chapter 3 introduced the data access and analysis services aspect of the SAP BW architecture. This section further explores these services. The data access services layer (as its name suggests) provides access to structured information stored in the SAP Business Information Warehouse. Structured information is retrieved through SAP BW InfoProviders, while unstructured information is retrieved from content management services. The integration of unstructured documents and structured documents has become an essential feature for business intelligence tools and is accomplished via shared metadata and the functionality available via the Enterprise Portal.

The main services in this layer are the InfoProvider interface, the Analytic Processing Engine, and the Analysis Process Designer (which encompasses the Data Mining Engine). These layers are categorized into request-handling services, processing services, and retrieval services. Each of these is discussed with attention on the request-handling interfaces in the "Information Distribution" section of this chapter. These services are a primary integration point for information distribution to third-party applications, specifically interfaces that expose the service of the Analytic Processing Engine.

Query Processing Overview

To better explain the data access and analysis services, let's first examine the query process used in SAP BW. The query process is a series of requests and responses, including requests for information, database selections, application caching, number crunching, information formatting, and ultimately responding to the requester by presenting results sets. From an end user's perspective, this process has been abstracted to the point that the end user's only concern is making a request for information that will lead him or her to solve the particular business problem at hand. Behind the scenes, however, the query process is busy at work, creating the optimal database access plan, locating aggregates, converting currency, applying hierarchies, filtering, and so on.

Let's look at the query request response process in the context of a typical business question. Consider the example of analyzing revenue and contribution margins across multiple geographies and customers to illustrate how the information request response process works. Figure 7-1 depicts the query process.

In this scenario, assume that this is the first time the corporate controller has requested contribution margin and revenue to be analyzed by geography and customer. After launching her favorite Web browser and navigating to her Portal homepage on the corporate intranet, the controller selects the Create New Query option of the Web Analyzer. After selecting this option, she invokes the metadata services to return a list of potential InfoProviders that may be queried. The controller selects the appropriate InfoProvider and again invokes the metadata services. The services return a list of dimensions that contain characteristic InfoObjects, as well as a list of key figures. The controller selects the `Revenue and Contribution` key figure as well as the `Geography` and `Customer` characteristics and assigns them to the rows or columns of the query result sets based on her preference. She then executes the query.

At the center of the data access, analysis, and, for that matter, an information distribution and presentation service is the Analytic Processing Engine. An information consumer application requests information from the Analytic Processing Engine in the form of a multidimensional expression or similar selection request. In this example, the controller requests revenue and contribution margin for the current period and fiscal year for all customers and all geographies.

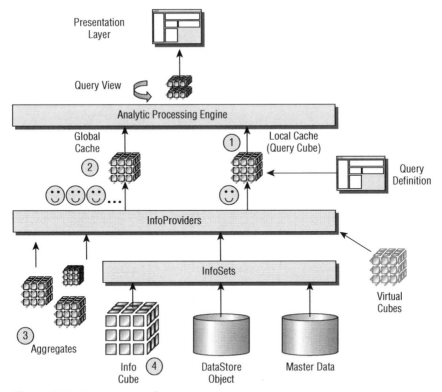

Figure 7-1   Query processing

Leading business intelligence tools generate selection expressions so end users do not need to know the specific syntax. The request is sent from the browser to the NetWeaver server. Consumers may be a browser, mobile device, Excel spreadsheet, or, as in this example, a third-party client application. The server takes the request through one of a number of standard interface techniques and hands it to the Analytic Processing Engine for fulfillment.

The NetWeaver server takes the initial request and determines if there is a cache in existence that may satisfy the request. There will be no local cache for the controller if this is indeed her first request. The global cache is then checked to see if this request has been cached for multiple users. If no global cache entry exists, the InfoProvider will search for aggregate cubes that may satisfy the request. In this example, an aggregate cube that summarizes customer or geographies may be a candidate for optimal retrieval. If no such aggregate cubes exist, the application server makes a request to the database server.

The database requests and selects records for an InfoProvider. The records selected from the database server may be returned to the application server. Depending on the query's read mode and cache settings, records are put into memory for the Analytic Processing Engine to process and, ultimately, to calculate and return a query navigation state to the presentation server. The caching of the selected data on the application server is sometimes referred to as a *query cube*, depending on the cache and read-mode settings set for the query. The Analytic Processing Engine will use the query cube to calculate and return result sets to the client for subsequent information requests, assuming the query cube contains the necessary data to respond to the request. The options for setting a query's read mode and the impact of global caching on performance are discussed in Chapter 12.

The controller in our example would receive a listing of revenue and contribution margins for all customers in all geographies. She notices that revenue, which is displayed in U.S. dollars (USD), is higher than she had planned and proceeds to investigate which geography is exceeding her expectations. Her request is sent from the client to the application server, where it is once again handled by the Analytic Processing Engine. Once the appropriate storage service returns the records, the engine creates the query data and proceeds as previously described. The controller learns that the UK is exceeding her sales expectations.

Note that the Analytic Processing Engine will take care of any currency translations based on the metadata of the InfoObjects included in the query, as well as the metadata of the query itself. In this case, the geographies are countries, and most countries have their own currency. The controller also may wish to analyze the revenue in the group currency of USD. Upon doing so, she notices that Argentina has failed to meet her sales expectation. Not satisfied that she has found the cause of the shortfall, she investigates further and requests that the currency be converted to local currency for all countries. A request is once again sent to the Analytic Processing Engine to be processed. The local currencies are either retrieved or calculated, depending on the modeling of the InfoProvider, and the newly calculated query slice is returned to the client. Now the controller realizes that Argentina did, in fact, meet sales expectation but experienced a significant foreign-exchange impact as a result of the rate dropping.

The process of requesting and responding to queries is the central concept of this chapter.

NOTE SAP BW attempts to limit the number of round trips from presentation server to database server by caching and reusing query results and navigation steps on the application server in a cross-transactional buffer after it has been selected from the database. This global caching technique was introduced with the goal of sharing memory across various users' sessions.

InfoProvider Interface

SAP has isolated and abstracted functionality and complexity throughout its software. Nowhere is this more evident than in the retrieval services, specifically the InfoProvider interface. The *InfoProvider interface* has been introduced to standardize access to the structured data available to SAP BW. The InfoProvider interface allows access to information stored in SAP, as well as data not stored in SAP. The interface enables the Analytic Processing Engine to treat all requests for information in the same manner, regardless of where and how data is physically stored. There are two generic types of InfoProviders: physical and virtual.

Figure 7-2 highlights the fact that both physical and VirtualProviders are accessed by the same set of analysis services. The InfoProvider may be thought of as an abstraction layer for all data flowing to end users, third-party business intelligence tools, other SAP applications, or custom-built analytic applications. The ultimate consumer of the information requested need not be concerned about how or where data is physically stored. While the Analytic Processing Engine accesses all different types of InfoProviders, the Info-Provider, in turn, accesses the data storage services in very specific ways.

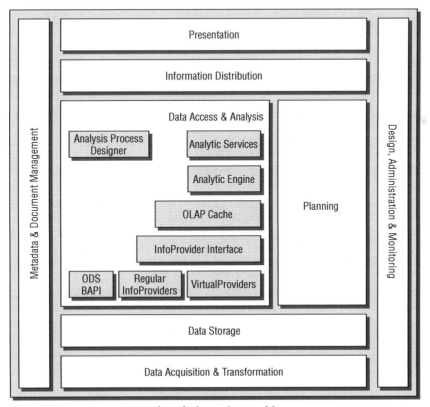

Figure 7-2   Data access and analysis services architecture

Physical InfoProviders

All queries passed to the Analytic Processing Engine are sent as either multidimensional expressions or, in the case of the BEx Analyzer, command codes. As discussed later in this chapter, there are multiple interfaces options, so the language and syntax of the expression may differ, but the essence of requests is the same. The Analytic Processing Engine handles the request the same way, regardless of the interface the request was received from, and passes it to the InfoProvider interface. The InfoProvider interface, in taking care to abstract the data source, handles all requests from the Analytic Processing Engine in the same manner and determines the InfoProvider type for the specific request.

Once the InfoProvider type is identified, query requests are handled in a specific manner, depending on how and where data is physically stored. For example, if the InfoProvider is abstracting a DataStore Object, the InfoProvider will flatten the multidimensional request for data. Remember from Chapter 4 that the DataStore Object is nothing more than a relational table. The flattened request will be passed to the InfoSet interface, which will, in turn, send a request to execute an actual InfoSet. The InfoSet will then hand the request to a storage service, which will, in turn, determine the optimal access plan. The same holds true for a master data InfoProvider.

The result set of the InfoSet will be retrieved and handed back to the Analytic Processing Engine, where (pardon the redundancy) analytical processing services are applied prior to handing the specified query view back to the original requester. The Analytic Processing Engine's ability to generate both multidimensional query cubes and tabular result sets has by and large enabled the InfoProvider interface to abstract both multidimensional and flat data sources. Note that both DataStore objects for direct update and standard DataStore objects are available as InfoProviders.

In the case of a physical InfoProvider for basic InfoCubes (real-time and standard), the requests are routed to the storage services. The so-called Data Manager uses its Aggregate Manager to identify aggregate cubes and ultimately find the optimal database access path. The InfoProvider abstracts the storage and access details from the Analytic Processing Engine.

VirtualProviders

Information requests flow into the InfoProvider layer in similar ways for both physical and VirtualProviders. The InfoProvider layer abstracts analytic processing logic from the Data Manager, and the Data Manager takes care to access the physical data storage if indeed the data is stored in SAP; if it isn't, the Data Manager hands off the request to a virtual system. The differences occur in how the requests are routed and how and where the actual data access takes place. It is important to understand that the end user requesting information from SAP need not know or care where or how the information is physically stored.

VirtualProviders can be thought of in two categories: remote and local. *Remote* VirtualProviders are useful whenever data residing on a remote system cannot (or should not) be copied to the local database. Sometimes external data may not be copied to a local system for licensing reasons, and other times there are functional or nonfunctional requirements that prohibit data from being copied from an operational system into SAP. This may be the case when real-time data from an operational system is needed but access to the data must be tightly controlled. VirtualProviders may be *local* if, for example, the InfoProvider does not directly interface with the Data Manager. Such is the case when MultiProviders are used as InfoProviders.

NOTE An *InfoSet* may be thought of as a VirtualProvider that has implemented an additional abstraction layer on top of the Meta Data Repository. InfoSets allow the defining of joins for multiple InfoCubes, DataStore Objects, and master data tables. InfoSets and MultiProviders are not the same. MultiProviders implement a union of the underlying InfoProviders, while InfoSets define joins of the underlying InfoProviders.

Local VirtualProviders

MultiProviders are typically used whenever information from different business processes (or parts of a business process) must be displayed and available for navigation within a single query. MultiProviders are an alternative to modeling overly complex InfoCubes or DataStore Objects. It is important to keep in mind that MultiProviders are unions of InfoProviders and do not allow defining joins. The MultiProvider takes the retrieval request it receives from the Analytic Processing Engine and determines, based on the metadata for the MultiProvider, the number of physical or VirtualProviders that compose the MultiProvider.

Remote InfoProviders

Remote InfoProviders are easily defined for data sources available on mySAP ERP and other SAP BW systems. In the SAP system requesting the data, an SAP VirtualProvider is defined with an InfoSource that points to another SAP system. The BW Service API is used to access the remote data on the SAP systems. For non-SAP systems, a generic VirtualProvider may be defined. This generic interface enables custom-developed programs to act like an SAP VirtualProvider and provide information to the requesting SAP BW system.

NOTE The data access interfaces that do not utilize the InfoProvider layer are the Persistent Staging Area (PSA) and DataStore APIs.

VirtualProviders are a powerful way to satisfy reporting and analysis requirements without the need to physically reconstruct InfoCubes or create new application-layer DataStore objects. VirtualProviders are InfoProviders that do not route data selection requests directly to the SAP BW Data Manager. For example, a VirtualProvider may represent a remote InfoCube physically stored on a remote system supporting the VirtualProvider interface definition; these can be flat database tables, ERP DataSources, and actual InfoCubes stored in a remote SAP BW system. The VirtualProvider merely hands off the request to another retrieval service, which takes care of data selection.

This type of remote InfoCube interface allows direct access to data stored in mySAP ERP systems (through the BW Service API) and external systems supporting this interface. Using the VirtualProvider interface, SAP BW users are able to define remote cubes for any type of data stored on any kind of system. There is also an option that allows for master data to be selected locally from SAP BW while data records are selected from a remote system.

DataStore Objects and PSA APIs

There are architectural modeling scenarios that may require data to be retrieved from DataStore Objects or the PSA without first accessing the Info-Provider interface. Some of these scenarios are covered in Chapter 5. The discussion here describes the APIs present not only to retrieve but also write records to the PSA and DataStore Objects.

Standard DataStore Objects are accessible via BAPIs. There are methods to change, create, activate, get, and read this type of DataStore Object. There are essentially four methods that may be called for a Direct Update DataStore Object through the programming interfaces: Insert, Modify, Update, and Delete. The function modules for these methods all start with RSDRI_ODSO_*. The Insert and Delete APIs are self-describing, while the Modify and Update APIs are a bit trickier. The Modify method allows for the creation of new records, should the key values being "modified" not already exist in the Direct Update DataStore Object. The Update method will only change records that have keys already in a DataStore object.

The PSA API consists of three methods that may be called: Get, Put, and Delete. The function modules for these methods start with RSAR_ODS_API_*. As the names indicate, records may be retrieved (GET), written (PUT), or removed (DELETE). System administrators should be aware that the PSA tables do not care to track changes to records written through this simple yet effective API.

Information Analysis

The information analysis portion of this chapter has been broken down into two sections:

- A brief discussion of the knowledge-discovery process

■ The details surrounding the analytic features of the software, including the Analytic Processing Engine, the Analytic Process Designer, with its Data Mining options, and a few other analytic services that do not necessarily utilize the Analytic Processing Engine

Knowledge-Discovery Process

Knowledge, according to en.wikipedia.org (at least it was defined this way at one time), "...is the confident understanding of a subject, potentially with the ability to use it for a specific purpose." The automated discovery of knowledge has moved from pie in the sky to dinner on the table. Advancements in predictive modeling, the interconnectedness enabled by the Internet, and the increase in computer processing power have come together to enable not only the automation of knowledge discovery but also the embedding of said knowledge into business processes. As briefly described in Chapter 1, in addition to an example application involving an online auction house and the selective ability to provide price-protect insurance to its buyers and sellers, many other business processes are awaiting this intersection of vision and value. Before describing what were once considered Holy Grail business applications, let's first define the steps in the knowledge-discovery process.

While many derivations to the steps are outlined here, the series of steps almost always starts with a definition of the problem at hand, or some type of task analysis. This step is often referred to as a *requirements gathering* exercise. This is followed by a preprocessing step where data is prepared, cleansed, and at times transformed to conform to a specific format required by the predictive modeling algorithms. The algorithms are often referred to as *data mining algorithms,* which must be developed, trained, and ultimately executed in order to make predictions. These predictions are often output in a type of postprocessing step and may be graphs or tables representing the executed model. The final step is the embedding of the results into a business process. This is often referred to as *closed-loop processing*.

Data mining is the term commonly used to describe a class of database applications that uncover previously unknown patterns from data. The goal of data mining is to identify golden nuggets of information in large volumes of data. Many terms have been used somewhat synonymously with data mining (for example, knowledge discovery, data archeology, information harvesting, and predictive analytics). Some of these terms represent types or components of data mining. Regardless of the terminology, data mining algorithms have found their way out of university research papers and into enterprise software applications.

SAP has delivered data mining methods and Business Content to help organizations identify potentially significant patterns, associations, and trends that otherwise would be too time consuming to uncover through conventional human analysis or that were missed (since analysts tend to see the information they are expecting or hoping to discover and may miss valid information that lies outside their expectation zone).

Analytic Services

There are three primary analytic tools delivered as BI capabilities of NetWeaver designed to assist in knowledge discovery: the Analytic Processing Engine, Analysis Process Designer, and the Data Mining Workbench. Each of these tools is described in the following sections, along with a description of a few more analytic tools that don't quite fit into one of these three buckets.

Analytic Processing Engine

Regardless of whether or not an organization decides to standardize on the Business Explorer front-end delivered as part of the NetWeaver, the Analytic Processing Engine provides all analysis and navigational functions. While there are several integration possibilities for third-party, so-called "alternative front-end packages," the Analytic Processing Engine is the analysis brain for NetWeaver. Later, this section discusses each option and the possibilities for certifying third-party software to the interfaces. For now, let's focus on functions supported by the engine itself.

The Meta Data Repository stores a list of all queries that have been defined, regardless of the tool that will ultimately present the results delivered from the Analytic Processing Engine. When a query is requested by a presentation service (whether the Business Explorer or a third-party program), the query definition is retrieved from the Meta Data Repository. The Analytic Processing Engine takes the query definition and generates, updates, and executes the queries by running the generated program. Once the selection request is handed to the InfoProvider interface, the InfoProvider may determine the type and invoke the appropriate service, be it a storage, analysis, or remote system service. The InfoProvider then returns the selected data records to the Analytic Processing Engine for runtime calculations, exceptions, conditions and authorization checks.

The Analytic Processing Engine checks the query definition of the so-called *query read mode*. There are three types of query read modes, each type controlling the behavior of the Analytic Processing Engine. The read modes are used to accelerate performance and are set based on a number of factors. The read mode and other performance optimization options (such as caching) are covered in greater detail in Chapter 12.

Analysis Process Designer

The Analysis Process Designer (APD) enables the exploration of data in an attempt to uncover relationships in the data by using advanced transformation and predictive analytic models. The APD may be used to prefill variables for subsequent queries to use when they are run. It may also be used to create data and fill master data attributes with newly created data. For example, a query may be run to determine the credit worthiness of customers, and that scoring may then be stored as a customer attribute to be used in further queries and business processes. The APD is tightly integrated with SAP CRM, which enables scenarios such as customer mailing list creation and marketing campaign planning and execution, as well as subsequent tracking of the campaign's performance. Automating this so-called *closed-loop analytic application* is one of the benefits of using the APD.

There are three main parts of the APD:

- Sources
- Transformations
- Targets

The APD provides a graphical work area much like the Visual Composer described in Chapter 2. There is a palette of icons representing data sources, transformations, and data targets that may be dragged onto the work area to establish a process. While this source-transformation-target process may sound like the ETL process described in Chapter 6, there is a great difference. The APD is designed to create insightful information from existing data and the newly created information in a business process or manual decision-making process, whereas the ETL process supports the movement and preparation of data so it may enter the data warehouse.

Sources

A variety of sources are available to the APD, including the following:

- Database tables
- Characteristics (Master Data InfoObjects)
- Queries
- InfoProviders
- Flat files

Any number of these sources that include data that is statistically relevant may be processed together. A source may have transformations applied prior to being joined or merged with another source. For example, the customer attributes ZIP code, gender, and age can be joined with customer sales records. A source may also be retrieved from the data returned in a query view or an InfoProvider (including MultiProviders), which allows for complex selection and preprocessing of records entering an analysis process.

Transformations

One of the challenges in uncovering unknown or nonintuitive insight from data is that a tremendous number of variables may or may not need to be evaluated in conjunction with one another. The variables must have consistent domain values, which SAP does a nice job of ensuring for its own data sources. However, if third-party sources are used, this so-called "coding process" may require a significant amount of manual intervention. Unfortunately, this preprocessing or preparation step is often the most time consuming and requires the most knowledge about the data and its relationship to other data objects and attributes, as well as expertise in statistics.

A variety of transformations are available when configuring the APD. They include the following:

- Filter
- Merge
- Sort
- Transpose Rows<->Columns
- Aggregate
- Drop/Hide Column
- Run ABAP Routine
- Launch External Data Mining Model

Several data mining methods are also considered "transformations," which will be described shortly. Transformation icons are placed onto the APD work area and linked to a data source or sources for which they are to be applied. With the goal of discovering meaningful information, the transformation steps allow for the display of intermediate results. Since the APD may include complex transformation of various data sources, statistics are available for each node in an analysis process. The statistics include information on the number of records, distinct values, and frequency of occurrence, as well as mean, median, mode, standard deviation, and the like. These intermediate statistics may be used to help determine which variables should be used in, for example, a data mining model.

Targets

There are several targets that the data created in the APD may be stored and forwarded to, including the following types:

- DataStore (Real-time) Objects
- InfoObjects (Master Data)
- OLTP systems (for example, SAP CRM system)
- Data mining models (Association, Regression, Clustering, and Decision Trees)

The ability to persistently store the results of the APD (be it a simple sub-query to prefill variables for a subsequent query or the results of a complex predictive model) in the data targets provides a mechanism for creating complex analysis processes.

Data Mining Engine

The goal in this discussion is not to provide a discourse on data mining but rather to sketch the methods that SAP delivers. NetWeaver is delivered with support for three categories of data mining methods:

- Classification (decision trees, scoring)
- Clustering
- Association analysis

Data mining analysis is configured via the APD or directly with transaction RSDMWB and comes with a data mining wizard to guide the user through the setup. The setup is performed by selection of the data mining methods (classification, clustering, and association analysis) from the Transformation toolbar. Note that classification methods are further broken down into decision trees and scoring methods in the Transformations toolbar. Based on the model selected, the parameters are different per data mining method and are covered in more detail later in the chapter. For each method, sources for the training, evaluation, and prediction must be configured.

Up to three sources of data are used in data mining: training data, evaluation data, and prediction data. *Training data* consists of a representative subset of data for the model to learn against before its learning is applied to historical data to make predictions. *Historical data* can be used for both evaluative and predictive purposes. Historical data for evaluation and prediction should be separate sources. *Evaluation* is used to validate whether or not a model has been appropriately trained before it is turned loose against historical data to make predictions. Note that model evaluation is not an explicit step in all mining processes. In some cases, evaluation means only viewing the results of the training, not running the model with a separate source, because only a classification needs to be made, not a prediction.

All data mining methods share similar processes:

- **A data mining model is created** — The configuration of the models differs, depending on the data mining method (especially the model variables). The model typically consists of two levels of configuration: one for the model itself and one for the modeling variables. The configuration settings for model variables and parameters differ per model.

- **The model is trained** — Training allows the model to learn against a subset of data. The source for the training exercise should take this into account by selecting enough data to appropriately train the model but not too much that performance is adversely affected. Where predictions are not needed (such as association analysis), training is not needed. A model has a status indicator used to identify whether or not it has been trained.

- **The model is evaluated** — After a model has been trained, it may be evaluated to determine whether it was trained appropriately. A sample of historic data is used to verify the results (but not the historic data to be used for predictions). A model has a status indicator used to identify whether or not it has been evaluated.

- **Predictions are made** — Once a model is appropriately trained and evaluated, it is ready to make predictions. Predictions may be performed either online or as a batch process, depending on the volume of data. Predictions should be made on yet another source for historic data, separate from what was used in training and evaluation. The actual output of data mining depends on the method picked. Decision trees output probability trees, while clusters show percentage slices of an overall pie. A status indicator shows whether a model has been predicted.

- **The results are stored or forwarded** — Predicted values may be stored in InfoObjects. For example, customer classifications generated by scoring models may be saved to customer master data. When loading the results as a characteristic attribute, you must take care to match the metadata of the master data with the metadata of the model fields. More explicitly, the domain values in the model must match the domain values of the master data. When loading cross-selling rules determined via association analysis to SAP CRM, you must specify the logical system name and target group to export the data. Predicted values may also be exported to file or another target type. Once these results are stored or forwarded, they may be used for operational purposes or "embedded" into decision points in a business processes. For example, a bank may decide to offer or deny credit to a potential customer based on the customer's attributes and behavior. This may be done in an automated fashion if, for example, the loan request is performed online.

The following sections detail the different types of data mining methods available.

Decision Trees

Decision trees classify historical data into probability hierarchies (based on attributes for a specific characteristic such as customer) for a specific key figure (such as a count of all customers lost in a given period). Decision trees are used in scenarios such as identifying which customers are more likely to churn (in order to improve customer retention) or which customers keep good credit (in order to screen prospects better). For example, in a number of cellular phone markets, the struggle for market share is won through customer retention. Churn behavior decision trees can be produced by data mining historical data such as telephone usage, service, and payments coupled with customer attributes such as the brand or model used and the locale. The results of the decision tree can then be used to initiate a customer-loyalty program.

The classifications of a decision tree are depicted hierarchically, which makes for good visual associations and linkages. Each hierarchy level of the decision tree represents a characteristic attribute (such as profession, age, membership status, marital status, and annual income of a customer) with associated probabilities for an outcome like churn. Based on the probabilities calculated for historical data, predictions can be made for other sets of data (such as the likelihood for churn on a different customer base or for a new customer). When a node of the decision tree is highlighted, the details behind the node percentage are given via a graph, such as the class distribution and node statistics showing the sample size.

The configuration for the decision tree consists of maintaining the parameters for the model and the parameters of the model. The model parameters control the decision tree calculation, such as how much data to use for training, how to determine which records are relevant, when to stop the calculation, and how to prune the tree. Pruning cuts out the records that do not significantly affect the accuracy of the decision tree. The parameters for each of the model fields control how to handle missing or junk values within that field.

The training process can be controlled by a *windowing technique*. Windowing is an iterative approach to growing the sample set of data used for training a decision tree model. If larger window sizes are specified, more data is used for training. Larger windows increase the accuracy of the trained model but have a greater impact on performance during training.

The settings for windowing are set in the parameters for the decision tree model. The settings dictate when windowing (or the growing of the sample set of data) should stop. Windowing settings consist of an initial window size, a maximum window size, and the number of trials to perform. The initial window size dictates the percentage of the sample data to use in the first iteration (or trial) of training. After the first trial of training, the decision tree is iteratively applied to the remaining data that is misclassified in the sample set until one of four things happens:

- The maximum window size is met.
- The number of trials is exceeded.
- There are no more misclassified records.
- The decision tree gets pruned.

Fields in a decision tree model may be excluded if they are irrelevant to classification. To perform the check for relevancy during classification, you must activate the check in the model, and settings must be maintained to tell the model what constitutes as irrelevant. There are two methods for defining irrelevancy: Either a threshold is maintained for how informative a field must be before dropping it from classification, or top-N analysis can be performed, where a field is dropped if it is not among the top-most informative fields.

Stopping conditions define the criteria for the decision tree engine to stop growing the tree. While windowing relates to the growth of training data, stopping conditions relate to the growth of the decision tree. Stopping conditions dictate how many nodes to allow on a decision tree before splitting the node into further nodes, as well as the percentage of accuracy needed on a node before splitting can stop. *Node accuracy* is the percentage number of cases at a node that have the majority classification. When either of the minimums is reached, the decision tree stops splitting.

Pruning is a technique to avoid decision trees from being "overfitted." It improves readability of the rules by eliminating nonessential information (such as redundant nodes) without having a negative impact on the calculation of the result. *Extended pruning* can be used, which checks whether more accuracy can be achieved when any given node can be replaced by its parent node. If this check is successful, the node and all its children are pruned. Extended pruning is a performance-enhancement feature for large data sets.

For the model fields, parameters and field values must be set to dictate what is junk, what to include, and how to include it. For example, the field parameters control how initial values in the model field are to be treated. A flag sets whether null values in the model field are informative (meaning null is a valid value). If the flag is not set, all initial values are treated as missing. Alternatively, a default value can be specified to replace all initial or missing values.

For specific values within a specific field, there are even more specific settings. For example, a particular value or value ranges can be configured to be treated as a missing or ignored value. This level of detailed specification is helpful when you want to single out a particular field value as junk (such as question marks, asterisks, or 9999).

Scoring

Although originally designed for SAP CRM, the scoring technique has many general applications that can run outside of CRM analytics (such as vendor scoring). In the context of CRM analytics, you might use scoring scenarios to identify customers of a particular market segment for a new product launch or to categorize customers most likely to cancel service to a subscription. One of three regression types must be picked to do scoring:

- **Linear regression** — Scoring is trained by performing linear regression algorithms against historical data. This option is ideal for attributes that exhibit linear dependencies with a prediction key figure (such as discretionary income with sales).

- The system creates a separate linear function for every combination of discrete values in the training source. For example, suppose a query is mapped to two discrete model fields in the training source. If each discrete model field has five distinct characteristic values represented in the query, 25 linear regression analyses are performed. This is also true of nonlinear regressions. Performance of the system must be taken into account when a scoring model generates a significantly sized Cartesian product.

- **Nonlinear regression** — This is the same type of scoring as linear regression, except the algorithm does not assume any direct linear relationship. More specifically (for the mathematicians), multilinear splines are applied to model the relationship. Multilinear splines are linear regression models glued end to end to explain nonlinear behavior.

- **Weighted score tables** — Scoring is done without the need for any historic data (hence, training can be skipped). Weighting factors are given to specific attribute values to come up with a score.

The scoring parameters for model and model fields are different from the parameters for decision trees. The parameters of the scoring model consist of setting the regression type and default scores. The default scores are optionally set for any outliers or missing data records.

The configuration within each regression type is different. For linear and nonlinear options, outliers can be excluded by specifying minimum threshold values. The threshold quantities exclude field values based on the number of records for that value. These records can be excluded entirely from a score value, or a default score can be assigned, depending on a configuration flag. More explicitly, counts are determined for every combination of values, and when the number of records for each combination is exceeded, regression analysis skips the combination.

For nonlinear regression, a smoothing factor can be specified additionally. The higher the smoothing factor, the closer the algorithm is to being linear, but overfitting to the training data where there are not enough records is prevented.

Following are additional field value parameters for linear and nonlinear regression types:

- **Most frequent, all, or selected values** — These options set whether all discrete values, specific discrete values, or the most frequent discrete values should be considered in the linear regression. If the most frequent values option is picked, a number up to 100 determines how many of the most frequent discrete values are to be included.

- **Full or specified data range** — This option is similar to the preceding one but is for continuous values. Therefore, ranges have to be set or all values be permitted for use in regression analysis.

- **Automatic or manual intervals** — Intervals within a continuous data range can be automatically generated or manually created. If the automatic option is picked, the number of intervals to generate must be specified. Data-range limits are then calculated by automatically rounding off the maximum and minimum values of the training data. If data in the prediction source falls outside the limits, it is treated as an outlier.

Table 7-1 illustrates the field value parameters for both discrete and continuous content types per regression type.

Table 7-1 Scoring Field Value Parameters

REGRESSION	DISCRETE TYPE	CONTINUOUS
Linear	Most frequent, all, or selected values	Full or specified data range
Nonlinear	Most frequent, all, or selected values	Full or specified data range
		Automatic or manual intervals
Weighted Score	Weight of model field	Weight of model field
	Partial scores	Threshold partial scores
		Function piecewise constant
		Left/right borders

Table 7-2 provides the model fields and their weights, as well as field values and their partial scores. Weighted score regression types are explained in more detail via calculation scenarios presented in Table 7-3. The information appearing in Table 7-2 is to be used in the calculation scenarios in Table 7-3. In the scenarios presented, the weighted score regression type scores customers to identify potential buyers for a new cocktail beverage based on two attributes: where they live and how old they are (or model fields "dwelling" and "age," respectively). The definitions for weights and partial scores are:

- **Weight of model field** — The calculation for weighted scores is calculated at two levels. Weightings are made at the field level (weight of model field) and at the field values level (partial scores). This parameter is for the first level.

- **Partial scores** — Partial scores can be given per discrete value or by thresholds for continuous values. These entries are made per discrete value. All remainder values explicitly specified can be assigned a default partial score.

- **Threshold partial scores** — For continuous values, thresholds can be maintained for partial scores that effectively work as intervals.

Table 7-2 Example Customer Scores

MODEL FIELD	WEIGHT	CONTENT TYPE	VALUE/THRESHOLD VALUE	PARTIAL SCORE
Dwelling	2	Discrete	City	25
Dwelling	2	Discrete	Suburb	15
Dwelling	2	Discrete	Town	10
Dwelling	2	Discrete	Remaining values	5
Age	5	Continuous	0	0
Age	5	Continuous	21	50
Age	5	Continuous	31	35
Age	5	Continuous	41	15
Age	5	Continuous	65	5

Table 7-3 Example Calculation Scenarios for Weighted Scores

CUSTOMER PROFILE	FIELD VALUE PARAMETER	CALCULATION
35 year old, suburb dweller	Piecewise constant set (left border)	$(2 \times 15) + (5 \times 35) = 205$
21 year old, suburb dweller	Piecewise constant set (left border)	$(2 \times 15) + (5 \times 50) = 280$

Continues

Table 7-3 Example Calculation Scenarios for Weighted Scores *(continued)*

CUSTOMER PROFILE	FIELD VALUE PARAMETER	CALCULATION
35 year old, city dweller	Piecewise constant set (left border)	$(2 \times 25) + (5 \times 35) = 225$
35 year old, suburb dweller	Piecewise constant not set	$(2 \times 15) + (5 \times 25) = 155$
21 year old, suburb dweller	Piecewise constant not set	$(2 \times 15) + (5 \times 50) = 280$
35 year old, city dweller	Piecewise constant not set	$(2 \times 25) + (5 \times 25) = 175$
21 year old, rural dweller	Treat as separate instance is set	$(2 \times 5) + (5 \times 50) = 135$
70 year old, city dweller	Constant extrapolation (for outlier)	$(2 \times 25) + (5 \times 5) = 75$
70 year old, city dweller	Extrapolation (for outlier)	$(2 \times 25) + (5 \times 1) = 55$

There are three discrete values for the dwelling model field: city, suburb, and town. All remaining values are treated as their own separate discrete value. For age, the continuous values are defined by the following intervals: 0 to 21, 22 to 31, 32 to 41, 42 to 65, and over 65. Partial scores are assigned to each of these values or intervals in the scoring model.

How a calculation is actually performed is dependent on the field value parameters (Table 7-1). The parameters influencing the calculation are:

- **Function piecewise constant** — This setting is only for continuous values and, if set, partial scores are applied based on the ratchet values of the interval. Otherwise, partial scores are interpolated from the left and right borders of the interval.

- **Left/right borders** — This setting is only for piecewise constant values (does not apply to discrete values) and specifies whether the left or right border is included in a numeric interval.

- **Outlier treatment** — How the system handles outliers can be controlled. For discrete values, outliers are any values not explicitly addressed. For continuous values, outliers are any values outside the threshold limits. You configure how outliers are treated by picking one of these options: "Treat as separate instance," "Cancel processing," "Ignore record," "Set default score," "Constant extrapolation," or "Extrapolation." The first option is only for discrete values where all outliers are treated as one value. The last two extrapolation options are only available for continuous values.

Table 7-3 illustrates how weighted score calculations are influenced by the aforementioned field value parameters. The formula for the weighted score calculation is the sum of the weight of the model fields times the partial scores of their respective field values.

All regression types support how missing values are treated. As a default, the system handles spaces or zeros as missing values. However, if an explicit value represents a missing value (for example, 9999), this value can be specified. For example, this might be useful when a distinction between null values and a zero value is needed for key-figure values. If missing values are found, the system reaction is configured to either stop processing, ignore the record, set a default score, or replace the value. A replacement value must be given for the last option.

Clustering

The clustering method groups data into segments based on associations among different characteristics in data. For example, an insurance company might want to identify the potential market for a new policy by segmenting their customer base according to attributes such as income, age, risk categories, policy types, and claims history. Clustering divides a set of data so that records with similar content are in the same group, while records with dissimilar content are in different groups.

Clustering is also known as *segmentation*, as the relationships it finds can be used to identify customer or market segments. For example, clustering might identify customers susceptible to specific marketing campaigns based on specific attributes or behaviors, like a book club searching for a cluster of customers that may be interested in home improvement or gardening books. Clustering might have determined the different customer profiles presented in Table 7-2. Because the categories of clustering are unknown before clustering is performed, it has also been referred to as unsupervised learning or knowledge discovery. The results of its discovery (for example, identified and validated customer segments) may then be stored to master data and may be passed on to other CRM analysis such as CLTV.

The configuration of clusters is straightforward. Configuration controls how many clusters should be generated and specifies criteria for pruning the calculation for enhanced quality and performance.

For example, a numeric threshold can be set for a model field so that if the number of distinct values in that field is exceeded, the additional records are ignored in the calculation. This improves the trainability and performance of the model, because if a model field with high cardinality is included for clustering, the system has to use more data from more dimensions to find associations. Other performance savers are putting a cap on the number of iterations to be performed on the data set, as well as defining a minimum threshold of change (expressed as fractions) required for clustering iterations to continue. If nothing much has changed, clustering stops.

For the model field parameters, weights can be assigned to skew clustering in favor of a particular field, as well as default replacement values for missing or initial values. Weights and treatment of missing values can also be controlled for individual discrete field values or continuous field value ranges. For model fields that contain continuous field values, there is an additional setting that influences the graphical view. The graphical view of clustering can be controlled by specifying the number of binning intervals for visualization. This has no impact on training the model. The binning intervals are broken into equal intervals between the minimum and maximum amounts. Each binning interval contains the frequency of values within the range.

Association Analysis

Association analysis is a type of dependency analysis and is sometimes also referred to as *market basket analysis* because of its heavy use in retail. However, there are practical applications in other industries such as a telecom company offering additional services to customers who have already bought a specific set of services.

Association analysis is used to develop rules for cross-selling opportunities. As a result, this data mining model has the unique output option of exporting the association rules it calculates to operational CRM (to applications such as the customer interaction center). The association analysis generates Boolean logic rules such as the famous association "If it is Friday, then male buyers of diapers also purchase beer."

To configure association analysis and understand its output, you must first understand certain data mining terms:

- **Support** — This is a percentage of how often a collection of items in an association appears. For example, five percent of the total purchases at an airport sundry shop support the sale of both toothbrush and toothpaste.

- **Confidence** — From a statistical perspective, confidence has a close association with conditional probability. It is the percentage likelihood that a dependent item occurs in a data set when a lead item has occurred. For the diapers (lead item) and beer (dependent item) association, confidence could be expressed as a 50 percent probability of beer being purchased given a sale of diapers. This number is observational rather than predictive.

- **Lift** — This is a measure of the effectiveness of an association analysis by taking the ratio of the results with and without the association rule. Lift can be used to eliminate records that do not have a true association but are picked up in the analysis because they appear frequently. More explicitly, lift is confidence divided by support for a given association. The actual mathematical formula the system applies is as follows: Lift is equal to the actual support of the lead and dependent items divided by the ratio of actual support for lead item to actual support of dependent item. Fractions are used in the equation rather than percentages.

The configuration curtails the association analysis by excluding records that fall below specified minimums for support, confidence, and lift or that fall above the maximums for the number of leading and dependent items used in any given association rule. These configuration settings improve performance and understandability of the association rules generated.

The model fields configuration for this analysis does not contain any parameters, although the content types are different, consisting of items, transactions, and transaction weights (instead of key, discrete, and continuous values).

Note that SAP appears to be taking a neutral approach to data mining algorithms. While they are delivering a core set of data mining methods, they are providing plenty of room in the sandbox for others to play. This is accomplished via mining interfaces that allow third-party data mining engines (such as IBM's Intelligent Miner, KXEN, SAS, and so on) to integrate into SAP's platform when standard methods are not sufficient. There is an ability to select external data as a source and run an external transformation (read as Data Mining Model) in the APD. While it would be nice to see SAP export its trained models for embedding in non-SAP systems, this flexibility hopefully will be forthcoming. Note that SAP supports interface standards for data mining such as the data mining extensions to OLE-DB and the Predictive Modeling Markup Language (PMML) for exchanging data models and result sets among different data mining engines.

NOTE For readers with investments in IBM's Intelligent Miner, transaction code `MINING_IBM` will take you to the customization options for integration with SAP BW.

More Analytic Services

A handful of analytic services are delivered with the BI capabilities of NetWeaver that are performed outside of the traditional Analytic Processing Engine and the APD data mining transformations. It is a common misconception (most likely promoted by competing vendors) that SAP BW supports only OLAP. This is not the case. As discussed in Chapter 9, tabular reporting, formatted reporting, and what could be categorized as generic analytical services are all supported. Examples of the so-called generic analytical services are customer lifetime value analysis (CLTV) and recency, frequency, and monetary (RFM) value analysis for campaign optimization.

There are also specialized transactions to configure analytic engines for RFM analysis and CLTV analysis. While these engines were designed to be used as part of SAP CRM, you do not have to install SAP CRM, although some calculations would lose their relevancy outside the CRM context. (Note that CRM data can also be furnished by non-SAP systems.) RFM and CLTV analysis stores the results of its calculations to Business Content DataStore Objects. These DataStore Objects need to be activated before these specific analytic techniques may be configured. CLTV analysis may be accessed via the command code RSAN_CLTV. Entering this in the OK command box takes you to the CLTV Modeling functionality. A prerequisite for this functionality is the availability and activation of ODS objects 0CRM_OLVM and 0CRM_OLVF.

Customer Lifetime Value Analysis

Customer lifetime value analysis goes a step beyond customer profitability analysis. It treats customers as investments and calculates their net present value depending on projections of the lifetime profitability of the customer. Predicted customer profitability and the predicted relationship life span of the customer are the primary factors for the analysis. Maximum lifetime profit for minimum investment is sought via CLTV analysis. The costs of acquiring and keeping a customer must be evaluated by the stream of profits the customer is expected to bring. The concepts applied here are similar in spirit to financial investment theory (albeit simplified). During the customer lifecycle, four types of customer interaction take place:[1]

- **Engage** — Finding prospects and turning them into customers
- **Transact** — Actually selling the customer products and/or services
- **Fulfill** — Delivering products and services
- **Service** — Keeping the customer happy through customer care

These interactions take place in a circular pattern in multiple cycles during the different stages of the customer engagement lifecycle evaluated in CLTV analysis (depending on the industry). In a sense, CLTV integrates the costs and revenues from customer interactions over several engage, transact, fulfill, and service (ETFS) cycles into a more or less homogeneous, time-variant profit curve.

The CLTV analysis engine is configured via a menu transaction for a customer value analysis role. The transaction is composed of configuring the CLTV model, its calculation settings, and then its prediction settings.

The CLTV calculation is centered on key figures for customer retention rates and customer profitability. Customer profitability can be sourced from CO-PA (mySAP ERP profitability analysis). Retention rates are sourced from queries or calculations. If rates are calculated, parameter settings must specify the number of periods for which data can be missing for a customer before that customer is deemed lost. When the CLTV engine finds no data for a given customer for the specified number of periods, it factors the lost customer into its retention rate calculation.

---

[1] SAP AG. 2001. "Analytical CRM." p. 7, SAP white paper, www.sap.com

CLTV calculations are done per customer segment (the segment is arbitrary but most typically comes from data mining clustering) per lifetime period. A lifetime period represents phases in a customer lifetime typically spanning years. Both the customer segment and the lifetime period are configured into the CLTV model.

Consequently, the query specified as the source for CLTV analysis must contain characteristics representing the customer, the customer segment (attribute of customer), and the period. Key figures for profit and customer retention can be delivered in the same or separate queries. Additionally, a special InfoObject must be an attribute of customer representing a "customer since" date used as the starting point that marks the beginning of a customer relationship. These InfoObjects have to be explicitly configured into the calculation settings.

NOTE Refer to InfoObject 0BPARTNER **and corresponding attribute** 0CRM_CUSSIN **as templates for customer and customer since date, respectively.**

Manual entries can be made for additional costs not picked up in the query sources as well as any other adjustments for the CLTV calculation. Furthermore, new entries can be manually entered into the CLTV calculation if data is missing. This can be an alternative to using queries for sourcing the data. The results of manual entries, data collection via queries, and the actual calculation are stored to Business Content DataStore Objects. Additionally, the results can be forwarded to the customer interaction center of operational CRM via a CRM alert modeler. Lastly, CLTV predictions can be performed based on the data stored to the CLTV DataStore objects.

The CLTV calculation itself calculates two key figures: CLTV and discounted CLTV (the difference being a discount factor applied to the second key figure for its net present value). The discount factor is configured in the CLTV model. In this example, the discount was 10 percent (Figure 7-3). When used in conjunction with prediction, these key figures can then be compared to the estimated cost of acquisition to determine if a customer in a given segment is worth it. How the cumulated retention rate and CLTV is calculated is provided in Table 7-4. These calculations and values relate to the CLTV model depicted in Figure 7-3.

The CLTV analysis starts its calculation on the execution date. If prior periods need to be picked up in the calculation, this can be configured in the calculation settings. The number of lifetime periods created depends on the time span of the source data and the length of the lifetime period. All customers in the query source can be considered or just the new customers. New customers are calculated by looking at the "customer since" attribute of the customer, determining the starting month of the calculation, and referencing a special configuration setting. The setting in question is the number of months from the start of a calculation that a customer can be considered "new." Restricting a CLTV calculation to new customers simplifies the results of the calculation and gives a picture of the complete customer lifecycle.

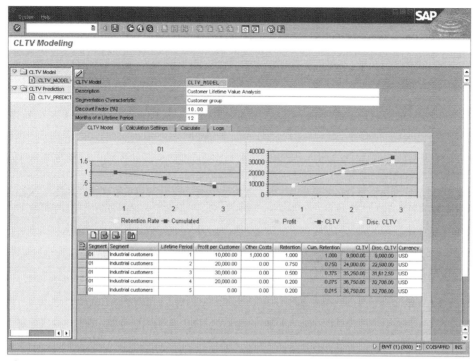

Figure 7-3   CLTV modeling

Table 7-4   CLTV Example Calculations

LIFETIME PERIOD PROFIT	RETENTION	CUM. RETENTION	CLTV	
1	9,000	1.000	1.000	9,000
2	20,000	0.750	0.750 = 1.000?0.750	24,000 = 9,000 + (0.750 × 20,000)
3	30,000	0.500	0.375 = 0.750?0.500	35,250 = 24,000 + (0.375 × 30,000)
4	20,000	0.200	0.075 = 0.375?0.200	36,750 = 35,250 + (0.075 × 20,000)
5	35,000	0.200	0.015 = 0.075?0.200	37,275 = 36,750 +(0.015 × 35,000)

When you are executing CLTV prediction, the calculation determines how many customers are retained and the expected profit on the remaining customers. When configuring the CLTV prediction, you must specify the number of lifetime periods to predict, as well as the query source. The query source of the CLTV model can be used for prediction, or a new query can be specified. The new query must have the same definition as the CLTV model query source, as well as contain the same segments. If data is missing, an option exists to reuse data from the last CLTV calculation.

RFM Analysis

RFM analysis evaluates the recency, frequency, and monetary value of customer purchases to determine the likelihood that a given customer will respond to a campaign. It is an empirical method that has long been applied to campaign planning and optimization as an alternative to segmenting a customer base by less-effective demographic means. The results of RFM analysis provide marketing departments the financial justification for specific marketing campaigns. RFM analysis provides the measurements for success from both planned and actual perspectives. The RFM analytic engine performs two processes:

- **Segmentation** — Similar to clustering, RFM analysis segments customers into different target groups. The main distinction is that RFM analysis is focused on specific aspects of customer behavior, namely:

  - **Recency** — When was the last purchase made? The most recent customers are sought based on the assumption that most-recent purchasers are more likely to purchase again than less-recent purchasers.

  - **Frequency** — How often were purchases made? The most frequent customers are sought based on the assumption that customers with more purchases are more likely to buy products than customers with fewer purchases.

  - **Monetary value** — What was the amount of the purchase? The biggest-spending customers are sought based on the assumption that purchasers who spent the most are more likely to purchase again than small spenders.

- **Response rate calculation** — Once segments have been established, the response rates for each customer segment is calculated based on historical data of actual response rates of past campaigns. The results of the response rate are then saved to Business Content DataStore Objects and can then be passed on to the Segment Builder tool in SAP CRM. The Segment Builder models target groups by specifying attributes and building customer profiles for use in marketing activities such as running a campaign.

For the analysis to be effective, representative data must be used from prior campaigns. A campaign is considered sufficiently similar if the nature of the campaign and the customer target groups hold similar attributes. If historical data cannot be found for the representative target group, investments in learning must be made by launching new campaigns targeting the desired representative group so that RFM analysis can be applied. Using random, nonrepresentative data for RFM analysis can render it useless.

The process of RFM analysis is configurable, and the settings for the calculation are accessed via a transaction in the roles-based menu for a campaign manager.

To segment the customers, the system has to know which customers to segment, how many RFM segments to determine, and where to get the values for RFM analysis. This is controlled via the segmentation model settings. The customer values used for segmentation are represented by the InfoObject for business partner. The business partner determination is made either via a query source or directly from the business partner master data for all business partners identified as customers. If the source of the business partner is a query, the available characteristics in the query have to be assigned to the model field for customer.

The number of segments for recency, frequency, and monetary value has to be set separately. The system will segment each based on the value configured (the default is five). The segmentation starts with recency, then frequency, and finally monetary value. First, customers are ranked into recency segments and given a score based on the number of segments. Within recency segments, frequency segments are then ranked and scored. Finally, within frequency segments, monetary value scores are determined. Figure 7-4 illustrates the RFM segmentation process.

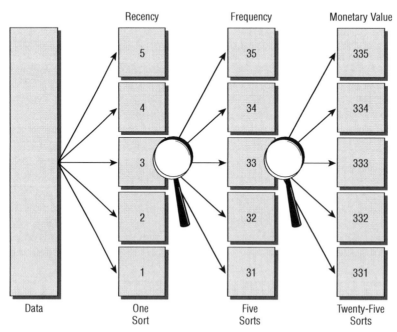

Figure 7-4 RFM segmentation process

Another consideration is the number of segments created vis-à-vis the number of records available and their impact on the response rate accuracy. For example, if the defaults of five segments per RFM were configured, 125 segments would be calculated ($5 \times 5 \times 5 = 125$). Out of a customer base of 1,250,000 (10,000 customers per segment), one response would affect the response rate calculated by a hundredth of a percent (1/10,000). Out of a customer base of 1,250 (10 customers per segment), the difference of one response could swing the response rate by 10 percent. For smaller customer bases, the number of segments should be decreased. There are two options for handling customers that do not have data for the evaluation periods under consideration. The first option is the default, where those customers fall to the bottom of the RFM analysis in the segment with the score of 111. The second option is to place these customers into a special segment with a score of 000 so that they fall out of the RFM analysis entirely (preventing any skewing of the segmentation results if there are enough customers missing data).

The queries used for the source of the RFM analysis must contain characteristic and key figures that map to the RFM segmentation model fields, namely business partner, RFM recency date, RFM frequency value, RFM monetary value, and currency key. A separate query can be mapped to each RFM key figure, or one query can cover all three. After these settings have been maintained in the RFM model, the segmentation can be executed, and response rates can be calculated.

For the response rate model, an RFM segmentation model must be assigned. Additional settings must be specified before you execute the calculations, such as whether or not the response rates should be viewable via the SAP CRM Segment Builder and the query sources for the representative target group and responding customers. During the response rate calculation, the first query is read to determine the campaign, the campaign start date, and the target customers, which are then segmented based on the RFM segmentation model. The second query selects the responding customers to each campaign. The response rate calculation outputs the RFM segment codes (for example, 335), the number of customers addressed (from the first query), the number of responses (from the second query), and the calculated response rates. This data is also written to a Business Content DataStore Object and is available via Business Content queries to check how effective the RFM analysis was in tying high response rates to the top-ranked RFM segments.

Report-to-Report Interface

The *Report-to-Report Interface* (RRI) is a feature that enables information surfing. The RRI works in a similar way as Internet surfing, where the user jumps from one page to another, following a path of predefined links from one Web page to the next. End users of queries may jump from one query to another query. The RRI enables linking information based on the context of an end user's analysis path. For example, a sales manager may be analyzing her most profitable customers in a given year and from the profitability query jump to an accounts receivable query to analyze payment behavior. In doing so she may find that her most profitable customer is indeed not as profitable as first thought, because of the drain on cash flow and increase in interest expense. The unique feature with the RRI is the ability to pass the context of the sending query — in this case, the specific customer number the sales manager analyzed the profitability of — to the receiving query as an input parameter. The RRI sender-receiver assignments are maintained in the Data Warehouse Workbench, which is not technically a part of the BEx Query Designer. The BEx Analyzer and the Web application's context menu use the *Go To* options in the context menu or toolbar to initiate the RRI.

The RRI is possible because of the common metadata definitions. The metadata objects in the sending query will be matched to the metadata objects in the receiver. When a characteristic is common in the sender and receiver, the value from the sender will be passed into the receiver if the receiver has a variable or input parameter. The RRI may help to avoid the problem of having particularly large or long-running reports, since information modelers may use a summarized report and still provide drill-down functionality into a more detailed query or transaction in mySAP ERP. For example, you may have modeled your master data attributes in such a way that they are not necessarily representing the current value (refer to Chapters 4 and 5 for information modeling options), but query users want to view or even maintain the master data for a certain characteristic. This may be accomplished by defining a receiver object for a query or InfoProvider that calls the appropriate maintenance transaction in mySAP ERP.

RRI allows you to call from a query (sender) to another object (receiver) by maintaining a sender-receiver assignment. The receiver may be any one or several of the following objects:

- BEx Query
- BEx Web Application
- Crystal Formatted Report
- InfoSet Query
- Transaction
- ABAP Report
- Web Address (URL)

Receiver objects may be located on remote systems or in the same logical system as the sending object. The technical settings on the remote system must be established with transaction SM59 so that the RRI will recognize the system as one with potential receiver objects. This functionality helps to support the scenario, where, for example, you have an InfoProvider for the finance department that contains highly summarized data and a central data warehouse layer with detailed transactional-level data. A query built on an InfoProvider in the finance area may contain data at the month/period level of detail. The central data warehouse layer may contain the daily detail data. The receiver object in this case may be called when a specific analysis path requires details of the transactions that occurred within a month. This type of drill-through to the daily records (query built on DataStore Object) from a summarized report (query built on InfoCube) is not uncommon.

As previously mentioned, mySAP ERP transactions and ABAP reports are valid receiver objects. However, jumping back to mySAP ERP might cause a few challenges. The metadata and Business Content in SAP BW has been transformed from the metadata that exists in ERP. This poses a bit of a challenge for drilling through to mySAP ERP, but in most cases, it is achievable without coding a customer exit or routine. One of the preconditions for jumping back to an ERP receiver object is that the data loaded into SAP BW was loaded through an InfoSource. The process of drilling back through to the ERP system uses a kind of reverse metadata and data transformation in order to determine the appropriate field mapping to pass into and the appropriate characteristic values. Only trivial data transformations can automatically be reversed. Complex transformation rules may need assignment details maintained with the expert function. In previous software releases, two customer exits were used in situations where not all of the information from the InfoSource definition was able to be derived: EXIT_SAPLRSBBS_001 and EXIT_SAPLRSBBS_002. The first exit was used for the metadata transformation and the second for the data transformation.

Currency Conversion

Support for foreign currency translation has always been one of the strengths of SAP. There are two primary places where currency translation is possible: during the update of a data target via the transformation rules as briefly described in Chapter 6 and during analysis and reporting. Currency translation during analysis and reporting also has two options: during query definition and ad hoc while analyzing a query. Readers familiar with the currency translation options and configuration found in mySAP ERP will recognize the terminology, configuration tables, and functionality.

Currency translation is the seemingly simple process of taking a specific value represented in a specified source currency, retrieving an exchange rate, and calculating the new value in a target currency. For example, revenue recorded in EUR may be translated into USD by looking up the exchange rate for the two currencies at a given time and multiplying the source currency by the exchange rate to determine the target currency. Figure 7-5 shows the four parameters that must be defined or derived to perform a currency conversion: source currency, target currency, translation date, and exchange rate type.

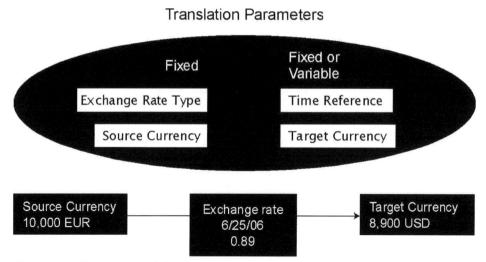

Figure 7-5 Currency translation

Several currency translations may be defined or applied to the same query. During query design time, a translation may be defined for each structure or key figure (restricted or calculated). During query execution, a business analyst may right-click and select from the context menu the currency translation option. From there, the analyst can select the currency translation type and target currency.

As is the case with mySAP ERP, SAP BW has a configuration table where exchange rates from one currency to another are stored with an effective date. This is referred to as an *exchange rate type*. Exchange rate types are fixed values. The next parameter is the source currency. The *source currency* is a characteristic value assigned to a specific key figure InfoObject in an InfoProvider. The currency of a key figure InfoObject may be fixed or assigned for each unique data record loaded into a data target, depending on the InfoObject definition in the Meta Data Repository. Regardless of the key figure InfoObject definition, the InfoProvider will send records to the Analytic Processing Engine for each key figure of type Amount. Query users will see this referred to as database currency in the BEx Analyzer.

Currency translation may be established explicitly during query design time or ad hoc during query analysis. The next two parameters may have their values dynamically set. The time reference and target currency may vary depending on the values present in the context of a query navigation state. Table 7-5 highlights the options available for defining or deriving all four of the parameters.

While the currency conversion functionality is quite powerful because of its flexibility, many organizations opt to design currency translation into the information model. In other words, they chose to store the data pretranslated as of a given time in a specific key figure.

Table 7-5   BEx Currency Translation Options

TRANSLATION PARAMETERS	PLACE DEFINED OR DERIVED	QUERY DESIGN OPTION	AD HOC OPTION
Source currency	Key figure in data record	X	X
Target currency	Fixed in trans. Type	X	X
	InfoObject attribute	X	
	Variable entry	X	X
Exchange rate	Fixed in rate tables	X	X
Time reference	Fixed date in trans. Type	X	X
	Current date	X	X
	Time characteristic value	X	

Conditional Analysis

Conditional result set processing allows the end user to limit the information returned to the query view to only the records that meet specific conditions (for example, a condition may be set to display only the top 10 customers from a revenue perspective or the bottom 15 percent of all employees based on their latest performance review). Conditions are an efficient way to zoom in on a specific subset of information.

A single query may have one or more conditions assigned to it, and a condition may have multiple preconditions assigned to it. Six condition types are applied to levels of navigational states:

- Top N
- Top percentage
- Top sum
- Bottom N
- Bottom percentage
- Bottom sum

When applied, the *top percentage* and *bottom percentage* and *absolute count* condition types act as their names imply. They reduce the list to display an absolute number, say the top 10 customers, from our revenue example and display the results line for the amount of revenue for all customers or a percentage. The percentage option works in a similar manner. In our performance review example, the scores would be looked at as a percentage of the total, and those with scores in the bottom 15 percent would be listed individually.

The *top sum* and *bottom sum* are a bit different from the percentage and absolute count. The top sum, for example, has a threshold set for a particular key figure. If you use the example of revenue as for the top 10 customers, this time you would set the condition not to the number of customers you are looking to analyze but to the amount of revenue for which you are looking. Let's assume 100,000 EUR. All of the customers would be sorted according to their revenues, in descending order. Moving down the list, customers would be selected and listed in the condition until the point that the 100,000 EUR total revenue threshold was broken. The customer that breaks the threshold is included in the list.

Along with the ability to create ranking lists, query designers and analyzers can create absolute lists that set thresholds that will either include or exclude individual rows of a query based on whether or not they meet the condition. For example, to support a physical inventory, a query may be set with a condition that displays all inventory positions that have negative stock quantities. Note that conditions may also be defined for combinations of characteristics — for instance, "show me the top 10 product/customer combinations."

There are also so-called *threshold conditions*. A condition row may be derived by evaluating a query structure and applying an operator and a value. For example, a condition may be set to show all customers that have revenue greater than $1 million. Eight threshold conditions may be applied to levels of navigational states:

- Equal to
- Not equal to
- Less than
- Greater than
- Less than or equal to
- Greater than or equal to
- Between
- Not between

Exception Analysis

Exception reporting is a bit different from conditional filtering. Exceptions allow for predefined or ad hoc. This discussion will focus on predetermined rules to be applied to a query that indicate how information should be highlighted to show that a threshold has been achieved. Up to nine different colors may be assigned to values that cross an exception threshold. These colors, in hues of red, yellow, and green, may be used to identify deviations visually.

There are three main areas of exception reporting that you should be aware of: the setting of exceptions, the online evaluation of exceptions, and the background processing of exceptions. The primary difference between the online exceptions and the background exceptions is that online exceptions highlight deviations within a query output, whether in the BEx Analyzer or in Web Analyzer created with the BEx Web Applications Designer, but they do not allow for the automatic handling of notifications.

The background scheduling of exception reporting is done via the *Broadcaster*. In the Broadcaster, the exception definitions that have been set in the BEx Query Designer are scheduled for evaluation and broadcast output types are defined. The Broadcaster options are explored in detail later in this chapter. This discussion concentrates on defining exception evaluations.

Exceptions are defined in the BEx Query Designer while defining the global query properties. The query designer must make three primary settings. The first setting is the key figure that the exception is to be applied to. The second setting is the threshold values and the alert level that should be used to highlight the exception, should the threshold be reached. (As mentioned, nine unique alert levels may be set.) The third setting is the aggregation level and combination of characteristic values by which the threshold should be evaluated. Figure 7-6 shows the characteristic combinations or *cell restrictions*.

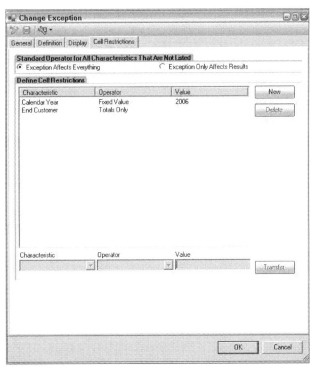

Figure 7-6 Exception definition

After the designer selects the appropriate characteristics, he or she must assign an operator for each characteristic. There are five options:

- **Totals Only** — The exception is only evaluated when a characteristic is aggregated.

- **Everything** — Exceptions are evaluated regardless of the level of aggregation for the characteristic.

- **Everything but Totals** — Exceptions are evaluated for nonaggregated values for a characteristic.

- **Fixed Values** — The exception is only evaluated for a preset characteristic value.

- **Hierarchy Level** — Exceptions are only evaluated for specific levels of a hierarchy.

A setting that query designers should be aware of is the default operator for all of the characteristics that do not have explicit cell restrictions defined. There are two options for characteristics that are not explicitly restricted: Totals Only or All. The *Totals Only* option is recommended when the key figure for the exception is an absolute number. The *All* option is recommended when the key figure for the exception is a relative number. The All setting is typically used for key figures that are percentages or ratios. The default operator is applied regardless of the drill-down level of the characteristics that are not explicitly defined in the exception.

The ability to set the operators by characteristic and to combine multiple characteristics enables query designers to create a powerful set of business rules that may be evaluated and subsequently trigger alerts via the Broadcaster. The triggering event is based on Broadcaster settings that determine if an exception has occurred or if one has occurred at a specific level of combined characteristics. Figure 7-7 shows exceptions as they may be viewed from the BEx Analyzer. If some of this seems a bit abstract, you may wish to return to this section after reading Chapter 8, which discusses the BEx tool suite.

Information Distribution

Information distribution takes on many forms in NetWeaver. This section discusses two primary options as related to the information distribution options found in the BI capabilities of NetWeaver. The discussion begins with information broadcasting and ends with the interface options available to presentation tools (delivered by SAP, custom developed, or purchased from a third-party software vendor). Figure 7-8 illustrates the information distribution services.

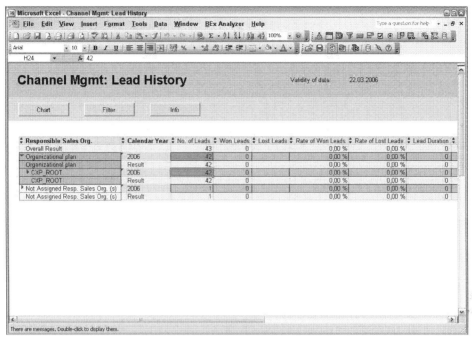

Figure 7-7 Displaying exceptions in the BEx Analyzer

Copyright © SAP AG

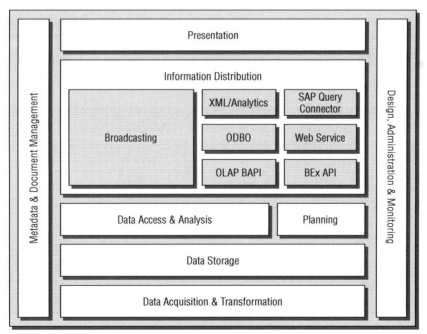

Figure 7-8 Distribution architecture

Broadcasting

The concept of information broadcasting has been realized in SAP software for more than a decade. It appeared as part of the Early Warning system in the Logistic Information Systems module of R/3 (now called mySAP ERP). The concept is to push information out to a person or group of people who will find the information relevant to their daily business so they may act upon the information and optimize business performance. SAP formally created a Broadcaster as part of the Business Explorer suite in the SAP BW 3.5 software release and has substantially developed the concept to what is now a powerful part of a comprehensive collaboration and knowledge management suite. The broadcasting capabilities support the precalculation or online distribution of information from BEx Queries, Query views, Web templates, Reports, and BEx Analyzer Workbooks to email recipients, the EP collaboration rooms and folders, printers, and more.

Broadcasting when used in conjunction with the knowledge management (KM) capabilities of NetWeaver enables the structured information often associated with BI tools to be utilized with, and as if it were, unstructured information. That is, KM features such as searching, discussing, providing feedback, subscribing, rating, application sharing, and so on are all available to business intelligence users.

The BEx Broadcaster may be accessed from various entry points, depending on the object you are attempting to distribute. Broadcaster settings may be maintained for each of the distribution objects supported. Distributable objects include the following:

- **Web template** — An HTML container for Web items (for example, grids, charts, and so on) that bind to queries or query views

- **Queries** — See the section, "Query Processing Overview," toward the beginning of this chapter.

- **Query Views** — See the section, "Query Processing Overview," toward the beginning of this chapter.

- **Workbooks** — An Excel container for BEx Analyzer Queries

- **Reports** — An HTML-structured layout and format for queries and queries views

From the Broadcaster, settings may be created, deleted, changed, scheduled, or executed immediately. The "settings" are named and scheduled for execution or immediately run. Once the settings are named, a distribution type is selected, which will determine the additional configuration options regarding recipients or destinations. For example, if the distribution type `email` is selected, recipient information will be requested, whereas distribution type `Enterprise Portal` will require information about the document that will be created or the collaboration room for which it is destined. Regardless of the distribution type selected, an output format will need to be set. Table 7-6 lists the output formats available for distributing information.

Table 7-6 Broadcaster Output Formats

FORMAT	DESCRIPTION
ZIP	Compressed file
PDF	Adobe's Portable Document Format
HTML	Hypertext Markup Language
MHTML	MIME encapsulation of aggregate HTML
PS/PCL	Postscript or Printer Control Language
URL	Universal Resource Locator is sent, which points to the object rather than a persistent file
MDX	The result set of a multidimensional expression
Exception	SAP alert is created and added to the Universal Work List (UWL)

The Broadcaster may be thought of as a calculation and publishing engine for BI objects (think Web templates) destined for the KM capabilities of NetWeaver. There are essentially three options when considering publishing Web templates:

- Calculated so that the pages are static
- Many views of the same Web template that may be generated and stored in the so-called precalculation stored as HTML documents
- Online links to live objects that may be published

While the first option precalculates HTML pages for Web templates, the second option precalculates data for Web templates, and the third option links back to live data.

Distribution Channels

There are several distribution channels supported by the Broadcaster, each able to be triggered in an ad-hoc, scheduled, or event basis. The following list contains the channels supported by the Broadcaster for distributing information.

- **Printer** — The Broadcaster is able to output to any printer that supports PS, PCL, or PDF. SAP has partnered with Adobe Systems and OEMd software to bring NetWeaver printing capabilities up to industry standards.

- **Email (with optional bursting)** — An email may be sent to any NetWeaver or non-SAP user with an attachment containing the object being broadcast (for example, Query). There is also an option to broadcast only the data in an object that is relevant to specific recipients, thereby showing them only their own data. A common example may be a national sales report that contains several regions. Regional sales directors would receive only the sales information for the regions for which they are responsible. This is used instead of specifying an email distribution list and is only possible if a master data attribute has stored the email address of the recipients (in this example, the regional sales directors).

- **SAP Alert** — The Broadcaster is integrated with the NetWeaver Central Alert Framework, which provides Portal users with a Universal Work List (UWL) in which to do, defer, or delegate business process work items. The idea behind the alert framework is that central management of all alerts generated by composite applications build on the NetWeaver integration platform.

- **Portal** — The KM features of the Portal combined with the analytic functions of the BI capabilities in NetWeaver bring services such as searching, discussing, providing feedback, subscribing, rating, instant messaging, Web conferencing, and application sharing to BI objects and users.

There is also the option for *multichannel distribution*. As the name implies, numerous distribution channels may be used simultaneously. This supports a scenario where a sales director may wish to have his or her report printed and on his or her desk every Monday morning but may also wish to have an electronic copy in email to support further analysis or collaboration.

Broadcast Timing

Unlike radio broadcasting (which sends its signal out to all receiving locations at once on a continuous basis), the Broadcaster in NetWeaver has a few more options:

- **Event driven** — The Broadcaster may be triggered based on system or administrative events. For example, you can evaluate an object type for possible distribution after data has been loaded into an InfoCube or a change is made to an InfoProvider.

- **Ad Hoc** — By using a so-called Broadcaster Wizard to initiate the distribution of objects, broadcasting may be initiated in an on-demand fashion. Information may be broadcast from the BEx design and presentation tools such as the Query Designer, BEx Analyzer, Web Application Designer, and Web Analyzer. This is typically found on the context menu when you are analyzing a query. For example, while analyzing a query, you may choose to send a colleague an email to seek explanation of an unusual figure. The Wizard would then be launched. From there, a few simple steps must be completed to distribute the query. The distribution type must be selected — in this case, email, the output format (for example, zipped HTML file), and the email content asking the colleague for assistance. It is also possible from the Broadcaster settings to execute objects in an ad-hoc fashion.

- **Scheduled** — Two methods of scheduling may be performed. The fist is *guided scheduling*, which is used to guide end users to execute broadcasts during predetermined, typically nonpeak times, so that system resources many be managed and balanced. These predefined times are set by the system's administrator. The other method is referred to as *flexible scheduling*, which is performed by administrators and/or power users and allows them to create jobs that run for a specific group of users. There is an option here to run the precalculations (described earlier in this chapter in the section, "More Analytic Services") based on the authorization profile of the target user of the information.

General Precalculation

It is in the general precalculation tab that settings related to how variables, exceptions, formatting themes, and navigation states should be handled when the Broadcaster is run. Depending on the object type being configured, the output format being broadcast, as well as the presentation tool being used at the time of distribution, these setting options will vary.

There are a few options for the transferring of navigation state when the Broadcaster is launched from a Web application. When queries are defined, they have an implied initial query view. The initial view is the first navigation state. As a user analyzes a query, the user navigates from one view to the next view and changes the navigation state. When the Broadcaster is called on to distribute a Web application, settings for transferring the existing navigation state or the default navigation state may be controlled.

The same concept holds true for the variables used to run the query. For example, a query may request the user to enter the period the user wants to analyze when the query is first launched. Queries may be defined to accept user input for variable values, as well as use a variant that has been preconfigured with values or even as a precalculated value set (described shortly). The settings for how the Broadcaster should handle variables are also configured in the Precalculation tab.

The settings for how Web applications that contain exception reporting also may be configured here. One option is to tell the Broadcaster to ignore the query's exception when precalculating or generating an online link. The other option is to indicate the level of exception that should be evaluated. For example, a query reporting gross revenue figures across North America should only be distributed if the region does not achieve its planned externally communicated revenue goals (think Wall Street), while the report may have exceptions set for the internally communicated tougher stretch revenue goals. In this case, if the internal revenue goals are not achieved, the report will not necessarily be broadcast. Up to nine alert levels may be configured as part of the exception functionality. The exception level (or a minimum level) may be set for the Broadcaster to evaluate and distribute accordingly.

Filter Navigation

There are situations where the same report should be run a number of times. For example, let's imagine that you have analyzed sales and identified the top five customers for the past month based on contribution margins achieved by selling to those customers. For each of these five customers, you would like to precalculate a detailed report listing order line items for each customer on a separate report. When preparing to distribute the line-item report, the Filter Navigation tab allows for the selection of specific characteristic values or the assignment of *control queries*. If the top five customers are known (as is the case in this example) at the time the Broadcaster is configured, you would simply select the customers from a list of characteristic values for the customer characteristic and a detailed order report would be run for each of the top five customers.

The `Control-query` option (if used) would determine the filter navigation values (formerly known as *bucket variables*) via another query. `Control queries` are ideal for scenarios where sophisticated condition logic must be applied for selection. For example, suppose you want to analyze if there is any correlation between the top ten customers for sales for last year and any exposure to late receivables this year. Two queries are devised: a top ten customers by sales query and an aged receivables query. The latter query uses a filter navigation that uses the former query as the `Control-query`. In this case, the first query must be executed before the second query has the customers to select its data against. In essence, the control query would run, determine the top 10 customers, and then use those ten characteristic values as a filter for the aged receivables report.

Technically, the `Control-query` is nothing more than a query without a key figure specified. Every characteristic combination in the rows of the `Control-query` serves to generate different views of data for the specified Web template.

Other Precalculation Functions

A few additional distribution types are available in the Broadcaster. While they may not exactly be distributing information, they play an important part in preparing data to be distributed. The same settings for broadcast timing, filter navigation, and general precalculation are applicable for the following distribution types:

- **Filling Precalculation Store** — A knowledge management folder where Web templates are stored as static HTML pages. Broadcaster settings ensure authorizations are adhered to for specific users.

- **Filling OLAP Cache** — This distribution type will cause the precalculation to fill the OLAP Cache with the goal of significantly reducing response times when users run queries, workbooks, reports, or Web applications that select data already in the cache.

- **Filling MDX Cache** — This distribution type will cause the precalculation to fill the MDX Cache, which is used by applications that call the OLAP BAPI. The cache is filled with an MDX result set. See the section "Interface Options for Third-Party Presentation Tools," later in this chapter, for further explanation).

- **Precalculating Value Sets** — Value sets are an alternative solution to using `Control-queries`. A *value set* is similar to a `Control-query` except the values are used to fill variables and are precalculated and stored and then may be shared across multiple queries. Value sets are used to fill variables of type `Precalculated Value Set` with values for characteristics. They are configured in the Broadcaster and use a special output format appropriately named value set. Value sets are typically used in scenarios where the characteristic values to be stored are used by many queries, or there is conditional logic in determining the characteristic values. Precalculated Value Sets may be used to replace variables that in former releases used the replacement path `from query`.

Interface Options for Third-Party Presentation Tools

SAP has come a long way in overcoming criticism that its software is only extensible by programming with its proprietary ABAP language and that it has closed or inaccessible APIs. Figure 7-9 shows the interfaces currently exposed for client programs to invoke. This section examines the interfaces available to third-party independent software vendors and Web application developers, as well as the interfaces used by the Business Explorer.

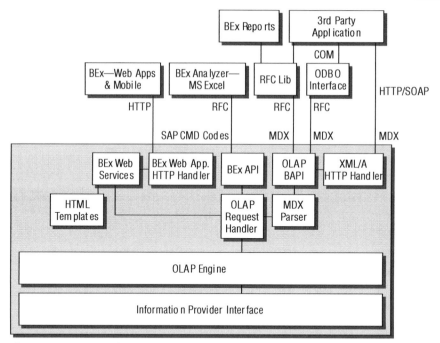

Figure 7-9   Integration options

There are three recommended methods for integrating so-called front-end presentation tools with SAP. The first method supported by SAP was the OLE DB for OLAP interface. This interface was published with the 1.2 release of the software, then named SAP BW, and gained wide acceptance by business intelligence tool vendors. However, this interface had several drawbacks, so a platform-independent business application programming interface (BAPI) was published with release SAP BW 2.0. While this interface provided greater flexibility in the choice of operating systems and platforms that the third-party tools could run on, it did not support access through HTTP. Next, the BEx Web API provided a command framework for accessing SAP BW information from a URL.

Note that regardless of the interface option chosen by the third-party software vendor, the Analytic Processing Engine performs the analytical processing and requests the data from the data provider as previously described in this chapter. The actual path that a request for data takes prior to arriving at the Analytic Processing Engine, however, is quite different.

NOTE ODBO is the acronym for the acronym OLE DB for OLAP or Object Link Embedding for Databases extended for Online Analytical Processing.

The connection protocols supported by SAP for third-party vendors to select from are COM, RFC, or HTTP. Most business intelligence tool vendors have chosen to support at least one of the protocols in order to meet the evolving demands of their customers. The leading business intelligence tool vendors support one or more of the interface protocols available for accessing SAP BW. For an up-to-date listing of certified vendors, refer to `www.sap.com/partners/software/directory`.

Now SAP NetWeaver extensively supports the use of the XML for Analysis (XML/A) and the Simple Object Access Protocols (SOAP) and provides a BI Java Software Development Kit (SDK). The BI Java SDK provides tools for Java developers to create applications that access SAP and non-SAP information. The SDK is composed of APIs and so-called "BI Connectors." The SDK assists developers in connecting to sources, accessing metadata, and handling query requests and responses from both relational and multidimensional sources. The connectors conform to J2EE Connector Architecture (JCA) standards and may be deployed on SAP Java WAS.

BI ODBO Connector — OLE DB for OLAP

To understand ODBO, you must first understand its foundation. OLE DB is a set of interfaces that Common Object Model (COM) objects expose to provide applications with uniform access to data regardless of the data's type or location (`www.microsoft.com/data/oledb/olap/faq.htm 2001`). The OLE DB protocol has consumers that request information and providers that provide information. The providers do so by exposing the interfaces of their objects to consumers. OLE DB for OLAP is the addition of two interfaces to the OLE DB protocol. These interfaces provide access to multidimensional data sources. The SAP ODBO driver is a provider in this protocol.

This major drawback in using OLE DB or its predecessor, the Open Database Connectivity Protocol (ODBC), is that they require a client component to be programmed to interface with a specific provider component. The provider component for SAP is delivered and installed on the client machine with the SAPGUI and SAP BW front-end add-on. The installation is necessary in order for the consumer application to access an SAP provider. This causes a number of client and server dependencies, such as version, platform, and in some cases programming languages.

Many of the third-party BI tools certified to this interface have run into significant challenges that prevent enterprises from fully deploying an alternative to the BEx front end. The challenges vary widely based on the architecture of the BI tool. The protocol definition left consumers and providers to interpret how certain functions should be supported. There were a few common areas where consumers and SAP, as the provider, had differing interpretations. For example, the support variable intervals, hierarchies, and calculated members were all different enough that either SAP or the BI vendors would need to rework their products or isolated portions of their products. These challenges limited the rollout of alternative front ends.

ODBO PROVIDER

There are two types of providers: data providers and provider services. The data provider owns data and exposes it to the consumer as a row set or table. The provider services make certain that data exposed by the BW server is returned to the third-party consumer, somewhat like a router sitting between a consumer and the ultimate data provider. The provider service in the case of BW is the mdrmsap.dll.

Several libraries and files are needed to support calls back to the SAP BW application server and to invoke an OLAP BAPI:

- `mdrmsap.dll` — The SAP BW OLE DB for OLAP Provider
- `librfc32.dll` — SAP/s main RFC library
- `wdtlog.ocx` — Dialog box for login parameters
- `mdrmdlg.dll` — Manager for the connection to an SAP system
- `mdxpars.dll` — Parser for multidimensional expressions so they may be sent to BW
- `scerrlklp.dll` — Error-handling routines

(*Source*: SAP AG ASAP for BW)

An enhancement to the level of protocol support by SAP has been encouraging and enabling third-party BI vendors to satisfy their clients and large installed bases with meaningful integration to SAP. When a third-party application requests data via the ODBO protocol, a mutidimensional expression (MDX) is used. One of the challenges application programmers familiar with MDX may have when working with SAP is terminology. SAP is notorious for creating new names for terms that are generally accepted in the industry. Table 7-7 contains a list of terminology differences between the Microsoft's OLE DB objects and SAP objects.

Table 7-7 OLE DB for OLAP Objects and SAP BW Objects

OLE DB FOR OLAP	SAP BW
Catalogs	InfoCubes
Schemas	Not Supported
Cubes	Query
Dimensions	InfoObjects (Characteristics)
Hierarchies	Hierarchies
Levels	Number Level or Name of Dummy Level
Members	Characteristic Values
Property	Display Attribute
Measures (Dimension)	Key Figures

SAP has included a tool to assist programmers in translating object definitions from one set paradigm to the next. Transaction code MDXTEST enables developers to test the result of their expression within the Data Warehouse Workbench. This transaction and other query-related administrational tools are briefly discussed in Chapter 11. If you are interested in more detailed information about how to write programs that access the ODBO interface, very detailed explanations may be found on the SAP public website at help.sap.com in the Business Intelligence section.

If you would simply like to execute queries from a certified third-party tool, keep the following in mind:

- Queries must first be defined in the BEx Query Designer. To date, it is not possible to create the query definition in the third-party tool.

- The BEx Query must be made available for OLE DB for OLAP. This is done during query design by selecting the Query Properties icon and checking the ODBO radio button.

- As of SAP BW version 3.0, it is possible to directly access an Info-Provider without first designing a BEx Query. A so-called *virtual query* that contains all characteristics and key figures of an InfoProvider is accessed in this case.

In the third-party tool, the end user would typically start by creating a query in that tool and selecting a data source. Selecting the SAP data source results in a list of BEx Queries (after the user has to be authenticated via the SAP login dialog). In the third-party tool, the end user will see the BEx Queries listed as cubes (the OLE DB terminology) with the naming convention <InfoCube name>/<Query name>. These cubes may be customized in the third-party tool by the end user but only within the framework of the originally defined BEx Query (that is, members and measures in the underlying InfoCube may not be added to the query cube by the third-party tool). Note that not all of the Analytic Processing Engine functions available in the BEx Analyzer are available via the ODBO protocol, and not all the ODBO functions are available in the BEx Analyzer.

NOTE If the BEx Query has not been released for OLE DB for OLAP, it will not be accessible via the OLAP BAPI, XML/A, or ODBO interfaces.

While the ODBO protocol has its advocates, it also has its critics. The tight coupling of client and server is not suitable for Web applications that are inherently stateless. This necessity (not to mention that the protocol is dependent on the Microsoft Windows platform) has caused the invention of additional integration options.

The BI ODBO Connector is delivered as part of the BI Java SDK and may be used to access SAP BI data, data stored in Microsoft Analysis Server, and Pivot-Table Services, as well as other vendors.

OLAP BAPI

There has been a bit of confusion about the number and type of OLAP engine interfaces that SAP supports. The confusion has been primarily caused by the term *OLAP BAPI*. When SAP first exposed the analytic functions of the OLAP engine, there was a recommended approach to integration: the OLE DB for OLAP interface (ODBO). As just described, application programmers would write to SAP's ODBO driver, and SAP would take care of the connection back to SAP BW and call the proper function via the OLAP API. The criticisms of the OLE DB of OLAP interfaces were varied, but the main issues were that the driver only supported Microsoft platforms and SAP's interpretation, and eventual extension, of the ODBO protocol was different from other vendors' interpretations. To alleviate platform concern, SAP decided to document and publish the OLAP API, thus turning it into a BAPI that would be supported through release changes. Up until SAP BW version 2.0 (when SAP added the B in front of API), vendors could write to the OLAP API, but they had no guarantee that SAP would not change the interface in subsequent releases. Figure 7-9 does not distinguish between the OLAP API and OLAP BAPI, as the latter is the more current terminology.

> **NOTE** Business Application Programming interfaces (BAPIs) are documented and supported methods of business objects that exist in SAP applications. BAPIs are the recommended method for integrating applications from independent software vendors with SAP applications.

You may notice in Figure 7-9 that all three supported connection protocols eventually access the OLAP BAPI. Two main groups of functions are supported by the OLAP BAPI. The first group is the browsing of metadata and master data. The second group is the fetching of data and execution of multi-dimensional expressions. The naming of the interfaces may be the cause of the confusion, since the ODBO, OLAP BAPI, and XML/A interfaces all access the OLAP BAPI. While XML for Analysis will probably become the interface of choice, ODBO has been a common method for third-party tools to integrate with the Analytic Processing Engine. Nearly all of the leading business intelligence tools on the market today have integrated their products with SAP BW via the ODBO interface and directly with the OLAP BAPI, as they both utilize the same object model and query request language (MDX).

Note that the ODBO interface calls the same underlying BAPIs that application programmers may call via the RFC libraries delivered by SAP. The primary difference is the amount of knowledge a programmer needs about the connectivity calls. With ODBO, the SAP BW-supplied driver abstracts many of the details, whereas the RFC library approach does not. While the interfaces have changed, the use of multidimensional expressions has remained constant. Table 7-8 highlights number of methods available via the OLAP BAPI.

Table 7-8   OLAP BAPI Methods

MDDATAPROVIDERBW	MDDATASETBW
GetCatalogs	CheckSyntax
GetCubes	CreateObject
GetDimensions	DeleteObject
GetHierarchies	FindCell
GetLevels	FindTuple
GetMeasures	GetAxisData
GetMembers	GetAxisInfo
GetProperties	GetCellData
GetVariables	SelectData

As is often the case, the added flexibility and breadth of functionality available when the BAPI is accessed directly comes at the cost of learning these methods. There are two business objects that contain the methods. The first is called MDDataProviderBW and exposes functions for browsing metadata and master data. The second is called MDDataSetBW and exposes functions for the retrieval of multidimensional result sets.

While it may seam a burden to learn the OLAP BAPI when written to directly form custom ABAP developments, the BAPI enables powerful applications to be created on any of the platforms SAP supports. It should be noted that a specific Unicode code page may be defined by the client application. While application programmers who want to utilize the BI Java SDK may at first glance be disappointed to learn there is no BI OLAP BAPI Connector, the next section shows how the same may be accomplished via XML/A.

BI XMLA Connector – XML for Analysis

XML for Analysis (XML/A) was originally defined by Microsoft and Hyperion Solutions and is said to advance the concepts of OLE DB that utilizes SOAP, XML, and HTTP. Since OLE DB is based on the Common Object Model

(COM) and XML/A is based on the Simple Object Access Protocol (SOAP), programmers must adapt their existing ODBO application to support XML/A. The communication API is designed to standardize access to an analytical data provider (OLAP and data mining) over the Web. It attempts to overcome the shortfalls of ODBO by decoupling the consumer and the provider. While ODBO was designed to standardize data access across data sources, and to some extent it did so, the technique required a client component to be deployed in order to expose COM or Distributed COM (DCOM) interfaces. XML/A is designed to eliminate this constraint.

The OLAP BAPI serves as a basis for the XML/A interface. The Web application requesting data from the SAP BW Application Server first passes through a so-called XML/A *request handler*. The request handler validates the inbound request, parses it, and passes the request to the OLAP BAPI. Both XML/A and ODBO send MDX commands to the OLAP BAPI and an MDX parser. The parser takes care to transform the expression into a format that the Analytic Processing Engine understands (that is, ABAP). Once parsed, the request is sent to the request handler, which in turn invokes the Analytic Processing Engine. The ABAP is generated and the appropriate InfoProvider is called.

In Figure 7-10, the provider Web service and data source represent a SAP system. Since SAP BI software is built into SAP NetWeaver, all necessary technology underpinnings are in place for organizations to expose BI-based, Unicode-supported Web services. Organizations would only need to describe the Web services they wish to expose to their trading partners by creating an XML document called a Web Services Description Language (WSDL) and registering the document with a Universal Discovery, Description, and Integration (UDDI) directory. Loosely coupled, stateless applications may run across platforms in a language-independent environment.

The BI XMLA Connector is available as part of the BI Java SDK and may be used to access any XML/A-compliant data sources from vendors such as SAP, Microsoft (Analysis Server), Hyperion, and MicroStrategy.

Web-Based Options for Query Data Access

When SAP first released the then-called SAP BW version 3.0, they made significant advancements in BI services supported by Internet protocols. New SAP BW web-based query access services are the greatest example of this. The Internet Communication Framework (ICF) takes care of requests from Web browsers or mobile devices that send requests via the Hypertext Transfer Protocol (HTTP). The services route the requests to the Analytic Processing Engine, which retrieves and assembles the request for delivery back to the requesting device (browsers, mobile phones, personal digital assistants, and so on). At that time, there were two options for custom web-based developments: the Web

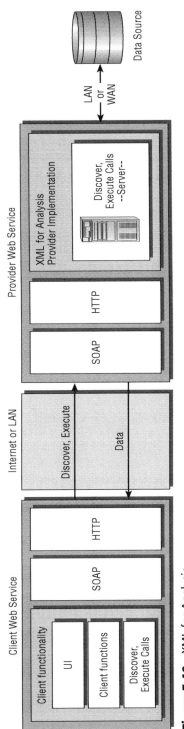

Figure 7-10 XML for Analysis
Source: Microsoft Corporation

Design API or XML/A. The Web Design API retrieves generated HTML at runtime (so-called web items) via URL requests while XML/A retrieves BI data via MDX statements. SAP left third-party Web application developers and independent software vendors (ISVs) confronted with an interesting option. They could use the BEx Web Design API or XML/A utilizing the OLAP BAPI to encapsulate the functionality of the Analytic Processing Engine in their products without creating a maintenance and upgrade nightmare for themselves and their customers. Back then, there was no statement from SAP on its intent to support the BEx Web Design API and its commands and parameters through release changes (as it does with its BAPIs). In addition to XML/A, SAP now provides an option to retrieve query data accessed through the BEx Web Design API for tables as a Web service. Unlike XML/A, an MDX statement is not utilized when retrieving Query views.

ICF services work with a request handler that receives requests from devices, validates those requests, and routes them to SAP BW services. Once the SAP BI services component receives a request, it disassembles it into its component parts, thereby separating content from format. The data requests for information are routed to the Analytic Processing Engine or a cache. When the Analytic Processing Engine returns the result set to SAP BI services, formatting and construction of the Web components are assembled. For example, say the Analytic Processing Engine retrieves a list of the top 10 customers for a given period. The requesting Web-based application asks for the results to be displayed as a bar chart. The Web Design API takes care of rendering the results in this format.

The Web service for accessing query data (through the Web Design Item for tables) may be created, released, and described for a query, query view, or the status description of a navigation step. The Web service uses an XML schema that corresponds to the aforementioned BEx Web API. To utilize this feature, transaction WSCONFIG must be called and the query_view_data service selected during the services definition. The path for the Web service is typically set to <Protocol>://<Server>:<Port>/sap/bw/xml/soap/queryview. When released for external usage, the WSDL may be retrieved by adding &wsdl to this path.

SAP Query Connector

SAP Query is a service that exists as part of NetWeaver and allows for queries to be created without ABAP programming knowledge. Formerly, this utility was referred to as ABAP Query. The SAP Query Connector is a part of the BI Java SDK that allows Java programmers to call existing queries from Java programs. This enables customer Java BI applications to include transactional data found in mySAP ERP or other applications created on the NetWeaver platform written in ABAP.

BI JDBC Connector

The BI JDBC Connector has been included in this section of the book, but you may have noticed the absence of the fourth connector in the BI Java SDK. Sun's Java Database Connectivity (JDBC) is generally accepted as the standard Java API for accessing relational database management systems (RDBMS). This API is incarnated as a driver much like the Open Database Connectivity (ODBC) protocol has done for years now on Microsoft operating systems. While the a JDBC Connector is typically used to cross various platforms and database formats (such as DB2, Microsoft SQL Server, Microsoft Access, Microsoft Excel, Oracle, Teradata, and even text file formats), the BI JDBC Connector may also be used to make available data stored external to SAP to the analytic engines within SAP. This is accomplished by utilizing the UD Connect option detailed in Chapter 6. So, while not exactly an interface option for third parties trying to access NetWeaver, it is available to draw information from JDBC-accessible sources.

The Business Explorer API

The Business Explore suite is discussed in detail in Chapter 8. Like the third-party interface options, the BEx tools have also evolved and undergone naming changes. The *BEx API* connects the BEx Analyzer and Web applications to the Analytic Processing Engine, allowing access to queries. The BEx API is not an open interface available to be used by other applications. Because it is not a BAPI, the BEx API is subject to change from one SAP BW release to the next. SAP has come under some criticism from leading business intelligence tool vendors for not exposing all of the functionality found in the BEx API in the OLAP BAPI. However, this was primarily a result of the loose interface definition by Microsoft. In fact, the OLAP BAPI has extended support for certain hierarchy, variable, and time functions. The BEx API, unlike the OLAP BAPI, supports a proprietary set of command codes in place of the multidimensional expressions used in the OLAP BAPI.

> **NOTE** SAP and Crystal Decisions (acquired by Business Objects) had integrated Crystal Reports with SAP BW utilizing the BEx API. It is unlikely that SAP will continue development partnerships utilizing this API.

There are two primary services that the Business Explorer front-end components utilize: the BEx API and the BEx Web API. The BEx API is nearly analogous to the OLAP BAPI; however, the interface is closed and utilized only by the BEx tools. The development philosophy appears to be first developing additional functionality for the Business Explorer components and then exposing those interfaces (if possible) through the OLAP BAPI.

The BEx API enables the BEx Query Designer to access metadata about Info-Providers and, as its name implies, the creation of queries. The BEx API also services the runtime requests generated by the BEx Analyzer as end users request query views and analytic functions. The BEx API, like the OLAP BAPI, interacts with the OLAP request handler so that it may send and receive commands to and from the Analytic Processing Engine. The most significant characteristic of the BEx API is that it enables the BEx Analyzer to expose functions that may not be exposed through the OLAP BAPI.

It is a much simpler process for SAP to extend a proprietary protocol than it is to extend and test an industry-standard protocol. For example, the use of variables is a powerful concept that has been pervasive across all SAP software components. The variable concept enables the filtering of a request by single values, a list of values, an interval, or list of intervals, while allowing the variables to have default values set based on an individual's personalized settings. This concept has been a part of SAP BW since the 1.0 version. However, it was not until 2.0b that SAP enhanced the ODBO protocol to expose the feature to third-party applications.

Summary

This chapter detailed the services for data access and touched on how these services interact with storage services. There are APIs for accessing data stored in the DataStore Objects as well as the Persistent Staging Area (PSA). These APIs support data access from the storage services. Information is retrieved via the InfoProvider interface and returned to the information consumer after it is processed in the Analytic Processing Engine. The information consumer will receive a view of the query cube for each step in the analysis navigation. The InfoProvider interface abstracts the storage and caching services from the information consumer. Alternatively, information consumers may utilize the Analytic Process Designer with its optional data mining services to discover hidden insight from the data.

There are several analysis options from OLAP to perform specialized calculations for determining the lifetime value of a customer. SAP has tackled the basics of data mining by including data mining methods. They include Decisions Trees, Scoring, Clustering, and Association Analysis in the standard software. SAP has taken an open approach to data mining by supporting industry standards and providing APIs for third-party algorithms to be easily embedded for advanced predictive analytics.

Information may be distributed via the Broadcaster or accessed via a number of interfaces. The Broadcaster acts as a precalculations and publishing engine for queries. The interface options for distributing information include the OLAP BAPI, XML/A, and ODBO, as well as the proprietary BEx API. The BI Java SDK assists programmers in accessing several interface options.

Chapter 8 examines the Business Explorer suite of tools and discusses the common functions across the tool set.

Information Presentation

The old saying that you can lead a horse to water but you can't make it drink is particularly apropos when discussing business intelligence presentation tools. Information access and presentation is often the center of great debate and controversy. Even if a tool delivers the right information to the right user at the right time, there is no guarantee that the user will use the tool. No single information-access tool can satisfy an organization's (or even an individual's) requirements. It is not uncommon for each department to insist on using a particular tool because of its unique requirements. SAP BI has and supports a broad range of presentation and access tools that turn data into information and deliver it to the desired consumer.

This chapter highlights the main capabilities provided in NetWeaver BI that retrieve data, turn it into meaningful business information, and deliver that information to an information consumer. The chapter has been organized into two main sections: one on the Business Explorer suite of tools and one on common functions across the tool set. If you have not read Chapter 7, now would be a good time to at least read the section titled "Query Processing Overview."

BEx Presentation Components

The Business Explorer (BEx) has come a long way since its first incarnation as an Excel add-in that provided access to information stored in SAP BW. It has evolved into a suite of independent tools that supports a wide range of usage types. For example, the SAP BI capabilities of NetWeaver support formatted reporting, mobile devices, HTML-based Web applications, and ad-hoc analysis via a Web browser, as well as Excel integration. Furthermore, the Business Explorer's integration with the Enterprise Portal enables a single point of entry for a wide spectrum of end-user roles and business-related information packs. This enables collaboration and integration with nonstructured information (such as documents that capture users' comments on such things as the explanation of variances, justification for changes in forecast figures, graphics, syndicated information available via the Internet, and the ability to embed analytics into highly flexible business processes). This functionality allows end users to dynamically create personalized analytic applications.

In Figure 8-1, you will notice that the Business Explorer consists of several tools: BEx Query Designer, BEx Analyzer, BEx Broadcaster, and BEx Web (which includes the BEx Web Application Designer, BEx Report Designer, and BEx Web Analyzer). BEx is designed to meet a vast range of business needs, from simple list reports (for example, all the customers in a range of ZIP codes) to the complex (for example, elimination of intrabusiness volume), while taking into account the local currencies and fiscal-year variants of the business entities. BEx is designed to appeal to a wide range of business users, from hunters and farmers to miners and explorers. Various end users will interact with the BEx tools. Farmers, for example, may request information via a Web browser by clicking a URL. Explorers, on the other hand, may use the BEx Analyzer to create and recreate complex queries based on their findings.

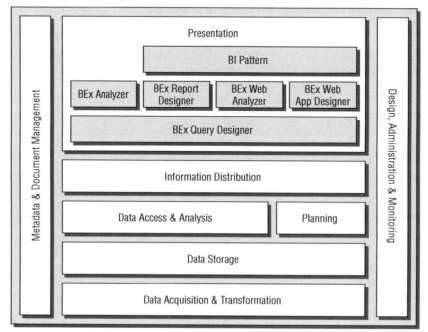

Figure 8-1 Presentation architecture

NOTE For an explanation of the various group types, see Bill Inmon's *Building the Data Warehouse, Fourth Edition* (Wiley Publishing, Inc., 2005).

BEx Query Designer

All multidimensional reporting and analysis performed in the BEx suite of tools is based on a query definition stored in the Meta Data Repository. Queries provide access to multidimensional information providers (InfoCubes), as well as flat information providers such as DataStore Objects and master data. The BEx Query Designer allows you to define queries in an interactive, standalone, .Net-based application by simply dragging and dropping the desired metadata objects into the query definition area.

For some readers, the term "query" may conjure up the image of a SQL generator that creates a simple list of records. The BEx Query Designer is a graphical tool for defining both tabular queries and multidimensional queries that the Analytic Processing Engine will execute and that any of a number of the BEx tools will visually render. The process of designing a query utilizes many of the available screen areas in the BEx Query Designer. Once opened, the tool will show a list of InfoProviders, a filter area, a properties window, a message area, and tab pages to access additional views.

The BEx Query Designer, while a standalone client program, interacts with the server (more specifically, the Meta Data Repository). Metadata about a query's Data Providers is passed to the Query Designer, so that the form and function of a query may be assigned to a design item. These Data Providers are then assigned to presentation items where properties are set to control the start view of a query as it relates to the design item it is being assigned to. More on these items in a moment.

All characteristics, navigational attributes, and key figures available through an InfoProvider are available for use in the Query Designer. Because queries will instantiate a multidimensional object, they effectively define subcubes (sometimes referred to as *query cubes)* on top of the InfoProvider. Query cubes define the degree of freedom available for query navigation in the presentation layer. Upon selection of an InfoProvider, the designer will see a list of metadata defining the following elements:

- **Structures** — These are collections of selections and formulas that provide layout criteria for a row or column that may be used by queries for a particular InfoProvider. Structures may contain a combination of key figures, characteristics, and formulas. A *reusable structure* is a particular, commonly used collection of key figures or characteristics stored in the Meta Data Repository for reuse in multiple queries (for example, a plan/actual variance or a contribution margin schema).

- **Filters** — Predefined filter criteria for the whole query that may be reused in all queries for a particular InfoProvider. A filter may contain any combination of characteristics and their filter values. A filter specifies the size of the subcube, as well as the initial navigation state displayed at query startup.

- **Key figures** — A type of InfoObject used to record quantitative facts or measures. All of the key figures for a particular InfoProvider are available for queries. A *calculated key figure* is a formula consisting of basic, restricted, or other calculated key figures available in the InfoProvider stored in the Meta Data Repository for reuse in multiple queries (for example, an average discount rate). A *restricted key figure* has an associated filter on certain characteristic values stored in the Meta Data Repository for reuse in multiple queries (for example, year-to-date sales of the previous year). A query consists of metadata elements arranged in rows, columns, and free characteristics.

- **Dimensions** — Dimensions refer to the grouping of characteristic InfoObjects in InfoCubes.

Elements may be assigned to the Rows/Columns screen area, which will indicate an initial display view. Free characteristics are aggregated in the initial query view. Free characteristics are available for navigation in the BEx Analyzer or in Web applications. Each navigational step (drill down, drill across, add/remove filters, and so on) in the analysis process provides a different query view, and the steps are controlled by the BEx Analyzer, BEx Web applications, or third-party tools.

Query elements include characteristics, key figures, calculated key figures (formulas), restricted key figures, and reusable structures. Queries may have filters on characteristic values or filters on key figure values (conditions) assigned to select a certain slice of information from the InfoProvider. They may be parameterized by query variables. Exceptions assigned to a query help identify key figure values regarded exceptional from a business point of view.

The simplest type of query is a *tabular query*. Tabular queries are often used to generate listings of master data (such as a listing of all customers in Illinois). For example, you could create such a query by locating the InfoObject for the characteristic `State` and dragging and dropping it to the column window. You could then right-click the state to restrict the query to just Illinois. You complete this simple tabular query by dragging and dropping the characteristic Customer to the column window.

NOTE Defining selection values that are valid for all the columns and rows of a query in the filter window will improve query performance.

Multidimensional queries provide more options but still are easy to define and use. Figure 8-2 illustrates the options a designer is presented with when working with multidimensional queries. Along with the rows definition window, there is also a Free Characteristics window. In multidimensional mode, the query creator drags and drops key figures and the characteristics desired in the query from a dimension to the desired column or row. As the InfoObjects are placed in a row or column, a preview of the query results is displayed. The designer may also place characteristics in the Free Characteristic or Filter window. Free characteristics are selected as part of the query's logic but are not displayed in the default view of the query. They may, however, be used for drill-down and drill-across functions by the user of the BEx Analyzer or Web application.

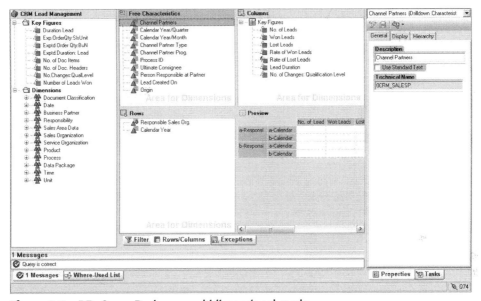

Figure 8-2 BEx Query Designer: multidimensional mode
Copyright © SAP AG

You use filters to limit the selection of data to a particular characteristic value or set of values. For example, the query "analyze revenue generated across all product lines that were sold to customers in Illinois during the month of July in the year 2006" may have three filter values: the state of Illinois, the month of July, and the year 2006. If you are familiar with any BI tool on the market today, you will notice a great deal of parity in the definition and handling of multidimensional queries.

Several good sources of information are available on SAP Web sites that detail the basic steps for building queries, so that information is not repeated here. The BEx Query Designer is simple enough to learn with a little practice. However, the key success factor is in understanding the information model.

With this in mind, instead of the absolute basics, let's focus on the functions that may not be obvious to the novice query designer. We have recognized a plateau that self-taught query designers reach in their learning. This next section should help those readers reach the summit.

> **NOTE** InfoCubes, Virtual Cubes, DataStore Objects, InfoSets, and master data are available to the query designer for either tabular or multidimensional analysis.

Designing Queries with Hierarchies

The concept of hierarchies was introduced in Chapter 4, and we detailed the impact that hierarchies have on information modeling. Hierarchies are used for data modeling, restricting data selection, navigation, and planning. For example, there are hierarchies for cost centers, profit centers, general-ledger accounts, customers, and products, to name a few. In most reporting and analysis applications, the concept of hierarchies exists. While it is not a new concept, it is an important one, because hierarchies are often the means of defining aggregation levels.

The BI capabilities of NetWeaver support three kinds of hierarchies: internal, external, and display. *Internal hierarchies* are modeled into a specific dimension. *External hierarchies* are called "external" because they are neither stored in InfoCube dimensions nor as navigational attributes; instead, they are stored in separate hierarchy tables associated to the base InfoObject (for example, 0CUSTOMER for a customer hierarchy). *Display hierarchies* are a convenient way to expand and collapse structures or characteristics found in either the x or y axis.

As mentioned in Chapter 4, there are several options for modeling hierarchies, including version and time dependency for the whole hierarchy tree, time dependency for the hierarchy structure, and the use of intervals instead of single values to assign a range of values to a specific hierarchy node. The hierarchy data model provides a means to store balanced and unbalanced hierarchies with different types of hierarchy nodes available at different levels or network structured hierarchies. These elements provide a tremendous amount of flexibility to the information modeler and query designer. Hierarchies may be explicitly assigned to a query at design time or may be entered by the query user at runtime when a hierarchy variable is used.

A query designer may set the hierarchy as fixed for a given query, thereby eliminating the possibility that a user of the BEx Analyzer or a BEx Web application may switch to an alternative hierarchy. The query designer may go so far as to fix the query to a given node within a given hierarchy. If the hierarchy assigned to a characteristic is time dependent and/or version dependent, the query designer may enable the query user to enter three variable properties for the hierarchy. The hierarchy name, version, and key date for data selection may all be prompted at query runtime, providing the maximum amount of flexibility.

The query designer sets the display attributes for an external hierarchy. For example, when a query is executed in the BEx Analyzer, the hierarchy is in either the rows or columns, depending on the placement of the underlying characteristic. The hierarchy may be expanded and collapsed at its node levels. Each node level may contain an optionally displayed results line. The results line (if calculated) is defined by the query designer, but it may be changed in an ad-hoc manner at runtime in the BEx Analyzer. Later in this chapter, a section titled "Local Calculations" describes the options for recalculating the results line.

Values selected as part of the query view that do not have a corresponding external hierarchy node assignment will be displayed as Not Assigned. Note that each node level in a hierarchy can have its own settings for how aggregation should be performed, displayed, and used in calculating results rows. This allows for one node level in a hierarchy to be used as a negative value. For example, if a hierarchy is created for general-ledger accounts, and all of the revenue accounts summarize to a node level, that node level may have a results line that is a negative number. This may be the case if your data model is tracking both debits and credits, since the revenue account is a credit in double-entry accounting. The hierarchy node may be set so the value is shown as a positive number.

End users may restrict the selection conditions of an external hierarchy at runtime or select a new hierarchy for the query. Selecting the local query navigation window, selecting the characteristic that has the hierarchy assignment, and then right-clicking the desired properties accomplishes this. The hierarchy window pane will appear, and a new hierarchy may be selected by name, as shown in Figure 8-3. This is, of course, assuming the query designer has not set any restrictions on the hierarchy or node within a hierarchy that is to be used in a given query.

Display hierarchies are powerful functions that allow end users to determine where and how hierarchies may be applied while in the BEx Analyzer. By selecting an axis (row or column), the Properties screen area will be filled. Under the General tab are settings for defining Display hierarchies on the fly at runtime. There is no need for a hierarchy to be previously defined and loaded as an external hierarchy when using the Display option. There are similar options for expanding and collapsing the hierarchy as there are for external hierarchies.

Display hierarchies work very well when internal hierarchies are modeled into dimensions. For example, profit centers and cost elements may be viewed together with the Display hierarchy options. It should also be noted that structures may be arranged into hierarchies at design time in the BEx Query Designer. These hierarchies behave in the same manner as display hierarchies, but they are defined prior to runtime.

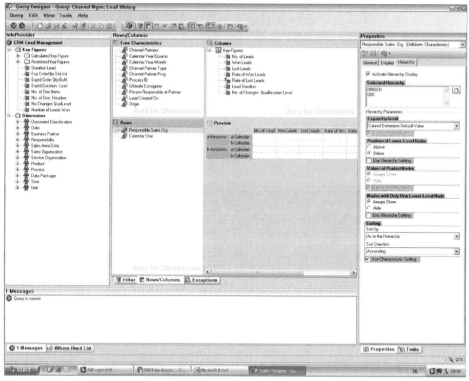

Figure 8-3   Hierarchy properties
Copyright © SAP AG

Variables

Variables are placeholders in a query definition that have their value defined at query runtime, thus enabling the parameterization of queries. There are five types of variables: characteristic, text, formula, hierarchy, and hierarchy nodes. A classic example of the use of hierarchies is found in a common financial query to display a profit-and-loss statement. The variables enable the query designer to create the profit-and-loss statement once and allow the end user to determine at query runtime the financial period for which the query should be run. In this example, the characteristic fiscal period is entered by the end user or defaulted, based on his or her personalization preferences.

Several processing types are available for the five variable types. The processing type sets the behavior of the variable. For example, if a variable has a processing type of "manual entry," a pop-up window will prompt the user to enter a value at the time of query execution. The five processing types are listed in Table 8-1. Each replacement path processing type will be described, since it may not be self-evident. This will be done as we describe the five variable types, specifically the text variable. Note that variables must be defined prior to being used in the BEx Query Designer and that the variables have a global scope. This means that once their properties are defined, those variable properties are inherited by every query that utilizes the variable, and all variables are available for all queries. Once variables are input, personalization options may be set to prevent the user from entering the variable values more than one time.

Table 8-1 Variable Processing Types

PROCESSING TYPE	DESCRIPTION
Manual/default entry	Prompts the end user to enter a value at query runtime.
Replacement path	Indicates that the value for the variable is to be found in the data of the query.
Authorization	Indicates that the value for the variable is to be extracted from the authorization storage.
Customer Exit	ABAP code that may be written by an SAP customer to fill a variable.
SAP Exit	ABAP code written by SAP to fill a variable value.

Characteristic variables are the most common type of variable and are used when an end user or group of end users would like to run the same query with a different set of parameter values, as described in the preceding example with the profit-and-loss statement. The characteristic value is commonly defined with a processing type of manual/default, with the settings ready for input so that at query runtime the characteristic value may be selected.

The entry for a characteristic variable is not necessarily limited to one value. For example, say an IT director is responsible for three cost centers. The director may run the same query definition for displaying direct costs as a sales manager responsible for one cost center. The sales manager will be prompted for her cost center numbers and the IT director for his.

The processing type authorization is an alternative to the manual entry processing type. The authorization processing type looks to the end users' authorization settings as defined with transaction RSMM and uses the value found there as input for the variable.

Text variables are commonly used in conjunction with a characteristic variable. In the profit-and-loss example, imagine there are two columns on the report: one column for the base period and another column for a forecasted period. When the end user of the report is prompted to enter a number for the base period to be analyzed, the value entered will populate the characteristic variable for the query, and the base period column on the report will be populated with the profit-and-loss values for that period. A text variable may be used in this situation to change the column header text for the base period, so when *0012007* is entered for the characteristic value, the column header may display the text Period 1 2007.

The text variable is commonly defined with a processing type of replacement path data, so at query runtime the characteristic value in the text variable's replacement path is used for the column header. Text variables using a replacement path have the option to use the characteristic value or the accompanying text value for a characteristic value. In the example, if the characteristic value is defined, the column header text would be set to 0012007. Text variables do not support the processing type authorization or exit. The replacement path is most frequently used for text variables.

Formula variables allow numbers to be passed to the query at runtime. This is especially useful for entering exchange, inflationary, or growth rates in a query at runtime. This may be used for simulations where the formula variable value is passed into the calculations of a column, row, or cell.

For example, the forecasted period in the previous example may take the base period and multiply the revenue for the base period by a factor that the user enters at query runtime to calculate the projected revenue in the forecasted period. In this scenario, the end user would enter a value (for example, five percent), and the formula in the forecasted period column would select the values in the base period column and multiply the values in the base period column by 1.05 to determine the forecasted period. Formula variables do not support the processing type authorization.

Hierarchy variables and *hierarchy node variables* behave in the same manner as characteristic variables. The hierarchy variable represents an entire hierarchy tree for a given characteristic. The hierarchy node represents a given substructure within a hierarchy. A difference between hierarchy and hierarchy node variables is the support of the authorization processing type. The hierarchy node is able to look to the settings in transaction RSMM for the default value for a given user. The hierarchy variable allows the query user to select entirely new hierarchies, versus simply selecting a different node within the same hierarchy.

Starting with the release of version 3.0, there is a wizard for creating variables that guides query designers through the process of defining all five variable types and the relevant processing types for each. It is worth noting that user-exits are available for each of the five variables, which allows for a completely customized business rule to be coded to determine a variable's value at the time of query execution.

Restricting and Calculating Key Figures

Queries are designed for InfoProviders in the sense that only the characteristics and their attributes defined in the InfoProvider are available for a query. Key figures are a bit different in that they may be used in one of three ways.

In the first way (often referred to as *basic*), the key figure is dragged from the InfoProvider area of the BEx Designer to a column or row. The basic key figure is calculated by the Analytic Processing Engine based on the query's aggregation settings and the key figure's attributes that were set when it was defined as an InfoObject in the Meta Data Repository. The other two options are restricted key figures and calculated key figures, both of which may be saved and reused in multiple queries.

Restricted key figures are the combination of a key figure with a filter value for a characteristic or set of characteristics. For example, a query designer wants to display in one column the net sales revenue key figure for the Northeast region and in the next column net sales for all regions. The designer drags and drops the net sales key figure to the column and then selects the Edit context menu option. Once done, a properties box appears, enabling the query designer to select the characteristic value or variable with which to filter the key figure selection.

Calculated key figures allow arithmetic formulas to be defined using one or more basic key figures or formula variables or calculated key figures. For example, a query designer wants to display in the column of a report the net sales revenue key figure and in the next column the cost of sales key figure. The reporting requirement is that the gross margin be calculated. If the gross margin is available in the InfoProvider, the designer can select it and drag it into a third column. If not, the designer can calculate it by using the basic key figures for net sales and cost of sales. To do this, after dragging and dropping the net sales key figure to the column and the cost of sales key figure, the designer selects the New Formula context menu option. A properties box appears, and the query designer can set the formula to calculate gross margin, in this case by subtracting cost of sales from net sales using the Selection/Formula properties editor. This editor contains a mathematically complete set of functions, as well as data functions and Boolean operators.

Exception Aggregation

You may recall that, during the definition of an InfoObject of type key figure aggregation, properties are set. The Analytic Processing Engine looks to the InfoObject definition as it determines how a key figure should be aggregated. Often, the InfoObject definition is set to SUM, and by adding all the selected values, the Analytic Processing Engine returns the value. For example, a query for fiscal year 2006 showing net revenue may aggregate net revenue for every customer for every period to determine the SUM of net revenue. That is fairly straightforward, but there are situations where summarizing figures is not appropriate, such as headcount.

Assuming headcount is stored each period as the period ending headcount, using SUM as an aggregation setting may at times create inaccurate results. Let's imagine the analysis being performed for the February period. Adding all the headcounts for every cost center is appropriate, but what happens when we are asked for the entire fiscal year's headcount? For these situations, there are settings in the InfoObject properties that determine how a key figure's exception aggregation should behave. In this case, a setting of LAST value may be more appropriate when aggregation is over several fiscal periods. In doing so, when a query is run for the entire year, headcount would only take each cost center's last period headcount.

Now let's take that concept a step further into the definition of formulas and calculated key figures. Calculated key figures and formulas have an option whereby the query designer may determine the timing of and type of exception aggregation to be performed. Keep in mind that a calculated key figure (as well as a formula) contains an InfoObject of type key figure in its definition and that key figures have aggregation properties. The Analytic Engine needs to know what order to perform the aggregation rules vis a vis the calculation. There is a tab page in the Selection/Formula properties area that, when selected, enables the setting.

By default, the aggregation key figure and the calculation (of, for example, the formula) occur at different times during the query process. With both calculated key figures and formulas, the Analytic Engine will collect and aggregate data as defined by the query plan. Key figures are aggregated over the relevant characteristic in the query either before or after the calculation of a formula or calculated key figure. More often than not, calculating prior to aggregation will have an impact on system performance. The ability to set the work plan for the Analytic Processing Engine is possible only if the calculated key figure was created in software release 3.5 or later.

There are situations where calculated key figures may need to be nested within other calculated key figures. For example, say the InfoProvider has only one key figure for net revenue, and you want to calculate the average number of different products ordered by different customers. A calculated key figure may be first configured using the net revenue key figure to determine the number of different products. The aggregation properties may be set to reference product and only count all nonzero orders. Next, a second calculated key figure for calculating the average number of different products sold to different customers would embed the first calculated key figure (different products) and set the aggregation properties to average all values while referencing the customer characteristic.

BEx Analyzer

The traditional tool for performing multidimensional analysis in SAP has been the BEx Analyzer. It was originally implemented as an add-on to Microsoft Excel with the idea of combining the power of SAP BW's OLAP engine with all the features Microsoft Excel. Query results had been stored in Microsoft Excel workbooks, allowing information to be used in an offline mode where users could add comments and send information to other users via email. During the first release of the software, BEx Analyzer (or, simply, BEx, as it was referred to) was the only tool for accessing information. Today, the BEx has evolved from a single tool embedded within Microsoft Excel to a full-blown suite of business intelligence tools, with the BEx Analyzer as the tool for the power users and analysts. It provides the typical functions of selecting a query, refreshing data, formatting the query layout, and, of course, navigating through the result sets generated by the Analytic Processing Engine.

The BEx Analyzer has two modes of operation: design and analysis.

In the *design mode*, query users are able to locally assemble workbooks by embedding reusable query components without affecting other users that may be running the same query at the same time. The design mode is where a query's design items are organized. Design items include such things as a list of available filters for the query, the analysis grid, and a navigation pane containing the characteristics and structures of the query. Table 8-2 lists the design items available to query designers.

Table 8-2   Design Items

DESIGN ITEM	DESCRIPTION
Analysis Grid	Central display area for query results. Analytic functions are performed on the data in this grid.
Navigation Pane	Contains the structures and characteristics available to the query user.
Buttons	Available for customized commands to be assigned.
Checkbox	Visual filter type.
Radio button	Visual filter type.
Condition list	Item displays a list of conditions active or deactivated, and indicates their current status.
Exception list	Item displays a list of exceptions active or deactivated and indicates current status.
Text	Item will display the text elements of a query.
Filters	Item lists all active filters.
Messages	Item will display any application-generated messages.

NOTE Map and Chart design items are not supported in the BEx Analyzer beyond version 3.5. Charts are inserted into workbooks by utilizing Microsoft Excel's chart engine. Maps, as of NetWeaver04s, are supported in the BEx Web tools; they are also able to be executed on the SAP BW 3.5 runtime environment.

Design items in the BEx Analyzer are analogous to Web items found in Web applications (which are described a bit later in this chapter). In *analysis mode*, the results of a query are displayed in the analysis grid within an Excel workbook. Analysis functions are performed on the analysis grid by selecting a context menu (right-click when over the grid). The navigation pane lists the structures and characteristics that may be dragged and dropped to add or swap out drill-down levels. There are also selectable icons that provide easy handling for common functions such as sorting and filter changes.

BUSINESS EXPLORER ADD-INS FOR MICROSOFT EXCEL

There are nearly 100 files in the BW subdirectory of the SAPGUI installation on a client workstation. A typical path, although this is customizable, is `C:\Program Files\SAPFrontEnd\BW`. When installing the SAP GUI, you must select the SAP BI options in order to install the BEx front-end tools. The following is a representative list of files found in the install directory:

- `BExAnalyzer.exe` & `BExAnalyzer.xla` – These files are used as a Microsoft Excel add-in and standalone executable and are launched either when the Start → Programs → Business Explorer → Analyzer menu path is selected in Windows environments or the Excel Add-in is initiated.

- `sapbex0.xla` – This file is used by SAP BW 3.5 when the BEx Analyzer is launched via the BEx Browser or the Administrator Workbench.

- `sapbexc.xla` & `sapbexc700` – These files provide a front-end installation check, depending on your front-end installation version. The former is valid for BW 3.5 and the latter for NetWeaver 2004s. It should be used after the SAP GUI is installed on a client workstation or for troubleshooting errors. The utility performs a check on the workstation to make certain the correct XLA, DLL, OCX, and EXE files are installed to ensure the Business Explorer suite, OLE DB for OLAP tools, and Microsoft core components will be able to function properly. Pressing the Start button in this spreadsheet initiates the check, and suggestions for corrective action are provided.

Once you have launched Excel with the BEx Analyzer add-in, you will see that a Business Explorer menu has been added to the standard Microsoft menu, as well as a BEx toolbar. The toolbar consists of icons to open, save, refresh, format, change, and navigate queries.

As described earlier in this chapter, queries are defined in the BEx Query Designer. However, the toolbar has an option for launching the BEx Designer.

Once a query is defined, it may be embedded into a workbook and analyzed in Excel. A workbook is a standard Microsoft Excel workbook with embedded references to query views and optional application elements built using Microsoft Excel functionality. For example, you may add charts to a query workbook, alongside the result area and filter-cell area of a query. You may also set the workbook template as a corporate standard so that all queries inserted into workbooks have the same look and feel.

Remember that a query is independent of the workbook it is attached to and that a workbook may have several queries attached to it. Business people may easily customize workbooks because they would be utilizing the standard formatting and formulas of Excel, as well additional features of the BEx.

Workbooks allow query results and any applications built within Microsoft Excel using Visual Basic for Applications to be saved and viewed offline and online. This is ideal for distributing the workbooks to a larger audience (say, via email), while still requiring proper authorization to review the workbook. One of the nice features in the BEx Analyzer is the ability to protect the workbook from changes, in addition to standard Excel-sheet protection. Excel-sheet protection limits the majority of the functions available to the end user. The SAP sheet protection password-protects not only the query areas from changes but the entire workbook, yet it still allows for ad-hoc navigation through the query.

The designer of a query determines the initial view of a query when the query is first defined. The properties of a query are considered global. That is, the designer of the query predetermines the rows, columns, filter values, variables, hierarchies, and free characteristics for all users who execute the query.

This does not prohibit a specific user from customizing the query. The changes made to a query by an end user may be done in the local analysis mode (see Figure 8-4) or in the BEx Analyzer design mode. Also, the global definition of a query can be performed in the BEx Query Designer, depending on authorization settings. Changes in the local analysis mode affect only the current user's session while analyzing a given query.

A common example of a local change is to swap the rows of a query with the columns by manipulating the analysis grid within a workbook. Hierarchies may also be added to a query in this mode, assuming the hierarchy definition exists for a characteristic in the query.

When in the design mode, changes to the query's design items may be made. For example, the location of a drop-down box may be moved or a chart added using Excel's charting functions. Changes made to the global definition of a query will affect all workbooks utilizing the query. As you might expect, the BEx Analyzer may launch the BEx Query Designer for such global definition changes.

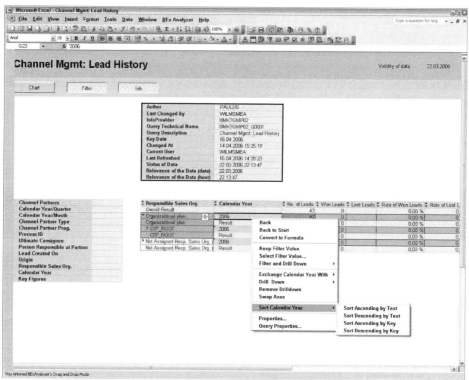

Figure 8-4   Analysis mode

Copyright © SAP AG

If a query is opened, the default workbook is loaded and the query is assigned to the Data Provider; then the workbook is refreshed. The default workbook may be customized in the system globally as well as locally at the user level. A query embedded into a workbook may be thought of in parts: title, filter, results area (analysis grid), and text areas. For example, the query name (title) and free characteristics (also known as *dynamic filters*) may be designed at the top-left portion of the Excel spreadsheet. This is referred to as the *filter cell area*. Once a query is executed and the results area is filled, the BEx Analyzer toolbar, Business Explorer menu bar, context-sensitive right mouse button, and drag and drop capabilities may be used to navigate through the query. The end user may easily filter, drill down and across, translate currencies, apply conditions and exceptions, and expand and collapse a hierarchy while navigating through the data. A series of navigation steps is often referred to as an *analysis path*.

The analysis grid contains four cell areas: characteristics, structures (key figures), characteristic values, and data values. The analysis grid will be filled according to the selection criteria set forth by the query designer in the BEx Query Designer. The title, filter, analysis grid, and text may each be moved any place on a worksheet independently of each other. All of the design items in the spreadsheet are under SAP's control.

While an end user may type a value into the data values cell, a refresh or navigation step will cause the typed value to be overwritten by the new view placed in the analysis grid. There is a setting to prevent this overriding called *formula mode*. This enables Excel to take over the calculation of values and essentially creates a local, offline analysis capability. Furthermore, as discussed in Chapter 9, the ability to enter planning values via the BEx Analyzer and have them stored on the server is now supported.

The BEx Analyzer can display a variety of technical metadata as well as business metadata for a query in a workbook. You display the technical metadata by selecting Business Explorer → Settings → Display → BW Server Information from within Excel or by selecting the Settings icon in the BEx toolbar. In doing so, you will be presented with technical information pertaining to the system ID, host, database, hardware, and IP address.

In addition, by switching the Trace option on, you can create a more powerful set of technical metadata. The trace option records all of the steps in an analysis path from connection to close. You can activate the trace log by selecting Business Explorer → Settings → Trace. To then view the trace log, you select Business Explorer → Settings → Display Trace. The BEx functions called from the Excel add-in are logged in the trace file. The log file helps programmers debug extensions to the front end that utilize the BEx Analyzer user exits.

BEx Web

This section describes the presentation capabilities of the BEx Web tools: BEx Web Application Designer, BEx Web Analyzer, and BEx Report Designer. Web applications may be configured in the BEx Web Application Designer or in HTML editors (such as Adobe's DreamWeaver or Microsoft's FrontPage). The BEx Web Application Designer is a visual-development environment that allows Web designers to create and tailor source code for Web applications, patterns, and cockpits that include traditional query elements such as structures, calculated key figures, variables, filters, and free characteristics, as well as documents and Web-content sources. Business charts, maps, and other graphical items are also integrated into the Web applications. These graphical items and the traditional query elements form the basis for BEx Web applications.

When a Web application is processed, the data providers used in this application are instantiated. First, the variables of the assigned queries are processed, and then data is read from the Analytic Engine. Next, each item renders the data provided by the data provider assigned to it. Note that the processing of a variable might lead to a selection screen prompting for variable values to be entered by the end user. Figure 8-5 shows the Web object model offered by SAP.

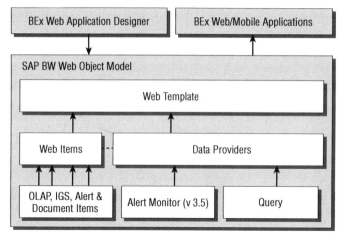

Figure 8-5   Web object model

The Web application is invoked by a URL. When the source code selects (or is bound to) data, a Web application is instantiated. Prior to the binding, it is simply a Web page with SAP-specific object tags. The application's Web items are instantiated and are bound to a specific data provider.

Note that the query-based data providers assigned to Web items will eventually call an InfoProvider, as queries are defined for a given InfoProvider.

> **NOTE** The use of the terms "data" and "information" may cause confusion for some readers, since "information" is generally considered data within a useful or relevant context and "data" usually is thought of as facts that still need to be processed to be useful. However, information to one service may be data to another.

BEx Web Application Designer

The process of defining a new Web application starts when a Web application designer logs in to the system from the BEx Web Application Designer. A Web item is dragged to the layout window in the BEx Web Application Designer, and the corresponding HTML source code is created. Figure 8-6 illustrates areas of the BEx Web Application Designer. They are the Web items, layout with overview and HTML tabs options, and the Properties windows.

On the left side of the figure is a list of all of the SAP-delivered Web items. Each of the standard Web items has a list of general and specific properties that control the behavior and appearance of the item. When a Web application designer drags the Web item to the layout window, an icon representing the web item (be it an analysis grid, a graph, a navigation block or a button) appears in the layout window. At the same time, the general properties for the web item are displayed. The designer is asked to name the data provider and to select a query or query view (created via the BEx Query Designer) for the newly created data provider. Each Web item has a list of general and specific properties that may be shown when the item is selected.

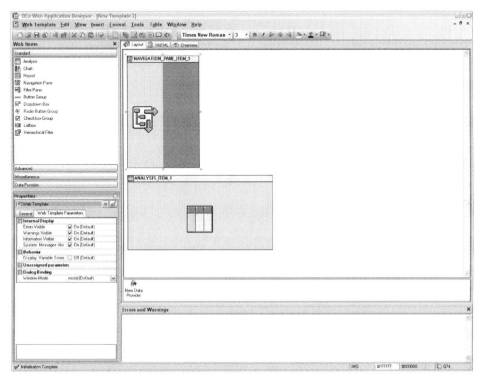

Figure 8-6   BEx Web Application Designer
Copyright © SAP AG

There are two types of data providers. First is the *query type*, which is either a query or a query view that provides data for Web items. This type of data provider may be also assigned to Web items commonly thought of as filter items such as Radio buttons and checkbox groupings. However, there is a second type of data provider specifically designed for filters.

The *filter data provider* does not fetch the entire results from a query but only data necessary to fill Web items that filter data. Typically, this type of data provider would select master data or characteristic values. A filter data provider may not be used for Web items such as charts and reports, because they only return characteristic values and the corresponding text elements.

The general settings of a Web item control such things as whether or not the title is to be displayed for a Web item, whether or not a border should be displayed around the item, whether or not the item should have links, whether or not the item's initial view should be closed or open, and what the initial size of the item should be set to. The general properties are the same for all Web items, with the exception of an additional sizing parameter for the Web items that represent graphical items.

There are two other powerful visualization Web items in addition to the Analysis Grid: charts and maps. The features are relatively simple to use and apply to query results sets. When the *chart Web item* is selected, a data provider will need to be assigned to it. A chart will adjust its rendering based on the current analysis being preformed by the user of the Web application. For example, if you attach a chart to a query that has a drill-down displaying countries and the revenue sold in those geographies, and you swap the country characteristic with the sold-to party, the chart would automatically adjust to the new characteristic.

When the *map item* is utilized, a map will appear in the Web application. The BEx map is attached to the query results area in a manner similar to the chart. The map Web item and its settings are a bit more flexible in that a specific key-figure column may be selected from a data provider, thereby allowing various mapping layers to be created.

A prerequisite to using the map Web item is that the data provider consists of at least one geo-relevant characteristic. In the InfoObject definition of a characteristic, geography-specific metadata is configured. There are two primary types of geographical settings for characteristics: static geo-types and dynamic geo-types. *Static geo-types* are used for characteristics that represent objects that do not change (for example, country or state borders). *Dynamic geo-types* are used to identify objects that may not be in the same locations (for example, vendors or store locations). Both the static and the dynamic types may derive their points from values stored as attributes for the characteristic.

Maps may have up to three layers of data displayed visually for a data provider. Each layer may contain separate images or color shading. For example, for revenue sold to all customers in Europe, each country may be shaded according to the total sales value, with the darkest states representing the highest sales value. Then a second layer may be defined to show a pie chart with a breakdown of profit by product type, where the size of the pie chart indicates the amount of profit relative to profit in the other countries. Figure 8-7 illustrates the map Web item at runtime.

There are Web items that cover everything from analysis and document handling to data filtering and graphical display. Every Web item is assigned to a data provider, or the data source is implied. Each of these Web items also has a set of specific properties. Again, there are exceptions, as the so-called *list of exceptions* and *list of conditions* Web items do not have specific object properties. The specific properties for the other Web items allow the Web designer to control how each item appears and the options each item represents to the end user. These properties may be set or replaced by the Web designer or at runtime by the Web application user by setting or replacing the parameter in the URL or object tag.

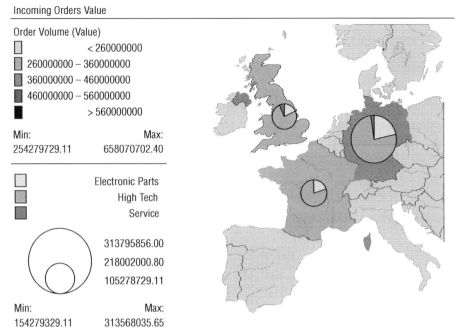

Incoming Orders Value

Order Volume (Value)

	< 260000000
	260000000 – 360000000
	360000000 – 460000000
	460000000 – 560000000
	> 560000000

Min: Max:
254279729.11   658070702.40

	Electronic Parts
	High Tech
	Service

313795856.00

218002000.80

105278729.11

Min: Max:
154279329.11   313568035.65

Figure 8-7   Map Web item at runtime
Copyright © SAP AG

Before diving into the object model, let's first make certain you are clear on what SAP means when it uses certain terms.

A BEx *Web application* is reasonably simple. A BEx Web application is an HTML page that contains one or more Web items and data providers that have rendered business information. The key word here is *have* rendered. It is with the BEx Web applications that the consumer of information interacts. Web applications are based on Web templates. The *Web application* is an HTML page that has at least one Web item and data provider defined as objects of the HTML page. SAP uses the term "Web applications" generically to represent everything from a static HTML page that renders precalculated information to complex, interactive, Web-based cockpits that retrieve information from various SAP and non-SAP software services.

Manipulating Web Applications

The Web application source code is the top level of the Web object model. The source code controls the structure, data sources, and properties of the Web application. Following is partial sample of HTML source code:

```
<bi:bisp xmlns="http://www.w3.org/TR/REC-html40"
xmlns:bi="http://xml.sap.com/2005/01/bi/wad/bisp"
xmlns:jsp="http://java.sun.com/JSP/Page" >
```

```
<html >
<head >
     <title >NetWeaver BI Web Application</title>
     <meta http-equiv="Content-Type" content="text/html; charset=utf-8"
/>
</head>
<body >
     <bi:QUERY_VIEW_DATA_PROVIDER name="DP_1" >
          <bi:INITIAL_STATE type="CHOICE" value="QUERY" >
               <bi:QUERY value="MBWTEST" text="MstrBW" />
          </bi:INITIAL_STATE>
     </bi:QUERY_VIEW_DATA_PROVIDER>
     <bi:ANALYSIS_ITEM name="ANALYSIS_ITEM_1"
          designwidth="400" designheight="200" >
          <bi:DATA_PROVIDER_REF value="DP_1" />
     </bi:ANALYSIS_ITEM>
<bi:TEMPLATE_PARAMETERS name="TEMPLATE_PARAMETERS" />
<!- Insert Data Providers, Web items and other template content here ->
</body>
</html>
</bi:bisp>
```

SAP has made significant advancements with Web applications in the latest software version. They take care of requests from Web browsers or mobile devices that send requests via HTTP. The services route the requests to the Analytic Processing Engine, along with the Internet Graphics Server (IGS) if necessary, and retrieve and assemble the requested Web items for delivery to the requesting device.

Web Applications now work with the Portal runtime environment and its request handler to receive requests from devices, validate those requests, and route them to the proper BI components. Once the Portal runtime environment receives a request, it is disassembled into its subcomponent parts, thereby separating content from format. Data requests are routed to BI engines (such as the Analytic Processing Engine) for execution. All requests with Web templates are routed in this manner. When the Analytic Processing Engine returns the result set, the formatting and construction are assembled and then rendered via the Portal runtime environment.

Following is a sample URL for Web applications:

```
http://<your domain>:<your port number>/irj/servlet/prt/portal/prtroot/
pcd!3aportal_content!2fcom.sap.pct!2fplatform_add_ons!2fcom.sap.ip.bi!
2fiViews!2fcom.sap.ip.bi.bex?TEMPLATE=WebApTempTest
```

Readers familiar with Web applications from SAP BW version 3.5 will notice that a significantly longer URL is used to access and manipulate Web applications. For those still running version SAP BW 3.5, a sidebar later in this chapter titled "Web Templates in BW 3.5 or Earlier" sheds some light on the URL and

Web-template handling differences. However, in the older and new version of the software, Web items may have their attributes altered at runtime, which creates a tremendous amount of flexibility to end users of the applications.

Let us first start by reviewing the fact that Web items and Web applications have predefined default values for their properties. For example, a chart Web item may have an SAP default width of 300 pixels. The chart Web item may be saved as a reusable item in a library, and the width of the reusable item may be set to 400 pixels. The properties of the reusable item would take precedence over the SAP default values. If a new chart Web item is defined and placed into a Web template, it may have a different width value still. Finally, at runtime, the user of the Web application may override the width of the chart Web item by altering the URL parameter for the chart's width.

This order of precedence and the ability to override URL parameters is available for properties of Web application, as well as web items. In the previous URL example, you will find near the end of the URL a question mark (?). The question mark indicates the beginning of the variable parameter section of the URL. In this example, you see that the Web TEMPLATE is set to =WebApTempTest. By adding another ? and a parameter to the URL, an application designer (as well as end user) is able to alter the properties of the template and or Web items at runtime.

Taking the parameter override concept back into the BEx Web Application Designer, SAP has developed a Command Wizard to assist Web designers in programmatically utilizing this powerful feature. The Command Wizard walks developers step-by-step through the process of creating a sequence of commands that may alter parameters of templates and Web items, reset data providers, or specify a planning function. A command or sequence of commands may be assigned to a pushbutton or other graphics element, thus creating highly customized, easy-to-use BI Web applications.

WEB TEMPLATES IN BW 3.5 OR EARLIER

When a Web application built in SAP BW version 3.5 or earlier is requested by a browser, the HTTP handler will identify the object tags within the template requested to find the objects in the template owned by SAP. The handler looks at the HTML and assesses the objects to identify which items are SAP BW and which are not. When an object is found, it is processed by the appropriate underlying engine (such as the Analytic Processing Engine). The other standard HTML tags are processed in the traditional manner (that is, the way any Web server would handle them). Let's walk through a simple example of how a version 3.5 Web application would access information, assuming the following URL was sent from a Web browser:

```
http://yourcompany.com:1080/SAP/BW/BEx?CMD=LDOC&TEMPLATE_
ID=MYSIMPLEWEBTEMPLATE
```

(continued)

WEB TEMPLATES IN BW 3.5 OR EARLIER *(Continued)*

The URL starts off with the HTTP protocol and the domain and port number assigned to the application server within NetWeaver. `/SAP/BW/BEx?` represents the path and program for the Business Explorer. Next, you will find the command being sent to the program, in this case `CMD=LDOC`, which is requesting that a Web template be loaded. The `&` symbol marks the beginning of a parameter. The value assigned to the parameter follows the equal sign. In the example URL, only one parameter, `TEMPLATE_ID`, is passed. The `TEMPLATE_ID` is set equal to `MYSIMPLEWEBTEMPLATE`.

Once requested, the template `MYSIMPLEWEBTEMPLATE` is retrieved and interpreted. The Web service looks for object tags owned by SAP BW and determines if the objects are data provider objects or Web item objects. The data provider object in this case has set the parameter `CMD` with the value `SET_DATA_PROVIDER` and named the data provider, appropriately enough, `DataProvider(1)`. The `CMD` command must be sent in order to instantiate a query. The other parameters of the object prove more interesting, because they set the value for the InfoCube and query. In the code sample, you will see that the query and InfoCube parameter values are set using the technical names for the desired query and InfoCube. In this example, standard business content for a sales and distribution InfoCube and query have been assigned to the data provider object.

You explicitly assign the data provider object for Web items in the BEx Web Application Designer by selecting a predefined query or query view. The behavior of a data provider may be changed by sending a URL containing the `CMD` parameter. For example, a Web template that has been designed and assigned to retrieve information about open sales orders from a query based on a sale, and a distribution query may reused to select data about sales deliveries from a different query and InfoCube. This is accomplished by calling the command `CMD=RESET_DATA_ PROVIDER` and assigning the parameters `INFOCUBE` and `QUERY` with the values of a deliveries InfoCube and query.

The data provider is a parameter of the Web items and is assigned in this example to the analysis Web item. This essentially binds the presentation item to a query assigned to the data provider object. The data provider object will route its request for information to the request handler and subsequently the Analytic Processing Engine. The analysis Web item object is instantiated and takes care of the presentation of the results returned from the Analytic Processing Engine and displays the results in the analysis Web item. Data providers may be manipulated by sending URLs that include commands and parameters. Web application designers may control such behavior as the filtering values, sorting, drill-down level, switching of characteristics, currency conversion, and exceptions. As you see, the lines that separate information access, analysis, and presentation are a bit challenging to draw. Web application designers may assign one or more data providers, as well as multiple Web items to the same. This enables the designer to create complex Web-based cockpits that source information from various information sources.

WEB TEMPLATES IN BW 3.5 OR EARLIER *(Continued)*

Access to static, stored, or live data is controlled by a parameter setting in the URL for the Web template itself. The difference among a standard Web template (which accesses a data provider directly), a precalculated Web template, and Web template that accesses precalculated data is the value set for parameter DATA_MODE. **The parameter** DATA_MODE **must be specified in the URL that accesses the Web template. There are three basic parameter values for** DATA_MODE**:**

- NEW — **This parameter value is optional, because it is the system default. The parameter value reads from the OLAP engine to get the most recent data.**

- STORED — **This parameter value reads from precalculated data. The hybrid parameter value is** HYBRID, **which uses precalculated data as long as stored data is available. Otherwise, it uses the** NEW **mode.**

- STATIC — **This parameter value reads from precalculated HTML pages. A hybrid parameter value is** STATIC_HYBRID, **which uses precalculated HTML pages as long as they are available; otherwise, it uses the** STORED **mode. If stored data is not available, the** NEW **mode is used.**

Regardless of whether the Web template is active, stored, or static, login is required, and hence security is ensured. If there are mandatory manual entry variables in the query, a variant must be specified. Alternatively, the variable values may be preassigned via URL parameters. Following is an example URL fragment specifying a variable value:

```
var_name_1=0COSTCNT&var_value_ext_1=10001000
```

This sets variable 0COSTCNT **to the value** 10001000. **As you can see, Web items may be set in a Web template or may be set and manipulated via URL. Together, these objects create the so-called *Web Design API*. The Web Design API is published and documented by SAP. The most comprehensive documentation may be found on the** help.sap.com **Web page.**

Usage Patterns

To create a consistent look and feel for the users of Web applications, SAP has introduced so-called *Patterns*. Part concept and part software, Patterns are Web applications that have been set up to meet the requirements of a group of end users. The Pattern provides for a consistent display of Web items, so an end user is able to interact with multiple Web applications the same way, with the same semantics.

The main concept behind Patterns is a Master Template. The Master Template is a Web template that defines the HTML, layout, Web items, and functionality for application-specific templates to inherit. The application-specific templates would take care of such things as query assignment, filter characteristics, text elements, and so on.

Many application-specific templates may be created from a Master Template by utilizing the Template Wizard. The Template Wizard installs as a client-side optional add-on and may be launched via the Windows Start menu. SAP delivers a few samples for the usage types Information Consumer, Casual User, and Analyst Patterns. The Wizard may open Templates stored locally or on the server and provides a maintenance interface for harmonizing Web templates.

BEx Web Analyzer

A new addition to the BEx suite is the Web Analyzer. SAP has positioned the Web Analyzer as an ad-hoc analysis tool. While much analysis may be done in an ad-hoc manner, the Web Analyzer currently does not support the creation of new query definitions. It may be difficult to call any analysis "ad hoc" when the underlying query must be predefined. Nevertheless, the Web Analyzer does play an important role as a zero-footprint alternative presentation option to the BEx Analyzer and a quicker alternative to using the BEx Web Application Designer.

The Web Analyzer displays information as either a table or graphic (or both). A navigation pane accompanies the three display options and handles this much like Web applications (including the drag-and-drop feature). There are context menus, pushbuttons, and links that may initiate deeper analysis functions, such as the following:

- **Open** — A previously saved analysis from favorites or a Portfolio iView
- **Save As** — Saves the current navigation state and corresponding elements (graphics and table) as an ad-hoc analysis
- **Display As** — Via a drop-down box graphic, table, or both, may be selected to display as a Web page
- **Filter** — A filter area is present if there are filterable characteristics.
- **Exceptions/Conditions** — If the data provider has reusable exceptions or conditions defined, they may be inserted into the ad-hoc analysis.

A nice feature of the Web Analyzer is its support for data providers bound to queries, query views, or InfoProviders from SAP systems, as well as those from non-SAP systems. Information about an InfoProvider may be viewed by selecting the Information pushbutton, which is part of the underlying analysis pattern. Metadata for the variable utilized, filter settings, date of last data refresh, time and person to last make a change, and the age of the data may all be viewed.

NOTE The Web Analyzer is technically based on the Web template
`OANALYSIS_PATTERN`.

There is also the ability to launch Excel and view the analysis in the BEx Analyzer. Likewise, the BEx Analyzer has the ability to launch the Web Analyzer. Like the other BEx tools, the Web Analyzer is integrated with the Broadcaster to support printing (and even the distribution) of ad-hoc analysis.

BEx Report Designer

The BEx Report Designer is a standalone tool that allows for the creation of formatted reports that have static and dynamic sections, may be viewed as Web pages, and are print-optimized. The addition of the Report Designer to the BEx suite fills a hole that was formerly filled by the Crystal Decisions integration. That legacy is discussed later in this chapter; for now, it is reasonably safe to assume that it is no longer necessary to license third-party software to meet business requirements that dictate highly formatted reports.

A report may be thought of a large grid of cells, with each cell containing formatting attributes. There are two main sections to the grid within a report: static and dynamic. The *static section* of the report supports the creation of uniform layouts, definition and placement of header and footer items, and the insertion of graphic elements. Furthermore, the static section allows static items to be freely placed anywhere within a static section. The layout settings include attributes to control font size, color, underlining, setting boarders, and so on. Header/footer information is considered to be in the static sections of the report and may contain such things as page number, date, time, and free-form text entered by the report designer and may be placed anywhere within a static section of a report. Graphic elements may be placed within a static section of a report as well.

The *dynamic section* of a report contains the query or query view and is bound by the use of a data provider, the same way Web application data providers function. Query and query views may contain several characteristics and varying numbers of characteristic values based on drill-down levels, hierarchy definition, and query selection properties. It is this variation in the number of rows that the dynamic section of the report facilitates. So, while the number of columns defined in a report is predetermined at design time, the number of rows is dynamic and determined at runtime.

Row Patterns and grouping levels determine the formatting options in the dynamic section of a report. There are three types of rows within the dynamic section of a report: Column Header Row, Detail Row, and Results Row. Each row may have its own settings to determine font color and size, the background color of the entire row, padding, and spacing, as well as alignment, border styles, wrapping, and column spanning. Row patterns contain a grid of cells each of which may contain specific display properties.

Group levels correspond to a row structure element of a query definition. Groups themselves contain header, detail, and footer areas. The detail area contains the innermost detailed characteristic values and key figure values of a query or a nested group. A row pattern is generated for each area of a group. Figure 8-8 illustrates the nesting of group levels.

Group 0 Header			[Country] Text	[Sold-to-Party] Text	[Revenue] Text	[Open Orders] Text
	Group 1 Header		[Country] Member Text			
		Group 2		[Sold-to-Party] Member Text	[Revenue] Value	[Open Orders] Value
	Group 1 Footer			[Result]	[Revenue] Sum	[Open Orders] Sum
Group 0 Footer			[Total]		[Revenue] Total	[Open Orders] Total

Figure 8-8   Report Designer group and row concept

Based on material with Copyright © SAP AG

NOTE It is also possible to include a query that contains two structures in the static section of a report, since a two-structure query has a fixed number of columns and rows.

The Report Designer may also be launched as part of the Web application. This is accomplished by utilizing the report Web item in the BEx Web Application Designer. The first step is to still define the report in the Report Designer and then embed that report into the report Web item. There are a number of properties to the Web item that allow the Web application designer to determine the display, interactivity, and data-binding options. Like reports executed with the Report Designer, Web applications containing report Web items may be distributed via the BEx Broadcaster.

Generic Presentation Options

This section details a few of the generic functions available as options to application designers and users of BEx tools. The discussion covers personalization options that increase ease of use for information consumers, local query calculation options that may take precedence over the Analytic Processing Engine, and the creation of versions of print settings. All of these functions are available across all of the BEx tools.

Personalization

Personalization is the customization of information based on previously known or real-time preferences set by the consumers of the information. Personalization may take on many forms but has the goal of efficiently serving or anticipating consumers' needs. While the personalization features in SAP BI are not only used by the BEx Analyzer but also in the BEx Web applications and the Administrator Workbench, the concept and its underlying components are examined here.

Prior to BW release 3.0, there was no useful server-side personalization for the Business Explorer Analyzer and very limited personalization available for Web-based tools. The personalization options were configured on the client within the BEx Analyzer plug-in for Microsoft Excel. The limitations created a burden on the data warehouse administrator, since the best way to achieve personalization was to create permanent variable assignments and limited access to queries and views through the use of authorizations and workbooks saved on the client. Current software versions not only overcome the personalization shortcoming of the previous releases but also layer a foundation for extension and integration with other applications.

There are three main areas of personalization:

- The automatic recording of previously accessed objects. This history is accessible to users of the BEx Analyzer, BEx Query Designer, and Web Application Designer. This is referred to as *open dialog personalization*.

- Web applications and their underlying queries and query views may be bookmarked or added to a Favorites menu. This is referred to as *Web template personalization*. Web templates and their usage will be discussed further in the next section in the context of the BEx Web Application Designer.

- *Variables* may be automatically filled with personalized default values.

Personalization provides information consumers with an experience customized to their preferences. The ease of navigation to specific Web queries from a Favorites list or a History list are not difficult to imagine and are analogous to bookmarking your favorite Web sites via your Web browser or adding a buddy to your buddy list in an instant messaging application. However, behind-the-scenes personalization also affects data warehouse administrators. The bad news is that they have another data set to monitor and manage. The good news is the impact that activating the personalization data is stored in specific DataStore objects and may be monitored and managed via the Data Warehouse Workbench like any other DataStore object.

Before using the three areas of personalization (open dialog, Web template, and variables), you must activate them. The activation process is straightforward and can be found in the implementation guide (IMG). Enter the transaction code

SPRO and in the reference **IMG** under reporting relevant settings. The process of activating a personalization option creates underlying DataStore objects that may be found in the Data Warehouse Workbench as part of the technical Business Content.

Personalizing History (Open Dialog)

When designing a query in the BEx Query Designer, the end user is prompted with a dialog window where he or she may select the InfoArea an existing query is stored in or create a new query. There are selection buttons for History and Favorites. These two options are similar in that they provide a customized list of queries to a query designer. They are different in that the history is automatically recorded based on the query user's most recent interaction with the Business Explorer, whereas the Favorites list contains queries that the user has explicitly designated as his or her favorites. The history is stored in the Data-Store object 0PERS_BOD. The DataStore object contains the history of all accessed queries, workbooks, and views for all users in the system. A user's Favorites are not stored in the DataStore object.

Personalizing Web Templates

When Web applications are accessed, a shortcut is automatically created in the user's Favorites menu. This shortcut stores not only information about the Web application but also information about specific viewing parameters selected by the end user.

For example, say a user is conducting a drill-down analysis path while analyzing global sales revenue. The analysis ends with a detailed drill-down of the Americas region and the country of Argentina. This information is stored in the bookmark. The bookmark is an SAP BI URL that contains the parameters and values to recreate the ending place of an analysis path. The DataStore object 0PERS_WTE contains the data for Web template personalization.

Variable Personalization

Variable personalization occurs automatically after the feature has been activated in the IMG. Once a query is executed and a value for a variable is entered, the value is stored in the DataStore object for the user/query/variable combination. When the query is subsequently executed, the values for the variables are retrieved from the DataStore object and automatically entered as the default values for the query. The DataStore object 0PERS_VAR contains the variable information. Since it also contains the variable history from cost and profit center planning, update rules automatically update the DataStore object with this new information.

Print Versions — PDF Output

From a Web application or Workbook, you are able to create so-called *print versions* that will determine the formatting for printed output. The print version controls essentially the following four things:

- **Scale** — Fit to Page Width, Fit to Page, or Poster. (Web applications will be printed with one area per page with the option of preserving the lead column.)
- **Page settings** — Theme (Display or Gray scale), orientation of paper (be that portrait or landscape), and paper size.
- **Margins** — Top, bottom, left, and right margin widths may be set.
- **Headers and footer information** — These are essentially the same in that they may contain information such as page number, date, and time of printing, as well as free text that may be entered by the person creating the print version.

Print Versions are applied to PDF output files and may be set in Web applications, in the Web Analyzer, and in the BEx Broadcaster. To utilize the Print Version functionality and generate PDF output files, the Adobe Document Services must be configured and managed. These services are available to NetWeaver applications, regardless of what the technology stack applications are written on (Java or ABAP). Customized forms may be created using Adobe LiveCycle Designer, which is embedded in both the NetWeaver Development Studio (Web Dynpro section) and the ABAP Workbench (form builder section).

Local Calculations

There are situations when it does not make sense for a query view to calculate a Totals line for a column. For these situations, a Results value may be calculated, or the Totals line may be removed. For example, if a query is configured using a formula to calculate the average selling price from the revenue number found in column one and a units-sold number found in column two, the Totals line for columns one and two may each be the sum of their respective columns. However, for column three, average selling price, it would not make sense to summarize the averages. There are a number of situations that may cause this results-line dilemma, including exception-aggregation settings (defined on a key figure InfoObject), when conditions are active for a query, or when a formula calculation exists.

A nice feature that may be found in the BEx Analyzer, Query Designer, and in Web applications is the ability to locally recalculate the results of a query view. This feature makes it possible to configure the behavior of the Totals line and turn it into a Results line. There are two types of local calculations. The first is the Calculate Results As (Table 8-3), and the second is Calculate Single Value As (discussed later in this section).

Table 8-3 Calculate Results As…

FUNCTION	DESCRIPTION
Summation	This function simply adds up all the values retrieved for the key figure according to the characteristics included in the query.
Maximum	The maximum function always returns the maximum values retrieved for the key figure, according to the characteristics included in the query.
Minimum	The minimum function always returns the maximum values retrieved for the key figure according to the characteristics included in the query.
Suppress	This function does not perform any aggregation and does not display a results figure.
Standard deviation	The standard deviation function returns the standard deviation of the values retrieved for the key figure according to the characteristics included in the query.
Variance	The variance function returns the variance of the values retrieved for the key figure according to the characteristics included in the query. The following formula is used when a selected area (N) has more than one value: $((\sigma2x^2 - (\sigma2\ x)^2 / N) / (N{-}1))$. Nonexistent is displayed when $N{=}1$.
First value	The first value function returns the first value retrieved for the key figure according to the characteristics included in the query.
Last value	The last value function returns the first value retrieved for the key figure according to the characteristics included in the query.
Summation of Rounded Values	Rounds each value first, then calculates the results of the rounded individual values. (Comes in handy when scaling factors are utilized.)
Count	The Count function returns the number of values retrieved for the key figure. The Count function comes in two different flavors: ■ Count all values unequal to 0 ■ Count all values
Average	The Average function returns the average of the values retrieved for the key figure according to the characteristics included in the query. The average function comes in four different flavors: ■ Average of all values not equal to zero ■ Average of all values

It should be noted that subsequent calculations and further analysis steps affecting a query column that formulaically determines a value (for example, actual to plan variance) will not utilize the results of a local calculation in determining its new values. Rather, it uses the results calculated in the Analytic Processing Engine. Said differently, local calculations utilize only figures that are in the current query's displayed view. When you call the Analytic Processing Engine to refresh or navigate through a query, the local calculations will be overwritten.

The second type of local calculation is referred to as the Calculate Single Value As function, which is a bit more complex. This function allows the query user to determine how percentage of totals, rankings, averages, and counts should be normalized. When you consider that a query view may be displaying values that have been drilled into the query views, results may be different from the overall result for a specific characteristic, which may be different from the overall result for the entire query. For example, if a query displays revenue for all customers, in all (two) regions, for two periods (halves) of a fiscal year 2006, the initial query view will show a list of customers and revenue values. If a drill-down to only view the eastern region of the query view is performed, there will be a different result from the query's overall results:

- **Results** — The figures calculated when there is only one characteristic in the drill-down.

- **Overall Results** — When there are several characteristics in a drill-down, the different results are calculated for the overall results.

- **Query Results** — For each key figure in a query, a query result is calculated over all the characteristics in the query.

Table 8-4 illustrates the normalization options available in the Calculate Single Value As local calculation function. Picking up on the previous example, imagine that the query's current drill-down state is the first half of the year and that a filter has been set for analyzing the eastern region.

Table 8-4 Calculate Single Value As… Normalization Options

CUSTOMER	REVENUE	NORMALIZED TO RESULT	NORMALIZED TO OVERALL RESULT	NORMALIZED TO QUERY RESULT
Customer 1	10	1.82%	0.91%	0.45%
Customer 2	20	3.64%	1.82%	0.91%
Customer 3	30	5.45%	2.73%	1.36%

(continued)

Table 8-4 Calculate Single Value As... Normalization Options (continued)

CUSTOMER	REVENUE	NORMALIZED TO RESULT	NORMALIZED TO OVERALL RESULT	NORMALIZED TO QUERY RESULT
Customer 4	40	7.27%	3.64%	1.82%
Customer 5	50	9.09%	4.55%	2.27%
Customer 6	60	10.91%	5.45%	2.73%
Customer 7	70	12.73%	6.36%	3.18%
Customer 8	80	14.55%	7.27%	3.64%
Customer 9	90	16.36%	8.18%	4.09%
Customer 10	100	18.18%	9.09%	4.55%
Result	550			
Overall Result	1100			
Query Result	2200			

The revenue figures for the first half of the year in the eastern region are listed and the Results line is calculated. The overall results would include the total revenue over the drill-down characteristic (in this case, the entire fiscal year), and the query results would represent revenue for all characteristics (including region). While the chance of selling the exact revenue amount to the same customers in different regions during the first half of the year as the second half is extremely rare, it does keep the math simple for our example.

NOTE The overall results and query results will be the same value if no filters are set.

The Calculate Single Value As function also supports local calculations for ranked lists, counts, and averages. Like the normalizing functions, these calculations are performed only on the local data in the query view. Counts and averages are fairly straightforward, and, with some experimentation during query runtime, end users will figure out how best to utilize these functions. Ranked lists are also straightforward, with one wrinkle (that is, what should be done in the case of a duplicate value). Table 8-5 illustrates the standard and Olympic-style ranked lists.

Table 8-5 Calculate Single Value As... Ranked Lists

CUSTOMER	REVENUE	STANDARD RANKING	OLYMPIC RANKING
Customer 1	10	8	10
Customer 2	20	7	7
Customer 3	30	6	6
Customer 4	20	7	7
Customer 5	50	5	5
Customer 6	60	4	4
Customer 7	20	7	7
Customer 8	80	3	3
Customer 9	90	2	2
Customer 10	100	1	1

You will notice that the highest revenue figures have the lowest (best) ranking. When utilizing the Ranking function, the characteristic values will be sorted according to the structure element you have selected. If a value appears more than one time in the structure element, all occurrences will receive the same ranking. The ranking assigned to the next lower value will depend on the ranking type you have selected. For standard rankings, the next lower ranking value will be assigned. The Olympic ranking will keep count of occurrences with the same ranking and add that number to the next lower values rank.

It should be noted that, like the Calculate Result As function, subsequent calculations (such as a column that formulaically determines a variance) will not utilize the results of a local calculation in determining its values but will rather use the results calculated in the Analytic Processing Engine. Likewise, any future navigation step or nonlocal calculation for the query view will utilize the results from the Analytic Processing Engine. Unlike the Calculate Results As function, the Calculate Single Value As function is not able to be used when a hierarchy is displayed for the query view.

Other Presentation Options

The Business Explorer suite may be extended with additional presentation options. This section covers four of these options. The discussion begins by detailing the Crystal Reports integration alluded to earlier in this chapter and then moves on to the options for displaying queries and Web applications on mobile devices. This section concludes with a discussion regarding integrating BI with Portal content and a brief discussion of the Visual Composer, a promising graphical modeling tool that adds the creation of Portal content.

Crystal Reports Integration

Another optional component in the Business Explorer suite is formatted reporting via integration with Crystal Reports. SAP partnered with Crystal Decisions to deliver a pixel-based reporting tool to extend the Business Explorer and meet the formatted output requirements that many organizations requested. Since that partnership was formed, Crystal Decisions was acquired by Business Objects, creating competitive uncertainties. SAP has subsequently developed its own solution for formatted reporting, the BEx Report Designer, as discussed earlier in this chapter. That development looks to solve many of the formatted reporting requirements organizations have and to reduce the total cost of owning and running SAP. With that said, Crystal Decisions may be a suitable option for those with significant existing investments in the software.

There are many reports for the public sector, in particular, that must be delivered in a specific format specified by different acts or amendments in government. These so-called legal reports need to conform to specific formatting requirements that are entered into law. Figure 8-9 shows an example from the Brazilian government called a "Mapa de Reintigrações" or "Map of Reintegration." This report describes the reintegration of funds into a program. The data in the third column of this report is sourced from a BEx query created for an InfoProvider abstracting a DataStore object. The data in the other columns is sourced from another DataStore object.

While custom development will accomplish the same results, the maintenance involved in supporting the solution would be too great. With the Crystal Reports integration option, the report designer is not required to have programming skills. The process of utilizing this option is reasonably straightforward once the additional software components are installed. Following are five steps for creating, publishing, and viewing a formatted report:

1. Create a tabular/single structure query in the BEx Query Designer.

2. Log in to the Crystal Reports Designer client software and select the tabular/single structure query from SAP based on your SAP authorizations.

3. Design the report in Crystal Reports Designer and save the formatted report definition back to SAP.

4. Publish the report from SAP to the Crystal Enterprise Server.

5. View the report via an Internet browser.

MAPA DE REINTEGRAÇÕES

METODO DAS QUOTAS DEGRESSIVAS

Firma

Activade principal

(a)

(1)	(2)	(3)	(4)	(5)	(6)	(7)	(8)	(9)	(10)	(11)	(12)	(13)	(14)	(15)	(16)
01	300000000000	KRL3	001	2000	100.00	90.25	0.01		0.75	9.00	91.00				0.00
01	300000000000	KRL3	002	2000	100.00	89.50	0.01		0.75	9.75	90.25				0.00
01	300000000000	KRL3	003	2000	100.00	88.75	0.01		0.75	10.50	89.50				0.00
01	300000000000	KRL3	004	2000	100.00	88.00	0.01		0.75	11.25	88.75				0.00
01	300000000000	KRL3	005	2000	100.00	87.25	0.01		0.75	12.00	88.00				0.00
01	300000000000	KRL3	006	2000	100.00	86.50	0.01		0.75	12.75	87.25				0.00
01	300000000000	KRL3	007	2000	100.00	85.75	0.01		0.75	13.50	86.50				0.00
01	300000000000	KRL3	008	2000	100.00	85.00	0.01		0.75	14.25	85.75				0.00
01	300000000000	KRL3	009	2000	100.00	84.25	0.01		0.75	15.00	85.00				0.00
01	300000000000	KRL3	010	2000	100.00	83.50	0.01		0.75	15.75	84.25				0.00
01	300000000000	KRL3	011	2000	100.00	82.75	0.01		0.75	16.50	83.50				0.00
01	300000000000	KRL3	012	2000	100.00	82.00	0.01		0.75	17.25	82.75				0.00
02	300000000000	KRL5	001	2000	100.00	74.11	0.01		0.00	25.89	74.11				0.00
02	300000000000	KRL5	002	2000	100.00	74.11	0.01		0.00	25.89	74.11				0.00
02	300000000000	KRL5	003	2000	100.00	74.11	0.01		0.00	25.89	74.11				0.00
02	300000000000	KRL5	004	2000	100.00	74.11	0.01		0.00	25.89	74.11				0.00
02	300000000000	KRL5	005	2000	100.00	74.11	0.01		0.00	25.89	74.11				0.00
02	300000000000	KRL5	006	2000	100.00	74.11	0.01		0.00	25.89	74.11				0.00
02	300000000000	KRL5	007	2000	100.00	74.11	0.01		0.00	25.89	74.11				0.00
02	300000000000	KRL5	008	2000	100.00	74.11	0.01		0.00	25.89	74.11				0.00
02	300000000000	KRL5	009	2000	100.00	74.11	0.01		0.00	25.89	74.11				0.00
02	300000000000	KRL5	010	2000	100.00	74.11	0.01		0.00	25.89	74.11				0.00
02	300000000000	KRL5	011	2000	100.00	74.11	0.01		0.00	25.89	74.11				0.00
02	300000000000	KRL5	012	2000	100.00	74.11	0.01		0.00	25.89	74.11				0.00
03	300000000000	KRL4	001	2000	100.00	91.00	0.01		0.00	9.00	91.00				0.00
03	300000000000	KRL4	002	2000	100.00	91.00	0.01		0.00	9.00	91.00				0.00
03	300000000000	KRL4	003	2000	100.00	91.00	0.01		0.00	9.00	91.00				0.00
					2.700.00	2.296.82			9.00	504.18	2.296.82				0.00

Figure 8-9 Crystal Reports example

First, you develop your reports by choosing your query, designing your report, and storing it within the Meta Data Repository. You then publish this report to the Crystal Enterprise Server. The integration between SAP and the Crystal Reports Designer includes a so-called *connector*. This connector makes it possible to launch the BEx Query Designer from within the Crystal Reports Designer, assuming both software components are installed on the same client machine. Information is passed from SAP to Crystal Enterprise after receiving a multidimensional expression from the Crystal Enterprise Server.

One of the current limitations with integration is the restriction to one structure in the query. This reduces the opportunity to use complex structures and single cell calculations in the published formatted report. From a query and report-design perspective, this may be its biggest limitation, and it is not very big. Query designers should look to see if creating more than one query and having them populate the formatted report will work around the limitation.

From a publishing and viewing perspective, the integration of the components leaves a bit to be desired, as shown in Figure 8-10. A potentially large drawback is that the Crystal Enterprise Server is serving the formatted reports to a Web server that is not integrated with the SAP Web Application Server. This means organizations must administer multiple Web servers and Web-security profiles to view formatted reports from SAP. While there is some security synchronization between the servers, this is a manual process that must be administered to keep in sync. Crystal Enterprise Server has its own security scheme that is quite different from the security scheme found in SAP.

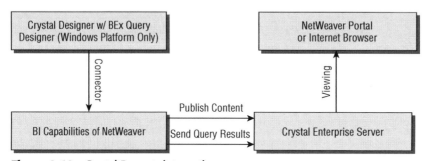

Figure 8-10 Crystal Reports integration

BEx Mobile Intelligence

Online access to BEx Web Applications and queries is only provided by BEx Mobile Intelligence utilizing the BW 3.5 Web runtime environment. This section highlights the Wireless Application Protocol (WAP) and PDA support. It should be noted that access to BEx is done in an online manner. There is the option to distribute via the BEx Broadcaster static HTML pages that contain information from a Web application, but this is a purely offline solution.

WAP

While not listed as a named distribution channel in the Broadcaster, there is implied support for WAP and General Packet Radio Services (GPRS) supported devices. Mobile phones that support WAP send requests for information to a WAP gateway that is typically hosted by the mobile service provider.

The request is translated by the gateway into an HTTP request and routed to the SAP server. The request from the gateway is a bit different from a request from a traditional Internet browser. The main difference is that the request is marked coming in from a specific WAP device type. The request uses the same SAP URL mechanism that the Internet browser would, and the data-selection process back in SAP is the same, regardless of the requesting device.

SAP BW 3.5 Web runtime uses its so-called *request handler* to determine the appropriate output format for the Web application output. For a WAP device, this would be the Wireless Markup Language (WML) instead of HTML for the Internet browser. The WML would be routed back to the gateway, where it would be translated into device-specific byte code and sent to the device for final rendering.

PDA Support

PDAs that support HTTP send requests for information to an Internet Service Provider (ISP). Unlike the WAP request, there is no need to translate the request prior to routing to SAP. The request uses the BEx Web Application URL mechanism the same as any Internet browser would. The data-selection process on the server is the same regardless of the requesting device. This time, SAP BW 3.5 runtime uses its so-called *request handler* to determine the appropriate output format for the Web application and generate the appropriate HTML.

Portal Integration

Certain aspects of the Business Explorer may be integrated into the Portal environment. Specifically, the BEx Web Application Designer provides options for easily publishing Web applications to Roles, Portal folders, and BEx Broadcaster. The following list contains the options for BI content within the Portal:

- **BEx Analyzer Workbooks** — BEx Analyzer Workbooks may be stored within KM as a document or as a link to a document. Either way, Excel will be launched in a separate window when the Workbook is requested.

- **Precalculated Web applications documents** — Utilizing the BEx Broadcaster (see Chapter 7), a Web application may be stored as documents in the KM capabilities of the Portal.

- **Web application links** — The information from the BI Meta Data Repository may by accessed from KM. Links to the Web application are associated with the metadata.

- **Web application iViews** — iViews act as containers for Web applications and provide access to current information by technically running the Web application when selected.

- **Metadata and Documentation** — The repository manager enables the integration of BI metadata and documentation with the Portal.

Integration with the Portal creates an extremely powerful combination where the traditional structured information found in BI environments may converge with unstructured information such as documents, recorded chat sessions, logs for meeting rooms, and other collaboration tools.

Visual Composer

Visual Composer is a visual modeling tool that enables content development for the Portal. The Visual Composer is entirely Web based and provides a debugging and testing environment, as well as support for the creation of documentation. SAP is converging many of the NetWeaver front-end presentation tools into the Visual Composer, but for the time being, the Visual Composer is used by the business-analyst user type rather than the professional developer. Not unlike the Web Application Designer, query views may be incorporated into an application built by the Visual Composer.

As mentioned in Chapter 7, SAP NetWeaver extensively supports the use of the XML for Analysis (XML/A) and contains the BI Java Software Development Kit (SDK). The SDK is composed of APIs and so-called BI Connectors. The SDK assists developers in connecting to sources, accessing metadata, and handling query requests and responses from both relational and multidimensional sources. The BI Java SDK provides tools for Java developers to create applications that access SAP and non-SAP information. Visual Composer uses a so-called BI query wizard to access these connectors. The wizard is installed as part of the default installation of Visual Composer.

Summary

The Business Explorer is now a suite of tools because no single information-access tool can satisfy an organization's or even an individual's requirements.

The Business Explorer has and supports a broad range of presentation and design tools that turn data into information and deliver it to the desired consumer. These include BEx Query Designer, BEx Analyzer, BEx Report Designer, and BEx Web, which includes the BEx Web Application Designer and Web Analyzer.

While each is a standalone tool, they behave as an integrated suite and interact with the BEx Broadcaster for printing and distribution functions, as well as the Portal for collaboration and document management capabilities. There are several functions that each tool in the BEx suite shares (such as the way they may create printed output, personalize favorites and history, as well as perform powerful local calculations).

This chapter concluded by highlighting additional integration points with presentation tools such as Crystal Reports, the Portal, and the graphical modeling environment called Visual Composer.

With the current software release, SAP has closed the gap on what was once a significant competitive knock on their solution: not having a core set of functions to support the input of planning data. Chapter 9 discusses the integrated planning capabilities within NetWeaver.

Integrated Planning

"Planning" is as generic a term as "information management" or "integration," conjuring a wide variety of presuppositions and connotations. As a result, this chapter introduces a specific definition of *integrated planning*:

> The process of formulating courses of action by setting quantitative measures that embody goals and objectives through systematic methods on enterprise and interoperable standards.

This definition is not to be confused with the SAP BW Integrated Planning tool. To make the distinction between integrated planning as a *process* versus a *tool*, the former will be referred to as simply "integrated planning," while the latter will be referred to as a coined acronym (SAP-IP) for this chapter.

The definition of integrated planning was crafted to position the SAP-IP tool itself. A further breakdown of the definition is provided after a historical context is given that explains why integrated planning is needed. This background and explanation should shed light as to how SAP-IP supports integrated planning.

In addition, the tool is further positioned vis-à-vis NetWeaver by introducing integrated planning design concepts from an Enterprise Architecture perspective before covering the technical functions and features of SAP-IP.

In summary, the first part of this chapter is dedicated to providing conceptual context to integrated planning, and the second half provides more detailed coverage of the SAP-IP tool.

Integrated Planning Positioning

To understand integrated planning, it is important to look at the following areas:

- History and trends
- Definition of planning
- Architecture considerations

History and Trends

The definition of integrated planning has strategy connotations but is broad enough so as not to exclude other levels of planning. For example, ERP itself has integrated planning capabilities of a more operational and tactical nature.

In turn, ERP can be thought of as a derivative or evolution of other predecessor integrated planning applications such as MRP. MRP, in turn, grew, expanding from "little MRP" (Material Requirements Planning) to "big MRP" (Manufacturing Resource Planning). And ERP itself has gone through mitosis, spawning other monolithic spin-offs such as customer relationship management (CRM) or supply-chain management (SCM), which, in turn, have integrated planning capabilities. In fact, all processes start with some sort of plan, decision, or agreement before actions are taken and must be managed against a plan to track performance.

mySAP ERPwas groundbreaking in replacing silo transactional systems with a unified and integrated one. SAP BW evolved the overall solution by increasing the transparency and integration of SAP and non-SAP enterprise applications. SAP-IP further leverages the SAP BW platform, offering the promise of breaking down planning system silos similarly to how mySAP ERP rationalized transactional systems. However, planning environments are probably an even more complicated ecosystem than transactional systems. In some sense, comparing the integrated planning story to the ERP story may be underestimating the task at hand.

Because planning is so pervasive and fundamental to organizational movement, many software applications support the process in myriad forms and manifestations. So, why move to integrated planning? What is missing today?

Birth of the Killer App

Aside from the advent of electronic word processing and database systems, one of the most pivotal "killer apps" for the business world was the digital spreadsheet. VisiCalc introduced the first commercially available digital spreadsheet in 1979. Several years later, digital spreadsheets quickly garnered business ubiquity with the introduction of more powerful PC versions. Leading the charge at the time was Lotus 1-2-3 spreadsheet software, but more than a quarter century later, the market is dominated by Microsoft Excel (anywhere between 60 percent and 90 percent of market share, with greater than 120-million licensed users).

The power of digital spreadsheets is the dynamic flexibility that can be shaped into all sorts of applications and can be wielded by business analysts (freeing them from IT support). This business-user empowerment allowed autonomy and self-service user productivity.

Not surprising, Excel is probably the most dominant and pervasive planning tool in the corporate world. Starting as a tool branded for accountants, it expanded its market footprint for anyone who had need for sophisticated formulas, graphic visualization, what-if analysis, long-term planning, and forecasting.

It is no small wonder that the front-end for SAP BW when it was first introduced was an Excel add-in (BEx Analyzer).

We have a lot to thank spreadsheet technology for. But we also have a lot to condemn: proliferation of planning silos, nonscalable capabilities, brittle systems that no one understands, competing methods and practices, and redundant applications with limited usage (that are often built, maintained, and used by the same individual). Planning systems can typically be characterized as stove-piped, chaotic environments rife with all the inefficiencies that come with rapid, unchecked, uncoordinated, fragmented, autonomous growth.

Rise of the EDW

Bill Inmon is often credited for fathering the concept of an enterprise data warehouse (EDW) to achieve semantic integration. The concept of an EDW was borne out of the need to take disparate data sources with differing semantics and create a central version of truth. One of his early criticisms of SAP BW was that it was just another data mart when it was first introduced. Not until SAP BW incorporated capabilities for supporting an EDW did Bill support SAP BW.

As many enterprises run their execution systems on SAP and as SAP support for EDW architecture becomes more robust, the decision to migrate legacy EDW solutions to SAP BW starts to make more pragmatic sense. Most of the effort in building an EDW is around ETL (that is, translating source system languages into a common enterprise definition). SAP BW Business Content already does the translating from SAP systems for you and was one of the key factors driving the growth toward using SAP BW.

In fact, the value proposition for integrated planning leverages the value proposition for enterprise data warehousing: the ability to plan on timely, accurate, and consistent information in an integrated environment on an enterprise scale. How SAP BW itself is positioned within an organization will, in large part, drive the discussion of how to use SAP-IP. If you're not an SAP shop (and hence not using SAP BW), this tool does not make sense, because it is part of the BEx suite that supports only SAP BW as the back-end. The question of how to position SAP-IP becomes more equivocal in SAP shops. Not only does SAP-IP need to be positioned vis-à-vis non-SAP capabilities, but there are plenty of architectural questions of how to use it vis-à-vis other SAP planning capabilities.

By building Excel-planning capabilities on top of an EDW, a number of advantages can be immediately derived:

- Consistent use of master data and hierarchies
- Access to consistent historical data
- A shared enterprise repository for plan and actual structures
- Central information system for plan and actual data
- Use of common services and tools for planning and reporting
- Shared security and infrastructure

However, nothing prevents integration advantages from being lost if BEx Analyzer workbooks are heavily customized. The additional flexibility of SAP-IP (the use of Excel and BEx) empowers business analysts. The very same killer app that got us into the hodge-podge mess to begin with can threaten to unravel the benefits of EDW integration if governance is not put into place.

Each governance model must strike a balance between global standards and local innovations. By giving business analysts a tool they are comfortable with, IT support is freed from the front-end development work load. Analysts can focus on globalizing internal best-practices planning models and functions (migrating Excel functions and data outputs to SAP-IP planning functions and real-time InfoProviders).

The Future of Analytics

EDW and BI concepts and topics have recently gravitated toward a more process-oriented approach and closed-loop analytics. Analytics must be driven back into other planning or execution systems. For example, market insights can power a statistical forecast used in demand planning that, in turn, drives supply-chain execution.

How the insights themselves are derived is typically through age-old statistical and mathematical models applied to new sources of data (such as consumer behavior patterns captured by loyalty cards or Internet click-streams). Simple statistic models not only can be applied to financials (such as revenue forecasting) but also to marketing research (such as product-preference probabilities). Old artificial intelligence and expert system concepts such as fuzzy logic and neural networks have found traction reborn as part of data mining. These concepts have been refashioned for finding patterns in large data sets, using mountains of facts to support decision-making rather than expert judgment calls. New-to-business-planning concepts (such as genetic algorithms, cellular automata, and chaos theory) promise to help model complex patterns (such as consumer or market behavior) that in turn can feed corporate planning or war-gaming tools.

Such applications promise to make planning more leading than lagging and more scientific than guesstimate. In parallel, business contributions such as balance score-carding, performance-based budgeting, activity-based costing, and value-based management influence the nature of how enterprise planning and budgeting will be done.

Annual budgeting cycles will move to agile and adaptive plans to better react to ever-changing business environments. Continuous planning cycles would call for dynamic and adaptive planning models that could either be reparameterized based on new business assumptions or remodeled based on new understandings of trends or behaviors.

As BI and EDW applications have matured, evolutionary stages have developed that have given rise to the importance of integrating data mining and planning processes into BI. Various BI pundits have different takes on BI maturity models, but all have elements that differentiate among traditional reporting, descriptive modeling, predictive modeling, and prescriptive modeling. Traditional BI reporting answers the question "What happened?" but offers no causes or relationships. Descriptive modeling addresses the question of "Why did it happen?" and is the basis of predictive modeling, which asks the question "What will happen?"

Here is where SAP-IP leverages the EDW and BI infrastructure: BI models and tools can be reparameterized and readjusted to predict potential outcomes and reveal causal insights. For example, a value driver model may predict the impact on profitability if customer service call center hours are cut. A prescriptive model is a heuristic or business rule that dictates how to "Make it happen." A prescriptive model executes on (or institutionalizes) insights like putting diapers closer to beer on Friday nights, because data mining association analysis discovered a buying correlation. SAP-IP can also be fashioned into an optimizer itself, such as cutting projects within a program portfolio that do not deliver the best expected value. Figure 9-1 shows the closed-loop nature of analytics.

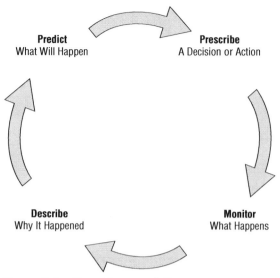

Figure 9-1 Closed-loop modeling

Definition of Planning

Our integrated planning definition is generic. Although fashioned for SAP-IP, it can also be applied to BW-BPS, APO-DP, and other SAP planning applications. The definition can be broken down into the following three points:

- Integrated planning is a formulaic process.
- Goals and objectives are quantitative and actionable.
- Data and functions are on enterprise and interoperable standards.

Each point and how it relates to SAP-IP will be covered in more detail.

Formulaic Process

Integrated planning should be thought of as a structured process, not an application bundle of interfaces (such as BEx Analyzer or Web Application Designer), data stores (such as InfoCubes), and calculations (such as planning functions). Although there are other SAP BW process-modeling tools (for example, Analysis Process Designer and Process Chains), the SAP-IP tool itself is not one of them. The traditional EDW and BI design paradigm is not business-process driven but rather information-output driven. End users of a traditional BI system interact with reports, not with a series of steps and transactions.

The SAP BW tools borne out of this paradigm are BEx Analyzer and BEx Web Application Designer, which now have write-back capabilities. Newer capabilities such as analytics tools (like Visual Composer) or NetWeaver development tools (such as Guided Procedures) can also be used to augment SAP-IP and enhance integrated planning applications. There have been a number of recent shifts in SAP BW to be aware of:

- The move toward closed-loop analytical processes
- The emphasis on embedding analytics into business processes
- The evolution of NetWeaver into a business process platform
- The growing notion of BI as a Web service instead of a report

What these shifts effectively mean is that more explicit process-modeling support scenarios will invariably converge with SAP-IP. SAP-IP designers need to be mindful that integrated planning is more a process than a data mart and still needs to be conceptually designed as such (irrespective of the technology).

The process should not only be thought of in workflow terms but in formulaic terms of how data is being transformed. Typical planning processes not only have calculation steps (such as price calculations) but also data manipulations (such as version copy). These formulaic procedures are best modeled in a spreadsheet rather than in any process model. Disciplined rigor is needed to break down a planning process into steps and formulas to derive the right data design. Getting the data design right as soon as possible should be an imperative during any SAP-IP implementation. The proper functioning of formulas and data procedures hinges upon the quality of the foundational information model. If the solution architect does not have a good handle on how the data design supports plan formulation, the process design is still conceptual, not engineered.

Quantitative and Actionable

The plan itself is an output of a process, but it should not end there in order to deliver value. The plan should not only set a goal but should steer what path to take. For example, activity-based planning not only derives a desired financial outcome but also details what level and kind of activity is needed to achieve a target.

As a result, plans must be quantifiable to measure actual performance against a target. Progress toward stated goals and objectives can't be monitored unless the drivers are being measured. As a result, SAP-IP is metric-centric in order to make a target actionable and track progress.

Furthermore, plans should not be static events that get dusted for performance reporting on obsolete assumptions but rather as statements of direction that continually lead execution activities. Annual budgets have drawn increasing criticism because of their static nature (that is, their snapshot picture at the beginning of a budgeting cycle). In contrast, continuous plans can reflect a more living and adaptive view of the world.

One of the advantages of having SAP-IP on an EDW and BI platform is the ability to continuously marry plan and actual data for measuring performance and forecast accuracy. Technically, the SAP-IP data basis is an InfoCube, which itself is a data schema that organizes around a central table of facts, the same type of data basis that can be updated continuously with actual data.

Note that our definition of integrated planning does not include unstructured data, qualitative goals and objectives, and collaborative interaction, because these features need to be integrated with SAP-IP. Although SAP-IP has document-attachment capabilities, it is better suited for small text attachments (for example, documenting brief assumptions for a metric) than for profiles and robust content management. Qualitative plans that include profiling mission, goals, objectives, and initiatives are better suited for solutions like SEM Balanced Scorecard or custom NetWeaver applications.

For example, document management of qualitative artifacts such as analyst research, market studies, and news and journal articles that help define and support a plan should be solution-mapped to SAP Enterprise Portals (EP) and SAP Knowledge Management (KM). Similarly, important collaborative interaction features such as discussion forums and virtual working environments are better suited for SAP EP collaboration rooms. Note that SAP-IP does have its own capability to support top-down and bottom-up collaborative planning, called *status and tracking*, explained later in this chapter in the section titled "Process Control."

Enterprise and Interoperable Standards

Mechanized and consistent procedures are important for repeatable results and baseline comparisons, especially in planning environments that necessitate a lot of cycles and scenarios as part of version control design. In many environments, the current planning systems are too manual and data intensive. Too much time is spent on gathering the information and compiling it even before calculations are run. SAP BW has acquisition and transformation automation capabilities that can speed the planning cycle. Furthermore, Business Content forms the basis of enterprise data standards.

Whether the plan is formulated on paper or in an enterprise application, there must be a standard program or procedure for defining it. Accomplishing this in an automated system like SAP-IP is more easily enforced than relying on human discipline.

Inconsistent planning methods destroy comparability and integrity. SAP-IP planning functions shift planning methods and calculations to the back-end, thereby improving enterprise scalability, performance, standardization, and control. SAP Business Content also promises to do for planning functions what it does for data semantics: offer out-of-the-box best practices and enterprise standards.

Not only must plan data and functions be on enterprise standards, they must also interoperate with other upstream or downstream processes, as well as integrate with actual data (for either priming plan data or for closing-the-loop comparison purposes).

For example, an SAP-IP advertising and media spend plan forecasts incremental sales by leveraging the data mining lift calculations derived from the results of past marketing campaigns. It then feeds sales to APO demand planning via a data mart interface and retracts back costs to R/3 overhead cost planning. Such seamless integration is enabled via enterprise semantic integration.

Note, however, that integrated planning retraction from SAP BW to SAP source systems needs to be customized. SEM-BPS predelivers "push" retractors (such as funds management or cost center planning) that can retract plan data from InfoCubes back into ERP. Similar retractors can be migrated to the SAP-IP platform with relative developer ease. In addition, SAP predelivers "pull" retractors triggered from SAP source systems that interface with BEx queries rather than planning interfaces.

Architecture Considerations

For architecting enterprise applications, any number of frameworks can be employed to solution designs. Although SAP has its own enterprise frameworks (most notably ARIS toolset and Composite Application Framework) neither has explicit integration with SAP-IP nor commercialized scenarios.

For the sake of understanding and communication, SAP-IP solution architecture will be explained with loose reference to the Zachman Framework for Enterprise Architecture perspective, as illustrated in Figure 9-2.

Generally speaking, the technology models and detailed representations in SAP BW systems are abstracted away from the designer. SAP BW applications are model-driven developments. System or logical models are developed that then generate the physical models.

For example, InfoCubes are logical models. Once they are logically defined in the DW Workbench, activating them will generate a physical star schema on the database, which the developer cannot access or control except through the logical model. As a result, the BI solution architect is free primarily to focus on the first two levels of the Zachman Framework in order to design.

First, the scope of the requirements must be set through business context (top level of the framework) through information gathering. Based on the requirements, business models must be developed: semantic models, business process models, landscape models, workflow models, planning cycle models, and business rule models. How each model is realized in integrated planning (logical or physical) not only depends on SAP-IP but on other NetWeaver model-driven development capabilities. Each area of modeling is addressed next.

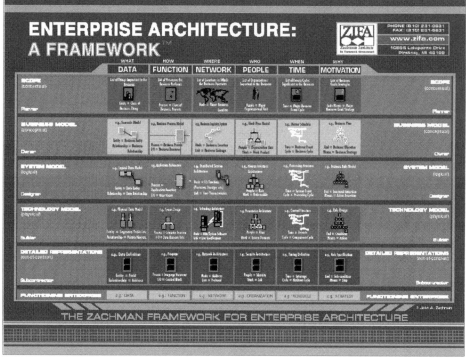

Figure 9-2 Zachmann Framework for Enterprise Architecture

Semantics

To achieve enterprise integration, there must be semantic integration. Without applications that can talk the same language, a lot effort goes into translating the different semantic languages through complex data mappings, lookups, and transformations. As simple and straightforward as this concept may seem, it is more often than not ignored on implementations.

Simple questions such as "What is revenue?" or "What is customer?" can trigger confusion and debates along the par of the famous blind men and the elephant parable (where everyone had individual definitions for the same thing).

When defining new planning applications, there is an opportunity either to create a new language or use a standard one. The model-driven nature of SAP-IP implementations is both an advantage (flexibility) and disadvantage (over-creativity). Because SAP-IP applications are custom defined, if no EA governance is in place, nothing prevents an architect from deviating from semantic standards (especially if the architect is not familiar with EA disciplines).

However, blind rigor to standards is not good either. Architects should understand the balance between customization and standardization. They should be aware of four typical and fundamental differences that naturally force semantic deviation in integrated planning applications:

1. Planning level of detail is more summarized than actual data.
2. Planning has processes separate and distinct from execution processes.
3. Planning models are simplified abstractions of reality.
4. Planning applications need forward-looking data structures.

EA discipline is needed to ensure that integrated planning semantics get properly translated (as well as the systems that it integrates to).

Business Processes

By evaluating an overall enterprise-level process model for a solution design, two things should start to unfold:

- Processes or steps that are redundant with other processes within the EA
- Processes or steps that are missing within the solution proposal or EA

For example, operational planning activities such as sales operations planning or cost center planning are capabilities that can be delivered either through mySAP ERP or SAP-IP. mySAP ERP planning is a lot more integrated and robust operationally than in SAP-BI but is on fixed structures and uses standard logic that is more difficult to customize. For example, the calculation engines in mySAP ERP are much more functional and scalable than what typically has to be SAP-IP custom-developed (such as product costing, activity allocations, capacity planning, activity rate calculations, sales pricing, or payroll processing). A project would be ill-fated to try to emulate all this detailed logic in SAP-IP. Either much simpler models and calculation engines should be employed, or data should be replicated back to the ERP system to leverage these engines (and the results extracted back into the SAP-IP system).

As another example, consider project planning. Standard project-planning capabilities already exist in SAP R/3 Project Systems, cProjects, xRPM, Solution Manager, or Microsoft Project. SAP solution maps should be evaluated to avoid potential planning-process redundancies.

As mentioned earlier, integrated planning should be viewed as a process, not as an input-ready report. In some cases, there are special planning steps with no operational execution equivalent (such as portfolio optimization or version control).

In addition, some planning processes should not be solution-mapped to SAP-IP but rather integrated. For example, planning processes for strategy management, activity-based costing, value driver trees, and balance score-carding are better solution-mapped to what is currently known as SAP SEM but require integrated planning in the background. Similarly, data mining processes should be mapped to the Analysis Process Designer but can be integrated and modeled along with SAP-IP.

Logistics

There is undoubtedly a pronounced trend to decouple and componentize applications led by vendor movements such as the SAP NetWeaver and ESA strategy. In the world of BI, Enterprise Information Integration (EII) and Enterprise Application Integration (EAI) are gaining increased adoption over extraction, transformation, and loading (ETL). EII and EAI architectural patterns enable distributed logistics models, while ETL patterns are more about consolidation. Master Data Management (MDM) technologies seem to have spun off a part of the traditional EDW. SAP BW technologies such as remote Info-Providers and Universal Data Connect enable federated querying, rather than having to replicate redundant data. In an increasingly networked world with fast adoption of Web standards, new paradigms in distributed logistics modeling are emerging (most notably is SOA).

For most NetWeaver applications, logistics modeling is an important component to consider, but for SAP-IP specific topics, it is less relevant, except to say that SAP-IP can leverage all the capabilities of SAP BW to take advantage of distributed logistics. For example, the data mart interface is not an SAP-IP specific capability but nonetheless can be leveraged as part of the BI platform. SAP-IP plans can readily distribute data to other InfoCubes in other systems (like SAP APO demand planning or a corporate consolidation system).

Newer solution offerings like SAP New Product Development and Integration (NPDI) (see Figure 9-3) leverage the Composite Application Framework (CAF) and are more logistically distributed. These solutions are more like broad processes or frameworks across a bundled set of applications rather than single monolithic applications like ERP or CRM. Note that the framework is closed-loop in nature and can start with SAP-IP and end with SAP BW for performance analysis.

As mentioned earlier, start-to-end processes more than likely span multiple systems. Strategic, operational, and tactical plans across all business functions more than likely will reside in different systems with different users and landscape considerations. There is no reason why an integrated planning solution cannot be distributed across multiple SAP BW environments as long as there is semantic integration.

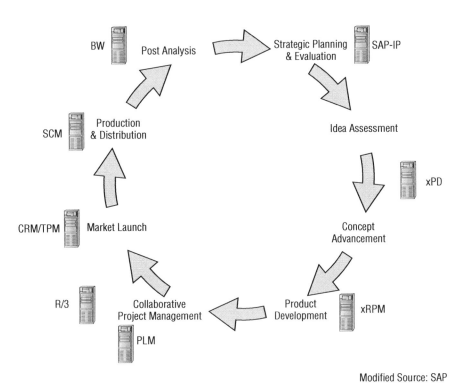

Figure 9-3 SAP NPDI
Based on material with Copyright © SAP AG

Workflow and User Interfaces

In the current release, Enterprise Portals is more ubiquitous and leveraged. Integrated planning designs can couple SAP-IP with collaborative and role-based SAP EP and KM capabilities like collaboration rooms, subscription services, and information broadcaster publishing. Collaboration rooms can be used as a central entry point for planners and a virtual working area to coordinate activities. KM folders can be used as a repository to share documents. Information broadcasting can be used to distribute plans with others at certain stages in the planning cycle.

SAP-IP comes with its own status and tracking workflow that works with SAP BW hierarchies to coordinate top-down and bottom-up workflow activities. In addition, SAP-IP can be augmented with other NetWeaver options for stepping a user through a process such as Guided Procedures, Web flow, and a heavier-duty workflow.

Because SAP-IP works against OLAP technology (that is, aggregated summarizations of data), it does not store audit details of changes made to data (such as user, date, and timestamp) typically found in transactional systems. SAP transactional systems employ the document principle: *Every entry gets a transactional document number.* In SAP-IP, every posting does not generate a document number but rather overwrites a total. As a result, audit-trail details of changes made are not stored as they are in documents.

Of course, SAP-IP is flexible enough to store such details in an InfoCube (some have tried this) via derivations (known as characteristic relationships) accessing system memory for the logged-in user ID and system date. However, tracking this level of detail is highly detrimental to the performance of the application because of the explosion of detail in an InfoCube. A better way to control and audit a planning environment is through BI analysis authorizations and workflow.

Roles-based design is not only important for workflows but central to Portals. Planning UIs can be either Web based and deployed as an iView to an Enterprise Portal or Excel based. The differences in designing planning and BI capabilities for applications with the BEx Web Application Designer or BEx Analyzer tools are negligible (sharing very similar design-time capabilities). As a result, planning layouts developed with either of these two BEx tools are either tabular or a list-oriented in format.

In contrast, BEx Report Designer and Visual Composer can support form-based layouts. Tabular UI patterns are helpful when metrics must be presented in the context of rows and columns like a spreadsheet. However, form-based UI patterns are better suited for other, more formatted types of data entry (such as profiles, applications, documents, or general forms).

The biggest difference between BEx Web Application Designer and BEx Analyzer planning applications is the runtime presentation-layer capabilities. (It is easier for business analysts to further manipulate output in their own local Excel workbook calculations than it is for them to do the same thing in JavaScript.)

As mentioned, electronic spreadsheets became ubiquitous as "killer-apps" because they put power in hands of the business analyst. For some environments, that loss of centralized control over what happens after information is served to the presentation layer is not a good thing. In those scenarios, the Web-based interface makes more sense (and offers a lower cost to deploy the front-end). Of course, governance and password protection can always prevent the casual end user tampering with template SAP-IP Excel workbooks.

Excel workbooks should be focused on customizations around the user interface. Any heavy logic should be saved for SAP-IP planning functions for better scalability and standardization. Reusable Excel calculations and logic should be migrated from front-end localizations to back-end best practices.

Master Schedule

Most collaborative planning processes have iterative cycles, be it a budget plan, annual operating plan, demand plan, sales forecast, and so on. These cycles, in turn, have phases and typically work on calendar schedules that change year to year. Large organizational plans may first work bottom-up or top-down or do both in parallel. Because of the collaboration and the various roles involved, deadlines must be set and scheduled. Version management is not just a matter of data design (versioning characteristics) and process design (version copy) but also a matter of scheduling or event-based modeling design.

Planning consists of cycles and scenarios before a direction is set. For this reason, modeling version-control processes is important part of SAP-IP designs, so as to continually refine a plan based on new information, insights, and collaborative feedback. Cycle-based versioning is used to manage the stages of the plan over time.

In contrast, scenario-based versioning is used to understand the impacts of differing assumptions at specific points in time. Integrated planning can be viewed as a process that actually generates a variety of proposals like a portfolio of options. The nature of most integrated planning processes whittles down the range of potential paths until one becomes the consensus target over a predetermined schedule.

As one plan phase gives way to the next, the planning application may require a number of things to happen. For example, in an early phase of budget preparation, a large number of users may need to have access to the system to do bottom-up planning. When the phase is over, these users should not have access to the system. Through the new BI analysis authorizations, these types of users can be assigned validity date ranges that control the window of time those users have access to the system (rather than manually updating their authorizations). Alternatively, the entire version phase can be locked via a *data slice* (however, this locks everyone and must be done manually rather than automatically, unless it is custom programmed). Finally, events can be scheduled via background jobs or process chains.

However, these scheduled methods lack a visual time-based modeling capability for scheduling (such as a Gantt charts or calendars typically found in project-planning tools). For more specialized planning applications like SAP CRM Marketing Calendar, business events such as a campaign or trade promotion can be planned along a time scale (with start and finish dates). Alternatively, the SAP CRM Marketing Planner tool has integration with MS Project so that campaigns can be viewed as projects within a project plan. Such features are not generically or explicitly available in NetWeaver (although something can always be custom developed), much less offered in SAP-IP (which is more quantitative-planning focused).

It is important for the architect to map out a schedule for any planning process being developed. Layering in roles and swim lanes with time-based phases integrates workflow and scheduling aspects for signaling where dependencies may be located in the planning process.

Business Rules

Pertaining to typical SAP-IP applications, two examples of general and broad categories of business rules for the scope of this discussion are:

- Decision-tree logic
- Validation checks

Decision-tree business rules can be embodied in an SAP-IP application in any of number of ways. It can be a predefined planning function (such as a constraint-based optimizer), or it can be the decision-tree results of a data mining clustering analysis.

Business judgments can also be applied explicitly to planning. For example, business rules can be within the configuration and definition of the planning function themselves (such as a revaluation of salaries by increasing them by 10 percent only for IT job roles, not to exceed their pay-grade maximum).

Most business rules can be captured when doing detailed process modeling that incorporates decision points or calculation logic. IF-THEN-ELSE commands in a planning function can model decision-tree rules.

What sometimes eludes SAP-IP architects is how to implement data quality and *validation checks* to ensure data integrity. For example, a planning modeler can design a solution where debits don't have to equal credits. While ERP financial applications enforce double-entry bookkeeping, SAP-IP applications don't necessarily impose the same rigor.

Furthermore, SAP-IP planning functions are not necessarily the best mechanism for performing such validation checking. Validation checking can be done in the presentation layer or in the BEx query definitions. These types of checks can be performed as conditions and exceptions within a query (highlighting in red any errors such as incorrect manual entries that must be corrected). However, such errors will be managed as soft errors (that is, the user can still ignore the alert and update data). Hard errors have to be handled via planning functions or custom UI development.

As an example, financial data validations and correcting adjustments of subsidiary trial balances are necessary before loading into a SEM-BCS (financial consolidation) InfoCube. BEx exception-reporting functions are well suited for performing data validation checks on key-figure totals. Rules might include the following:

- The trial balance must equal zero.

- Change in equity must equal net income.

- Assets must equal liabilities plus equities.

- Intercompany receivables must always have a breakdown by trading partners and never have a value of 999999.

- Asset accounts must always have a breakdown by transaction type.

- Profit center DUMMY doesn't have a value for any account except cash.

Because planning applications and their information models are entirely custom developed, many implementations run into data-quality problems because of poor design. Testing may reveal numbers doubling, disappearing, or simply wrong. The best way to ensure data quality is to preventatively catch errors before they are saved to the database on smaller data sets. Continuous data-quality checks on large data sets are more expensive to the system.

Sarbanes-Oxley has also heightened concern around financial integrity, increasing the need for better checks, reconciliation, and validation. Data in planning can constantly change with no audit trail. Financial integrity must be designed into the solution.

Integrated Planning Technology

SAP-IP really just represents the planning capabilities of SAP BW. It is not a separate tool but rather a set of BI functions or features integrated into the existing platform. Just as SAP BW can be fashioned into an EDW, it can be crafted into an integrated planning application.

As a result, building integrated planning applications requires the same or similar SAP BW tools and resources required for other scenarios such as constructing an EDW or an analytic application. For example, a typical SAP-IP application leverages the following BI capabilities:

- SAP BW Business Content

- BEx Web Application Designer

- BEx Analyzer

- Process Chains

- Data Warehousing Workbench

- Analysis Authorizations

That is not to mention all the NetWeaver capabilities that can be employed such as collaboration rooms, Visual Composer, Guided Procedures, Web-Dynpros, and so on.

However, specific components and functionality distinctly for integrated planning are embedded into SAP BW. These capabilities are covered in the remainder of this chapter, as well as how it relates to design. After some architectural context is given for SAP-IP, its details are explained from data, function, UI, and process-control perspectives.

Architecture

SAP-IP does add some architectural components to SAP BW. Although it shares the same OLAP services and Analytic Engine that the data access and analysis layer uses, it adds some planning-specific services as well. For example, to enter or manipulate plan data, aggregation levels are needed that load planning data into cache memory for faster processing. The Analytic Engine either serves this data to the presentation layer or a planning function. Planning data services such as locking are called before data is retrieved and processed, while semantic rules are applied after data is processed (either manually in the presentation interface or via planning functions). Multiple planning functions can be combined into a planning sequence for automation and background scheduling.

Figure 9-4 shows the architecture components and their relationships. The next half of this chapter focuses on providing more explanation behind these architectural components and how they relate to solution design.

Evolution

The first BI planning tools started in financial and supply-chain applications (SEM-BPS and APO-DP, respectively). SEM was an add-on component to SAP BW, while APO was built on a modified version of SAP BW. SEM-BPS steadily grew content, delivering prepackaged planning applications (similar in spirit to Business Content) such as the following:

- Capital Market Interpreter
- Balance Sheet Planning
- Profit Planning
- Investment Planning
- Cost Center Planning
- Liquidity Planning
- Personnel Planning
- Simplified Resource Planning
- Category Management Consumer Products (CMCP) Planning
- Profit Center Analytics in Retail
- Merchandise and Assortment Planning

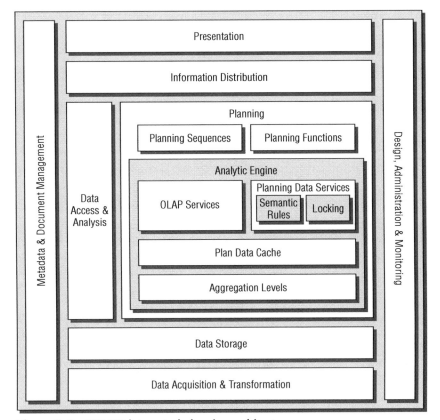

Figure 9-4 SAP BW integrated planning architecture

Then CRM Analytics incorporated prepackaged planning scenarios that leveraged the SEM-BPS infrastructure for planning such as the following:

- Sales Planning
- Strategic Service Planning
- Sales and Promotion Planning for the Consumer Products Industry
- Quotation Planning in the Utilities Industry (IS-U)

SEM, SCM, and CRM analytic applications are discussed in Chapter 10.

While SEM-BPS came prepackaged with business applications, it was possible to develop your own applications with the tool (that was how it was originally positioned). Because SAP SEM was a financial application, financial planning functions (for example, depreciation, NPV, and allocations) were added to its capabilities, along with the generic ones (for example, copy, delete, and repost).

Eventually, as EDW and BI evolved and shifted emphasis toward analytics, planning became a prominent capability missing in the SAP BW suite. So, SAP

BW development essentially moved the generic planning capabilities in SEM-BPS to SAP BW and renamed it BW-BPS. It was virtually the same capability of SEM-BPS, except the aforementioned planning applications were left behind, as were the financial planning functions.

BW-BPS was positioned as a generic planning tool only. Because it was a separately developed application, BW-BPS suffered from a lot of redundant capabilities (for example, planning layouts) and superfluous metadata (for example, planning areas) with SAP BW.

As a result, SAP BW was enhanced with planning capabilities (leveraging the lessons learned from SEM-BPS) and exploiting tight integration with existing BEx tools and, more broadly, SAP NetWeaver. This new capability is officially called SAP Netweaver 2004s BI Integrated Planning (which we shortened to SAP-IP). SAP-IP also benefits by sharing reusable functionality and services from BW-BPS, such as status and tracking, locking services, and FOX (an acronym for *FOrmula eXtension*, which is an SAP-IP formula language). In addition, SAP-IP benefited by leveraging many of the same concepts and capabilities of BW-BPS, only changing the underlying technical implementation (for example, data slices and planning functions). Almost every architectural component in SAP-IP has roots in SEM-BPS, with the exception of the planning UI, which BEx now replaces.

In fact, probably the largest impact to the SAP BW architecture was a change to the OLAP engine to allow expanded write-back capabilities. As a result, the OLAP Engine has been renamed the Analytic Engine. The Analytic Engine is not only composed of the well-established OLAP services in prior releases but now includes the planning services.

For example, because queries and planning functions access the same Analytic Engines, changes to the data in the planning cache are available immediately for querying and analysis before saving. Being able to visualize data while you are planning is an important usability feature in order to understand the impacts that manual adjustments are making.

In the past, because planning was done in a separately developed application (that is, SEM-BPS and BW-BPS), data had to be saved and queries refreshed in order to view planning changes. Now that planning and OLAP services have been integrated into the same Analytic Engine, queries are automatically updated when plans are. As discussed earlier, this is significant advancement, especially in the area of data-entry validation, where exception reporting can catch business-rule violations.

Of secondary impact were the changes to the BEx Query Designer, BEx Analyzer, and BEx Web Application Designer, which were all rewritten for Unicode and the new release anyway. Each of these tools now has planning enabled. The call to SAP-IP services such as planning functions is done via the presentation layer (that is, either the Web or Excel), versus the data access and analysis layer.

Planning Modeler

The back-end modeling of SAP-IP applications is no longer performed through an SAP GUI but rather through the Web, thereby enabling the easier deployment and usability of the tool. Planning modelers do not need access to the Data Warehouse Workbench to do their work. The Planning Modeler can be deployed as a standalone application on the SAP J2EE engine.

There are two ways to maintain planning models: through the Planning Wizard or through the Planning Modeler. Both are Web-based interfaces for maintaining the data and logic designs for integrated planning. Both are fairly straightforward and easy-to-maintain UIs and look similar.

The Planning Modeler works with tabs, while the Wizard works with Guided Procedures. The tab-driven approach for the Planning Modeler is ordered by InfoProvider, aggregation levels, filters, planning functions, and planning sequences. The Planning Wizard works in the same order but is more sequentially and step-by-step driven, with documentation on each step along the way (while in the Planning Modeler, the sequence is not predefined for modeling activities).

The Planning Wizard is for more casual users, while the Planning Modeler is for more advanced users (providing additional functionality for debugging and tracing of planning functions and sequences, as an example). How information is displayed on screens is configurable (such as columns displayed).

Figure 9-5 shows the look and feel of the Planning Modeler.

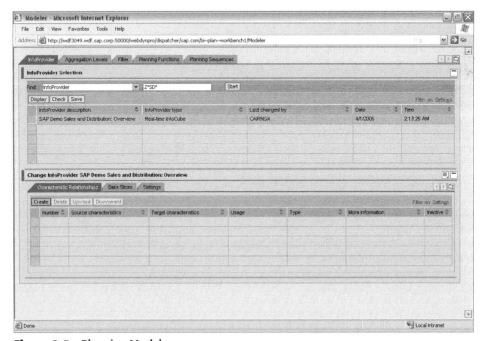

Figure 9-5 Planning Modeler

Integrated Planning Data

As indicated earlier, the data design is foundational to the planning application. A good data design must have a high degree of the following:

- Simplicity
- Adaptability
- Performance

Often, there is a tradeoff to be made among simplicity, adaptability, and performance, as well as impacts on process, calculation, and UI designs. Simple information models are easier to reconcile and reduce data-quality risks but may limit planning-function functionality. Adaptable information models are typically generic and force planning functions to be more abstracted and complicated. Specific data and function designs generally support better performance, while generic ones do not.

Every planning application faces some key information modeling decisions that have tradeoffs. The challenges of evolving requirements come with the dynamic nature of planning. The right balance of design tradeoffs today may not be the right balance tomorrow. In addition, innovations in BI technology itself tip the balance as well. For example, the BI accelerator offers breakthrough performance improvements that may require less discipline and rigor around information modeling for performance.

Nonetheless, fundamental data-design questions still must be asked and considered specifically for integrated planning, such as the following:

- How to model plan versus history?
- Distributed information model or centralized information model?
- Key figures as totals or incremental values?
- Shared or separated aggregation levels?
- Account-based or key figure-based information model?
- How to model a data version concept?
- How to handle large data volumes?
- How to use lock services, data slices, and authorizations vis-à-vis each other?
- Hierarchies as dimensional attributes, navigational attributes, or presentation hierarchies?
- Automatic derivations via attribute, hierarchy, data store, or custom table?
- Realignments as planning functions or transformations?

What follows is an introduction and explanation of the SAP-IP relevant metadata objects, as well as data design considerations (addressing the previous questions).

Information Logistics

Among the first architectural and design questions that must be asked before implementing any information models in any BI system is how many and what kind of data structures are needed to support a planning application? Should star schemas or flat tables be used for transaction data? Should data objects be master data or transaction data?

Some information modeling questions are fundamental to BI, but others are more specific to SAP-IP. For example, the question as to whether or not a star-schema data mart should be read-only or write-enabled is an SAP-IP consideration. However, to be able to address the information logistic design questions, BI metadata objects and their technical features must be understood as well.

Real-Time InfoProviders

InfoProviders were first introduced in Chapter 3. This discussion introduces the concept of a *real-time InfoProvider* for integrated planning. Although there are "real-time" or write-optimized DataStore Objects, SAP-IP only currently supports "write-optimized" InfoCubes as a real-time InfoProvider. (SAP-IP support for real-time DataStore Objects and master data is slated for the next release.)

Real-time InfoCubes are defined at creation by flagging a real-time indicator. Once flagged as real-time, an InfoCube behaves a little bit differently in order to optimize frequent updates to the InfoCube for performance. For example, since each planning update to an InfoCube may contain only a limited set of records (versus large data sets during data loads), the request in a real-time InfoCube is held open until a default threshold (for example, 50,000 records) is reached before automatically closing the request. These InfoCubes were formerly called *transactional InfoCubes*.

Additional performance optimizations include how the InfoCube is indexed and partitioned (which depends on the database). For example, on Oracle databases, there are no fact-table bitmap indices or automatic partitioning on data packets, as there are with standard InfoCubes. Aggregates can still be defined for real-time InfoCubes but cannot be rolled up until each request is automatically closed.

There are some design scenarios where it is necessary to both perform data loads and plan on real-time InfoCubes. It is not possible to simultaneously load an InfoCube while planning on it, but it is possible to toggle a real-time InfoCube (when no one has locked the InfoCube for planning) to allow for staging data. Converting the InfoCube between planning mode and staging mode is done via an InfoCube context menu setting in the DW Workbench.

The need to stage data into a real-time InfoCube depends on design. For example, if a planning InfoCube needs to be primed with history or actuals, it must convert its mode to allow data staging before the planning cycle begins. Or, for scenarios where planning functions cannot handle the data volumes involved (for example, version copy), an InfoCube staging into itself (and applying transformations) can supplant the planning functions for better performance. In this case, toggling the update mode is required.

Converting a standard InfoCube into a real-time InfoCube is a lot more involved (versus switching the update modes on a real-time InfoCube). There are two methods: Delete the data contents and flag the InfoCube as real-time or execute an ABAP program (SAP_CONVERT_TO_TRANSACTIONAL_ABAP). For large data volumes, this program should be executed in background.

Because the read performance of the real-time InfoCube is diminished, it is recommended that the reference data (that is, read-only data) be stored in a separate InfoProvider.

MultiProviders

Although write-back is only currently supported against real-time InfoCubes, data can be read from both master data and DataStore Objects via Multi-Providers. MultiProviders are essential for information logistic models where plan and reference data is split into separate InfoCubes. Examples of reference data are actual data, plan history, baseline, or planning function lookups (such as rates, percentages, or prices). More conceptually, active data (real-time Info-Provider) and static data (standard InfoCube) should be separated from each other in order to keep write and read optimized for performance and brought together for integrated planning via a MultiProvider.

MultiProviders will also parallelize data access to underlying InfoProviders, thereby helping performance. Another reason to split InfoCubes is to help eliminate sparsity or duplicate data. For example, if a top-down annual plan and a bottom-up periodic plan are simultaneously needed, separate InfoCubes can be used to separate the granularities (annual and periodic key-figure values). As another example, revenue and cost plans might be split into separate InfoCubes to eliminate sparsity but be brought together via a MultiProvider for profit planning.

Furthermore, key-figure totals themselves might be split across InfoCubes. The baseline for a plan can be stored as a reference in one standard InfoCube and the incremental changes in another real-time InfoCube (provided users want to enter incremental changes in a separate column from baseline amounts). A separate query can display the aggregated results as sum totals.

Note that input-ready values always must be restricted to a specific Info-Provider (SAP-IP needs to know which InfoProvider to write changes to). As a result, if the user typically enters plan amounts as sum totals, the baseline reference InfoCube is not helpful as it is not possible to plan on an amount that is the summation across two InfoCubes.

The MultiProvider enables the designer to push information model sparsity into a virtual InfoProvider layer, rather than in the database (thereby keeping InfoCubes dense). MultiProviders should be leveraged to logically partition the information model to eliminate database sparsity, increase performance, and improve modeling flexibility.

Information Modeling

One of the most fundamental information modeling considerations is picking between what SAP calls an *account-based* (or *key figure-based) information model*. Those who know the CO-PA module of SAP R/3 (Profitability Analysis) already know the technical difference between account-based CO-PA and costing-based CO-PA. Those who have read Chapter 4 already understand the difference between generic versus specific information modeling. The concept here is very similar. Figure 9-6 offers a review.

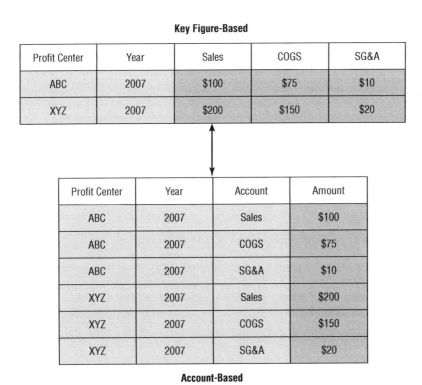

Figure 9 6   Key-figure versus account-based models

The intention is not to cover the same ground but to highlight some reasons why we recommend the use of an account-based model over the key-figure model for planning. The primary reason is the additional flexibility it affords in prototyping and iterative design. By keeping the key-figure dimension generic, the information model structure does not have to change every time a new fact is introduced. A characteristic value that represents a fact should be entered as a master data value (a data record to a table is more easily added than a field to a structure). This adaptability is important to support the dynamic nature of planning.

Furthermore, cheaper disk space and advances in data access performance (such as BI accelerator) make the data volume impacts of an account-based model less of an argument. Lastly, there are some additional points specific to SAP-IP to consider.

First, the rules of planning design have changed with BEx as the UI for integrated planning. Constraints in the BW-BPS planning layouts made a key-figure model attractive, but that is now obsolete with SAP-IP (more explained in the section titled "BW-BPS Coexistence," later in this chapter). The ability to use restricted key figures for input and calculated key figures for reference eliminates the need for key-figure information models for planning UI purposes. In addition, account-based models are needed for financial planning functions (such as allocations, offsets, net present value, depreciation, and so on). The possible exception advantage for key figure models is that some may find that it is easier to work with certain planning functions (but we would argue it is not necessary). However, that point leads to a guideline recommendation.

Because of the difficulty in auditing and tracing all the changes made to a planning InfoCube, extra care should be taken in keeping the data design simple for transparency purposes. Always opt for making a planning function more complicated by keeping the information model simple (as opposed to complicating the information model to keep a function simple). It is easier to iteratively change and fix a planning function than it is to iteratively change and fix an information model (especially when the information model has been logically partitioned and is filled with large data volumes).

Another fundamental information modeling consideration is version control. Typically, the SAP version control concept in SAP R/3 systems is not sufficient for SAP-IP application needs (in SAP, it is usually simply a three-digit field). There may be many dimensions to versioning, such as the planning cycle (for example, the budget year), the phase within the cycle (for example, a first draft submit stage), the planning scenario (for example, a working version within a phase), or the planning type (for example, top-down planning versus bottom-up planning). In contrast, actual data has no version concept and, as a result, should have its own information model sans version. Version control also has significant process modeling and master scheduling implications as discussed earlier in this chapter.

Aggregation Levels

Input-ready queries and planning functions do not actually work directly against the real-time InfoCubes or the MultiProviders. Instead, they work against *aggregation levels*. Aggregation levels can only be defined for either a real-time InfoCube or a MultiProvider. Aggregation levels are themselves a type of InfoProvider.

An aggregation level represents a subset of the characteristics contained in the real-time InfoProvider. In addition, any given aggregation level will always contain all the key figures of an InfoProvider on which it is based. Conceptually speaking, there are three dimensions to any data subset: the *projection*, the *aggregation*, and the *selection*. In this case, the level of aggregation (summarization) is controlled by the projection (subset of characteristics). In other words, the level of summarization is controlled by the characteristics available to avoid duplicate entries (versus passing all the unsummarized records into an aggregation level). Put differently, key figures in an aggregation level are always summarized over all the characteristics not defined in that level.

When input-ready queries execute against aggregation levels, the OLAP cache instantiates a "delta cache" for planning (that is, the plan cache and OLAP cache are essentially the same thing). Planning-function data changes and user inputs fill the delta cache. Saving data does not release the cache but compresses these "requests" kept in the delta cache. The advantage of creating queries against aggregation levels is the ability to read this cache. Designers should be aware of how much memory an OLAP session can consume for performance reasons.

Aggregation levels are important for information modeling the planning granularity. For example, a sales planning application may have a top-down planning process where sales targets are set by region based on InfoCube history data that is by sales office, as shown in Figure 9-7.

In this example, the sales planning InfoCube is primed with detailed historical data for Miami and Atlanta. The regional sales manager sets a target for the Southeast region (summarized across sales offices) for $40 million (overwriting the OLAP-summarized historical value of $35 million). This planning scenario requires an aggregation level that includes the characteristic for region but excludes sales office. Note that all the characteristics not included in an aggregation level cannot be assigned an explicit value. As a result, these unassigned characteristics are left blank (explicitly denoted by the application as a pound or "#" symbol). If bottom-up planning is needed for sales estimates by sales office, a separate aggregation level that includes sales office characteristics would need to be created.

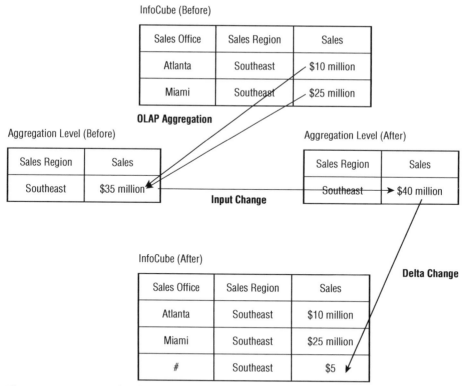

Figure 9-7 Aggregation-level sparsity
Based on material with Copyright © SAP AG

On one hand, care should be taken not to have too many aggregation levels. It creates a lot of data sparsity (characteristics left out of aggregation levels are never filled in). Such sparsity and aggregation makes comparisons with actual data difficult, because planning is usually more summarized than actual data. Most actual document postings consist of two levels (header and line item), and most of the time all the key figures are on the line items. A conscious effort should be made on the designer's part to be as consistent as possible with aggregation levels of detail.

On the other hand, creating separate aggregation levels decouples input-ready queries from planning functions and planning functions from themselves. In other words, if input-ready queries and planning functions do not share the same aggregation level, then changes in one should not impact changes in the other. If too many input queries and planning functions share the same aggregation level, a change in granularity affects them all. Put differently, if a net present value calculation (planning function) is by project but the sales assumptions needs to also be broken down by product (input-ready query) then adding product to the aggregation level should not impact the calculation if it has its own aggregation level. Otherwise, aggregation levels should be standardized and rationalized. The tradeoffs should be weighed.

Further complicating the marrying of plan and actual data into the same aggregation level is the possibility that different characteristics may be used for the same dimension. For example, some applications use a different account-dimension characteristic for planning data from what is used for actual data. Sometimes this relationship is many-to-many (meaning that sometimes the planning account is more detailed than the operational account and sometimes more summarized). As a result, neither can be a navigational attribute of the other. Such concepts make the possibility of comparing plan versus actual data at the account level difficult to achieve.

Lastly, requirements that necessitate manual planning on any level of large complicated hierarchies pose an information modeling challenge because each level of the hierarchy must be modeled as its own aggregation level if it is to be planned on.

Filters

If aggregation levels represent both the projection and aggregation of a data subset, *filters* represent the selection. Filters have been integrated into BEx queries for use in data selections. Filters can use BEx variables, hierarchies, or navigational attributes, as well as mix these types of restrictions (such as single values and variables together) for defining data selections. BEx variables allow for runtime parameterizations. Filters themselves are mandatory at runtime when planning functions are executed, because there can be many filters to an aggregation level. In other words, the application needs to know what combination of characteristic values to use in order to write to the aggregation level. At runtime execution, the selection space of a filter cannot be expanded.

Additional settings include specifying a key date in the filter for time-dependent data. Three options exist: standard key date (from the query or real-time InfoProvider), a manually specified fixed value, or a variable. Advanced settings permit additional controls by characteristic. Normally, the selection set is fixed in a filter and cannot be adjusted. However, if a characteristic is flagged to permit change, a filter can be narrowed at runtime.

In conjunction, it is also possible to force the user to restrict such a characteristic one value at a time. These settings pertain only to input-ready queries. For planning functions, they are ignored and the entire filter selection space is used instead. Furthermore, locking is done via the filter selection space as well, irrespective of whether the filter is further narrowed at runtime.

Finally, if any variables are used in the filter, they can only be set once per planning function execution and then are fixed in memory. Variable variants can be used to set variables and are mandatory when scheduling planning sequences as batch jobs.

Data Access and Locking

One fundamental and nontrivial information modeling challenge that BI planning designers face (but that traditional BI designers do not normally face) is how to handle lock contentions. Solution architects who fail to understand the significance of locking and its impact on data design invariably run into big challenges late in a project lifecycle (especially if the plan was not iterative) when concurrent users of the system discover they cannot simultaneously plan. Testing concurrency with rich, meaningful, and diverse planning scenarios is a test-plan challenge, even with a good automated test tool. Good, upfront lock design will alleviate locking problems downstream.

Even if a design can support a high-level of concurrency, the planning designer must understand how lock design affects performance. Each lock has associated system overhead to manage and check against that the SAP-IP solution architect must address.

In the SAP context, the term "lock" has a specific technical meaning. But in requirements gathering, the term "locking" may have a broader sense and take on a more business-functional meaning, especially for how users want to talk about planning. For data-design considerations, we apply a broader context to the locking discussion by referring to it as *data access and locking*. Data access and locking can be loosely and broadly defined as any functional device or mechanism for securing data from change. Following are the three types of mechanisms for controlling data access and locking behaviors:

- **Lock Services** — BI mechanism for locking data by user session to avoid concurrent changes.

- **Data Slices** — BI mechanism to protect data subsets from change by making them display only to avoid changes universally.

- **Analysis Authorizations** — BI mechanism for granting access to data by users or roles to avoid changes by the wrong users.

The reason why SAP introduced the notion of BI-specific lock services is that the selections for multidimensional data access can be a lot more complex than those typically found in transactional systems.

In addition to lock services, there are two application-oriented methods for securing data from change in the BI IP context: data slices and analysis authorizations. Data slices are covered in this chapter, while analysis authorizations are covered in Chapter 11. Before providing an example of how a solution architect might incorporate lock services, data slices, and analysis authorizations into an SAP-IP data access and locking design, consider Table 9-1, which compares the different approaches.

Table 9-1 Comparison of Data Access and Locking Approaches

CHARACTERISTIC	LOCK SERVICE	DATA SLICE	AUTHORIZATIONS
Purpose	Prevent "dirty reads'"	Freeze data	Grant access
Change Effect	One at a time	Not at all	If you have access
Data Basis	Per InfoProvider	Per InfoProvider	Across InfoProviders
User Basis	User-specific	Across users	User-specific
Design Context	Session-driven	Process-driven	Data-driven
Maintenance	Automatic	Operational	Configuration
Control	System	Administrator	Designer
Life Time	Session	Long-term (modeled)	Stable

A version management example is probably the best way to compare and illustrate how lock services, data slices, and analysis authorizations work together. Imagine a responsibility center planning application. At the start of the planning process, estimates are entered into the system bottom-up. Because each manager has an individual responsibility center at the lowest level of the hierarchy, there is no lock-service contention. Analysis authorizations prevent any manager from altering or even viewing another manager's estimates.

When the bottom-up plan is finished, it is data-sliced and copied into a new version to support the next stage in the planning cycle. The data slice ensures that no one can change the bottom-up estimates (no changes in analysis authorizations are needed for this business event). However, the managers can still view data as display only. If need be, the data slice can be deactivated. Deactivation is useful for any last-minute updates (without the need to change anything around analysis authorizations).

The next stage is a top-down planning process. Each line-of-business executive references the bottom-up estimates and then overwrites the estimates by setting targets at any level of the organization. Analysis authorizations prevent access to this version of the plan for anyone other than executives.

The executive version is then data-sliced and copied into a top-down planning new version, where middle management distributes the targets reconciling differences between targets and estimates. Because there are various levels of middle management, distributing targets must be done by each management level to avoid lock-service contention. This prevents "dirty reads," meaning that data is not being mucked with during the course of a middle manager planning session.

After a higher-level manager unlocks a planning session, a lower-level manager can distribute the target, thereby locking the data at a lower level (which then prevents the higher-level manager from going back to make changes until the lower-level manager is finished). Lock services prevent changes to higher-level aggregation levels (totals), while lower-level aggregation levels (details) are changed. Status and tracking (explained in the section titled "Process Control," later in this chapter) can help manage this locking workflow across hierarchy levels and the data-slicing versioning process. This example also illustrates the importance of releasing locks and analysis authorizations to prevent users from locking data irrelevant to their role.

In summary, lock services ensure that a certain set of data can only be changed by one user at one point in time (that is, short-term "lock"). Data slices ensure that a certain set of data can only be viewed by all users for as long as it is active (that is, long-term "lock"). Authorizations grant read or write access to data relevant for a role or user (that is, does not change over time). To put it differently:

- Lock services prevent users from "dirtying" each other's data during their planning sessions.

- Data slices are designed for "freezing" entire planned versions for historical-reference purposes.

- Analysis authorizations are for "furnishing" access to data sets by specific users and roles.

As the example portrays, data access, locking, and version control are interrelated concepts. Your information modeling exercises for version control should account for data access and locking scenarios.

For example, in more complicated planning environments, top-down and bottom-up planning stages are not sequential processes but rather occur simultaneously. A more sophisticated version and locking design would use separate versions or key figures for top-down and bottom-up planning (to prevent locking) and synchronize the different plan versions (for example, publish and subscribe planning functions) with business rules to handle conflicts.

Planning functions can be designed to use *reference data* (read-only inputs to data outside the function) so as to prevent locking of data that the planning function is not going to change. Reference data is covered in more detail later in this chapter.

Lock Services

Lock services are not something that you want to turn off (nor can you, because they are system controlled). Otherwise, users can stomp on each other's work without knowing about it. Lock services prevent users from colliding into each other inadvertently. They necessitate an orderly workflow or versioning process to facilitate collaboration.

Lock service concepts for OLAP have small (but significant) differences to OLTP locking concepts. The key differences are data granularity and complex data selections. Planning typically takes place at higher levels than OLTP transactions. OLAP engines efficiently aggregate data into totals on levels that planners need. OLTP transactions are typically incremental postings stored as self-contained documents.

Document numbers uniquely identify a record for locking in OLTP systems, which keeps the locking algorithm lean; only key fields need to be registered with the lock service and the lock is released when a new document needs to be posted. In contrast, BI planning data sets can represent much more complicated data selections that are both wide (across multiple dimensions in a star schema) and deep (for large hierarchies). Every field is evaluated as a key field in multi-dimensional OLAP data marts. As a default, the locking service accounts for every InfoObject used by a real-time InfoProvider.

Further compounding matters is the nature of planning versus transaction session. The data within a planning session requires a bird's-eye view of the data, while a transactional session requires a worm's-eye view. How this technically translates is that large volumes of data must be summarized and locked for OLAP planning sessions (data retrieved for both planning functions and input-ready queries), while OLTP transactional sessions lock only the document being modified at any given moment. The length of a planning session is relatively long, while the length of a transactional session is short. Before data is unlocked in OLAP planning, the input-query session must be exited. Before data is unlocked in an OLTP document posting, the document needs to be saved as the user moves on to the next document.

To illustrate a lock-contention scenario and recommend solutions to avoid locking, consider Figure 9-8. Imagine that a sales planning aggregation application has two roles: office managers (creating estimates) and regional managers (setting targets). Office managers have their own aggregation level that only consists of estimating their sales for their office and region. They do not plan on which customers they are targeting, because that guidance comes from regional managers. Regional managers set targets at the region level, irrespective of the office. As a result, their aggregation excludes sales office in order to plan the total. In addition, sales targets are set by customer, if at all.

If both regional and office managers concurrently planned, a locking conflict would immediately ensue, as there is an overlap in the data records needed. Note that even if there is not data, one manager cannot create new records while another manager is in the system, because of a logical lock (that manager might choose to create records in that data set). The two characteristics that overlap in question are sales office and customer. Even though sales office is not in the regional managers' aggregation level, the system needs to lock all the records that relate to the Southeast sales region. Similarly, even though the aggregation level for Atlanta sales office planner does not contain customer, it nevertheless locks all records that relate to Atlanta (customer details or not).

Aggregation Level	Sales Office	Sales Region	Customer	Sales
Sales Estimates	Atlanta	Southeast	*(All Values)	$10 million
Sales Targets	*(All Values)	Southeast	ABC, Inc.	$25 million

Aggregation Level	Sales Office	Sales Region	Customer	Estimate	Target
Sales Estimates	Atlanta	Southeast	*(All Values)	$10 million	
Sales Targets	*(All Values)	Southeast	ABC, Inc.		$25 million

Aggregation Level	Version	Sales Office	Sales Region	Customer	Sales
Sales Estimates	Estimate	Atlanta	Southeast	*(All Values)	$10 million
Sales Targets	Target	*(All Values)	Southeast	ABC, Inc.	$25 million

Figure 9-8 Lock conflict

Based on material with Copyright © SAP AG

There are two ways to resolve this locking contention: by process or by data. *By process* means coordinating the effort such that office and regional managers plan at different times. *By data* means changing the information model for planning in one of two ways: by characteristic or by key figure. Both approaches are illustrated in Figure 9-8. *By characteristic* entails using a versioning to separate by data records used by the regional manager, versus those used by the office manager. *By key figure* entails using a separate key figure for estimates and targets, since locking is done by key figure (not across all key figures). Both approaches require planning functions to synchronize and reconcile estimates with targets.

True data record locking occurs at the database level, but SAP has its own lock concept that abstracts database locks. These logical locks are database locks managed by ABAP programming and dictionary objects that will be generically referred to as *lock services*. These database lock abstractions are represented by ABAP metadata objects.

The standard SAP locking mechanism is called the *enqueue server,* consisting of ABAP dictionary lock objects and function module programming around it. However, SAP BW has introduced two alternative lock-service options that leverage memory (either ABAP shared objects or LiveCache) for better performance. What these different lock services share in concept are their own lock tables (where lock arguments are registered) and their own servers (either run on a central instance or separate servers). These alternatives effectively perform the same thing from a functional design perspective. As a result, we have and will continue to refer to them as if they were the same thing, unless otherwise distinguished.

The SAP-delivered default is the ABAP shared objects memory option, which has both low administration effort and high performance (working off of memory). This defaulted approach will more than adequately handle the preponderant share of SAP-IP implementations. Only in very large implementations should the LiveCache option be considered. It also uses memory for fast performance, but has a lot more administrative overhead associated with it (requiring its own dedicated hardware). These options can always be changed, as no planning-session locks are registered in the system. Table 9-2 provides a comparison of the options.

Table 9-2   Locking Service Options

CRITERIA	ENQUEUE SERVER	SHARED OBJECTS MEMORY	LIVECACHE
Size of Implementation	Small to Medium	Small to Large	Very Large
Administration	Low	Low	Medium
Performance	Medium	Fast	Fast
Table Name	RSPLS_S_LOCK	RSPLS_S_LOCK_SYNC	LCA_GUID_STR
Related Transactions	SM12	SHMA (cl_rspls_enq_area)	LC10
Profile Parameters	Enque/table_size	ABAP/share_objects_size_MB	

(Source: SAP)

Administration of the locks is handled via their own transaction (RSPLSE) and consists of configuration settings and monitoring tools. There are two types of configuration settings: one to determine the type of lock service the system should use (just described) and one specifying which characteristics the system should use to define locks. Lastly, there are two monitoring tools: one to view the locks for an InfoProvider or user and one to compare the locks between two users in conflict.

The characteristics relevant to locking can be controlled via configuration per InfoProvider. The default is to evaluate all characteristics in the InfoProvider for locking. If a characteristic is restricted, its selection is registered with the lock service. If a characteristic is unrestricted, it is assumed that all its records are to be locked and not registered with the lock service. Locking-relevant characteristics get registered to the locking service only if there is a relevant filter. Otherwise, all values are automatically locked (for unrestricted selections).

In configuration, you remove characteristics from a list of locking-relevant ones (since the default is all characteristics). This affects the behavior of the system in the following way: If a characteristic is not locking-relevant, it is *always* locked for *all values* but does not have a separate lock for *each value* because the characteristic is excluded from the locking service for that Info-Provider.

For example, imagine that you have a profit center balance sheet planning process where planners do not cross into each other's profit centers. The system will, by default, lock both the profit center and each general-ledger account that is planned on. Locking-service performance can be improved by eliminating the general-ledger accounts as a lock-relevant characteristic. After the account characteristic is removed, all accounts will be locked by profit center, which is the desired behavior, as each profit center plans its own data.

As another example, suppose planning is always done at the lowest granular level (without the need for summarized planning), such as position-based budgeting. Suppose a salary amount is always planned for a specific position (requiring a mandatory variable selection in the input-ready query). If this is always the case, the locks on job, pay grade, pay scale, and other summarizations of position are unnecessary. These characteristics can be eliminated as locking-relevant in configuration.

Finally, locks and lock conflicts can be monitored to determine if there are data-design issues or operational issues (such as orphaned or dead locks). The first view allows you to see all the SAP-IP locks by InfoProvider, by user, or by both. The second view allows you to enter two users for a given InfoProvider and compare their lock arguments. When planning, the system always does a check to see if another user has the data locked. If the system finds that the data you requested for planning is locked, it will issue an error message. The message will inform you of who is locking you out. By going to the locking service monitor, you can find out what data selections you were requesting compared to the data selections that the other user has locked. This level of detail is useful for identifying data-design flaws, user-entry errors, and operational system issues.

If an orphaned lock must be deleted, the standard method for deleting lock entries in SAP can be followed (transaction SM12). The locking table to use depends on the locking service. Table 9-2 gives the locking table names to use in order to find the lock arguments to be deleted.

Later in this chapter, you will learn how BW-BPS can coexist with SAP-IP, but it is worthy to note here that both planning tools can work on the same InfoCube without any danger, because they both share the same locking service.

Data Slices

Another way of controlling data access is to use an SAP-IP mechanism called *data slices*. Data slices are similar to filters but are used to freeze data. Data slices are data selections that work similarly to lock services but are a BI planning mechanism defined universally (independently of the user). Similar to the lock service (or even characteristic relationship checks), data slice locked data is still viewable by a user (it just becomes display only), while executed planning functions will end in error. Additionally, if variables are defined in the data slice, the selection values can be specified by users at runtime (so the data slice is flexible enough to be either dynamically determined by user or statically predetermined across all users).

There is another dynamic way that data slices can be defined. Instead of manually entering selection criteria, they can be programmatically derived. The programmatic method is based on an exit class (that is, configured to a custom ABAP object class). Figure 9-9 shows an example data slice (based on an exit class).

Data slices themselves can be activated and deactivated. If data slices do not have any restrictions, the entire InfoProvider will be locked. Lastly, single values, intervals, hierarchies, and variables can be used as part of a characteristic selection.

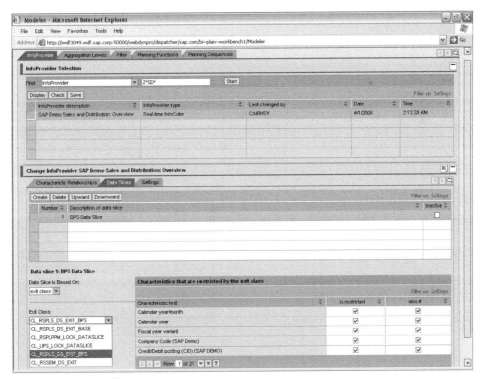

Figure 9-9 Data slice

Data slices are defined per real-time InfoProvider (and pertain only to real-time InfoProviders, since all other InfoProviders are automatically display only). If a MultiProvider is used, the underlying real-time InfoProviders and their corresponding data slices are called.

Semantic Rules

Semantic rules represent the relationships between data entities and the business rules in data. Primarily, this is modeled as characteristic relationships in integrated planning applications.

Because SAP-IP has been historically tied to InfoCubes, the ability to model semantic rules is important for data consistency. This is because information modeling options for planning have been constrained to fully denormalized models (star schemas).

For example, to plan on master data attributes or transitive attributes (i.e., an attribute of an attribute), those attributes must be included as dimensional attributes of the real-time InfoCube. In addition, any other data entity relationships or mappings (such as many-to-many relationships) also must be included into the denormalized data of the real-time InfoCube (that is, they cannot be planned on if the data is external to the InfoCube).

Because it is not possible to plan on key figures as attributes of master data or in normalized DataStore Objects, these relationships must be modeled as InfoCube dimensional attributes to be able to plan on the various levels of granularity. The same is true of presentation or characteristic hierarchies. Data must be flattened into the InfoCube to be able to plan on any hierarchy level.

SEM-BPS has the capability of planning on hierarchy levels either as a postable node hierarchy or as a runtime presentation hierarchy (building the hierarchy from the transaction data). Currently, presentation hierarchies in SAP-IP can only be planned at the leaf nodes (branch nodes are display only) which will be addressed in a future release. As a result, the answer is straightforward as to how to model hierarchies to support planning on any level: The only real option is to model characteristics for each level of the hierarchy as dimensional attributes of an InfoCube.

To support such planning design considerations, SAP-IP comes with functionality and mechanisms to maintain and enforce data consistency with volatile planning data in one of two ways:

1. Prevent users from creating bad semantic relationships while planning (that is, semantic rules are constant) as a validation or derivation.

2. Handle existing planned data with obsolete semantic relationships while planning (that is, semantic rules change over time) as a planning function.

The first scenario occurs during normal data input while the second scenario handles data that was inputted when the semantic rules were different.

The second scenario occurs in a planning environment where master data and hierarchies are changing as part of the planning process that creates the need for realigning the planned data (provided the change occurs in an unlocked version). In traditional data warehousing terms, this phenomenon is known as "slowly changing dimensions." SAP-IP characteristic relationships not only handle changing dimensions (that are more referential integrity driven) but can also handle many-to-many entity relationship rules and data enrichment logic.

For example, beyond referential integrity, characteristic relationships can handle semantic rules such as the following:

- Valid combinations of transaction types to asset, inventory, and equity accounts
- Valid combinations of cost elements to specific cost centers
- Validate that balance sheet records do not have cost centers
- Validate that profit and loss accounts do not have dummy profit centers
- Valid combination of innovation projects and products
- Valid combinations of customers and distribution channels
- Validate that the final version does not have any pseudo-master data

Valid combinations of many-to-many characteristic relationships can be stored in a DataStore Object, or semantic rules can be programmed. The DataStore Object option should handle most scenarios. Examples where programmatic logic might be needed are data-enrichment scenarios that do not require data lookups but rather string manipulations.

More specifically, a typical derivation needed is concatenating fiscal year and fiscal period into time characteristic 0FISCPER or doing the reverse by splitting 0FISCPER into separate fiscal year and periods (the system actually automatically handles this scenario, but there may be a need for custom ones). Another custom example may include deriving the system date, time, and user to store the details on changed data records for audit purposes. Applying such detailed runtime data enrichment logic should be closely scrutinized to prevent uncontrolled growth in data volumes.

SAP-IP works well for planning applications focused on manipulating aggregated facts. Where challenges occur is when planning applications are focused on manipulating more granular and normalized structures such as master data. For example, HR planning scenarios usually necessitate a lot of changes to employee, position, and job attributes or transitive attributes such as changes to a new job or pay grade or pay scale. These relationships must be completely denormalized into an InfoCube, and any transitive attribute change such as a change in pay grade must trigger a reposting that realigns the entire InfoCube for the new master data change for every instance of that relationship.

A planned event such as an employee switching jobs has data-consistency repercussions. Not only is master data updated, but planned transactions must be updated. In turn, not only does every new planning entry for that employee have to reference the new job, but every reference to the old job must either be deleted or moved to the new job. There are special planning functions to handle this scenario (explained later in the section titled "Basic Functions"). Because employee is very low-level granularity, and because version control usually explodes the number of records in an InfoCube, such a reposting function can be resource intensive.

An alternative realignment approach that some implementations take is to do a data mart load (loading the real-time InfoCube back into itself). Normally, this type of a data load would double the values in an InfoCube. However, if transformation rules were defined to multiply values by negative one, the effect would be to reverse out the values, which would net to zero. Compression with zero elimination would delete the records. This would simulate a characteristic relationship-delete planning function. If additional logic were added to the transformation to clone the records into the new characteristic relationships, the load would effectively behave like a repost planning function. This approach is more scalable but requires a process chain that switches the InfoCube loading mode (from planning to loading and then back), while data transfer processes run the load in background.

When master data planning and key-figure attribute updates are included in a future release, this type of scenario will be a lot easier to design. In the meantime, characteristic relationships are needed to keep external data (such as master data) consistent with internal data (such as transactional data).

Characteristic Relationships

Characteristic relationships do not exist for specific MultiProviders but rather exist at the underlying real-time InfoProvider level. So, if one MultiProvider consisted of two real-time InfoProviders, each real-time InfoProvider would have its own characteristic relationship logic. Figure 9-10 shows the configuration for characteristic relationships.

Characteristic relationships can either validate or derive characteristic combinations or values. A characteristic relationship is either configured with derivation or without derivation (which makes it a validation).

As the name implies, characteristic relationships do not validate or derive key figures (better served by exceptions and calculated key figures, respectively). Characteristic relationships are mostly used for data-integrity purposes or characteristic-combination purposes.

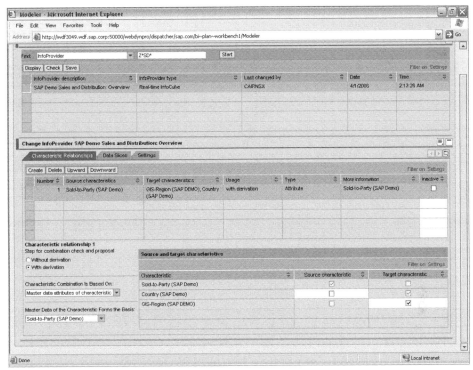

Figure 9-10 Characteristic relationships

There are four types of sources for characteristic relationships:

- Master data attribute
- Characteristic hierarchy
- DataStore Object
- Exit class

For each type, the metadata object that represents the source must be maintained (such as an InfoObject name, hierarchy name, DataStore Object name, or ABAP object class name). For each source, the source characteristic and target characteristic must be flagged.

Existing data stored within the BI metadata objects represent valid combinations (that is, whatever is missing is considered invalid data). If hierarchies are used, the target characteristic must be a characteristic within the source characteristic hierarchy. If DataStore Objects are used, they must be standard (not real-time). If an exit class is used, the ABAP object class must use an explicit interface (IF_RSPLS_CR_EXIT) or inherit from a specific parent class (CL_RSPLS_CR_EXIT_BASE).

If the designer wants to use characteristic relationships to do automatic derivations (such as product group from product), the derived attribute (in this case, `product group`) must be excluded from the aggregation level. Otherwise, a validation check will be performed instead.

Multistep derivations are possible as well. For example, a first step may include deriving `region` from `city`, which then feeds a derivation that determines the `country` from `region`. Multiple characteristic relationships can be defined to build one derivation off of the other.

From a user-input perspective, if inconsistent data (old characteristic relationships) appears in an input query, it is shown as display only, blocking any changes. Any planning functions that use obsolete data will error. To make data available for planning-function use, two special planning functions can be employed: one to delete data based on characteristic relationships and one to repost data on characteristic relationships. The former should be used if transactional data is no longer needed, while the latter should be used for realignment of data (similar in concept to an attribute change run for aggregates).

While entering data, if a user enters an invalid combination such as an inconsistent `product` and `product group` combination, the system will block the user from making this entry with an error message.

For time-dependent relationships, a standard key date can be specified in the characteristic relationships used not only for deriving time-dependent attributes of master data in characteristic relationships but also in filters.

These characteristic-relationship checks can be performance intensive (using logic that goes cell-by-cell within an input-query). So queries with a lot of real estate (that is, rows and columns) might suffer if there are too many characteristic relationships defined and activated (they can be turned off for performance-testing purposes). In particular, any significant combination proposals should be closely monitored. The design risk is generating a Cartesian product (that is, a multiplicative explosion of all value combinations) that consumes too much memory.

Planning Functions

SAP-IP data manipulations, transformations, and calculations are done via planning functions. Planning functions use two types of data: transaction data and reference data. *Transaction data* is the data that planning functions manipulate and must be written against real-time InfoProviders. Meanwhile, *reference data* is a read-only input to the planning function.

Reference data can be sourced from any type of InfoProvider (master data, DataStore Object, InfoCube, and so on). The key distinction between transaction and reference data is that the former gets locked based on the aggregation level and filter, while the latter does not. Planning functions either perform transformations (such as reposting records) or calculations (such as revaluations) against transaction data. All planning functions run in memory (plan cache) for performance reasons and are only committed to the real-time Info-Provider when data is explicitly saved.

Planning functions work against aggregation levels with filters being applied at run-time. The configuration of the planning functions differs depending on the planning functions. Some commonalities are in configuration, which will be generically discussed and applied to all the planning functions.

Controlling Function Behavior

Planning functions have two conceptual levels of metadata associated with them:

1. Metadata that controls how a particular planning function executes
2. Metadata that controls how types of planning functions are defined

The first level of metadata is called a *planning function,* while the second is called a *function type.* Planning functions are composed of the following metadata components:

- Function type (see Figure 9-11)
- Aggregation-level assignments (see Figure 9-11)
- Characteristics usage (see Figure 9-12)
- Parameter values (see Figure 9-13)

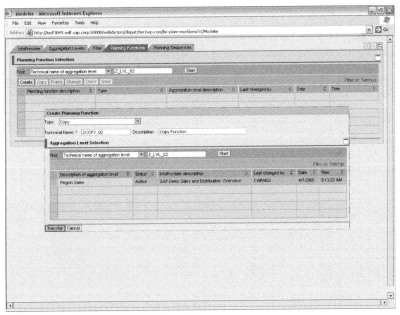

Figure 9-11   Creating a planning function

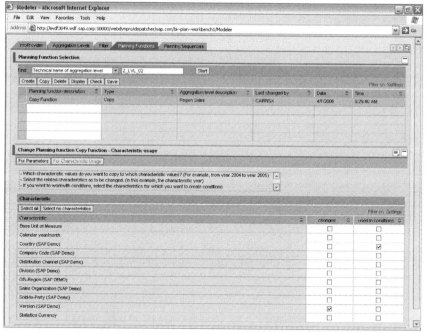

Figure 9-12   Configuring characteristics usage

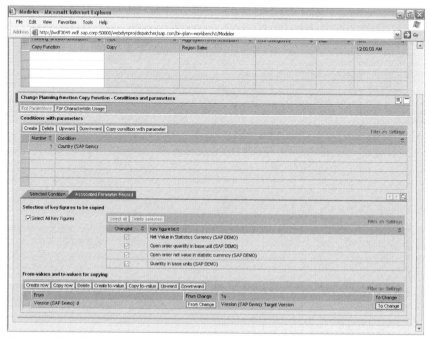

Figure 9-13   Configuring parameters

Function types are core to planning functions and are what differentiates them. In another sense, planning functions are the physical realizations of function types. Function types are composed of the following metadata components:

- An ABAP object class
- Properties settings
- Web Dynpros assignments for designing planning functions
- Parameter definitions

Generally, most planning functions have a number of parameterizations that must be specified to control the behavior of the planning function, depending on the function type. First, every planning function must be given a function type (that is, copy, delete, repost, and so on.) and must be assigned to an aggregation level. Figure 9-11 shows a planning function of type copy being created for a regional sales aggregation level.

Second, how characteristics in the aggregation level are used must be specified. Either characteristics are to be changed (which usually makes them available for further parameterization), are to be used in conditions (for further filtering of records before being passed to the function), or are not to be used at all (known as *block characteristics*). In Figure 9-12, the characteristic to be changed is version, so as to change the versions from source to target during the copy. In addition, country is used as a condition (to control the copy by country). The restrictions for conditions are configured in the parameters of the planning function (Figure 9-13).

Last, parameters for a planning function must be set. Typically there are two activities: defining the restrictions for conditions and configuring associated parameter records. If a planning function supports conditions, the configuration behavior for it is pretty universal. The configuration for associated parameter records is more unique per function type.

Figure 9-13 shows the associated parameter records for a copy function. First, the key figures to be updated by the function must be selected. Second, because version was flagged as a characteristic to be changed (see Figure 9-12), it is available here to be parameterized (specifying a source and target version). BEx variables can be used in parameters to control the behavior of the function at runtime. You can see at the bottom of Figure 9-13 that the source version is zero (representing a baseline version) and that the target version is a BEx variable (a user-specified value at runtime). Note that multiple sources and targets can be specified by creating additional rows. Not shown is that, in the Selected Condition tab strip, the condition characteristic (country) was also restricted by a BEx variable.

The way data is grouped when passed to the planning function is controlled via *block characteristics*. Block characteristics are all the characteristics not flagged as characteristics to be changed. In other words, these characteristics are unchanged by the planning function. Each unique combination of these characteristics form a *data block*. Data blocks can be thought of as subset groupings (similar in concept to data packages but more aggregated). Each of the block characteristics per data block is always constant; the data records in a data block vary by the characteristics to be changed.

For custom planning functions, it is important to know how data will be passed into the function. If all characteristics are flagged as characteristics to be changed, the entire dataset for the filter is loaded into the planning function at once. If none of the characteristics is flagged as a characteristic to be changed, each record in the filter selection is passed to the planning function one record at a time. Passing each record at a time is generally not good for performance, because of the memory overhead associated with each call to the planning-function logic. Figure 9-14 illustrates an example.

Customer	Sales Office	Sales
A1	1000	20
A1	1001	10
A2	1000	5
A2	1001	7

Fields to Be Changed	Number of Calls
Empty	4, one record per call
Sales Office	2, (1+2) and (3+4)
Customer	2, (1+3) and (2+4)
All	1, all records

Figure 9-14   Block characteristics
Based on material with Copyright © SAP AG

Additionally, some planning functions use reference data. Reference data can read records outside the aggregation level and filter of a planning function. Although reference data is an additional selection, it keeps the locking algorithm lean, following the "only-use-what-you-need" principle, and does not have the overhead of lock entries. Using the version copy example, the source version can be read as reference data (baseline version 0) because it does not change. The filter of the aggregation level assigned to the copy function can be restricted to the target version (the same BEx variable used in the parameter record of the copy function). The aggregation level is then filled whenever the function is executed.

It is also important to note that most planning functions do not read records with zero amounts nor generate records that have zero amounts. The exception to this is the copy function (in order to overlay or refresh the target with new amounts) and the generate combinations function.

Planning functions can be called via BEx Web applications or BEx workbooks. If the planning function must be scheduled in the DW Workbench or called from the Planning Modeler, it must be configured into a planning sequence. A *planning sequence* is nothing more than a bundle of functions that get sequentially executed.

Planning sequences can be integrated into process chains for background scheduling, as well as be executed in the foreground as part of a test mode in the Planning Modeler. For this reason, Input templates can be configured into planning sequence (for testing purposes). Input templates are otherwise ignored (if not run in test mode).

Putting an input layout into a sequence allows you to follow in test mode how data is being manipulated in each step. It is enough to have one input layout per planning sequence, since the input grid stays open when you step through the sequence. During rapid iterative prototyping, you should break a planning function into simpler components. By functionally decomposing a complex calculation into its atomic planning functions and combining them into a planning sequence, the logic design becomes more flexible and adaptable. Furthermore, the planning functions are easier to debug because each component can be run one at a time until the bug is found (and each function is modularized into easier-to-understand blocks of logic).

If requirements change, these building blocks can be quickly reassembled to support new capabilities. The downside is that this configuration is not optimal for performance. However, after iterative design and testing, these functions can be continually collapsed once they have stabilized and requirements have been frozen.

Function Types

Function types control design-time behaviors of configuring planning functions, which, in turn, control runtime behaviors. In addition, function types are assigned to an ABAP object class that not only controls planning function design-time logic but runtime execution logic as well. The ABAP object class has definition and execution methods. Note that the only required method for any custom function type ABAP object class is an execution method; the system will default the parameterizations for configuring a planning function.

Similar to other SAP BW repository-related metadata, function types are delivered as part of Business Content. They are modifiable, and custom ones can be developed. But note that the assigned ABAP class itself cannot be changed without being considered a modification (although it can be copied and customized). Similar to extractors, the code behind the Business Content should not be modified and comes with the system whether or not the Business Content is actually activated. In addition, new Business Content function types are expected in the future without having to wait for the next release of NetWeaver (similar to the rapid waves of Business Content add-on releases for SAP BW 3.0B).

As abstractions, function types are to planning functions what InfoObjects are to master data values. Just as InfoObjects have ABAP dictionary tables supporting them, each function type has its own ABAP object class. Just as every SAP BW master data table has its standards, so do the function type classes (which leverage a set of interfaces for defining, checking, and executing planning functions that come with standard methods and attributes). The standard interfaces are listed in Table 9-3.

Table 9-3   Function Type Interfaces

INTERFACE	LEVEL OF CONTROL	OPTIONALITY
IF_RSPLFA_SRVTYPE_IMP_DEF	Design	Optional
IF_RSPLFA_SRVTYPE_IMP_CHECK	Design	Optional
IF_RSPLFA_SRVTYPE_IMP_EXEC	Execution	Depends
IF_RSPLFA_SRVTYPE_IMP_EXEC_REF	Execution	Depends

At least one of the two execution interfaces must be assigned to any given ABAP object class assigned to a function type. One interface uses reference data, and the other does not. Which interface to use depends on whether or not reference data is flagged as mandatory in the function type configuration. Another flag determines whether or not blocks will be passed to the function (effectively setting all characteristics to be changes).

After a planning function is assigned a function type and an aggregation level, characteristic usage and parameters must be defined. The behavior of the characteristic usage and parameter screens is controlled by the function type. For characteristic usage, a flag can be set to determine whether or not the characteristics to be changed are hidden and whether the characteristic usage screen should be shown before the parameter screen. Either characteristic usage or parameter screens can be replaced with a custom Web Dynpros. Otherwise, the system will automatically generate the configuration screens. Figure 9-15 shows the configuration for the function type properties.

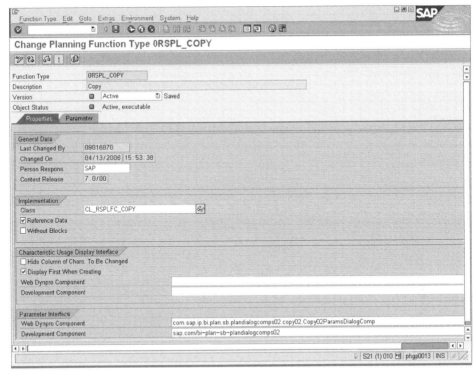

Figure 9-15   Function type properties

To generate the parameters screen, parameters for a function type must be defined. Each parameter defined has an associated parameter type consisting of the following options (shown in Figure 9-16):

- **Elementary** — An elementary parameter type is a characteristic value or a key-figure value. If this parameter type is picked, an InfoObject must be specified.

- **InfoObject-of-the-InfoProvider** — The InfoObject-of-the-InfoProvider parameter type is a characteristic name or key-figure name in the aggregation level.

- **Data Selection** — Data selection parameter types represent multiple characteristic selections as they relate to filters as part of a selection table.

- **Structure** — Structure parameter types are not ABAP dictionary structures but rather collections of parameters assigned together. These structures can then be made tabular (via a flag) to generate table-driven configuration (like source and target versions for version copies).

- **Key Figure Selection** — Key figure selection parameter types are simply key figure names. Other settings include whether or not variables are allowed in the parameter.

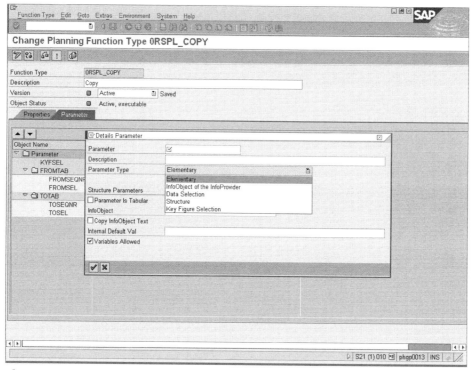

Figure 9-16 Function type parameters

Through function types, customers can develop planning functions the same way SAP develops planning functions (similar to all SAP BW Business Content). This was not the case with the previous SEM-BPS and BW-BPS technologies. Function types were predelivered and fixed; only the planning functions themselves were configurable.

Customer-defined planning logic and calculations could only be controlled by planning function parameterizations. FOX and user-exit function types made the calculation logic extensible but had inflexible parameterization structures that limited the ways a developer could influence how a planning function was designed.

The function type concept enables new capabilities such as controlling the interface to parameterize the planning function. The ABAP object class associated with a function type can use interface methods that extend its execution-time capabilities well beyond that of the SEM-BPS and BW-BPS user-exits, not only providing initialization and execution methods but also finishing, reference-data-reading, and adding-new-block methods.

Although function types can be delivered as part of customer, partner, or SAP Business Content, they still must be parameterized. The logic may be predelivered, but your data is not. Furthermore, predelivered function types should be viewed as building blocks. It is up to the solution designer to figure out how to wield the technical functions into something business meaningful.

In the current release of SAP-IP, the Business Content planning functions are mostly generic and abstracted, with the exception of forecasting functions. The SEM-BPS business planning functions have yet to be migrated but in the interim can be used in parallel to SAP-IP if needed (such as retractors or financial functions). Currency translation and unit conversion are more business specific but can also be employed in BEx. Furthermore, enhancements in FOX include currency-translation commands.

What follows is an explanation of the function types available. The standard function types are arbitrarily categorized as basic and advanced, depending on the level of sophistication.

Basic Functions

For the most part, simple planning functions lack business context. They are focused on different technical ways of manipulating characteristics and calculating key figures. Normally, they serve as building block functions that can be used in a planning sequence in conjunction with other functions (such as deleting data before a custom recalculation in order to eliminate orphaned records). The simple functions have been logically presented as data operations, characteristic relationship, and valuation planning functions.

Data Operations

In most cases, this set of functions should work against an aggregation level that includes all the InfoObjects in the real-time InfoProvider. Otherwise, unexpected results may occur (each planning function scenario is explained shortly). For this reason, be mindful of the performance impacts these functions may have on the system if performed on large data sets.

Following are the planning functions that perform data operations:

- **Delete** — No SAP-IP data operation actually ever physically deletes records in InfoCubes. This function simply zeroes out records for specific key figures by creating reversal deltas. When values zero out, they then "disappear" from planning because zero records are normally not read. No characteristics are changed; only key figures are revalued to zero. As a result, characteristic-usage configuration is grayed out in the parameterization for this function. Instead, you must specify the conditions and which key figure is affected or select all of them. Single values, intervals, hierarchies, and variables can be used in the conditions. If a summarized aggregation level is used to support a delete function, be mindful that the deletion might not work as you expect it. It will create a reversal at a summarized level rather than at a detailed level. This means that the details don't get reversed but net to zero at a summarized total. The summarized total is set to zero via a residual that offsets underlying details.

- **Copy** — This function is most popularly used for version management but has other applications as well. Note that this function copies only records, not key figures, on the same record (that is, copying a sales target key figure to a sales estimate key figure — this would be done in FOX). However, the parameters for this function do control which key figures are updated in the copied records and for what conditions. It also includes characteristic-usage criteria for controlling how the target of the copy will differ from the source. For version management, the versioning characteristics would be flagged as characteristics to be changed (that is, multiple characteristics can be simultaneously flagged). Then, in the parameterization, source and targets must be defined. It is possible to copy a source to multiple targets and collect multiple sources into a target. Single values, intervals, hierarchies, and variables can be used to define the source and target. Also, note that the copy completely refreshes the target data sets (instead of overlaying the records); this means that if a target has no corresponding match from the source, it is set to zero instead of left alone. In BW-BPS, there were two different copy functions that would either overlay or refresh. In SAP-IP, there is only one copy option, and it refreshes (which is what most people expect). Also, be mindful that if a summarized aggregation level is used to do the copy, all the details not included in the aggregation level will be truncated and summarized when copied into the target records (refer to the earlier discussion on sparsity in the section titled "Aggregation Levels").

- **Repost** — Repost configuration is very similar to copy configuration. It also behaves similarly to a copy function, except that the source is deleted after the target is updated. If no preexisting target records with amounts exist, a repost function could be simulated by combining copy and delete functions into a planning sequence (but repost does this as one operation, for better performance). Otherwise, such a planning sequence could be used in lieu of a repost if target values need to be refreshed. The reposting function augments target records instead of refreshing them. More explicitly, it adds the source key-figure amounts to the target records if values already exist on target records instead of overwriting. Multiple repost steps can be configured, but each source and target step must be limited to a single value. Furthermore, since source and target must be locked, the filter used with this planning function needs to have both values. Reposting can be used as a realignment tool. In other words, amounts and quantities do not change, but the associated characteristic combinations do change based on parameter configuration. Unexpected results can occur if a summarized aggregation level is used; totals would be reposted to other characteristic combinations, but the details would not follow.

Characteristic Relationships

As explained earlier, a set of planning functions is delivered that works with the semantic rules of characteristic relationships to ensure consistency between outside semantic relationships and the transactional data stored in planning. In addition, because characteristic relationships are defined per real-time Info-Provider (and do not exist on MultiProviders), these planning functions operate only against aggregation levels assigned to them. They do not work otherwise.

The following are the planning functions that work with characteristic relationships:

- **Delete invalid combinations** — This function is like the delete function but only deletes records that do not map to characteristic relationships as defined as part of the real-time InfoProvider. Consistency is maintained by purging the system of obsolete entries every time master data, hierarchies, or some other configured relationship changes.

- **Repost (characteristic relationships)** — This function is like the repost function, except instead of controlling how records are reposted in the parameters of the function, it is controlled from characteristic relationships. It effectively realigns the data to be consistent with the characteristic relationships. For small subsets of data, this function can be used to effectively handle slowly changing dimensions during the planning process. The result is similar to how attribute change runs work for aggregates if the characteristic relationships were based on master data. Other scenarios might include aggregating details no longer needed, based on a status change.

- **Generating combinations** — Because most functions cannot read zero records, this function can be used to create blank records based on the characteristic relationship combinations configured against the InfoCube. These records then can be further manipulated and valuated. This function is helpful for initializing an input-query with records for usability. This is also helpful in a planning sequence where a subsequent planning function must be called, irrespective of whether data is in the aggregation level or not (such as a validation of reference data).

Valuations

Valuation planning functions do not change characteristics on planning records but rather update key-figure values. As a result, characteristic-usage configuration does not apply for these planning functions, except for revaluation (which uses conditions).

Following are the planning functions that explicitly update key figures:

- **Currency translation** — This function updates a target key figure from a source key figure after applying a currency translation. This function can perform multiple translations at once (such as translating transaction currency into both local currency and group currency on a plan record). The target currencies (in this case, local and group) are overwritten each time the translation is performed (even if the source key figure is zero). For each source and target key-figure pairing, a currency translation type must be specified to drive how the translation is performed. This is very similar to and consistent with how currency translations are applied in transformation rules and in BEx. Also, note that FOX can perform currency translations. Finally, note that currency keys are not changed by this translation; only amounts are updated.

- **Unit conversion** — This unit conversion function is very similar to currency translation, except that it uses conversion types instead of currency translation types. It also updates one key figure from another. Since the unit of measure is not changed (only key figures values are updated), there are no characteristics to be changed within this planning function.

- **Revaluate** — This function changes the values of key figures, not characteristics. Nevertheless, it does use characteristics as conditions so as to be able to configure a revaluation percentage per key figure per conditional characteristic value. This way, multiple revaluations (per condition) can be performed without the necessity of multiple planning functions. Each condition created can be a value, interval, variable, or hierarchy. The revaluation fixed percentage can be applied to specific key figures or across all key figures per condition. In addition, the revaluation percentage can be dynamically derived via a variable.

Advanced Functions

This section arbitrarily defines advanced functions to mean any planning functions that require a little more effort and thought in designing and configuring.

Distribution

Distributions are primarily for pushing-down values from higher levels of a planning hierarchy to lower levels via aggregation levels that represent each level of the hierarchy. An example has already been already given whereby regional sales managers are distributing sales targets to two sales offices (Atlanta and Miami). This example will be used to elaborate on the distribution planning function.

There are two different function types for distribution: one for distribution by key and one distribution by reference data. *Distribution by key* requires manual weighting factors, while *distribution by reference data* is automatically derived from existing data (such as another year's data).

To distribute data from region to office, the aggregation level used by the planning function needs both characteristics. The region is used as a condition, while the office is a characteristic to be changed. The condition represents the source of distribution, and the characteristic to be changed represents the target. For each source and target combination, a weighting factor must be manually maintained. Distribution can be per key figure or across all key figures.

In addition, how key figures are to be totaled and distributed is configurable. There are a number of options:

- Create entries manually.
- Top-down distribution: Distribute all.
- Top-down distribution: Only distribute unassigned values.

The first option is not for top-down distribution scenarios (that is, across characteristics) but rather a form of manual allocation (that is, within a characteristic). For example, if a sales office shuts down and its sales pipeline must be picked up by two other sales offices, this distribution option allows you to manually specify the closed office as the source and the other two offices as targets in the parameters.

The second option rolls up all values into a calculated total for the sales region (including sales office estimates and any residuals created by target setting) and then distributes the total back down to the sales offices. Residuals are any values not assigned to a sales office but fall under the region (that is, blank or "#" values).

The third option only distributes residual (or unassigned) values on the region to the sales office.

All three options apply to both distribution planning function types (that is, by key and by reference). After the distribution is finished, the source values are reposted to the target values based on a split (either by weighting factors or reference values).

For distribution by key, weighting factors are manually entered (or derived via formula variable) per target (which can represent multiple values). For distribution by reference data, a block characteristic and characteristic value must be specified. A reference key figure can be optionally specified as well.

If a key figure is not chosen, each key figure references itself to determine the distribution. For example, if the reference characteristic is fiscal year and the value is this year, and the reference key figure for headcount is used, regional sales are distributed to a sales office based on the current year's sales office headcount. However, if the reference characteristic is fiscal year and the value is last year, and no reference key figure is used, regional sales are distributed to a sales office based on last year's sales office sales.

Forecasting

Currently, the forecasting planning function is the only example of statistical planning in SAP-IP, and it employs the same statistical forecasting algorithms that SAP APO uses. Other forms of statistical analysis (such as decision trees and association analysis) are more appropriate for data mining applications. Forecasting concepts and techniques is a broad subject with many collegiate texts supporting it. The intention of this section is to give a quick overview and glossary of what types of forecasting are possible within SAP-IP.

First, when configuring a forecasting planning function, a forecasting strategy must be decided on. The options are as follows:

- **Automatic model selection** — This option will automatically pick an optimal forecasting strategy but must be used carefully because of the performance impacts that optimization has on forecasting. All the forecast methods use history as a baseline to forecast the future, and each strategy has its own minimum set of data to do its calculations.

- **Average** — This option takes the straight average of history and forecasts that number forward.

- **Moving average** — This option takes an average but specifies how many sequential time intervals to use (specified in forecast configuration) in the calculation.

- **Weighted moving average** — This option is the same as moving average, but different manual weightings can be given to specific periods.

- **Simple exponential smoothing (constant model)** — This option is like the moving average option, except it applies an alpha factor that weighs more-recent periods more heavily than less-recent periods.

The degree of the smoothing is dependent upon how the alpha factor is parameterized.

- **Linear exponential smoothing (trend model)** — This model is like the constant model but introduces a beta factor for exponential smoothing. The beta factor is used to weigh in trends (such as growth or shrinkage) into the smoothing. Both alpha and beta factors can be configured.

- **Seasonal exponential smoothing (seasonal model)** — This model is like the constant model but introduces a gamma factor for exponential smoothing. The gamma factor is used to weigh seasonal cycles into the smoothing. Both alpha and gamma factors can be configured.

- **Trend-seasonal exponential smoothing (multiplicative seasonal component)** — This model combines both the trend and seasonal models together but with multiplicative effect (meaning that seasonality and trends are amplified). In other words, beta and gamma factors are multiplied together in this model. Alpha, beta, and gamma factors can be configured to adjust the multiplying effects.

- **Trend-seasonal exponential smoothing (additive seasonal component)** — This model is the same as the previous one, except that trends do not amplify the seasonality trends but rather incrementally add to them. In other words, beta and gamma results are added together in this model. Here again, alpha, beta, and gamma factors can be configured.

- **Linear regression** — This is a classic, ordinary, least-squares regression.

Each forecast strategy can be additionally parameterized for behaviors such as how to handle outliers, how to handle negative forecasts, and how to handle historical amounts with zeroes. If the forecast strategy is a trend model, a factor for dampening (or amplifying) the trend can be configured. In addition, optimizers for auto-determining alpha, beta, and gamma factors can be employed using various methods such as mean-absolute error, mean-absolute deviation, mean-square error, or exponentially smoothed absolute error and step-sizing the factor in increments between zero and one. Finally, for all the statistical forecast strategies there is additional logging that provides the technical details behind the calculations.

Figure 9-17 shows an example parameterization for an automatic model selection forecasting strategy. Note that the parameterization screen changes depending on the forecast strategy picked (only showing the relevant parameters). Automatic model selection was chosen as an example to illustrate most of the parameterizations across all forecast strategies at once.

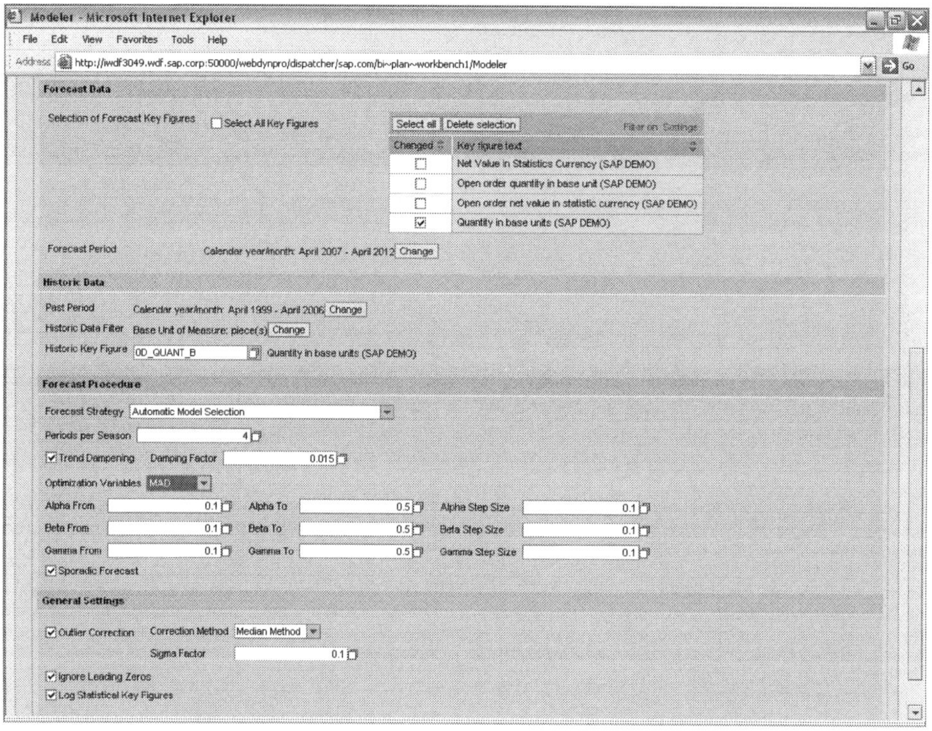

Figure 9-17   Forecasting parameters

Formula

If a standard function does not meet requirements, before jumping to a custom function type and ABAP programming, another option should be evaluated: formula functions. Even though a formula function uses its own programming language, it is simplified logic that abstracts away the complexities of ABAP you might find in coding a custom planning function type (such as deep structures and field-symbol logic).

Another reason to use a formula function is to combine multiple standard functions for performance gain. In this case, the formula function does not add new capability; it simply replaces what simple standard functions do in one function instead of in many.

Syntax

Formula functions are programmed in FOX, which can be thought of as meta-ABAP or an SAP-IP scripting language (although it is compiled into ABAP for parity performance). Put differently, it is a language specific to planning functions that abstracts ABAP for simpler logic constructs. FOX was first introduced by SEM-BPS, but the language can also be used in SAP-IP. It can perform logical expressions, mathematical operations, loop logic, string-processing, data retrieval, financial functions, messaging, and ABAP function calls.

FOX has its own editor in the parameters for a formula planning function shown in Figure 9-18. FOX programs can be written from scratch or built via program elements and operands. Program elements represent programming commands and operators, while operands represent the data structure elements to be processed.

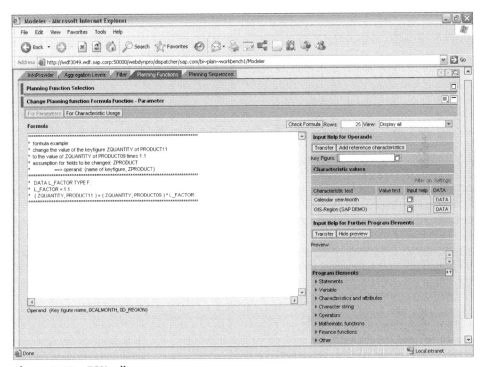

Figure 9-18 FOX editor

The operands available are contingent upon characteristic-usage configuration. The characteristics to be changed become the operands in a FOX formula and have a specified order listed at the bottom of the editor. Key-figure name is always an operand because aggregation levels always automatically include all key figures. The form of the operand can have the following two variations:

- **Only key figure name** — {'Key figure name'}.
- **Key figure name and one or multiple characteristics values** — {'Key figure name', 'Characteristic value', 'Characteristic value'…}.

Note the similarities in the structure of the operands for the two variations and that the first operand is always the key-figure name. Four example scenarios will be given to illustrate FOX formula syntax:

1. Only specific key figures are updated.
2. Only one characteristic is updated (across all key figures).
3. Multiple characteristics are updated (across all key figures).
4. Multiple characteristics and specific key figures are updated.

Looping logic will be introduced here (across key figures) to illustrate the scenarios but explained in more detail later in this chapter in the section titled "Programming Logic." Note that this looping is necessary because the key-figure name is automatically part of the operand in SAP-IP FOX formulas (since aggregation levels automatically include all key figures).

Imagine that an information model for a top-down and bottom-up sales planning application has two key figures: one custom InfoObject for sales estimates (named ESTIMATE) and another custom InfoObject for sales targets (named TARGET). Estimates are entered during bottom-up planning and then must be copied into targets at the initiation of top-down planning. To initialize the targets, the copy planning function will not work, because this scenario requires copying data across key figures, not data records. The operand for this FOX statement follows the first variation (only contains the key-figure name). The statement would look like this:

```
{TARGET} = {ESTIMATE}.
```

Now, for the second scenario, suppose that after the targets have been properly updated for the upcoming year, another year is added to the planning horizon. For this scenario, you want both target and estimate key figures to be updated in the copy. The only thing that changes in the data records is the fiscal year. As a result, in this planning function configuration, the characteristic to be changed is flagged as fiscal year. Since all key figures are automatically included, they need to be looped through in the FOX formula by declaring a variable for the key-figure name, and looping through each instance of key-figure in the aggregation level. If the current year is 2007 and both target and estimates are to be copied into the next year, the FOX statement would look like this:

```
DATA KF TYPE KEYFIGURE_NAME.
FOREACH KF.
    {KF, 2008} = {KF, 2007}.
ENDFOR.
```

The system knows that the values 2007 and 2008 are for the fiscal year operand because it is the only characteristic to be changed. However, for the third scenario, multiple characteristics are flagged to be changed. In this case, the order of the operands is important and is displayed at the bottom of the FOX editor.

For example, suppose that in this example there are two versions: One is a working version and the other is a final version represented as the alphanumeric codes WORK and FINAL, respectively. If the aforementioned FOX formula is used, both versions are copied into the following year, which is undesirable (record explosion). As a result, a versioning characteristic is added in the fields to be changed. At the bottom of the editor, the following text is displayed:

```
{Key figure name, Fiscal year, Version}
```

This tells you the order of the operands. In addition, you want all key figures to be updated. The corresponding FOX statement would look like this:

```
DATA KF TYPE KEYFIGURE_NAME.
FOREACH KF.
     {KF, 2008, WORK} = {KF, 2007, FINAL}.
ENDFOR.
```

As with the previous scenario, you want to control which key figures are updated as well. In this scenario, you decide that targets should not yet be set in the following year but that only estimates should be initialized (and targets left blank). Furthermore, you believe that next year's estimates should be initialized as this year's targets. In this planning function, the fiscal year, version, and key-figure name are all included as characteristics to be changed. The form of the operand as displayed below the text editor is as follows:

```
{Key figure name, Fiscal year, Version}
```

As a result, the FOX statement is as follows:

```
{ESTIMATE, 2008, WORK} = {TARGET, 2007, FINAL}.
```

As another more complicated variation of the previous example, imagine that you want to update both target and estimate next year but also include a new key figure in your aggregation level for sales quantity (InfoObject 0QUANTITY). Because populating sales quantities from target sales amounts would be nonsensical calculation, you must exclude that key figure from the copy. The statement is as follows:

```
DATA KF TYPE KEYFIGURE_NAME.
FOREACH KF.
     IF KF <> '0QUANTITY'.
          {KF, 2008, WORK} = {TARGET, 2007, FINAL}.
     ENDIF.
ENDFOR.
```

The examples covered are statements applied to characteristics that can be changed in the formula function. It is also possible to access reference data (that is, a block characteristic value). Any part of the formula on the right-hand side of the "equal" sign is considered reference data.

For example, suppose that in the previous example, instead of copying the final target version in the current year, you want to copy the target work version in the current year to a work-version estimate in the following year. Since the version does not change, it can be used as a block characteristic (that is, left out of the fields to be changed) so that the operand form is as follows:

```
{Key figure name, Fiscal year}
```

Supposing you use a custom InfoObject for a version called STATUS, your FOX statement would then be:

```
{ESTIMATE, 2008} = {TARGET, 2007|STATUS = WORK}.
```

You could also apply mathematical operators (addition, subtraction, multiplication, division, and so on) to a FOX formula. For example, you can increase our estimate by 10 percent:

```
{ESTIMATE, 2008} = {TARGET, 2007|STATUS = WORK} * .10.
```

Note that FOX always uses the internal format for characteristic values (meaning they haven't passed through any conversion routines). For example, alphanumeric conversions that apply leading zeroes would be applied before characteristic values are used in FOX formulas (that is, FOX references version "001" as simply "1"). Finally, a period at the end of every statement is essential.

Functions

Besides simple mathematical operations, all the other mathematical functions available in ABAP can be used in FOX formulas (such as absolute values and logarithmic functions). There are also additional BI-specific commands such as minimums and maximums. Here is a brief listing of the functions: ABS, CEIL, FLOOR, FRAC, TRUNC, SIGN, MAX, MIN, SQRT, LOG, LOG10, EXP, COS, SIN, TAN, COSH, TANH, ASIN, ACOS, and ATAN.

There are also FOX-specific, financial-related functions such as DECL (straight-line depreciation), DECD (declining-balance method of depreciation), DISC (discounting), and PERP (perpetual bond). These functions typically need to be properly parameterized to calculate the results. Similarly, FOX contains some recently included valuation functions such as CURC (currency translations that require parameterizations for exchange rate date, type, source currency, and target currency) and ROUND (rounding) as well.

Besides calculations, there are FOX commands for data retrieval and string processing. For example, master data lookups are possible using functions such as ATRV for attribute lookups and ATRVT for master data text lookups. Reference data can be referenced with functions TMVL (for time characteristics) and OBJV (for block characteristics). String processing commands include REPLACE (for replacing values), CONCAT (for concatenating values), SUBSTR (outputs substrings), and STRLEN (outputs the length of the string).

Probably one of the more flexible extensions to FOX is the ability to call ABAP function modules. Function modules to be used by FOX must be registered in table RSPLF_FDIR. There are a number of restrictions on the function module that can be called. Although FOX supports importing, exporting, and changing parameters, they must be simple data types. Structures and tables are not supported as function module parameters. Only InfoObject data types or program variables defined as floating point, integer, or decimal are supported. Exceptions can be raised and handled. The FOX command for calling the function module is similar to how you would call it from ABAP (that is, CALL FUNCTION).

Programming Logic

To make FOX more dynamic, programmatic constructs can be employed such as program variables, loops logic, and conditional statements. Program variables can be created for simple data types (such as integer, floating point, or decimal), characteristics, and key-figure names:

```
DATA KF TYPE KEYFIGURE_NAME.
DATA CHA_VERS TYPE STATUS.
DATA PERCENT TYPE F.
```

These program variables can then be used within loop constructs or FOX functions. Six types of loop constructs can be used in FOX:

- FOREACH *<characteristic variable>*...ENDFOR.
- FOREACH *<characteristic variable>* IN REFDATA...ENDFOR.
- FOREACH *<characteristic variable>* IN SELECTION...ENDFOR.
- FOREACH *<characteristic variable>* IN VARIABLE...ENDFOR.
- DO *<number>* TIMES...ENDDO.
- DO...ENDDO.

The first loop command loops through all the records in the current block being passed to the planning function for every distinct value of the characteristic to which the variable belongs. With each loop pass, the characteristic value is filled with a value that can then be used inside the loop for dynamically setting values.

For example, in the FOX formula scenarios provided earlier, the syntax could have been made more dynamic through the use of a loop construct and programming variables for characteristics. Suppose a planning horizon must be initialized or refreshed with current-year data. The following FOX code could be programmed:

```
DATA KF TYPE KEYFIGURE_NAME.
DATA YEAR TYPE 0FISCYEAR.
FOREACH KF, YEAR.
    {KF, YEAR} = {KF, 2007} * .10.
ENDFOR.
```

At runtime, the values for the FOX program variable YEAR are taken from the records in the planning function selection. The InfoObject 0FISCYEAR is a characteristic to be changed.

Furthermore, assume that there is data for a two-year horizon consisting of fiscal years 2008 and 2009 and that a condition is configured in the planning function to restrict the function to apply only to the years 2008 and 2009. In the first loop, the FOX program variable KF and YEAR will dynamically fill with the estimate key figure and fiscal year 2008, which would be effectively the same as programming the following FOX statement:

```
{ESTIMATE, 2008} = {ESTIMATE, 2007} * .10.
```

In the second loop, the effective statement is as follows:

```
{ESTIMATE, 2009} = {ESTIMATE, 2007} * .10.
```

The second loop command does the same kind of loop logic, but instead of using the current block, it loops through the reference data used in a formula function. The system determines and fills reference data via the FOX formula definition. It evaluates all the data needed for the right-hand side of the equations as reference data. In this scenario, fiscal year 2007 could have been left out of the filter for the planning function, because it was reference data and did not need to be locked for update. If this reference data loop construct was used in the scenario, there would only be one loop pass for fiscal year (that is, 2007).

The third loop command loops through all values in the filter assigned to the planning function. In this example, this could be three loop passes for all three years (2007-2009).

The fourth loop command is very similar to the one just described, except it is technically sourced differently. Instead of using the filter, it gets its list of values from the BEx variable, which may or may not be the same as the filter list of values.

Finally, the last two loop constructs do not relate to any data. They are generic loops that can be called for a fixed number of loop passes or endlessly. For the last loop, it is important to use a conditional statement (IF...THEN...ELSE...)

and a command to terminate the loop (EXIT). The conditional statement and exit commands can be used for all the other loop-processing logic as well. However, you should use planning function conditions in lieu of the FOX conditional statement commands, if possible. This keeps the logic more readable and reusable.

Loops can be nested into each other, but use this option sparingly because unexpected and undesirable results may occur. If possible, try to perform all your operations in one loop. Figure 9-19 shows the difference between including every characteristic combination in one loop versus doing nested loops for each characteristic. The former loops through the data, while the latter creates a Cartesian product for every combination of characteristic values. Solution designers who do not understand the difference between the two loop constructs can inadvertently create large data volumes and performance problems via improper use of nested loops.

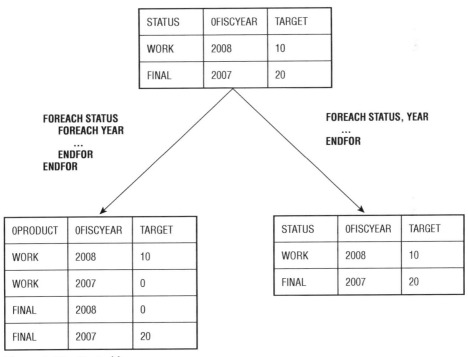

Figure 9-19   Nested loops

Based on material with Copyright © SAP AG

For rigorous testing and visibility into FOX formula functions, there are two other commands that you should liberally use: BREAK-POINT (for stopping the code at runtime to step through what might be going wrong) and MESSAGES (to document known errors and exception scenarios).

Integrated Planning User Interface

Probably the largest advance in SAP-IP capabilities is around the UI. By simply making well-established tools like BEx Analyzer and BEx Web Application Designer planning-enabled, immediate synergies are achieved. BEx comes with a lot of functions and services that SAP-IP applications can leverage. The intent of this section is not to rehash topics covered in Chapters 7 and 8 but to build on them with planning-specific scenarios.

By leveraging native BEx capabilities, a number of new-use scenarios are possible to enrich the user planning experience.

Runtime Capabilities

Whether the planning application is in Excel or on the Web, a number of BEx standard capabilities are now available that can enhance a planning application. The robust ad-hoc and self-service capabilities of BEx can be leveraged by planners during the planning session without the need for predefining or constraining the steps a planner might take. Furthermore, planners no longer must change sessions to shift their activities from planning to analysis in order to evaluate the impact of their inputs. The planner is able to plan and see the reporting results simultaneously. Table 9-4 lists some example BEx capabilities and their planning relevancies.

Table 9-4 BEx Runtime Planning-Relevant Capabilities

FUNCTION	PLANNING-RELEVANT EXAMPLES
Context Menu	Because there are many functions available at runtime after a query is executed, a context menu is provided to list the functions available, depending upon where you are in the query and the navigation state. This makes planning sessions more dynamic instead of predefined, static planning UIs. Furthermore, input-ready queries have additional context options (such as transfer values and save values).
Drag and Drop	In addition to the context menu, many of the same functions can be performed via simple drag and drop, thereby improving usability and navigability in a planning session to dynamically change how the data must be sliced for planning. This enables planners to get to the data they need to change quicker and more intuitively, as well as better find data anomalies.
Properties	Planners can make self-service changes to their planning session "look and feel" by taking advantage of such runtime settings as zero suppression, data formatting, display options, presentation options, currency conversion, number format, sorting, text display options, and result row suppression for planning usability.

Table 9-4 BEx Runtime Planning-Relevant Capabilities *(continued)*

FUNCTION	PLANNING-RELEVANT EXAMPLES
Drilldown and Filtering	The ability to start with aggregated information (for the birds-eye view) and then drill down to the details (worms-eye view) to make changes (and vice-versa) is now possible. Swapping axes to plan the data in a different order is also possible. The ability to drill down and filter alleviates the need to create too many areas for plan-inputs and display-outputs on screen at the same time (thereby improving performance). Instead of having separately designed static inputs and outputs that take up memory and real-estate, navigation can enable both sets of information within the same session, but at different times and eliminate the need for separate grids for input versus output. A change can be made and its aggregated effects reviewed by simply removing drill-down characteristics. Filtering allows characteristic values to be swapped out in place of each other (such as profit centers or accounts) in order to traverse the data.
Hierarchies	A lot of planning is hierarchy-driven, and it is another way via drill-down to visually rollup amounts into hierarchal subtotals. Hierarchies can either be added or removed from the planning session at runtime, and can be represented in both the rows and columns (such as an account hierarchy by a time-based hierarchy rolling a five-year horizon by quarter and year summaries).
Local Calculations	In addition to drill-down summarizations, exception aggregation and OLAP functions can also be called to evaluate plan data entry (such as averages, counts, variances, minimums, maximums, first values, last values, result normalizations, ranked lists, and so on) to evaluate the reasonableness of what you planned.
Query Jumps	If separate planning sessions are needed, but with the same planning data context (such as different queries or different aggregation levels), the report-report interface can be leveraged for seamless integration of planning sessions. In some scenarios, this can be very helpful. For example, in a sales planning, two aggregation levels are needed: one for regional sales and one for office sales. A planning session for a regional sales manager might entail entering a target adjustment by a region, distributing it to sales offices, and query-jumping to an input-query on the sales office aggregation level to view the results of the distribution (and make further manual adjustments).

When executing an input query, there are a number of things to be mindful of at runtime. First, it is possible to slice and dice on aggregation levels, but it is not possible to plan on cells that represent aggregations or summations (such as hierarchy node rollups, subtotals, and totals). Until the level of granularity of the query is the same as the aggregation level, input cells will be display only. If the aggregation level is on a MultiProvider, this lowest-level granularity has to explicitly identify the real-time InfoCube to be updated. Furthermore, navigational attributes are included as part of the aggregation level if it is restricted to a value in a filter or a restricted key figure; otherwise, it is ignored.

Once a cell is ready for input, it will be highlighted and can be modified. From a context menu, there are two planning options: transfer values and save values.

The option to *transfer values* writes the data changes to the planning cache. All subsequent OLAP functions (such as drill-down) will read the values from the planning cache. For BEx Analyzer workbooks, there are additional options to automatically transfer data during navigation (with or without a confirmation message pop-up). Otherwise, the context menu option to transfer values must be manually selected after each change and before the next navigation step.

The *save values* option commits the changes to the database. All changes will be lost if the session is exited and the user chooses not to save the data.

For BEx workbooks, it is possible to perform offline planning by saving the workbook locally as a file and entering the data offline. After going back online, data can then be synchronized and persistently saved in SAP BW. Functions that involve the back-end are not available offline, such as working in design mode or navigating in analysis mode (that is, slicing and dicing). From this perspective, the BEx workbook goes static when offline until a connection is reestablished. This feature is also helpful for reconnecting to the SAP BW system if the connection is lost for any reason.

For the most part, the look and feel of SAP-IP planning applications is almost indistinguishable from the look and feel of BEx reporting and analysis applications and is just as varied. Following are the possible distinctions:

- Whether or not cells are presented in a workbook or Web application that are ready for input

- Whether or not buttons are included to call planning commands

- The messaging passed back from the planning application (such as a custom warning from a FOX planning function)

Figure 9-20 illustrates a hypothetical planning application demonstrating the following planning-enhancing features:

- Highlighted input ready cells (thick cell borders)

- Buttons for refresh, save data, planning function, and planning sequence commands

- Planning function messages notifying the planner of successful execution and how many data records were generated and changed

- Input-ready query and display-only query, as well as a chart working in tandem.

- Exception reporting on variances between plan and actuals

- Statistical details of when data was last refreshed

- Navigation block for filtering the data selections and navigation buttons to other planning applications

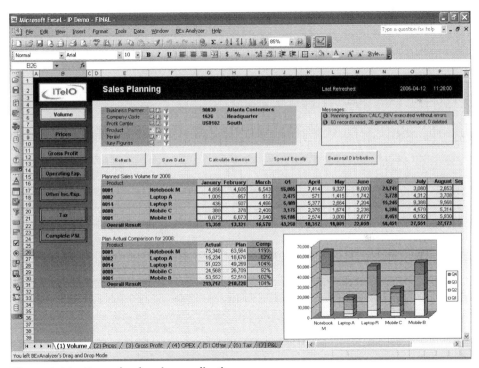

Figure 9-20   Example planning application

Design-Time Capabilities

There are two levels (and sets of tools) for designing a planning application: the query level (that is, BEx Query Designer) and the presentation level (that is, BEx Analyzer or BEx Web Applications Designer).

Queries

The query definition controls readiness for input. In turn, there are two levels of settings: one associated with the query properties and the other associated with the structural components of the query (that is, key figures or restricted key figures in the query definition, as shown in Figure 9-21). A planning tab in the query properties simply allows you to determine whether a query starts in change mode or display mode. It is nothing more than a checkbox option. For each structural component, there is a choice of three radio buttons: input ready, not input ready (but changeable via a planning function), or not input ready (and not changeable via a planning function). Note that these settings affect only the modifiability of planning data for the structural element (such as a key figure) at the query level (that is, they don't affect or interact with data slicing and lock services).

Table 9-5 highlights some selected BEx query capabilities (typically defined at design time). These reporting and analysis capabilities can be leveraged in planning applications. For example, modeling business rules, validation checks, and calculation logic do not necessarily have to be done via planning functions. OLAP functions (as shown in Table 9-5) or Excel and Web functions (explained shortly) can be employed in SAP-IP.

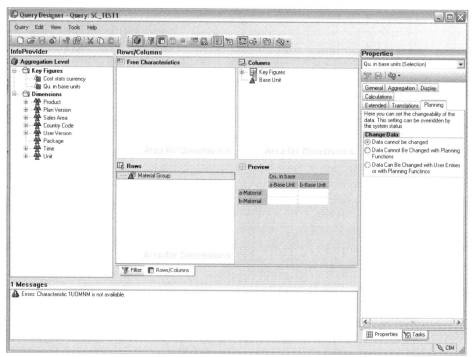

Figure 9-21　Structural component properties

Table 9-5   BEx Query Design-Time Planning-Relevant Capabilities

FUNCTION	PLANNING RELEVANT EXAMPLES
Conditions	Plan data can be validated quickly by finding bad data conditions (such as finding sales offices that do not yet have a distribution amount after a top-down planning process is data-sliced). Or outliers can be found through ranked lists (such as an errant planning function that doubles sales office projected revenue). Ranked lists and thresholds can be mixed to find specific data scenarios (good or bad) or monitor the progress of a planning process.
Exceptions	Exceptions can work with conditions or separately. Exceptions can also set thresholds, but assign alert levels that can visually display (via traffic light colors) where data is good or bad. Business rules or quality checks can also be employed that set thresholds such as capping the percentage increase in requested budget from one version to the next. Exceptions can visually display where data needs attention with "soft-error" alerting. Typical planning applications have a plethora of business rules that can be checked via conditions and exceptions. Exception reporting can also be scheduled as a background job to send alerts to an alert monitor (useful for periodic large data set checks such as the end of a planning cycle stage). Lastly, exceptions can be graphically displayed in charts for further transparency.
Calculated Key Figures	For some scenarios, calculated key figures can displace planning functions for calculations, especially for reference or reporting purposes that do not need re-use in other downstream planning functions. In addition, calculated key figures may be helpful for reconciling planning function calculations. For example, complex networked calculations may not get recomputed in its entirety (that is, someone in the calculation chain forgets to recalculate based on new input). A calculated key figure can either displace or reconcile such a planned key figure. Calculated key figures can also be used in conditions and exceptions.
Restricted Key Figures	The use of restricted key figures keeps a planning model dynamic without the need to remodel or reload an InfoCube whenever data definitions change. Generic information models can be made specific via restricted key figures and then used in planning. Restricted key figures are especially useful in iterative prototyping.
BEx Broadcaster	Another tool to make the planning process more transparent is through collaboration methods like BEx Broadcaster. BEx Broadcaster allows distributing or publishing the results of planning to a wider audience (for example, through email or a Portal).

Presentation

The BEx workbook and BEx Web applications control what and how information is displayed, as well as how the user interacts with integrated planning. As it relates to planning, there are two ways to control the UI: through BEx development and through custom development. For Excel workbooks, development is either done in the BEx Analyzer or by Visual Basic for Applications (VBA). For Web applications, development is either done in the BEx Web Application Designer or typically by Java or JavaScript. BEx support for custom programming development is increasingly sophisticated, and treating them as separate topics will be an increasingly artificial delineation than has been historically the case.

BEx Development

As discussed in Chapter 8, the presentation layer can be highly customized into cockpits. The presentation outputs do not have to be tabular grids but can be a variety of graphical outputs such as pie charts, bar charts, line charts, area charts, radar charts, maps, Gantt charts, scatter plots, portfolios, histograms, speedometers, and so on. Data-visualization techniques can be used by planners to immediately assess the downstream impacts of their planning sessions (especially when sophisticated calculations are involved) to make better business judgments while in the planning process. In addition, graphics can be used to monitor the aggregated progress of an overall planning process to spot problems and evaluate data quality.

The tabular grids for planning data entry are either known as *analysis Web items* or *design items* that have additional properties relevant for write-back (such as input-ready new rows, input style of editable cells, and selectable rows). The property for input-ready new rows allows you to enter additional entries in an analysis grid for new characteristic combinations, versus simply updating input-ready cells of existing records. The formatting options of editable cells in an analysis (such as borders, background color, and font) can be controlled via an input style property. The selectable rows property enables the user to choose rows in an analysis grid to control data manipulations to a limited set of data, such as clearing its values, deleting the rows, or executing a planning function (if the user doesn't want a planning function applied across the whole filter or data selection).

In addition, an analysis grid has a property that is very useful in developing Excel-based planning applications called *formula mode,* which will be discussed in more detail shortly in the section titled "Custom Development."

The BEx presentation tools also control planning commands accessible in the UI. Planning commands can consist of planning functions, planning sequences, or planning operations. Table 9-6 provides a list of command names available for planning.

Table 9-6   Planning Commands

COMMAND NAMES	DESCRIPTION
REFRESH_DATA	Refresh data
SAVE_DATA	Save changed data
RESET_DATA	Reset changed data
SET_DATA_ENTRY_MODE	Set data entry mode
EXEC_PLANNING_FUNCTION_SIMPLE	Execute a planning function (simple)
EXEC_PLANNING_SEQUENCE_SIMPLE	Execute a planning sequence (simple)

The REFRESH DATA command updates any planning changes to the plan cache, thereby making it the data available to the rest of the planning application (such as reporting). The SAVE DATA command commits planning changes to the InfoCube, thereby making all the data in plan cache persistent. The RESET DATA command undoes any changes that are not yet saved (helpful for starting over planning scenarios without reversing persistent data). SET DATA ENTRY MODE enables toggling between edit and display mode for an Info-Provider.

Besides planning commands, other BEx Web API commands are shared by both the BEx Analyzer and Web Application Designer that can be leveraged to enhance a planning application such as data provider, Web template, and Web item commands. Some specific examples include (but are not limited to) the following:

- Setting drill-downs, conditions, and exceptions
- Setting data cell properties and local calculations
- Setting filter values
- Creating new documents or opening the document browser
- Setting Web item parameters
- Calling the BEx Broadcaster

Commands are typically assigned to and triggered from buttons but don't have to be. There is a lot of flexibility in how to trigger planning commands. The standard method is via buttons by properly configuring the properties of Web application button group items or workbook (see Figure 9-22). In the BEx Web Application Designer, the Web item properties for button group have a parameter for a button list. Each button in the button list, in turn, has properties of which one is the action (command trigger) that launches the command wizard for the Web Design API (shown in Figure 9-22). The planning functions, planning sequences, and planning operations are configurable from the command wizard. The command wizard then passes back the command line for the action. This same command line can be used to trigger a planning function for an Excel workbook button by configuring its properties.

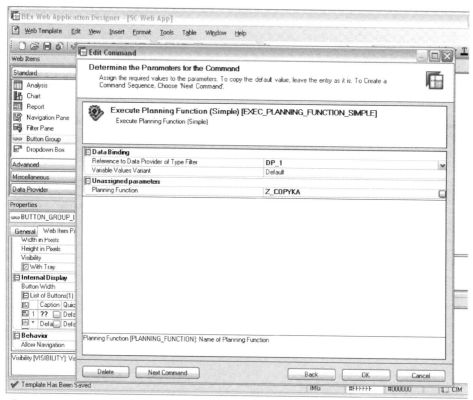

Figure 9-22 Command parameters

In addition to static parameters, command ranges can be used for button design items in BEx Analyzer. Command ranges reference three-column ranges in worksheets that store the same information captured in static parameters (that is, the name of the command, the order of execution, and value of the command). This worksheet range can be manually entered or dynamically derived for an added level of sophistication.

For the Web, the design possibilities for calling planning commands in the planning UI can get interesting. More explicitly, a drop-down box with a list of commands (planning functions and sequences) or an associated Go button instead of a group of buttons are implementation alternatives.

For automated execution of commands, there can be an automated execution of a command *sequence* (that can be a planning function) triggered by events such as before opening a tab and upon leaving the tab panel.

Lastly, the data passed to a planning function can be controlled and restricted in a variety of different ways. Not only can planning functions be bound to filter objects and query data providers, but the selection can also be defined per characteristic (fixed value, variable, input field, and row selection of an item). Such methods are more flexible for dynamic binding methods of data selection than the assignment of a filter to a planning function.

Custom Development

The standalone nature of BEx workbooks (that is, BEx Analyzer is an Excel add-in) opens the potential to push planning logic to the front-end for more rapidly developed, localized, and specialized deployments.

In addition, the introduction of the formula mode property for analysis grids further expands possibilities by replacing the analysis grid with formula cells.

Typically, the BEx Analyzer controls all the formatting of cells in the analysis grid. Any local manual adjustments to cells (such as a font change) are overwritten when the workbook is refreshed (replaced with the template formatting settings). In this scenario, the entire analysis grid and its formatting is passed to the workbook on each refresh.

The formula mode changes the nature of the refresh by converting every cell into a separate formula (technically utilizing the function BExGetCellData). In formula mode, the data is retrieved cell by cell instead of refreshing the entire grid, which has significant planning design implications. For example, in formula mode, it is possible to cut and paste cells anywhere in the workbook without being undone on the next refresh, as well as apply local formatting that "sticks."

For input-ready cells, these formulas can then be changed with new parameterizations or functions. This is an important feature for developing Excel-based capabilities — important to planning such things as prepopulating data entry cells, performing local data validations checks, and executing local planning functions. Formulas available for input-ready cells can be accessed via the Office Assistant in Excel. Formulas can be defined for individual or multiple cells. The formula calculation then updates the query output. The planning-relevant function in question is BExSetData.

Alternatively, VBA can be used more extensively to develop a planning application. The following is a sampling list of BEx Analyzer functions and their parameters that can be used in VBA applications:

- BExGetData(iDataProv As String, ParamArray iParam() As Variant)

- BExGetCellData(iMemberX As String, iMemberY As String, iDataProv As String)

- BExSetData(iValue As Double, iDataProv As String, ParamArray iParam() As Variant)

- `SAPBEXgetErrorText() As String`

- `SAPBEXsetVariables(varValues As Range) As Integer`

- `SAPBEXsetDrillState(newState As Integer, Optional atCell As Range) As Integer`

- `SAPBEXgetDrillState_CurrentState() As Integer`

- `SAPBEXgetDrillState(currentState As Integer, Optional atCell As Range) As Integer`

- `SAPBEXsetFilterValue(intValue As String, Optional hierValue As String, Optional atCell As Range) As Integer`

- `SAPBEXgetFilterValue_IntValue() As String`

- `SAPBEXgetFilterValue_HierValue() As String`

- `SAPBEXgetResultRangeByID(ByVal queryID As String, Optional ByVal charName As String) As Range`

- `SAPBEXreadWorkbook(wbID As String) As String`

- `SAPBEXgetWorkbookID(wbName As String) As String`

Note that functions prefixed as SAPBEX (versus BEx) are from earlier releases of BEx Analyzer, and that not all of those earlier VBA functions are supported in the new release. Earlier VBA developments in BEx workbooks may need to be manually reprogrammed if a function is no longer supported.

In Web applications, there is a JavaScript API that can be leveraged in one of two ways: to JavaScript within Web items or for executing commands within JavaScript functions. This feature opens up the custom development possibilities for BEx Web applications. Furthermore, outside of BEx, there is BI Java SDK for Java-based developments (although, as of this writing, there is yet to be write-back capabilities, but that is expected to come).

Integrated Planning Process Control

As NetWeaver has evolved from a composite platform to a business process platform, its process modeling capabilities and tools will continue to become more robust and complement SAP-IP capabilities (such as Guided Procedures, workflow, universal worklists, the alert framework, XI, and so on). Furthermore, there are additional tools explicitly integrated into SAP-IP for process control:

- Process chains
- Status and tracking

The integration of planning functions and sequences with process chains enables resource-intensive planning functions to be scheduled as background processes. Meanwhile, foreground schedule-driven planning processes can be controlled and monitored via status and tracking. Process chains are discussed in Chapter 11.

Status and Tracking

The *Status and Tracking System* (*STS*) capability enables the coordination, control, and monitoring of bottom-up (such as funding requests or operational plans) and top-down (such as budget approvals or strategic targets) planning processes. STS puts a more process-oriented design approach to SAP-IP, which is usually more focused on data, UI, and calculation designs because of the nature of its functions. Status and tracking features scheduling (setting due dates), user-driven task management (identifying who is responsible for which planning task), event-driven triggers (planning sequence based on status changes), workflow (email notifications to the next responsible person in the hierarchy), version control processing (data locking upon plan completion), and monitoring (hierarchical and graphical depiction of tasks).

STS supports as many iterative cycles of hierarchy-driven planning tasks as needed. The elements needed to set up status and tracking are the following:

- Subplan
- Planning sessions
- Organizational hierarchy

A *subplan* is associated with a real-time InfoProvider and, as a result, should represent a functional domain or subject area (such as a cost center or investment or sales planning). *Planning sessions* should be associated with versions and represent an iteration or stage of a planning cycle. Status-relevant tasks occur within a planning session such as new, in-process, for-review, back-to-revision, approved, and completed activities. After all tasks within a planning session are approved, the planning session is considered completed. The associated versioning data slice is then locked from data entry. The *organizational hierarchy* represents all the users and tasks needed to complete the subplan across all planning sessions.

The configuration of these elements is straightforward. Subplans and planning sessions are merely table entries. The organizational hierarchy is a BW hierarchy with some specific restrictions. The top node must be a text node, while the rest of the nodes must be characteristic or postable nodes. As a result, existing hierarchies may need to be copied and modified or custom maintained. This hierarchy is then assigned to a subplan.

Each planning session must be configured separately. The main requisite configuration tasks are logically grouped as follows:

1. Controlling the planning session behavior
2. Mapping the planning session to a data slice
3. Identifying and controlling users and task assignments

First, the system must know the direction of planning (either top-down or bottom-up sessions) and what features to enable during the planning session or the configuration of the planning session. Additional statuses are available for top-down planning than for bottom-up planning (such as for-review, back-to-revision, and approved).

More specifically, you must identify how to control the following system behaviors:

- Whether planning sequences triggered by status changes are executed in the foreground or background
- Whether automatic notifications are made at each status switch
- Whether task deadlines should also have time associated with them
- Whether cascading status switches should be available (for easier status-setting for those responsible for several levels of the hierarchy)
- Whether a custom SAPscript text should be used instead of the standard
- Whether a style sheet should be used to modify the Web interface

Second, a planning session is mapped to data-selection criteria that it logically represents. After a planning session is completed, this data-selection restriction is locked from data entry via a data slice. For example, this data restriction could assign a planning session to a specific version and a specific time frame.

Third, each user and task assignment is controlled within the planning session via an organizational hierarchy. Each hierarchy node is assigned the following core settings:

- A person responsible and an email address for notification
- The completion due date (and time if configured)
- The URL of the Web-based planning application
- The URL of the Web-based control report
- A planning sequence per status switches

There are two runtime views of the planning session: one for the planning coordinator and one for person responsible. The *planning coordinator* initiates the planning session by sending a start email, which either emails the person responsible at the top of hierarchy (top-down planning) or the people at the bottom (bottom-up planning). The coordinator can view the overall planning session as a hierarchical or tabular view of all the tasks and their associated statuses, persons responsible, expected completion dates, and hyperlinks to the task details. In turn, the task details show the same information, but for a particular task, with buttons to initiate the Web-based planning application, call the control report, maintain comments, and set the status.

The *person responsible* view shows the same task details view, unless there is more than one task for the person responsible. In that case, a tabular view is presented of all person-responsible tasks and corresponding hyperlinks to task details. The core activities that each person responsible in the hierarchy performs during a planning session can be summarized as follows:

1. Execute the planning application

2. Run a control report

3. Maintain comments

4. Switch status

For those responsible for many tasks, an additional cascading status switch can be used (the option is configurable via the settings for the planning session) to update many tasks below a hierarchy node at the same time.

STS was a planning-related capability introduced with SEM-BPS but has been made to integrate with SAP-IP (with minor enhancement). STS is a fairly independent capability with its own BSP-based UI with a few integration points to integrated planning: the planning session-to-data-slice assignment, the planning sequence-to-status-switch assignment, and the URL assignments (for planning application and control report).

The decoupled nature of STS makes it independent enough to integrate with both SEM-BPS and SAP-IP. First, to prepare the system to use STS for integrated planning, a data slice based on a special ABAP object class (CL_UPS_LOCK_ DATASLICE) must be configured in SAP-IP. This data slice then uses the data-slice assignment of a planning session. Second, a separate column for SAP-IP planning sequences was added (next to SEM-BPS planning sequences), where status switch options are configured. Finally, the URL assignments can either point to an SEM-BPS Web application or a SAP-IP Web application. A new search help (F4-Help) was added to find the appropriate URL by popping up a list of either SEM-BPS applications or SAP-IP applications.

BW-BPS Coexistence

Conceptually, there is very little difference between the integrated planning capabilities in BW-BPS and SAP-IP. The only significant conceptual difference is that there is now just one UI and one engine for planning, as well as for reporting and analytics. From a capabilities perspective, all the functions and features of BEx (front-end and OLAP) are available for planning applications instead of being constrained by the limitations of a separate, more static mechanism for rendering the UI (for example, planning folders, planning layouts, Web interface builder, and so on). This major step forward was one of the advantages that motivated the shift from SEM-BPS to SAP-IP.

Another advantage gained by enabling the BI capabilities of SAP BW was a streamlined back-end. Fewer metadata objects are now needed to accomplish the same capability.

Because SAP-IP is an evolutionary step for integrated planning, it shares a lot of concepts and services with its older sibling, BW-BPS. Both applications can still play with each other in tandem. Migration is not mandatory. As a result, very little in the way of migration utilities has been delivered, but in their place are configuration options on how to integrate both applications.

From a data storage layer perspective, nothing really changes. The same real-time InfoCubes used in BW-BPS for planning can be used for SAP-IP. No data migration is needed. Furthermore, BW-BPS and SAP-IP share the same enhanced locking services and analysis authorizations.

In contrast, the metadata objects in integrated planning that represented the virtual data layer have changed. These BW-BPS metadata objects will require manual migration if needed (with the exception of planning areas). More explicitly, planning areas are displaced by underlying real-time InfoCubes. Meanwhile multiplanning areas are replaced by MultiProviders. Planning levels have been superseded by aggregation levels, while planning packages have been supplanted by filters.

Conceptually, characteristic relationships and data slices have not changed. However, technically, they have changed but can be leveraged. SAP-IP characteristic relationships and data slices can be configured to point to BW-BPS characteristic relationships and data slices. SAP-IP predelivers standard exit classes (ABAP object classes that can be used as user exits) that can be configured into characteristic relationship and data slices (ABAP object classes CL_RSPLS_CR_EXIT_BPS and CL_RSPLS_DS_EXIT_BPS, respectively). Some additional configuration is needed for characteristic relationships so as to ensure that the source and target characteristics in SAP-IP are consistent with BW-BPS.

Similarly, from a business capability perspective, the standard planning functions have not changed much from BW-BPS to SAP-IP, but the technical details have. Significant changes have been made that make planning functions more extensible and customizable.

The planning function and planning sequence concepts remain the same in both BW-BPS and SAP-IP, although they are technically different. As a result, planning functions also must be manually migrated. Some of the technical changes that planning functions have undergone are that now they are associated with an ABAP object class and are delivered as business content (as explained earlier in this chapter). In BW-BPS, custom planning functions were function module calls to a user-exit function type. In SAP-IP, no user-exit function type exists; you just create your own function type and assign it a custom ABAP object class.

However, a custom function type can be created that calls BW-BPS user-exit functions. In fact, a standard ABAP object class is delivered for this purpose (CL_RSPLFC_BPS_EXITS) and can be used as a function type. However, there are enough differences between the BW-BPS planning functions and SAP-IP planning functions so that problems can arise when wrapping this ABAP class around a user-exit function module (such as pop-up handling, calls to BPS functions or APIs, and tight coupling with BPS parameters and configuration). Furthermore, the user-exit function is the only function type in BW-BPS that can be directly called from an SAP-IP planning function.

BW-BPS planning functions must be separately executed or manually migrated. SAP-IP runs against its own cache, which is not shared with the BW-BPS cache. As a result, the runtime integration possibilities are limited, especially from the UI. Data generated from BW-BPS planning functions will not update an SAP-IP planning session already in progress.

However, there is one design-time integration consideration. Both BW-BPS and SAP-IP formula functions can employ FOX syntax. Enhancements in FOX syntax and capabilities are enjoyed by both BW-BPS and SAP-IP applications. However, that is where integration stops. In order for SAP-IP to use the BW-BPS FOX code, the program logic must be cut and pasted to SAP-IP in order to be migrated because they are separate instantiations. Similar to the other standard planning functions, SAP-IP cannot directly call a FOX function in BW-BPS.

Meanwhile, long-established technologies in the SAP-IP front-end render BW-BPS technologies superfluous. For example:

- Input-ready queries supplant planning layouts.
- BEx workbooks and Web applications displace planning folders.
- BEx variables supersede SEM variables.
- Web Application Designer replaces Web Interface Builder.

All of these changes in technology require a manual migration (that is, currently no tools will perform the conversion automatically). But the scaled-down nature and simplistic power of SAP-IP begs the question of whether or not there is any design benefit in straight migration (versus reimplementing in SAP-IP while taking advantage of new capabilities unavailable before). For example, one input query can potentially replace several planning layouts, which makes the migration easier.

SAP recommends building any new planning applications with SAP-IP. Old BW-BPS applications should eventually be migrated and rebuilt in SAP-IP.

This should be done over time — application by application and step-by-step (as SAP-IP rapidly evolves to make the business case increasingly compelling).

Best and Worst Practices

The shift to model-driven application development mandates a new set of SAP skill sets to deliver integrated planning applications. The advent of new tools and a paradigm shift toward model-driven development creates a climate vulnerable to worst practices.

Business analysts, SAP application analysts, SAP BW modelers, program developers, and SAP infrastructure (traditionally known as BASIS) all must collaborate and rediscover engineering disciplines to deliver the integrated planning solutions.

Those with an ERP background are accustomed to having SAP engineering and SAP best practices handed to them. In model-driven applications such as integrated planning, there is no such benefit (at least, not yet). Furthermore, the design paradigm between configuration and modeling is worlds apart. Configuration typically presents a finite set of options, while modeling is a lot more open and flexible to a much greater range of possibilities.

Integrated planning (like any custom enterprise application) requires a lot of modeling upfront along various dimensions (such as data, process, schedule, business rules, roles, and workflow). Organizations with Enterprise Architecture initiatives must comply with governance standards and policies. Most BI architects tend to think only in terms of data when they should be holistically blueprinting around who, what, when, where, how, and why perspectives of the solution from various levels of business and technology vantage points.

Two examples of common design challenges follow. The first is around advanced data modeling techniques for handling delta change capture in planning applications. It is an information modeling topic that typically confounds novice planning designers. The second is more of a story regarding the challenges around architecting enterprise integration. The first topic steps deeper into SAP-IP design specifics, while the second topic steps back for a broader look at enterprise design.

Delta Change Modeling

Novice integrated planning designers typically fail to take into account how to model for delta change capture. The ramifications of such an oversight can manifest itself in a number of ways:

- Broken functions that change key-figure values each time they are reexecuted on static data

- Poor-performing planning functions because of excessive use of data
- Unexplained data sparsity and poor data quality

There are two fundamental ways to address delta capture, depending on the usage scenario: modeling change capture in key figures and modeling change capture in characteristics.

Key-Figure Change Capture

As an example, the SAP BW developer designs an InfoCube that contains a characteristic for employee and a key figure for annual salary. In turn, the planning function developer creates a formula that calculates annual salary by multiplying it by a factor. Both are surprised to discover that every time the salary calculation function is run, the annual salary continues to grow by the factor specified, even though it has not changed. They conclude that the information model should have had a separate key figure for baseline (as a "before-image") that applies the factor to the baseline and stores the calculation result in another key figure (as an "afterimage"). By having a shared key figure for salary, the planning function continually overwrites the amount each time it is executed with the results, thereby losing the original baseline amount. Table 9-7 illustrates the incorrect calculation where both result columns represent the same key figure ("before" and "afterimages," respectively).

Table 9-7 Incorrect Calculation

ITERATION	RESULT	FACTOR	RESULT
1	$100,000	1.1	$110,000
2	$110,000	1.1	$121,000

By having a baseline key figure for the original amount, the situation can be fixed, as shown in Table 9-8. Since the baseline is frozen, the salary calculation should not change the salary each time the function is run.

Table 9-8 Corrected Calculation

ITERATION	RESULT	FACTOR	RESULT
1	$100,000	1.1	$110,000
2	$100,000	1.1	$110,000

Unfortunately, in many implementations such simple information modeling oversights are not realized until late in the project (and they have high impacts).

Information model changes and fundamental changes in how calculations are done (incremental rather than total) usually translate to a significant amount of rework because of all the design dependencies on the information model. To avoid this problem, iterative methodologies and tighter collaboration can catch this early.

Characteristic Change Capture

Information modeling considerations for the sparsity that aggregation levels can create was discussed earlier in this chapter. This discussion expands the concept to take advantage of the sparsity for two scenarios:

1. Improved performance through delta change capture of incremental planning records
2. Reconciling top-down and bottom-up planning differences using delta change capture

The first scenario determines how to identify newly created records. Such delta change capture handling is helpful for improving the performance of planning functions. However, note that this approach should not be used for certain types of calculations (that require a total instead of an incremental amount).

Figure 9-23 shows a scenario of an incorrect calculation (where the calculation is supposed to be on a total amount instead of an incremental one). Where this delta capture technique is more helpful is around data processing functions such as version copies (where the entire set of data in one version does not need to be copied over into the next version but rather only the incremental changes). The example in Figure 9-23 illustrates how the use of aggregation levels can be used to generate delta change records (so a planning function only picks up the changed records). Again, the example also illustrates how a recalculation (in this case a 10-percent revaluation) might bring unexpected results. Replacing the revaluation function with a copy function is an example of a better way of using this information modeling technique.

First, an information model has a characteristic added to it called a *delta change indicator*. The two values for the delta change indicator are blank (which represents the incremental change) and CALCULATED (which represents records that had already been picked up in a calculation). Two aggregation levels are created: the first one without the delta change indicator (used by the input-ready query for manual entry) and the second one with the delta change indicator included (used by planning functions).

For example, say the user makes a $10.00 sales entry against the first aggregation level. Because the delta indicator does not exist in the first aggregation level, it is saved with a blank (denoted by the "#" symbol). The second aggregation level is for a revaluation function for incremental changes in sales.

User Action	Data View

Manually Enter $10
1st Aggregation Level

Delta Indicator	Sales
#	$10

Execute 10% Revaluation
2nd Aggregation Level

Delta Indicator	Sales
CALCULATED	$11

Change $11 to $30
1st Aggregation Level

Delta Indicator	Sales
#	$19
CALCULATED	$11

Execute 10% Revaluation
2nd Aggregation Level

Delta Indicator	Sales
CALCULATED	$31.90

Figure 9-23   Delta change capture

The revaluation function employs a filter or condition that only runs the function if the record has a delta indicator of blank. In this case, the incremental change of $10.00 has a blank delta indicator, and the revaluation function picks up this record and increases sales by 10 percent to yield $11.00. After the revaluation function is run, a reposting function changes the delta indicator on that record from blank (representing a changed record) to CALCULATED. That way, if the revaluation function is run again, no records are selected, because there are no more records with delta indicator blank ("#") on them.

The user then sees $11.00 for sales and changes it to $30.00. Again, because the aggregation level is missing the delta change indicator, the incremental difference between the entered amount and what is in the database is written to delta indicator space ($19.00). The revaluation function is executed once again picking up the $19.00 and calculating 10 percent against that record, which yields a result of $20.90. A reposting function adds $20.90 to $11.00 to yield an incorrect total of $31.90. The user was expecting a total of $33.00. A better scenario would be to run the revaluation after the delta was copied and summarized into another plan version.

This example not only illustrates a useful information modeling technique but also how it could go wrong if not well understood.

Note that some forms of calculations are possible with this technique, such as proportional distributions (for example, a 50/50 distribution split will yield the same result if it is performed against a total or against incremental changes). To understand the distinction, you must grasp the significance of the difference between the *formula of sums* and the *sums of formulas*. The revaluation example is a formula on sum totals (10 percent of sales), while a distribution is a sum total result of splitting each record by the 50/50 formula.

The second scenario is a more simplistic one that illustrates an information modeling technique for a hierarchical planning process. Imagine you are a sales manager setting sales targets for a region consisting of two sales offices that are concurrently planning.

Each sales office estimates $10 million in sales. The aggregation level that sales office plans against contains a characteristic for the office so that they can plan estimates for Atlanta and Miami separately. The regional sales manager views an input-ready query that totals the estimates to $20 million for the region by using an aggregation level that leaves out the characteristic for office. The regional sales manager believes this estimate is not aggressive enough and sets a target of $25 million at the region level.

The total of $25 million is not actually stored on the database; it represents a calculated total. Instead, a residual difference of $5 million is created on the database, as shown in Table 9-9. A distribution planning function could then split the difference down the middle, so that both Atlanta and Miami target $12.5 million in sales.

Table 9-9 Residual Example

REGION	OFFICE	SALES
Southeast	Atlanta	$10 million
Southeast	Miami	$10 million
Southeast	#	$5 million

Enterprise Design

Recent public sector mandates such as the President's Management Agenda have spurred the EA discipline in public sector IT initiatives. In this context, imagine the following public sector enterprise initiative: a headquarters budgeting application that must integrate with R/3 Funds Management and Overhead Management in order to perform midbudget cycle updates of actual data and retract the approved budget.

For illustrative purposes, a semantic world of a budgeting system is created consisting of characteristics (see Figure 9-24) and key figures (see Figure 9-25) that do not completely line up with SAP Funds Management and Overhead Management. Note that the data structures in the custom budgeting application are freely defined, but in packaged ERP applications (such as Funds

Management and Overhead Management), they are not. In this scenario, custom InfoObjects were created that either do not exist in SAP Funds Management and Overhead Management or were designed differently. As a result, semantic integration nuances and challenges must be addressed.

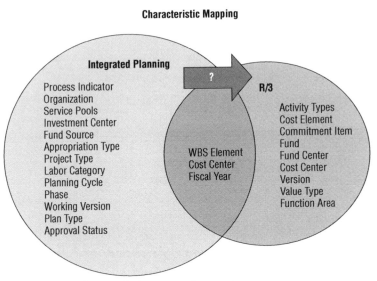

Figure 9-24 Characteristics semantic mapping

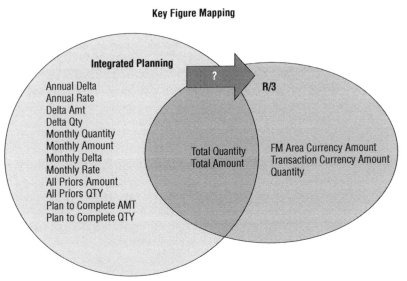

Figure 9-25 Key figures semantic mapping

In this case study, the first set of scenarios will be data design challenges and semantic differences introduced by too much creativity (artificial differences) rather than differences introduced by the nature of planning (natural differences). Artificial and natural differences are illustrated with example design decisions. Lastly, a hypothetical process integration miscommunication is chronicled. The purpose here is to illustrate how subtleties in design decisions can lead a project astray.

Artificial Differences

In the first scenario, the solution architect decides to track process flows in the data by storing a process ID number in the information model. At first glance, the idea seems to be sound; it gives process visibility to the application. In reality, however, this causes a number of data design and semantic problems.

First, the process model is continually changing and evolving, which would force data realignments. Second, massive data redundancies and multiple versions of truth are created when process variants share the same data (each process variant would have its own version of data by process indicator). Lastly, in mySAP ERP, there is no concept of process indicators. At best, there are transaction codes or value types to determine the origin of a data record. As a result, semantic integration of plan and actual data is thwarted (complicated process-indicators-to-value-types mappings would have to be constructed, assuming a bridge existed).

In a second scenario, the budgeting application has maintained a master data list of service pools that are supposed to conceptually link to levels of the cost center hierarchy. But if there is no systemic enforcement (such as master data management or data replication), master data values can quickly get out of sync. In this example, the codes are compared to the cost center hierarchy, and, although a visual relationship can be inferred, technologically, the values do not line up, as shown in Figure 9-26.

In a third scenario, key figures are defined that are not consistent with R/3. mySAP ERP models its key figures generically. This hypothetical SAP-IP architect decides to use both generic and specific key figures to do a number of things:

1. Show annual and periodic figures in separate buckets.

2. Show a time horizon where the first and last column is a calculation of all prior and future years summed up respectively (that is, `'all priors'` and `'time to complete'` key figures).

3. Be able to illustrate totals and incremental values.

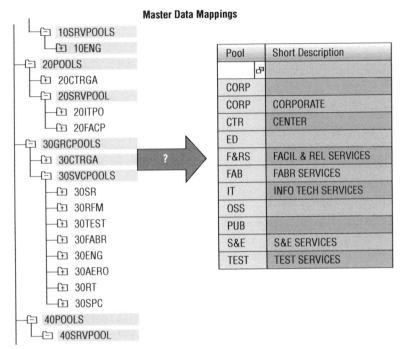

Figure 9-26 Master data mapping

Such a model causes confusion when semantically trying to integrate. First, annual and periodic amounts should be in separate InfoCubes with different time granularities (for example, fiscal year versus fiscal period) that share the same generic key figures because they represent the same thing to eliminate sparsity. In addition, the aggregated amounts at both ends of the horizon can be stored on the first and last years of the planning horizon without the need for separate key figures, thereby simplifying the model (although the values sitting on the first and last year records truly represent multiple years).

In contrast, having separate key figures for totals versus incremental values is a natural and helpful mechanism for separating baseline amounts from delta changes. To get a total, a calculated key figure can be defined that adds incremental changes to baseline. Alternatively, the result total can be stored persistently as a key figure, and the original amount can be calculated by subtracting the incremental changes. The latter approach has the added advantage of enabling planning on either totals or deltas. Otherwise, if persistent results of calculations are stored that can be easily displaced by calculated key figures or OLAP aggregation, artificial complexity will be introduced to the information model (such as `'all priors'` and `'time to complete'` key figures).

Natural Differences

In this scenario, there are other examples of how the nature of planning forces design differences with underlying OLTP systems. The first one occurs when planning data structures are more summarized or differentiated than execution data structures. In this scenario, new InfoObjects were created for concepts based off of cost center, fund, and project. InfoObjects called organization (who gets funded and is responsible), service pools (who indirectly supports), and performing centers (who actually does the work) all represent different partner roles for cost objects (for example, WBS element or cost center). Funds source and appropriation type are substring components of a smart naming convention for fund. Project type is a natively defined categorization in budgeting for WBS elements groupings.

By creating custom InfoObjects that represent summary-level detail for cost center, WBS element, and fund, these underlying master data InfoObjects would need to be extended to incorporate the custom InfoObjects as navigational attributes. Mappings would be needed to fill those attributes. This would solve loading midplanning cycle updates with actual data. Plan data is written to the custom (less granular) characteristics, and actual data must be rolled up to that level through navigational attribute assignments to make comparisons at the matching levels of granularity. Additionally, greater slicing and dicing capabilities of actual data are enabled through such custom categorizations. The challenge is retraction, since the execution data structures are at a lower level detail than planning. A process of distributing the aggregated amounts would need to be designed to accommodate the gap.

Even when there is semantic integration, there can be even more complicated scenarios for matching levels of detail. In the case study, consider WBS element or cost center. Both are shared and semantically integrated across the budgeting and ERP system. Both also have hierarchies, but here is where the similarities end. There may be requirements to model all the levels of the hierarchies as post-able nodes so as to be able to plan at any level. In transactional execution systems, amounts collect on the lowest leaf nodes of the hierarchy. Here is where there is a mismatch in levels of detail.

Currently, this capability of planning on hierarchical nodes is part of SEM-BPS top-down or bottom-up budgeting capabilities and is not currently available in SAP-IP (which allows planning only at the lowest leaf nodes). For example, the ability to set a control at a hierarchical level that is not to be exceeded in a budgeting hierarchy is "smart logic" that can be achieved only in SEM-BPS presently. Workarounds may involve shortened hierarchies at the right levels and queries collapsed at the corresponding levels for comparable results. Otherwise, hierarchies must be modeled as flat dimensional attributes of the InfoCube.

In rarer cases, planning has lower-level detail than the execution system. For example, in this scenario, the labor indicator represents the difference between civil servants and contractors. This distinction and detail is not directly captured in Funds Management nor Overhead Management and is a case where planning is more granular than execution.

A second natural difference can occur when a planning has distinct incomparable processes from other planning or execution processes. For example, actual data flows have no version control concepts, while most planning data flows do. Or, as another example, the process of requesting and approving funding is different after it is approved.

The third natural difference relates to processes simplified for modeling purposes. Cost center allocation is a good example that was provided earlier. In this example, cost center is a characteristic shared by the budgeting system and SAP R/3, as well as the generic key figure for amount. However, in this hypothetical scenario, the planned costs cannot be reconciled to actual data, because an enterprise method of allocating was employed in planning, while the allocation methods configured in Overhead Management are configured by departments and uncontrolled (and, hence, done differently, depending on the allocation cycle). Furthermore, the budget planning application does an even distribution of cost center costs to projects while R/3 employs more exact methods. Because of the lack of enterprise consistency in the ERP system, and the simplified allocation model in budget planning, variance analysis is less meaningful if at all useful. Further compounding the reconciliation issue, the fully burdened project budgets are retracted back to Funds Management. Some projects will be overfunded, while others will be underfunded because of inconsistencies in allocations methods.

Finally, the last natural difference can be one of the biggest challenges with semantic integration. Stating that plan data is forward-looking and actual data is backward-looking may seem to be an overobvious observation, and yet many implementations fail to fully grasp this important master data management nuance early enough. Traditional BI implementations are EDW-focused. Most of the data is historical. And, after all the pain of realizing an enterprise standard, they may find that many of the hierarchical categorizations that have been defined are not useable for planning. This is most notably the case with organizational structures.

In many forward-looking planning scenarios (for example, a 10-year horizon) require new entities (new customers, new products, new profit centers, new employees) or changed hierarchies (new segments, new categories, new organization, new jobs). In short, an integrated master data planning system must be implemented as part of integrated planning. In many engagements, master data that does not yet exist in execution systems is referred to as *pseudo-master data*. Typically, there are two fundamental options for pseudo-master data management: One is to maintain data in the source system, and the other is to maintain data in integrated planning.

On the one hand, entering pseudo-master data into the source system (as opposed to the SAP-IP system) keeps the source system as a consistent version of truth for master data (not true for all environments). In addition, it minimizes the SAP-IP change management impact by leveraging source system master data management processes and procedures. Furthermore, if the pseudo becomes "real," nothing more needs to be done. This approach eliminates the complication of retracting pseudo-master data back to R/3 if it becomes "real."

On the other hand, entering pseudo-master data in the source systems potentially puts a lot of junk into it, thus jeopardizing its quality. Furthermore, how do you know the difference between what is pseudo and what is real in the source system? How do you delete or block or hide pseudo-master data that is no longer needed? How do you turn off the mandatory fields needed for real entities (pseudo-master data usually has less rigor and fewer attributes)?

Our recommendation is to design pseudo-master data in the SAP-IP system with its own naming convention and a navigational attribute flag that identifies it as a pseudo. When it becomes "real," another navigational attribute should be filled in with the real number, used in place of the pseudo for retractions. Alternatively, the use of global keys and qualified local keys can do the same trick as explained in Chapter 5. In future releases of SAP-IP there will be master data planning support for this scenario.

Process Integration

As a separate scenario for the same example, Enterprise Architecture research and assessment is performed for a headquarters budgeting application that requires retraction into SAP R/3 Funds Management. In this scenario, the technical development team discovers that the information model for planning does not include information about the appropriation (represented by fund). And yet, it is a required field in SAP Funds Management for retraction.

A misunderstanding and confusion quickly ensues between the headquarters budgeting and ERP teams. The SAP R/3 team insists that budget planning application must include funds in its information model, but headquarters flatly pushes back, seeing no need. Weeks pass and ultimately the technical team researches enough on the federal budgeting and funding process to make a realization. The team realizes that the budgeting application being developed is only used to submit a budget request to Congress, after which it is finished until the next planning cycle.

The technical team learns that, in the meantime, the budget does not disappear but gets deliberated on for months as part of Congressional hearings before it is officially passed back as an appropriation (that is, with the fund). The Congressional pass-back, they later learn, goes into a separate legacy operational planning system that performs apportionments of the appropriated funds.

This process step was where the "missing" fund got lost. Both the headquarters budget planning team and the SAP R/3 Funds Management team were right. Neither owned the operating plan or the system that housed it (which needed to be enhanced with a retractor so as to pass back the apportioned budget into SAP Funds Management, where the budget could be executed). In this scenario, early enterprise process modeling and more business involvement would have quickly identified the missing process step in the integration effort, salvaging time, resources, and scope.

Summary

This chapter started off with a definition of integrated planning as the process of formulating courses of action by setting quantitative measures that embody goals and objectives through systematic methods on enterprise and interoperable standards. Integrated planning was then positioned, giving historical context and an outlook for the future, before the definition was broken down further, explaining how SAP-IP tools supported it.

Then integrated planning was positioned within an Enterprise Architecture context, comparing SAP-IP capabilities with other NetWeaver capabilities before diving into the technical aspects of the tool.

The discussion around SAP-IP started with the solution architecture and then examined topics around the architectural components and their design implications (starting with data, then planning functions, then the UI, and finally process control). How SAP-IP coexists with BW-BPS was then explained, followed by examples and scenarios around best and worst practices in SAP-IP design.

In Chapter 10, the story around SAP analytics moves out of integrated planning and into other SAP solution offerings in business analytics and how they relate to SAP BW.

Business Analytics

Henry Morris of IDC Research defines an analytic application as a packaged software application that performs the following tasks:[1]

- **Process support** — This consists of organizing and automating tasks and activities oriented toward business process optimization and control. Process support can manifest itself in SAP BW in such ways as predefined analysis paths that lead to a decision or any type of planning, simulation, and risk assessment. Process support should close the gap between analysis and execution.

- **Separation of function** — The analytic application must be able to stand separate from any operational transaction system. Of course, any analytic application is heavily dependent on transactional systems for information and must have a closed-loop backflow to feed its results, but there must be a clear demarcation between the systems.

- **Time-oriented, integrated data** — These are essential characteristics for any data warehouse or data mart that must always have a time dimension and the capability of integrating data from multiple internal and external sources.

Based on Henry Morris' definition, SAP NetWeaver is the ideal platform on which to build analytic applications, providing separation of function and time-oriented, integrated data. However, there are shades of gray as to what scenarios constitute enough process support to be considered an analytic application.

For example, does a Web application with drill-down to mySAP ERP constitute a feature of an analytic application? Or is it part of Business Content or, more simply, Business Explorer (BEx) functionality? As a guideline, if there is a feedback-and-response scenario along a predefined closed-loop analysis path (for example, a hiring freeze after a headcount assessment), the answer should be yes. What about data mining? Data mining would be deemed a tool, not an analytic application. However, when used in conjunction with customer lifetime value (CLTV) analysis, data mining becomes a feature of an analytic customer relationship application. Again, the degree of process support is the deciding criterion.

Analytic applications themselves are often divided along business processes such as the following:

- Financial analytics

- Human resource analytics

- Customer relationship analytics (CRA)

- Supply-chain analytics

- Web analytics

The NetWeaver integration platform and its Composite Application Framework put SAP BW at the heart of SAP analytic applications. The architecture of an analytic application consists of more than Business Content and its information models. Analytic applications have their own builders, models, and engines. *Builders* are used to construct analytic *models*, and *engines* are then run against those models. For example, although data mining is closely integrated with SAP BW to read information, it still has its own builder, model, and engine. As a more specific scenario, a customer behavior analysis may use a Business Content query to pass information to the data mining engine, which segments customers based on a decision tree model parameterized in the Data Mining Workbench.

This chapter provides three different examples of analytic applications in the business areas of customer, supply-chain, and financial analytics: the technology components mySAP CRM, SAP Advanced Planner and Organizer (APO), and Financial Analytics, respectively. All of these areas are composed of operational, collaborative, and analytic technologies that are tightly integrated and support closed-loop analytic scenarios. The NetWeaver integration platform provides the technical underpinnings for these applications.

CRM supports marketing, selling, and customer service. CRA is the application that measures those processes. CRA comes integrated with SAP BW and consists of analytic engines such as data mining that can be used for customer behavior analytics, CLTV analysis, and customer segmentation analytics (such as recency, frequency, and monetary value of purchases made by customers in marketing campaigns). Data mining methods in customer behavior analytics include decision trees, scoring, clustering, and association analysis.

Supply-chain supports sourcing, making, and delivering products. Likewise, the application that measures those processes is Supply Chain Analytics (SCA). SCA is heavily influenced by the Supply-Chain Council's Supply-Chain Operations Reference (SCOR) model. This chapter describes the SCOR model in more detail, explaining its significance to SCA before providing a summary of the SAP APO application and its architecture. This chapter then explains the three ways that SAP BW interacts with SAP APO to deliver analytics, namely:

- Through the supply-chain cockpit
- Through interfacing with planning-book-based applications such as demand planning
- Through Business Content, where SAP APO works to deliver analytics for more operationally based planning applications

In addition, the discussion provides an SAP BW implementation case study for demand planning that details how data from SAP APO was loaded into SAP BW, what business logic was applied to the data in the update rules, and how analysis on the information is performed.

The financial capabilities of mySAP ERP are used to tie all the enterprise-wide pieces together for consolidation, financial analysis, strategy management, corporate performance measurement, and stakeholder relationship management. The three major subject areas of corporate performance management, enterprise planning, and consolidation were historically part of what SAP called Strategic Enterprise Management (SAP SEM). Today, these applications are part of the financial analytics found in mySAP ERP. Corporate performance management is built on the principles of the balanced scorecard. The *balanced scorecard* is a strategy management system that strives to achieve two objectives: to change the way performance is measured and to change the way strategy is implemented. This chapter highlights how SAP works to achieve these two objectives and then touches on enterprise planning and the capital market interpreter. Next, business consolidation is discussed, detailing its history and current status. Finally, this chapter discusses the information modeling impacts for using the consolidation engine.

Before diving into these analytic applications, let us first look at an overview of the architecture and examine SAP's Business Content. There is a great deal of Business Content and possibly even more misinformation on the topic. The discussion attempts to dispel some of these Business Content myths.

Analytic Application Architecture

SAP BW is at the heart of SAP's analytic applications. Because it provides separation of function and time-oriented, integrated data, it is the ideal business intelligence platform for analytic applications. Figure 10-1 shows the various components of analytic applications, including the following:

- **Builders** — These tools allow you to build the analytic application environment. They may consist of data warehousing administration tools, visual modeling tools, and planning environments.

- **Models** — These designs are either standard-delivered or custom-developed via the Builders. Models, such as data mining models or simulation models often utilize an object model or an enterprise's information model.

- **Engines** — These represent the application-specific logic that must be applied during runtime (such as specialized calculations). OLAP, data mining, and planning calculations are all performed by their respective engines during runtime.

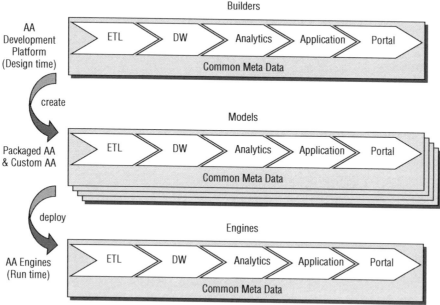

Figure 10-1 Analytic applications architecture
Copyright © SAP AG

The adjoining components in Figure 10-1 are as follows:

- **ETL services** — These can be provided by software that connects to source systems to extract data, provides transformation functions and libraries to format the data and seamlessly handles the loading process behind the scenes.

- **Data warehouse** (DW) — A data warehouse is a time-variant, subject-area-oriented, nonvolatile collection of data used to support business decision making.

- **Analytics** — These are the analytic calculations, exceptions, conditions, currency conversion, triggered alerts, planning functions, and data mining engines that process and present information for business decision making. Analytic models may either be preconfigured or custom-built applications. The builders for analytics can fall into any one of a number of toolsets by literally hundreds of vendors.

- **Applications** — These are now being built in as composite applications that take data from various systems and add process support. The legacy terms may include "cockpits" or "dashboards," but today's applications are closed-loop and enable you to drill through to the underlying applications either for reporting or executing a transaction.

- **Portals** — These create a framework that analytic applications pass through. Portals are no longer just places to view a collection of Web pages; they now support information and business processes needed to perform roles within organizations. This is accomplished by combining worksets from various underlying business applications into runtime environments that handle services such as single sign-on, personalization, role-based menus, authorization checks, and so on.

The glue that binds all the components together is common metadata. Common metadata enables tighter integration such as drill-through scenarios or the passing of data between applications. Consistent metadata jump-starts the building of new analytic applications. Metadata has evolved from rather low-level technical metadata (which described field lengths and valid character sets) to high-level metadata (which defines objects commonly used by any given industry or describes entire business processes even as they cross enterprise boundaries into the supply or demand chain).

Business Content is a type of metadata delivered by SAP. It should be viewed as a collection of different types of building blocks that can be used to create analytic applications. The building blocks themselves are either individual, low-level metadata elements (like InfoObjects) or preassembled sets of metadata objects (such as an analytic application). Business Content supports analytic applications by providing information models used for monitoring processes, as well as the analysis paths to optimize processes in a feedback-and-response system (also referred to as a *closed-loop application*).

This chapter demonstrates how analytic applications can be built on the SAP NetWeaver platform in mySAP CRM, SAP APO, and mySAP ERP, exploring specific builders, models, and engines in each application. For the purposes of this discussion, how these builders, models, and engines are technically implemented in each of these applications is a less important lesson than learning how analytic applications can be built and evolved on the SAP platform.

The analytic application technologies are subject to change themselves. Application subcomponents roll in and out of what has traditionally been called different components. For example, CRM sales planning has used the historic SEM planning engine, while SAP APO had its own separate planning engine. CRM development had created the data mining engine that was packaged with SAP BW. The data mining engine was used in customer relationship analytics purely for customer behavior analysis, but the engine was generic enough to be used for other applications. Currently, SAP is moving even more toward shared engines and reusable software components and services to support a wide variety of business applications.

How mySAP CRM, SAP APO, and mySAP ERP interact with SAP BW differs as well. The builders, models, and engines for CRM analytics come predelivered as part of Business Content with SAP BW. In contrast, the builders, models, and engines for SAP APO are not in SAP BW. Instead, they are built directly into the SAP APO application, while the SAP BW itself is directly embedded into SAP APO as part of a merged NetWeaver environment. The builders, models, and engines for mySAP ERP come more as an add-on application as part of the mySAP offering, while technically utilizing the SAP BW capabilities of NetWeaver.

Figure 10-2 shows how these applications converge for certain business scenarios such as closed-loop planning, where all three applications interact with each other. (The process starts with financial market analysis to gauge market growth feeding CRM sales planning. CRM sales planning then passes sales quantities to SAP APO demand planning, which then drives supply network planning to provide sales quantities for profit planning.)

Business concepts for analytics also converge. The SCOR model (employed in SAP APO) and the balanced scorecard share many of the same high-level concepts and complement each other.

The forces for standardization and integration will merge the SAP technologies themselves. At the very least, how these applications interact with SAP BW is subject to change as fast as the underlying technologies themselves. Consequently, the most important thing to take away from this chapter is how

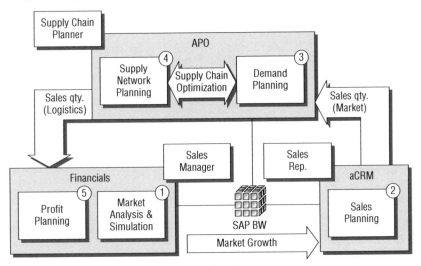

Figure 10-2 Integrated, closed-loop planning
Copyright © SAP AG

analytic applications such as mySAP CRM, SAP APO, and financial analytics provide additional business process support over SAP BW Business Content. These applications augment Business Content building blocks in order to deliver their business analytics. For each application, the discussion in this chapter provides an explanation of different technical approaches (in SAP BW, merged with SAP BW, or as an add-on to SAP BW for mySAP CRM, SAP APO, and mySAP ERP, respectively) toward the same goal (process support). You should not infer that these distinct approaches are starting to disappear, or are at least being deemphasized, as NetWeaver converges what used to be separate components into a unified technology stack. While this convergence has yet to be completed, it is well underway.

What Is Business Content?

Business Content is a roles-based, predelivered set of information models. As a result, when Business Content information models are used out of the box, the BI capabilities of NetWeaver become a turnkey data warehouse and analytic application solution. When the prepackaged information models do not entirely meet business requirements, they can be flexibly extended via configuration and program enhancements. Additionally, Business Content information models consist of fundamental metadata elements that can be used as building blocks to quickly forge custom information models such as the following:

- InfoObjects (that is, characteristics and key figures)
- InfoCubes
- VirtualProviders
- DataStore Objects
- InfoSets
- MultiProviders
- InfoSources
- DataSources (and their corresponding extractors)
- Transfer and update rules
- Queries (and their corresponding formulas, structures, calculated and restricted key figures, exceptions, conditions, and so on)
- Workbooks
- Web applications (and their corresponding Web templates, Web items, and data providers)
- Roles

Chapter 3 includes the descriptions of the metadata object types.

Roles-based information models organize Business Content around delivering information needed to accomplish specific tasks. When used within analytic applications, Business Content enables business process support to accomplish the tasks necessary for analytic activities.

Tasks are the different physical or mental work assignments necessary to carry out a specific objective. A collection of tasks and information available for a group of users holding similar positions is called a *role*. From a Portals perspective, a role can be further broken down into *worksets*, which are the tasks and information pertaining to specific activities. Worksets can be redundantly used across several roles that share similar tasks and activities. For example, a workset may consist of a series of tasks to perform a success analysis on a marketing campaign. The task-oriented workset Campaign Success Analysis could be simultaneously assigned to a campaign manager and a sales manager. Another example is the workset Cost Center Controlling, which can be assigned to all manager roles. Additionally, other applications can be integrated to the same manager roles, such as Human Resources worksets.

However, the impact of roles on Business Content is much more than on the organization of information deployment; it influences information modeling design and spawns analytic applications (more on analytic applications coming up later in this chapter). There is an interrelationship between the processes being modeled, the key performance indicators (KPIs) that measure the processes, and the roles that evaluate the KPIs to plan, monitor, and control processes. The circular interrelationship forms a feedback-and-response system where roles not only monitor processes but also optimize them.

From a Business Content information modeling perspective, the impact of this interrelationship is such that:

- The processes drive what subject areas are being modeled. They determine the data sources and corresponding extractors needed.

- The KPIs dictate what queries and their InfoMarts should look like. Note that KPIs do not necessarily fall within a single process but can cross multiple processes for ratios (such as inventory days of supply or cycle times like order to cash).

- Roles drive what KPIs are needed.

Because roles may need to plan, monitor, and control non-SAP processes, Business Content is being pushed outside the SAP domain. Heterogeneous system landscapes are a reality that a roles-based BI solution must contend with. By necessity, SAP Business Content is strategically moving in this direction, and SAP has created process modeling tools like the Visual Composer to enable such solutions.

For example, a purchasing manager may need to measure supply-chain processes sourced from i2 or Manugistics (such as inventory-days supply or material-cycle time). Figure 10-3 shows how the purchasing manager may need KPIs sourced from different processes such as business-to-business e-procurement, materials management, quality control, human resources, cost management, and sales and marketing. These processes can potentially reside in differing non-SAP systems.

Similarly, KPIs can be used in more than one role. For example, a bottling facility measures the performance of its production process by monitoring the cost of scrap. Potential problems in the production line include running out of glue or labels in the labeling work center. Such a problem might not be identified until after bottles are put into cases and palletized. Mistakes in labeling mean bottles have to be scrapped. Because of the significant impact to product cost, many roles in the bottling organization (spanning production managers, production planners, quality control managers, and supply-chain planners) evaluate the cost of scrap as a KPI to minimize. Figure 10-4 illustrates how a scrap KPI for measuring a production process can be used in several roles.

Besides the impact of roles-based information modeling, Business Content has grown horizontally across systems, applications, and processes, as well as vertically into different industry sectors.

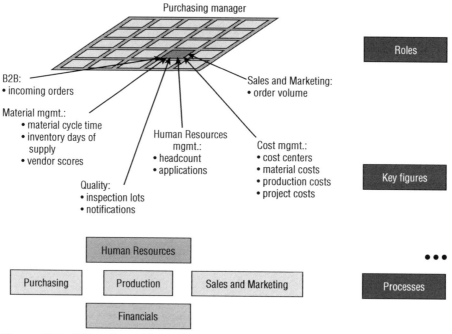

Figure 10-3 KPIs collected into roles

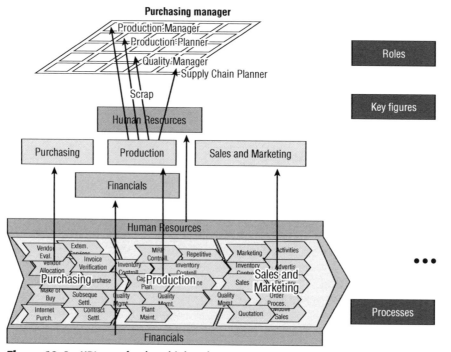

Figure 10-4 KPIs can feed multiple roles

Business Content Progression

From the beginning, SAP BW was meant to be a BI platform that was source-system agnostic. In other words, there were native tools that supported the loading of non-SAP data into SAP BW. More explicitly, the file and BAPI interfaces were loading options present at the advent of the product. Furthermore, early Business Content scenarios included non-SAP data such as the information models for Dun & Bradstreet information. Nevertheless, before the recent proliferation of analytics and the incorporation of SAP BW into SAP's NetWeaver offering, Business Content had a distinctly mySAP ERP flavor. This propagated the myth that SAP BW was a mySAP ERP-only reporting server.

Business Content has come a long way. In the earliest days of SAP BW, the most popular subject areas were sales and profitability analysis. Not only have these mySAP ERP application sources become less dominant, but mySAP ERP itself is not as central. New SAP and non-SAP applications are shrinking mySAP ERP's share of the information in SAP BW. In addition to mySAP ERP, Business Content supports SAP sources such as SCM, CRM, and non-SAP sources through the use of tools (from companies such as TeaLeaf Technologies and Informatica Corp.) and provides support for XML. It is by no means a stretch of the imagination to envision all the major non-SAP applications (such as Oracle and Manugistics) being supported by Business Content, especially through Business Content developed by systems integrators and partners.

Additionally, Business Content has become more specialized, catering to the information needs of industry sectors. Because SAP industry solutions have their own unique processes, these systems are typically separate solution offerings. These SAP industry-specific applications not only require separate information models but also distinct new extractors.

Horizontal Growth

Before the emphasis on roles, Business Content was application oriented. Business Content development took an inside-out approach; mySAP ERP applications were identified and corresponding extractors were written, passed to SAP BW InfoSources, and mapped to InfoCubes.

Business Content development then evolved into a more sophisticated outside-in approach. This approach focused on all the business processes available in SAP's solution map (SAP processes or a partner process). Using this approach, the interrelationships among roles, key figures, and processes were balanced.

The inside-out approach had limitations but created the foundation for an efficient implementation of the outside-in approach. Put differently, the inside-out approach provided what information was available, while the outside-in approach made that information more business relevant and meaningful for supporting the tasks of a role.

With the outside-in approach, SAP Business Content encompasses processes that extend across applications and systems and encapsulates integrated information to deliver the relevant KPIs for specific roles. To reiterate, there is a circular and tight relationship among processes, roles, and KPIs. Examples of non-SAP Business Content include the following:

- **e-analytics** — Clickstream analysis of Web logs
- **Market analytics** — ACNielsen and Dun & Bradstreet InfoCubes
- **Benchmarking analytics** — Benchmarking InfoCubes for the Corporate Performance Monitor (CPM)

SAP's development work with TeaLeaf Technologies has had an accelerating effect on the growth in e-analytics. Business Content now consists of specialized metadata with corresponding master data and transaction data. The Web content loads into DataStore Objects that make heavy use of transfer rules. The transfer rules parse the data into InfoObject values.

Third-party data provider information may be accessed via InfoCubes loaded from flat files. There are specialized flat files in Business Content that may be loaded prior to executing queries. ACNielsen examples align with industry solutions such as mySAP Consumer Products. Dun & Bradstreet scenarios have broader usage, being more geared toward customer relationship management and supplier relationship management.

For measures defined within CPM, benchmark data (such as market research studies) can be loaded into a fixed InfoCube by third-party benchmark providers. Whether benchmark data is available and who the benchmark provider is depends on the measure. Benchmark information can then be used for comparability purposes.

Business Content goes beyond providing non-SAP content; it also integrates it. For example, spend-optimization analytics merge Dun & Bradstreet data with purchasing data across purchase orders, confirmations, goods movements, and invoices. In sales analytics Business Content for mySAP Pharmaceuticals, industry-specific content is merged with mySAP CRM and external data from the third-party data provider IMS Health.

Vertical Growth

Instead of developing Business Content as one size fits all, SAP also develops industry-specific Business Content. More specifically, specialized Business Content can be found in the following verticals:

- mySAP Aerospace
- mySAP Defense and Security Forces

- mySAP Automotive

- mySAP Banking

- mySAP Insurance

- mySAP Chemicals

- mySAP Consumer Products

- mySAP Retail

- mySAP Media

- mySAP Utilities

- mySAP Oil & Gas

- my SAP Pharmaceuticals

- mySAP Public Sector

- mySAP Healthcare

In some cases, industry-specific Business Content simply enhances the standard content rather than replacing it. For example, the Business Content for mySAP Media augments the standard extractors with media-specific extensions (or, more technically, appends the extraction structures).

In other cases, for example, where there are no mySAP ERP counterparts, entirely new and separate metadata objects are introduced. Two examples can be found in the mySAP Automotive and mySAP Healthcare Business Content. In the former, there is a new InfoObject for vehicle, with requisite new master data extractors. For the latter, there is a new InfoObject and requisite extractors for diagnoses.

Industry-specific Business Content has taken more advanced forms than simple augmentation of metadata. More specifically, some industry-specific requirements have borne whole new techniques for extracting data out of mySAP ERP and using SAP BW. For example, the SAP Apparel and Footwear (SAP AFS) solution of mySAP Consumer Products introduced a new concept for extraction transformation that breaks down data fields into elementary fields. *Elementary fields* (a term coined by SAP AFS Business Content) represent any piece of information contained in grids and categories of the SAP AFS solution (such as color, size, origin, and quality). Specialized function modules read information from SAP AFS tables to break down the fields for grid value and category into more elementary ones.

For mySAP Retail, SAP BW has been used to correctly derive the valuation of materials for the Retail Method of Accounting (RMA), functionality that was not available in mySAP ERP. A specialized application called the RMA Engine must be configured to revalue the financial postings in InfoCubes.

Lastly, more advanced industry-specific scenarios have integrated Business Content across several applications (examples include mySAP ERP and mySAP

CRM). These so-called *composite applications* were the rationale for SAP's large investment in the development of the NetWeaver integration platform. One example is the case for mySAP Consumer Products' integrated sales planning application for key accounts. This particular solution includes specialized services that allow for planning and synchronization with online SAP applications for transferring plan and historical sales key figures. An application such as this must be flexible and easily changed as the business's needs change. Business Content becomes a key building block within the CAF (described in Chapter 2) to model and deploy analytic applications quickly.

Using Business Content

Business Content is a vital part of every SAP BW implementation. However, the degree to which you should use Business Content varies. To understand what to expect from Business Content, let's look at its value proposition, as well as evaluate its usability, postulate its challenges, and dispel some myths along the way.

More usable Business Content translates into greater savings in design and implementation costs by reducing the time to delivery. Business Content is also easily extendable so that its information models can still be leveraged even for highly customized solutions. The Business Content extractors alone save an implementation costly programming efforts. SAP initiatives such as Quick Start or Best Practices are predicated on Business Content usage to make implementations turnkey.

Business Content keeps the data warehouse in the SAP vernacular. Using the predelivered contents of the Metadata Repository standardizes everyone on a common set of business semantics. In addition, implicit in Business Content are best-practice information models and extractors.

The end result of utilizing Business Content is ensured data consistency and integrity. SAP-delivered InfoObjects are shared across many of its InfoCubes, thereby reducing data redundancy and minimizing the possibility of mismatched values. As a result, you can iteratively deploy Business Content InfoCubes without too much concern over metadata and information modeling impacts. Business Content InfoCubes and their designs are independent of other InfoCubes, but are linked by common InfoObjects.

Following are further advantages of Business Content:

- Fewer skilled resources needed to implement SAP BW
- Automatic improvements to the information model when Business Content is reactivated or replaced with newer information modeling versions
- Easier environment for SAP to support
- Predocumented information models

- Tight integration with SAP applications
- Ensured data quality, since the extractors revalidate the data before transmitting to SAP BW

Business Content has another impact on the nature of the project cycle: It enables BI to be implemented in reverse. Instead of implementing the SAP data warehouse using the traditional software development lifecycle (SDLC), the SAP can be implemented via the iterative CLDS ("SDLC" in reverse) approach. In the CLDS approach, the data warehouse is implemented first and then backward-mapped to requirements.

There are a number of advantages to the CLDS approach:

- A "quick win" data warehouse can be immediately deployed (that is, immediate progress can be demonstrated to the user community and project stakeholders, thereby increasing trust and confidence in the system and its implementation).
- If requirements are not met by Business Content, the process of gap analysis is accelerated, because users have an actual "live" system for evaluation. The real requirements can be deconstructed with concrete Business Content examples.
- Change management is accelerated, as users have a system they can touch and feel rather than having to conceptualize what may appear to them as a straw-man system. Users get immediate exposure to the information analysis environment and can more quickly shift away from traditional operational reporting to adopt more analytic reporting.

Not surprisingly, Business Content has grown multiplicatively with each new release and is a cornerstone to any SAP implementation.

Myths

The technology industry is rife with jargon and exposure to catachresis, and Business Content is no exception. Following are some of the myths that belittle the value of Business Content:

- **Business Content is merely a collection of precanned reports** — Business Content's most valuable offering is information models made of DataStore Objects, InfoCubes, queries, extractors, and so on.
- **Business Content is SAP-specific** — Many of the information models are generic enough to be source-system agnostic. For example, the CRM information models can be used for Oracle data. Business Content for Web site monitoring may come from any of a number of Web log file formats. Then there is Business Content exclusively for non-SAP sources such as Dun & Bradstreet. Furthermore, the partnership with

Informatica promises explicit Business Content for popular business applications such as Oracle, Manugistics, and i2.

- **Business Content is just predelivered metadata** — Business Content consists of not only metadata, but complete information models and associated extraction programs. Furthermore, Business Content information models are not just designs but can be quickly implemented via a simple activation process.

- **Business Content is simply an example or a demonstration** — Business Content should not be confused with demo content. *Demo content* is a very small subset of Business Content. In contrast to most standard Business Content, demo content is not to be used in production, and usually comes with its own master data and transaction data for demonstration purposes only. Demo Business Content information models are exclusive of all other Business Content, and are oversimplified versions of standard content. Standard Business Content is ready to run and is extensible. Business Content can be used in production systems for real business scenarios as is, or enhanced. The extent to which Business Content is enhanced depends on requirements and source-system customization. Business Content does not have to be used only as a template.

Usability

Business Content's usability can be organized into a pyramid, as shown in Figure 10-5. Certain universal reporting needs (such as balance sheet and profit-and-loss reporting) are commonly found requirements that make up the foundation of Business Content and its usability pyramid. As reporting requirements become more specific, the usability of Business Content decreases. SAP does deliver industry-specific Business Content. If the needs become any more specific (such as a unique requirement for a specific corporation, or even for an individual user), customization should be anticipated. In reality, your organization may be such that the Business Content usability pyramid is inverted. In such organizations, Business Content is only helpful as examples and templates.

Business Content usability can also be alternatively viewed as a scale, as shown in Figure 10-6. A relationship exists between where Business Content is situated in the information flow and how usable it is. As data transforms into information (from source to provider), Business Content becomes less usable without customization. Standard-delivered workbooks and queries are typically used as templates, since these metadata objects are often personalized and easy to develop. On the other hand, standard-delivered extractors are almost always adopted, because they can serve a gamut of information needs and are very difficult to custom-develop.

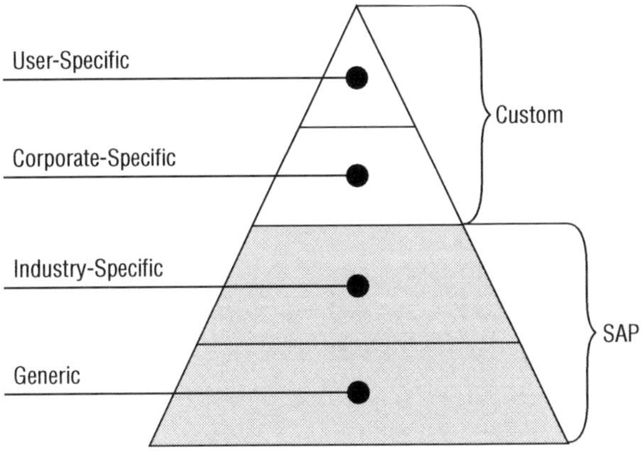

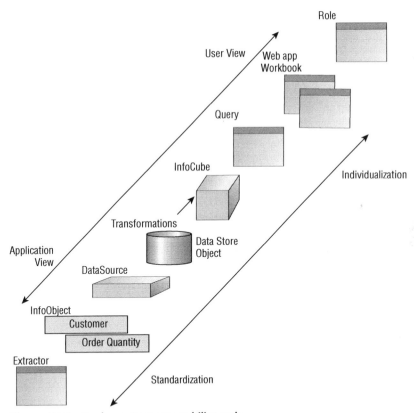

Figure 10-5   Business Content usability pyramid

Figure 10-6   Business Content usability scale
Based on copyrighted material from SAP AG

The popular adoption of Business Content extraction should not come as a surprise. Thousands of tables are relationally modeled in mySAP ERP. The entity relationship diagrams are complex and difficult to understand. Who else knows SAP like SAP? The SAP extractors are application specific and can handle transforming the data in lots of tables into meaningful business information to SAP BW DataSources.

Business Content extractors employ sophisticated delta change capture techniques as well. In many cases, SAP altered core mySAP ERP posting modules to effect a delta change management technique for extraction. Custom delta change capture is difficult to duplicate independently or with a third-party tool without modification. Often, change logs are read for custom delta extraction, which can be expensive from a performance perspective. As a result, you should unequivocally use Business Content extractors whenever available to spare an implementation the cost of development, the chance of poor performance, and the risk of poor data integrity. Chapter 6 discusses extraction and delta change capture in more detail.

Business Content is biased by application area. Some applications have greater Business Content support than others. These tend to be the more popular mySAP ERP processes such as sales, distribution, or financials or the more compelling scenarios such as analytics in mySAP CRM or mySAP SCM. The current trend is heavily tilted toward analytic applications, because this is where the current demand is.

Challenges

Business Content information models have been growing in sophistication with the increased capabilities of SAP NetWeaver. For example, the introduction of object types such as DataStore Objects, Visual Composer, and virtual InfoProviders has opened the gamut of information modeling options. The development trends have influenced Business Content design from both ends of the information-flow spectrum. At the front end are the innovations in presentation and information deployment options; at the back end is the steady increase of more detailed and frequent data extraction.

Keep in mind that not all Business Content is up to date. As SAP applications evolve, Business Content naturally becomes obsolete. Migration to improved information models is then required.

The two biggest challenges to managing Business Content result from SAP's fast-paced growth, namely maintaining conformity and controlling obsolescence.

Conformity

Business Content works best when metadata may be centrally defined and shared. Business Content is predicated on centrally defined, consistent metadata.

Typically, a high cost is associated with the discipline of designing information models that get consistently used in an organization. Business Content saves that expense. However, in reality, specialized organization and user needs will drive metadata away from Business Content (and, in fact, away from all forms of centralized consistency) and into inconsistent and disparate directions. This happens in any data warehouse, and SAP's is no exception.

Two basic conceptual levels of centralized metadata exist: the information models and the metadata building blocks that compose the preassembled information models. Business Content supports both forms. The building blocks are metadata objects (such as InfoObjects, DataStore Objects, and InfoCubes). Centralized information models incorporate the building blocks to ultimately deploy information-delivery components such as queries, workbooks, and Web applications. Sharable metadata building blocks are more essential than conforming to a particular information model. However, undisciplined management of both levels of metadata will result in a data warehouse environment full of redundant or fragmented building blocks and information models. You should take care when extending Business Content with custom developments by enforcing consistent metadata governance, and by utilizing Business Content whenever present.

Conceptually, sharable metadata and autonomous metadata are mutually exclusive forces that push at diametric odds. However, you shouldn't conclude from this that Business Content is more successful among user groups that require running precanned queries than among user groups that create ad hoc queries. This might be true for Business Content predelivered information models. However, it is not true for Business Content building blocks. Centrally defined, sharable metadata building blocks are necessary for any ad-hoc analysis to ensure that information across applications and systems are easily combined.

Bill Inmon, our coauthor, breaks the user community into groups, namely information tourists, farmers, explorers, and miners. The metadata needed for each user group is different. Predefined information models meet the needs of the information tourists (who sporadically peruse what is available) and the farmers (who have a set repertoire of analysis they conduct). In contrast, predefined information models are a futile effort for information explorers (who may not know what they are looking for until they find it) and information miners (who depend on the explorers to determine what information to mine). Consequently, Business Content information models have a greater likelihood of success with tourists and farmers than with explorer and miner roles. However, all user groups benefit from the use of consistent, centralized metadata building blocks. Business Content at the very least provides this vital service.

There may always be a need for autonomous metadata outside of Business Content (or any centralized metadata for that matter) — for example, creating on-the-fly metadata while building ad-hoc queries from unique user-specific data sources. More specifically, third-party OLAP tools are available that support scenarios where users want to merge data from files on their desktops. In essence, these tools bypass the centralized Meta Data Repository — a benefit that is debatable. Such scenarios do not leverage consistent and sharable centralized metadata that Business Content delivers.

Where the force for autonomy has had a divergent effect on Business Content is the specialized metadata needs of different applications for common business entities. For example, the Business Content for customer and material has spawned numerous InfoObjects that more or less represent the same thing. Not only is there separate customer and material InfoObjects for the different views of the same object (sales view, financial view), but each analytic application has its own version of the InfoObjects (the primary culprits being mySAP CRM and mySAP SCM). mySAP CRM alone has more than two dozen InfoObjects that represent product, which are, in turn, different from mySAP SCM materials.

In these cases, delivering centralized metadata and information models is a double-edged sword. On one hand, development could resign itself to supporting only generic information models. This would foster an easier-to-understand repository of centralized and shared metadata but would not address specialized needs. On the other hand, Business Content creation has been opened up to partners and customers who are creating a rich repository of information models at the expense of metadata chaos. The price of such chaos would be an overabundance of unneeded metadata, inconsistent information models, and decreased flexibility in data integration. In reality, both options are being explored further. A project has already commenced to implement a more generic data model for central entities such as product and customer, and industry standards for metadata are evolving.

Additionally, there are other techniques for handling metadata proliferation. For example, you can hide or unhide Business Content metadata depending on the components being used in SAP BW, and you can activate Business Content components to use its associated metadata. Tools such as the Content Analyzer and the Content Browser have helped to reduce pain typically involved in the trade-offs between centralized and decentralized metadata. Another way of handling the proliferation of attributes in InfoObjects is to allow more than one instance of the same InfoObject. For example, material could actually consist of several InfoObjects with different attributes (for CRM or for APO or for ERP) that all share the same surrogate ID.

There is yet another dimension to our discussion about conformity. Some processes and related applications are less conformed to begin with. For example, logistics applications tend to be more divergent than accounting applications. Hence, a generalized information model for financials is more likely to be successful than a logistics information model. The more potentially divergent the process models, the harder it is for SAP to deliver generic content to meet specific information needs.

NOTE The SCOR model (explained further later in this chapter) has taken on the challenge of standardizing the performance metrics for evaluating supply chains. Even in this area, there is a convergence toward standardization.

Finally, there are practical limits to Business Content:

- Business Content does not follow enterprise data warehousing standards and architectural guidelines very closely.

- Business Content cannot anticipate any customization or enhancement work in mySAP ERP. Every mySAP ERP implementation we have been involved in has required significant customization and enhancement work.

- Business Content does not include custom dynamic summary structures in mySAP ERP such as CO-PA, Financial Accounting-Special Ledger (FI-SL), and custom Logistics Information System (LIS). Although there are tools to generate extractors for these data sources, there are no delivered Business Content information models (it is possible, however, to generate all the requisite InfoObjects).

- Business Content is devoid of any logic based on organization-specific characteristic values or hierarchies. There are no predelivered organizational hierarchies or master data in SAP BW. Hence, no predelivered query can be hard-coded to any organizational hierarchies or master data values (although Business Content can work around this via variables in BEx queries). Similarly, there are no update rules that can take organizational or special characteristic values into consideration (although examples do exist where Business Content includes hierarchies for generic analysis such as age classifications in HR). For example, financial profitability metrics are often predicated on the company's chart of accounts. SAP examples of calculated financial performance indicators must be based on an SAP-delivered chart of accounts and must be adapted to your own chart of accounts.

Fortunately, Business Content is easily extensible to accommodate such scenarios. After customizing Business Content, you must take special consideration before performing a functional upgrade of the Business Content. To take advantage of new Business Content, you must reactivate the metadata with the new version of Business Content. When doing so, you have the option of merging the new version of Business Content with the older or customized version of Business Content or adopting the new Business Content entirely (effectively discarding the older version and any associated customizations). Business Content versioning is an ongoing maintenance consideration with each new SAP BW release.

Versioning

Not all Business Content stands the test of time. There are two drivers for versioning: new analytics tools and new information modeling options. The BEx has constantly evolved from being an Excel add-in to now a full BI suite. Furthermore, the advent of data mining tools supports mySAP CRM Business Content that utilizes decision trees, association analysis, and clustering. While in former times SEM Business Planning and Simulation (SEM-BPS) introduced planning tools that had specific information modeling impacts, these planning services are now a core part of SAP BW.

Along similar lines, since Business Content was introduced to SAP BW, numerous improvements have been made in the information modeling options available, including DataStore Objects, line-item dimensions, time-dependent aggregates, MultiProviders, and VirtualProviders. These improvements have enabled more sophisticated and powerful Business Content scenarios. The downside is that some Business Content becomes obsolete or no longer best business practice. In such scenarios, you must upgrade Business Content to take advantage of the new features. Fortunately, SAP has proactively provided new information models in many cases. To do a functional upgrade, you must reactivate the Business Content with the new Business Content version, or adopt a new information model.

For example, the first Business Content InfoCube delivered for costs and allocations in Cost Center Accounting of Controlling (CO-CCA) has been replaced with a new InfoCube for the same subject area. Both InfoCubes have the same text description and coexist, but the newer one should be used. The newer Business Content information model is mapped to the delta line-item extractor for actual costs, while the older Business Content information model is mapped to a summary-level extractor for actual data. In this case, migration is simply cutting over to the new information model.

Additionally, even delta line-item extractors can become outmoded. For example, there are two accounts receivables and accounts payable delta line-item extractors. One is an older version than the other. These extractors coexist, but only one extractor should be employed. The older version handled the deltas for accounts payable and accounts receivable in a decoupled and unsynchronized manner. Each could be loaded on separate schedules. The newer extractors are tightly coupled with a third delta line-item DataSource for general-ledger accounts that guarantees that all three extractors are in sync with each other.

LIS extractors have a similar versioning story. Newer delta extractors replaced the older summary-level LIS extractors. The migration path to new Business Content does not have to be immediate. At first glance, you might think that upgrading a SAP BW system entails the same level of effort for upgrading a mySAP ERP system. This is true to a certain extent, but note that there is a difference between a technical upgrade and a functional upgrade.

When upgrading an ERP system, you are typically doing both a technical upgrade and a functional upgrade at the same time. In a *technical upgrade,* the system is upgraded to the next release. A *functional upgrade,* on the other hand, means that your design and implementation of the system must be changed to adopt the new functionality in the system.

When upgrading SAP BW systems, you do not have to change all existing information models, including Business Content. You can keep the existing Business Content information models without upgrading to the new Business Content. A technical upgrade can be performed with very little impact to the design and implementation of the system. To take advantage of any new functionality in the system, you must perform a functional upgrade that involves much more effort in evaluating the potential impact. However, you can perform this more or less separately by each business area. Chapter 11 provides more information on upgrades.

While Business Content has its challenges, it does provide great value in accelerating the speed to value in modeling and deploying analytic applications. The remainder of this chapter will focus on how Business Content may be put to use and provide business analytics.

Customer Relationship Analytics

Customer relationship analytics come delivered with SAP NetWeaver as specialized analysis techniques. These analysis techniques are typically targeted for specific scenarios, but are reusable for custom designs. Briefly, the following are the topic areas for analytic CRM:

- **Customer analytics** — These analytic applications center on your customers and your customer knowledge base in order for you to gain greater understanding of who your customers are and their behavior. Customer behavior analysis digs deep into the buying habits and loyalties of your customers to find patterns via data mining techniques. CLTV analysis measures the worth of a customer from a lifetime relationship perspective. The results of an ABC analysis (which ranks data into A, B, and C segments) can be written back to the master data of an analyzed characteristic such as the customer.

- **Marketing analytics** — These analytic applications evaluate the effectiveness of campaigns, lead generations, marketing management, and the market in general. Techniques such as RFM analysis can be applied to optimize the target groups selected for a campaign based on the recency, frequency, and monetary (RFM) value of their purchases. Market exploration analysis helps to identify new market opportunities and size the market for its potential. Product and brand analysis makes use of data mining association techniques to derive rules for cross-selling.

- **Sales analytics** — These analytic applications assist in planning, predicting, and simulating sales and profits. Under the covers, this application integrates with SAP BW and its planning engine to do its simulations. Sales analytics is a component that can fit into a more holistic, integrated sales planning process. Sales analytics involves not just planning but also quite a lot of reporting such as pipeline analysis around objects available in operative processes (for example, opportunities, contracts, orders, and quotations). These parts of sales analytics are covered by standard Business Content. Sales cycle analysis takes apart the sales cycle from lead to sales order processing to uncover any deficiencies.

- **Service analytics** — These analytic applications track service contracts, service processes, confirmations, and complaints to help ensure optimal levels of customer service. Customer satisfaction, product quality, and complaint patterns can be derived from such analysis.

- **Channel analytics** — These analytic applications track the effectiveness of varying sales channels such as the CRM Customer Interaction Center (CIC) or a Web site. Alerts can be provided to the CIC via a CRM alert monitor, for notifications such as cross-selling opportunities or particular promotions that match the customer profile. Web site analysis is part of e-analytics and allows for behavioral analysis of a customer based on his or her clickstream.

CRM-specific analytic techniques will be covered in more detail later.

Analytic Engines

SAP BW comes with specialized transactions to configure analytic engines for CRM calculations such as customer behavior analysis (data mining), RFM analysis, CLTV analysis, and ABC analysis. To use these techniques, you do not have to install mySAP CRM, although some calculations would lose their relevancy outside the CRM context (note that CRM data can also be furnished by non-SAP systems). The transactions to configure these analytic CRM engines are accessible via role-based user menus. RFM and CLTV analysis stores the results of its calculations to Business Content DataStore Objects. These objects need to be activated before these specific analytic techniques can be configured. The techniques and their configuration are described in Chapter 7.

Customer Behavior Analysis

Customer behavior analysis is based on data mining methods such as classification, clustering, and association analysis to find patterns and hidden relationships in a customer knowledge base. Customer behavior analytics center on buying habits and churn (customer loyalty) behavior.

Data mining analysis is configured via a Data Mining Workbench and comes with a data mining wizard to guide the user through the setup. The setup is by data mining method (classification, clustering, and association analysis). Classification is further broken down into decision trees and scoring methods. The model parameters are different per data mining method and are covered in more detail in Chapter 7. For each method, sources for training, evaluation, and prediction must be configured. These sources relate to ODBO-enabled queries.

Data mining is highly integrated into SAP BW. In addition, mySAP CRM provides data mining interfaces to allow third-party data mining engines (such as KXEN, IBM's Intelligent Miner, and others) to integrate into the system when standard methods are not sufficient.

From an integration standpoint, SAP BW queries are used as sources for the training and mining processes. The data mining results can be stored back into the SAP BW system (as master data, for example) or forwarded to another system (such as cross-selling association rules to operational CRM).

Up to three sources of data are used in data mining: training data, evaluation data, and prediction data. *Training data* consists of small but representative subsets of data for the model to learn against before its learning is applied to historical data to make predictions. Historical data can be used for both evaluative and predictive purposes. Historical data for evaluation and prediction should be separate sources. *Evaluation data* is used to validate whether or not a model has been appropriately trained before it is turned loose against historical data to make predictions. *Prediction data* need not be historical data, but may be real-time business events. Note that model evaluation is not an explicit step in all mining processes. In some cases, the evaluation only means viewing the results of the training but not running the mining model with a separate mining source (because only a classification needs to be made, not a prediction).

All data mining methods share similar processes:

- **A data mining model is created** — The configuration of the models differs depending on the data mining method (especially the model parameters). The model typically consists of two levels of configuration: one for the model itself and one for the modeling fields. The configuration settings for model fields and parameters differ per model.

- **The model is trained** — Training allows the model to learn against small subsets of data. The query specified as the source for training should take this into account by selecting enough data to appropriately train the model but not so much that performance is adversely affected. Where predictions are not needed (such as association analysis), training is not needed. A model has a status indicator used to identify whether or not it has been trained.

■ **The model is evaluated** — After a model has been trained, it may be evaluated to determine whether it was trained appropriately. You should use a sample of historical data to verify the results (but do not use the historical data that is to be used for predictions). A model has a status indicator used to identify whether or not it has been evaluated.

■ **Predictions are made** — Once a model is appropriately trained and evaluated, it is ready to make predictions. Predictions can be performed either online or as a batch process, depending on the volume of data. Predictions should be made on yet another source for historical data separate to what was used in training and evaluation. The actual output of data mining depends on the method picked. Decision trees output probability trees, while clusters show percentage slices of an overall pie. A status indicator shows if a model has been predicted.

■ **The results are stored or forwarded** — Predicted values may be uploaded to SAP BW. For example, customer classifications generated by scoring models can be saved to customer master data. When loading the results back to SAP BW as a characteristic attribute, you must take care to match the metadata of the master data with metadata of the model fields. More explicitly, the keys of the model must match the keys of the master data. The master data load is triggered directly from the prediction and can be done online or in the background. When loading cross-selling rules determined via association analysis to a CRM system, you must specify the logical system name and target group to export the data. Predicted values can also be exported to file. Once these results are stored or forwarded, they can be used for operational use to drive decisions. For example, a bank may decide to offer or deny credit to a potential customer based on their attributes and behavior.

Following are the different types of analytics available for customer analytics. (Chapter 7 provides a more complete description of these methods.)

■ **Decision Trees** — Decision trees classify historical data into probability hierarchies. They are used in scenarios such as identifying which customers are more likely to churn (in order to improve customer retention), or which customers keep good credit (in order to screen prospects better). The results of the decision tree can then be used to initiate a customer loyalty program.

■ **Scoring** — Scoring scenarios may be used to identify customers of a particular market segment for a new product launch, or to categorize customers most likely to cancel service to a subscription. One of three regression types is used to perform scoring.

- **Clustering** — Clustering divides a set of data so that records with similar content are in the same group, while records with dissimilar content are in different groups. Clustering is also known as *segmentation,* since the relationships it finds can be used to identify customer or market segments.

- **Association Analysis** — Association analysis is a type of dependency analysis and is sometimes also referred to as *market basket analysis* because of its heavy use in retail. However, there are practical applications in other industries such as a telecom company offering additional services to customers who have already bought a specific set of services.

- **Customer Lifetime Value Analysis** — Customer lifetime value analysis treats customers as investments, and calculates their net present value depending on projections of the lifetime profitability of the customer. Predicted customer profitability and the predicted relationship life span of the customer are the primary factors for the analysis. Maximum lifetime profit for minimum investment is what is sought via CLTV analysis. The costs of acquiring and keeping a customer must be evaluated by the stream of profits the customer is expected to bring.

- **RFM Analysis** — RFM analysis evaluates the recency, frequency, and monetary value of customer purchases to determine the likelihood that a given customer will respond to a campaign. It is an empirical method that has long been applied to campaign planning and optimization as an alternative to segmenting a customer base by less-effective demographic means.

Supply Chain Analytics

One of the core technology components to supply-chain analytics is SAP APO. Most of the SAP BW support for SAP APO comes through the embedded SAP BW system or as standard Business Content on a remote SAP BW system. In contrast to CRM analytics, SAP APO does not provide SAP BW with separate analytic engines for its content.

The discussion in this section begins with an explanation of the SCOR model before briefly covering the applications and architecture of SAP APO. SCOR has modeling and analysis aspects that are topically covered with skewed emphasis on analysis. Finally, the discussion explains how SAP APO uses the SAP BW platform. SAP APO integrates with SAP BW in three basic ways: through the supply-chain cockpit, through customizable planning book-based applications (such as demand planning), and through Business Content for fixed operational planning applications (such as production planning and detailed scheduling).

SCOR Model

Independent of SAP, a SCOR model has emerged as an industry standard. The SCOR model is largely the work of the Supply-Chain Council (SCC), a non-profit corporation (`www.supply-chain.org`) founded in 1996 by Pittiglio Rabin Todd & McGrath and AMR Research. It has grown from its initial 69 volunteer members to more than 1000, testament to its importance to the industry. SAP now takes active involvement in the SCC.

The standardization movement facilitates the delivery of Business Content for supply-chain analytics. Because SCOR includes standardized key performance metrics for every detailed process in its model, SAP has a business model on which to build Business Content. For SAP, Business Content for SCOR metrics becomes more a matter of how to technically implement it than to devise useful business scenarios. Although there is some Business Content residing outside the SCOR model, much of the new development around Business Content is to deliver SCOR metrics. SCOR is not yet fully covered by Business Content, but the number of SCOR metrics supported grows. SAP furnishes a list of SCOR metrics supported by Business Content out on the SAP Service Marketplace.

A standardized operations reference model provides significant benefits. Standardized models provide companies' maps toward business process engineering, establish benchmarking for performance comparison, and uncover best business practices for gaining a competitive advantage. By standardizing supply-chain operations and metrics for managing such operations, companies can compare their results against others and also gain visibility of operations over a supply chain that may cross corporate borders. Partners in a supply chain can communicate more unambiguously and can collaboratively measure, manage, and control their processes. Greater visibility over complicated orchestration of supply-chain activities lets you fine-tune targeted problem areas and identify the cause-and-effect relationships in a supply-chain network.

SCOR and its corresponding performance metrics span supply chains from the supplier's supplier to the customer's customer. The process reference model contains:[2]

- Standard descriptions of management processes
- A framework of relationships among the standard processes
- Standard metrics to measure process performance
- Management practices that produce best-in-class performance
- Standard alignment to features and functionality

As shown in Figure 10-7, the SCOR model crosses all functions, incorporating business-process reengineering (BPR), benchmarking, and best-practice analysis. The process model is the idealized "to be" model for any BPR project and can serve as industry benchmarks for practices and software solutions that embody best-in-class management principles.

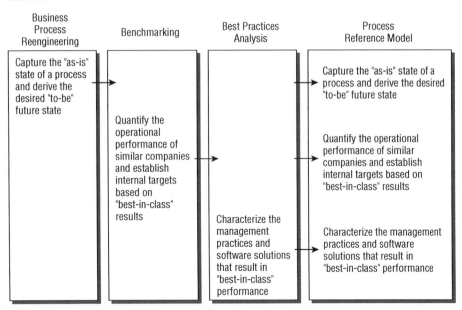

Figure 10-7 Process reference model
Copyright © Supply-Chain Council, Inc. www.supply-chain.org

The SCOR model consists of five management processes:

- **Plan** — This area encompasses demand-and-supply planning, which consists of balancing aggregate demand and supply to forge the optimization of sourcing, making, and delivering activities. Metrics on the actual planning process itself are not as robust as in the other areas.

- **Source** — Analytics in this area revolve around performance attributes of the processes of procuring goods and services to meet planned or actual demand.

- **Make** — Here analytics revolve around performance attributes of the production processes to develop finished goods to meet planned or actual demand. Production processes can be make-to-stock, make-to-order, and engineer-to-order.

- **Deliver** — This area's analytics revolve around performance attributes of order, warehousing, transportation, and distribution management processes, providing goods and services to meet planned or actual demand.

- **Return** — Analytics in this area revolve around performance attributes of the processes to return goods to suppliers or receive returned goods from customers for reasons such as defective products, maintenance, repair, and operating equipment (MRO) supplies, and excess, including post-delivery customer support.

The SCOR model (see Figure 10-8) processes are stratified into three levels of detail. The top level consists of the aforementioned processes (plan, source, make, deliver, and return), which are further subdivided into process types of planning, execution, and enable. Enable is the process of managing the information on which planning and execution rely and are categorized into *performance attributes*. All process metrics are an aspect of a performance attribute. The performance attributes for any given process are characterized as either customer-facing (reliability, responsiveness, and flexibility) or internal-facing (cost and assets) metrics. Table 10-1 shows a listing of all the top-level attributes defined by the SCOR model. Typically, only one metric should be focused on within a performance attribute. For example, for the reliability performance attribute, delivery performance, fill rate, or perfect order fulfillment should be picked as a metric but not all three.

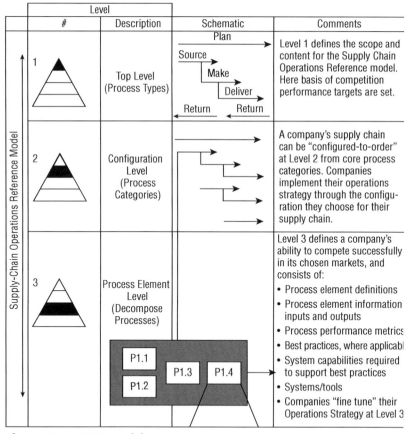

Figure 10-8   SCOR model

Table 10-1 SCOR Performance Attributes

PERFORMANCE ATTRIBUTE	CUSTOMER-FACING			INTERNAL-FACING	
	RELIABILITY	RESPONSIVENESS	FLEXIBILITY	COSTS	ASSETS
Delivery performance	x				
Fill rate	x				
Perfect order fulfillment		X			
Order fulfillment lead time		X			
Supply-chain response time			X		
Production flexibility			X		
Supply-chain management cost					X
Cost of goods sold				X	
Value-added productivity				X	
Warranty cost or returns processing cost	x				
Cash-to-cash cycle time					x
Inventory days of supply					x
Asset turns					x

Copyright © Supply-Chain Council, Inc. (www.supply-chain.org)

At the second level, the intersection of process and process types forms process categories. Not all process categories are represented in a company's supply chain. Only the relevant process categories are chosen before decomposing them into process elements at the bottom level. A company can pick and choose from a menu of process categories to configure its own SCOR model (such as make-to-order, engineer-to-order, or make-to-stock categories).

The bottom level consists of the actual process elements and their process flows. This bottom level of the SCOR model is most significant to analytics. Process elements are the most granular detail of the SCOR model and serve as the first level of process decomposition. Each process element has its inflows and outflows, as well as its own definition, features, best practices, and, most notably, performance metrics. Any further process decomposition into lower levels of detail is outside the domain of SCOR. How a company uniquely implements the SCOR model is reflected as lower levels to the model consisting of more detailed process decompositions. The process element "Schedule Product Deliveries" and its corresponding performance attributes and metrics are listed in Table 10-2 as an example. For instance, the process element has a performance metric that measures the percentage schedules generated or changed within the supplier's lead time. The performance metric is characterized as a reliability performance attribute in the process element.

Table 10-2   Schedule Product Deliveries Process Element*

PERFORMANCE ATTRIBUTE	METRIC
Reliability	Percent schedules generated within supplier's lead time; percent schedules changed within supplier's lead time
Responsiveness	Average release cycle of changes
Flexibility	Average days per schedule change; average days per engineering change
Cost	Product management and planning costs as a percentage of product acquisitions costs
Assets	None identified

"Supply-Chain Operations Reference Model: Overview of SCORE Version 5.0," p. 11. SCOR, Supply-Chain Council, Inc. www.supply-chain.org

The performance metrics of process elements can equate to the SAP APO key performance indicators. SAP APO key performance indicators are integrated with BEx. At this level, the Business Content (in the form of queries or calculated key figures) can meet the SCOR model. More information about the SCC and the SCOR model can be found at www.supply-chain.org.

Supply-Chain Cockpit

The *supply-chain cockpit* is a gateway-monitoring tool that spans all the major SAP APO processes and allows access to the most granular details. The tool is graphical in nature, consisting of instrument panels to monitor and control different aspects of the overall supply chain (such as demand planning, manufacturing, distribution, and transportation). The supply-chain cockpit is an analytic application in its own right and is integrated with SAP BW.

Via context menus, the supply-chain cockpit can call both SAP APO queries and SAP BW KPIs. The context menu of the supply-chain cockpit is the integration touch point between SAP BW and SAP APO. To configure the supply-chain cockpit, you must configure the following items:

- **Context menus** — Context menus allow user-defined menu items for queries and KPIs for any given SAP APO planning object (such as locations, products, resources, and so on). A default context menu and default SAP BW destination can be assigned to SAP APO planning objects if a context menu is not explicitly assigned. The context menu is configured via radio-button selections determining if SAP APO queries or KPIs (sourced from SAP BW) will be assigned to the context menu. SAP BW queries are listed for drag-and-drop selection to the context menu for SAP APO key-performance indicators. Note that KPIs link to specific SAP BW workbooks and not to a specific query. The implication is that the Excel Add-In for Business Explorer Analyzer must be installed on the SAP APO user's desktop.

- **Work areas** — Work areas are ways to manage the view to the overall supply chain a section at a time. Two types of queries can be launched from a work area: SAP APO queries and SAP APO KPIs. SAP APO queries are native to SAP APO, while KPIs are actually SAP BW queries. These queries are organized into query-object pools that represent subsets of all the supply-chain elements (or SAP APO metadata objects) composed of the following object types: locations (for example, plants, customers' receiving points, distribution centers, or suppliers' warehouses); resources (such as those utilized during production, storage, handling, and transport); products; production process models; and transportation lanes. The queries or KPIs are called for these supply-chain elements. The supply-chain elements and their values or value ranges used in a work area are configured into the work area itself.

- **User profiles** — The user profile controls how the navigation tree is displayed in the cockpit. This profile has settings such as the default context menu, if SAP APO hierarchies should be used in the navigation, how work areas should be displayed, how alerts should be displayed, and the planning calendar to use for time-dependent query data.

- **Control panel** — The control panel is located at the bottom of the supply-chain cockpit and contains individual context menus. These configurable monitoring options represent individual applications in SAP APO and are windows to alerts in the respective areas. Alerts can be monitored by products, resources, or locations. The configuration of the control panel is a matter of dragging and dropping the desired applications into the slots for the control panel.

If SAP APO has its own monitor and its own queries, apparent questions to ask are: "Why is SAP BW needed?" or "What additional functionality does the supply-chain cockpit offer?" SAP APO queries can be displayed in the supply-chain cockpit on the map, in graphics, in lists, or in tables. They are ABAP reports that select data by pointing to an object in the supply-chain cockpit or through the data-entry screen of a transaction.

Beyond SAP APO queries, BW queries have OLAP functions such as drill-down to details, integration to ERP data with drill-through, geographical information system (GIS) queries, Web reporting, and Web cockpits. The SAP BW queries are more flexibly maintained and configured. Example SAP BW queries for SAP APO demand planning *case study* for a consumer goods company will be detailed later in this chapter to provide a specific sample of the types of analysis that SAP BW can offer.

Demand Planning (DP)

This application is used to develop a market forecast for the demand of the goods that a company provides. Many causal factors can be taken into consideration, as well as many forecast types generated (such as statistical, field, marketing, consensus, and so on). This application facilitates more accurate demand predictions.

Typically, sales history is loaded into SAP APO to extrapolate forecasts, and actuals are loaded to test forecast accuracy. No Business Content InfoCubes are delivered for demand planning (DP), because of the customized nature of the planning application. Because of its focus on historical data as input, DP is not immediately updated through the core interface. DP is either directly loaded via Business Content extractors or indirectly loaded via the data mart interface from a sales history InfoCube. After DP data is performed, it is extracted out of SAP APO via the data mart interface back to an SAP BW InfoCube. Typically, the InfoCubes reside on a separate SAP BW instance.

DP is done in Live Cache. To plan data (for example, for statistical forecasts), you load sales history from SAP BW. Since data is only temporary in DP, data must be extracted back out to SAP BW InfoCubes, where data may more permanently reside. History can be matched with forecasts to do sales analysis. Business Content (InfoCube 0SD_C03) does, however, exist for such reporting.

Figure 10-9 shows the information logistics for such an information model. The sales analysis InfoCube can either be done as a single InfoCube or as a MultiProvider (splitting history and forecasts into separate InfoCubes, since these records typically are at different levels of granularity).

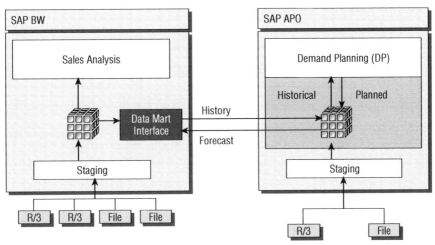

Figure 10-9   SAP APO demand planning information flow
Copyright © SAP AG

Design Impacts

Analysis on data extracted from SAP APO Live Cache planning data has special design considerations. Irrespective of whether SAP APO or a separate SAP BW system is picked for reporting, some SAP APO information modeling considerations must be taken into account because of how its planning data is stored. Following is a list of these design considerations:

- **Noncumulative key figures** — Only the most recent information is available in Live Cache. Live Cache does not store history. Its data can be backed up to hard disk for disaster recovery, but the data available is only a snapshot at the specific moment in time. As a result, transactional history or delta amounts are not available. This information must be extracted this way as well and cannot be cumulated over time. The key figures from planning are snapshots in nature. However, noncumulative key figures cannot be used to model this snapshot data, since it depends on delta increments to do its noncumulative calculation. Consequently, the snapshot quantities and amounts must be stored in a cumulative key figure with an exception aggregation (for example, a "last value" exception aggregation). This has a profound impact on how reporting InfoCubes should be modeled so as to avoid cumulating snapshot amounts over time.

- **Data Mart** — The data residing in Live Cache cannot be accessed directly. An export DataSource must be generated from the SAP APO planning area. The export DataSource can be assigned an InfoSource. The data can then be extracted out of Live Cache and into an InfoCube for reporting via the data mart interface.

- **VirtualProvider** — If Live Cache must be read directly, a Virtual-Provider may be built directly on top of the Live Cache InfoSource. If history is needed, saving the plans to a InfoCube is recommended.

- **MultiProvider** — Plan and actual data necessarily belong to two different InfoCubes. Typically, plan data is much less granular and has much less history than actual data. Plan data may be accessed via a Virtual-Provider or RealTime InfoCube, while actual data resides in a InfoCube for which aggregates should be built. MultiProvider technology allows you to unite plan and actual data together for variance analysis. Technically, it is possible to unite plan and actual data into a InfoCube.

- **Master Data** — SAP APO has its own master data. The planning model in SAP APO is separate from the information model in SAP BW. The planning model and associated metadata are created in the Supply Chain Engineer in SAP APO; in SAP BW it is the Data Warehousing Workbench (DWB). The master data may not only differ in values, but the metadata properties may differ as well. For example, SAP APO product is 40 characters long (identified by a generated ID), while materials in SAP BW are 18 characters long, since they are in mySAP ERP. To reconcile the ERP master data values loaded into SAP BW with SAP APO master data values, a crosswalk is needed between SAP APO and SAP BW for those values. This is done via navigational attributes on SAP APO master data. For example, the SAP APO product has material as a navigational attribute (technically, InfoObject 0APO_PROD has the navigational attribute 0MATERIAL). Similarly, SAP APO location number is cross-linked with plant (technically, 0APO_LOCNO has the navigational attribute 0PLANT). Additionally, InfoObjects like SAP APO location number are predelivered with integration to the GIS.

Case Study

A consumer goods company has a rolling forecast cycle. Each forecast cycle plans demand for the next 12 periods on a rolling basis (that is, a June forecast projects demand July through June of the following year). Within each forecast cycle, different forecast types are planned at different points within the period. Following are the forecast types:

- **Statistical** — This forecast uses sales history available in the first phase of the period to forecast demand based on forecasting algorithms such as regression analysis. This forecast is the first made in the second phase of the forecast cycle.

- **Marketing** — This forecast is made by the marketing department in the third phase of the forecast cycle.

- **Field** — This is the aggregated forecast made by individual field sales representatives for their respective customers and products. This forecast is also made in the third phase of the forecast cycle.

- **Consensus** — All the forecast types are evaluated, including the previous consensus forecasts, in order to come up with a new consensus forecast. This forecast is formulated in management team working sessions based on the analysis of specialized reports.

After the consensus forecast, the forecast cycle starts all over again in the next period when new history is available. Figure 10-10 shows the forecast cycle.

History is then compared to the previous period forecasts to check for accuracy. Forecast accuracy is measured in four different lags (one through four period lags). *Lag* is calculated as the difference in periods between the forecast cycle (the period the forecast was made *in*) and the period forecasted (the period the forecast was made *for*). Forecast variances should decrease as the lag shortens. SAP APO and SAP BW were implemented in order to shorten the forecast cycle within the month and to enable better forecasting through improved reporting and analysis.

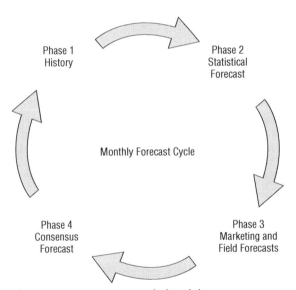

Figure 10-10 Forecast cycle breakdown

Data Loads

Forecast accuracy cannot be calculated until history is available. As a result, some forecast accuracies cannot be computed until more than a year has passed (that is, a four-period lag for the last month forecasted in a forecast cycle). As history becomes available, forecast accuracies must be calculated for four different forecast cycles to determine the lags (one, two, three, and four periods) that have already been posted to InfoCubes.

For example, a forecast in May is made for the months of June through May of the following year. The next month, another forecast is made for the months of July through June of next year. With each new forecast cycle, the previous period's history becomes available for forecast accuracy variance calculations. Not only can the accuracy of a previous forecast (one period lag) be calculated, but variances can be determined for the accuracy of the forecast in two periods, three periods, and four periods.

Figure 10-11 shows the waterwheel schedule of the data flow for actuals and forecasts coming into the SAP BW. The x-axis represents the forecast cycles, while the y-axis represents the forecasted periods. The value F in the cells represents the forecast data for that month. An asterisk (*) represents the period that the forecast was made in. The value H represents the history as it becomes available. History is not shown in the figure until it coincides with a forecast to highlight when lags are available.

12 Month Rolling Forecast Generated in Jan.

	1	2	3	4	5	6	7	8	9	10	11	12	1	2	3	4	5	6
1	.	F	F	F	F	F	F	F	F	F	F	F	F					

12 Month Rolling Forecast Generated in February and History Loaded for January

	1	2	3	4	5	6	7	8	9	10	11	12	1	2	3	4	5	6
1		F	F	F	F	F	F	F	F	F	F	F	F					
2		.	F	F	F	F	F	F	F	F	F	F	F	F				

12 Month Rolling Forecast Generated in Mar. and History Loaded for Feb.
4 Week Lag Calculated for January Forecast

	1	2	3	4	5	6	7	8	9	10	11	12	1	2	3	4	5	6
1		F&H	F	F	F	F	F	F	F	F	F	F	F					
2			F	F	F	F	F	F	F	F	F	F	F	F				
3			.	F	F	F	F	F	F	F	F	F	F	F	F			

12 Month Rolling Forecast Generated in Mar. and History Loaded for Apr.
4 and 8 Week Lags Calculated for Mar. and Feb. Forecasts, Respectively

	1	2	3	4	5	6	7	8	9	10	11	12	1	2	3	4	5	6
1		F&H	F&H	F	F	F	F	F	F	F	F	F	F					
2			F&H	F	F	F	F	F	F	F	F	F	F	F				
3				F	F	F	F	F	F	F	F	F	F	F	F			
4				.	F	F	F	F	F	F	F	F	F	F	F	F		

12 Month Rolling Forecast Generated in Mar. and History Loaded for Apr.
4, 8, and 12 Week Lags Calculated for Apr., Mar., and Feb. Forecasts, Respectively

	1	2	3	4	5	6	7	8	9	10	11	12	1	2	3	4	5	6
1		F&H	F&H	F&H	F	F	F	F	F	F	F	F	F					
2			F&H	F&H	F	F	F	F	F	F	F	F	F	F				
3				F&H	F	F	F	F	F	F	F	F	F	F	F			
4				F	F	F	F	F	F	F	F	F	F	F	F			
5				.	F	F	F	F	F	F	F	F	F	F	F	F		

12 Month Rolling Forecast Generated in March and History Loaded for February
4, 8, 12, and 16 Week Lags Calculated for May, Apr., Mar., and Feb. Forecasts, Respectively

	1	2	3	4	5	6	7	8	9	10	11	12	1	2	3	4	5	6
1		F&H	F&H	F&H	F&H	F	F	F	F	F	F	F	F					
2			F&H	F&H	F&H	F	F	F	F	F	F	F	F	F				
3				F&H	F&H	F	F	F	F	F	F	F	F	F	F			
4				F&H	F	F	F	F	F	F	F	F	F	F	F			
5					F	F	F	F	F	F	F	F	F	F	F	F		
6					.	F	F	F	F	F	F	F	F	F	F	F	F	F

Figure 10-11   Rolling forecast data loads

   Figure 10-11 starts the first forecast cycle in January of a new year. A one-period lag accuracy variance is not available until two forecast cycles later (in March). In each subsequent forecast cycle, older lag accuracy becomes available (in period increments) until finally, in June, all lags are available for the month of May. Going forward, all lags (for the four periods) will be available for each previous month. The missing lags for the first five forecast cycles occur only when starting the system.

Update Rules

The forecast accuracy variance calculation requires special programming in the update rules if the variance is to be stored with the detailed records of the InfoCube. Figure 10-12 illustrates how the variance records are generated (records in *italics*). The first four request IDs represent records loaded for four different forecast cycles. Only the records forecasted for May are displayed. The lag is calculated as the difference between the period forecasted and the period of the forecast cycle. Forecast, history, and variance are saved as separate key figures. When the forecasts are loaded, history and variance are left blank.

Request ID	Product	Forecast Cycle	Period	Lag	Forecast	History	Variance
1	Chewing Gum	1	5	4 period	55		
2	Chewing Gum	2	5	3 period	85		
3	Chewing Gum	3	5	2 period	90		
4	Chewing Gum	4	5	1 period	105		

Request ID	Product	Forecast Cycle	Period	Lag	Forecast	History	Variance
5	Chewing Gum		5			110	
5	Chewing Gum	1	5	4 period			55
5	Chewing Gum	2	5	3 period			25
5	Chewing Gum	3	5	2 period			20
5	Chewing Gum	4	5	1 period			5

Figure 10-12   Lag and variance calculation

When history is loaded, the InfoCube is read for all the lags for the period in question. In this scenario, history is loaded for May, so the forecasts for forecast cycles 1, 2, 3, and 4 are read into the memory of the update rules so as to calculate variances on these same records. In this case, four new records are generated for each history record loaded.

This logic is repeated for each forecast and variance key figure pairs (one for each forecast type of statistical, field, marketing, and consensus).

Analysis

The purpose of the DP queries in SAP BW is to report on the forecasts generated in SAP APO. The queries give insight into forecast accuracy by comparing the different forecast types with the related actual and target data. Example SAP APO queries include the following:

- **Forecast accuracy** — This query gauges the accuracy of forecasts by calculating the variance between forecast and actual data. Variances are shown for one-, two-, three-, and four-period lags to show any trends in accuracy over the forecast development stages. The query can be run for different forecasts (such as marketing, field sales, consensus, and statistical), and it can drill down on different sales organization levels (such as division, sales groups, and so on).

    The query can also rank sales organizations by forecast accuracy. The rankings are based on a comparison between target and actual forecast accuracy per lag (one, two, three, or four). The target and actual forecast accuracy are measured as variance percentages.

- **Consensus** — This is a query designed to assist with forecast consensus meetings every period. Several drill-downs are available in this report. The query provides history, previous consensus, statistical, field, and marketing forecasts. The query also provides the variance between the previous consensus and each of the current statistical, field, and marketing forecasts.

    The query displays the consensus forecasts generated in the specified previous period (the forecast cycle minus a period) and all other forecast types generated in the current forecast cycle. History up to the forecast cycle is displayed as well. Furthermore, the query displays the variance of forecasts relative to the previous period consensus forecasts.

- **Consolidated demand** — This query provides a list of all products forecasted in a specific forecast cycle. It reports each product's forecast by period, by sales organization, and in total. The results of the query are shared with the production planning department, deployment managers, and other operational individuals as a reference.

  The query looks at the consensus forecasts generated for a specific forecast cycle. The query can filter the data by the period of the forecast cycle and specified products so as to gain an overview of the 12 periods (of consensus) forecasts.

Network Design and Production Planning

Although no Business Content is delivered for the highly customizable planning applications such as DP, there is Business Content for the fixed planning applications in the planning hierarchy. Two examples of fixed applications are network design and production planning/detailed scheduling (PP/DS). Both operational planning applications are explained in more detail later in this section. Although there are SAP APO reports to access the data within these applications, SAP BW Business Content delivers queries that are more analytic in nature.

Network design assists the strategic decision-making process around the design of a supply-chain network, maximizing the utilization of a network's assets. In an environment with many products, many facilities, and many trading partners, strategic questions arise such as the following:

- What is the most effective way to set up manufacturing, transportation, and distribution networks?

- What changes can be made to the network design with the best cost impact?

- How can the network be expanded or contracted?

- What is the best sourcing strategy?

This component also interfaces with SAP BW via Business Content. The Business Content for network design is broken into three InfoCubes for location, shipment and transportation, and production analysis. The queries for these InfoCubes can be GIS-enabled for geographic reporting output via the Web Application Designer.

The first InfoCube breaks down location-specific information for products, delivering key figures such as cost and quantities for procurement, production, goods issue handling, goods receipt handling, and so on. The second InfoCube breaks down product-specific information surrounding shipments such as transportation durations, shipment quantities, and shipment costs. The last InfoCube is for analyzing production planning delivering key figures around production capacity such as percentage utilization, availability, expected costs, and consumption.

(PP/DS supports order-to-shop-floor planning and scheduling for multisite manufacturing operations. Collaboration among multiple production plants and outsourced manufacturing sites is optimized to maximize the return on manufacturing assets. Following are example strategic questions addressed:

- What happens if an unexpected event occurs such as a production-down scenario?

- How can production throughput be maximized?

This component also interfaces with SAP BW via Business Content. The Business Content InfoCubes delivered for this component are for resource and operations data, order data, and order/customer assignment.

The first InfoCube differs from the others because its data comes from two InfoSources: one for resource data and one for operations data. The resource InfoSource delivers to the InfoCube key performance indicators such as total resource capacity, resource availability, and capacity loads. The operations InfoSource delivers key performance indicators such as operation durations (gross and net) and quantities for original, open, operational yields, scrap, and so on. The merged view of resource and operations in this InfoCube provides meaningful information around the resource situation and how it got there.

The second InfoCube holds all of the order data in the SAP APO system, providing status information and key performance indicators such as order lead time, setup time, delay time, work-in-process time, open orders, late orders, yield, and scrap. The last InfoCube provides pegging data. One is provided with picking and packing data per order per customer. Analysis can be done on which orders are late, their percentage of total orders, and quantities produced for specific customer, and so on.

Financial Analytics

The financial capabilities of mySAP ERP provide other examples of analytic applications built on top of the SAP BW platform. These analytic applications are delivered as what is essentially an add-on application to SAP BW. Contrast this with mySAP CRM and SAP APO. Analytics for mySAP CRM comes pre-bundled with SAP BW. The analytic applications for SAP APO come from an embedded SAP BW system.

In addition, financial analytics comes with its own builders, models, and engines to extend the BI platform for building analytic applications such as planning and performance measurement tools. In former times, SAP marketed these applications as part of SAP Strategic Enterprise Management (SEM). The main applications for stakeholder relationship management, strategy management, performance measurement, business consolidation, and strategic planning (shown in Figure 10-13) were all aligned along the concepts of value-based management. The functions of corporate performance management, enterprise planning, and consolidation will be covered in this chapter.

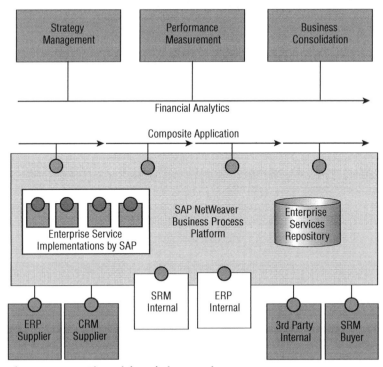

Figure 10-13   Financial analytics overview
Copyright © SAP AG

Corporate Performance Management

Corporate performance management can be logically subdivided into three distinct areas: strategy management, performance measurement, and stakeholder relationship management. *Strategy management* consists of a suite of applications and tools that support the formulation of strategy and creating a framework for communicating it through an organization. Applications such as the balanced scorecard, capital market interpreter, risk management, and value-based management aid strategy formulation, implementation, and operationalization.

In contrast, *performance measurement* relates to applications that output the results of corporate performance. Performance measurement tools help link measures to strategies and present them visually for ease of understanding. Here, the native functions of SAP BW offer the most value, but additional functionalities offered by the SEM suite extend BI through tools such as the management cockpit, measure builders, and value driver trees.

Lastly, *stakeholder relationship management* controls how performance measurement gets communicated to the outside world, keeping stakeholders well informed of performance so that the market does not get caught surprised by anything that would have an adverse impact on shareholder value. Stakeholder relationship management pushes stakeholder communications beyond sharing traditional financial measures through conventional channels.

Most of these applications are predicated on academic theories and are closely tied to the works of Alfred Rappaport (shareholder value), Stern and Stewart (economic value added) and David Norton and Robert Kaplan (balanced scorecard).

Balanced Scorecard

This application relates heavily on the body of work established by Norton and Kaplan. The origin of the balanced scorecard traces back to 1990 when a multiple company study was conducted predicated on the notion that over-reliance on financial performance measures was hurting more than helping value creation. The study revealed that some companies were using scorecards to overcome the limitation of financial performance metrics. These group discussions evolved into a more balanced approach by introducing the notion of adding four perspectives to scorecards. The new balanced scorecard then translates mission and strategy into objectives and measures organized into these perspectives.

The balanced scorecard addresses the needs for linking value creation to metrics other than financial, a more effective way to implement strategies, and more dynamic budgeting linked to strategy. Consider the following statistics:[3]

- Tangible book assets as a percentage of market value have been rapidly declining over the past three decades. For example, in industrial organizations, it has dropped from 62 percent in 1982 to 38 percent in 1992 and then to 10 to 15 percent in 2000. In other words, 85 percent of the value of these companies is now intellectual. How do traditional financial measures capture the value of human capital?

- In the 1980s, a Fortune survey was conducted that revealed fewer than 10 percent of all strategies formulated were implemented successfully.

- Twenty percent of organizations spend more than 16 weeks to prepare the budget, 78 percent of organizations don't change their budget within the fiscal year, 85 percent of management teams spend less than 1 hour per month discussing strategy, and 60 percent of organization don't link their budget to the strategy.

The balanced scorecard has evolved even further. Not only is it a *performance measurement* system, but it is a central *strategy management* system used to accomplish critical management processes and enable effective strategy implementation. A common misconception is that a balanced scorecard is just another type of visualized report. The formulation of management strategy is a process just like any other process, such as sales, distribution, procurement, production, or accounting. The balanced scorecard not only supports strategy formulation but also the process of pushing strategies and objectives top-down in an organization. By translating strategies into measurable objectives, performance can be measured. When performance can be communicated and measured throughout an organization, the organization becomes more transparent and operations become more aligned with management objectives. Strategy management can be broken down into four main processes that feed into each other in a perpetual loop:[4]

- **Translating the corporate vision** — This entails clarification of the vision and consensus building.

- **Feedback and learning** — This is composed of vocalizing the consensus vision, receiving strategic feedback, and promoting strategy review and learning.

- **Business planning** — Here, targets are specified, strategic initiatives aligned, resources allocated, and milestones set.

- **Communication and linking** — Here, goals are set, rewards linked to performance, and communications and education takes place.

All these management processes revolve around the balanced scorecard framework. The balanced scorecard has two objectives:

- Change the way performance is measured and managed.
- Change the way strategy is implemented and how it is translated into actions.

Performance Management

To achieve the first objective, the balanced scorecard introduced two major distinctions to traditional financial performance measures: the addition of four perspectives to scorecards and the linking of performance measures to strategy. The four perspectives ask different strategic questions, such as:

- **Financial** — To succeed financially, how should we appear to our shareholders?

- **Customer** — To achieve our vision, how should we appear to our customers?

- **Internal business processes** — To satisfy our shareholders and customers, what business processes must we excel at?

- **Learning and growth** — To achieve our vision, how will we sustain our ability to change and improve?

The balanced scorecard does not do away with financial performance metrics but augments them with different perspectives. These different perspectives add nonfinancial indicators and qualitative measures into the system of strategy formulation and evaluation. Nonfinancial measures may consist of measuring important (but intangible) assets such as employee motivation, customer satisfaction, operational efficiencies, and product-quality or service-quality levels. The balance scorecard marries the conventional accounting measures, which gives an enterprise a historical perspective with measures for intangible assets. This, in turn, gives an enterprise a future performance outlook. The perspectives do not have to be limited to the categories given or limited only to four. For example, a scorecard used in the public sector may consist of goal (mission goals of an agency), customer (citizens, taxpayers, and beneficiaries), and employee perspectives. Figure 10-14 illustrates the balanced scorecard and how it is rendered in SAP.

The SAP balanced scorecard functionality allows for the formation of scorecard hierarchies and groups. These scorecards are assigned to organizational elements of your organizational structure, including integration to human resources, allowing for employee-specific scorecards. Higher-level scorecards can drill down to lower-level scorecards, allowing for navigation throughout the organization. Scorecards can even be compared to each other. Scorecards are time dependent, allowing for time-variant comparisons and creation of validity dates.

The linking of balance scorecard measures to strategy is done through cause-and-effect analysis. The different perspectives build on each other to influence financial key performance indicators. The perspectives can be viewed as a pyramid where learning and growth drive internal business process improvement, which, in turn, drives customer satisfaction. This ultimately improves the bottom line.

Cause-and-effect analysis links the outcomes and performance drivers of other perspectives to the financial perspective. Along the rows of cause-and-effect analysis are the perspectives. Along the columns are the strategies. In the bubbles are the strategic objectives. These objectives have measures associated with them (which can be displayed with an alternate view). Figure 10-15 illustrates cause-and-effect analysis in SAP.

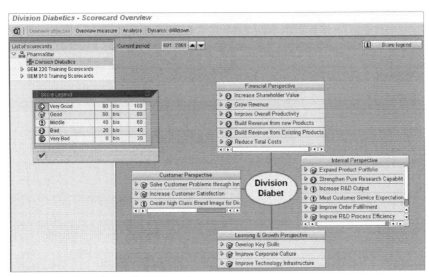

Figure 10-14   Balanced scorecard

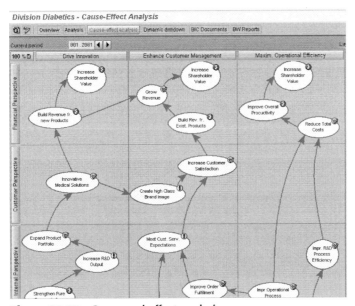

Figure 10-15   Cause-and-effect analysis

Copyright © SAP AG

The balanced scorecard perspectives can be alternatively displayed in the management cockpit, where each perspective can be represented by different color-coded walls (blue, black, red, and white) with different graphic types per measure (such as speedometer, tachometer, quadrant, chart, and so on) configurable in a so-called *measure builder*.

Strategy Implementation

The second objective of the balanced scorecard (to change the way strategy is implemented and how it is translated into actions) distinguishes it from traditional methods in two ways. The first way is that the balanced scorecard should bridge the traditional gap between strategy formulation and implementation. Balanced scorecards should avoid four main obstacles:

- Nonactionable vision and strategies
- Strategies unlinked to goals at all levels of the organization (whether departments, teams, or individuals)
- Strategies unlinked to resource allocation
- Feedback that is tactical instead of strategic

The second way is how the balanced scorecard provides the framework for overcoming these obstacles. The first and second obstacle is bridged by creating organizational alignment top-down by fostering shared commitment and understanding of corporate strategies among all employees. The third obstacle is avoided by incorporating the balanced scorecard into strategic planning and operational budget formulation processes. The last obstacle is overcome by a process known as *double-loop learning*, illustrated in Figure 10-16.

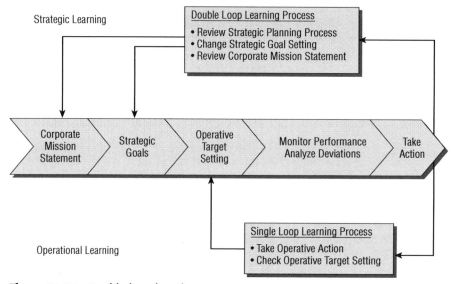

Figure 10-16 Double-loop learning
Copyright © SAP AG

A company should not expect to implement a balanced scorecard by simply implementing the SAP software application. Before configuring this application, a corporation should already be well versed in balanced scorecard theory and know corporate strategies.

Two challenges to implementing a balanced scorecard solution are using the correct measures and measuring correctly. The implementation process can take years and, hence, should be done incrementally.

The first challenge of using the correct measures relates to strategy formulation consisting of determination of what the strategies, objectives, initiatives, and measures are for an enterprise. This has to be accomplished before the application can be configured. From an SAP BW perspective, the second and more difficult challenge is capturing the measures correctly once they have been determined. Ironically, CPM is typically the last application to be implemented after mySAP ERP and BI capabilities have been implemented, when in an ideal world, it should be considered first. The balanced scorecard will have a potential impact on how OLTP source systems are configured and how information is modeled to support analytics. For example, one of our clients had found themselves with a *finished* implementation of mySAP ERP only to discover they needed to reimplement some areas in order to support the design of their CPM application and thus align their ERP implementation with their overarching business strategy.

Once an enterprise is organizationally prepared for the balanced scorecard, the SAP application can be configured. The advantage of building an electronic scorecard in SAP is the integration capabilities to structured information (queries), unstructured content (information gathered by SEM batch information cockpit, or BIC), and planning (SAP BW planning layouts).

The SAP balanced scorecard has its own scoring engine to give data residing in SAP BW a qualitative context of whether a key performance indicator is bad or good. You can assign status symbols to a range of scores (which can be weighted) to measures based on performance levels, thereby giving a visual means for gauging performance.

Creating a scorecard in SAP consists of building measures, creating a pool of balanced scorecard elements, maintaining general settings such as the creation of CPM variables, and then constructing the actual scorecard by assembling the balanced scorecard elements.

The configuration of measures via the measure builder is a central activity to CPM. Measures are not only used for the balance scorecard, but are also used in value driver trees, risk analysis, and the management cockpit. The measures are configured via the measure builder, which includes a measure catalog containing a large number of predefined measures with detailed descriptions. The definition of measures consists of settings such as the definition, a formula if relevant, assigning it benchmarks, and mapping technical key figures available via ODBO-enabled queries. The integration with SAP BW is achieved via value fields. Multiple value fields (such as plan and actuals) can either be assigned to objectives or measures that represent multiple query cubes.

Once measures have been configured, balanced scorecard elements can be configured. Balanced scorecard settings exist at two levels: balanced scorecard-independent settings and balanced scorecard-dependent settings. The independent settings must be maintained first.

The balanced scorecard (BSC) elements are centrally maintained and used as building blocks to balanced scorecards. When configuring BSC elements, the relationships between the elements have not been established. The basic elements consist of strategies, strategy categories, perspectives, objectives, and common objectives.

Then, general settings such as CPM variables (which reduce the need for hard-coding values in the balanced scorecard), value fields (which link to queries), and technical settings for the integration to SAP BW (such as serial versus parallel processing of data requests) must be maintained. Status symbols and scoring methods are also configured at this point.

Finally, the balanced scorecard-dependent settings are maintained when scorecard elements are assigned to a specific scorecard, as well as general scorecard parameterizations (such as its time dimension, graphics, documents, and links). The configuration of the scorecard itself takes only a fraction of the time it takes to design it.

Enterprise Planning

Planning applications are an important aspect of business intelligence. Performance measurement relies heavily on the variance analysis of plan versus actual. Planning is an essential activity to the forward-looking organization. Strategic enterprise planning closes the loop between strategic and operational planning.

The planning process typically covers multiple reporting areas on both a corporate and operational level. Corporate plans include capital investment plans, free cash flow plans, tax plans, profit-and-loss plans, and balance sheet plans. Operational plans include a sales plan, expense plan, profitability plan, cost center plan, production plan, and so on.

The planning cycle typically involves the following methods:

- **Research and prognosis** — Estimating future situations and assessing the impact on the enterprise.
- **Target setting** — Setting goals and milestones.
- **Budgeting** — Allocating resources for the achievement of targets.

The reality is that the planning infrastructure for many corporations is a fragmented environment consisting of heterogeneous data using different technologies supported by many interfaces. The reality of many planning cycles is that by the time the plan gets formulated, it is already obsolete. Enterprise planning addresses the need for timely, consistent planning data. Integration across all the reporting areas and methods is needed.

SAP utilizes the SAP BW planning engine, which works quite differently compared to the current SAP APO planning engine. Planning, therefore, works against real-time InfoCubes, while SAP APO planning works against Live Cache. Real-time InfoCubes are within the configuration domain of SAP BW, while Live Cache is not. InfoCubes are set for real-time at time of creation, thereby changing the way data requests are updated. Planning and real-time InfoCubes have an impact on information modeling.

Planning Applications

As discussed in Chapter 9, planning applications may be custom-designed from scratch or predelivered. The predelivered planning applications are analytic applications in their own right. If used, the predelivered planning applications speed up the time of an implementation. These planning applications come with test data for master data and transactional data to jump-start familiarization with the applications.

The planning applications are configurable and extensible. These planning applications also consist of specialized functions and logic built into the application. For example, the *capital market interpreter* has its own specialized logic and configuration settings, which will be explained in more detail later in the section of this chapter with the same name. In reality, all these planning applications may be integrated into one comprehensive planning application:

- **Balance sheet planning** — This planning application actually is composed of income statement planning, balance sheet planning, and cash flow planning steps. Each step has an impact on the balance sheet amount, and all the interdependencies are demonstrated via an integrated planning folder with all the components. As a result, a cash flow change after data entry in balance sheet planning can be immediately assessed. The relationships among income statement, balance sheet, and cash flow are captured in this application. For example, receivables are calculated as a quotient of net sales (the quotient being calculated as the ratio of receivables to net sales in the prior year), so that when net sales are adjusted, so are receivables. Special planning functions for accumulating balances, depreciating, and discounting are also included.

- **Investment planning** — Investment planning allows for preinvestment analysis of planned investments, or planned investment programs (a hierarchical structure of planned investments in investment management). There are two types of preinvestment analysis available: static and dynamic.

Static preinvestment analysis holds cash inflows and outflows static over the duration of the investment timeframe measured in years. *Dynamic preinvestment analysis* varies the cash inflows and outflows per period in the investment timeframe. Hence, dynamic preinvestment analysis involves more data entry, but offers more precise preinvestment analysis. Furthermore, the cash flows in dynamic analysis can be discounted in order to calculate net present value. Additionally, a conventional interest rate can be specified, or an internal rate of return can be calculated for the net present value formula. Static preinvestment analysis should be considered only for small investments with a short investment timeframe (such as relatively inexpensive replacement or expansion investment).

Since investment planning consists of adding assets to the balance sheet and an expected return on investment. This planning application is integrated with balance sheet planning and profit planning, respectively. The integration is achieved via multiplanning areas. For example, the profit planning application has unit prices such as the cost of goods per unit, which can be read into investment planning. Investment planning may then drop the unit price, which in turn updates profit planning.

- **Sales planning** — This planning application ties into analytic CRM. It has two versions: online and offline. The *online version* is performed for top and middle management. The *offline version* is for the planning of key accounts by sales representatives in the field. The offline version is still Excel-based and is used to upload to the online version. This planning application starts with top sales management to establish performance targets that get distributed down the organization. Finally, once targets are set, the target plans are passed to operational sales planning. The operational sales plans are performed by sales employees who forecast expected sales orders based on current sales volumes and expected opportunities. Once complete, the consolidated sales plan can feed subsequent plans (potentially in other applications such as SAP APO) like production and supply and then come full circle to financial budgeting and profit planning.

- **Profit planning** — Profit planning works against two InfoCubes: one for the planning results and one to read the values that will influence the profit planning results. The latter InfoCube contains key figures such as average prices like price per unit or cost of goods per unit (fixed and variable), percentages like direct sales costs or reductions, and quantities like sales units. By changing the key-figure values in this second InfoCube, the profit planning results in the first InfoCube are influenced. Many scenarios and iterations can be performed to simulate different profit plans based on changes in prices or percentages in the second InfoCube. The calculations can be performed at various different levels of detail and can then be subsequently distributed either top-down or bottom-up.

- **Liquidity planning** — This planning application allows planning of cash flows in multiple currencies. The data is posted by period to different organizational planning units and to account structures referred to as *liquidity items*. Plan and actual data can then be consolidated at a group level for analysis.

- **Simplified resource planning** — This application is a standalone and simplified product-costing application to determine the overall cost of goods sold for given planned sales quantities. Product-costing InfoCubes are loaded as a basis for its calculations. One InfoCube has the itemization breakdown of a product and its quantities. The itemization represents a kit of materials, services, and overhead costs that compose a saleable good. The itemization is a much more simplified version of a bill of materials and routings in that it is nonhierarchical. A second InfoCube contains the resource prices for each of the itemizations. The overall cost of goods sold is then calculated by multiplying sales quantities by the price of goods (which, in turn, is calculated by multiplying the planned quantities of itemized resources by their respective planned resource prices). Because of its simple design, this planning application has numerous restrictions compared to other SAP planning applications. For example, it doesn't take inventory levels into effect, resources are consumed at time of sales, and the itemization cannot change (although quantities can be adjusted). However, this application does illustrate that if some SAP planning applications are overengineered for a particular set of business requirements, a simplified version can be custom-built.

Capital Market Interpreter (CMI)

There are several competing theories on value-based management such as McKinsey's economic profit calculations and Stern and Stewart's economic value-added analysis. The capital market interpreter (CMI) incorporates the concepts of value-based management as set forth by Alfred Rappaport. CMI attempts to valuate the market impact of management decisions. CMI aids in maximizing shareholder value by evaluating the discounted cash flow effects of management decisions. CMI is one of the many tools available for analyzing the market value of an enterprise. The CMI has a number of different analyses available:

- **Shareholder value analysis** — This is the primary function that the capital market interpreter performs. The calculations made here are reused in value gap and sensitivity analysis. This analytic engine calculates corporate value and shareholder value. The corporate value is a representation of the market value of the corporation by calculating the net present value of the discounted cash flows. The shareholder value is the corporate value minus debt. This calculation is made for a particular version of plan data representing the valuation (in Figure 10-17 the version is C01). The timeframe for shareholder value calculation is from the current start date to the competitive advantage period (CAP) specified in planning. The CAP can be up to 15 years. To perform the calculation, the following key figures (or value drivers) are necessary: sales, EBITDA (earnings before interest, tax, depreciation, and amortization), taxes, depreciation, asset investment, working capital, and the WACC (weighted average cost of capital). These values can be manually entered by planning layouts specified in CMI configuration.

The results of the calculation can be displayed in absolute amounts or as percentage comparisons to the previous year.

The analysis calculates two types of cash flows: free cash flow and discounted cash flow. The definition of the free cash flow calculation as well as the corporate value, debt, and shareholder value are all configured. After configuration, the value drivers within a shareholder value equation can be graphically charted (see Figure 10-17).

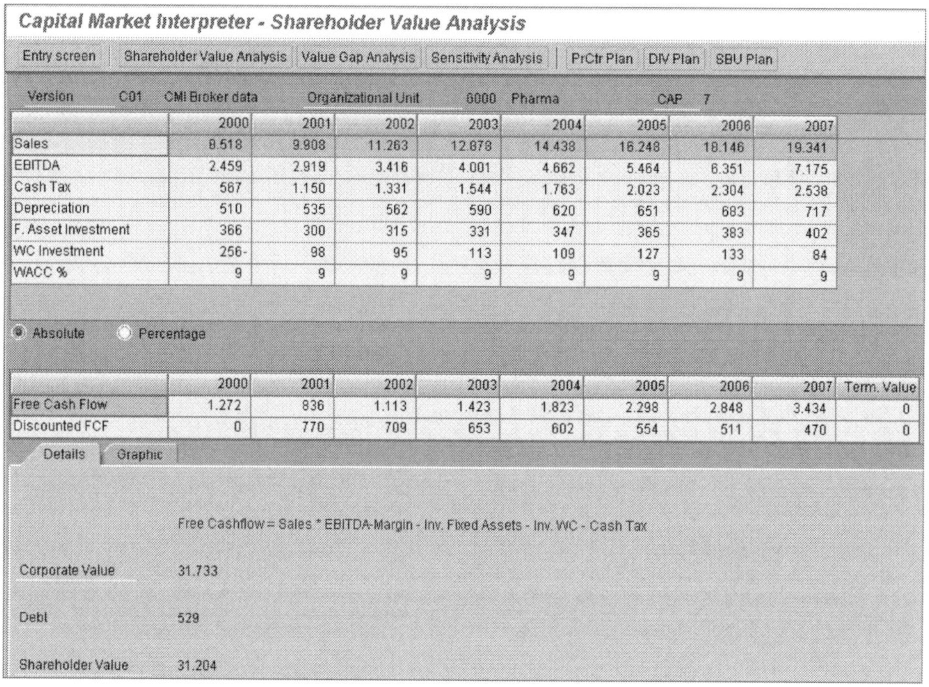

	2000	2001	2002	2003	2004	2005	2006	2007
Sales	8.518	9.908	11.263	12.878	14.438	16.248	18.146	19.341
EBITDA	2.459	2.919	3.416	4.001	4.662	5.464	6.351	7.175
Cash Tax	567	1.150	1.331	1.544	1.763	2.023	2.304	2.538
Depreciation	510	535	562	590	620	651	683	717
F. Asset Investment	366	300	315	331	347	365	383	402
WC Investment	256-	98	95	113	109	127	133	84
WACC %	9	9	9	9	9	9	9	9

	2000	2001	2002	2003	2004	2005	2006	2007	Term. Value
Free Cash Flow	1.272	836	1.113	1.423	1.823	2.298	2.848	3.434	0
Discounted FCF	0	770	709	653	602	554	511	470	0

Figure 10-17 Shareholder value analysis

■ **Value gap analysis** — Different shareholder value calculations can be made for different versions and then compared. For example, if a broker's expectations for shareholder value must be compared with an internal valuation, two versions of data can be created and then compared against each other to ascertain the value gap. Significant value gaps can assess exposure to hostile takeover risks, for example.

When executing the value gap analysis, you must specify the two different versions along with a simulation version called the variation version. The *variation version* is different from the *comparison version* in that its values can be overwritten and manipulated during analysis to do on-the-fly what-if scenarios. The version comparison is then performed for each of the value drivers in each version (first, second, and variation). An absolute and relative value gap for the shareholder value difference is calculated and outputted; then the second and variation versions are compared against the first version.

■ **Sensitivity analysis** — The shareholder value calculation is a complex one. All the component or value drivers that factor into the equation may have greater influence on shareholder value than others. This analysis tool facilitates identifying which value drivers have the most sensitive effect on the shareholder value calculation. Finding that shareholder value is particularly susceptible to a value driver (such as WACC) may lead to new strategies such as looking for lower-cost means of financing.

Sensitivity analysis is compared against the variation version for its analysis. During the initialization of the analysis, the variation version value is copied from the version specified for sensitivity analysis. The variation version values can then be manipulated for analysis either directly (by changing the value driver values in the variation version manually) or indirectly (by specifying a percentage change for a value driver in the comparison version). The indirect method multiplies the percentage amount entered against the comparison version in order to overwrite a new variation version value. After changes are made and the sensitivity calculation is performed, the shareholder value percentage deviation is output and can also be visualized in a bar chart.

CMI comes with predelivered user-exit code (for the calculation functions and variables). The user-exits must be configured because the CMI logic is not hard-coded to any Business Content. Consequently, the CMI engine can work against any information model. CMI consists of the following configuration items:

■ **Data source** — Any InfoCube can be used with the CMI. As a result, the planning objects to be used for CMI analysis must be specified here (planning area and planning level, as well as the initial data entry layout used strictly for data access). Planning layouts for data entry are a separate configuration item. Recall that the planning area equates to a specific InfoCube.

- **Evaluation groups** — Three characteristics must be specified for CMI calculation: an organizational unit, a version, and (optionally) an account (depending on whether or not accounts are modeled as characteristic values in the InfoCube or as key figures). Here, the InfoObject name is specified.

- **Key figures** — These are the value drivers for the shareholder value calculation. For each CMI key figure or value driver, a SAP BW key figure must be specified. If account values such as sales are not modeled as discrete key figures but rather as characteristics of an account dimension, the account InfoObject must be specified in the evaluation group and then restricted per CMI key figure. Because there are a large number of value drivers, further details can be found in the measure catalog about each key figure.

- **Versions** — Versions are used in sensitivity analysis. Sensitivity analysis involves changing each value driver used in the equation for shareholder value, while holding all other value drivers constant, and ultimately identifying the value drivers with the most impact to shareholder value. Key figures represent each value driver (seven in total), and an additional key figure is needed for competitive advantage period (CAP). Each value driver key figure must be assigned a version so that its results can be saved separately. The sensitivity analysis can then be used to compare the different versions to evaluate which value driver was the most sensitive to changes. An InfoObject must be specified and characteristic values representing separate versions assigned to each value driver. The characteristic used to represent version is specified in the evaluation group.

- **Calculations** — This tabstrip, shown in Figure 10-18, represents the configuration mapping of planning functions and their corresponding parameter groups to the different calculations for CMI. As a general rule, each planning function (except for the copy versions) must refer to user-exit functions that refer to user-exit function modules belonging to the specific function group for CMI calculations. These function modules can be used or replaced with custom user-exits if other calculations are desired. The user-exit function modules that are provided for the CMI calculations are based on Alfred Rappaport's definition of shareholder value.

- **Data entry layouts** — This tabstrip is optional. It can be used to allow the entry of data such as sales, profit-and-loss, and balance sheet values that link to CMI calculations.

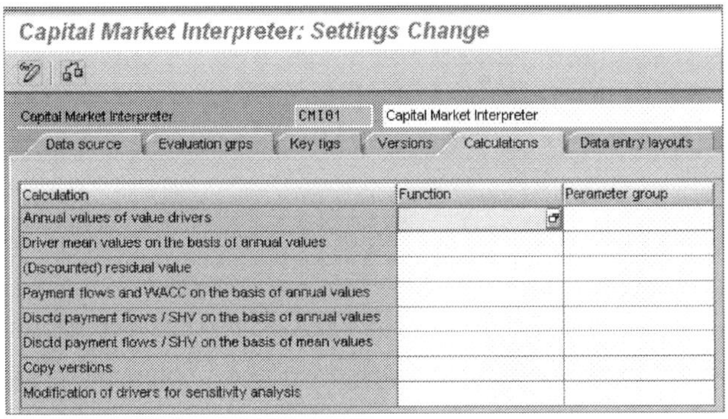

Figure 10-18 CMI configuration
Copyright © SAP AG

Financial Consolidation

Financial consolidation may be the most mature of all the financial analytic applications, because it has long been a part of mySAP ERP. The first consolidation application was part of financial accounting (FI), and was designed to perform legal consolidation. It was an application that was originally based on the special ledger platform, taking advantage of the data transformation and reporting capabilities embedded in the platform.

The consolidation functionality was then expanded to include management consolidation. As opposed to legal consolidation, where statutory requirements dictated the application's functionality, management consolidation had to be more dynamic, especially to accommodate management reporting. The most popular way to perform management consolidation was to eliminate inter-profit-center activities, such as profit in inventory transfers. However, the intent of the application design was that the application could source from anywhere, whether from an application such as profitability analysis or from non-SAP systems via flexible upload of flat files.

As the consolidation product matured, it has grown more extensible. At first, the tables were fixed and could not be changed. Then three additional fixed fields were added to the table to allow for custom use. The application also changed its tables and moved under the enterprise controlling module, allowing rollups from applications such as profit center accounting. Currently, management consolidation has transformed into a generic consolidation engine that can sit on Special Ledgers in mySAP ERP or custom InfoCubes in SAP BW.

The first version of SEM Business Consolidation and Sourcing (BCS) utilized the enterprise-controlling architecture, but added a real-time extractor to SAP BW. The consolidation application still resides in mySAP ERP, but updates (such as intercompany eliminations or consolidation of investments) can be posted to SAP BW in real time to achieve a faster month-end closing of the financial books via the same interface business planning used to write to InfoCubes. Alternatively, real-time reporting options were then added, such as a VirtualProvider that read the consolidation postings in mySAP ERP that have not yet been loaded to SAP BW. Then closed-loop integration was added, allowing retraction back from SAP BW to consolidation using its flexible upload technology, so that different versions of plan data could be consolidated. Figure 10-19 illustrates and example of an integrated information logistics model for the historic SEM architecture.

Now that the consolidation engine sits on top of SAP BW, real-time postings from mySAP ERP or VirtualProviders or retractions are no longer necessary, since all data manipulations can be performed directly in SAP BW. The consolidation engine supports management consolidation activities (such as standardizing entries, reclassification, and intercompany elimination) and specialized currency translation functions for consolidation reporting as well as full consolidation functionality (both legal and management) and functionalities such as value-based management adjusting entries. Figure 10-20 shows an example information logistics model for the current architecture (where the business consolidation engine can sit entirely on SAP BW but is delivered as part of mySAP ERP).

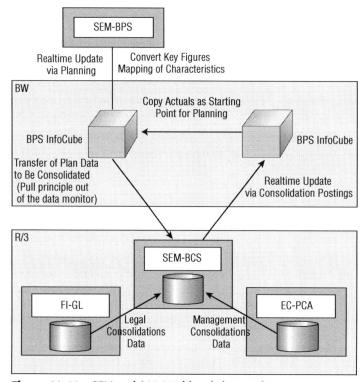

Figure 10-19   SEM and SAP BW historic integration

Based on copyrighted material from SAP AG

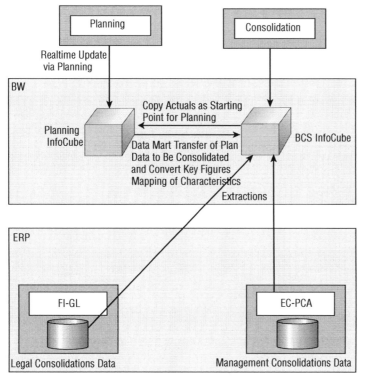

Figure 10-20   Financial capabilities current integration

Based on copyrighted material from SAP AG

Information Model

The consolidation application has a number of important master data components that are vital to its consolidation logic. As opposed to other typical consolidation systems, SAP performs eliminations on pairs of trading partners within a consolidation group, versus eliminating specific accounts. A *trading partner* represents the entity in a consolidation group to which a transaction is made (and then subsequently needs to be eliminated). Typically, the trading partner can be derived from the general-ledger account that the transaction posted to or from the customer or vendor on that transaction. These transformations are important to have already reflected in the records consolidations uses to make its eliminations.

Trading partners are essentially *consolidation units*. In legal consolidation, consolidation units are legal entities (companies) or lines of business (business areas). In management consolidation, consolidation units could be divisions, profit centers, or any other responsibility unit. Companies and profit centers (or a combination of both) must be mapped into consolidation units for the consolidation. Consolidation units can represent parents or subsidiaries. The collection of parent and subsidiary consolidation units that need to be consolidated is termed a *consolidation group*. Consolidation groups can belong in other consolidation groups, effectively forming hierarchies that can also often reflect complicated ownership structures and cross-holdings.

Another element that must be mapped into consolidations is the *financial statement item*. Financial statement items are what make up the consolidated profit-and-loss and balance sheet statements. They represent consolidated account structures. Potentially, each consolidation unit could have its own separate chart of accounts (especially when dealing with consolidation of entities in different countries). These different charts must be standardized. As a result, each account must be mapped to a financial statement item that represents the conformed and consolidated account structures of all the subsidiaries into the parent unit's books.

Management and legal consolidation are typically kept separate via different *dimensions* representing different data feeds. Different *versions* of data can also be kept for different planning and simulation scenarios in consolidation such as what-if reorganization analysis (like mergers, acquisitions, or divestitures). Reorganizations in consolidation typically present interesting restatement reporting scenarios where all data has to be realigned and reported as if a new organizational structure or hierarchy had always been in effect. Sometimes such restatements are simple to simulate via reporting tricks, but other times they can be much more complicated, forcing changes in the data set. Restatements in consolidation, much like realignments in SAP BW, have always been one of the more difficult areas to information model for reporting.

Adding to data complexities in consolidation is the *posting level* concept. The posting levels allow for the creation of a consolidation worksheet to view the different levels of consolidation postings that reconcile the consolidation statements with the simple summation of all the subsidiaries' statements into the parent's financial books. The consolidation worksheet gives the user an overview of the consolidation process. For example, a four-posting-levels worksheet could show the user what the trial balance of all the reported data submitted by the subsidiary plus the parent unit trial balance for a given consolidation group. Posting levels for all standardizing entries (such as GAAP adjustments), interunit eliminations (such as receivables and payables), and consolidation of investments (that is, investment and equity eliminations) could be displayed in separate columns. The final result of adding all these posting levels together then yields the consolidated trial balance.

The posting level concept is very useful detail information for reporting, but it introduces data complexities in the consolidation information model. Each posting level has a different relationship to consolidation units, trading partner units, and consolidation groups.

The first basic posting level represents data as it comes into consolidation (as reported by subsidiaries). No consolidation entries have been made at this point. This data is consolidation-unit dependent.

Any consolidation unit can belong to many consolidation groups. As a result, this data has to be repeated for every consolidation group it exists in. The same goes for consolidation-unit-dependent standardizing entries.

In contrast, the posting levels representing interunit eliminations are con-solidation-unit and trading-partner dependent. These data entries must repeat themselves in all consolidation groups that contain the consolidation unit pairs. Finally, consolidation-of-investment postings are consolidation-group dependent. Since these data entries only pertain to one consolidation group, the data does not need to be repeated. Figure 10-21 illustrates the posting level impact on data redundancy.

The posting level's impact on data redundancy depends on how the consol-idation group hierarchy is modeled. In this example, consolidation units are repeated in multiple consolidation groups. This might happen for any number of business scenarios, such as a consolidation unit belonging to more than one parent, multiple alternate hierarchies for management and legal consolidation, or modeling consolidation hierarchies as concentric consolidation groups.

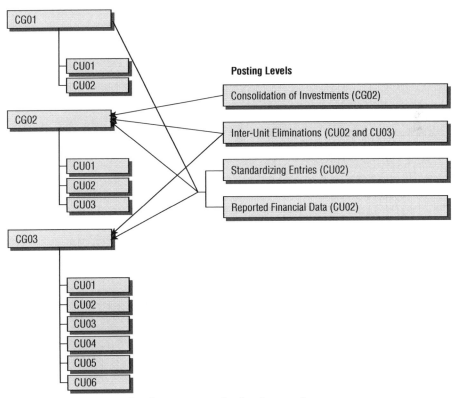

Figure 10-21   Data redundancy per posting level example

Another important consolidation reporting topic is currency translations. Currency translations in consolidation are different than in SAP BW. The purpose of currency translation in consolidation is to report all subsidiary balance sheet and profit-and-loss activities in the parent currency so that they can be added into the parent's accounting books. Currency translations in consolidation typically must translate records differently based on the type of the financial statement item. Typically, the currency translation must be performed as follows (or some variant):

- If the financial statement item is a balance sheet account, its balances must be translated using a month-end spot rate.

- If the account is a profit-and-loss item, translation must be at an average rate.

- If the account is an investment or equity item, the translation must be at a historical rate.

More details on the reporting requirements for currency translations for consolidation can be found in Financial Accounting Standards Board Statement No. 52 and 95 (for cash flow reporting). The differences in the balance sheet and profit and loss must be then plugged to a currency translation adjustment item to keep debits equaling credits. SAP BW currency translations are not designed for this type scenario. The SAP BW is only meant to translate values straight from one currency into another.

Summary

Analytic applications provide separation of function, provide for process support, and utilize time-orientated, integrated data. SAP BW is at the center of the BI capabilities of NetWeaver when it comes to building analytic applications. SAP BW is delivered with a set of building blocks called Business Content that accelerates the speed to value when implementing analytic applications. The building blocks may be used by the NetWeaver Composite Application Framework to model and deploy business analytics.

Three examples of analytic applications built on the SAP BW platform were highlighted in this chapter:

- **Customer relationship analytics (CRA)** — CRA consists of customer behavior analysis, customer lifetime value (CLTV) analysis, and recency, frequency, monetary (RFM) analysis. Customer behavior analysis consists of the data mining techniques decision trees, scoring, clustering, and association analysis. RFM analysis is primarily used for campaign optimization.

■ **Supply-chain analytics (SCA)** — SCA is mainly influenced by the SCOR model. Analytics can be performed within SAP APO via the supply chain cockpit, which can be integrated with SAP BW or can be performed by a separate SAP BW environment using Business Content analysis. Some applications (such as demand planning) interact with SAP BW to get sales history and to return the demand plan for historical analysis.

■ **Financial analytics** — What was formerly known as SEM is now part of the financial capabilities of mySAP ERP. Corporate performance management largely centers on the balanced scorecard framework. Enterprise planning is part of SAP BW with which planning applications may be built. Capital market interpreter was explained as an example of a prepackaged planning application. The consolidation application history and migration path to the SAP BW platform was then summarized, as well as design considerations for information modeling.

Next, we turn attention toward administering the system and options for improving performance. Chapter 11 focuses on administration.

Notes

1. Morris, Henry. 1997. "Analytical Applications and Market Forecast: Changing Structure of Information Access Markets." IDC # 14064 Vol. 1 (August). IDC Research. www.idc.com.

2. "Supply-Chain Operations Reference-model: Overview of SCORE Version 5.0," page 2. SCOR, Supply-Chain Council, Inc. www.supply-chain.org.

3. Norton, D. P., R. S. Kaplan. 2000. *The Strategy Focused Organization: How Balanced Scorecard Companies Thrive in the New Business Environment.* Harvard Business School Press.

4. Harvard Business Review. 1998. *Harvard Business Review on Measuring Corporate Performance.* Harvard Business School Press.

Administration

SAP BW administration tasks can be divided into two conceptual categories: application-oriented tasks and system-oriented tasks. While *application-oriented administration* tasks focus on EDW and BI application processes, *system-oriented tasks* are more oriented toward underlying infrastructure operations that are typically found in any SAP system.

The first section of this chapter is focused on application-centric batch processing and monitoring capabilities (namely, process chains and monitors). This section is primarily focused on configuring, monitoring, and troubleshooting tasks. Performance tuning is a large enough topic to be covered on its own in Chapter 12, "Performance Planning and Management."

The second section centers on system-related tasks (such as analysis authorizations, information lifecycle management, transports, metadata management and upgrades).

Most all of this work can be performed via the Data Warehousing (DW) Workbench as back-end activities. The DW Workbench is not only used for modeling but is also used for controlling, monitoring, fixing, and tuning application processes, as well as for administering infrastructural activities. From a design perspective, it is used to maintain the modeling layers for data acquisition, transformation, information storage, and access, as well as information distribution. Each modeling layer has corresponding application administration and monitoring tasks and tools, such as the extraction monitor for data acquisition, the data transfer monitor for transformations, and the query monitor for information access and distribution.

The application processes themselves are continually being traced by BI performance statistics and the CCMS Alert Monitor. The Batch Monitor controls how application processes behave in the background.

Not all administration-related activities are done on the back-end, however. Such activities as information distribution via BEx Broadcaster or monitoring via the BI Administration Cockpit are performed in the front-end. Information broadcasting empowers end users to schedule their own jobs and the BI Administrator Cockpit makes BI statistics and CCMS alerts more transparent and centralized through a Web-enabled cockpit. Instead of the DW Workbench, these capabilities are largely BEx- and Portal-driven. The BI Administrator Cockpit is an example of SAP NetWeaver leveraging its own infrastructure (Portal and BEx) and Business Content to deliver a new capability.

System-oriented tasks are typically the same in any SAP system, but there are SAP BW-specific twists and capabilities that warrant special consideration and coverage. For example, SAP BW provides additional functionality for authorizations, transports, and metadata management. In this new release, the authorization concept has been redesigned for planning, reporting, and analysis (replacing standard authorizations with analysis authorizations). This chapter explains SAP BW security from a design perspective, detailing the decisions to make when building authorizations (such as making them user-based versus role-based, or object-centric versus data-centric). The discussion then explains the SAP BW transport and its additional transport options, as well as special considerations that come with the transport and management of metadata. In addition, the coordination of transports on SAP source systems is considered. Finally, upgrade considerations for a multilayered application environment are highlighted.

All of the aforementioned tools, tasks, or capabilities are encapsulated as architectural components as shown in Figure 11-1.

Application-Oriented Administration

The application-administration tasks can be viewed as processes with lifecycle-related delineations of control, monitor, fix, and optimize. This chapter delves into the first three activities, while the last task (optimize) will be touched on from an administration perspective (the performance aspects is grist for Chapter 12).

Any activity in an IT system (SAP or non-SAP) that has a clear beginning and a clear end can be referred to as a *process*. Usually, processes cannot be viewed in isolation; complex interdependent networks of processes need to be configured, scheduled, and monitored to accomplish a certain system task. While scheduling has always been a core part of the SAP NetWeaver Application Server, these scheduling capabilities were generic and were not designed to suit application-specific needs.

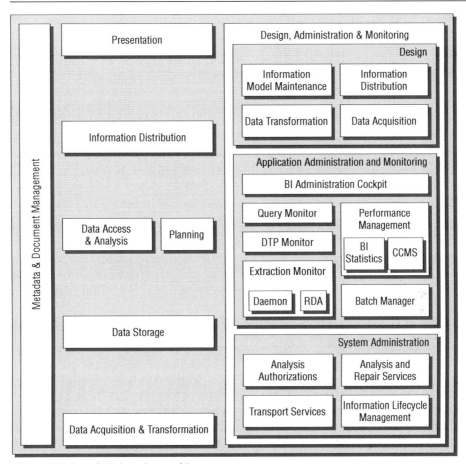

Figure 11-1 Administration architecture

There are two application-specific needs in question: back-end and front-end. *Back-end scheduling* is handled via process chains, and *front-end scheduling* such as information distribution is handled via BEx Broadcaster.

Process chains are designed to handle the complex dependencies in data staging and loading. In addition, process chains schedule and monitor a variety of other data management and application processes such as index maintenance, data compressions, data realignments, data exports, custom programs, workflows, operating system commands, and so on.

On the other hand, BEx Broadcaster handles batch reporting activities such as alerting, mass-distributing reports, batch printing, filling query cache or pre-calculating Web templates (thereby retiring the older reporting agent functionality and its use within process chains). Batching complex analysis processes (such as data mining) is covered by the Analysis Process Designer (part of the DW Workbench). Both BEx Broadcaster and the Analysis Process Designer are explained in more detail under "Information Distribution" and "Analytic Services" in Chapter 7, respectively.

The monitoring, troubleshooting, and performance tuning of queries is still handled by the BEx Monitor within the DW Workbench, however.

Process Chains

Process chains were designed to be a centralized tool to support complex networks of processes and their dependencies. The advent of the process chain technology and related extensions to the SAP BW Meta Data Repository enabled administrators to use a scheduling tool that was more application-aware of realistic day-to-day scenarios and complexities but still leveraged the robustness of the time-tested functions of the SAP NetWeaver AS. In addition, process chains are extensible with hooks for custom developments and open interfaces. Third-party job-scheduling tools can interface with process chains and connect them to even more complex global scheduling needs across multiple heterogeneous systems.

The basic concept behind the process chain implementation is to have an additional abstraction layer on top of the basic batch scheduling functions with more sophisticated application logic. Technically speaking, process chains automatically generate *events* and automatically schedule subsequent processes waiting for those generated events (thereby gluing the application processes together). The process chain technology is completely modularized and built upon an object-oriented programming model where each process is an object, described by the following attributes:

- **Process category** — All the processes are broadly grouped by process categories such as general services, data load and subsequent processing, data target administration, and miscellaneous others.

- **Process type** — A process type is a specific type of application or system process such as a data transfer process, an InfoPackage, a BI accelerator index rollup, or a master data change run.

- **Variant** — Each process has its own variant (a parameterization that controls the process, such as limiting a change run to a particular characteristic or limiting a dropped index to a particular InfoCube). A variant can sometimes directly equate to a metadata object such as an InfoPackage for extractions, or a DTP for data loads. While many variants may be available for a specific process, only one gets assigned to any particular process within a process chain.

- **Instance** — The instance describes a specific running of a process. It consists of all messages and information relevant to the process at runtime, which are read and passed on to other processes.

While the currently available process types cover most applications in SAP BW the list of process types is configurable and custom new ones can be added via the process chain administration transaction. Process types control process instance behaviors through either ABAP or configuration. Custom process types can be controlled via custom object classes that use predelivered process chain interfaces (prefixed with 'IF_RSPC_') that influences functions such as variant maintenance or scheduling. Configuration of the process type controls behaviors such as the following (see Figure 11-2):

- **Only in SAP BW clients** — A flag determining whether a process is client dependent or independent (relevant for bolt-on applications that utilize the client concept such as SAP SCM).

- **Possible Events** — A list of possible events for a process such as successful, failed, or always (ignoring the failed or successful state). A newly added option of outcome of complex status allows for more dynamic execution paths where subsequent processes can be based on many different outcomes (up to 99). `Workflow` and `Decision` are both examples of process types that have complex status outcomes.

- **Repeatable** — A flag enabling processes to restart after error under a new process instance. InfoCube compression is an example of a repeatable process.

- **Repairable** — A flag enabling processes to resume under the same process instance even after errors. Data transfer process is an example of a process that has the capability of repairing data requests after errors midstream (depending on how the DTP was parameterized).

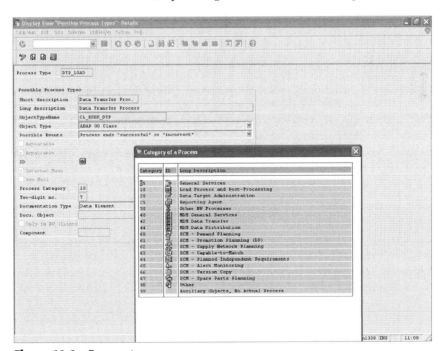

Figure 11-2   Process types

Process types are also assigned to process categories (which include but are not limited to):

- **General services** — Includes process types for a start process; for logical AND, OR, XOR and complex decision operations; ABAP programs; system commands; workflow; as well as local and remote process chains, which are referred to as meta chains, since SAP allows you to implement chains of process chains.

- **Load processes and subsequent processing** — Includes application processes related to loading data, such as execute InfoPackages, execute DTPs, read PSA and update data target, save hierarchy, update DataStore Object for further update, data export to external system, delete overlapping requests, and trigger event data change for Broadcaster.

- **Data target administration** — Includes data maintenance processes such as Delete/Generate indexes, Construct database statistics, Fill aggregates, Rollup aggregates, Compress InfoCube, Activate DataStore Object data, and Delete data target contents.

- **Other SAP BW processes** — Includes general SAP BW processes, such as Attribute change run, Adjustment of time-dependent aggregates, Deletion of requests from the PSA, and Reorganization of attributes and texts for master data.

When a specific process is executed, first its predecessors and their corresponding variants are determined. Then the process object is instantiated, asking for additional information from the predecessor process if required before actually executing the process. After finishing the process, it returns its status and instance to the process chain.

This approach allows for flexibility in defining subsequent processing, which may be triggered, based on a variety of outcomes for a process: successful, failed, always, or complex status. In addition, process chains themselves can be assigned an attribute so that if they are used as a subchain, they don't fail an overall process chain if errors occur (useful in scenarios where the subchain is not important enough to stop the overall process chain).

In summary, the process chain approach is more results driven and object oriented, and it makes use of complex criteria for starting each subsequent process. In addition to event handling (which is an SAP NetWeaver AS service) application-specific, complex Boolean logic is available. From a usability point of view, process chains provide a higher degree of automation, centralized maintenance, and control, and much improved visualization where complex relationships and hierarchies of dependencies are maintained and depicted graphically.

The background scheduling behavior of process chains can also be controlled and checked. There are optimization features such as specifying the background user determination logic (for load balancing and traceability) and automatic batch process consumption checks (to prevent process chain paral-lelization from grabbing too many background work processes).

Although process chains are designed to be run in the background, they can now be scheduled synchronously or as a simulation (that is, as an online dia-logue process instead of batch). This is to enable debugging and troubleshoot-ing. Be aware that only one dialogue process is consumed, so any parallelization will have to be serialized and queued until the dialogue work process is freed. As a result, only small data sets and simple process chains should be run in this mode.

The following three different maintenance views are available in the process chain maintenance transaction:

- **Planning view** — How process chains are modeled.

- **Check view** — How process chains are validated for the integrity of their design.

- **Log view** — How the process chains are monitored. Monitoring process chains is now also integrated into the Computing Center Management System (CCMS).

In the planning view, there is also an expert mode that turns off application checks for those who know what they are doing. Figure 11-3 shows the planning view of the process chain maintenance transaction for a simple process chain.

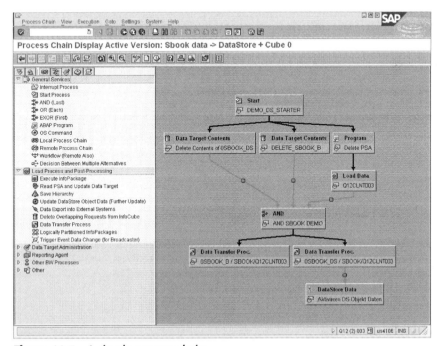

Figure 11-3   A simple process chain
Copyright © SAP AG

The need for process chains stems from the many dependencies of any sophisticated information model run in a productive data warehouse system. Defining a process chain requires planning and preparation, taking application logic, operational processes, availability of system resources, performance, and technical dependencies into account. (Many times, these various factors work against each other and must be balanced.)

Types of Dependencies

Table 11-1 lists several different types of conceptual dependencies that can drive the design of the process chain execution paths. The system itself is actually aware of some of the generic application dependencies and provides corresponding consistency checks to ensure that process chains are defined appropriately. Otherwise, most of the dependencies listed are purely conceptual dependencies to consider in process chain blueprinting exercises.

NOTE All the process dependencies that the system enforces and checks against are stored in table RSPCTYPESDEP, which can be used as a reference when you are planning a process chain design.

Table 11-1 Types of Conceptual Dependencies

DEPENDENCY	DESCRIPTION
Application process dependencies	Certain processes always need to be (or should be) executed in a specific sequence. Examples of these types of dependencies are attribute change runs after a master data load, or dropping and creating indexes before and after transaction data loading. The process chain maintenance transaction provides checks to ensure that all required processes are included and are defined in the correct order. When you are defining a simple process chain such as the one shown in Figure 11-3 (where a data load is dragged and dropped into the planning view), the system automatically inserts a process of process type delete_index as a predecessor and one of type create_index as an antecessor. Note that these automatically inserted processes are removable and configurable (acting only as defaults). Additional wait times can be added to honor timing or performance dependencies.

Continued

Table 11-1 Types of Conceptual Dependencies *(continued)*

DEPENDENCY	DESCRIPTION
Alert dependencies	If an individual needs notification on the completion status of a certain process within a process chain, you can configure an alert message via the central alert framework. The recent integration with the SAP NetWeaver AS central alert framework enables new capabilities beyond email notification (such as Short Message Service, that is SMS, and pager text messaging, faxing, and subscription features) while enabling centralized maintenance of all system alerts. Custom alert categories can be created and mapped to process chains. Otherwise, predelivered defaults are used.
Referential integrity	Business Content for Asset Accounting has prebuilt checks that ensure asset master data is loaded before transaction data (0ASSET and 0ASSET_AFAB). HR also has similar dependencies for employee master data loads where predecessor master data loads (four levels) had to be loaded before employee masters could be loaded. This was because the employee master had navigational attributes referring to other characteristics, which, in turn, had other navigational attributes, and so forth. If referential integrity checks for master data are activated, any compound characteristics or navigational attribute has to be preloaded. If referential integrity checks for transactional InfoSources are activated, all master data must be preloaded. Another option for referential integrity checking for individual InfoObjects of an InfoSource can be configured in the InfoSource. Process chains must be defined according to the dependencies imposed by referential integrity checks.
Transformation dependencies	These dependencies arise from transformation logic such as data lookups in the update rules. If an attribute is to be derived from an attribute of a characteristic, then that characteristic must be loaded. Otherwise, an old or blank value will be derived. This is different from referential integrity, which merely checks if the value already exists. Another example (for key-figure derivations) is having the most recent exchange rates loaded before executing currency translation in the update rules. Typically, these transformation dependencies need to be taken into account to ensure data quality and correctness of custom business logic. Other examples might include proper unit conversions on the most recent conversion factors or derivations that read a preloaded hierarchy to determine an attribute, or an update rule that reads a custom table that must be loaded with the most recent and correct values before derivation.

Continued

Table 11-1 Types of Conceptual Dependencies *(continued)*

DEPENDENCY	DESCRIPTION
Business cycle dependencies	There are time-dependent scenarios in data loading that go beyond the generic job scheduling capabilities of triggering a load based on a calendar date and time. For example, BI integrated planning and budgeting applications typically are planning-cycle driven with entirely separate processes depending on the stage or version of the cycle (such as a refresh of actual data just before a final submission of the plan or budget or a top-down push to a detailed operating plan). The actual calendar date of when such loads occur may vary, and there could be complex dependencies (predecessor preconditions and antecessor branching processes) that render the generic job scheduling capabilities limited.
Performance-enhancing sequences	Certain sequences may be better for performance, such as scheduling jobs after other jobs to avoid too many work processes contending with each other, causing bottlenecks or, worse, deadlocks. For example, if you have multiple transaction data loads for the same InfoCube, it may make sense to drop the indexes once, do all the loading, and then rebuild the indexes once at the end, rather than dropping and re-creating for each data load. Or, some parallelization scenarios might be built to improve performance (for example, loading PSA and DataStore Objects at the same time or loading master data and transaction data simultaneously). Or perhaps parallelization is achieved by breaking up a data load job into various data selections (for example, by company code for a large delta initialization). Finally, parallelization can be achieved by separating process-chain work processes onto separate servers (identified as part of scheduling).
Quality checks	There may be a need to insert manual intervention steps into the automated flow of process chains for quality checking. For example, before automatic loading of PSA to an InfoCube, administrators might want to execute data-consistency checks on the PSA level to ensure that the data loaded into the InfoCube is correct before changing the read pointer and making the data available for reporting.

Note that these process dependencies can span across multiple SAP and non-SAP systems. Within the SAP sphere, remote process chains can integrate processes in other SAP systems into the current process chain. In addition, third-party external systems can be called from within a process chain (in this case, it is a matter of designing a custom process type by developing a class with the proper interface or using an appropriate third-party job scheduling tool).

It is good practice in process-oriented administration to document all processes, dependencies, and error-handling procedures in an operations guide. While process chains support the administrative processes by visualizing complex dependencies, they are not a replacement for documentation.

Process Chain Service Processes

Process chains provide special process types used for generically modeling the initiation of a process chain, and Boolean logic operators for collecting the results of multiple processes in a process chain. The process chain service processes are as follows:

- **Start process** — Every process chain must have a start process that acts as the initial trigger to start the whole chain. Start processes never have predecessors (with the exception of other process chains within a meta chain or via an API), and only one exists per process chain. The variant for the start process simply contains scheduling parameters, such as the time a process chain must be executed, or a specific event that causes the process chain to execute.

- **Collection processes** — Collection processes collect the results of several parallel processes and merge those into one single result by applying simple Boolean operators:

  - AND (Last) — The work process starts when all events in the predecessor process have finished.

  - OR (Each) — The work process starts each time an event in a predecessor process finishes.

  - XOR (First) — The work process starts when the first event from one of the predecessor processes finished.

- **Decision** — The work process is based on conditional logic built in a formula builder that has special variables and functions for use in formulas. There are up to 99 potential outcomes on which subsequent processes can be scheduled.

Dynamic Execution Paths

The processes chain type for workflow and decision leverage the new functionality for process outcomes of complex status (with the capability of defining up to 99 possible outcomes without the need for code). As a result, process chain logic can become a lot more flexible and dynamic based on conditional logic built as formulas in the formula builder. The formula builder is the same technically as the one used in transformation rules. All the same functions and capabilities are available, including Boolean logic constructs, date conversion functions, string manipulation functions, mathematical functions and system variables (that is, system, date, time, and user). However, these are enhanced with process chain functions. Specifically, process chain parameter values (as well as runtime values for the current and predecessor processes) can be accessed via a process chain function in a formula.

This formula is defined as part of a process variant and is used as a condition as part of IF-THEN-ELSE logic dictating outcomes. Each outcome is given an event number (with the option of defining one error event) on which subsequent process can be scheduled. In workflow processes, this event number can be manually determined without the need for formula conditions.

This functionality is particularly useful for modeling complex business cycle and process chain dependencies.

Data Management Processes

Naturally, data management processes are the most common and most intensive processes in a data warehouse environment. Different types of data management processes are available in SAP BW. Each requires a different set of parameters. For example, index maintenance processes require the name of an InfoCube; DataStore Object activation processes require the name of a DataStore Object. The required parameters are stored in so-called *variants* (readers familiar with SAP systems will already know the concept of variants used to store different sets of parameters for ABAP reports).

The configuration of variants in the SAP BI context either depends on specifying metadata objects, variants for other process types, or the actual configuration of the metadata object, as well as process-type-specific settings. Table 11-2 provides an overview of the data management processes in SAP BW and their parameters.

Table 11-2 Variants for Data Management Processes

DATA MANAGEMENT PROCESS	PARAMETERS
Data loading	InfoPackage
Data export	InfoSpoke
Initial fill of new aggregates	Aggregate
	InfoCube

Continued

Table 11-2   Variants for Data Management Processes *(continued)*

DATA MANAGEMENT PROCESS	PARAMETERS
Attribute change run	Hierarchy
	InfoObject
	Variant of an ABAP report
Compressing the InfoCube	InfoCube
Constructing database statistics	InfoCube
Deleting data target contents	InfoCube
	DataStore Object
Deleting index	InfoCube
Saving hierarchy	(None)
Generating index	InfoCube
Activating DataStore Object data	DataStore Object
Further processing of DataStore Object data	DataStore Object
Further processing of DataStore Object data	DataStore Object
Deleting requests from PSA	PSA table
	Data request
PSA update/reconstruction	Data request
Deleting overlapping requests	(None)
Rollup of filled aggregates	InfoCube
Adjusting time-dependent aggregates	(None)

The most complex set of parameters is required for the extraction and loading of data and is contained in metadata objects of themselves: the InfoPackage and DTP, respectively. The different configuration options available for both InfoPackages and DTP are described in the following sections, "Extraction Process" and "Data Load Process," respectively. A description of the variants of the remaining process types follows under "Subsequent Processes" at the end of this section. Also, note that some processes do not require variants (such as adjusting time-dependent aggregates).

Extraction Process

As explained earlier, the introduction of DTPs has made some of the functionality of InfoPackages obsolete. Specifically, InfoPackages have been repositioned for extraction purposes only. InfoPackage functions are more limited now; they only control and schedule the portion of the data flow that moves data from external source systems into the PSA of the SAP BW system. All subsequent data-flow processing in the SAP BW environment is handled by the DTP. The only exception to this is the use of InfoPackages for scheduling data mart interface loads (that is, loading data targets back into themselves). As a result, settings for controlling how data targets are updated and processed is no longer parameterized in the InfoPackage but rather in the DTP. Additionally, error-handling settings have shifted from the InfoPackage to the DTP.

The settings available to control an InfoPackage are dependent on the type of DataSource. Special InfoPackages are needed to handle the new DataSources for real-time data acquisition and Web services. In addition, some control settings are set via the DataSource, as in the case for extraction settings.

The use of InfoPackages and DTP in a process chain is the variant itself. InfoPackages can be maintained either as a process chain variant, or outside the process chain maintenance transaction in the DW Workbench.

When creating an InfoPackage for transaction data, there are new flags for transaction data for real-time data acquisition (specifically for push and pull scenarios). For push scenarios, the system will automatically flag the InfoPackage as a push InfoPackage and as real-time. This is for information purposes and is derived from the Web service DataSource definition. For pull scenarios, the real-time flag must be set. An existing transactional data source can be configured to supply real-time updates by simply flagging the real-time indicator upon creating an InfoPackage for that DataSource.

When creating an InfoPackage for master data, you must choose whether the InfoPackage is for scheduling the text, attributes, or hierarchy extractions. A separate InfoPackage is needed for each DataSource type of master data (where applicable).

Figure 11-4 shows a typical InfoPackage. Parameterization options for InfoPackages are listed and are detailed in the following sections:

- Data selection
- Extraction options
- Processing options
- Update parameters
- Third-party selections (only for Staging BAPI DataSources)
- Scheduling options

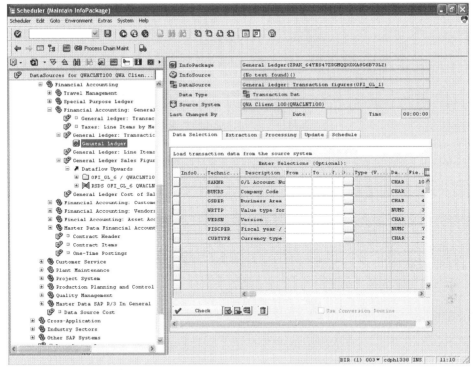

Figure 11-4   InfoPackage
Copyright © SAP AG

Data Selection

The availability of fields for selection is controlled by the DataSource definition in the source system or in the SAP BW system for manually maintained
source system types (for example, for file source systems).

> **NOTE** If the InfoPackage is for a data mart export DataSource for an archived
> data target, a button to the left of the conversion exit switch appears that
> allows you to alternatively select an archive file to load from. More on archiving
> can be found later in this chapter in the section titled "Information Lifecycle
> Management."

For dynamic or more complicated selections (especially for the time dimension), reporting variable selection criteria of the types listed in Table 11-3 can
be specified.

Table 11-3   Types of Dynamic Selection Criteria

TYPE	DATA TYPE	SELECTION	DESCRIPTION
0	DATS	Yesterday	Midnight to midnight
1	DATS	Last week	Monday through Sunday
2	DATS	Last month	First to last day of previous month
3	DATS	Last quarter	First to last day of previous quarter
4	DATS	Last year	First to last day of previous year
5	NUMC	User defined	Recurring time series
6	ANY	ABAP routine	Custom-defined ABAP routine
7	ANY	BEx variable	SAP- or custom-defined OLAP variable

The last three variable values require additional configuration. Type 5 selection criteria are used to specify a user-defined period of time for the fiscal year period characteristic. In this scenario, bimonthly plan data is loaded into profit center accounting. Other parameters are detailed in Table 11-4.

Table 11-4   Maintenance of Variable Selections

PARAMETER	VALUE
Fiscal year/period from	2007001
Fiscal year/period to	2007002
Next period from value	2007003
Period Indicator	1
Number of periods until repetition	12

Using this configuration, the first time the InfoPackage is executed, the first two periods in the fiscal year are loaded. The next time the InfoPackage is scheduled, the next two periods are loaded (that is, 2007003 to 2007004). After 12 periods have repeated themselves, the period resets itself back to the first period. If the period indicator was set to zero, the cycle would restart itself in the same year. The period indicator of 1 was specially designed for rolling the year over into the next year so the new start would be 2008001. The period indicator 0 was designed for InfoObject time characteristics (like 0FISCPER3) that do not have a year in them.

For type 6 (ABAP routine) the Detail pushbutton generates an ABAP routine framework. The code that follows is an example where the current fiscal year and period is derived via the system date (assuming a fiscal year variant of K4):

```
*$*$ begin of routine - insert your code only below this line     *-*
 data: l_idx like sy-tabix.

* Find entry for fiscal period in selection criteria table
 read table l_t_range with key
   fieldname = 'FISCPER'.
 l_idx = sy-tabix.

* Initialize fiscal period selection criteria
 l_t_range-sign = 'I'.
 l_t_range-option = 'EQ'.

* Determine fiscal period for current date
 CALL FUNCTION 'DATE_TO_PERIOD_CONVERT'
  EXPORTING
    I_DATE = sy-datum
    I_PERIV = 'K4'
  IMPORTING
    E_BUPER = l_t_range-low+4(3)
    E_GJAHR = l_t_range-low(4).

* Update selection criteria table
 modify l_t_range index l_idx.
 p_subrc = 0.
*$*$ end of routine - insert your code only before this line    *-*
```

The same effect could be accomplished without code by using an OLAP or BEx variable value. Table 11-5 illustrates the same selections described previously implemented with type 7 selection criteria using the BEx variable 0FPER.

Table 11-5 Use BEx Variable

PARAMETER	VALUE
BEx Variable of the OLAP	0FPER
Fiscal year variant	K4

The use of conversion exits for selections may be turned on or off. Conversion exits may be required to ensure correct formatting of the selection values passed to the source system. The extraction process first tries to apply the conversion exit in the source system, and, if unavailable, it calls the conversion exit in SAP BW.

The data selection for hierarchies works a little different from flat data selections. Instead of data selection options, a list of all hierarchies available in the source system are be retrieved from the source system via RFC. A button push refreshes this list. A limitation of loading hierarchies is that only one can be parameterized at a time (that is, an InfoPackage cannot simultaneously load multiple hierarchies at once). Additional parameterizations allow specifying additional options (such as automatically renaming the hierarchy, or merging subtrees or inserting subtrees). The ability to update subtrees rather than loading the complete hierarchy tree is a performance-enhancing feature, allowing targeted refreshes.

Extraction Options

This is a new parameter set for InfoPackages. As mentioned earlier, the extraction settings in the InfoPackage are primarily derived via the DataSource definition. For example external files, extraction settings used to be in the InfoPackage (for example, filename and path), but are now part of the Data-Source definition. The options differ depending on the DataSource. Some of the parameters can be overtyped, depending on the DataSource. For example, for real-time data acquisition push scenarios, Web service profiles can be adjusted in the InfoPackage to be either basic authorization for SOAP or secure SOAP. Basic authorization for SOAP requires user and password login for caller authentication, while secure SOAP uses client certificates and transfers encrypted data (via the SSL protocol).

Processing Options

Processing options allow you to specify update processing options and whether or not additional consistency checks are performed in the transfer rules. If the flag for additional consistency checks is turned on, data will be verified for valid date and time values, permissible special characters, capitalized letters, and conversion routine compliance.

For the new DataSource concept, the only data target processing option is loading into the PSA. The rest of the data target load options are obsolete and are only useful for the older DataSource concept.

Transaction data basically provides the same processing options. However, for master data (in this case, cost center master data) there are additional options. The system is able to identify DataSources that potentially return duplicate records by identifying the primary key of the underlying DataSource and matching it up with the key of the transfer structure. If the DataSource potentially returns duplicates, the DataSource `Transfers Double Data Records` flag is set. This flag allows you to treat duplicate records as an error or ignore them by checking the `Ignore Double Data Records` indicator.

For real-time data-acquisition InfoPackages, there are additional options, such as setting the threshold for closing a request (either by time or by number of records), the threshold for failed attempts before a daemon issues an error, specifying the daemon to do the processing, and adjusting the periodicity of the daemon (also set in the monitor for real-time data acquisition).

Update Parameters

Update parameters are used to control the update mode (full update, delta initialization, and delta update), referential integrity handling, and the separation of delta transfers. Delta initialization and delta update options are only available for delta-enabled DataSources. For real-time data acquisitions, only the delta update option is available. Note that delta extraction must be initialized by either a delta initialization request, or an initialization request (`Initialize without data transfer` flag). Once initialized, deltas can be loaded as required.

For time-dependent data, additional options are available for selecting date ranges for the extraction process. Similar to data selection options, the options for using ABAP routines or BEx variables are available here. These options work exactly the same as they do for data selection options.

Error handling is no longer the domain of InfoPackages, but is now handled by DTPs. If data errors occur within an extraction, that data must be reextracted after the errors are corrected in the source system.

Third-Party Options

Third-party selections are used for Staging BAPI source systems. The parameters here heavily depend on the third-party tool or custom program using the Staging BAPI. IBM (formerly Ascential) DataStage, for example, requires the name of a DataStage job to be entered here.

Scheduling Options

InfoPackages can be run independently of process chains, as they include scheduling options and parameters that allow executing extraction loads immediately or as a batch schedule. For scheduling in batch mode, the same scheduling options as found in the standard SAP batch scheduling dialog are available, such as periodical execution of data load jobs, execution at a specific date and time, execution after a specific event, or execution after completion of a specific program. A Gantt diagram is available for display in the InfoPackage to provide a simple graphical representation of scheduled processes.

Note that the process starting the extraction load normally only issues a data load request to the source systems (for example, by sending a request IDoc to an SAP R/3 system) and terminates, thereby making the internal scheduler (as well as external job-scheduling tools) believe that the process has terminated successfully, when, in fact, it has just started the extraction process. Setting the `Request Batch Process Runs until All Data Has Been Updated in BW` flag can be used to keep the process active until all data has been uploaded completely.

For real-time data acquisitions, scheduling either activates or deactivates the daemon.

Data Load Process

All movement of data from a source to target within the SAP BI environment is controlled via DTPs. The source and targets can either be persistent (for example, PSA to InfoCube) or virtual (for example, direct access DataSource to a VirtualProvider).

There are three types of DTPs: Standard, Real-Time Data Acquisition, and Direct Access. Additionally, there is a special Error DTP that can be created for loading errors from a standard DTP error stack. DTPs have the flexibility of loading directly from PSA into data targets without the need of InfoSources (which are now optional).

Data transfer rules are defined for a transformation and, as a result, the transformation itself must be created before a DTP is configured. The source and target objects for a DTP are derived from the transformation itself, and then further parameterized for data flow control. An important flexible design feature is that multiple DTPs can be created for any given transformation; the significance is explained in the following section, "Extraction Options."

There are three sets of parameters for a DTP: the extraction options for the source, the update options for the target, and the execution options for scheduling. Note that for direct access DTPs, all the settings are specific, streamlined, and predetermined.

The options explained in greater detail in the following sections pertain more to standard and real-time data acquisition DTPs.

Extraction Options

An extraction mode must be selected (either full or delta), filters defined (that is, data selection), and data package size specified (for performance tuning). Data selection and separated scheduling for delta change records is an important new capability of the DTP. Previously, it was a limitation that delta data loads from the PSA or DataStore Object could not be separately loaded and filtered, except via a cumbersome custom workaround.

This hampered the ability to model global scheduling scenarios. For example, many global BI environments have the need to decentralize load schedules by regions or countries, especially if they are in different time zones. For example, a failed load in Asia should not have to affect Europe. Furthermore, when North America loads its data, Asia data shouldn't have to be updated as well. Figure 11-5 shows a DTP filtered by a specific legal entity (company code).

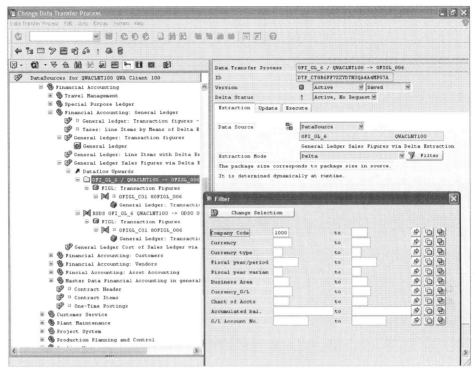

Figure 11-5   DTP Extraction options
Copyright © SAP AG

In the past, the need to decouple delta change management into separate load schedules necessitated various custom workaround information modeling (such as separating InfoCubes by region) and logic (such as filtering regions in custom update rules) tricks. However, the new DTP capabilities eliminate the need for custom workarounds through the use of separate DTPs with separate filters on different decentralized delta load schedules. In other words, different DTPs with different data selections can be used in different process chains for the same source and target.

Update Options

The update options are primarily for configuring how data loads can be restarted and how errors are to be handled and potentially fixed. These are newly available capabilities. To enable both data load restarts and error handling, persistent database tables were needed for each scenario. These tables are called *temporary storage* and the *error stack*, respectively.

Temporary storage not only facilitates restarting a process; it also helps in finding records with errors. Temporary storage saves the data state of every stage of a DTP. Every stage of a DTP is known as a *substep* (for example, extraction, filter, and transformation) and must be flagged for temporary storage if the DTP is to be restarted at that point or detailed record-level information is needed for that substep. Furthermore, the level of detail to be traced in temporary storage can be parameterized (either by data package, by erroneous record, or by data record).

Because of the volumes that temporary storage can create, parameters are available that tell the system when to delete the contents for temporary storage for a given DTP (either for successful loads, deleted loads, or after a period of time).

The error stack, as well as how it is updated and used, is also defined in the DTP. The error-handling options are as follows:

- **No update, no reporting** — This option means that if there is an error, no records are updated and, hence, will not be available for reporting. All incorrect records are highlighted in red in the Data Monitor and can be manually corrected and loaded individually. The error stack is not updated.

- **Valid records updated, no reporting (request red)** — This option specifies that if an error occurs, all valid records will still be updated but will not be available for reporting. The request will stay in a red status, which will not update the reporting read pointer. All invalid records are physically separated from valid records in a new request written to the PSA for error handling and subsequent update. The error stack is updated.

- **Valid records updated, reporting possible (request green)** — This option specifies that even if errors occur, the data loaded in the request should update the reporting read pointer to make it immediately available for reporting. All invalid records are physically separated from valid records in a new request that is written to the PSA for error handling and subsequent update. The error stack is updated.

- **Termination by number of records** — This parameter is a threshold for the number of invalid records that are permitted before the data load aborts and no records are updated.

- **No aggregation allowed** — If this flag is set, an additional check is made to ensure that the number of records read into BI must equal the number of records that are updated. If any records are generated, deleted, or aggregated, an error ensues.

- **Update type** — Lastly, there is an option to either perform (or not perform) referential data-integrity checks against master data via two update types: update without master data or no update without master data.

The error stack itself is technically the same as a PSA table and, as a result, stores information by request that can be extracted using DTP technology. This error DTP can be created from the update options within a standard DTP. When the error records are corrected, this error DTP can be scheduled into a process chain, and will merge into the same target as the standard DTP from which it was created.

The amount of records stored within the error stack can be one-to-one with the error records. However, if additional nonerror records are needed along with the erroneous ones (for evaluation or transformation purposes), there is a mechanism for grouping such records together. The mechanism in question is called a *semantic group* and represents an evaluative key for the error stack. In most cases, it should be at the same level of granularity as the target (which the system defaults). This can be overridden by specifying a less granular key. Any data record that shares the same key as the error records will also be written to the error stack (within or outside the data package). As a result, the less granular this key, the more records will be written to the error stack. Figure 11-6 shows how the semantic group is defined.

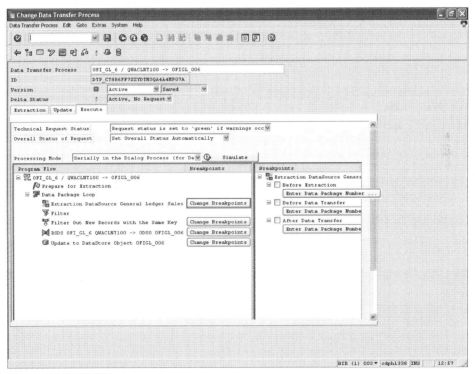

Figure 11-6   DTP Update options

Copyright © SAP AG

Execute Options

As part of execution, there are control parameters that influence two behaviors: how warnings should be handled (that is, stop-light color for the technical status, which is either green or red) and how the overall status should be set (that is, manually or automatically). The system will automatically default the processing mode (that is, serial or parallel loading) and display the process flow (that is, the DTP substeps as a tree). For troubleshooting purposes, the processing mode can also be set for debugging (serially in the dialogue process). Breakpoints can be set at each substep in program flow such as the extraction, the filter, the transformation, and the update. The number of breakpoints available for each substep depends on the substep itself (see Table 11-6).

Table 11-6   DTP Debugging Breakpoints

SUBSTEP	BREAKPOINT
Extraction	`Before Extraction`
Extraction	`Before Data Transfer`
Extraction	`After Data Transfer`
Filter	`Before Accepting Data`
Filter	`Before Filtering New Records`
Transformation	`Before Transformation`
Transformation	`After Transformation`
Update	`Before Insert`
Update	`After Insert`

If a breakpoint is specified, a specific data package number can be explicitly identified for the breakpoint to occur. (For large data loads, this is an important feature so that a breakpoint is not called for every data package loop.) Figure 11-7 shows how the breakpoints discussed are set.

Other Processes

In addition to extractions and data loads, there are a variety of data management processes that may be needed for regular scheduling and maintenance as part of an optimally run SAP BW system. These process types are explained in greater detail in Table 11-7.

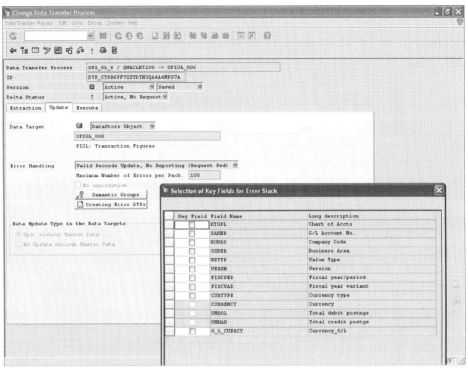

Figure 11-7   DTP Update options
Copyright © SAP AG

Table 11-7   Data Management Processes

OPTION	DESCRIPTION
System Commands	Not only can operating system commands be executed, now there is additional functionality to evaluate the result string (through a parsing search). This added capability helps support process chain scenarios where it is necessary to search for a file before uploading it. Additionally, there is an option to repeat the command until it is successful (so when the file does arrive, it gets loaded, for example).
Trigger Event Data Change (for Broadcaster)	This variant will automatically populate a list of all other process variants defined within the same process chain that are either InfoPackages, DataStore activations or updates, or PSA-to-data target updates (that can be flagged). Otherwise, a data target can be explicitly selected. This process works in conjunction with a broadcaster scheduling setting, which dictates a job trigger upon update of an explicit data target.

Continued

Table 11-7 Data Management Processes *(continued)*

OPTION	DESCRIPTION
Data Export into External Systems	This variant is a DTP that contains relevant parameters on the Open Hub destination (that is, the table or file details). The only restriction on the use of the Open Hub services for process chains is that file outputs must be to an application server. To download data to the presentation server, the Open Hub services must be run as a dialogue process (which can be done directly from the Open Hub destination maintenance).
InfoCube compression	This variant has additional options controlling which requests are compressed (for example, all requests of the last n days, or all but n requests), how they are compressed (delete zero value records or not), and if the marker for noncumulative key figures should be updated. This marker stores the latest snapshot for noncumulative values and should be updated with latest snapshot for better performance. This should only be flagged for scenarios where past noncumulative value changes are being loaded.
Construct database statistics	This variant also requires a parameter that specifies the percentage of InfoCube data that should be used for compiling the database statistics.
Save hierarchy	A flag must be checked if the hierarchy load is to be activated after loading. If the hierarchy is used in an aggregate, it can only be marked for activation and the process type for attribute change run must be subsequently executed.
Activate DataStore Object data	This process type has two additional configuration settings in the variant for overriding performance enhancement defaults. The first flag prevents the compression of requests in the DataStore Object change log after activation so as to keep the details for additional data targets to be updated. The second flag loads requests in a serial (rather than parallel) manner to have stricter control over the work processes being used.
Deletion of requests from PSA	A date or the number of days as a threshold for PSA request deletion can be specified. In addition, you can specify that only successful requests, unsuccessful requests, or requests no longer available in a data target should be deleted.

Continued

Table 11-7 Data Management Processes *(continued)*

OPTION	DESCRIPTION
Rollup of filled aggregates	As with other process types, cutoff points must be maintained for which requests are updated. The rollup will only update those requests that are older than a specified number of days, or the remainder requests after a specified number of requests. The same exact programs for aggregate rollup are used to rollup BI accelerator indexes as well.
Initial fill of new aggregates	This variant can be configured by aggregate, InfoCube, or DTP. This process is the first filling of the aggregates, which can also be done manually. As opposed to rollups, the build of BI accelerator indexes is not included here but is done manually.
Attribute change run	This variant can be configured to an InfoObject, a hierarchy, an InfoPackage, or a report variant. Attribute change runs mainly do two things: realign aggregates predicated on an affected navigational attribute, and activate the newly loaded master data. Because there can be a lot of data associated with the navigational attribute and its use within the dimension table of an aggregate, attribute change runs can become resource-intensive. BI accelerator attribute change runs are a lot faster because only the index needs to be adjusted (more shortly under "BI Accelerator").
Delete overlapping requests from an InfoCube	Automated deletion of data, for example, is required where every upload into an InfoCube needs to be a full upload because the extractor is not capable of providing delta loads. Deletion options can be specified based on: how the request was loaded (full or delta load), what selection conditions were used — InfoPackage selection conditions, when the request was loaded, and when the deletion is being requested. Finally, there are special criteria for preventing deletion depending on the day that the new request is loaded. Even more complex criteria can be implemented in an ABAP routine, returning a list of requests that must be deleted from the InfoCube.

Unlike extraction and loading, many of the aforementioned data management processes are optional. They provide additional design and performance-optimization options and should be evaluated as part of every process chain design discussion.

Application Management Processes

While most of the administrative effort centers on designing and scheduling data management activities via process chains, there are a number of tasks that involve more back-end application set up and tuning, including the following:

- **Batch Manager** — How data management processes can be better administered by the newly introduced Batch Manager.

- **BI accelerator** — The administrative tasks associated with maintaining this new performance-boosting capability.

- **Information broadcasting** — What needs to be set up and configured before information broadcasting functionality can be deployed to end users.

Batch Manager

The Batch Manager serves as a central transaction (RSBATCH) for managing background processes. The Batch Manager has reporting and message cleanup capabilities around background jobs. For example, information related to background work processes (such as number of failed jobs and utilization) can be obtained from the Batch Manager. Jobs themselves can also be listed as well as displayed, or you can delete messages associated with executed ones. In addition, all the application logs, system logs, traces, runtime errors, transport logs, and monitors can be accessed via this central transaction.

However, there two other more important capabilities that the Batch Manager introduces: controlling parallel processing and converting data load request tables for improved performance and ease of administration.

Parallelization of work processes is controlled by process type and process chain variant. The parameters control whether the process is run serially or in parallel. If the process is to be distributed over several work processes, the number of splits can be set, as well as on which servers or server groups the parallel work processes should be run. This not only works with extractions and data loads but with other data management processes such as aggregate rollups and attribute change runs.

Before using this functionality, be sure there are enough background work processes to accommodate the increased use of background parallelization.

The Batch Manager can also convert request details registered against data targets and PSA with special programs that read this information into new tables (one for data targets and the other for PSA). The benefits for converting are improved performance in viewing and managing the request details of a data target or PSA table. In most environments, the data requests and monitor logs can take up a lot of space quickly. Coupled with large data volume, frequently closed-out requests and lots of monitor messages in the log make the need for this administration feature imperative. Other scenarios where high-volume requests can occur are frequent delta load updates or custom verbose logging or planning applications that continually toggle the real-time data target between planning and loading modes.

Once the request tables have been converted, administration and logging data can be regularly archived using standard archiving functionality. The archive object BWREQARCH was specifically developed for these tables and can be accessed either through archive administration or the Data Warehouse Workbench.

BI Accelerator

Those who have worked on squeezing out as much performance as possible with aggregates can appreciate the never-ending and time-consuming nature of analyzing user behavior and creating optimal aggregates for their use (while balancing the impacts this has on data management activities such as aggregate rollups, attribute change runs, and dreaded reinitialization scenarios.

Aggregate optimization strategies for end-user performance are a subject for the section on "Aggregates" in Chapter 12. From an administrator's perspective, optimizing aggregates might consist of a rollup hierarchy plan (filling aggregates from aggregates). From a modeler's perspective, aggregate optimization may consist of aggregating data into separate data targets to avoid the performance impacts that attribute change runs have on aggregates.

The BI accelerator simplifies this world by eliminating a lot of data redundancy through the use of an innovative indexing scheme leveraging SAP's proprietary search engine technology called TREX. There is only one conceptual "aggregate," and that is the BI accelerator index. InfoCubes can have both aggregates and a BI accelerator index simultaneously, but only one or the other can be active at any given time (that is, one can toggle between the two to evaluate which option is preferred).

From a data-maintenance perspective, the BI accelerator is very similar to an aggregate rollup. There is the build and fill of the index, as well as rollups. However, there are differences to be noted.

From a performance-tuning perspective, the differences are a lot more apparent. While aggregates must be manually optimized based on end-user behavior, the plan is for the BI accelerator to automatically adjust it and to index accordingly (that is, zero administration from this perspective). The goal of the BI accelerator is to deliver automatic monitoring, configuration, optimization, and self-repair of the index and TREX-based BI accelerator engine.

The build and fill of a BI accelerator index is done manually via the data target context menu, while the rollups can be scheduled as process chain variants (the same exact ones used for aggregates). Like aggregates, BI accelerator indexes can be toggled active and inactive manually, and need an attribute change run scheduled after navigational attributes are changed via a master data load.

The data management impact of an attribute change run is very small in comparison to aggregates. This is because aggregates store navigational attributes inside the extended star schema (like a mini-InfoCube), while the BI accelerator index is predicated on the InfoCube data model, where navigational attributes are stored outside the extended star schema. As a result, adjusting the BI accelerator index is like adjusting master data (no need for realignments).

From a different perspective, InfoCube compressions work differently for aggregates and the BI accelerator index. Again, aggregates are like mini-InfoCubes and have a request dimension and use compressed (the E table) and uncompressed (the F table) fact tables just like their underlying InfoCube. This makes deletion of a specific request out of an InfoCube easy before compression is run (otherwise, aggregates must be rebuilt). After compressing an InfoCube, it makes sense to compress the corresponding requests in the aggregates for data conservation and performance reasons.

Data compression is not necessary for BI accelerator indexes, and if compression is run frequently enough, it may prompt the need to rebuild the BI accelerator index. This is because the index is not updated when compression is run. As a result, it is possible to have a state where there are more entries in the BI accelerator index than in the InfoCube fact table. To keep the index optimized, at some point it makes sense to rebuild the BI accelerator index to synchronize it with compressed data.

The concepts and use of OLAP cache and precalculation stores for Web applications still remain the same and can be leveraged on top of BI accelerator-based analysis. It is also important to note that BI accelerator sits on its own server that leverages adaptive computing concepts such as blade servers so as to flexibly scale. As a result, the connection to this server must be configured in the DW Workbench global settings. In addition, because the BI accelerator is TREX-based, it comes with a TREX administration tool to monitor the BI accelerator environment as well as directly administrate the engine and index itself.

Information Broadcasting

Information broadcasting functions require a measure of integration set up and maintenance to leverage functionalities of other NetWeaver components such as SAP Portal collaboration services, KM subscription services and SAP NetWeaver AS mail server services. These NetWeaver infrastructure elements must be in place before exporting to a Portal collaboration room, publishing to a KM folder, or distributing an email, respectively.

For the precalculation and distribution of BEx workbooks, a precalculation server must be created on a PC. This is done by installing a special Windows service off of the NetWeaver installation. After installing the SAP BW Precalculation Service, it should appear in the management console. Then you should log into the SAP BI system on that same PC and create a precalculation server in the

Implementation Guide under SAP BI report-relevant settings for BEx Broadcaster. The server should show a red light until you start the Windows service, thereby taking the server online and making it ready to support precalculation and distribution of BEx workbooks.

In terms of ongoing administration and batch scheduling, there are two ways to schedule a broadcaster setting: upon any data changes of a specified InfoProvider or upon a date and time schedule. The former requires a process chain, while the latter can be simply scheduled as a background job.

These SAP background processes work in conjunction with end-user broadcaster settings. Any broadcaster setting can have settings of both kinds and can have multiple date and time settings scheduled to occur once, daily, weekly, or monthly (hourly not supported).

Once an end user has scheduled a broadcaster setting, the setting can be picked up and processed via a background job. If the setting is scheduled upon an InfoProvider data change, a process of that corresponding process type needs to be included at the end of the process chain that loads the InfoProvider in question.

For date and time broadcaster schedules, an ABAP program (RSRD_BROADCAST_FOR_TIMEPOINT) must be scheduled in the background with a similar schedule so as to poll the system for matching broadcaster date and time schedules and to activate the execution of these settings.

Monitoring

To make BI and EDW processes more transparent, monitoring tools are needed to check on their progress or status, fix or troubleshoot any errors and performance tune or optimize them. The definition of a "monitor" is loosely applied here; it is simply where you go to get information on a process, be it a log, report, or transaction.

A variety of monitors can be accessed from various points, some specific to a particular activity, while others are more generic (like system monitors). SAP BW delivers a set of application-specific monitors tailored to the context of specific application functions. Typically, these application monitors can also call generic system monitors. For example from the extraction monitor (transaction RSMO), you can jump to a job process overview (transaction SM50).

Business Content for technical data is also playing a much more prominent role for application monitoring with the addition of new BI statistics tables and the incorporation of the CCMS central monitoring system data into Business Content. Not only has the back-end of Business Content been enriched, but so has the front-end with the introduction of the new BI Administration Cockpit, positioned to be the central Portal for all BI monitoring and administration activities.

What follows is a rundown of available application monitors, system monitors, and Business Content in the BI Administration Cockpit.

Application Monitors

Generally speaking, you can categorize SAP BW application monitors into two groupings: one that gives summary and end-result status and another that gives in-progress details of an active process. Let's call the former a *status monitor* and the latter a *process monitor*.

Table 11-8 shows examples of status monitors.

Table 11-8 Status Monitor Examples

MONITOR	DESCRIPTION
Aggregate Status	This monitor gives a listing of all the aggregates with information on its activation and fill status, details about the who and when of the last change and rollup to the aggregate, statistics of how many records are in the aggregate, the average summarization multiple, its usage and a valuation score. This is important input for the ongoing administrative activity of optimizing the use of aggregates.
BI accelerator Index Status	Similar to aggregates, this monitor lists by BI accelerator index its activation and fill status, the who and when of the last change, and the number of records in the index. Additionally, there is a multiple-usage column that indicates if master data SID tables are being shared by another index. Behind each listed BI accelerator index there is information about the index properties such as its RFC destination, block size, degree of parallelization, auto loading into main memory and number of parts the fact table index is split into.
DataStore Object Status	This monitor lists the DataStore Objects and corresponding request and status information for the last load, the last activation, and the last data mart update. If there are incomplete statuses or errors, you can jump into the transaction to manage the DataStore Object from the monitor.
Managing InfoProviders	Alternatively, each InfoProvider has a request management display where a listing of all loaded requests is provided with status and technical details of the request (such as number of records added and transferred, request and update times, selections used, and so on).

Continued

Table 11-8   Status Monitor Examples *(continued)*

MONITOR	DESCRIPTION
Delta Queue Status	This monitor is found in the source system and gives the delta queue status by DataSource. If the delta queue is for a generic delta, then there is an option to view the field being used as the selection criteria for the delta, as well as the date stamp to be used for next extraction. From the monitor, you can also view the entries in the delta queue, or repeat delta queue via the qRFC monitor, delete delta queue data, or the queue itself.

Process monitors are more common. The most actively used ones in the SAP BW environment are the extraction and data transfer process monitors. Table 11-9 provides a brief explanation of process monitors.

Table 11-9   Process Monitor Examples

MONITOR	DESCRIPTION
Extraction Monitor	The monitor details all the information associated with a data load. It comprises three levels: header, status, and details. To reduce the number of data load requests displayed in the monitor, various filters can be applied (such as time selections or metadata object selections like data target, InfoSource, and InfoPackage). Typically, when data loads fail, an express mail notifies the initiator of the data request. The request overview screen can be displayed as a tree, overview list, or planning table. The default is the tree display. The tree display for the monitor is configurable and is organized by the details about the request. From the status level, a wizard is available for Step-by-Step Analysis. The Step-by-Step Analysis Wizard walks through the steps of the data load process to pinpoint any errors that have occurred.
Real-time Data Acquisition Monitor	This lists the daemons and their status. Under each daemon is a hierarchy that can show both the upstream PSA and its request, as well as the downstream data target and its request. For the extraction request, data source and source system are also displayed. The monitor displays the scheduled periodicity of the daemon, number of errors, date and times for the last load and next load. InfoPackages with unassigned daemons are grouped under a not-assigned tree. All the metadata objects listed including the daemon itself can be maintained from this monitor.

Continued

Table 11-9 Process Monitor Examples *(continued)*

MONITOR	DESCRIPTION
Data Transfer Monitor	The DTP monitor consists of header and detail levels. The header consists of request details, while the details show all the messaging and status by steps and substeps in the DTP with corresponding timestamps and durations. Before processing the data packages in the request, there is a message for request generation and the setting of the status as executable. After processing, there are the steps for setting the technical and overall status. In the processing of the data package, the same substeps are displayed in the form of the execution tab of the DTP parameterizations. If temporary storage was flagged for any of these substeps, a data display button will appear next to it in the monitor and can be displayed from here. Additionally, if errors are written to the error stack, it can be viewed from the monitor.
Open Hub Monitor	A hierarchical listing is displayed essentially by Open Hub and date and timestamp a status indicator, the request and all of its technical details (that is, source and destination, changed by, and so on)
Analysis Process Monitor	Similar to extraction and DTP monitors, the hierarchy displayed is configurable. You can hierarchically arrange by status, analysis process, start date, version, user, and data target. The results can also be flexibly filtered. General information is stored in a header display, while messages are in a log display.
Process Chain Log	Process chains have a log view where a listing of log ids are provided by date and time for the process chain with a graphical depiction of the process chain itself in another pane with color-coded statuses per process. From each process the associated messages can be displayed. Messages are organized by process, background and chain. Process messages are integrated into the underlying process monitor (such as the extraction or DTP monitor) or application log. Background messages are integrated with the background job logs. The process chain details are more status and technical details focused on providing information on the instance and start and end triggers (such as technical ids and date and times).
BEx Monitor	The BEx Monitor consists of both the Query Monitor and OLAP Cache Monitor, which are both performance-tuning centric and covered in more detail in the section on "Optimizing Query Performance" in Chapter 12.

System Monitors

Aside from the application monitors, universal system monitors can be found in any SAP system. CCMS introduced a new central monitoring framework as part of SAP NetWeaver AS (available from 6.20 on). Referred to as simply the *Monitoring Architecture*, it is designed to centrally monitor and administer any system (SAP or non-SAP) across any landscape (simple or complex). However, because the CCMS Monitoring Architecture comes with SAP NetWeaver AS, it is also part of every local NetWeaver system. If the Monitoring Architecture is used truly as the Central Monitoring System (CEN), it probably should be centrally designed and reside on a separate server (especially if it's monitoring a complex, heterogeneous landscape), but doesn't have to be.

The Monitoring Architecture is not a tightly coupled monolithic application but rather an abstracted framework that is designed to be flexible and extensible. Similar to Business Content, it comes with its own predefined templates (such as a Data Archiving Monitor). The most notable template from a BI perspective is the BI monitor. Aside from generic system monitoring objects, there is an application-specific monitoring object for process chains. Process chains come preintegrated with the CCMS Monitoring Architecture and are preconfigured to send alerts to the framework. This can be turned off by process chain via its attributes for monitoring, where it can be exempted via a flag. The CCMS BW monitor can be directly accessed via the attribute setting, as well.

Alternatively, it can be accessed by the Alert Monitor (transaction RZ20), the CCMS tool for analyzing the data in the CEN. The Alert Monitor is a central repository for displaying alerts (such as events that are errors or exceed thresholds or have a particular status). Figure 11-8 shows the CCMS Monitoring Architecture.

Performance values are only temporarily stored in the Alert Monitor (default is last 24 hours). In the longer term, data is moved into the Central Performance History (CPH) to meet reporting needs historical data such as IT service-level agreements. Because of the data volumes involved, CPH allows you to manage the storage periods and granularity of the data with data management tools. This is particularly relevant for understanding CCMS Technical Content (explained in more detail under "BI Statistics" in Chapter 12).

The following examples are additional system monitoring tools particularly relevant to monitoring SAP BI activities (and are, in fact, usually accessible via the application monitors):

- **Job Process Overview** (SM50) — This gives a listing of all active dialogue and background jobs running with associative administrative functions and reporting. This is a universal transaction for all SAP background jobs.

- **Internet Communication Manager Monitor** (SMICM) — This monitor is important for Web applications and is very similar in layout to the aforementioned job process overview transaction, except instead of work processes you have worker threads.

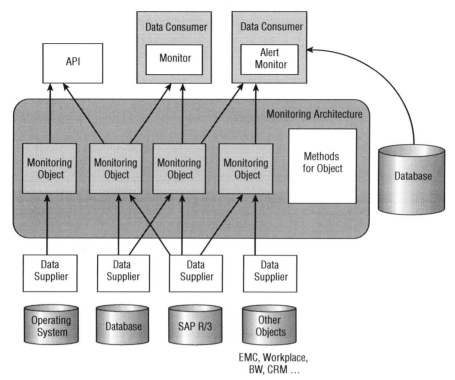

Figure 11-8   CCMS Monitoring Architecture

Copyright © SAP AG

- **ABAP Runtime Errors** (ST22) — All abnormally ended programs caused by a bug or error in syntax that the SAP system did not catch are logged here. This log that has a lot of trace details for troubleshooting purposes, and is vital for any error analysis.

- **System Log** (SM21) — All SAP system errors, warnings, and process messages go into the system log. This is particularly useful when ABAP runtime errors do not lead to a problem cause, as might be the case for database errors and issues.

- **CCMS Monitors** — The CCMS is actually composed of other monitoring display tools aside from the Alert Monitor. The more notable and often used ones are for the operating system with Workload Analysis (ST03) or for the database system with the Database Monitor (ST04).

BI Administration Cockpit

The *BI Administration Cockpit* can be thought of as Business Content itself. It is a predelivered template for monitoring the SAP BI environment from a Web-based cockpit. The BI Administration Cockpit itself consists of Business Content Web applications deployed through SAP Portals. It is yet another NetWeaver application built out of itself.

The BI Administration Cockpit has two primary sources of Business Content: *Technical Content* (mostly in the way of BI statistics) and *CCMS content* (which is optional).

Technical Content is mostly composed of BI performance statistics data, which, again, has been recently enriched with more details. Installing this technical Business Content is important because there isn't really a way to evaluate BI statistics other than directly viewing the underlying BI statistics table contents via the Data Browser (SE16).

BI statistics can be categorized into three categories: OLAP statistics, EDW statistics, and EDW status. The first two categories are performance-centric and will be covered in more detail in Chapter 12 under "BI Statistics." The last category simply covers load status details for process chains and for data requests (either InfoPackages or DTPs). The information capabilities are similar to what is available in the application monitors described earlier, except that this cockpit monitor centralizes the details and is Web deployed. Another form of Technical Content available that can be delivered to the BI Administration Cockpit is analysis authorizations details.

The inclusion of CCMS content can be significant. It enables the BI Administration Cockpit to become something much bigger — a central and universal administrator cockpit for the CEN (provided the Monitoring Architecture is central and universal). Figure 11-9 shows the data flow architecture for the CCMS Business Content.

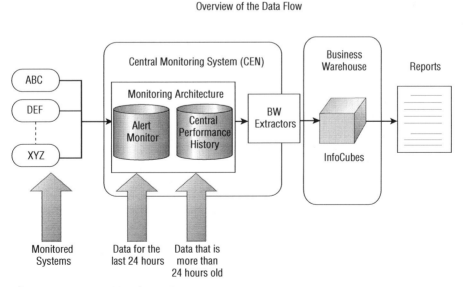

Figure 11-9 CCMS Business Content
Copyright © SAP AG

The CCMS Alert Monitor and CPH are not to be confused with the central alert framework that is more about distributing alerts through various channels (email, fax, cell phone, and so on) than it is about bringing alerts together. The central alert framework is integrated into both SAP BI and the CCMS. Either application can call the central alert framework, which, in turn, can publish to the BI Administrator Cockpit via a Universal Work List iView. In brief, a Universal Work List is a SAP Portal tool to centralize all tasks and activities into one Web-deployed list. Figure 11-10 illustrates the BI Administrator Cockpit Architecture.

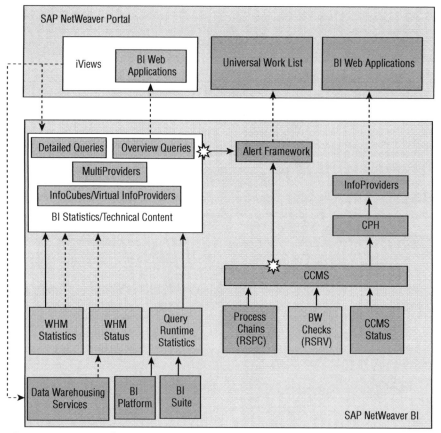

Figure 11-10   BI Administrator Cockpit Architecture
Copyright © SAP AG

Troubleshooting

Besides the Extraction and DTP Monitors, other commonly used transactions are available for troubleshooting. Typically used after loading data, these transactions are as follows:

- LISTCUBE — This transaction allows you to view the contents of an Info-Provider without having to design a query. Additional functions include:
  - Viewing the SQL plan
  - Viewing the surrogate identifier keys (SIDs) instead of characteristic values
  - Avoiding aggregation
  - Output the number of record hits
  - Storing the results to either a table or a file
  - Turning off conversion exits

- LISTSCHEMA — This transaction allows you to view the underlying data dictionary tables an InfoCube comprises (whether an aggregate, remote cube, MultiCube, and so on). From there, you can drill down into the data dictionary definitions or display the table contents to view technical data (such as the SID tables).

- RSRV — This transaction contains a collection of reports to check the consistency of the metadata and data in the system, and offers repair programs for most inconsistencies. These reports should be periodically run as a preventative maintenance measure to catch any data corruption, especially during stabilization exercises like a test phase, and can raise alerts to CCMS (similar to process chains). Figure 11-11 shows an example report where the dimension keys are compared with the surrogate identifier keys for sold-to customer in the sales transaction data InfoCube. Instead of having to manually compare the dimension tables with the SID tables in transaction LISTSCHEMA, you can execute this reporting utility. All errors are logged and can be viewed in a separate session. Each report has its own parameters to conduct its tests.

- RSRT — The BEx Analyzer is not the only way of viewing the output of a query. You can use transaction RSRT to view the results of a query instead. This transaction is normally used for troubleshooting purposes and for maintaining technical query properties.

- RSRT2 — This is a Web version of the Query Monitor that allows you to troubleshoot Web queries. This transaction is similar to RSRT, except the Web query URLs must be specified in this transaction. This transaction is particularly relevant for any enhancements to the Web table interface.

■ MDXTEST — If the ODBO interface or the OLAP BAPIs is being used to access SAP BW data, query statements must be specified using a query language called MultiDimensional eXpression (MDX). MDX is the equivalent of Structured Query Language (SQL) but is intended for multidimensional structures rather than relational tables. This transaction allows testing the syntax of MDX statements. This transaction can also autogenerate MDX to jump-start familiarity with MDX syntax.

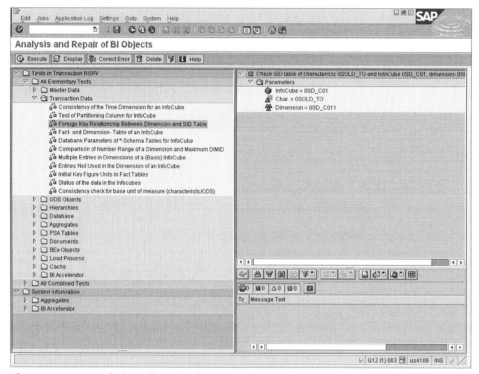

Figure 11-11 Analysis and repair of SAP BW objects
Copyright © SAP AG

System-Oriented Administration

System administration functions are part of every SAP system, but SAP BW systems have unique design implications and specific functions to consider. Again, the intention of this chapter is not to review general concepts. In some instances, knowledge is presumed in these areas so that the SAP BW-specific topics can be more readily addressed. Chapter 3 introduced many of the high-level concepts (see the section titled "Administration"), and this chapter gets into more detail. The system administration topics differ from the process topics in that the former are less batch-job intensive. Instead of focusing upon data management scheduling activities, system-oriented administration is more about technical design and maintenance. More specifically, this section deals with information lifecycle management, security, transports, and upgrades.

Information Lifecycle Management

As its name implies, information lifecycle management (ILM) is a broad concept. It looks at appropriately leveraging and optimizing all the applications, processes, and tools associated with information management during the various stages of the useful life of information.

According to general industry consensus, business records decay at the rate of 2.5 to 3.5 percent per month. Combine that with the explosive growth in new data sources and mediums, coupled with the data redundancies inherent in a corporate information factory (that is, information marts and corresponding aggregates), and near-line storage (NLS), and archiving quickly becomes an important post-implementation consideration.

The primary driver for defining useful life is (predictably) stakeholder needs (whether that's the end user or a regulatory need). End-user needs differ in an ERP system (transactional focused) versus a BI system (analysis focused). Regulatory factors differ by industry (such as SEC, FDA, Basel II, HIPPA, and so on). The other side of the equation is the cost of keeping information that is continually in flux because of technological innovations.

Generally speaking, the more frequent an information asset is updated and the more granular and comprehensive its details, the faster its data growth will be. Whether or not that information can be aggregated, deleted, archived, stored near-line, kept, or loaded into memory depends on its usage and retention value.

The intention here is neither to go into varying ILM cost-benefit scenarios and strategies nor to discuss data modeling options. Instead, this chapter highlights two BI administration options for aging data: standard data archiving functions and the newly introduced the NLS capabilities.

Archiving

SAP BW archiving is not a new technology. Archiving was available in earlier releases for purging unnecessary IDocs out of the SAP BW environment. It is based on the already-established archiving technology prebuilt into all SAP systems called the archive development kit (ADK). The ADK is a service of mySAP Technology, meaning that it is a core component of all SAP systems. It provides an API that not only SAP but also customers and partners can use to develop their own archiving solutions. The ADK provides the following features:

- **Administration** — The ADK can schedule, monitor, and administer archiving sessions.

- **Reporting** — The ADK has its own information system. To view the contents of an archive file, you must manually create an InfoStructure for the SAP BW-generated archiving object via customization.

- **Change handling** — If structural changes are made to an InfoProvider after data has been archived, the ADK is not affected. The data is simply displayed in the new structure. Note, however, that this is not the same thing as converting the data into the new structure.

- **Platform-independent** — Different code pages (ASCII, EBCDIC, Unicode, and so on) and number formats are supported.

- **Compression** — The ADK supports data compression algorithms, allowing compression down to one-fifth the original size.

The standard ADK has been enhanced to support SAP BW InfoProviders. As a result, this section focuses on the SAP BI-specific aspects of archiving. The more general topic of SAP archiving is beyond the specialized scope of this book.

Because all the tables where transaction data is stored are generated and extensible, predelivered *archiving objects* do not exist as they do in other SAP systems (such as SAP R/3, where tables are usually fixed). An *archiving object* is logical. The archiving object consists of business data that can be grouped and treated for reading, archiving, and deleting. The central piece of SAP BW-specific configuration for archiving entails creating the archiving object based on the data target definitions, as well as some design considerations. This SAP BW metadata that encapsulates the archiving object is termed *Data Archiving Process* and includes configuration for NLS as an example. Currently, archiving supports only the InfoCube and DataStore Object data targets. Master data, PSA, and documents are not yet supported.

Once the archive object has been generated, archiving can be scheduled as a standard batch job or can be incorporated into process chains via a DTP variant. The DTP configuration for an archiving purge consists of appropriately setting the extraction mode for loading into an archive. For background processing, there are dependencies and sequencing considerations. The process of archiving consists of first writing all the data out to a file and then deleting it from the data target.

Once archived, the data file can be reloaded into SAP BW if necessary. The export DataSource for the data targets archived has special archive features. As mentioned earlier, in the InfoPackage data selection for the export DataSource, archive selections can be enabled to read records from a file. When reloading data into SAP BW, you should update a new data target specifically for archived data and create a MultiProvider for marrying new data with archived data.

Figure 11-12 illustrates the regular archiving data flow. The archiving object itself generated via a piece of metadata is also called an *archiving process*. The archiving process is configured within the maintenance of the data target. It provides the following configuration parameterizations:

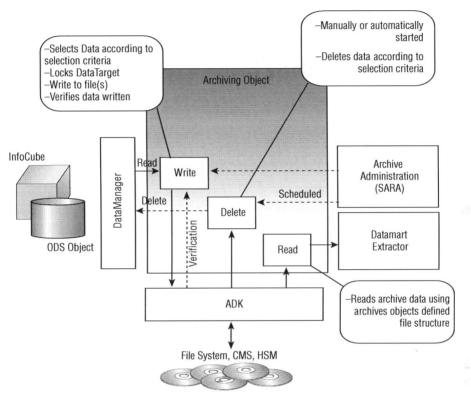

Figure 11-12 Archiving data flow
Based on copyrighted material from SAP AG

- **Selection profile** — The characteristics used for data selection as part of an archiving process must be parameterized as part of the selection profile. For example, when data is written to a file, you may want to restrict the archive deletion by a specific calendar year. If the data target is partitioned, this characteristic must be the partitioning characteristic. Otherwise, a time characteristic must be used. DataStore Objects may be the exceptions where alternative characteristics may be used if a time characteristic is not available.

- **Semantic group** — In the semantic group, the *data object* is maintained. The data object is the most atomic unit of data in the archive. The data records read into the archive file are grouped and sorted by the characteristics specified here. If nothing is specified, all records will be written unsorted into the file. This tabstrip also controls the size of archive files in one of two ways: by maximum size of the file or by maximum number of data objects per file. If the maximum is exceeded for a file, a new file is created until the same maximum is exceeded. If these fields are left blank, all data is written to one file.

- **Folder** — The storage settings for the folder archived to must be dictated to the system. If the archive storage is in SAP, a logical filename is given. Otherwise, third-party-specific settings must be maintained for the storage system.

- **Delete** — How the archiving process subsequent data deletion job will be scheduled must be controlled via configuration. The options are not scheduled but rather are started automatically or after an event.

Once the archive object is created, archive administration can be called from the DW Workbench (just a context menu option from the InfoProvider), and the process of archiving is the same as in any other SAP system. As mentioned earlier, any InfoPackage created for the export DataSource of an archive-enabled data target will have an additional option in the data selection to extract from a specific archive file.

Near-Line Storage

Until recently, there had been no standard solution for SAP BW NLS information access. Archived data had to be reloaded into the SAP BI environment if its data needed to be accessed as just explained. Even though archiving data is recoverable, because it was purged from the system, users had to wait for this information to be reloaded into the system before it was available. The NLS solution does not require any data to be reloaded. The data is online but with slower response times (being on lower-cost and lower-performing hardware).

The NLS hardware architecture and medium options vary and include tapes, optical libraries, Network Attached Storage (NAS), Storage Area Networks (SANs), and so on. An NLS adapter interface abstracts away the NLS hardware infrastructure for housing the data. The NLS interface is an open one, but there are certified partners (namely, PBS software, File Tek, OuterBay and SAND Technologies). Figure 11-13 provides an architectural overview of NLS and archiving.

From an SAP BI application perspective, the administration, maintenance, and setup of NLS is the same across NLS platforms, and the procedures are similar to those of archiving. For example, archiving objects still must be generated via Data Archiving Processes. Data Archiving Processes control such things as the archiving type (for example, Offline and ADK-based, Near-line

ADK-based and Near-line Standalone) as well as the selection schema (either by data request, by data selection parameters, or by time slicing on application events such as compression or delta loads). From an NLS perspective, an NLS connection must be configured and NLS-specific parameterizations made within the Data Archiving Process

To migrate data into an NLS archive, a DTP must be created so as to extract the data from the data target into an NLS archive. The extraction mode of the DTP controls this load behavior. Special InfoPackages for archiving data reloads are not necessary, because the data will still be online. Finally, queries must be parameterized to read from NLS archives. This setting is accessible either via the query properties in the BEx query definition or via the Query Monitor (transaction RSRT).

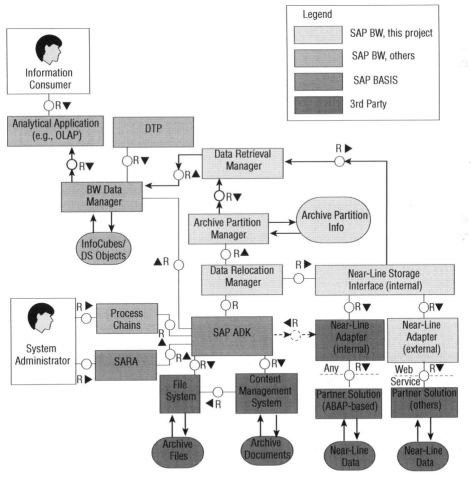

Figure 11-13   NLS architecture

Based on copyrighted material from SAP AG

Similar to archiving, NLS support is currently only for InfoCubes and Data-Store Objects.

Authorizations

Until recently, authorizations in SAP BW were primarily handled the same way as authorizations in any other SAP system — based on the standard SAP authorization concept. To deliver improved authorization capabilities for reporting and analysis, a new authorization concept has been introduced in addition to the standard authorization concept.

Before reading this section, you should already be familiar with the standard SAP authorization concepts and terms such as users, roles, object classes, authorization objects, profiles, profile generator, and authorizations. This discussion deals with the SAP BW authorization concepts and design issues.

SAP BW authorizations are fundamentally different from SAP R/3 authorizations and must be designed and created separately. A large part can be attributed to the fundamental differences between a data entry (OLTP) system and a data access (OLAP) system. The roles, applications, and processes are all different as well. Consequently, the authorization objects and associated object classes are different (except for cross-application components and Basis).

The fundamental differences between OLAP and OLTP systems from an authorizations perspective are highlighted in Table 11-10.

Table 11-10   OLTP versus OLAP Security

CRITERIA	OLTP	OLAP
Application area	Within	Across
Transaction-oriented	Yes	No
Data focus	Master data	Transaction data sets

From a design perspective, authorizations are designed along two perspectives: *who* and *what*. From the *who* perspective, security designers have the choice of assigning authorization profiles to either users or generating ones for roles. From the *what* perspective, security designers can authorize by SAP BI metadata *objects* and DW Workbench tasks or by *data* sets.

The design decision on securing an SAP BI system either by metadata *objects* and DW Workbench tasks or by analysis *data* must be weighed before implementing authorizations. Typically, administration tasks and metadata object security control are handled by standard authorizations (with predelivered authorization objects for BI-related objects and tasks). The authorization objects themselves vary by the SAP BW metadata objects and tasks themselves (for example, InfoCubes, DataStore Objects, InfoObjects, queries, and so on).

Standard authorizations control access to specific SAP BW objects and tasks. These authorization objects group under an object class for administration in standard authorizations. The standard authorization concept found in any SAP system has not significantly changed in the current release.

For reporting and analysis authorizations, there is not necessarily a need for the use of standard authorizations. The use of custom and generated reporting authorization objects for restricting data access has been replaced with a separate analysis authorization mechanism and tool for restricting analysis data access. Data authorizations restrict user access to report output controlled by specific characteristic or key-figure values (for example, for cost centers or a salary amount). There is now only one standard authorization object if used at all (depending on if you define authorizations by role instead of by user). This standard authorization object is for all analysis authorizations and is assigned to a role. It defines which analysis authorization to use. Otherwise, it is not needed, because an analysis authorization can be directly assigned to a user.

As security design goals move from user-centric to role-centric and from a focus on BW metadata objects to a focus on analysis data sets in reporting, simplification is compromised for tighter and more targeted security control. Authorization design options are shown in Figure 11-14.

User versus Role

Authorizations (whether standard authorizations by object or analysis authorizations by data) can be assigned either directly to users or indirectly via roles. For complex designs, you should design authorizations by role for flexibility. Where this approach breaks down is when reporting scenarios require the roles to be at the same level of detail as the individual users.

For example, say an organization has 1,000+ cost centers (let's be conservative), with a manager assigned to each cost center. Should 1,000+ roles be created one-to-one with the users? Such a design is maintenance intensive. If broad roles are created with many users assigned to those roles (say, to a specific cost center hierarchy node), maintenance is alleviated. Changes to a role affect many users.

In many cases, this is desirable. But in such a design, how do you handle exceptions (for example, one user needs access to a cost center outside the hierarchy node that no one else in the role should have access to)? If the roles were one-to-one with the user, individual user exceptions would be easier to handle. However, when many users share a role, an alternative is to assign the new authorization profile directly to the user rather than the role.

When broad reporting roles are defined, the standard SAP transaction for administering role authorizations (transaction PFCG) should be sufficient. When reporting authorizations need to be assigned to individual users, the SAP BW transaction for central analysis authorization management should be used (transaction RSECADMIN). This transaction will be covered in some more detail under "Analysis Authorizations," later in this chapter.

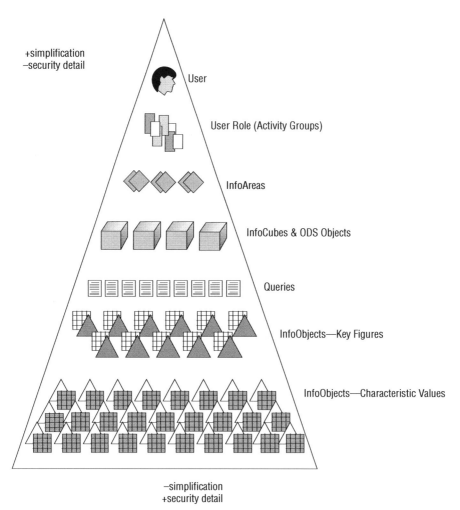

Figure 11-14 Authorization design considerations
Based on copyrighted material from SAP AG

Typically, when authorizations are designed using standard authorizations, it is to restrict access to particular BI metadata objects. Roles can be defined broadly enough to restrict user access to a particular query or InfoCube. However, when authorizations are based on dimensional values in analysis authorizations, they are typically more user-centric than role-centric. In other words, analysis authorizations typically lend themselves to user assignments, while standard authorizations lend themselves to role assignments (although it's possible to mix and match). To assign an analysis authorization to a role, special authorization objects for analysis authorizations must be assigned (and parameterized to the technical name of the analysis authorization). The difference between object and value definitions in authorizations will be covered in more detail in the section titled "Object Versus Data," later in this chapter.

The advantage of using roles over users for authorizations is that roles have additional features not available to user definitions, such as user menu configuration and Portal integration. One simplistic way of providing security is restricting access to a query or a transaction via user menus. In other words, this design approach assumes that if a user cannot see it in the system, he or she is not sophisticated enough to find it and access it by other means. You should also design roles with Portals in mind, even if there are no immediate plans to implement them.

There is a mechanism and tool to facilitate the mass maintenance of user-centric authorizations through the use of generated authorizations. If SAP HR authorizations exist in mySAP ERP extractors can load this information into Business Content DataStore Objects that, in turn, can be used as basis for automatically generating analysis authorizations and assigning them to users. Another approach is to use a value set BEx variable populated by an InfoCube with all the assignments. This approach restricts access by query design rather than by authorizations. These authorization design alternatives will be covered in the section titled "Object Versus Data," later in this chapter. Table 11-11 summarizes the design considerations for user-centric versus role-centric authorizations.

Table 11-11   User versus Role Authorizations

CRITERIA	USER	ROLE
Number of authorizations	Many	Few
Metadata object authorizations	Not typical	Typical
Analysis value authorizations	Typical	Not typical
Administration transaction	RSECADMIN	PFCG
Restrict access by menu options	No	Yes

Object versus Data

As mentioned before, authorizations can be used to restrict each component of an information model, such as InfoSources, InfoCubes, InfoObjects, individual queries, and even their components (such as calculated or restricted key figures). If metadata objects are shared within other metadata objects, restriction can be enforced at higher levels. For example, the InfoObject 0PERSON is used both in HR Business Content and CO Business Content. Access to the InfoObject can be centrally controlled by assigning the InfoObject to an InfoCatalog and restricting access to the InfoCatalog.

Another way to categorize SAP BW information modeling objects is by naming conventions. Authorization values can accept asterisks as wildcard values (such as 0CRM* for all CRM Business Content). If you are planning on using security by metadata object approach, you should design a naming convention at the beginning of a project before too many custom SAP BW objects are created.

SAP BW delivers role templates that contain a series of authorization objects and corresponding default values such as the following:

- S_RS_RDEAD — Role: Administrator (development system)
- S_RS_RDEMO — Role: Modeler (development system)
- S_RS_ROPAD — Role: Administrator (production system)
- S_RS_ROPOP — Role: Operator (production system)
- S_RS_RREDE — Role: Reporting developer (production system)
- S_RS_RREPU — Role: Reporting user

Figure 11-15 shows the types of activities and BW metadata objects assigned to such role templates.

Role	Query	InfoCube	InfoSource	InfoObject
Reporting User	R E			
Reporting Developer	R E M			
Reporting Power User	R E M D	R M		
Data Manager	R E M	R M		M R
Data Modeler	R E M	R E M D	R E M	R E M
System Admin.				

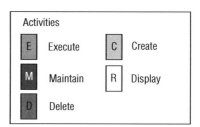

Activities

E	Execute	C	Create
M	Maintain	R	Display
D	Delete		

Figure 11-15 Example roles by object

Based on copyrighted material from SAP AG

Analysis Authorizations

The security designer has a more sophisticated option for restricting access to reporting data other than by restricting access to a metadata object (such as query or query element) via standard authorizations. A more advanced approach is to restrict access by data sets via analysis authorizations. Analysis authorizations replace the old reporting authorizations, providing more flexibility and functionality such as the following:

- An unrestricted number of InfoObjects to define a data set (versus 16 before)

- Simplified relevancy settings by InfoObject (versus by InfoObject and InfoProvider)

- Integrated hierarchy authorization configuration (versus separate configuration)

- Expected union logic for composite authorizations (versus unexpected intersection logic every time a new authorization is added)

- Characteristic-dependent navigational attribute authorizations (versus global use)

- Maintainability after implementation and in production (versus deletion and reimplementation)

There are migration tools and processes to convert the older authorizations mechanism into the newer one and a configuration switch to start using the new analysis authorizations or stay with the old approach (it is not automatic with upgrade).

Defining analysis authorizations consists of defining sets of data that a user or role needs to possess to view BI content. Analysis authorizations do not act as filters unless a BEx authorization variable is explicitly employed in a query definition. Instead, the system checks that an authorized data set resides completely within an OLAP request for information. If any portion of the OLAP data request resides outside the authorized data set, an authorization error is returned.

The data set itself is identified by defining an authorization structure consisting of an unlimited number of characteristics and navigational attributes. The way characteristics are defined is by InfoObject name, while navigational attributes are the concatenation of the InfoObject name the attribute belongs to and the InfoObject name of the attribute itself. For example, an authorization for cost center is `0COSTCENTER`, while an authorization for cost center as a navigational attribute of asset is `0ASSET__0COSTCENTER`.

Key figures are handled differently from characteristics in an authorization. A characteristic InfoObject by the technical name of `0TCAKYFNM` is used to represent the key figure. In the authorization structure, the InfoObject `0TCAKYFNM` has to be used and cannot be coupled with a hierarchy (but rather a value authorization). The actual key-figure name is fixed in the authorization in the same way that characteristic values are fixed.

If a key figure or an attribute is display only, the system behavior is a little different. If authorizations are missing, instead of an authorization error, the display-only attributes are hidden. The restriction for display-only characteristics attributes is all or nothing. Either the display-only attribute is made visible by giving the attribute the value asterisk (*) in the user or role authorization, or it is hidden. For key-figure attributes, identifying the requisite key-figure name should suffice.

Not all characteristics and navigational attributes are available for use in reporting authorization objects. Only the characteristic InfoObjects flagged as authorization-relevant and their corresponding navigational attributes are available for use in defining an authorization structure. This flag is found in InfoObject maintenance via the BEx Explorer Settings and the Navigational Attribute settings. The SAP BW authorizations can be centrally maintained (via transaction RSECADMIN), or they can be maintained via the Profile Generator (transaction PFCG). The considerations for using one transaction over the other were explained earlier in this chapter.

The central maintenance for authorizations is divided into the following task categories:

- **Defining Authorizations** — Here authorizations can either be defined, generated, or transported. Defining authorizations consist of configuring the authorization structure by defining dimensions (essentially characteristics or navigational attributes) and dimensional values (hierarchies, fixed values, ranges, BEx variables, or wildcards). Generating authorizations is contingent upon the proper Technical Content being filled for authorization purposes. HR and CO extractors can populate these DataStore Objects for use in mass generating authorizations and user assignments. Transports are covered as part of the next section on "Transports."

- **User Assignments** — Here, user assignments to authorizations can be made and transported. Central system transactions for user and role maintenance can be made here. A where-used report can be executed to provide a listing of which authorizations have been created and which users were assigned. Users are assigned indirectly to authorizations via named groupings of authorizations called *authorization selections*, which can also be grouped via a BI hierarchy on the InfoObject OTCTAUTH.

- **Authorizations Analysis** — Here authorizations can be monitored either via simulation as another user, checking the error logs, or reviewing the generation logs (if using generated authorizations). If simulating another user, that user name must be specified as well as the transaction to be used (such as the Query Monitor or the DW Workbench).

Besides the characteristics, navigational attributes, and key figures, there are three special metadata InfoObjects that are mandatory for inclusion into every analysis authorization but are optionally restricted with a value: 0TCAACTVT (activity), 0TCAIPROV (InfoProvider), and 0TCAVALID (validity range). The ability to limit data authorizations by activity (display or change) is not new, because it was needed for planning authorizations (that is, not all activities in an SAP BI environment are for reporting). In addition, limiting authorizations to a particular InfoProvider was mandatory in the earlier release because an InfoProvider flag was the mechanism for activating the authorization. The analysis authorization restriction to a specific InfoProvider is now optional (but recommended). The most significant new capability of analysis authorizations is the ability to specify a validity date range.

There are many scenarios in a BI environment where information access or planning access needs to be limited to a time window such as period-end close or a planning cycle phase. This is much more dynamic than having an authorizations maintenance activity to activate and deactivate authorizations during the requisite time windows.

Besides restricting characteristics and navigational attributes by explicit characteristic values or ranges, other special authorization values such as wildcards can be employed. There are two wildcard options: the asterisk (*) that represents any number of arbitrary characters and the plus (+) that represents only one character. The former wildcard can be universally applied, while the latter only works with 0TCAVALID (time range validity). When using wildcards, the option identifier to be applied (EQ for "equals" on single values and BT for "between" on ranges) is CP for "contains pattern."

The asterisk wildcard is helpful when there is a smart naming convention for a characteristic such as cost center. For example, if a user is authorized for all cost centers that belong to a particular sales department and there is an intelligent coding scheme where all cost centers that belong to that function area have the value 010 for the first three characters in the technical code for cost center, an authorization value 010* simply needs to be maintained. Alternatively, plus signs can be used as wildcard characters (such as 010++20*).

The plus wildcard is available only for specifying validity ranges. So, if users need to be able to have limited planning access to during a bottom-up planning phase in the overall planning cycle in September every year, the range might look like 09.01.++++ to 09.30.++++.

If more advanced logic is needed in place of wildcards (for example, a master data lookup of function area 010 via cost center master data), BEx user-exit variables can be used in authorizations as well. The convention is to prefix the variable name with a dollar sign ($) instead of specifying a value.

Lastly, there is the use of a colon (:), which allows for aggregated access to a particular characteristic or navigational attribute. So, for example, you might want to be able to view total salary costs for a cost center without viewing the salary costs broken down by employee.

In addition, hierarchies can be used for restricting data access. The hierarchy and hierarchy node must be specified, as well as the type of authorization and a hierarchy determination strategy currently termed a *validity period*. The hierarchy is explicitly identified while the hierarchy node can be explicitly determined or derived dynamically via a BEx variable.

The type of hierarchy authorization must be specified to tell the application how to use the hierarchy node within an authorization. The most obvious logic is to select all the branches and leaves under a hierarchy node branch. So, for a cost center hierarchy, if a hierarchy branch represents a sales geography, this authorization type would give access to all the sales office details that rolled up into the sales region.

Another authorization type option is to provide access only to the node itself. Under this authorization type, the same cost center hierarchy would provide access only to the branch of that node (in this case, regional sales cost centers excluding sales office cost center details).

Another authorization option is to ignore the node and grant access to the entire hierarchy.

Lastly, there are two more sophisticated authorization types that give access to an entire hierarchy node except to a predefined level in relative terms or absolute terms. With this option, you must specify the hierarchy level to count to. With the absolute hierarchy authorization type, the counting begins at the top of the hierarchy. With the relative hierarchy authorization type, the counting starts at the top of the specified node. So, if there is reorganization that redistributes all hierarchy leaves simply for reporting purposes, the absolute level counting option would probably be undesirable, but the relative one might work (especially if the hierarchy nodes or branches stay relatively untouched at higher levels).

If access to all analysis data needs to be granted, a predelivered authorization (0BI_ALL) is regenerated each time a new InfoObject is flagged as authorization relevant. This is a handy authorization to have for development and testing tasks.

Because of increased legal auditing needs such as the Sarbanes-Oxley Act, enhanced auditing capabilities come with new analysis authorizations. All change documents associated with changes made to user assignments and authorization value or hierarchy changes can be viewed via Technical Content VirtualProviders, which, in turn, can be deployed to the BI Administration Cockpit.

Although maintaining authorizations is an administration task, the design of security is an important information modeling consideration that must be addressed at the beginning of a project, not saved until the end, especially with today's increased corporate compliance requirements.

Transports

Chapter 3 introduced the *Transport Connection* tool and Chapter 5 discussed system landscape design consideration. This section presumes some familiarity with the SAP Transport Management System (TMS). This section discusses considerations specific to SAP BW. A number of features make SAP BW transports different from traditional SAP R/3 transports:

- Most of the transported objects are metadata definitions as opposed to configuration data or programs. *After-import methods* are called to generate the metadata object environment (such as database tables and ABAP programs) as part of metadata activation.

- SAP BW supplements the standard transport mechanism by the Transport Connection tool, which automatically handles dependencies between different SAP BW metadata objects. The Transport Connection tool is available as part of the DW Workbench.

- SAP BW object transports and related source system object transports must be synchronized.

- As opposed to SAP R/3, SAP BW does allow changing certain types of objects (for example, InfoPackages) in the production environment.

Transport Connection Tool

The TMS distinguishes between local (assigned to a temporary package named $TMP) and transportable objects (assigned to a permanent package). The TMS is used to record changes to all transportable objects. Changes recorded by the TMS include creation, modification, and deletion of objects. While most SAP applications (for example, the ABAP Workbench) require explicit assignment of a package to a transport object (which may be $TMP), SAP BW metadata objects are always initially assigned to the temporary package $TMP. This keeps them out of reach of the TMS until they need to be transported to the quality-assurance or production system. Once an SAP BW metadata object is transported for the first time using the Transport Connection tool, a package name has to be assigned explicitly and the metadata object is put under control of the TMS, which begins recording the changes.

The Transport Connection tool allows you to collect SAP BW metadata objects along two dimensions: metadata object cross-references (for example, InfoObjects used in InfoCubes) and data flow (for example, InfoSources feeding an InfoCube and queries defined for an InfoCube). Object collection ensures correctness and completeness of transport requests. The Transport Connection tool utilizes standard TMS functionality, thus enabling use of all standard TMS transactions in conjunction with SAP BW metadata transports. However, the Transport Connection tool is not able to identify and honor dependencies between SAP BW and non-SAP BW objects (such as ABAP programs and dictionary structures).

BEx queries are similar to other SAP BW metadata objects in that newly created queries are initially assigned to the temporary package ($TMP) until ready to transport. However, BEx queries can be explicitly assigned to their own transports in the transport connection as an option for managing these transports separately. Once released, a new standard transport request must immediately be defined and assigned for BEx queries, or any additional changes will result in an error.

Table 11-12 illustrates the differences between the SAP BW Transport Connection tool and the standard TMS.

Table 11-12 SAP BW Transport Connection Tool and the SAP TMS

CRITERIA	TRANSPORT CONNECTION	TMS
No tracking of changes until first transport	Yes	No
Metadata object authorization necessary	Yes	No
ABAP development or configuration	No	Yes

Transport Dependencies

The SAP BW Transport Connection tool handles a great deal of complexity. However, by shielding this complexity from the user, it makes it more difficult for administrators to understand why transports might go wrong. It is still important to understand what the Transport Connection tool is actually doing for you in order to troubleshoot and resolve transport errors (which, most of the time, relate to sequencing issues). You need to understand the following fundamental dependencies:

- Dependencies between different SAP BW metadata objects (for example, the InfoObjects required by an InfoCube)
- Dependencies between SAP BW metadata objects and ABAP Workbench objects (for example, includes, macros, or ABAP dictionary structures used in update rules)
- Dependencies between metadata stored in SAP BW and metadata stored in the source systems

Because of the nature of these dependencies, there is no easy technical solution. Instead, organizational solutions must be defined that help to avoid transport problems with SAP BW metadata objects. An organizational solution approach for the first two problems is using collective transport requests, where all developers working on a specific part of the project use the same (therefore, *collective*) transport request to record their changes.

NOTE Custom ABAP code references to SAP BW-generated ABAP structures can be eliminated if sophisticated methods are used to make the code more dynamic and generic (such as the use of field symbols or runtime type identification). This makes custom code less maintenance intensive when changes are made to metadata, and it eliminates any dependencies in transport.

Although the Transport Connection tool can handle dependencies among multiple metadata objects, it is still possible to define multiple transport requests and spread interdependent SAP BW metadata objects across these multiple transport requests. Centrally maintained collective transport requests help to avoid metadata spreading and allow for keeping control of non-SAP BW metadata objects required, although they do not offload the responsibility of taking care of such dependencies from the developers.

The most frequently ignored dependency, however, is the source system dependency. Figure 11-16 illustrates those dependencies and the sequence of steps that must be taken for a safe and reliable transport. The steps are as follows:

1. The first step is to transport the information model (consisting of InfoCubes, DataStore Objects, InfoSources, InfoObjects, update rules, queries, and other SAP BW metadata objects not related to any source system) and non-SAP BW transport objects in an initial transport request. The Transport Connection tool can be used to collect all required SAP BW metadata objects.

2. While export DataSource for InfoCubes and DataStore Objects are generated automatically, SAP BW releases 2.0B and 2.1C did not automatically generate export DataSources for master data. These needed to be transported separately via maintenance of the DataSources (using the SBIW transaction).

3. The third step is to transport all required DataSources from the source system development landscape to the source system quality-assurance landscape.

4. This step involves replicating all metadata for all source systems, including the SAP BW system itself, to ensure that all (export) DataSource definitions are up to date. Obviously, all relevant source systems need to be created at this time.

5. The last step is to transport all staging objects, such as DataSources (transfer structures), transfer rules, and InfoPackages.

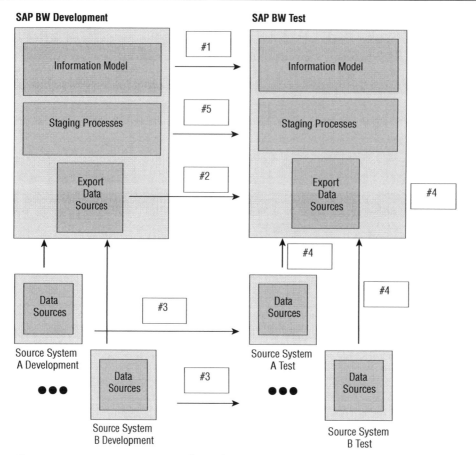

Figure 11-16   SAP BW transport dependencies

In addition, two important configuration steps must be completed prior to performing Step 5. The first configuration step is to select the source systems for which the Transport Connection tool should collect metadata. This avoids transporting metadata for source systems merely used in the development system for testing or sandbox purposes.

The second step is to ensure that all source system mappings (mappings of different technical source system names in the development and quality-assurance environments) are defined correctly in the target system. This second configuration step is much more important. As part of the import procedure, the original source system name is mapped to the name specified in this mapping.

Activation

Various object versions typically belong to metadata: delivered, modified, and active. The only version that can be transported in customer systems using the

TMS is the active version. SAP BW transports the active version of metadata definitions to downstream systems. The metadata environment (such as master data tables) is generated as part of the activation performed by so-called *after-import methods*, where applicable (for example, currency types can be transported without a separate activation step).

NOTE After-import methods can be called manually in a quality-assurance system to debug the activation of a BW metadata object. The function module for the after-import method is RS_AFTER_IMPORT. **Never transport the underlying generated ABAP dictionary objects directly.**

Most SAP BW objects are not supposed to be changed in a production environment. The TMS prevents such changes or records them in special "repair transport requests" depending on its configuration. However, some SAP BW objects must be changed in a production environment, such as queries, workbooks, Web templates, InfoPackages, or process chains. The SAP BW TMS extensions allow changing the settings for these objects types to one of the following:

- **Not changeable** — All SAP BW object types with this setting must be changed in the development system and promoted to production using the TMS.

- **Changeable original** — As a result, if an object (like a query) is transported from development to production, that query cannot be maintained in production even if the changeable option has been set. All changes to the object must be done in development and transported. Meanwhile, if the object is created directly in production, it can be changed freely.

- **Everything changeable** — Regardless of whether or not an object type was transported, the object can be maintained. This option is not recommended, since changes made in production can be overwritten by changes transported from development. This option is accessible via the context menu of the Object Changeability pop-up.

Decisions must be made regarding whether these object types should be directly maintainable in production.

Upgrades

Upgrades are changes to an SAP system that bring it to a new release or patch level. These upgrades typically introduce code, data changes, and new functionalities that must be applied in sequential fashion. *Release upgrades* are more involved than *patch upgrades*. To apply a release upgrade, typically a couple of days must be scheduled to do the work.

In contrast, patch upgrades are much quicker and require only an hour or two of downtime. Patch upgrades typically consist of bug fixes (but can also introduce new functionality) packaged as independent units for application to a system. Technically, patches are nothing more than transport requests developed in SAP development systems and are applied much in the manner that a transport is imported into a system but via a special transaction (SPAM). Patches typically come out on a regular cycle of a month or two.

Upgrades are also similar to transports in that they must be applied following the same transport route of the system landscape. Any upgrade should first be performed on the development system and, after it has been tested, moved downstream to quality assurance and production. Upgrades to the SAP BW system and source system can be done in parallel, but you should study the release notes for the upgrade carefully before doing so.

There can be many independent levels to which an upgrade may be applied, and each level has dependencies on the other levels to be at a specified release and patch level. Figure 11-17 shows a sampling (not the inclusive list) of the different levels that upgrades can apply to. With the exception of Business Content, all the different levels have separate release and patch cycles that must all be coordinated.

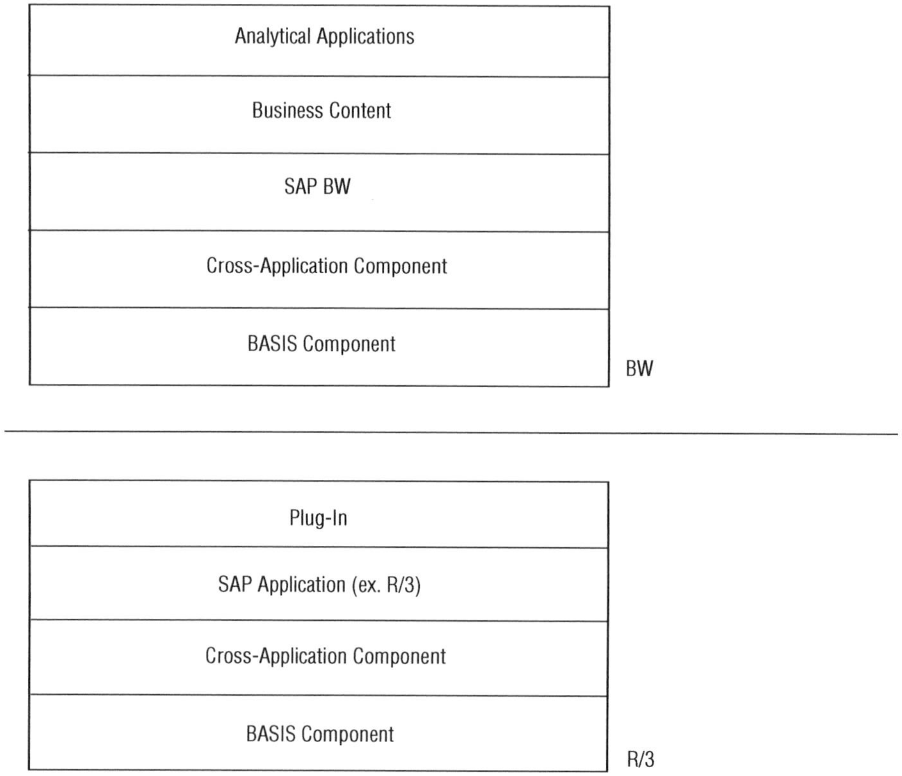

Figure 11-17 Different levels for upgrades

At the top of all levels, we have the analytic applications such as supply-chain analytics or customer relationship analytics which interacts with Business Content, as discussed in Chapter 10. Underlying Business Content is the SAP BW, which in turn sits on a core SAP system composed of a kernel and any cross-application components (such as the ADK, TMS, batch scheduling, and so on). A source system like SAP R/3 itself sits on the same core SAP system, but the application layer is different (and can actually be many different layers for different applications). To extract from this system, a plug-in must be added on to the source system (containing the BW Business Content DataSources).

There is another dimension to the coordination of different upgrade levels that are the front-end components. Deploying upgrades to front-ends for a large, geographically dispersed organization is no small task. Matters are compounded when the front-end upgrades are add-ins to popular products such as Excel, which may be different from desktop to desktop (on different operating systems, on different releases, with different add-ins). Third-party solutions such as Citrix alleviate the problem by providing users a window to the server where the front-end is installed. These products have been successful with deploying the BEx Analyzer to large organizations.

However, the Web is changing all the rules. With the jump in reporting functionality, Web applications are a very attractive alternative to the BEx Analyzer, especially from a deployment and upgrade perspective.

Two types of patches can be applied to a system: a functionality patch and a stabilization patch. If the patch is a *functionality patch*, you should stay a patch behind. If the patch is a *stabilization patch*, the patch consists only of notes to fix bugs and errors. These patches should be applied as the need warrants. SAP has an aggressive patch schedule, and your implementation should not fall too far behind to avoid the application of too many manual note corrections to the system and to avoid falling into the unfortunate circumstance of being on a patch level that is no longer supported.

In SAP BW, a conceptual distinction should be made between technical upgrades and functional upgrades. A *technical upgrade* of an SAP BW system does not change any of the preexisting information models in the system. A *functional upgrade* does so either by taking advantage of new functionalities or information modeling options or reactivating Business Content. Upgrading Business Content requires reactivation of the Business Content on the new BW release or patch level. When reactivating, you have the option of accepting changes per metadata object. More explicitly, you have the option to overwrite the existing objects with the new Business Content, keep the existing content, or merge the new changes to existing content (the last option is ideal when content has been custom-extended and you want to incorporate new Business Content). You should have a plan on how to adopt new Business Content and select options carefully in order to avoid losing work.

Information on new Business Content can be found in a variety of sources on the Web. If Business Content belongs to a vertical, each industry has its own area where industry Business Content can be described. There is also application-specific Business Content that can be covered by application-specific areas, such as SAP SCM or SAP CRM. The SAP BW help portal has extensive coverage on Business Content. The release and patch schedules (availability and maintenance), as well as cross-compatibilities, are well documented on the SAP Service Marketplace.

Summary

This chapter described the most important aspects of SAP BW-related administrative topics, categorizing them into application-oriented and system-oriented administration.

Application-oriented administration consists of process chains, data management tasks, application management activities, monitoring and troubleshooting. Data management tasks are central to SAP BW administration comprised of extraction and data load processing.

System-oriented tasks consist of the regular maintenance activities found in any SAP system such as information lifecycle management, authorizations, transports and upgrades. SAP BW specific functionalities were covered in relationship to the standard system tasks involved.

In addition, the current release of SAP BW offers significant enhancements consisting of new process chain types, near-line storage, analysis authorizations and BI administration cockpit that extend the SAP BW administration management functionality and ease the duties of SAP BW system administrators.

Chapter 12 picks up on system administration with a specific focus on performance optimization, especially performance management.

Performance Planning and Management

Performance is one of the key success factors of every IT system or application. It requires careful planning and constant attention, even more so for data warehouse systems and reporting and analysis applications. In contrast to operational environments, data warehouse administrators are confronted with large or very large amounts of data that must be handled, as well as a discontinuous, unpredictable user behavior.

For a data warehouse project to be successful, performance considerations have to be part of every single project phase, from requirements analysis (via design, implementation, and testing) to deployment and finally when administering and maintaining the deployed applications. This chapter looks at performance as a two-step process: performance planning and performance management.

Performance planning is part of the system-development process and involves critical reviews of the requirements and the chosen information models from a performance point of view. This includes designing an appropriate information flow and corresponding system landscape; implementing efficient transformations; defining highly parallel data-load and data maintenance process chains; and, finally, managing user expectations. Performance planning lays the foundation for the overall system performance; correcting mistakes made in performance planning can be very expensive and may involve redesigning parts of the application. In particular, managing user expectations should not be underestimated; losing user acceptance because of insufficient performance, or performance just perceived as being insufficient, is easy. Winning the users back is a very cumbersome task, if possible at all.

Performance management, on the other hand, is part of ongoing system administration and maintenance activities. It involves proactive monitoring of the relevant processes and resources in the system and utilizing the available tools and techniques to optimize performance. These tools and techniques include building aggregates, use of OLAP cache, use of precalculation, as well as system administration steps (such as tuning DB or OS parameters) and capacity planning measures (such as adding application servers or upgrading hardware components).

Much of performance planning and performance management centers on the trade-offs between space/flexibility/load time on the one hand and reporting time on the other (Figure 12-1).

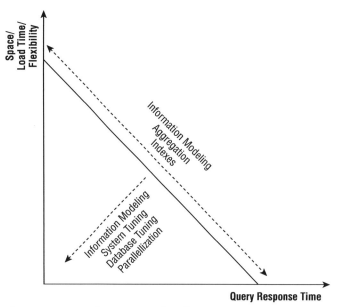

Figure 12-1 Performance trade-offs

The first trade-off is between time and space. Allocation of additional space can take the form of redundant storage of different aggregation levels of data, redundant storage of precalculated query sets, additional indexes on Data-Store Objects, and an additional index in the BI accelerator; this allows you to optimize query response times by choosing the most cost-effective manner of providing the desired result.

Along with this trade-off is a second trade-off between data-load time and query response times — the more redundant objects are created to optimize reporting performance, the more time is required to load data and maintain the redundant storage objects.

A third-trade off is between flexibility (or functionality or user requirements) and query response times, where functionality, flexibility, or both are sacrificed to improve reporting time.

Two types of performance optimizations are shown in Figure 12-1. The first one moves along the trade-off line, either sacrificing or saving space, load time, and flexibility versus query response times. The second one actually moves the trade-off curve itself to a more optimum level, closer to the lower-left corner of the diagram. Information modeling is the only performance optimization technique that influences both types of optimizations to a certain degree: the first one by affecting flexibility and functionality, the second one by, for example, designing an information model that ensures a high degree of parallel processing.

There is no silver bullet for performance optimization of data warehouse systems. Building a high-performance data warehouse application requires careful planning, monitoring, and optimization. The goal here is to enable you to effectively plan for and manage performance. The first half of this chapter introduces the options in planning for optimal performance, covering the impacts of information modeling and information flow, as well as system landscape and process design. The second half focuses on the performance management process and the tools SAP BW and SAP NetWeaver offer in support of these processes.

Recommendations for configuring specific parts of your system and other detailed information relevant for performance planning and optimization are available from the SAP Service Marketplace (`http://service.sap.com`), from database vendors, and from hardware/system software vendors. These recommendations are highly dependent on your specific combination of hardware, operating system software, and database management software, and their respective versions or release levels and, therefore, cannot be covered in this book. Generally, you should have experienced consultants support the performance planning and management activities.

Performance Planning

Planning for optimal performance already starts in the early phases of a data warehouse project — the project planning and requirements analysis phases, where initial infrastructure decisions are prepared and user expectations and requirements are collected and addressed. Technical design and implementation are crucial project phases for performance planning, where an information model, transformation processes, and queries are designed and implemented. The testing and rollout phases finally yield valuable assumptions on user behavior and allow advance planning for redundant storage of aggregates, the need for utilizing the BI accelerator or additional indexes.

The most important focus of performance planning is to ensure that all the things that are painful to change after going live with the system are designed properly (namely, the information model, batch processes, and the system infrastructure). In addition, when conducting any performance planning, you should adhere to the following two general guidelines:

- **Only use what you need** — Store everything you may need in the data warehouse layer. Keep the amount of data stored in the InfoMart layer to what you need for reporting and analysis on a regular basis, thus keeping storage requirements and processing time low.

- **Do as much as you can in parallel** — Try to maximize the utilization of your system by planning for as high a degree of parallelization as possible.

Managing User Expectations

As a rule of thumb, the user community of a data warehouse is composed of the following:

- About 75 percent occasional users who mainly execute queries customized to their needs

- About 20 percent frequent users who mainly execute existing parameterized queries and navigate through the query result set

- About 5 percent power users or analysts performing complex analysis tasks

There are different challenges attached to estimating the system load for each group of users. For the group of occasional users, the system load distribution is usually pretty stable, with relatively low system loads most times and peak system loads at certain times (for example, beginning of a new week or month or early in the morning). Knowing the peaks for this group is an important part of effective planning of resources, to ensure that the system can support the workload during these peak times without major performance degradation. In addition to these predictable peak times, frequent users may cause additional peak times whenever a certain business event or trend requires further analysis along the predefined analysis paths.

The most difficult group to deal with is the power user or analyst group, which tends to have a fairly erratic system load distribution. This is caused by the use of more advanced analytic functionality on a broader and more granular spectrum of data outside the expected analysis paths.

To achieve a maximum of user acceptance for a data warehouse implementation, you should be sure to collect and assess user expectations about performance, identify gaps, and then set expectations appropriately. Managing user expectations does not actually improve performance; it helps to close the potential gap between the user's performance expectations and what is achievable with a reasonable amount of money and time spent on the project.

Information Modeling

The biggest potential for performance improvement lies in the requirements analysis and design phases, ultimately resulting in an information model and information flow. This chapter extends the discussion of information modeling from Chapter 4, focusing on the performance impacts of available modeling options for the different types of InfoProviders: InfoCubes, DataStore Objects, master data, MultiProviders, and VirtualProviders.

As with other commercially available BI applications, the options to optimize performance by changing the physical data model used to store InfoCubes, DataStore Objects, or master data are very limited and only indirectly available through SAP BW configuration options like line-item dimensions. Using the right objects and techniques for your requirements from those available (and setting these objects up correctly) still has a huge impact on your system performance.

InfoCube Modeling

InfoCubes are still the most important and most visible InfoProviders for reporting and analysis purposes. Developing the best possible information model for InfoCubes has a significant impact on user acceptance of the data warehouse. Much of this whole section is, therefore, focused on evaluating the different modeling options available from a performance point of view.

How Does SAP BW Execute Queries?

To fully understand the pros and cons of the different InfoCube modeling options available, let's look more closely at how SAP BW actually executes queries. The following pseudocode illustrates this from a 10,000-foot perspective. Note that the purpose of this code is to illustrate the process rather than describe the actual programs (which obviously are much more sophisticated) and that the following description does not apply to query execution when there are BI accelerator indexes available for query execution. The BI accelerator will be discussed in more detail in the section titled "Optimizing Query Performance," later in this chapter.

```
*** STEP 1 – Prepare query execution
Convert selections into surrogate key representation.
Generate optimized temporary hierarchy table.
```

```
*** STEP 2 - Prepare query execution
Generate query view
Open query cursor

*** STEP 3 - Execute query
Loop at cursor.
  Execute user exit for virtual characteristics / key figures.
  Apply dynamic filters.
Endloop.

*** STEP 4 - Complete query result
Read key values, texts, display attributes, hierarchies.
Format query results.
```

The first step of query execution converts selection criteria specified in the query definition into the surrogate key format. For restrictions on characteristic values, this basically means determining the surrogate keys for all key values used in the selection. In case of selections on hierarchies, a temporary table is generated containing the surrogate key values for all relevant nodes of the hierarchy.

Step 2 generates an SQL statement used to create a temporary database view, which is then used to open an SQL cursor for the required result set. In Figure 12-2, #1 shows the access path of such a generated SQL statement for a simple query not using any hierarchies or navigational attributes.

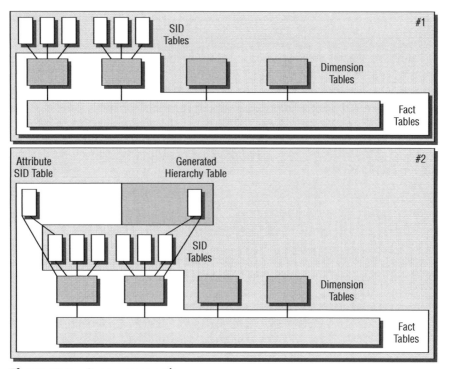

Figure 12-2 Query access paths

A standard query effectively generates and executes a join of the dimension tables required (through characteristics used in the query definition) to the two fact tables. Keep in mind that no nonessential dimension table is used in the join and that no surrogate key table is used at this time, as illustrated in #1 of Figure 12-2. The generated SQL query returns surrogate key values for all characteristics and (usually) aggregated values for all key figures used in the query definition.

The third step reads the data set retrieved for the open cursor and applies user exits and dynamic filters (such as conditions and exceptions) to each data record.

Step 4 completes query execution by reading texts, display attributes, and hierarchies from the respective tables (using the surrogate key values retrieved in Step 3) and formats the output accordingly.

Use of Line-Item Dimensions

The SAP BW concept of line-item dimensions corresponds to what is known to the data warehouse community as *degenerate dimensions* — dimensions where the key has a significant cardinality. *Cardinality* refers to the number of distinct values represented in a set or table column. A relatively high cardinality results in dimension tables that are large, sometimes nearly as large as the fact table itself. A join operation on high cardinality table columns represents a higher-than-normal process workload because of the large number of combinations that must be evaluated to execute the join.

Data warehouse developers developed various ideas of how to effectively support line-item dimensions. SAP BW provides the ability to designate dimensions (with one and only one characteristic) as line-item dimensions. The result is that instead of generating a dimension table holding the surrogate keys of the characteristics of that dimension, the surrogate key for the characteristic's semantic key is directly stored in the fact table.

Line-item dimensions are an effective means to speed up both data loads and query execution. Data-load performance is improved by eliminating the need for dimension key handling for a large number of values during the load processing. On the query-execution side, the join operation is much more efficient because it avoids the expensive join of the high cardinality of the dimension table to fact table. SAP recommends using line-item dimensions only for very large dimensions (as typically found in line-item-level data, hence the name). However, line-item dimensions have successfully been used for applications with large numbers of customers and large numbers of products or product variants or even in scenarios with a small number of characteristics in the InfoCube and no large volumes at all.

As will be seen later, the same concept of storing surrogate keys in the fact table is used in maintaining special types of aggregates — so-called *flat aggregates*. Note that a limitation of line-item dimensions is that only one single characteristic can be assigned to that dimension. Line-item dimensions can only be modeled prior to loading data.

Use of High Cardinality Dimensions

Another option to control query performance is the "High Cardinality" flag that can be assigned to dimensions. Depending on the underlying DBMS, SAP BW generates different types of indexes for the dimension fields of the fact table. In Oracle-based systems, the standard index type for dimension fields is a bitmap index, while for high cardinality dimensions BTree indexes are used. BTree indexes can provide faster access to columns with high cardinalities. BTree indexes can be assigned for dimensions that have more than one characteristic and can be assigned even if data already exists in the InfoCube. In general, dimension tables that are 10 percent or greater of the InfoCube fact table size should be considered candidates for either line-item dimensions or cardinality flag.

Use of Navigational Attributes

Navigational attributes are special because they are not stored in the dimension tables but in the attribute tables of characteristics used in the InfoCube definition (for example, `material group` as a navigational attribute of `material` and is stored in the `material` master data tables). Attributes must be marked as navigational attributes when modeling both the InfoObject and InfoCube definition in order to make them available for reporting. Setting this flag for at least one attribute causes the system to create one of the navigational attribute SID tables discussed in Chapter 4 and to store the surrogate key values for this attribute in this table. Note that SIDs of navigational attributes are not stored in any of the InfoCube tables. Changing the value of a navigational attribute, therefore, does not require any realignment of the InfoCube. It may, however, require realignment of aggregates containing the navigational attribute.

The access path of a generated SQL query for this scenario is shown in Figure 12-2, #2. The navigational attribute SID table is joined to the dimension table (for example, `product dimension`) that contains the anchor characteristic (`material`), which itself is joined to the fact tables. The performance implications of using navigational attributes are clear. Joining additional tables to a query increases query response times. The actual impact on reporting performance corresponds to the cardinality of the master data attribute tables involved, the number of navigational attributes used in the query, and, of course, the selectivity of the query. The smaller the cardinality, the lower the number of navigational attributes, and the higher the selectivity of the query, the better the performance will be. Because of the consistent use of surrogate IDs in these tables, however, the effect of using navigational attributes in an InfoCube on query execution performance are kept to a minimum. Possible performance problems can be addressed by defining appropriate indexes or aggregates (discussed in the section titled "Optimizing Query Performance," later in this chapter) at the cost of having to maintain that extra index or aggregate.

NOTE Defining additional indexes on the navigational attribute SID tables improves performance in cases where medium- to high-cardinality tables are read with high selectivity.

While performance for InfoCube data loads is not affected by the use of navigational attributes, they definitely add some overhead to the master data load process, which now needs to maintain one or two additional tables (plus indexes if defined). This may significantly decrease data-load and data maintenance performance in applications such as CRM analytics, where many navigational attributes are required to perform complex analysis on millions of customer master data records. Right from the start of the modeling process, you should differentiate priorities for navigational attribute requirements and factor those in to your modeling decision.

Use of Hierarchies

Using hierarchies leads to similar query access paths as using navigational attributes. This is shown in Figure 12-2, #2, where an additional, generated hierarchy table is joined to the fact table. While the core query access plan is similar, two additional steps are required in the overall query execution process to retrieve the query results.

In Step 1 of our high-level algorithm, a temporary hierarchy table holding all hierarchy nodes selected by the filter associated to the query is created on the fly by reading the hierarchy, applying the selections to the hierarchy, and storing the remaining nodes in the temporary tables. The time required to execute this part of the operation depends on the size of the hierarchy and on the complexity of the selection criteria defined. In Step 4 of that algorithm, the query results must be rehashed according to the actual structure of the hierarchy.

When a hierarchy is accessed in a query, the performance is largely dependent upon the number of nodes in the hierarchy and the number of levels of the hierarchy. The higher the number of nodes and levels, the more time it takes to compute the query results. In general, using hierarchies is more performance intensive than using navigational attributes.

Hierarchies do not affect load performance for InfoCubes or master data texts or attributes. Of course, it takes some extra time to load hierarchies into the system.

Use of Virtual Characteristics and Key Figures

Virtual characteristics and key figures allow you to replace stored values of characteristics and key figures with dynamically calculated values. Looking back at our query execution algorithm, it is obvious that this functionality must be used with extreme care because of its potential impact on performance. First of all, the corresponding code is executed for every single record retrieved from the InfoCube, so ensure that it is optimized from a performance point of view. Secondly, using virtual characteristics and key figures may force the Analytic Engine to add characteristics to the query, increasing the size of the dataset in the query operation and, in many cases, the granularity — or number of records returned by the query. Carefully review the requirements. In many cases, virtual key characteristics or figures can instead be computed during staging or during query execution with less impact on performance.

Modeling DataStore Objects

Performance-relevant modeling choices for DataStore Objects include SID generation for DataStore Objects, additional indexes, and three different types of DataStore Objects: write-optimized, direct-update, and standard. SID generation for DataStore Objects causes the Staging Engine to compute and store surrogate keys for the fields of the DataStore Object and effectively slows down the data-load process. This option should only be used for DataStore Objects frequently used for reporting purposes. Reporting on DataStore Objects will still be possible without enabling this option, although with lower reporting performance.

Indexes can be built on DataStore Objects using the application's utilities, resulting in BTree indexes on the active table at the database level. Indexes speed up query performance for queries that contain the characteristics defined in the index by accelerating the read operation for relevant values. Adding indexes on a DataStore Object affects data-load performance in that new records must also be inserted into the indexes (in addition to the active data table). Thus, be conservative in building indexes on DataStore Objects, and bear in mind the data-load performance tradeoff.

As already discussed in Chapter 4, standard DataStore Objects basically are collections of similarly structured flat tables with key fields and data fields, allowing you to keep track of changes in a so-called *change log*. The change log is generated after the actual upload of data in a second step called *activation*. Activation performs an after-image handling by identifying inserted and updated data records and tracking both in the change log.

Write-optimized and direct-update DataStore Objects are both updated directly, either through transformation rules (as for the write-optimized DataStore Object) or through an API (as for the direct-update DataStore Object), and do not require an activation step. In scenarios where no change log is required, using write-optimized or direct-update DataStore Objects can significantly speed up the upload process. Figure 12-3 illustrates the load process for the different types of DataStore Objects.

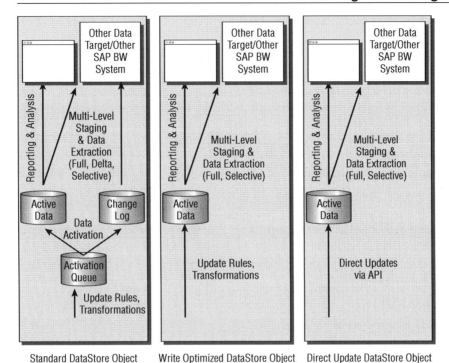

Figure 12-3   Different types of DataStore Objects

General performance improvements of recent releases of SAP BW include an optimization of the activation process, tools supporting user-defined database partitioning (see the section titled "Database Partitioning," later in this chapter) and improvements in the parallelization of load and activation processes.

Master Data Modeling

The most important performance aspects of master data modeling are related to time dependency and the navigational status of attributes, which have already been discussed in the section titled "Use of Navigational Attributes." Time-dependent master data attributes, texts, and hierarchies should be used with care. Time-dependent master data tables can grow rapidly, because every change of a single time-dependent attribute creates another record in the time-dependent master data tables.

The introduction of time-dependent aggregates (see the section titled "Aggregates," later in this chapter) provides some (limited) options for performance optimization. Still, you should make sure to estimate the expected number of changes before deciding to flag a particular attribute, the texts, or a particular hierarchy as time dependent, and you should make certain it is required to be time dependent. An average change rate of 10 changes per year brings a customer master data table from 1 million records to 10 million records per year. Also, consider reducing the update frequency and the granularity required for validity periods down to minimum. If those average 10 changes per year all occur in, say, three months and the granularity of the validity period is one month, the system only needs to store three different records instead of 10.

For some applications, many or most of the queries actually request the current value of an attribute, while only a portion request the historical values. In these cases, modeling the same attribute twice in two different manners (as a time-dependent and as a non-time-dependent attribute) may help speed up query performance of the non-time-dependent attributes. This approach avoids heavy use of time-dependent aggregates and allows non-time-dependent queries to access the smaller non-time-dependent master data tables and should be considered when there is a potential for significant data volumes.

VirtualProviders

VirtualProviders are used to avoid redundant storage and staging of operational data and to provide real-time access to information stored in the operational system. Using VirtualProviders may positively affect overall system performance by eliminating some data-load processing and its associated resource utilization.

From a reporting performance point of view, VirtualProviders based on the data transfer process usually can't provide the same kind of performance compared to when data is stored persistently in the BI system, for two main reasons. First, queries against VirtualProviders are executed on the source system, using data structures optimized for transaction processing instead of reporting.

Second, SAP VirtualProviders are calling data-extraction programs available through the BW Service API. Most of these extractors are not capable of performing dynamic aggregations according to the query definition. Granular data is sent from the source system to the requesting SAP BW system, and aggregation is performed there as part of the query processing. VirtualProviders should be used with caution wherever real-time access to operational data is required. Queries against VirtualProviders should be highly selective to avoid long runtimes. Performance of accessing VirtualProviders can be optimized by adding indexes to the underlying database tables in the remote system. However, be sure to consider the performance impact that adding indexes has on update processes in the remote system.

For VirtualProviders based on BAPIs or function modules, reporting performance highly depends on the implementation of the BAPIs or function modules used as well as the underlying data structures.

MultiProviders

MultiProviders define a dynamic union of InfoProviders such as InfoCubes, DataStore Objects, master data tables, InfoSets, or aggregation levels. As the first step when a query is executed against a MultiProvider, it is decomposed into subqueries to be run against the underlying InfoProviders. The second step executes the resulting subqueries either sequentially or in parallel, depending on the settings for this MultiProvider. The final step applies a *union* operation to all query results, providing the final query result set.

Using MultiProviders is an important information modeling technique for speeding up performance, in that parallel execution of the decomposed query can help to improve reporting performance by better utilizing available system resources — at the cost of additional overhead required for decomposing queries and computing the union of the query results. The system resource requirements for processing parallel subqueries should be considered. In cases where system resources are scarce, switching the MultiProviders to sequential query execution should be considered. However, note that the significant performance benefits of MultiProviders are not fully realized in this case.

The total overhead of using MultiProviders compared to physical InfoProviders for reporting performance is low and can be ignored for most cases.

Whenever a certain query is defined in a way that only a subset of the underlying InfoProviders is required to provide correct query results, you should add a filter on the required InfoProviders using the special characteristic 0INFOPROV to avoid running subqueries on the other InfoProviders. More details on optimizing query execution on MultiProviders are available in the SAP Service Marketplace.

> **NOTE** MultiProviders do not require additional storage; they just define a view across multiple InfoProviders.

Although SAP BW does not directly support aggregates for MultiProviders, it does use aggregates defined for underlying InfoCubes wherever possible.

Logical Partitioning

In many cases, performance of data maintenance functions such as data loads, aggregate rollups, or InfoCube compression and reporting functions can be significantly improved by splitting the overall data volume into several manageable pieces. While the application provides the ability to utilize database partitioning features for InfoCube fact tables using time characteristics, partitioning on other characteristics values, such as organizational characteristics, can only be achieved by defining several standard InfoProviders — one for each value or range of values defining a certain partition — together with a

MultiProvider combining the partitions. This approach is called *logical partitioning*. Note that logical partitioning does not make use of any database partitioning features.

An example of logical partitioning by region is shown on the left-hand side of Figure 12-4. A side effect of logical partitioning is an increased degree of flexibility regarding the data models of the underlying InfoProviders because these InfoProviders don't need to be identical in structure. The sales InfoCube for Europe might actually provide slightly different information compared to the Americas sales InfoCube (for example, additional characteristics or key figures), as long as it provides all information required for the MultiProvider. You could even replace an InfoCube with a DataStore Object or add a Virtual-Provider for real-time data from an operational system. A drawback of this approach is that there are multiple sets of transformation rules to be maintained, one for each participating InfoProvider.

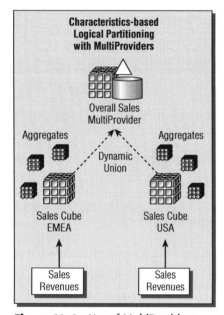 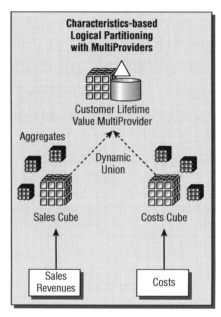

Figure 12-4   Use of MultiProviders

The right-hand side of Figure 12-4 shows a cross-application information model using MultiProviders that can be used instead of defining a single large InfoCube storing the same information. Again, the same performance considerations discussed earlier apply, in addition to achieving an easier-to-understand and easier-to-use information model. Note that because of the nature of the "union" operation performed as part of queries executed on MultiProviders, characteristics not available in all underlying InfoProviders will have an initial value, usually represented as "#."

Database Partitioning

The basic idea behind database partitioning is to split a physical table and its indexes into several smaller physical tables and indexes. In SAP BW, database partitioning is used for InfoCube fact tables, DataStore Objects, and the Persistent Staging Area (PSA). For InfoCubes and DataStore Objects, partitioning can be defined using the DW Workbench and is completely transparent to information modeling, data loads, or reporting and analysis. Different partitioning techniques such as range partitioning (shown in Figure 12-5) or hash partitioning are offered by different DBMSs. Changing this setting in a production system requires deleting the contents of the InfoProvider, adjusting the setting, reactivating it, and finally reloading it with data. Following are the main advantages of partitioning from an SAP point of view:

- **Faster inserts/updates** — Mass inserts/updates on single or several smaller partitions run faster than inserts/updates on a single large table, mainly because of reduced effort for index maintenance. Another positive effect on performance can be achieved by parallelizing mass inserts/updates on partitioned tables.

- **Selective reads** — Data warehouse queries commonly include some time characteristic in their selection criteria. Figure 12-5 shows an InfoCube with range partitioning by calendar month and a query requesting information about the last three months of 2005 using range partitioning. Whenever the partitioning criterion is part of the filters of the query, the DBMS recognizes that it only has to read a subset of the partitions. In this example, the DBMS reads only three out of 24 partitions. Depending on the application, selective reads may dramatically speed up query execution time.

- **Faster deletes** — For deleting a contiguous range of data, tables partitioned using range partitioning allow using the DROP PARTITION statement whenever the partitioning criteria is contained in the selection criteria for the delete operation, instead of having to use the DELETE FROM statement.

NOTE There are cases where the query does not specify the actual partitioning criterion (for example, month) but instead specifies a filter on some other time characteristic (for example, quarter or day). Normally, this would prevent the DBMS from performing selective reads. However, adding redundant filters on the partitioning criterion — eventually filled by a user exit, based upon the actual filter values — will allow the DBMS to perform selective reads.

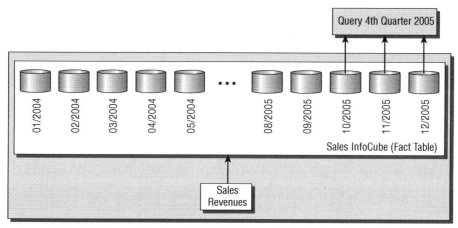

Figure 12-5 Database range partitioning

NOTE Aggregates containing the partitioning characteristic automatically take on the same partitioning properties as the parent InfoCube at the time of aggregate definition.

Database partitioning may already make sense for relatively low data volumes (for example, a couple of million records). However, the more partitions the database system creates, the higher the overhead for decomposing, executing, dispatching, and merging query results.

Complex Aggregations

Where aggregates clearly provide the advantage of being completely transparent to the end user, the aggregation functions available are restricted to summation, maximum, and minimum. Additional aggregation functions (such as average, counting, deviation, and variance) are available under certain restrictions, but more complex aggregation functions are required in many applications, such as balanced scorecards. The definitions of high-level key performance indicators (KPIs) such as customer lifetime value and return on investment are based on multiple low-level key figures sourced from different applications using different aggregations paths.

High-level KPIs typically require cross-application information models like those shown in the text that follows. The dynamic aggregation variant stores data in two InfoProviders and merges those in a single MultiProvider, while the static aggregation variant stores precalculated values on a higher aggregation level in a single standard InfoCube. Figure 12-6 illustrates both variants of implementing aggregations.

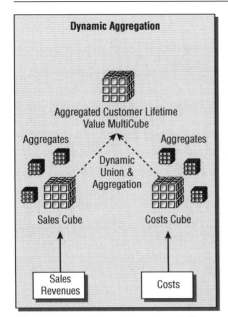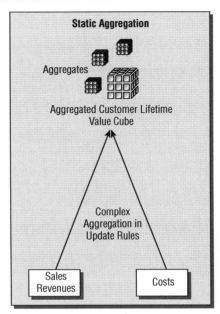

Figure 12-6   Dynamic versus static aggregation

Static aggregation allows more complex, aggregated key figures to be calculated at load time, reducing the time required for online calculations at query runtime. Dynamic aggregation is more flexible because of a higher level of granularity in the standard InfoCubes, but it requires all (or most) calculations and aggregations to be executed during query runtime, which can significantly increase query response times. Of course, all considerations of cross-application information models mentioned previously still apply here.

Multiple Staging Levels

Multiple staging levels are an integral part of today's layered data warehousing architectures discussed in Chapter 5. Another important reason for adding staging levels above the data warehouse layer are complex, application-level transformations, sometimes requiring intermediate storage of data in a specific format.

At first glance, an improvement of data-load performance is not expected after adding staging levels, because additional processing is required to load into multiple levels. However, if you take a step back and look at the whole picture, you see that adding staging layers may actually improve the performance of the overall load process, as the comparison of single-level and multi-level staging approaches in Figure 12-7 shows.

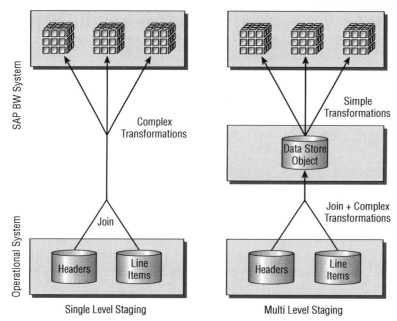

Figure 12-7 Multilevel staging performance

Surprisingly, transformations can be very CPU-intensive processes with most of the time spent processing data rather than reading or writing it. The more complex the transformation rules are for each of the InfoProviders, the more effective a multilevel staging approach can be. The key here is applying complex or expensive transformation rules (such as database lookups) only once before writing into the first staging level and only leaving simple transformations for the second staging level. As a side effect, the multilevel staging approach easily allows more flexible scheduling of the individual transformation processes. Some InfoProviders may need to be updated daily or even more frequently, while others are updated on a monthly basis, although all are using the same data sources.

Reporting performance is usually not affected by the number of staging levels. Reporting users and analysts usually just access the highest level. Multilevel staging may, however, enable you to choose a less granular information model, thereby reducing the size of the InfoProviders used for reporting purposes and letting the users access the data warehouse level for integrated, granular data where necessary. This way, multilevel staging may indirectly help improve reporting performance.

Staging data into the operational data store layer is not discussed in this context, because the ODS layer is typically used for operational reporting purposes rather than as a source for the staging process. However, if used in such a way, the same considerations apply for the ODS layer as well.

In summary, there are situations where multiple staging levels actually help to improve both load and reporting performance. Overall, however, in most situations, single staging levels provide better data-load performance without affecting reporting performance.

Process Design

Process design primarily involves scheduling the various data-load and data management processes (such as aggregate rollups, InfoCube compressions, index creation, and calculation of database statistics) as well as information broadcasting related batch processes (such as precalculation of queries, batch printing, and so forth) in such a way that the total runtime required to perform all tasks is minimized, all dependencies between different processes are accounted for, and all processes are aligned with processes on other systems in the overall system landscape. For all local processes, process chains, introduced in Chapter 3 and discussed in more detail in Chapter 11, are used to organize and schedule processes. For cross-system scheduling, SAP BW provides interfaces to external job-scheduling tools.

The main guideline for process design is to utilize as many resources available as possible. Experience shows that SAP BW data-load jobs scale pretty well with multiple CPUs, allowing you to schedule as many parallel data-load jobs as there are CPUs available in the system. I/O-intensive jobs such as aggregate rollup, InfoCube compression, and index creations can be scheduled for parallel execution as long as there are no I/O bottlenecks and enough temporary disk space for simultaneous sort operations is available.

System Landscape Design and Setup

Besides information modeling, another cornerstone of performance planning is system landscape design and setup, which requires a basic understanding of the technology used. This is especially true for standard software, where, compared to custom systems, the options to change or exchange parts of this technology are limited. Figure 12-8 shows the SAP application server multitier architecture of all SAP systems.

The core of an SAP BW system landscape consists of a database server, a number of application servers, and a number of clients communicating with one of the application servers. Additional servers (such as separate EP servers or BI accelerator servers) are usually part of a complete system landscape.

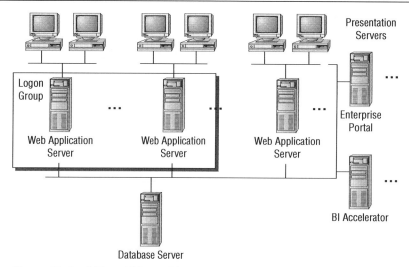

Figure 12-8   SAP multitier architecture

Starting an SAP BW implementation requires planning the system landscape; sizing the database and application servers; estimating network bandwidth requirements; and making sure the front-end systems match the system requirements. SAP provides detailed information on how to size, install, configure, and monitor all these different systems in their Service Marketplace, updating this information on a regular basis. Rather than merely restating that material, the next sections provide a basic understanding of the performance-relevant aspects of the functionality of these different components of an SAP BW system landscape.

Database and Application Servers

Scalability is a key requirement for all SAP BW systems where an exact sizing approach is not feasible. Scalability can be achieved in two different ways: by adding application servers to the multitier system landscape or by increasing the performance of the underlying hardware by adding resources.

Adding application servers in combination with the dynamic load balancing across the application servers of a logon group addresses bottlenecks on the application-server side (typically all CPU heavy processes). Dedicated application servers or logon groups allow managing response times for mission-critical applications separately. Overall, SAP BW actually scales fairly linearly with the amount of main memory used for buffering by both the database server and the application server, with the number and speed of the CPUs available in both types of servers and finally with IO throughput.

While sizing application servers is a less critical part of planning for a system landscape, sizing the database server and making sure the database server is scalable, on the other hand, are among the most critical parts. All actual database requests from all application servers — and, in turn, all client requests — are performed by and on the database server. The SAP architecture utilizes extensive buffering of frequently used data in the main memory of application servers to bridge this potential bottleneck on the application servers.

However, in SAP BW systems, database buffering is less effective than in operational systems, because the amount of data read from the database and transferred to the application servers (for example, fact table data) is too large for typical buffers, and the buffering algorithm has limited or no visibility of the actual application requirements. Buffering is supplemented by query-caching algorithms explained later in this chapter. Support for distributed databases, allowing you to distribute the load to multiple servers, is currently limited and has rarely been used.

Sizing an SAP BW system (or any other data warehouse, for that matter) requires reliable information about a number of parameters, such as the number of users, the amount of disk space needed, and a reliable forecast of the actual user behavior. While the user behavior may be relatively easy to predict for standard application scenarios (for example, the sales controlling department checking the results of last month at the beginning of a new month), it is virtually unpredictable for ad-hoc analysis performed by business analysts or power users. Another issue with predicting user behavior is that a successful implementation drags a lot of interest by other business areas, potentially increasing the amount of data and the number of users.

A good starting point for all sizing efforts is the SAP QuickSizer available in the SAP Service Marketplace (`alias  /quicksizer`). Results of the sizing process will then need to be mapped to hardware components available. Seeking support from hardware vendors at this point is strongly recommended.

Concrete recommendations for a specific setup of the different components of the system landscape are beyond the scope of this book. SAP supports many combinations of hardware architectures, system software, and database management systems and continuously develops the configuration options of its own software. You should follow the information offered in the SAP Service Marketplace and corresponding offerings of the vendors of hardware, system software, and database management software when setting up the system. Periodically monitoring changes to this information and adjusting the systems accordingly helps ensure optimal performance.

Operation Modes

As discussed previously, SAP BW system performance scales pretty well with the number of CPUs. While determining the required number of CPUs is part of the sizing process, administrators must ensure that CPUs can actually be utilized by defining how many so-called *work processes* of what type are available at a specific point in time. The SAP application server distinguishes five types of work processes:

- **Dialog processes** (type DIA) — These are used for processing dialog programs, such as the DW Workbench, the extraction monitor, online analysis and reporting requests, and data-load processes submitted online.

- **Batch processes** (type BTC) — These are required for any kind of process submitted for batch processing. Typical batch processes are data-load processes, aggregate rollups, and InfoCube compression.

- **Update processes** (type UPD and UP2) — These are used for asynchronous updates (known as V1 and V2 updates), update processes are not used by SAP BW. Still, at least one process must be available for technical reasons.

- **Enqueue processes** (type ENQ) — These are used for locking and unlocking objects. One process of this type will usually be sufficient.

- **Spool processes** (type SPO) — These execute print requests. Because most reports are usually printed from the client workstation, only a small number of spool processes are required (in many cases, a single process will be enough).

The so-called *operation mode* of an SAP system defines how many processes of what type are available. Different operation modes can be defined by the administrator and can be selected at runtime, allowing you to optimize the distribution of process types for specific needs. Different operation modes can be defined on different application servers so that you can easily set up specific application servers for batch-processing purposes.

Buffers and Memory

Supplemented by high-level query caching, buffering data and programs in the main memory of application servers is one of the keys to the performance of both the database and the application servers. Therefore, a general recommendation is to have as much main memory available as possible (and reasonable) and to use as much of that as possible for buffers and caching. Configuration recommendations again are available in the SAP Service Marketplace.

The most important buffers on an application server are the table buffers used to reduce the number of database accesses by buffering data on an application level. Two types of table buffers are available: a single record buffer and a generic key buffer. The *single record buffer* is used to buffer all access operations to master data tables, except for the hierarchy table (for example,

/BIO/HMATERIAL). The hierarchy table is buffered in the *generic key buffer* using the hierarchy identifier and the version as the generic key, effectively buffering a complete hierarchy. Buffering master data speeds up the retrieval of master data in reporting and analysis, as well as looking up surrogate keys during the loading process. InfoCubes, DataStore Objects, or PSA tables are not buffered at all. These are mostly used in complex database joins where the SAP application buffers are not applicable.

Another buffer relevant for load performance is the *number range buffer*, which is used to identify available surrogate keys from the number range table NRIV. In addition, a couple of buffers are used by the application server. However, the effect of these buffers on performance is small compared to that of the table buffers. Monitoring the utilization of buffers is discussed in the section titled "System Performance," later in this chapter.

General Database Setup

Having discussed buffering on the application-server side, it is obvious that buffering on the DBMS side also has a serious impact on performance. Additional configuration considerations on the database-server side include optimizer settings (such as star schema awareness), parallelization, and distributed data access.

Every SQL statement executed by the database management is optimized by a component usually referred to as the *optimizer*. To find the most efficient way of executing the statement, the optimizer needs information about the data model, found in the database schema, and statistical information about the actual field values of records stored in the database. Information about the data model allows the DBMS to take the specifics of the star schema data model into account. Statistical information (or *database statistics*) is used to estimate the cost of a specific database operation and the total cost of possible ways of executing a specific SQL statement.

Modern DBMSs allow you to execute data retrieval and manipulation operations in parallel, fully utilizing as many CPUs and IO channels as possible. Some DBMSs also allow you to distribute data to several physical servers, utilizing even more resources.

Physical Distribution of Data

Today, most SAP installations use SANs or comparable technologies for storage. These systems take care of optimizing many of the aspects of storing and retrieving data and hiding the actual physical distribution of data from the administrators of SAP systems.

However, to be able to optimize physical access to data, it is still worthwhile to understand the different types of data maintained in a typical SAP BW installation and how different processes make use of this data. The following six clusters of data are illustrated in Figure 12-9:

- InfoCube and DataStore Object data, stored in fact tables, dimension tables, and DataStore Object tables
- InfoCube and DataStore Object indexes
- Master data, stored in attribute, text, and hierarchy tables
- Temporary data, internally used by the DBMS (for example, for sorting purposes)
- Database transaction logs, internally used by the database management to allow rolling back or reprocessing transactions
- System data, such as configuration data, customization data, SAP BW metadata, program source code, and application logs

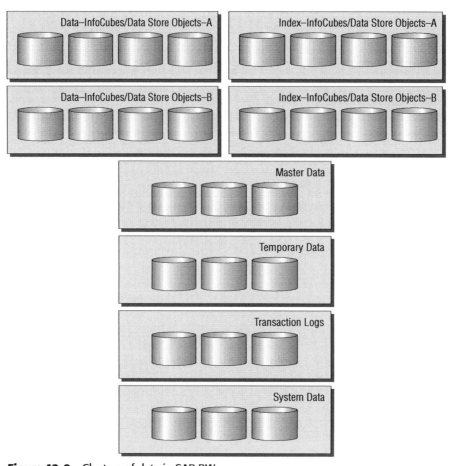

Figure 12-9 Clusters of data in SAP BW

Temporary data is heavily used as part of query execution, mostly for sorting processes inside the database. Database transaction logs are used to keep track of changes to data in the database to allow rolling back update transactions and for online backups. Separating physical access to these two data clusters from the physical access to the other data clusters can significantly help to resolve IO bottlenecks. More sophisticated approaches to improving IO performance are beyond the scope of this book. At this point, you should refer to the information provided by the vendors of storage subsystems.

Enterprise Portal Server

Sizing of the Enterprise Portal Server is not covered in this book. From a Portal point of view, SAP BW is just another content provider and does not affect the overall system load of the Portal server more than any other content provider.

BI Accelerator Server

The BI accelerator (discussed in the "Optimizing Query Performance" section, later in this chapter) can dramatically improve query performance for certain types of queries by maintaining specialized indexes. The BI accelerator requires separate, highly parallel (blade) servers. As of this writing, there is only little experience available as far as sizing of BI accelerator servers is concerned. More detailed information will be available on the SAP Service Marketplace.

Client Systems

Today, client systems no longer represent a major challenge in improving the overall performance, regardless of the choice of front end. Detailed information about hardware and software requirements for client systems is available in the SAP Service Marketplace.

Network Considerations

Driven by multimedia consumer applications, bandwidths available in local and global networks have increased dramatically during the last couple of years, so that the significance of network performance considerations has decreased. Still, it is worthwhile to keep an eye on the extra load that a data warehouse solution imposes on network traffic. Figure 12-8 not only shows the different systems participating in the SAP BW system landscape; it also shows some of the relevant network connections between those systems:

- **Between database server and application server** — This is the most critical network path in the system landscape. Every database request that cannot be served out of the buffers of the application server is transferred to the database server, and the resulting data set is transferred back to the application server. Network performance can seriously degrade when queries that return large result sets or massively parallel data loads are executed. In most cases, however, these systems are located in the same computing center and are connected by high-bandwidth local area networks. Application servers connecting to the database server using a slow network connection should not be used for massive data loads. On the other hand, client access to an application server through a slow network connection will not be able to return large query result sets with the same performance as local application servers.

- **Between application server and client workstation** — Client workstations executing queries via the BEx Analyzer usually require three to five times the bandwidth of standard SAP GUI applications. Client workstations using the Web to access queries or Web applications are comparable to other typical Web applications.

- **Between application server and Enterprise Portal (EP) servers** — In typical SAP BW installations, an EP server will serve as the main entry point for most users. The network communication load between these two servers still is low, as the actual Portal content and the query result sets are directly sent from the respective server to the client workstation.

- **Between application server and BI accelerator servers** — During data uploads to InfoCubes utilizing the BI accelerator, this server requires access to all data to update its indexes. The network connection between the BI accelerator server, the application server it communicates with, and the database server should be very fast. During query execution, the same considerations as between application and database servers apply for the BI accelerator server.

- **Between application server and source system** — Network traffic between the application servers and the source systems is determined by the amount of data extracted on the source system and transferred to the SAP BW system. The total network load may be everything from very low to very high additional traffic for large data volume applications.

- **Between application server and target system** — The data mart interface and the Open Hub Services allow you to create complex information-flow scenarios between multiple operational and data warehouse systems. This additional information flow in turn adds traffic to the network. The impact of this additional traffic needs to be considered on a case-by-case basis.

Performance Impact on Source Systems

Although not shown in Figure 12-8 as part of the system landscape architecture, source systems must be considered as part of your performance considerations when you are setting up the SAP BW system landscape. Source systems run extraction programs on a regular basis, adding to the normal system load caused by transaction and batch processing.

This may not be a problem from an overall system-load perspective. A successful implementation normally alleviates some of the load of the operational systems by taking over most of the system load caused by reporting and analysis. On the other hand, timing of extractions may become a problem. Operational systems often are occupied with running batch processes during the typical extraction time windows. High peak loads during these time windows may have an impact on sizing there.

Finally, there is a transition period from starting live operation of the SAP BW implementation to finally shutting down reporting services in the operational system, where the operational system may have to deal with both the reporting load and the extraction load. Performance planning must cover both scenarios to warrant the source system's performance standards.

Performance Management

Even if all performance-planning efforts are successful and the application initially presents itself with great performance, managing performance is crucial. It is even more so for data warehouse applications, where user behavior tends to be more dynamic compared to operational environments because the user's focus of analysis is constantly shifting, following the business issues that must be solved. Finally, the more successful the data warehouse, the more users from the same or other business areas it will attract.

Simply stated, managing performance means to constantly monitor the performance of all system components, starting with the application (reporting, analysis, and data-load performance) and including hardware, system software, database management system, and database server software, as well as application server software. Then it's just a matter of waiting for the squeaky wheel and fixing it.

System administrators already running an SAP NetWeaver-based system — the majority of SAP BW customers — will immediately feel familiar with the multitier architecture and the Computing Center Management System (CCMS) tools available for monitoring and tuning. Additional services around performance management available from SAP include Go Live Checks and periodical automated system checks called Early Watch sessions. Parts of the Early Watch sessions can be scheduled for low-utilization periods of time and evaluated by the administrator without the help of SAP.

This chapter is organized along the priorities of performance management. The higher the visibility of a potential performance problem from an end user's point of view, the more important it is to fix it quickly. Let's begin with a discussion of analysis and reporting performance, continuing with data loading and data management and concluding with the more technical topics.

BI Statistics

On request, SAP BW generates a comprehensive set of statistical information about all relevant reporting and data maintenance processes summarized under the term *BI Statistics*. The so-called *Technical Business Content* composed of a set of DataSources, InfoCubes, MultiProviders, Queries, and Web applications provides easy access to information query runtimes and warehouse management runtimes.

The information available through the Technical Business Content is available through the BI Administrator Cockpit summarizing the critical issues and through BEx Queries. *Time series queries* allow you to identify performance trends, make increased use of queries or performance degradation over time visible, or prove that perceived performance degradation does not exist. *Detail queries* allow detailed analysis of the specific queries, data load, or data management processes. The next two sections provide an overview of performance-relevant information available. A complete documentation of the Technical Business Content and the BI Administrator Cockpit is available as part of the SAP BW documentation. A step-by-step guide to installing the BI Administrator Cockpit is available as part of the customizing transactions Implementation Guide (IMG).

NOTE The Technical Business Content (like all other Business Content) must be activated prior to using it for monitoring and analysis purposes; regular data loads have to be scheduled to make sure the information displayed is up to date.

Query Statistics

Query statistics provide detailed information about what queries have been executed at what time by what user, what navigational steps the user executed, and what InfoObjects, hierarchies, and aggregates have been used in those navigational steps. Query statistics are divided into three areas:

- *Front End statistics* cover the rendering of Web items, the execution of Web applications, the rendering of BEx Analyzer workbooks, or the time a user spent waiting between different navigational steps.

- *OLAP statistics* cover the processing times of the Analytic Engine, caching runtimes, hit rates, and master data access times.

- *Data Manager statistics* cover data retrieval times for InfoCubes, aggregates, BI accelerator indexes, DataStore Objects, and other InfoProviders.

Table 12-1 shows some of the most important key figures available. Additional key figures are available to provide more details or information about other steps of the query execution process. All key figures can be used to provide average values, deviations, rankings, and other higher-level analysis. An analysis of the information available from query statistics usually provides a good indication of where exactly an observed bottleneck is located. Long database runtimes, for example, indicate a potential problem with database statistics or the I/O subsystem or indicate a need for additional aggregates or the use of the BI accelerator.

Table 12-1 Important Key Figures in Query Statistics

KEY FIGURE	DESCRIPTION
0TCTDBSCTR	Number of database selects executed
0TCTNAVCTR	Number of navigations performed
0TCTCHAVRD	Number of attribute values read
0TCTNCELLS	Number of cells transferred to the front end
0TCTNDBSEL	Number of records selected from the database
0TCTNDBTRA	Number of records transferred from the database to the server
0TCTNTEXTS	Number of texts read
0TCTTAUTH	Time spent for authorization checks
0TCTTDBRD	Time spent for reading from the database
0TCTTDMCACC	Time spent by Data Manager for InfoCube access
0TCTTDMDBB	Time spent by Data Manager for reading from standard InfoCube
0TCTTDMDBO	Time spent by Data Manager for reading from DataStore Object
0TCTTFRONT	Time spent for front end operations
0TCTTNAVIG	Time spent between navigational steps
0TCTTOLAPAL	Total time spent for OLAP processing
0TCTTOLINI	Time spent for OLAP processor initialization
0TCTTRDMDA	Time spent for reading texts / master data
0TCTTREST	Time spent for what the system was unable to assign
0TCTTVARDP	Time spent for inputting variables
0TCTTOLAP	Time spent for OLAP processor

Warehouse Management Statistics

Warehouse management statistics provide information about all data maintenance processes (for example, the number of records processed and the time
spent on loading data, maintaining aggregates, or compressing InfoCubes).
Warehouse management statistics cover another three areas:

- *DTP statistics* cover the runtimes and statistical information about data-
  load processes using data transfer processes.

- *InfoPackage statistics* cover the runtimes and statistical information
  about data-load processes using InfoPackages.

- *Process Chain statistics* cover all different types of processes scheduled
  through process chains, including (but not limited to) aggregate rollup,
  InfoCube compression, DataStore Object activation, and attribute
  change runs.

Table 12-2 shows the most important key figures available in this part of the
Business Content.

Table 12-2 Important Key Figures in Warehouse Management Statistics

KEY FIGURE	DESCRIPTION
0TCTMNRECO	Records (WHM process) for a particular processing step when loading data
0TCTMTIME	Time (WHM process) for a particular processing step when loading data
0TCTNAGGRRD	Number of records read for aggregation
0TCTNAGGRWR	Number of records written to the aggregate
0TCTTAGGIN	Time spent for aggregation during rollup
0TCTTAGGRD	Time spent for reading data during rollup process
0TCTNCNDDEL	Number of deleted records
0TCTNCNDINS	Number of added records
0TCTNCNDRAT	Summarization proportion
0TCTNCNDRPI	Number of added markers
0TCTNCNDRPU	Number of marker updates
0TCTNCNDSEL	Number of selected records
0TCTNCNDUPD	Number of update records
0TCTTCNDALL	Overall runtime

The Technical Business Content for data loading and maintenance helps to identify performance trends or exceptions; it does not provide sufficiently detailed information for an analysis of performance issues. This kind of analysis can be done in the extraction monitor (transaction RSMO).

Optimizing Query Performance

Besides correctness of information, reporting and analysis performance is the most important prerequisite for users to accept a data warehouse solution. Consequently, most of the performance management efforts should be invested in this area. While constant monitoring using BI statistics allows you to manage performance proactively, there still are occasions where the reporting and analysis wheel starts squeaking. Action against query performance issues should follow a systematic approach; the first step is a thorough analysis, followed by a consideration of measures in order of complexity or effort required to implement.

- **Analyze query execution to identify bottlenecks** using the BI statistics Business Content transaction if a number of queries show slow performance, or the Query Monitor (transaction RSRT) to analyze a single query.

- **Analyze SQL execution times** whenever database performance seems to be causing the problems (long database runtimes). Some anomalies may actually require checking overall system performance. Possible fixes in these cases include system parameter reconfigurations (hardware, operating system, DBMS, or the application server) or hardware upgrades.

- **Check query properties** in the Query Monitor (transaction RSRT) to ensure that the query read mode and the query optimization mode are set correctly.

- **Check if parallelization is possible** in query execution. This is usually only possible for MultiProviders and partitioned InfoProviders.

- **Check if InfoCube is compressed** in the DW Workbench. Too many uncompressed requests in an InfoCube slow down query execution, especially for partitioned InfoCubes.

- **Check if additional indexes can solve the problem.** Defining additional indexes may help in cases where queries access navigational attributes in large master data tables or where large dimension tables are used.

- **Check if query caching is an option.** Query caching can be defined in the Query Monitor (transaction RSRT). Because of the amount of memory required, query caching must be used with care and in scenarios where the same or similar queries are used multiple times by multiple users.

- **Optimize the query definition** using the BEx Query Designer; see the section titled "Optimizing Query Design" for more details.

- **Check adding aggregates.** The Query Monitor debugging functionality allows checking the validity of aggregates for certain queries or navigational states of queries. In some cases, a modification of a specific aggregate or the definition of a new aggregate may resolve the problem. Keep in mind, however, that aggregates also have a significant impact on data maintenance performance because the aggregate rollups required for every time transaction data are loaded or the full or partial rebuilds after master data changes.

- **Check adding the BI accelerator.** The BI accelerator can dramatically speed up query execution times but requires additional hardware investments. See the section titled "BI Accelerator," later in this chapter, for more details.

- **Check the information model** for compliance to the guidelines presented earlier in this chapter. Eventually, modify the InfoProvider definition or parts of the information model. The remodeling tool available since the SAP NetWeaver 2004s release facilitates implementing the changes required.

- **Check for partitioning options.** As explained earlier, logical or physical partitioning may improve query performance. Switching to partitioned objects after data has been loaded can be a costly process if it requires reloading the InfoProvider — but then, this hurts only once.

- **Check if dormant data can be archived.** Reducing the amount of data stored in the InfoProvider by archiving or introducing NLS systems speeds up database access times.

- **Revisit performance planning covering data retrieval times for InfoCubes, aggregates, BI accelerator indexes, DataStore Objects, and other InfoProviders**. The final resort for performance optimization is revisiting performance planning — reviewing the information model, reviewing the system landscape, and eventually adding one or more application servers, upgrading hardware, reorganizing disk space, and, finally, reviewing your user's expectations.

Analyzing Query Execution

Once a low-performance query has been identified, you have several options to analyze query execution: the Query Monitor (transaction RSRT), query tracing (transaction RSRTRACE), and, of course, the CCMS. Figure 12-10 shows the query debugging options available in the Query Monitor.

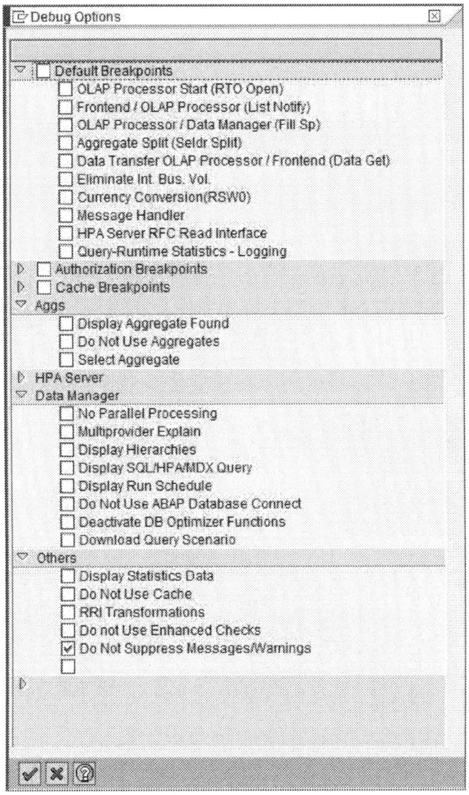

Figure 12-10   Debugging options in the Query Monitor
Copyright © SAP AG

The Display Statistics Data option essentially provides the same information as the Technical Business Content and is helpful whenever the Business Content has not been activated or a single query must be analyzed in more detail. The Display Aggregate Found option shows a list of applicable aggregates for the query executed. Display SQL/HPA/MDX Query displays the generated SQL statement used to retrieve relevant data from the InfoProvider. Ultimately, query execution can be debugged using the breakpoint options available.

The query trace (transaction RSRTRACE) allows you to further analyze the query execution details. For experienced users, it is possible to analyze the aggregate determination process. The CCMS provides additional options for query analysis on a technical level. Finally, transaction RSRV provides a number of options for low-level analysis and consistency checks, including:

- Plausibility of DBMS parameters
- Existence and consistency of SAP BW standard database indexes
- Existence and consistency of database statistics

Defining the Query Read Mode

SAP BW queries can be executed in different read modes causing the Analytic Engine to follow different strategies in retrieving data from the database and composing query result sets. The query read mode can be defined for each query separately:

- Mode H (Read on navigation/hierarchy drill down) — The Analytic Engine retrieves all data required to create the result set for the initial query view or the current navigation step. Subsequent navigation steps or hierarchy drill-downs will require reading additional data or rereading the data read before.

- Mode X (Read on navigation) — This is the same as Mode H, except for hierarchies. The Analytic Engine reads and buffers all information required for hierarchy drill-downs in advance. Because the complete hierarchy must be read, providing the initial query view takes more time. Subsequent hierarchy drill-downs are performed faster, because they are read from buffers instead of from the database.

- Mode A (Read all in one step) — All data available through the query definition is read and buffered when creating the initial query view. All subsequent navigational steps are executed reading from buffers instead of from the database. Note that this option adversely affects performance of bringing up the initial query view, especially for queries with a large number of free characteristics or large hierarchies.

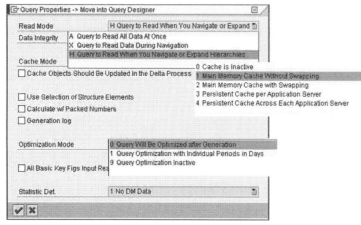

Figure 12-11 Query modes and caching options

Query Caching

Query caching stores result sets of query executions in main memory, flat files, or cluster tables. Query caching also stores result sets to be able to serve subsequent executions of the same or similar queries (partly or entirely from the cache, instead of having to read all query result data from the database). Query caching is turned on per query using the query properties function in the Query Monitor (transaction RSRT). The query cache mode, delta caching, and partitioning for MultiProviders define the query caching strategy applied. In all scenarios, information broadcasting functionality can be used to fill a cache in batch mode (for example, after uploads, after system restarts, or just periodically).

Query Cache Mode

The query cache mode defines how SAP BW handles query caching and where the cache is stored. Five different query cache modes are available:

- **Cache inactive** — Selecting this cache mode deactivates caching for the query. It is recommended in scenarios where data is changed frequently, many different types of queries are executed against an InfoProvider, or many ad hoc queries are used.

- **Main memory without swapping** — The cache is kept in main memory and swapping for this part of the memory is disabled. This cache mode is recommended whenever there are frequent executions of the same, stable set of queries with result sets of a limited size.

- **Main memory with swapping** — The cache is kept in main memory and swapping for this part of the memory is possible. This cache mode applies in the scenario described previously and additionally in scenarios where many different queries are executed or the result sets can be larger.

- **Persistent cache per application server** — The cache is kept persistently in cluster tables or flat files per application server. Keeping a cache per application server helps optimize caching in scenarios with dedicated logon groups for certain groups of users. The use of cluster tables or flat files decreases the performance of query execution compared to main memory use but is still significantly faster than without caching.

- **Persistent cache across all application servers** — The cache is kept persistently in cluster tables or flat files available to all application servers. Keeping a cache across all application servers helps optimize caching in scenarios with dynamic load balancing.

Delta Caching

Delta caching enables dynamic addition of data to a cache based upon data uploaded into an InfoCube. This avoids having to reexecute queries to refresh the cache whenever additional data has been uploaded.

Partitioning Type

In the context of caching, *partitioning* refers to how caching is handled for queries against MultiProviders. Four partitioning types are available:

- **No Partitioning** — Caching is performed on the level of the Multi-Provider. Subqueries to the underlying InfoProviders are not cached. This partitioning type is useful when most queries are executed on a MultiProvider level and the underlying InfoProviders are not referenced by multiple MultiProviders.

- **Partitioning in Groups** — Separate caches are kept for the group of all standard InfoCubes, the group of all standard DataStore Objects, and groups of other types of InfoProviders (for example, VirtualProviders).

- **Partitioning in Groups with separate standard InfoCubes** — Separate caches are kept for each standard InfoCube, the group of all standard DataStore Objects, and groups of other types of InfoProviders (for example, VirtualProviders).

- **All separate** — Separate caches are kept for each InfoProvider. This partitioning type is recommended where the underlying InfoProviders of a MultiProvider are used in multiple MultiProviders.

Optimizing Query Design

The most common mistake in query design probably is using queries for list reporting, producing a large number of pages with detail information. This is not what SAP BW is made for. In fact, the software is made for getting rid of list reporting by providing interactive, slice-and-dice analysis capabilities. Running list reports — even in batch using information broadcasting — typically is evidence of a poorly managed transition from operational batch reporting to modern data warehouse-based analysis and a lack of analysis of the actual business requirements for information. The following is a checklist to keep in mind when optimizing query design:

- **Use filters** — Filters in the query definition are added to the SQL statement generated to retrieve the required data from the InfoProvider, reducing the amount of data that needs to be read at its very source. Using as many filters as possible can dramatically reduce query runtimes — especially in the query view shown initially when executing a query.

- **Avoid using conditions and exceptions** — While filters are evaluated by the database, conditions and exceptions are usually evaluated by the application server, resulting in a much larger volume of data being transferred between both servers. Always try to use conditions and exceptions in conjunction with filters.

- **Use free characteristics** — Use as few characteristics as possible in the rows and columns of the initial query view, or at least be careful about increasing the granularity of an initial query result set. The more granular the result set, the larger it will be and the more unlikely it is that an appropriate aggregate can be found. Use the characteristics required for navigation as free characteristics.

- **Use restricted key figures with care** — Restricted key figures either require more complex SQL statements to be executed in order to retrieve the desired results, or they add to the complexity of creating the query result in the Analytic Engine. Restricted key figures specifically hurt when there are overlapping ranges of characteristic values used as restriction criteria.

- **Use more than one structure with care** — While one structure for all key figures is obligatory in query design, additional structures usually include some restrictions similar to those used in restricted key figures. Additional structures should be used carefully for the same reason as restricted key figures.

- **Characteristics/Navigational attributes are more efficient than hierarchies** — Evaluating hierarchies requires generating an additional temporary hierarchy table and increases the complexity of query evaluation. Consider replacing hierarchies with characteristics or navigational attributes. If hierarchies need to be used (as in many cases), make sure appropriate aggregates are defined and consider using a variable to select a number of specific hierarchy nodes for query execution.

- **Avoid complex queries** — Don't define queries showing everything in the InfoProvider. Consider using the Report-to-Report interface to offer analysis paths rather than complex queries.

How far a query can be optimized using the preceding checklist, of course, heavily depends on the user requirements and on the information model in place. Not all of the optimizations discussed may be applicable in a specific scenario.

Aggregates

Typical queries request an aggregated selection of data from the system. Selections are supported by database indexes where additional information is stored to allow quick retrieval of selected data sets without having to access all data records. Analogously aggregated data is supported by aggregates that redundantly store aggregated views on InfoCubes. Aggregates can be defined for InfoCubes at any point of time, are automatically maintained, and are transparently used without the user even being aware of a specific aggregate.

Aggregates for VirtualProviders may actually be supported by remote systems, as SAP BW does for standard InfoCubes accessed by a remote SAP BW system. While aggregates for MultiCubes are not supported, the system automatically recognizes and uses the aggregates of the underlying standard InfoCubes. SAP BW does not support aggregates for DataStore Objects or other types of flat InfoProviders.

Generally speaking, SAP BW uses the same data model for storing aggregates as it does for storing InfoCubes. Common dimension tables are shared between InfoCubes and aggregates wherever possible. For aggregates with a maximum of 15 characteristics and without hierarchies included in the aggregate definition, SAP BW automatically uses a flat table instead of a multidimensional data model for storing the aggregates. This flat table is composed of the SIDs (surrogate keys) of all characteristics included in the aggregate definition and of aggregated values of all key figures available in the InfoCube. Flat aggregates speed up both aggregate maintenance (rollup and rebuild) and querying.

Aggregates are defined in the DW Workbench by simply dragging and dropping the required characteristics and navigational attributes into the aggregate definition area. SAP BW automatically takes care of creating dimensions according to the original dimensions of the InfoCube. Figure 12-12 shows the aggregate definition dialog. Three options are available for including characteristics or navigational attributes values in the aggregate:

- Include all characteristics/navigational attribute values in the aggregate (no filtering of records).

- Include all records with a specific value for a characteristic or navigational attribute value in the aggregate. This option allows you to create aggregates (for example, for a specific part of an organization, for a specific region, or for a specific group of customers).

- Include all records on a specific level of a selected hierarchy of a characteristic or navigational attribute. This option increases the performance of queries that make use of external hierarchies.

From an aggregate data maintenance perspective, there are three types of aggregates:

- **Type 1** — Aggregates not including navigational attributes or hierarchies

- **Type 2** — Aggregates including time-independent navigational attributes or hierarchies

- **Type 3** — Aggregates including time-dependent navigational attributes or hierarchies

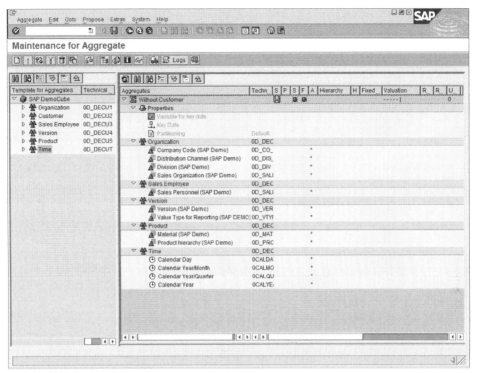

Figure 12-12   Defining aggregates
Copyright © SAP AG

For all types of aggregates to be up to date, all data records that have been added to the corresponding InfoCube since the last aggregate maintenance are applied to the aggregates, a process called *aggregate rollup*. It is up to the system administrator to schedule aggregate rollups as part of the staging process or as a separate process.

In addition to the rollup, Type 2 and 3 aggregates must be realigned every time the master data attributes or hierarchies used in the aggregate change. This task is performed during master data activation. Based on a threshold value defined by the system administrator, SAP BW dynamically decides if this realignment is performed by dropping the aggregate and re-creating it, or if it just realigns the aggregate based on the changed master data or hierarchy records. The default threshold value is 20 percent. If more than 20 percent of the master data or hierarchy records have changed, the aggregate is dropped; otherwise, the deltas are computed.

Type 3 aggregates require a reference date as part of their definition. All navigational attribute values and hierarchy nodes are retrieved using this reference date. In typical applications, this reference date needs to be adjusted from time to time (for example, a reference date referring to the last day of the previous month needs to be adjusted on a monthly basis), and with a changing reference date, the aggregate itself needs to be adjusted.

SAP BW automatically identifies hierarchical relationships between the aggregates defined for a specific InfoCube. Figure 12-13 shows a simple aggregate hierarchy for four aggregates: Aggregates 2 and 3 can be derived from aggregate 1, and aggregate 4 can be derived from aggregate 2 but needs additional hierarchy data. All aggregate data maintenance (creation of aggregates, rollup, and realignment) is automatically performed along this hierarchy reusing already aggregated data.

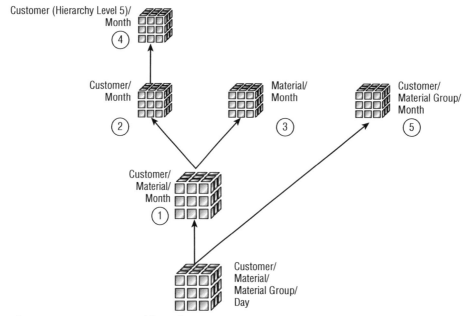

Figure 12-13   Aggregate hierarchy

Optimizing the set of aggregates is a continuous process following the changes in user behavior and user requirements. An initial set of aggregates should be created before going live, based on user requirements, information about user behavior, and information about the actual distribution of data values collected up front. It is very important for gaining and retaining user acceptance to have the most important aggregates in place before going live. Aggregate adjustment is supported again by the Technical Business Content. The following discussion provides some high-level guidelines and tips for aggregate design. Further information about aggregates can be found in a detailed how-to guide on aggregates, available in the SAP Service Marketplace (http://service.sap.com/bw).

SAP BW allows generating proposals for aggregates either based on static query definitions or on actual user behavior. This proposal is usually too extensive and should be reviewed very critically according to the guidelines discussed here.

Developing an optimal set of aggregates requires having the trade-off between reporting time versus space, and load time in mind. The most important prerequisite for optimizing the set of aggregates is intimate knowledge of the actual distribution of data values. Aggregate number 1 shown in Figure 12-13 is only useful for optimizing reporting performance, if there are multiple records per customer, material, and month (for example, if a customer buys the same product more than once a month). While SAP recommends an aggregation factor of at least 10, aggregates with smaller aggregation factors have proved to be useful in many cases. Even large aggregates may be useful, as aggregate 1 in Figure 12-13, with an aggregation factor of only 2, shows. Several other aggregates can be derived from this large aggregate. These kinds of large aggregates are called *base aggregates*.

As shown in Figure 12-12, the aggregate definition dialog provides statistical information about the aggregate, including the setup, maintenance, usage, and a rating of the aggregate's usefulness. The rating is based on the aggregation factors along the aggregate hierarchy and the actual usage of the aggregate. While this rating provides a first indicator on aggregate quality, it needs further consideration. Base aggregates will always be rated very low, because they are not frequently used for query execution.

A mistake frequently made in aggregate definition is to not include characteristics that depend on another characteristic already included in the aggregate. For example, `quarter` and `year` should be included in an aggregate that includes `month`, or `material group` should be included in an aggregate that already includes `material`.

Including dependent characteristics is important for two reasons. First, as illustrated in Figure 12-13, aggregate 5, for example, could be derived from aggregate 1 instead of the underlying InfoCube, decreasing the time required for computing aggregate 5 roughly by the aggregation factor of aggregate 1. Second, InfoCubes and aggregates share common dimension tables, as long as they are composed of exactly the same fields. If the `material` dimension of the InfoCube shown in Figure 12-13 contained just `material` and `material group`, this dimension table could be shared between the InfoCube and aggregates 1 and 5.

NOTE The `quarter` and `year` **characteristics never change for a given** `month`, **as opposed to** `material group` **and** `material`. **However, as long as changes in the assignment of materials to certain material groups are rare, including** `material group` **in the aggregate will not significantly increase the number of records in the aggregate.**

BI Accelerator

The BI accelerator is a recent addition to SAP BW and has shown some impressive performance gains with typical improvement factors between 10 and 100. It is based upon the TREX search engine for unstructured data applying its technology to structured data stored in the InfoCubes of an SAP BW system. Figure 12-14 shows the architecture of the BI accelerator in the context of the overall SAP BW architecture. The BI accelerator replaces the MOLAP aggregate option available in earlier releases of SAP BW.

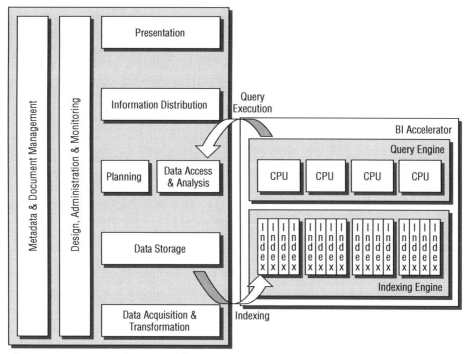

Figure 12-14   BI accelerator architecture

The BI accelerator achieves these performance gains by creating special types of additional indexes — also called *BI accelerator indexes* — and using these indexes as the basis for massively parallel query execution. Both indexing and query execution run on a separate, highly parallel blade server.

The underlying technology is actually not new but has been part of the TREX search engine, which itself is part of the SAP NetWeaver suite. SAP BW uses a special instance of the TREX search engine, enhanced to better support searches in structured data of a business intelligence system. Creating a BI accelerator index involves three steps:

1. **Vertical decomposition** decomposes the data to be indexed by attribute (or database column) instead of by record (or table row), as it is done in

traditional database indexes. This approach has been known from other search engines for nonstructured data — only now applied to structured information stored in SAP BW

2. **Smart compression** involves recoding the attribute values found in the indexed data to smaller integer values using a directory, which is generated on the fly. Typical reductions in the size of the indexed data reach a factor of 10-20.

3. **Horizontal partitioning** divides the generated index into multiple partitions in such a way that query execution using these indexes can be run in parallel without having to share data.

BI accelerator indexes are not stored in a database but are stored in flat files residing on the BI accelerator server. Query execution using the BI accelerator again involves up to three steps:

1. **Load index to memory.** When starting the execution of a query, the system checks if the corresponding index is already (or still) available in the main memory of the BI accelerator server. If the index is not available, it is loaded into main memory. Alternatively, loading critical indexes can be triggered by external processes to ensure that these are instantly available at all times.

2. **Aggregation.** BI accelerator indexes also contain key-figure values corresponding to the requested characteristic values. These key-figure values are used for highly parallel on-the-fly aggregations.

3. **Merge and return results.** The final step before returning query results to the BI server is to retrieve and merge all subresults from the different parallelized query execution processes.

Using the BI accelerator has a couple of advantages over other traditional performance optimization methods. First of all, using it does not require any changes to existing information models or queries. Considerations around logical partitioning, line-item dimensions, or additional database indexes could even be ignored in the development of information models for use with the BI accelerator — although you should still aim for the best possible information model. As opposed to traditional aggregates, one BI accelerator index serves all queries of an InfoCube, regardless of the granularity of the result set or the actual filters used. Therefore, the manual effort for tuning aggregates is kept to an absolute minimum while the system still provides stable, predictable query response times. Because BI accelerator indexes are not stored in a database, there's also no need to optimize database queries or parameter sets.

On the other hand, hardware resource requirements (especially for main memory) are too demanding to allow for using the BI accelerator for all InfoCubes of the overall information model. In many applications, classic aggregates will be sufficient to provide good performance for query execution at much lower hardware requirements. Typically, the BI accelerator will be deployed in scenarios with very high data volumes (hundreds of millions or even billions of records in the fact tables), incalculable query requirements that are hard to optimize for, or scenarios with tight service-level agreements regarding average or maximum query runtimes. The BI accelerator does not optimize the Analytic Engine itself, nor does it help to cut down network transmission times. It can, however, substantially optimize database-intensive query execution.

Finally, as of this writing, the BI accelerator does have some restrictions. First of all, the BI accelerator only supports InfoCubes with cumulative key figures and does not support DataStore Objects or other InfoProviders. Initially, the available hardware platforms were limited to Windows- or LINUX-based highly parallel blade servers. The BI accelerator could not be installed on standard TREX installations. You should refer to the SAP Service Marketplace for updates.

Data Loading and Data Management

Performance of data loads and data maintenance is crucial to providing information in a timely manner. The main entry point for performance analysis in data loading and data management again is the BI Administrator Cockpit. Detailed information is available through the DW Workbench or through transaction code RSMO (a screenshot of the SAP BW data load monitor is featured in Figure 3-6). Five major steps are taken in processing a request, as shown in Table 12-3, along with a typical distribution of the runtimes required for each of these steps.

Table 12-3 Data Staging Steps

STEP #	DESCRIPTION	TYPICAL SHARE OF TIME
1	Request a data package	0 percent
2	Extract data from the source	10 percent of the ETL process
3	Transformations	60 percent of the ETL process
4	Surrogate key generation	30 percent of the ETL process database updates
5	Subsequent steps	(varies)

The runtimes given here may largely vary, depending on the complexity of the transformations and the information model, but still the numbers are helpful as a reference in comparison to actual numbers shown in the extraction monitor. As described in Chapter 6, there are two different staging processes available as of the SAP NetWeaver 2004s release: the classic InfoSource staging process with transfer and update rules and the new DataSource staging process with transformations. In the classic staging process transfer, rules will typically take some 30 percent of the time of this step, and update rules will take 70 percent of the total time.

Many performance problems in the extraction and staging process are actually caused by careless use of user exits, transformations, transfer rules, or update rules. Expensive database operations or calculations should either be avoided or carefully reviewed and optimized from a performance point of view (for example, by replacing single record database reads by multiple record database reads in the start or end routine). While much of the data transformation performance is under the control of the user, subsequent data maintenance steps such as DataStore Object data activation, attribute change runs, or aggregate rollups are predefined by the system and can usually be influenced only by changing the information model or optimizing database performance.

Data Extraction

Data extraction performance obviously largely depends on the data model and data volume of the source system application. Still, a few things can be done to improve overall data extraction performance:

- **Check performance of custom code in extraction** — Custom code can be used in user exits or in the implementation of generic function module extractors. Ensure that all custom code is implemented in the most efficient way. Transaction SE30 can be used to further analyze the runtime of delivered or custom extraction programs.

- **Check data transfer parameters** — In transaction SBIW, a number of parameters (including the size of data packages, the frequency of sending status information, or the maximum number of parallel processes to be used) can be defined. Depending on the availability of system resources, you may want to increase the number of processes and the size of the individual data packages and reduce the frequency of status IDocs to improve the performance of the extraction process. Again, specific recommendations for parameter settings are available at the SAP Service Marketplace. The potential for improving extraction performance by manipulating these parameters is limited, however.

- **Check application specific setup** — Transaction SBIW also covers a variety of application-specific options and settings that influence data extraction performance for the corresponding applications. Refer to the documentation available for the application, to subject matter experts available to your project, or to the SAP Service Marketplace.

- **Check extractor** — A more detailed analysis of the actual extractor performance can be done using the debug mode in transaction RSA3 (extractor checker). Using this transaction allows testing the extractor without having an SAP BW system requesting data.

- **Analyze database performance** — See the section titled "System Performance," later in this chapter. Adding indexes to extracted database tables and making sure the database statistics are up to date will, in many situations, help improve extraction performance.

- **Analyze system performance** — See the section titled "System Performance," later in this chapter.

Data Staging

As mentioned previously, the most common causes of bad performance in the data staging process are flaws in the information model or in custom transformations. Again, a systematic analysis helps to get to the bottom of the performance issues at hand:

- **Check data load and other parameters** — Use transaction SPRO (customizing) to set data load and other parameters according to the SAP recommendations. Also note that the defaults settings for data package size and other parameters can be overridden by settings made in the InfoPackage or data transfer process. This may, for example, help to increase the overall data package size where certain memory-intensive extractors or data staging processes need to run with a lower data package size.

- **Check if tRFC option can be used instead of IDocs** — Although normally not used anymore, be sure to switch the data transfer mode to tRFC where it is set to IDoc to reduce the overhead implied in IDoc processing.

- **Check if PSA is required** — If the PSA is used for intermediate storage, check if storing the data packages in the PSA is really required (for example, for error-handling purposes) and turn it off eventually. Especially in an Enterprise Data Warehousing setup with a separate data staging layer, using the PSA is not necessarily required.

- **Use plain ASCII files instead of CSV format** — If CSV files are used to load flat-file data, consider changing the file format to plain ASCII files with fixed field lengths.

- **Check performance of custom transformation rules** — As stated previously, custom transformations implementing complex, data-driven business logic are common causes of performance problems. Keep in mind that transformations are executed for every single record. All parts of the custom code that can be implemented as part of the start or end routines should be implemented there. As always, common ABAP performance guidelines should be followed when implementing the code. Transaction SE30 can be used to connect to a running update process and perform a runtime analysis.

- **Ensure availability of master data prior to loading other data** — Loading master data prior to transaction data reduces the need for creating new surrogate keys for master data and may significantly improve data-load performance.

- **Check number range buffering** — Efficient number range buffering reduces the time required to create new dimension keys and SIDs. Number range buffering can be switched on in transaction NRIV.

- **Parallelize multiple data loads** — Data staging processes in SAP BW scale very well with the number and speed of CPUs. While increasing the degree of parallelization does not speed up individual data staging processes, it does reduce the overall time required to load data. Try to maximize use of existing CPU, I/O, and memory resources.

- **Delete indexes prior to data load and re-create afterwards** — In many cases, index maintenance (for example, for fact tables) can slow down database updates significantly. Try deleting indexes before the data load and re-creating indexes after all data loads have been completed. This will also help to prevent the occurrence of degenerated indexes that will also slow down reporting performance.

- **Check database statistics** — SAP BW must read existing master and transaction data as part of the update process. Without up-to-date master data indexes and statistics, these operations can cause dramatic performance drops.

- **Analyze database performance** — See the section titled "System Performance," later in this chapter.

- **Analyze system performance** — See the section titled "System Performance," later in this chapter.

Information Lifecycle Management

Dormant data is the subject of ongoing discussions in the data warehouse community. *Dormant data* can be defined as data still available in the reporting structures of the data warehouse but no longer (or very rarely) used for reporting purposes. The most obvious cause of data becoming dormant simply is time. Many reporting and analysis applications focus on a two- to three-year period; only few business areas (for example, some marketing applications) require data for a longer period of time. Other reasons include organizational changes (for example, if part of the organization is sold to another organization) or a shift of focus to another area of interest.

The implementation of a data warehouse layer that is not used for reporting purposes and new database features like partitioning may already help to reduce the impact of dormant data on query performance. However, hierarchical storage management concepts and archiving are the ultimate means to remove dormant data from the system without actually losing it. While previous releases of SAP BW only supported classic archiving of data, SAP BW now supports hierarchical storage concepts based upon NLS subsystems.

For more information on information life cycle management please refer to the information life cycle management section of Chapter 11.

System Performance

In a way similar to BW statistics, the SAP NetWeaver application server also collects statistical information about system performance (hardware, database, and operating system) and provides Business Content DataSource, InfoProviders, queries, and Web applications for high-level analysis purposes. A number of transactions bundled in the CCMS component of the SAP application server allow in-depth analysis of performance problems for both dataload and query execution processes. This section briefly describes the most important functionality available — more information is provided in the SAP Service marketplace at `http://service.sap.com/systemmanagement`. All performance-relevant transactions are accessible by entering menu code STUN.

Application Server

On the application-server level, buffering and user workload have the most significant impact on performance. This section provides a brief overview of the most important transactions available for monitoring the application server.

Buffers

Transaction ST02 is the entry point for information about main memory and buffers maintained by the application server. Information available includes size of the buffer, available space, hit ratios, and the number of database accesses related to the buffer. Critical buffer parameters that may cause performance problems are highlighted in red. Figure 12-15 shows transaction ST02, where, for example, the single record buffer and the generic key buffer are in a critical state. Administrators might consider increasing the size of these buffers in this situation. More detailed information is available by pressing the "Detailed Analysis menu" button.

Another buffer relevant for SAP BW load performance is the number range buffer. Information about this buffer is available via transaction SM56. The number range buffer is used for determining surrogate keys.

Tune Edit Goto Environment Monitor System Help

Tune Summary (us4419_B73_50)

Current parameters   Detail analysis menu

System   us4419_B73_50   Tune summary
Date + Time of Snapshot 23.02.2006   16.11.42   Startup   14.02.2006 12:11.24

Buffer	HitRatio %	Alloc KB	Freesp. KB	% Free Sp	Dir Size	FreeDirEnt	% Free Dir	Swaps	DB Accs
Nametab (NTAB)								0	
Table definition	98.19	67.972	30.617	53.68	200.000	107.369	53.68	0	291.850
Field definition	99.41	175.625	43.756	27.35	200.000	117.625	58.51	0	85.075
Short NTAB	99.74	10.250	3.316	82.90	50.000	47.376	94.75	0	2.661
Initial records	87.00	18.250	496	4.13	50.000	28.653	57.31	0	25.693
								0	
program	77.13	1.500.000	4.775	0.33	375.000	326.202	86.99	10.153	291.759
CUA	99.60	24.000	15.273	79.87	12.000	11.755	97.96	0	583
Screen	99.59	33.203	27.247	84.65	10.000	9.469	94.69	1	1.193
Calendar	100.00	488	361	76.48	200	50	25.00	0	300
OTR	33.33	4.096	3.274	99.79	2.000	1.999	99.90	0	
								0	
Tables								0	
Generic Key	99.97	234.375	8.849	4.22	80.000	10.759	13.45	2.256	473.328
Single record	95.59	60.000	19.188	31.98	800	664	83.00	1.589	5.225.487
								0	
Export/import	68.17	40.000	26.974	75.07	10.000	6.743	67.43	0	
Exp./ Imp. SHM	58.56	4.096	3.259	99.33	2.000	1.975	96.75	0	

SAP Memory	Curr.Use %	CurUse[KB]	MaxUse[KB]	In Mem[KB]	OnDisk[KB]	SAPCurCach	HitRatio %
Roll area	1.48	3.886	101.535	262.144	0	IDs	99.70
Page area	0.50	1.299	44.584	124.800	137.344	Statement	99.89
Extended memory	18.52	757.760	1.961.984	4.091.904	0		0.00
Heap memory		0	0	1.569.708	0		0.00

Call Stati	HitRatio %	ABAP/4 Req	ABAP Fails	DBTotCalls	AvTime[ms]	DB Rows Aff
Select single	92.31	209.858.883	11.767.851	2.499.824	0	198.091.032
Select	73.73	179.243.835	0	7.639.302	0	983.340.128

Figure 12-15 Application server buffers
Copyright © SAP AG

Workload

Several transactions are available for monitoring the application server workload from a user, process, and task type point of view. From a user point of view, transactions SM04 and AL08 list all active users on the local application server and all users on all application servers. Transactions SM50, SM51, and SM66 give information about the number and types of processes available on the local and global application servers, as well as their current status. Current status information includes (but is not restricted to) the name of the active program, CPU time, elapsed time, number and type of database access operations, and the current database operation performed. More detailed information about the application server workload is available via transaction ST03N (or its older version ST03), shown in Figure 12-16.

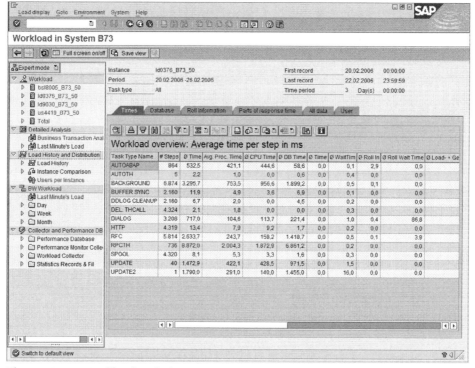

Figure 12-16 Workload analysis

Copyright © SAP AG

Transaction SE30 allows analyzing the performance of an ABAP program either started under the control of that transaction or of separate processes (for example, update processes) running in parallel that this transaction is able to connect to.

Database Server

Much of the effort required to optimize the performance of the DBMS has already been done by SAP as part of the ongoing development and software maintenance activities. For example, different indexing schemes and parameter sets are used for different DBMSs and their different versions. Because SAP BW is a generic data warehouse solution, however, there may still be some work left to do to further optimize the database. Adding indexes, maintaining database statistics, and adjusting database buffers are the most prominent examples of these optimizations. The next sections provide a generic discussion of the indexing scheme SAP BW uses, the implications of database statistics, and how the CCMS supports monitoring the DBMS.

Database Indexes

The most important indexes for standard SAP BW operations are generated automatically when activating an InfoCube, DataStore Object, or InfoObject. The exact layout and type of theses indexes varies with the DBMS used and may change with later releases of the database management software or the SAP BW software. Refer to the SAP Service Marketplace for further information about indexing.

Common indexes for fact tables are one index per dimension key field in the fact table. Dimension tables use a composite index composed of all SIDs. Master data tables use a primary key index. Additional indexes on dimension tables or on the navigational attribute SID tables may help to increase performance in cases of dimension tables or navigational attribute SID tables with a high cardinality. To identify where an additional index could be helpful, an analysis of the SQL trace (transaction ST01) or the query execution plans available through the database performance monitor (transaction ST04) have proven to be helpful — typically, repeated execution of full table scans on larger tables indicate that either an index is missing or another common cause of performance problems such as indexes that have degenerated through frequent update operations. Whenever an index is added to the database, keep in mind that additional indexes cause additional data maintenance efforts. To avoid index degeneration, indexes should be deleted and re-created periodically.

Database Statistics

Database statistics are statistical information about the data stored in a database table — for example, the number of distinct values in a specific field, the distribution of these values, or simply the total number of records in the table or its indexes. This information is used by the DBMS to identify the most efficient way to execute a specific SQL request. What kind of statistical information is maintained and used in the optimization strategy again depends on the DBMS.

In general, up-to-date database statistics are very important to warrant a high-performance system. Outdated database statistics can cause a simple query that could be executed in seconds to take several hours, just because of the DBMS choosing the wrong query execution plan.

Again, information about the query execution plan helps to identify outdated database statistics. You should update database statistics on a regular basis, depending on the frequency and data volume of uploads. The more frequent and the more volume, the more often an update of database statistics is required. In most cases, a monthly update should be sufficient. Functionality to maintain statistics is integrated into the DW Workbench transactions, supplementing the functionality available in CCMS.

Monitoring

CCMS includes a number of transactions for monitoring the DBMS and identifying bottlenecks and other issues. The most important transactions are the database performance analysis transaction (ST04) and the database allocation transaction (DB02). Figure 12-17 shows transaction DB02 for a Microsoft SQL Server database. Note that all the screenshots in this section may look different in your system, depending on the DBMS you use. The CCMS performance functions allow you to track down database operations and their use of system resources, even below the SQL request level. The "Explain" function shows the query execution plan, which allows you to check if the optimizer of the underlying DBMS has chosen an efficient query execution plan. As mentioned earlier, inefficient execution plans are mostly caused by missing or out-of-date database statistics or by missing indexes.

Sometimes information about SQL requests is hard to catch, especially in systems with many users. In these cases, transactions ST01 (System Trace) and ST05 (Performance Trace) are helpful to get a hold of the SQL requests executed by the database, its query execution plans, and other valuable information.

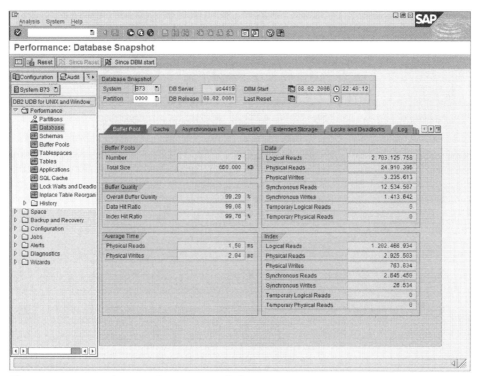

Figure 12-17   Database performance analysis
Copyright © SAP AG

Hardware and Operating System

Finally, hardware bottlenecks may cause your SAP BW system performance to degrade. Again, the CCMS is the place to go for further analysis with transaction OS06 being the main entry point for operating system analysis. And again, the layout and content of the screenshots in this section depend on the operating system used and may look different in your system. Aggregated information about CPU, memory, and IO usage is available on a single screen; additional detailed information can be reached by selecting the "Detail analysis menu." The same information is available for remote SAP servers using transaction OS07. Figure 12-18 shows transaction OS06.

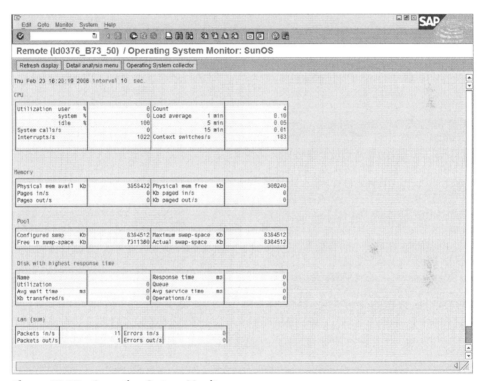

Figure 12-18 Operating System Monitor
Copyright © SAP AG

Alerts

Although not always directly related to performance management, analysis of alerts sometimes provides helpful information. The main transactions available for alert analysis are RZ20 (Alert Monitor), SM21 (System Log), and ST22 (Dump Analysis). The Alert Monitor is a one-stop-shopping solution for critical conditions in your SAP BW system. It allows for a quick high-level assessment of the overall system before you dive into the details of the analysis process. The system log available in transaction SM21 provides information about serious error conditions that cannot be handled or reported otherwise, including login failures, database error conditions, aborted transactions, and ABAP runtime errors. The latter can be examined in detail in transaction ST22, showing all information available in dumps of the aborted ABAP programs.

Transaction and Menu Summary

Table 12-4 provides an overview of the transactions discussed in the context of performance monitoring. Of course, many more transactions are available for analyzing and enhancing performance that have not been covered in this chapter, especially when actually changing the system setup is involved. Consult your system documentation for additional information.

Table 12-4   Collection of Important Transactions for Performance Management

TRANSACTION	DESCRIPTION
AL08	Active users on all application servers
DB02	Database administration
OS06	Local operating system monitor
OS07	Remote operating system monitor
RSMO	SAP BW extraction monitor
RSRT	SAP BW query execution monitor
RSRTRACE	SAP BW query execution trace configuration
RSRV	Analysis and Repair of BW Objects
RZ20	CCMS Monitoring
SE30	ABAP runtime analysis
SM04	Active users on local application servers
SM21	System log
SM37	Batch job management
SM50	All processes on local application server
SM51	Application servers
SM56	Number range buffer

Continued

Table 12-4 Collection of Important Transactions for Performance Management *(continued)*

TRANSACTION	DESCRIPTION
SM66	Global process overview on all application servers
ST01	System Trace (SQL, Authorizations, Table Buffers, RFC Calls, …)
ST02	Application server buffers and memory
ST03, ST03N	Application server workload and performance statistics
ST04	Database performance monitor
ST05	Performance trace
ST22	Short dump analysis
STUN	Provides access to all performance-relevant transactions (Menu)

Summary

Performance optimization is divided into two categories: performance planning and performance management. Performance planning accompanies the project team developing the SAP BW solution through all phases of the implementation project — from project definition via requirements analysis, information modeling, and implementation, to testing, where performance planning overlaps with performance management. The most important steps in performance planning are information modeling, system landscape definition and sizing, and, finally, management of user expectations. Although managing user expectations does not actually improve the performance of a system, it does help to set user expectations appropriately and avoid disappointment and consequently fading acceptance of the system.

Performance management is a continuous process and part of system administration and maintenance procedures. SAP BW offers a wealth of tools for system administrators to monitor performance and identify bottlenecks: the BI Administrator Cockpit with high-level monitoring; the SAP BW Technical Business Content with detailed information on an applications level; and various tools to identify database, operating system, and hardware bottlenecks.

One of the greatest enhancements in recent releases of SAP BW from a performance management point of view is the addition of the TREX search engine BI accelerator technology that has yielded some dramatic query runtime improvements for queries (especially on large data volumes). Requiring additional hardware components, using the BI accelerator should already be considered as part of the performance planning process; considerations to actually utilize the functionality for certain InfoCubes will mostly be part of performance management.

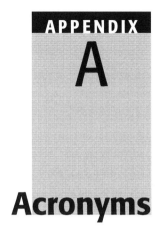

Acronyms

Table A-1 provides a handy guide to commonly used acronyms and their meanings.

Table A-1 Common Acronyms

ACRONYM	TERM
ABAP	Advanced Business Application Programming
ADK	Archive Development Kit
AFS	Apparel and Footwear solution
ALE	Application Link Enabling
APD	Analysis Process Designer
APIs	Application Programming Interfaces
APO	Advanced Planner and Optimizer
BADI	Business Add-in
BAM	Business Activity Monitoring

continued

Table A-1 Common Acronyms *(continued)*

ACRONYM	TERM
BAPI	Business Application Programming Interface
BC	Basis Component
BCS	Business Consolidation
BEx	Business Explorer
BI	Business Intelligence
BIA	Business Intelligence accelerator
BIC	Business Information Collector
BI-IP	BI Integrated Planning
BON	Business Object Navigation
BOR	Business Object Repository
BPEL	Business Process Execution Language
BPR	Business Process Reengineering
BPS	Business Planning and Simulation
BSC	Balanced Scorecard
BSPs	Business Server Pages
BTEs	Business Transaction Events
BW	Business Information Warehouse
CA	Cross Application component
CAF	Composite Application Framework
CAP	Competitive Advantage Period
CBS	Component Build Services
CCMS	Computing Center Management System
CEN	Control Monitoring System
CIC	Customer Interaction Center
CIF	Corporate Information Factory
CLTV	Customer Lifetime Value
CMCP	Category Management Consumer Products
CMF	Content Management Framework
CMI	Capital Market Interpreter

Table A-1 Common Acronyms *(continued)*

ACRONYM	TERM
CMSM	Cross-Media Storage Manager
CO	Controlling Module
COC	Center of Competence
CO-CCA	Cost Center Accounting aspect of Controlling
CO-PA	Controlling Profitability Analysis
CPH	Control Performance History
CPM	Corporate Performance Monitor
CRA	Customer Relationship Analytics
CRM	Customer Relationship Management
CSV	Comma-Separated Values
CWMI	Common Warehouse Metadata Interchange
DBMS	Database Management System
DBSL	Database Shared Library
DIS	Data Item Set
DP	Demand Planning
DQE	Distributed Query Engine
DSI	Day Sales Inventory
DSO	Day Sales Outstanding
DSS	Decision-Support System
DTD	Document Type Definition
DTP	Data Transfer Process
DTR	Design Time Repository
DW	Data Warehousing
Dynpro	Dynamic Program
EA	Enterprise Architecture
EAI	Enterprise Application Integration
EBCDIC	Extended Binary-Coded Decimal Interchange Code
EBITDA	Earnings Before Interest, Tax, Depreciation, and Amortization

continued

Table A-1 Common Acronyms (continued)

ACRONYM	TERM
EDW	Enterprise Data Warehouse
EII	Enterprise Information Integration
EJB	Enterprise JavaBean
ERD	Entity Relationship Diagram
ERP	Enterprise Resource Planning
ESA	Enterprise Service Architecture
ETL	Extract/Transform/Load
FI	Financial Accounting module
GIF	Government Information Factory
GIS	Geographical Information System
GPRS	General Packet Radio Service
GSM	Global System for Mobile Communications
GUI	Graphical User Interface
HRIS	Human Resources Information System
HRNP	Hyper-Relational Navigation Protocol
HTTP	Hypertext Transfer Protocol
HTTPS	HTTP with Secure Sockets
IDE	Integrated Development Environment
IDoc	Interchangeable Document
ILM	Information Lifecycle Management
IM	Instant Messaging
ITS	Internet Transaction Server
IVR	Interactive Voice Response
J2EE	Java 2 Enterprise Edition
J2ME	Java 2 Mobile Engine
JCA	Java Connector Architecture
JCo	Java Connector
JDBC	Java Database Connectivity
JRE	Java Runtime Environment

Table A-1 Common Acronyms *(continued)*

ACRONYM	TERM
JSPs	Java Server Pages
JVM	Java Virtual Machine
KM	Knowledge Management
KPI	Key Performance Indicator
LDAP	Lightweight Directory Access Protocol
LIS	Logistics Information System
MDM	Master Data Management
MDX	Multidimensional Expression
MOLAP	Multidimensional OLAP
MRO	Maintenance, Repair, and Operating
MRP	Materials Requirements Planning
NAS	Network Attached Storage
NLS	Near-Line Storage
NPV	Net Present Value
ODBC	Open Database Connectivity
ODBO Interface	OLE DB for OLAP Interface
ODS	Operational Data Store
OLAP	Online Analytic Processing
OLE	Object Link Enabling
OLTP	Online Transaction Processing
PBO	Process Before Output
PCD	Portal Content Directory
PIA	Process After Input
PLM	Product Lifecycle Management
PMML	Predictive Modeling Markup Language
PP/DS	Production Planning/Detailed Scheduling
PSA	Persistent Staging Area
RDA	Real-time Data Acquisition

continued

Table A-1 Common Acronyms *(continued)*

ACRONYM	TERM
RDBMS	Relational Database Management System
RFC	Remote Function Calls
RFID	Radio Frequency Identification
RFM	Recency, Frequency, and Monetary
RMA	Retail Method of Accounting
ROMI	Return on Marketing Investment
RRI	Report-to-Report Interface
SAN	Storage Area Network
SCA	Supply Chain Analytics
SCF	Synchronous Collaboration Framework
SCM	Supply Chain Management
SCOR	Supply Chain Operations Reference
SD	Sales and Distribution module
SDLC	Software Development Lifecycle
SDN	Software Developers' Network
SEM	Strategic Enterprise Management
SID	Surrogate ID
SLD	System Landscape Directory
SNC	Secure Network Communications
SOA	Service Oriented Architecture
SOAP	Simple Object Access Protocol
STS	Status and Tracking System
TMS	Transport Management System
UDConnect	Universal Data Connect
UDDI	Universal Description, Discovery, and Integration
UDI	Universal Data Integration
URL	Uniform Resource Locator
UWL	Universal Worklist
VBA	Visual Basic for Applications

Table A-1 Common Acronyms *(continued)*

ACRONYM	TERM
VODS	Virtual Operational Data Store
WACC	Weighted Average Cost of Capital
WAP	Wireless Application Protocol
WAS	Web Application Server
WSDL	Web Services Description Language
XI	Exchange Infrastructure
XML	Extensible Markup Language
XML/A	XML for Analysis
XSD	XML Schema Definition
XSLT	Extensible Stylesheet Transformation

Index

8666434R0

Made in the USA
Lexington, KY
28 February 2011